A Companion to Modern
Chinese Literature

Blackwell Companions to Literature and Culture

This series offers comprehensive, newly written surveys of key periods and movements and certain major authors, in English literary culture and history. Extensive volumes provide new perspectives and positions on contexts and on canonical and post-canonical texts, orientating the beginning student in new fields of study and providing the experienced undergraduate and new graduate with current and new directions, as pioneered and developed by leading scholars in the field.

Published Recently

A COMPANION TO

MODERN CHINESE LITERATURE

EDITED BY

YINGJIN ZHANG

WILEY Blackwell

This edition first published 2016
© 2016 John Wiley & Sons, Ltd.

Registered Office
John Wiley & Sons, Ltd, The Atrium, Southern Gate, Chichester, West Sussex, PO19 8SQ, UK

Editorial Offices
350 Main Street, Malden, MA 02148-5020, USA
9600 Garsington Road, Oxford, OX4 2DQ, UK
The Atrium, Southern Gate, Chichester, West Sussex, PO19 8SQ, UK

For details of our global editorial offices, for customer services, and for information about
how to apply for permission to reuse the copyright material in this book please see our website at
www.wiley.com/wiley-blackwell.

The right of Yingjin Zhang to be identified as the author of the editorial material in this work has been
asserted in accordance with the UK Copyright, Designs and Patents Act 1988.

Library of Congress Cataloging-in-Publication Data

A companion to modern Chinese literature / edited by Yingjin Zhang.
  pages cm
 Includes bibliographical references and index.
 ISBN 978-1-118-45162-5 (cloth)
1. Chinese literature–20th century–History and criticism. 2. Chinese literature–21st century–
History and criticism. I. Zhang, Yingjin, editor.
 PL2303.C616 2016
 895.109'005–dc23

             2015014604

A catalogue record for this book is available from the British Library.

Cover image: Zao Wou-Ki, Untitled, 2005. © DACS 2015 / ProLitteris.

Set in 11/13pt Garamond by SPi Global, Pondicherry, India

Printed and bound in Malaysia by Vivar Printing Sdn Bhd

1 2016

Contents

Notes on Contributors

Mark Bender 馬克·本德爾 received his PhD in Chinese from Ohio State University, United States, where he is Professor of Chinese Literature and Folklore and Chair of the Department of East Asian Languages and Literatures. He is the author of *Plum and Bamboo* (Illinois, 2003), a co-editor of *The Columbia Anthology of Chinese Folk and Popular Literature* (Columbia, 2011), and a translator of *Butterfly Mother* (Hackett, 2006). His interests include traditional oral literature and folklore in several regions of China, and contemporary indigenous poetry in East Asia.

Yomi Braester 柏右銘 received his PhD in Comparative Literature from Yale University, United States, and is Professor of Comparative Literature, Cinema, and Media at the University of Washington, Seattle, United States. He is the author of *Witness against History* (Stanford, 2003) and *Painting the City Red* (Duke, 2010), and a co-editor of *Cinema at the City's Edge* (Hong Kong, 2010) and of a special issue on Taiwan cinema for *Modern Chinese Literature and Culture* (2003), in addition to other publications. He is the recipient of a Guggenheim Fellowship for his forthcoming study of cinephilia in the PRC.

Sung-sheng Yvonne Chang 張诵聖 received her PhD in Asian Languages from Stanford University, United States, and is Professor of Chinese and Comparative Literature at the University of Texas, Austin, United States. She is the author of *Modernism and the Nativist Resistance* (Duke, 1993) and *Literary Culture in Taiwan* (Columbia, 2004), and a co-editor of *Bamboo Shoots after the Rain* (Feminist Press, 1990) and *Columbia Sourcebook of Literary Taiwan* (Columbia, 2014), in addition to other publications.

Angie Chau 周安琪 received her PhD in Comparative Literature from the University of California, San Diego, United States, and taught Chinese literature and world literature there for 2 years before taking up a postdoctoral fellowship at Arizona State University, United States. Her dissertation deals with Chinese artists and writers studying in France in the early twentieth century. Her article on Han Han and the Internet culture appeared in *Chinese Literature Today* (2014).

Jianhua Chen 陳建華 received his first PhD in Chinese Literature from Fudan University, China, and his second PhD from Harvard University, United States. He taught at Hong Kong University of Science and Technology for many years, and is Zhiyuan Chair Professor of Humanities at Shanghai Jiao Tong University, China. His recent publications cover revolution and modernity, popular literature, print culture, and cinema from early modern to contemporary China.

Lingchei Letty Chen 陳綾琪 received her PhD in Comparative Literature from Columbia University, United States, and is Associate Professor at Washington University in St. Louis, United States. She is the author of *Writing Chinese* (Palgrave Macmillan, 2006). Her recent publications cover diaspora and Sinophone, memory and postmemory, Cultural Revolution memoirs, Chinese global cities, and Chinese modernism and modernity.

Chen Sihe 陳思和 received his PhD in Chinese Literature from Fudan University, China, where he is Changjiang Scholar Distinguished Professor and was a longtime Chair of the Chinese Department. He was a pioneer in rewriting literary history in the 1980s. His numerous influential Chinese publications include *A View of New Chinese Literature as a Whole* (Shanghai Literature & Arts, 1987) and *Textbook History of Contemporary Chinese Literature* (Fudan, 2008).

Xiaomei Chen 陳小眉 received her PhD in Comparative Literature from Indiana University, Bloomington, United States, and is Professor of Chinese Literature at the University of California, Davis, United States. She is the author of *Occidentalism* (Oxford, 1995; expanded edition, 2002), *Acting the Right Part China* (Hawaii, 2002), and the editor of *Reading the Right Text* (Hawaii, 2002) and *The Columbia Anthology of Modern Chinese Drama* (Columbia, 2010; abridged edition, 2014), in addition to other publications.

Chen Xiaoming 陳曉明 received his PhD in Literary Theory from Chinese Academy of Social Sciences, and is Changjiang Scholar Distinguished Professor in the Chinese Department of Peking University, China. His numerous Chinese publications cover contemporary Chinese literature, literary theory, aesthetic criticism, and cultural studies, including *A Boundless Challenge* (Epoch Literature and Art, 1993), *Derrida's Bottom Line* (Peking, 2009), and *Major Trends in Contemporary Chinese Literature* (Peking, 2009).

Amy Dooling 杜愛梅 received her PhD in Chinese Literature from Columbia University, United States, and is Associate Professor of Chinese at Connecticut College,

United States. She is the author of *Women's Literary Feminism in Twentieth-Century China* (Palgrave Macmillan, 2005), the editor of *Writing Women in Modern China: The Revolutionary Years, 1936–1976* (Columbia, 2004), and a co-editor of *Writing Women in Modern China: An Anthology of Women's Literature from the Early Twentieth Century* (Columbia, 1998), in addition to other publications and translations.

Jin Feng 馮進 received her PhD in Asian Languages and Cultures from the University of Michigan, Ann Arbor, United States, and is Professor of Chinese and Orville and Mary Patterson Routt Professor of Literature at Grinnell College, United States. She is the author of *The New Woman in Early Twentieth-Century Chinese Fiction* (Purdue, 2004), *The Making of a Family Saga* (SUNY, 2009), and *Romancing the Internet* (Brill, 2013), in addition to other publications.

Ari Larissa Heinrich 韓瑞 received his PhD in Chinese Literature from the University of California, Berkeley, United States, and is Associate Professor of Chinese Cultural Studies at the University of California, San Diego, United States. He is the author of *The Afterlife of Images* (Duke, 2008), and a co-editor of *Embodied Modernities* (Hawaii, 2006) and *Queer Sinophone Cultures* (Routledge, 2013), in addition to other publications and translations.

Hu Ying 胡纓 received her PhD in Comparative Literature from Princeton University, United States, and is Professor of Chinese Literature at the University of California, Irvine, United States. She is the author of *Tales of Translation* (Stanford, 2000) and *Burying Autumn* (Harvard, forthcoming), and a co-editor of *Beyond Exemplar Tales* (California, 2011), in addition to other publications.

Nicole Huang 黃心村 received her PhD in Chinese Literature from the University of California, Los Angeles, United States, and is Professor of Chinese at the University of Wisconsin, Madison, United States. She is the author of *Women, War, Domesticity* (Brill, 2005), and a co-editor of *Written on Water* (Columbia 2005), and of a special issue on Taiwan cinema for *Modern Chinese Literature and Culture* (2003), in addition to other publications. She is currently completing a book manuscript on the auditory culture of late Mao China.

Haili Kong 孔海立 received his PhD in Comparative Literature from the University of Colorado, Boulder, United States, and is Professor of Chinese at Swarthmore College, United States. He is the author of *Life of Duanmu Hongliang* (Yeqiang, 1998; Fudan, 2011), a co-author of *Beijing* (Palgrave Macmillan, 2007), and a co-editor *One Hundred Years of Chinese Cinema* (2006), in addition to other publications.

Ping-hui Liao 廖炳惠 received his PhD in Comparative Literature from the University of California, San Diego, United States, where he is Chuan Lyu Endowed Chair in Taiwan Studies and Professor of Literature after teaching in Taiwan for many years.

He is the author of a dozen of books in Chinese—including *Keywords 200 in Literary and Critical Studies* (Ryefield, 2003)—and hundreds of articles, which cover a wide array of areas such as postmodernism, postcolonialism, music and culture, and modern Taiwan literature and film. He is a co-editor of *Taiwan under Japanese Colonial Rule* (Columbia, 2006), *Comparatizing Taiwan* (Routledge, 2015), and several other critical volumes in Chinese, Japanese, and English.

Paul Manfredi 魏樸 received his PhD in Chinese Literature from Indiana University, Bloomington, United States, and is Associate Professor of Chinese and Chair of Chinese Studies at Pacific Lutheran University, United States. He is the author of *Modern Poetry in China* (Cambria, 2014) and has published in *Journal of Modern Literature in Chinese, Modern Chinese Literature and Culture*, and *Yishu: Journal of Contemporary Chinese Art*, among others. His research has been supported by fellowships from the National Endowment for the Humanities (2003), the Chiang Ching-kuo Foundation (2006), and the AsiaNetwork (2014).

Qian Suoqiao 錢鎖橋 received his PhD in Comparative Literature from the University of California, Berkeley, United States, and is Professor (Chair) of Chinese Studies at Newcastle University, United Kingdom. He is the author of *Liberal Cosmopolitan* (Brill, 2011), and the editor of *The Little Critic* (Jiuzhou, 2012) and *The Cross-Cultural Legacy of Lin Yutang* (Berkeley Institute of East Asian Studies, 2015), in addition to other publications.

Qin Liyan 秦立彦 received her PhD in Comparative Literature from the University of California, San Diego, United States, in 2007 and is Associate Professor at the Institute of Comparative Literature and Culture, Peking University, China. Her research interests include the relationship between Chinese and American literatures, Chinese cinema, and modern English poetry. She has contributed chapters to critical volumes such as *The Chinese Cultural Revolution as History* (Stanford, 2006) and *Art, Politics, and Commerce in Chinese Cinema* (Hong Kong, 2010).

Carlos Rojas 羅鵬 received his PhD in Chinese Literature from Columbia University, United States, and is Associate Professor of Chinese Cultural Studies, Women's Studies, and Arts of the Moving Image at Duke University, United States. He is the author of *The Naked Gaze* (Harvard Asia Center, 2008), *The Great Wall* (Harvard, 2010), and *Homesickness* (Harvard, 2015), a co-editor of *Writing Taiwan* (Duke, 2007), *Rethinking Chinese Popular Culture* (Routledge, 2009), *The Oxford Handbook of Chinese Cinemas* (Oxford, 2013), and *The Oxford Handbook of Modern Chinese Literatures* (Oxford, 2016), in addition to other publications and translations.

Tze-lan D. Sang 桑梓蘭 received her PhD in Comparative Literature from the University of California, Berkeley, United States, and is Professor of Chinese Literature and Media Studies at Michigan State University, United States. She is the author of

The Emerging Lesbian (Chicago, 2003) and a co-editor of *Documenting Taiwan on Film* (Routledge, 2012), in addition to other publications.

Weijie Song 宋偉杰 received his first PhD in Comparative Literature from Peking University, China, and his second PhD in Chinese Literature from Columbia University, United States, and is Associate Professor of Chinese Literature at Rutgers University, United States. He is the author of *Mapping Modern Beijing* (Oxford, 2016) and the author, in Chinese, of *From Entertainment Activity to Utopian Impulse* (Jiangsu People, 1999) and *China, Literature, and the United States* (Huacheng, 2003), in addition to several translations of English scholarship in Chinese.

Tao Dongfeng 陶東風 received his PhD in Literary Theory from Beijing Normal University, China, and is Zhiyuan Chair Professor of Humanities at Shanghai Jiao Tong University, China. He is the editor of *Chinese Revolution and Chinese Literature* (Cambridge Scholars, 2009) and the author of numerous Chinese books, including *The Publicness of Literary Theory* (Fujian Education, 2008), *Literary and Cultural Trends in Contemporary China* (Peking, 2008), and *Chinese Literature in the New Era, 1979–2009* (China Social Sciences, 2008). His interests include literary theory, cultural studies, intellectual history, and contemporary Chinese literature.

Nicolai Volland 傅朗 received his PhD in Modern Chinese Studies from the University of Heidelberg, Germany, and is Assistant Professor of Asian Studies and Comparative Literature at the Pennsylvania State University, United States. He is the author of *Cold War Cosmopolitanism* (forthcoming), and a co-editor of *The Business of Culture* (British Columbia, 2014) and a special issue on "Comic Visions of Modern China" for *Modern Chinese Literature and Culture* (2008). He has published articles on cultural exchange, translation, print culture, media, and the Internet in China.

Ban Wang 王班 received his PhD in Comparative Literature from the University of California, Los Angeles, United States, and is William Haas Professor in Chinese Studies at Stanford University, United States. He is the author of *The Sublime Figure of History* (Stanford, 1997) and *Illuminations from the Past* (Stanford, 2004), editor of *Words and Their Stories* (Brill, 2011), and co-editor of *Trauma and Cinema* (Hong Kong, 2004), *China and New Left Visions* (Lexington, 2012), and *Debating the Socialist Legacy and Capitalist Globalization* (Palgrave Macmillan, 2014), in addition to other publications.

Yiyan Wang 王一燕 received her PhD in Chinese Studies from the University of Sydney, Australia, and is Professor of Chinese and Director of the Chinese Program at the School of Languages and Cultures at Victoria University of Wellington, New Zealand. She is the author of *Narrating China* (Routledge 2006), in addition to other publications.

Alvin Ka Hin Wong 黃家軒 received his PhD in Cultural Studies from the University of California, San Diego, United States, and served as Mellon postdoctoral fellow at the

University of California, Los Angeles, United States, before taking up a position as Assistant Professor of Chinese Literature and Film at Yonsei University, South Korea. His articles on Sinophone culture have appeared in *Journal of Lesbian Studies* (2012) and critical volumes such as *Transgender China* (Palgrave Macmillan, 2012) and *Queer Sinophone Cultures* (Routledge, 2013).

Michelle Yeh 奚密 received her PhD in Comparative Literature from the University of Southern California, United States, and is Professor of Chinese and Chair of the Department of East Asian Languages and Cultures, the University of California, Davis, United States. She is the author of *Modern Chinese Poetry* (Yale, 1991), five books in Chinese, and numerous articles. She has also edited or co-edited *Anthology of Modern Chinese Poetry* (Yale, 1992), *No Trace of the Gardener* (Yale, 1998), *Frontier Taiwan* (Columbia, 2000), and *Columbia Sourcebook of Literary Taiwan* (Columbia, 2014), and has translated hundreds of classical and modern Chinese poems, short stories, and essays.

Zha Mingjian 查明建 received his PhD in Translation Studies from Lingnan University, Hong Kong, and is Dean of the School of English Studies at Shanghai International Studies University, China. He has published numerous books and articles on translation studies and comparative literature, including *A History of Translated Foreign Literatures in Twenty-Century China* (Hubei Education, 2007).

Zhang Longxi 張隆溪 received his PhD in Comparative Literature from Harvard University, United States, and is Chair Professor of Chinese and Comparative Literature at the City University of Hong Kong. He is the author of *The Tao and the Logos* (Duke, 1992), *Mighty Opposites* (Stanford, 1998), *Allegoresis* (Cornell, 2005), *Unexpected Affinities* (Toronto, 2007), and *From Comparison to World Literature* (SUNY, 2015); and the editor of *The Concept of Humanity in an Age of Globalization* (V & R Unipress, 2012), in addition to other publications.

Yingjin Zhang 張英進 received his PhD in Comparative Literature from Stanford University, United States, and is Distinguished Professor of Comparative Literature and Chinese Studies at the University of California, San Diego, United States, where he serves as Chair of the Department of Literature. He is also Visiting Chair Professor of Humanities at Shanghai Jiao Tong University, China. He is the author of *The City in Modern Chinese Literature and Film* (Stanford, 1996), *Screening China* (Michigan Center for Chinese Studies, 2002), *Chinese National Cinema* (Routledge, 2004), and *Cinema, Space, and Polylocality in a Globalizing China* (Hawaii, 2010); a co-author of *Encyclopedia of Chinese Film* (Routledge, 1998) and *New Chinese-Language Documentaries* (Routledge, 2015); the editor of *China in a Polycentric World* (Stanford, 1998), *Cinema and Urban Culture in Shanghai, 1922–1943* (Stanford, 1999), and *A Companion to Chinese Cinema* (Wiley-Blackwell, 2012); and a co-editor of *From Underground to Independent* (Rowman & Littlefield, 2006), *Chinese Film Stars* (Routledge, 2010), and *Liangyou, Kaleidoscopic Modernity and the Shanghai Global Metropolis* (Brill, 2013).

He has also published a dozen books in Chinese and hundreds of articles in Chinese, English, German, Italian, Korean, Spanish, and Portuguese.

Yi Zheng 鄭怡 received her PhD in Cultural and Critical Studies at the University of Pittsburgh, United States, and is Associate Professor of Chinese and Comparative Literature at the University of New South Wales, Australia. She is the author of *From Burke and Wordsworth to the Modern Sublime in Chinese Literature* (Purdue, 2011) and *Contemporary Chinese Print Media* (Routledge, 2013), the editor of *Traveling Facts* (Campus Verlag, 2004), and a co-editor of *Motion and Knowledge in the Changing Early Modern World* (Springer, 2014). Her articles have appeared in journals such as *Journal of World Literature*, *Modern Chinese Literature and Culture*, and *Positions* as well as in critical volumes.

Acknowledgments

As with my previously edited *A Companion to Chinese Cinema* (Wiley-Blackwell, 2012), this book too provides a historical overview, tracks the current development, and envisions the future of a relatively young discipline. First and foremost, I express my gratefulness to all those who have contributed to the growth of modern Chinese literature and culture around the world. I commend scholars whose research has collectively made this book possible, and I particularly thank my twenty-eight contributors for their cooperation, insight, and persistence. Second, for institutional support, I acknowledge the University of California, San Diego (UCSD), United States, for a sabbatical leave in Fall 2013; the UCSD Center for the Humanities for a faculty fellowship in Winter 2014; the UCSD Academic Senate for research and conference travel grants from 2012 to 2015; and the School of Humanities at Shanghai Jiao Tong University, China, for a visiting chair professorship that has facilitated my field research since 2011. Third, on the personal side, my gratitude goes to all my colleagues and friends in San Diego and elsewhere for sharing my interest in moving interdisciplinary scholarship forward; to anonymous press reviewers of this book for timely suggestions; to Emma Bennett, Bridget Jennings, Ben Thatcher, and other Wiley-Blackwell staff for their confidence and guidance along the way; to my former doctoral students Angie Chau, Qin Liyan, and Alvin Wong for translating relevant chapters from Chinese into English; to Chen Yi, Wu Yuyu, and Paul Ricketts for their assistance with the references, the glossary, and Japanese names, respectively; to Jun Lei for her meticulous work on the index. Last but not least, I owe my deepest appreciation to my family—Jean, Mimi, and Alex—for their love, understanding, and sustenance through all these decades.

1

General Introduction

Yingjin Zhang

This introduction constructs, in four steps, a general framework for approaching modern Chinese literature. First, it seeks to reenvision the boundaries of modern Chinese literature by broaching critical issues embedded in key designations of this evolving field over time. Second, it traces the processes whereby the institutionalization of modern Chinese literature has taken shape, particularly in North America. Third, it delineates the structure of this volume—*A Companion to Modern Chinese Literature*—and briefly summarizes its subsequent 29 chapters in relation to pertinent topics in English scholarship. Fourth, it identifies areas not adequately covered in the companion and tracks new research directions. Overall, this introduction is designed to review the history and state of the field of modern Chinese literature, which emerged as a discipline in the early 1950s and has experienced rapid expansion since the early 1990s.

Modern Chinese Literature: Reenvisioning the Boundaries

We begin with an examination of the term "modern Chinese literature" and its three composite keywords. The first keyword is "modern." Unlike its European counterparts, China claims a short span of the "modern," especially relative to its history of thousands of years. What we now understand as "modern Chinese literature" initially refers to "New Literature" (*xin wenxue*), which arose in the New Cultural Movement (1917–1927), and the "new" here forms a sharp contrast to the "old"—either literature written in the old linguistic form of classical Chinese (*wenyan*) or a mixture of it with the modern vernacular (*baihua*) in traditional literary forms of fiction and prose (*sanwen*). "New Literature" is differentiated in this case from "old literature" and "popular literature" (*tongsu wenxue*), especially the type of "middlebrow" urban

A Companion to Modern Chinese Literature, First Edition. Edited by Yingjin Zhang.
© 2016 John Wiley & Sons, Ltd. Published 2016 by John Wiley & Sons, Ltd.

romance known as "Mandarin Ducks and Butterflies" (*yuanyang hudie*) or "butterfly fiction" for short (T. Liu 1984). In the 1950s, "modern literature" (*xiandai wenxue*) gradually replaced "New Literature" when the former was recognized as a new discipline in the People's Republic of China (PRC). Since the mid-1980s, "modern literature" also tends to subsume "early modern literature" (*jindai wenxue*), as scholars extend the boundary of modernity to late Qing literature (1840–1911). In the PRC, a related concept of "twentieth-century Chinese literature" (*ershi shiji Zhongguo wenxue*) is theorized to incorporate post-1949 "contemporary literature" (*dangdai wenxue*), but its inability to encompass either the pre-1900 late Qing decades or post-2000 developments makes this new term less desirable than "modern Chinese literature." In English scholarship, "modern Chinese literature" is a standard term that covers from the late Qing all the way to the present, rather than the PRC's compromised term "modern and contemporary literature" (*xiandaingdai wenxue*).

The second keyword is "Chinese." As a linguistic designation, "Chinese" refers to *Zhongwen* or *Hanyu* (Chinese language), the script used by the majority Han people in China as well as overseas, despite the fact that many Chinese—Han or otherwise—may speak different dialects or languages, the latter in the case of ethnic minorities. The term "Chinese literature" used to refer to literature written in Chinese only, but more recently there is a tendency to include literature written in minority languages such as Tibetan, and "Chinese" in this sense becomes a broader ethnic–national designation whereby *Hua* or *Zhonghua* encompasses ethnic minorities as well as Han people in mainland China. However, as a geopolitical designation, the otherwise innocuous English term "Chinese literature" becomes problematic because its Chinese equivalent *Zhongguo wenxue* means "literature of the Chinese nation-state"—carrying with it an implied privilege of *guo* (the nation-state) that writers and scholars outside mainland China may find offensive. While PRC scholars sometimes resort to *Huawen wenxue* (literature written in Sinitic languages) or *haiwai Huaren wenxue* (literature by overseas Chinese) to cover Hong Kong literature, Taiwanese literature, Malaysian Chinese (Mahua) literature, and so on, people outside mainland China often prefer these geopolitically distinct designations to the umbrella term "Chinese literature." Such a politics of naming addresses questions of Chineseness (R. Chow 2000: 1–25) and the power geometries of center versus periphery in transnational or transregional contexts, and the most recent contender in this debate is the Sinophone or *Huayu yuxi*, a concept that intends to destabilize the entrenched habits of literary studies in the PRC, as well as China studies and diaspora studies in North America and elsewhere in the West (Shih 2007; Shih, Tsai, and Bernards 2013)—to which we shall return in the concluding section.[1]

The third keyword is "literature." Although *wen* (writing) has long been theorized in traditional Chinese aesthetics (Owen 1992), *wenxue* is a new term imported from the West into modern China. As in Western literary taxonomy, Chinese literature is divided into major genres—fiction, poetry, drama, and prose essay. Contrary to traditional Chinese literature in which poetry reigned supreme, in modern Chinese literature, fiction quickly assumed a leadership position as it proved more effective than poetry in serving China's urgent needs of cultural, social, and political reforms or revolutions. From "New Literature" to "modern Chinese literature," literature largely includes only elite literature, whereas literature of other types (e.g., folk literature, popular literature) is routinely excluded from the modern literary canon. It is after the advent of new media in the 1990s that the elite monopoly of literary institutions becomes ineffectual, and Internet or Web literature has swiftly spread to cultivate tastes and values alternative or even oppositional to elite culture. As long as we keep in mind that "modern Chinese literature" designates diverse literary genres and types, ethnic origins, and geopolitical territories, there is no need to pluralize "literature."[2]

As we shall see later, many issues broached in this brief examination of the three keywords that make up the term "modern Chinese literature" have received critical attention in literary scholarship—in Chinese as well as in English. Given the limited space, *A Companion to Modern Chinese Literature* cannot adequately represent Chinese scholarship, but it has commissioned prominent scholars in mainland China to share their views on select topics (e.g., Chen Jianhua, Chen Sihe, Chen Xiaoming, Tao Dongfeng, and Zha Mingjian), in addition to featuring many scholars who have published extensively in Chinese as well—for instance, Ping-hui Liao (Liao Binghui), Michelle Yeh (Xi Mi), and Zhang Longxi. Although parallel developments in Chinese and English scholarship occurred in the late 1980s without trans-Pacific coordination (e.g., rewriting literary history), since the 1990s there have been more exchanges between Chinese and English scholarship as scholars increasingly engage in bilingual research and sometimes participate in collaborative projects (Chen Sihe and Wang 2011). To better contextualize such exchanges and engagements, we now turn to a concise institutional history of modern Chinese literature in English scholarship before delineating individual chapters in this companion.

The Institution of Literary Scholarship: Polemics and Paradigms

This section divides the institutional history of modern Chinese literature in English scholarship into three parts—the founding moment (1951–1963), the initial growth (1960s–1980s), and the rapid expansion (the 1990s to the present). Again, the limited space does not allow for a comprehensive overview, and the following selective sampling should be supplemented with my elaboration on literary modernity in English scholarship in Chapter 30 and Chen Sihe's brief survey of Chinese scholarship in Chapter 29.

The founding moment, 1951–1963: literary historiography

In Chinese as in English scholarship, modern Chinese literature is a relatively new field, and its two founding acts transpired by coincidence in 1951: first, Wang Yao, a scholar of medieval Chinese literature, published the first volume of *A Draft History of*

New Chinese Literature (*Zhongguo xin wenxue shigao*) in the PRC; second, C. T. Hsia (Xia Zhiqing), a PhD student in English literature at Yale University, was recruited to research on modern China. These two acts would yield drastically different results. In the PRC, modern Chinese literature was officially instituted as a new discipline, but literary historiography was subjected to strict ideological supervision (Y. Zhang 1994: 358–364). In response to official criticism of his "petty bourgeois" stance and his "purely objective" method of privileging art over politics in 1952, Wang Yao quickly revised his first volume and reissued it with his second volume in 1953. Still, he failed to keep up with the frenetic speed of political changes, and after a few more rounds of public criticism and self-criticism, he saw his history removed from circulation in 1955 (Y. Zhang 2016) and banned until a revised edition was approved for publication in 1982. Meanwhile, C. T. Hsia served as research assistant to David N. Rowe, professor of political science at Yale, who was compiling *China: An Area Manual*, a three-volume handbook funded by the US government and intended for US military officers (C. T. Hsia 1979: 3–4). With further funding from the Rockefeller Foundation, Hsia completed much of his book, *A History of Modern Chinese Fiction*, by 1955 (D. Wang 1999: viii), published it in 1961, and released a second edition in 1971.

Historically, Wang Yao and C. T. Hsia represent two belated responses to an even earlier moment in the institutionalization of modern Chinese literature—the first comprehensive selection of representative works of New Literature published by Shanghai's Liangyou Press in a 10-volume compendium (Zhao Jiabi 1935), each edited by a preeminent scholar or writer of the time (e.g., Hu Shi, Lu Xun, Mao Dun). The 1935 compendium constructs an inclusive, humanist vision of a new field of national literature (L. Liu 1995: 214–239) that covers a wide range of genres (fiction, drama, poetry, prose) and types (theory, polemics, research materials). Although this incipient humanist vision is still traceable in Wang Yao's inclusion of a large number of writers and his generous quotations of their original works, it would soon be repressed and replaced by an exclusive political vision of a teleological progression of New Literature toward the goals legitimized by Mao Zedong, which Wang Yao was forced to adopt in his history, and which would become more pronounced in subsequent PRC literary historiography (Ding Yi 1955; Liu Shousong 1956). Perhaps unknowingly, Hsia returned to this abandoned humanist vision of the Liangyou compendium by "rediscovering" authors who had been marginalized in official historiography, and his alternative canon in modern Chinese literature might not have been so controversial if scholars such as Wang Yao were allowed to pursue an even-handed treatment of writers of competing ideological persuasions. Published a decade before Hsia's, Wang's history contains more fiction writers than Hsia's, and Wang's artistic foresight is reaffirmed by the 1980s project of rewriting of literary history, which has since restored a large number of writers already mentioned in Wang's history but overlooked in Hsia's.

David Der-wei Wang (Wang Dewei) acknowledges the "Cold War cultural politics" when he praises "Hsia's monumental groundbreaking work" (1999: ix, xxxii) in justifying the publication of a third edition of Hsia's history. The Cold War exigency explains why C. T. Hsia (1961: 498) found it necessary to declare his intention "to contradict rather than affirm the communist view of modern Chinese fiction" and why Jaroslav Průšek (Pu Shike), "the monumental figure among the sinologists working under European communist regimes" (D. Wang 1999: xxvii), immediately launched a trenchant critique of Hsia's "failure to grasp the social significance of literature" (Průšek 1961: 361). Hsia's rebuttal (1963) appeared in the same Leiden-based Sinology journal, *T'oung Pao*, and this ferocious cross-Atlantic debate constitutes an early example of ideological confrontations between orthodox Marxism in the East and bourgeois liberalism in the West, although each side pretended to adhere to "objective," "scientific" principles of literary scholarship and accused the other of propagating "extrinsic political standards" (Průšek 1961: 358).

The initial growth, 1960s–1980s: between leftists and non-leftists

In the institutional history of literary studies, polemics often mark moments of ruptures and paradigm shifts (Hohendahl 1989). The Průšek–Hsia polemic of the early 1960s signals two contradictory movements: on the one hand, close textual analysis as perfected by New Criticism, which dominated North American academia and was Hsia's doctoral training, found an entry into modern Chinese literature, which was tacked on as a modern-day supplement to the millennia-long tradition of classical Chinese literature and thought in pre-1950s China and overseas Sinology; on the other hand, modern Chinese literature acquired new relevance in the expansion of area studies, where the Cold War imperative was to "know thine enemy" in the Communist bloc, literary texts were treated merely as "historical source materials" (Link 1993: 4–5), and the disciplines of history, sociology, and political science came to prominence. Given such contradictory movements in area studies and Sinology, the development of English scholarship on modern Chinese literature did not follow a straightforward path. Indeed, C. T. Hsia himself was compelled to retreat into classical Chinese fiction (1968), whereas his brother Tsi-an Hsia (Xia Ji'an) moved in the opposite direction by examining modern leftist writings (1968), a topic for which C. T. Hsia had little patience but which was nonetheless explored by Eastern European Sinologists (Gálik 1969; Průšek 1969).

It took two decades of sporadic publications before English scholarship on modern Chinese literature reached critical mass in the early 1980s. Following C. T. Hsia's author-oriented history of modern Chinese fiction, where an alternative canon consists of non-leftist writers such as Eileen Chang (Zhang Ailing), Shen Congwen, and Qian Zhongshu, the majority of early North American scholars approached authors either individually or in groups. In addition to the Twayne monograph series,[3] one book concentrated on Ba Jin (Lang 1967), another on Cao Yu (J. Lau 1970), one on Hu Shi (Grieder 1970), two on Lao She (Slupski 1966; Vohra 1974), and another one on Zhou Zuoren (Pollard 1973). Leo Ou-fan Lee (Li Oufan) was attracted to "the romantic generation" (1973) and Edward Gunn (Geng Dehua) to a wartime group of "unwelcome muses" in Beijing and Shanghai (1980). Admittedly, Hsia's influence is evident in these author studies, but we see an equally strong interest in leftist and socialist literature: Merle Goldman studied literary dissent in Communist China (1967), David Roy published on Guo Moruo (1971), William Lyell on Lu Xun (1976), Paul G. Pickowicz (Bi Kewei) on Qu Qiubai (1981), and Yi-tsi Mei Feuerwerker (Mei Yici) on Ding Ling (1982). Besides these monographs, a critical volume on May Fourth literature came out (Goldman 1977), along with three literary anthologies, respectively, on revolutionary literature (Berninghausen and Huters 1976), PRC literature through the 1970s (K. Hsu 1980), and the literature of the Hundred Flowers (Nieh 1981).[4]

By the mid-1980s, C. T. Hsia's diminishing influence was discernible in Leo Lee's collection of Průšek's works (1980) and Lee's own monograph on the realist master Lu Xun (1987). Similar to Lee, realism was a central concern for Yu-Shih Chen (Chen Youshi) in her study of Mao Dun (1986), and the momentum was carried further when Marston Anderson (An Mincheng) confronted the limits of realism (1990) and David Wang (1992) traced the divergence of fictional realism in Mao Dun, Lao She, and Shen Congwen. Besides realism, scholars ventured into other subjects in this phase of initial growth. In the area of comparative literature, Douwe Fokkema (Fokema) traced the Soviet influence on Chinese literary doctrine (1965); Bonnie McDougall (Du Boni) tracked the introduction of Western theories into modern China (1971); and Marián Gálik (Gao Like) explored the genesis of modern Chinese literary criticism (1980) and located milestones in Sino-Western literary relations (1986). In the area of literary genres, Perry Link (Lin Peirui) provided a sociological perspective on popular urban fiction (1981), and Chang-tai Hung (Hong Changtai) examined intellectuals and folk literature (1985). Two signs clearly show that English scholarship finally came of age in the second half of the 1980s: one is the appearance of edited volumes on such topics as a survey of the field (Kubin and Wagner 1982), late Qing fiction (Doleželová-Velingerová 1980), popular literature in the PRC (McDougall 1984), Lu Xun studies (L. Lee 1985), and women writers (Duke 1989), which showcase the results of collaborative research; the other is the increasing attention to post-Mao China (Duke 1985; Kinkley 1985), which demonstrates that scholars were no longer confined to history but were ready to tackle contemporary issues.

The rapid expansion, 1990s to the present: politics and theory

By the late 1980s, English scholarship on modern Chinese literature was poised for a rapid expansion more in line with North American literary studies in general than with either area studies or Sinology. With the advent of critical theory from Europe in the 1960s, ideological criticism informed by Neo-Marxism steadily transformed North American academia, where New Criticism's emphasis on the literary integrity and aesthetic excellence of genius authors soon fell out of favor. Terry Eagleton (1983: 51, 199) reassessed New Criticism as "a convenient pedagogical method" and "a disinterested reconciliation of opposing impulses" that had "proved deeply attractive to sceptical liberal intellectuals disoriented by the clashing dogmas of the Cold War," and in the early 1980s he doubted "how many students of literature today read them." In Chinese studies, Link (1993: 5) describes the 1980s as a moment of "catching up" when "scholars of modern Chinese literature began increasingly to read Western criticism and theory." One early example was a 1982 conference where participants were instructed, as Theodore Huters (Hu Zhide) recalls, "to apply various theories about narrative developed outside of China to fiction created in China" (1990: vii).

In hindsight, the outcome of reaching out to Western theory resulted in yet another moment of rupture, as evident in a 1993 forum of *Modern China* dedicated to "paradigmatic issues in Chinese studies" that involved two generations of scholars. Representing the younger generation, Liu Kang (1993: 13) reminds us that "modern Chinese literature studies in the West have only very recently been recognized as an independent field, after decades of hard battle with the academic sinological hegemony dominated by classicists, historians, and sociologists." Fully aware of "the danger of overstatement, incompleteness, and generalization" (K. Liu 1993: 15), Liu first credits C. T. Hsia for challenging "the predominance of the sociological approach" in both China and the West, but dismisses his "critical paradigm that is avowedly Eurocentric, formalist, and ahistorical" (K. Liu 1993: 17–18). Liu then interrogates Leo Lee's "romanticist" vision and his "historicist" approach that "searches for a dominant Zeitgeist" but "fails to come to grips with ... the struggle of modern Chinese writers for the discursive power of representation in bringing about their visions of China's modernity" (K. Liu 1993: 28).

Three responses were published in the same issue of *Modern China*. First, Link (1993: 6–7) sees Liu Kang as belonging to "a cohort of bright young students" from the PRC who is "a most welcome addition" to the field but whose "rush to critical theory" resulted in "an excessive self-absorption that diverts attention from literary works," "the excessively facile labeling of viewpoints," and the use of "modish but sloppy language." Michael Duke admits that, perhaps surprising to Liu Kang, he would have been "far more likely to side with" Průšek than with C. T. Hsia in the early 1960s (Duke 1993: 42); yet, in a radically changed circumstance decades later, Duke sounds very much like Hsia when he makes repeated claims on behalf of literature (Duke 1993: 64): "Literature is art... Literature is primary. Theory is secondary... Literature is not politics... Literature is art." A scholar who has systematically introduced Western theory to China (L. Zhang 1986), Zhang Longxi does not share the kind of theory-phobia that Duke and Link have, but he nevertheless cautions against Liu Kang's theoretically uncritical acceptance of omnipresent politics as Zhang (1993: 88) suspects that Liu "meant to confirm the validity of Mao's views by connecting them with Foucault's," thereby collapsing historical and cultural differences between China and the West. For Zhang (1993: 79), "To think critically of Western theory thus means to rely on the aesthetic experience of reading a Chinese text, and in a broader context, to rely on the experience of real life in China, the experience of that economic, political, and cultural environment we call China."

As with the Průšek-Hsia polemic three decades earlier, the 1993 debate in *Modern China* marks a moment of rupture whereby liberal humanism found itself on the defensive, unable to articulate itself theoretically, thus hiding behind the untenable claim to the "universal" values of literature.[5] In hindsight, the 1993 debate announced the retreat of reputedly disinterested textual criticism and the arrival of "the age of theory" (R. Chow 2000), an age in which different types of ideological criticism contend for dominance, as represented by several critical volumes published since then (Larson and Wedell-Wedellsborg 1993; Liu and Tang 1993; Widmer and Wang 1993; Hockx 1999; R. Chow 2000; G. Davies 2001; Laughlin 2005; Jie Lu 2007). Indeed, the 1993 debate witnessed the formation of three groups of scholars—"the liberal, humanist critics" (Duke 1993: 65) such as Duke and Link, "the radical, oppositional" critics such as Liu Kang, and "the critical, self-reflexive" scholars such as Zhang Longxi (Y. Zhang 1993: 827–828). Since the early 1990s, different critical interventions have sought to advance modern Chinese literature in different ways, and their achievements in English scholarship are enumerated in the subsequent sections.

Part I: History and Geography

Now that we have a framework of keywords and an institutional history in place, we can move on to comprehend modern Chinese literature by directing attention to its four major parts: "History and Geography," "Genres and Types," "Cultures and Media," and "Issues and Debates." In general, this introduction is focused more on literature (themes and subjects) than on criticism (issues and debates), for the latter presents some of the challenges to be taken up in Chapters 29–30, dealing with Chinese and English scholarship, respectively. Nonetheless, critical views are indispensable to our multilayered mapping of modern Chinese literature, so references to selective monographs and critical volumes are made whenever relevant.[6]

Part I establishes the structure for approaching modern Chinese literature by presenting overviews on literary history and geography. In terms of history, modern Chinese literature is divided into late Qing literature (1840s–1910s), Republican literature (1920s–1940s), socialist literature (1950s–1970s), and postsocialist literature (1980s–present). In terms of geography, Taiwanese literature and Sinophone literature (including Hong Kong and elsewhere) are brought into view so as to foreground multiple temporalities, spatialities, identities, and textualities in different geopolitical territories.

Chapter 2, "Literary Modernity in Perspective," institutes a comparative, historical perspective on modernity that transcends the rigid divide of premodern and modern literature. Zhang Longxi (1992a; 1998; 2005; 2007), a prominent scholar of China–West comparative literature and traditional Chinese poetics, insists that modern Chinese literature needs to be understood in its sociohistorical conditions at the turn of the nineteenth century to the twentieth, which witnessed the end of Chinese dynastic history and the rise of modernity in China. The concept of "modernity" was defined against the old imperial system; literary modernity manifested itself as the vernacular that replaced the classical language, and a whole set of new genres, ideas, and values prevailed over the traditional ones. In a very different world today, there is much rethinking of modern Chinese literature and literary history since the May Fourth Movement, a revaluation of Chinese tradition, and a revived interest in Confucianism. This must be understood in the global context economically, politically, and culturally, in particular with regard to the critique of modernity in Western postmodern and postcolonial theories. To understand literary modernity in China, therefore, calls for a contextual approach that puts the concept in perspective and sees it in its historical circumstances, past and present.

Zhang Longxi's contextual approach reveals, not without irony, the contrasted fates of Chinese tradition in the two *fin-de-siècles*—from the late Qing's painful realization of the inadequacy of Chinese tradition in a world of modern nation-states to the post-socialist reinvention of "national learning" (*guoxue*) in a new era of globalization—both measured against China in a changing world order of specific times. Recent scholarship (D. Wang 1997; Hu Ying 2000; Huters 2005) shows that, rather than a dark age before the May Fourth enlightenment era, the late Qing was actually a time of culture ferment, characterized by audacious experimentations and flourishing creativity. In Chapter 3, "Late Qing Literature, 1890s–1910s," Hu Ying revisits the last decades of the Qing dynasty as a time, paradoxically, of great anxiety—the fear of China's dismemberment by Western imperialist powers after a series of disastrous encounters—and of great hopes—for a new political and social order and a new historical era. Everywhere one looked, something "new" was happening: leading reformists called for "making new" the people; the burgeoning newspaper industry carried stories from around the world; and the Qing court proclaimed its new policy and abrogated the 1,000-year-old system of the civil service examination (*keju*) in 1905. A new literature was being imagined. It is against such paradoxical impulses of anxiety and hopes that Hu Ying surveys the trends and changes in the three major genres of late Qing literature—prose, poetry, and fiction.

In Chapter 4, "War, Revolution, and Urban Transformations: Chinese Literature of the Republican Era, 1920s–1940s," Nicole Huang (Huang Xincun) uses three inter-twined themes as a window into the myriad of voices and styles of literature from Republican China. The literary landscape of the period was both closely integrated and sharply divided, as various literary schools and societies negotiated through various discourses and ideologies. The progressive literature, from the iconoclastic May Fourth to leftist writings of the 1930s–1940s, was often set against the violent background of urban and rural reform, revolutions, and wars, and revolutionary romances sometimes directly engaged the plagued relations between Chinese cities and their surrounding countryside. While literature produced in Communist-controlled rural areas in the 1940s anticipated a new literary landscape to emerge after the 1949 transition, the urban literature of the period thrived in a flourishing print culture and sustained an ever-growing middlebrow readership through the turbulent era. A postwar emphasis on individual subjectivity and aesthetic experimentation, however, would soon be suppressed in the socialist period.

Similar to Chinese scholarship, English scholarship on modern Chinese literature has consistently favored May Fourth literature (Goldman 1977; Doleželová-Velingerová and Král 2001) and leftist literature (T. Hsia 1968; W. Wong 1991), and wartime literature has only periodically come into view (Gunn 1980; Y. Shu 2000; N. Huang 2005; Fitzerald 2013), while postwar literature is almost invisible. Similarly, socialist literature—previously labeled "Communist literature" (C. T. Hsia 1971: 509–532)—has largely been overlooked in book-length studies until recently (Link 2000; Button 2009; K. Hang 2013; King 2014). In line with a more sympathetic reading of socialism in current English scholarship, Chen Xiaoming argues that only when we understand socialist literature as the product of radical modernity can we better situate it in the modern formation of world literature. In Chapter 5, "Socialist Literature Driven by Radical Modernity, 1950–1980," Chen shows how heavily involved socialist literature was in a quick succession of political campaigns (e.g., the Anti-Rightist Campaign) and to what extent the literary development was driven by political movements. Socialist revolutionary literature tried to blaze a trail alternative to modern capitalism, albeit such blazing took a radical form that exposed all its difficulties and complications. Socialist literature was dictated by politics and had paid a dear price, but its experience of blazing a trail outside bourgeois literature represents a miracle in world literature, and for that reason its failure merits our continued deliberation.

Chen Xiaoming's chapter overlaps slightly with Chapter 6, "Thirty Years of New Era Literature: From Elitization to De-Elitization," where Tao Dongfeng begins with the immediate post-Mao years of the late 1970s. Rather than focusing on radical politics and its rationale as Chen does, Tao investigates a cultural dynamic of "elitization" (*jingyinghua*) and "de-elitization" (*qu jingyinghua*) that has fundamentally altered the literary landscape in the "New Era" (*xin shiqi*), and he extends his scope beyond literary production to include literary criticism and culture trends. Tao divides the 30 years of postsocialist literature into two phases: the pre-1989 phase of elitization is marked by sociocultural critique (e.g., roots-searching literature, reflection literature, reform literature) and aesthetic experiments (e.g., Misty Poetry, modernism, avant-garde literature), whereas the post-1989 phase of de-elitization is driven by the market and mass media and represented by hooligan literature, private writing, parody literature, Internet literature, and flamboyant young writers born after 1980. Still, Tao's concluding discussion of elite writers (e.g., Mo Yan) and their recent works proves that serious literature continues to flourish, although it no longer monopolizes the literary institution.

Tao Dongfeng's dialectic model provides an effective means of evaluating contemporary cultural transformation in the PRC in a period that has moved far away from Mao's socialism. Consequently, fewer scholars now reference Mao in their English titles as was the case in the 1980s (Duke 1985; Kinkley 1985), and postsocialism has remained a fascinating concept for critics (Dirlik 1989; Pickowicz 1994; X. Zhang 2008; McGrath 2008; H. Gong 2012). Two related keywords in postsocialist literature are postmodernism and postmodernity (Larson and Wedell-Wedellsborg 1993; Dirlik and Zhang 2000; S. Lu 2001; X. Yang 2002), and they are often explored in conjunction with avant-garde fiction (T. Lu 1995; J. Wang 1996; X. Zhang 1997; Y. Huang 2007; Jianguo Chen 2009) as well as modernist poetry and drama (X. Chen 1995; M. Yeh 1999). As typical of current scholarship, many scholars examine post-socialist literature in relation to other fields of cultural production, in particular cinema and visual culture (Barmé 1999; K. Liu 2004; S. Lu 2007; McGrath 2008).

The final two chapters of this part direct attention to literary history and geography outside mainland China. In North America, Taiwanese literature received academic attention generally as part of modern Chinese literature (C. T. Hsia 1971: 555–586) and was often anthologized as such (Hsia and Lau 1971; Lau, Hsia, and Lee 1981), except for a few separately issued titles (Lau 1976; Lau 1983). Although an edited volume on Taiwanese literature was launched relatively early on (Faurot 1980), single-authored monographs are still rare (S. Chang 1993; S. Chang 2004; E. Teng 2004), and so are the comprehensive surveys of this vibrant field (Chi and Wang 2000; D. Wang and Rojas 2007). As many Taiwan-based scholars have done in the new century, Sung-sheng Yvonne Chang (Zhang Songsheng) revisits Taiwan's colonial period in Chapter 7, "Building a Modern Institution of Literature: The Case of Taiwan," but she offers a regional comparative perspective. In her judgment, colonial Taiwanese launched a Mandarin vernacular movement as well as a campaign for a "nativist literature" in written Taiwanese in their efforts to build a locally based modern literary institution. Both movements were aborted after 1937 when the Japanese tightened their monolingual policy in the colony. Despite their brevity and atrophied forms, both movements were properly modernist projects generated by the same historical impulses as those behind similar processes in other parts of East Asia. Chang highlights the structural affinities between these processes and their full-fledged counterparts in modern Japan and Republican China, and contends that disparities among their evolutionary trajectories are explained by different types of historically wrought disjuncture. After the mid-century transition, Taiwanese writers transplanted and subsequently brought to fruition a major strand of modern Chinese vernacular literature that had evolved during the Republican period on the mainland but was suppressed in the PRC's socialist era.

A distinct contribution of Chang's comparative approach is its exploration of the difficult linguistic choices presented to literary reformers at a critical historical juncture in building a modern literary institution that is locally based but regionally connected, and Chang's specific Taiwan case therefore foregrounds the "Japanophone" as an issue that is now obscured by the increasing emphasis on the Sinophone. In Chapter 8, "Sinophone Literature," Ping-hui Liao reminds us that, as emergent or minor literature, Sinophone writings have been studied in conjunction with the Chinese ethnoscapes in "dis-semi-nation" or with an agenda to debunk cultural nationalism and to rethink the notion of "Middle Kingdom" and even that of "Cultural China" in terms of the center and periphery dichotomy. Whereas "overseas Chinese literature," "world literature in Chinese," "Chinese immigrant literature," "literature by Chinese ethnic minorities," and so forth have been used over the years, Sinophone discourse is proposed as an alternative to address the hybrid, expressive cultures that have been developed across a rich diversity of Chinese-speaking communities. Scholars attend to the differential and multiple ways in which Chinese scripts as well as Chinese heritages have been appropriated and cultivated to entertain new visions of being Chinese along the direction of exile and creativity, linguistic creolization and critical multiculturalism, and centrifugal and contrapuntal forces in connection with the imaginary homeland. Liao places Sinophone discourse in relationship to its more established counterparts in the Anglophone, Francophone, and other traditions, and traces the historical trajectories of Sinophone writings and Chinese diaspora to map out the imperial and post-contemporary conjectures. He ends the chapter by examining critical debates around this provocative terminology and reflecting on the most recent coercive attempts by PRC scholars to incorporate it into new Sinology or global Chinese literature.

Part II: Genres and Types

Part II covers key genres—poetry, drama, fiction, and prose—and types of literature—translated literature, women's literature, popular literature, and ethnic minority literature—in modern Chinese literature. Poetry is the best genre with which to measure the seismic change in the time-honored Chinese literary tradition since the late Qing, when poetry started to lose prestige to fiction. In Chapter 9, "Modern Poetry in Chinese: Challenges and Contingencies," Michelle Yeh presents the development of modern poetry written in Chinese from the early twentieth century to the present. She begins by examining the distinct differences between modern poetry and its revered predecessor, classical poetry with a history of almost three millennia. Modern poetry not only represents changes in form, language, and aesthetic orientation but also embodies the fundamental transformations of social, political, and cultural structures unfolding in the late nineteenth and early twentieth centuries. Despite these historical challenges, modern poetry has created a highly original "minor tradition," which runs parallel to, rather than countering, the "major tradition" of classical poetry. Modern poetry has come a long way from the earnest yet somewhat simplistic attempts of the first generation of modern poets in China in the 1910s–1920s, to the various experiments in romanticism, symbolism, and modernism in the 1930s–1940s, to the thriving modernist movement in Taiwan and Hong Kong in the 1950s–1960s, to the poetry renaissance in post-Mao China in the 1980s–1990s, and finally to an impressive array of styles today. Each phase has given us outstanding works and influential poets. Together, they have established a new aesthetic paradigm that enlarges and enriches the formidable canon of Chinese poetry.

Michelle Yeh's succinct review reflects both the diversity of modern Chinese poetic expressions (K. Hsu 1963; W. Yip 1970; M. Yeh 1992) and the sophistication of modern poetry studies in English scholarship (J. Lin 1972; J. Lin 1985; M. Yeh 1991b; Hockx 1994; Van Crevel 1996; J. Mi 2004; J. H. Zhang 2004; Van Crevel 2008; Crespi 2009; Kunze 2012; Manfredi 2014). In comparison, modern Chinese drama remains rather marginal in English scholarship (Wagner 1990; Conceison 2004; Ying and Conceison 2008; Ferrari 2012; Hsiung 2013), except for studies of Gao Xingjian (to be enumerated in the conclusion). Xiaomei Chen has published on modern Chinese drama (2002a; forthcoming) and edited comprehensive drama anthologies (2002b; 2010), and in Chapter 10, "Modern Chinese Theater Study and its Century-Long History," she recommends an approach that combines *huaju* (spoken drama) and *xiju* (theater) and uses three major playwrights—Cao Yu, Hong Shen, and Ouyang Yuqiang—to illustrate how these dramatic forms worked together in their careers and how concepts of Greek tragedy found their ways into new Chinese narratives of class struggle. Modern Chinese drama refers to spoken drama, which was introduced from the West (e.g., William Shakespeare, Anton Chekhov, and Henrik Ibsen) at the turn of the twentieth century as an alternative to traditional operatic theater. The history of modern Chinese theater, however, shows a gradual acceptance of traditional opera as an equally important genre both in aesthetic form and in social function, as seen in the successful use of opera for wartime mobilization in the 1930s–1940s and in socialist construction (1949–1979), when the state-sponsored Peking opera reform succeeded in establishing a "revolutionary model theater" during the Cultural Revolution (1966–1976) as the dominant artistic mode. In the post-Mao period, the theatrical concepts, techniques, and aesthetics of Chinese opera likewise found their way into the experimental performances of spoken drama and inspired the initial trend toward avant-garde theater. In the twenty-first century, both operatic theater and spoken drama are equally present in university curricula, scholarly research, and stage performance, although they have suffered from a declining audience base because of fierce competition with commercial culture, television shows, and touring Western theater troupes.

As with drama, prose is another marginal genre in English scholarship (Wagner 1992; Daruvala 2000; Woesler 2000; Laughlin 2008; S. Qian 2011). In Chapter 11, "Literariness (*Wen*) and Character (*Zhi*): From *Baihua* to *Yuluti* and *Dazhongyu*," Qian Suoqiao points out that prose as a distinctive literary genre with its significance comparable to fiction, poetry, and drama is a modern Western construct mapped onto Chinese modernity. When the age-old literary language was denounced as incompatible with modernity, writing itself has become a *problematique* in Chinese modernity. The successful promotion of *baihua* (vernacular) as the national (written) language is probably the defining feature of Chinese modernity. However, the *yuluti*-versus-*dazhongyu* debate in the 1930s highlights the continuing disagreement as to what counts as written *baihua* in modern prose. Qian identifies the nexus of *wen* (literariness, embellishment) and *zhi* (substance, character) as the key *problematique* of modern Chinese prose and discusses its accomplishments and contentions through an examination of theories and practices of such diverse modern Chinese prose writers as Hu Shi, Lin Yutang, Lu Xun, Zhou Zuoren, and, more recently, Zha Jianying, Su Wei, and Li Chengpeng.

Compared with poetry, drama, and prose, the ascendance of fiction in the modern Chinese literary hierarchy is remarkable. In Chapter 12, "Fiction in Modern China: Modernity through Storytelling," Yiyan Wang maps the enormous body of fiction in modern China written in Chinese since the late nineteenth century. By tracing the evolution of this genre against the sociohistorical and cultural changes taking place at the same time, Wang observes Chinese modernity as reflected through innovations and transformations in fiction, including its form, content, thematic concern, and narrative language. She demonstrates how politics, social change, international influences, and technology have altered the production, distribution, and reception of fiction. Fiction in modern China is understood as both an active agent advocating ideals for modernity and as an integral part of China's modernization process. Wang demonstrates that the arrival of Chinese modernity is marked by storytelling as new expressions of political ideas, public histories, and individual trajectories in addition to the legitimation of fiction as popular entertainment.

Similar to Yiyan Wang, Zha Mingjian provides a sweeping overview in Chapter 13, "Modern China's Translated Literature." It is a critical consensus in Chinese comparative literature that translated literature (*fanyi wenxue*) has not only motivated the modernization of Chinese literature but has also exerted a great influence on contemporary Chinese society and culture (M. Zha and Xie 2007; Song Binghui 2013). Translated literature has enriched and expanded the production and reception of modern Chinese literature, forming the relationship of heterogeneous isomorphism with creative literature, and thus making itself an indispensable part of the Chinese literary system. Zha tracks the development of China's translated literature in the context of modern Chinese culture, analyzes the selection and purpose of translation in different historical periods, and evaluates its influence on mainstream ideology and literary styles. It is significant to see which foreign writers are translated, what rationales are offered, and which consequences are intended or unintended. In short, it is productive to investigate the mutual influence and interaction between translated literature and original literature, and the sheer impact of translated literature on modern Chinese literature and literary studies is undeniable.

The imbrication of translated literature and original literature in late Qing fiction has received much critical attention (Doleželová-Velingerová 1980; Hu Ying 2000; Hanan 2004; Huters 2005). In Chapter 14, "Writing Chinese Feminism(s)," Amy Dooling (Du Aimei) examines a group of late Qing feminist novels (by male and female authors) in which women's transformed mindset is depicted as enabling them to embark on revolutionary courses of action. Embedded in these gendered narratives of revolution-to-come is a new politics of writing that called for engagement in social change. Late Qing progressive fiction about women deployed an array of discursive strategies—fantastic plotlines, larger-than-life heroines, bold rhetoric, and stark imagery—all of which aimed at shifting the female reader's horizon of expectation and possibility through alternative ways of imagining future selves and polities. Dooling's revisit of individual elite literary women (e.g., Qiu Jin) writing at the turn of the twentieth century demonstrates that their creative engagement with gender and genre not only predates the much-celebrated literary revolution of the 1910s–1920s but also productively complicates the influential May Fourth paradigms of tradition and modernity that have long impeded research on Chinese women's forgotten pasts.

While Amy Dooling concentrates on the late Qing here, she and other scholars have explored many relevant issues in women's literature in different historical periods and geopolitical territories (R. Chow 1991b; H. Kao 1993; Larson 1998; Lieberman 1998; J. Feng 2004; Dooling 2005; H. Yan 2006; A. Zhu 2007; Schaffer and Song 2013). Just as gender and sexuality—a cluster of issues to be further explored in Chapter 25— are instrumental in researching women's writing, so is space an illuminating approach to rethink popular fiction in modern China. In Chapter 15, "The World of Twentieth-Century Chinese Popular Fiction: From *Shanghai Express* to *Rivers and Lakes of Knights-Errant*," Yi Zheng develops Chen Sihe's concept of *minjian* (folk realm) to map the evolving landscape of popular fiction in modern China. She examines the urban plebeian configuration in Zhang Henshui's early Republican butterfly romance and the spatial imagination in Jin Yong's mid-century émigré martial arts novels. Through an analysis of the construction of a modern *jianghu* in these genre novels, she argues that the spatial as motif and structure—from the social to the topographical—in the modern Chinese popular novel is closely related to the dislocation of culture and home as a modern Chinese experience, because the geopolitics of revolutions and wars, particularly the Cold War, have shaped the affective perimeters of Chinese writers and readers. Along the way, Zheng also suggests that the emotional and cultural geography of these novels embody the *minjian* judgment on and aspirations for modernity.

An immensely popular writer, Jin Yong, and his type of literature—new martial arts fiction—came under critical scrutiny only recently in Chinese and English scholarship (Hamm 2005; Huss and Liu 2007; P. Liu 2011). Indeed, popular culture (McDougall 1984; N. Huang 2005; Rojas and Chow 2009) remains rather challenging in a field where elitism still prevails, albeit in a new theoretical disguise. Given such entrenched elitism, it is understandable that ethnic minority literature stays off the academic radar most of the time, even though it is geographically widespread, as Mark Bender illustrates in Chapter 16, "Ethnic Minority Literature." Since 1949, the existence of 56 minority groups has been officially recognized in the PRC. All of them have traditions of oral literature, some have traditions of written literature dating back centuries, and writers in many groups have employed standard Chinese as their medium of expression. Since the 1980s, a significant amount of poetry, fiction, and dramas has been produced by a growing number of ethnic minority authors, and some of them draw on their bilingual specialties. Bender introduces them by major ethnic groups (e.g., Uygur, Hui, Korean, Mongolian, Tibetan, Yi) and references their representative works.

Given the limited space, this companion does not cover subgenres such as autobiography (Larson 1991; L. Wang 2004), children's literature (Farquhar 1999; K. Foster, 2013), the political novel (Kinkley 2007), reportage (Laughlin, 2002), and travel writing (Teng 2004). Additional subgenres (e.g., detective stories, science fiction, and eco-writing) have yet to receive sustained scholarship in English, while other types of writing such as urban literature, regional literature, and Internet literature are considered in the next part on cultures and media.

Part III: Cultures and Media

Part III explores modern Chinese literature in relation to various cultures and media. In his deliberation on aesthetics and literature in modern China, Ban Wang reconfirms the primacy of the political function of literature through aesthetics in Chapter 17, "Use in Uselessness: How Western Aesthetics Made Chinese Literature More Political." Wang contends that, in the introduction of Western aesthetics into Chinese literature, a narrow notion of aesthetic qualities as transcendent of history and politics has become the mainstream. Taking issue with this aesthetic view, he shows that, rather than seeking intrinsic qualities in literature, critics schooled in aesthetics and concerned with China tended to engage aesthetics in a manner that links literature to the broad horizons of culture, morality, and politics. Following the classical imperative that literature must carry the *Dao*, pioneer writers such as Wang Guowei, Huang Moxi, and Lu Xun are shown to engage aesthetics in their literary criticism in response to the moral and political crises of their times.

In a sense, Ban Wang revisits an earlier tradition of aesthetic politics in the late Qing that would become dominant from the May Fourth all the way to Mao's aesthetics. Elsewhere, Wang has identified a sublime figure of history running through modern China (B. Wang 1997), and Liu Kang (2000) has further explored the intricate connection of this branch of Chinese aesthetics to Western Marxism. Switching the focus from aesthetics to language itself, Chen Jianhua takes a more cautious view of literary revolution than Ban Wang in Chapter 18, "The Linguistic Turns and Literary Fields in Twentieth-Century China." It is well known that the centrality of vernacular language established in the May Fourth period dominated the literary field in modern China, yet by contextualizing this radical "linguistic turn," Chen excavates its repressed other: the writers of "national essence" (*guocui*) who lost their voice after the early 1920s debate with May Fourth writers mainly because they stood by the classical language. Chen's analysis of linguistic polemics involves Lu Xun, Mao Dun, Zhou Shoujuan, Wang Zengqi, and Zheng Min, and shows their diverse linguistic and literary theories and practices with regard to issues of tradition and modernity, revolution and reform, politics and aesthetics, and nationalism and print capitalism. From the 1980s onward, in a climate of "farewell to revolution," the classical language is revived as a new cultural fashion. Along with collective critiques of May Fourth radicalism, a new Han language consciousness has emerged as a paradoxically local response to the pressure of globalization.

Chen Jianhua's discussion of the fates of Chinese tradition echoes Zhang Longxi's contextual approach to literary modernity and Yvonne Chang's comparative perspective on Taiwan's search for a locally based literary institution during the colonial period. As with aesthetics, language is equally enmeshed with a local or regional culture, and dialects, accents, and linguistic styles are developed to enrich literary or other artistic expressions and to articulate distinct local and regional consciousness (Gunn 1991; Gunn 2006; G. Zhou 2011; Jin Liu 2013). One of the earliest groups of regional writers to attract critical attention in modern China came from Northeast

China. In Chapter 19, "The Significance of the Northeastern Writers in Exile, 1931–1945," Haili Kong examines the emergence of this group in relation to both regional culture and the particular pattern of literary sponsorship in Republican China. Kong delineates the trajectory of literary careers of three major Northeastern writers—Xiao Jun, Xiao Hong, and Duanmu Hongliang—that intersect with national, ideological, and personal crises. The Japanese occupation of Northeast China drew national attention to the region, but the leftist patronage (e.g., Lu Xun, Mao Dun, and Zheng Zhenduo) played a decisive role in promoting these young writers, who brought a new type of realism to Shanghai's literary circles. Kong's approach is author studies, which portrays these writers as idiosyncratic and which enumerates their aesthetic contributions to the subgenres of the epic novel, pastoral–elegiac fiction, and stories of the war. Their native-soil flavor and panoramic description of Northeastern life brought in refreshing perspectives on the lost Manchuria and further cultivated patriotism among general readers in South China.

Haili Kong's chapter touches on the mechanism of literary sponsorship through literary journals and literary societies, which was an important aspect of literary culture in Republican China (Hockx 2003; Denton and Hockx 2008), and which often concentrated in urban centers. The crucial importance of Shanghai to the literary field in the late Qing and Republican periods has been proven time and again (L. Lee 1999b; Des Forges 2007; S. Shen 2009), and the rural–urban continuum in Chinese urban imagination is often filtered through the contrast between Beijing and Shanghai (Y. Zhang 1996; Shih 2001), although this contrast has found new configurations in postsocialist China (Visser 2010). The challenge of writing cities, therefore, runs through the entire history of modern Chinese literature.

In Chapter 20, "Writing Cities," Weijie Song charts modern Chinese literary representations of major cities from the late nineteenth century to the present. He addresses a wide array of issues specific to different cities, such as literary modernity, urban awareness, historical consciousness, individual/collective memories, and nationalist perceptions regarding the old and new capital, Beijing; the semi-colonial metropolis and socialist Shanghai and their remnants; the traumatized and decadent Nanjing; the abandoned capital, Xi'an; Taipei under Japanese colonial rule and the subsequent Nationalist Party dominance; and Hong Kong from a British Crown Colony to a Special Administrative Region of the PRC. Concentrating on the nexus of the city in literature and literature in the city, Song provides a nuanced mapping of modern Chinese literary narrative, urban imagination, and cultural memory against the downfall of the Manchu Empire, the rise of the modern nation-state, the 1949 great divide, and the formation of a post–Cold War world of globalization. As more and more Chinese now live in urban areas, the city will surely take on more importance in Chinese literature.

In Chapter 21, "Divided Unities of Modern Chinese Literature and Visual Culture: The Modern Girl, Woodcuts, and Contemporary Painter–Poets," Paul Manfredi (Wei Pu) conceives of "divided unity" as a paradoxical concept predicated on the fundamental confluence of literary and artistic practices in traditional China, the relative disparateness of the two media in early modernity, and a resurgence of word–image overlay in the new century. He illustrates such divided unities with three specific instances of word–image interaction: first, literary images of the Modern Girl in the early twentieth century whose meanings are contested through gendered configurations; second, the woodcut movement of the mid-twentieth century in which an indigenous art form was expediently reinvented to serve the urgent goals of national salvation (*jiuwang*) and Communist revolution; third, the phenomenon of the poet–painter since the 2000s when China's drastically changed socioeconomic condition has compelled a group of avant-garde artists to reclaim a lost tradition of word–image symbiosis and contemplate on a globalizing world in new media. Evocative in his analysis, Manfredi demonstrates that modern Chinese literature's relation to visual culture is an intriguing area in need of further exploration (L. Lee 1999b; Kuo 2007; X. Tang 2008; Visser 2010; Pickowicz, Shen, and Zhang 2013).

Moving beyond the literary and visual realms, the last two chapters in this part deal with the technological impact of media on literature. In his deliberation on literature and print media, Nicolai Volland (Fu Lang) offers an alternative print-centered view of literary history in Chapter 22, "All the Literature That's Fit to Print: A Print Culture Perspective on Modern Chinese Literature." The rise of modern Chinese literature has been closely intertwined with the evolution of the print media. The new platforms for the publication and dissemination of literary works not just altered the economics of literary consumption, but had direct impact on the aesthetic, formal, and social dimensions of literary production in modern China. Volland focuses on two problems: the rise of new media, and the emergence of new sites of organization. Since the late nineteenth century, new channels of publication, such as newspapers, journals, and collectanea (*congshu*), provided new outlets for creative writing; meanwhile, the physical shape of the book changed fundamentally. The availability of diverse media increased the choices available to both writers and readers, while having a direct impact on literary forms and styles. At the same time, the rise of new institutions, such as the modern publishing house and the editorial offices of journals, created unprecedented opportunities for writers to interact and participate in the larger processes of literary production and circulation. Volland traces the role of print culture in the making of modern Chinese literature from the late Qing through the 1920s–1930s, the socialist period, and the postsocialist era. He reassesses the importance of print culture for a new understanding of modern Chinese literature by focusing on some key moments in the history of both print culture and modern Chinese literature as a whole.

In the new millennium, the print media still plays a significant role in generating bestsellers (S. Kong 2005) and cultivating middleclass taste (Y. Zheng 2013), but the representative new media this time is the Internet, and its impact on literature is tremendous (J. Feng 2013; Hockx 2014; S. Kong 2014). In Chapter 23, "The Proliferating Genre: Web-Based Time-Travel Fiction and the New Media in Contemporary China," Jin Feng uses a subgenre of Internet literature as a revealing case to explore the effects of technology and new media on modern Chinese literature and culture. She first traces the origin and evolution of Chinese Web literature, including a discussion of the politics and economics of Web publishing. She then outlines salient characteristics of Web novels, such as their common plots, tropes, and devices. Finally, she examines new writing and reading practices that the Internet has inculcated and the unique aesthetics and ethos that Web fiction embodies. Despite the perceived lack of social consciousness and writing skills often associated with it, Feng argues that Chinese Web fiction is characterized not only by sheer enthusiasm and the social energy it generates, but also by narrative innovations and border crossings that it makes possible.

Part IV: Issues and Debates

Given a great variety of issues and debates related to modern Chinese literature, Part IV only selects a few of them for scrutiny. One large issue is the classification of realism, romanticism, and modernism. Constructed respectively as *liupai* (school), *sichao* (trend), and *meixue* (aesthetics), realism has long been canonized as the mainstream in modern Chinese literature; modernism, on the contrary, was overlooked in literary scholarship until the 1980s (Fitzgerald 2013). In Chapter 24, "The Persistence of Form: Nation, Literary Movement, and the Fiction of Ng Kim Chew," Carlos Rojas (Luo Peng) uses a small case to glimpse at the big picture. Through a detailed analysis of "The Disappearance of M" (1990), a short story by Sinophone author Ng Kim Chew (Huang Jinshu), Rojas examines the relationship between literary movements such as modernism, realism, and nativism on the one hand, and national literary formations such Chinese, Taiwanese, and Malaysian Chinese literature on the other. While these two sets of categories might appear to obey very different taxonomical logics, with literary movements reflecting a process of imitation while national literatures are assumed to be determined by the work's origin and the identity of the author, Rojas asserts that the logic of imitation actually plays a critical role in shaping national or transnational literary formations as well.

Similar to Carlos Rojas, Tze-lan Sang (Sang Zilan) tackles the big issue of gender and sexuality through a close reading in Chapter 25, "The Modern Girl in Modern Chinese Literature." In the large body of research on gender and sexuality in modern Chinese literature, the literary representation of the Modern Girl in Republican China stands out as one of the most generative questions. Instead of focusing on visual representation as Manfredi does in Chapter 21, Sang revisits the Modern Girl first by providing an overview of existing scholarly approaches. She then reminds us that the representation of the Chinese Modern Girl occurred not only in literature but also in a multiplicity of representational genres and media (e.g., fiction, cartoons, films, advertisement drawings, journalistic reports). She reestablishes the linkages between fictional representation and some of the most common motifs that ran through the cacophonous mass media debate over the Modern Girl during the 1930s–1940s, and contends that the Modern Girl was a chameleon-like enigma over whose definition intense ideological struggles were waged. Her analysis of modernist writers such as Ye Lingfeng reveals that the Modern Girl is depicted as an unhappy heterosexual: she is either under pressure to settle for financial security rather than true love or is betrayed or misunderstood by her male lovers. If the Modern Girl was a product of both capitalist consumer culture and a modern sexual ideology that lionized women's desire for men, Chinese literary depictions of the Modern Girl nevertheless foregrounds the discontents of both capitalist material culture and modern heterosexual liberation.

There is a substantial body of English scholarship on gender and sexuality in modern Chinese literature (R. Chow 1991b; Barlow 1993; T. Lu 1993; Lieberman 1998; J. Liu 2003), and, besides femininity and feminism (Dooling 2005; H. Yan 2006; A. Zhu 2007), critics have also examined questions of masculinity (X. Zhong 2000; Louie 2002), homosexuality (T. Sang 2003), and queer representations (F. Martin 2003; Chiang and Heinrich 2013). More recently, these issues have also been investigated from the new perspective of the body and science. In Chapter 26, "Body as Phenomenon: A Brief Survey of Secondary Literature of the Body in Modern Chinese Literature and Culture," Ari Larissa Heinrich (Han Rui) introduces existing approaches to science, corporeality, and modern Chinese literature with an eye toward suggesting a critical genealogy of methodologies leading into the present day. The chapter begins with a discussion of critical approaches to the body in Chinese literature from the 1980s onrward (looking in particular at feminist approaches to gendered corporeality in analyses of writing by women). It then examines intersections between science studies and humanities scholarship from the 1990s, and finally reviews recent key contributions to the increasingly sophisticated application of science history and history of the body to literary studies in modern Chinese literature. Some of the issues surveyed include realism and the body, women's bodies, gendered bodies from a science perspective, and the pathological body.

The next two chapters form a cluster on memory and trauma, two interrelated issues in modern Chinese literature that have engaged several scholars (X. Yang 2002; Braester 2003; B. Wang 2004; M. Berry 2008). In Chapter 27, "The Post-Maoist Politics of Memory," Yomi Braester (Bai Youming) suggests that the post-Maoist period may be characterized by three main approaches to memory. The state-sponsored media reappropriate remembrance in a highly selective form; dissidents repudiate the collective amnesia brought about by the repeated erasure of public records; and others endorse a cynical view, whereby forgetting becomes playful and noncommittal. Postsocialist literature has closely followed these trends, and Braester discusses the political, social, and cultural implications of reportage, memoirs, and especially fiction, and provides a detailed analysis of Chan Koonchung's *Fat Years* and Wang Shuo's *Playing for Thrills* as two very different approaches to memory.

While Yomi Braester presents remembrance and forgetting as equally viable responses to issues of memory, Lingchei Letty Chen (Chen Lingqi) emphasizes the tremendous efforts of contemporary PRC writers in retrieving repressed memories and confronting devastating traumas of revolution and repression in Chapter 28, "Writing Historical Traumas in the Everyday." She examines innovative new ways in which these writers represent impacts of trauma on individuals who are caught in the midst of violence or who live in the aftermath. Through reading selected literary texts, she shows how Chinese avant-garde fiction delineates the juncture of violence and the everyday life in which cruelty and irrationality are witnessed repeatedly, especially through children's eyes. Experimental writing in this case becomes an effective means of historical testimony and personal remembrance.

The last two chapters of this companion offer overviews of Chinese and English scholarship, respectively. In Chapter 29, "A Brief Overview of Chinese-Language Scholarship on Modern Chinese Literature," Chen Sihe divides the development of modern Chinese literature as a new discipline in mainland China into three phases. The first phase of New Literature studies (1917–1949) pursued literary criticism at the same time when new trends in literary production occurred, and *The Compendium of Chinese New Literature* (*Zhongguo xin wenxue daxi*, 1935) was a major achievement then (Zhao Jiabi 1935). The second phase of modern literature studies (1949–1985) refashioned "modern" as a political concept, defined literature as part of state ideological apparatuses, and instituted modern Chinese literature as a discipline where a group of specialists were produced. The third phrase of modern and contemporary literature (1985 to the present) has witnessed the spread of "twentieth-century literature" as a concept that seeks to transcend the rigid demarcation of modern and contemporary literature and enables scholars to study the literary development of the entire century as a whole, stretching all the way to current trends and future orientations.

Compared with Chinese scholarship, English scholarship is much more obsessed with literary modernity. In Chapter 30, "Toward a Typology of Literary Modernity in China: A Survey of English Scholarship on Modern Chinese Literature," I differentiate five phases of modernity in China as they are formulated in recent critical works. First, incipient modernities in the late Qing are marked by its cultural logic of heteroglossia and its wishful indulgence in decadence and mimicry. Second, translated modernity of the May Fourth period is characterized by its enlightenment rhetoric and its radical binarism of revolution. Third, urban modernities of the Republican era—especially in its "semicolonial" configuration in Shanghai—are energized by an ever-renewed fascination with the glossy surfaces of materiality and an unabashed display of hybridity along with cosmopolitan sensibility. Fourth, socialist modernity excels in staging glorious life as a grand spectacle and inducing the ecstatic experience of the revolutionary utopia, thereby aspiring to an alternative to capitalist modernity. Finally, aesthetic modernity of the postsocialist era began in its first decade with a return to the May Fourth rhetoric of enlightenment by championing culture over politics, but only to depart, since its second decade, from utopian intellectualism into a sober, at times cynical or even pessimistic, confrontation with an all-powerful consumer culture. This typological survey shows how critical endeavors have evolved in the field since the early 1990s, where debates on modernity, postmodernism, and postsocialism have positioned scholars to new challenges posed by globalization.

Conclusion: Tracking Scholarly Trajectories

After a summary of all 29 chapters in the preceding sections, it is fair at this point to admit what this companion does not aspire to be. First, it is not a comprehensive overview of all conceivable aspects of modern Chinese literature, including movements, schools, genres, authors, texts, styles, and themes, although such efforts have been made occasionally (Doleželová-Velingerová 1987; Slupski 1987; Haft 1988; Eberstein 1989; Mostow 2003: 285–616; Denton forthcoming). Second, it is not a general narrative literary history, although such a volume is urgently needed half a century after C. T. Hsia's pioneering attempt on fiction (1961).[7] Third, it is not a selective guide to representative authors and works, which is obtainable from biographical dictionaries (Moran 2006; Moran and Ye 2013), interviews (L. Leung 1994), and self-portrayals (H. Martin and Kinkley 1992).

With this caveat in place, we can now take another look at author studies as one major area of literary studies that is not adequately covered in this companion.[8] A salient feature of English scholarship in its moment of initial growth, author studies has remained a reliable, albeit by now secondary method. In Lu Xun studies, scholars have revisited his old-style poems (Kowallis 1996), his prose collection *Wild Grass* (Kaldis 2014), his fictional character Ah Q and Ah Q progeny (P. Foster 2006), his love lives (McDougall 2002), his contemplations on the past (E. Cheng 2013), revolution (G. Davies 2013), evolution (Pusey 1998; A. Jones 2011), and violence (E. S. Chou 2012). Contrary to a veritable boom of books in Chinese scholarship, Eileen Chang has received no exclusive monograph treatment, although two volumes came out recently (Louie 2013; Peng and Dilley 2014), and discussions of her works are scattered in various English books. Significantly, except for Ding Ling (Alber 2002; Alber 2004), Guo Moruo (Xiaoming Chen 2008), and Tian Han (L. Luo 2014), the majority of recent monographs on a single author from the late Qing and Republican periods deal with "conservative" or non-leftist writers, such as Dai Wangshu (G. Lee 1989), Lao She (Witchard 2012), Lin Shu (Hill 2012), Lin Yutang (S. Qian 2011), Shen Congwen (Kinkley 1987), Wu Zuxiang (P. Williams 1993), Zhang Henshui (McClellan 2005), and Zhou Zuoren (Daruvala 2000). Several post-Mao writers have been graced with exclusive attention in a monograph—Bei Dao (Dian Li 2006), Dai Houying (Pruyn 1988), Gao Xingjian (H. Zhao 2000; Quah 2004; Łabędzka 2008; Yeung 2008; M. Lee 2012), Haizi (Kunze 2012), Han Shaogong (Leenhouts 2005), Jia Pingwa (Y. Wang 2006), Su Tong and Yu Hua (Hua Li 2011).[9] As the first ethnic Chinese to win the Nobel Prize in Literature, considerable critical limelight on Gao Xingjian is understandable, but so far there is only one English monograph on Mo Yan (S. W. Chan 2011), the first Chinese national to win the Nobel Prize in Literature.

Regardless, this sample list of monographs does not fully represent the scholarly trend because many writers, such as Eileen Chang and Mo Yan, are discussed in single-authored books (e.g., X. Wang 2013) and critical volumes (e.g., Duran and Huang 2014) that address specific issues across historical periods and geographic areas, which is a preferred approach in English scholarship after the early 1990s. Judging from the titles of recent English books, we notice that these key issues cover a wide spectrum, ranging from agency (Knight 2006), identity (L. L. Chen 2006; Tsu 2006; Shih 2007), self (Denton 1998; Tam and Yip 2010), subject (R. Cai 2004; P. Liu 2011), love (J. Liu 2003; H. Lee 2007) to power (Feuerwerker 1998), justice (Kinkley 2000), evolution (Pusey 1998; A. Jones 2011), and the past (B. Wang 2004; Choy 2008; M. Gao 2008; Stuckey 2010), although ideology, politics, and revolution still occur most frequently in book titles.

Finally, we may conclude this introduction by returning to literary polemics, which often signal paradigmatic changes in the literary institution, as suggested in my survey of pre-1990s English scholarship earlier in this introduction. Three critical exchanges are related to the 1993 *Modern China* debate. First, in his response to Liu Kang's predisposition for politicization, Zhang Longxi discusses a prior polemic triggered by Stephen Owen's dismissal of Bei Dao's poems as belonging to a derivative kind of world poetry, which appears to the Western audience as "translations of a poetry that originally grew out of reading translations of our own poetic heritage" (1990: 29). In her rejoinder, Michelle Yeh questions Owen's rigid conceptualization of China and the West "as mutually exclusive" and his own anxiety—both "the anxiety of difference (between tradition and modernity)" and "the anxiety of the dissolution of difference (between China and the world)" (M. Yeh 1991a: 95–96). Second, Zhang Longxi critiques Rey Chow (Zhou Lei) for relying on Western theory when she responded to the shock of the Tiananmen Incident in 1989 with "a set of questions that pertain more closely to us in the U.S., where … China is … a spectacle for the West" (Chow 1991a: 82–83). For Zhang (1992b: 127), precisely due to "the skeptical and sometimes even agnostic attitude characteristic of much of contemporary Western theory," Western or Western-centered critics often indulge in their own rhetoric while failing to understand Chinese reality. Third, a 1995 critical debate in the Hong Kong-based journal *Twenty-First Century* (Ershiyi shiji) concerns Western theory—especially the so-called "post-isms" (*houxue*, including postmodernism and postcolonialism) that is relabeled as "Chinese new conservatism" (H. Zhao 1997)—and Chinese identity, as Chinese critics began to differentiate between those educated inside and outside the PRC. In her intervention, Michelle Yeh (2000: 272) cautions against the rise of cultural nationalism in Chinese academia and advocates "a transnational identity or positionality that challenges and problematizes the reification of China and the West, inside and outside, native and foreign."

In the twenty-first century, the generality of Chinese reality versus Western theory no longer preoccupies the majority of scholars because theories—now understood to encompass both Chinese and Western—are considered part of the institution of modern Chinese literature on both sides of the Pacific, although there is no consensus as to what theory is most needed for further developing the field. In the PRC, a persistent contention exists between two large ideological camps—the Neo-Liberalism (*xin ziyou zhuyi*) versus the New Left (*xin zuopai*)—whose disciplinary coverage extends beyond the humanities into social sciences. Curiously, there has been no corresponding debate in North America, even though as a leading New Left proponent, Wang Hui, has published books in English (2003; 2009; 2011). Whether a few recent books on the socialist legacy and New Left visions (B. Wang 2011; B. Wang and Lu 2012; X. Zhong and Wang 2014) would change the situation remains to be seen.

Just as English scholarship in North America shows little interest in the New Left debate in the PRC, Chinese scholarship pays scant attention to a new polemic on Sinophone studies in English scholarship. The polemic started when Shu-mei Shih (Shi Shumei) offers a controversial definition of the Sinophone as "a network of places of cultural production outside China and on the margins of China and Chineseness, where a historical process of heterogenizing and localizing of continental Chinese culture has been taking place for several centuries" (2007: 4). For Shih, the Sinophone "subverts fixed identities," "interrupts fixity," and "disrupts the symbolic totality" (2007: 35), while "foregrounding the value of difficulty, difference, and heterogeneity" (2007: 5). Critical of Shih's narrow territorial vision (S. Lu 2008), Sheldon Lu (Lu Xiaopeng) further contrasts these two definitions of the Sinophone (2012: 24): one includes China, as does his work on Sinophone cinema (S. Lu 2007: 161–163), whereas the other excludes China, as does Shih. After a subsequent elaboration of the Sinophone as both theory and history (Shih 2011), Shih clarifies that her definition of the Sinophone as situated "on the margins of China and Chineseness ... was never intended to exclude China, but to give space for minoritized and colonized voices within China, be they Tibetan, Mongolian or Uyghur" (2012: 5). Nonetheless, Shih's passing mention of ethnic minorities in the PRC does not alter the fact that the predominant examples of her Sinophone articulations (2007) come from the United States, Taiwan, and Hong Kong.

In Sheldon Lu's characterization (2012: 22), Shih's vision of the Sinophone carries an ideological bent—"anti-Sinocentrism"—but Shih would rather save "Sino" for the Sinophone and sets as her target "Han-centrism" and "China-centrism" (2007: 23, 31), since she prefers "the heterogeneity of Sinitic languages" and intentionally avoids "such constructs as 'China', 'Chinese', and 'Chineseness'" (2007: 4), all of them judged to be "terms of conflation and manipulation" (2007: 25). However, China cannot be simply wished away because it is more than a mere construct; historically and theoretically, China and the Chinese are more heterogeneous than Shih's definition of the Sinophone allows. For better or worse, Jing Tsu (Shi Jingyuan) affirms, "the ethnicizing marker 'Chinese' in Western academic discourse ... survives its conceptual contradictions as a necessary specter for comparisons and contestations" (2010: 714). Again, the Chinese is more than a specter that haunts a scholar's conscience, for it carries with it all the complexities of history, geography, identity, and textuality that have shaped modern Chinese literature and literary scholarship around the world. As Arif Dirlik (De Like) perceptively observes in his rejoinder to the polemic that further involves Asian American studies, "If there is any point to the Sinophone ... as a criterion for mapping literature and culture, it is to call for a spatiality that enables dialogue between different, place-based, histories in the creation of a new cosmopolitan space of 'Chineseness'" (2013).

Notwithstanding rhetorical flourishes, it is encouraging to see the positive outcome of Sinophone studies in bringing into view Southeast Asia, especially Sinophone Malaysian literature (Groppe 2013; E. K. Tan 2013). Yet, whether Hong Kong and Taiwan would benefit from this new development remains unclear. After all, even though Taiwanese literature was introduced to North America as early as the 1960s, very few Taiwan writers have received an exclusive monograph treatment in English scholarship (Ross 1974; L. Wong 2009). In light of this imbalance, the Sinophone is a welcome addition in the critical approaches to modern Chinese literature and culture. Indeed, the fact that the Sinophone polemic has attracted participants mostly from within modern Chinese literature and culture—some doubled institutionally in comparative literature—reaffirms that the field is now mature enough to accommodate different scholarly approaches and critical positions.

NOTES

1   As a linguistic designation, the Sinophone does not cover *Huaren wenxue* (literature by ethnic Chinese in a language other than Chinese), which includes "Chinese literatures in English" (Khoo and Louie 2005).

2   Carlos Rojas is perhaps the only exception in English scholarship because he prefers pluralization in "Chinese cinemas" (Rojas and Chow 2013) and "modern Chinese literatures" (Rojas and Bachner 2016).

3   Issued 12 years apart, these Twayne monographs deal with individual writers such as Ba Jin (N. Mao 1978), Cao Yu (J. Hu 1972), Feng Zhi (D. Cheung 1979), Li Boyuan (Lancashire 1981), Shen Congwen (Nieh 1972), Su Manshu (W. Liu 1972), Xiao Hong (Goldblatt 1976), Qian Zhongshu (Huters 1982), Wen Yiduo (K. Hsu 1980), Zeng Pu (P. Li 1980), and Zhou Zuoren (Wolff 1971), in addition to one writer from Taiwan, Jiang Gui (Ross 1974). Significantly, this series already included late Qing writers as part of modern Chinese literature.

4   Literary anthologies are indispensable to the institutionalization of literary studies in Chinese as well as in English. The earliest English anthologies that feature selections of modern Chinese literature include Birch (1972); another important anthology is Lau, Hsia, and Lee (1981). For a survey of modern Chinese literature in English translation, see Kinkley (1994).

5   As Duke (1993: 64; emphasis added) claims, "Literature is always concerned with abiding moral problems and value conflicts that arise between and within individual human beings in their living experience of the *universal*

human emotions of love and hate, the *universal* human conflicts between self and other, humanity and nature, and the *universal* human predicament of good and evil."

6   Regrettably, the limited space makes it impossible to cover a great number of articles in academic journals and critical volumes, but readers are advised to consult, in particular, *Modern Chinese Literature*, edited by Howard Goldblatt (Ge Haowen), which changed to *Modern Chinese Literature and Culture*, edited by Kirk Denton (Deng Tengke). In addition to an early list provided by Jeffrey Kinkley (Jin Jiefu) that includes *Australian Journal of Chinese Affairs* (now *China Journal*), *China Information*, *China Quarterly*, *Chinese Literature: Essays, Articles, Reviews* (*CLEAR*), *Modern China*, *Positions*, *Tamkang Review*, and *World Literature Today* (1994: 1265), other journals such as the following also publish English articles on modern Chinese literature and culture: *Boundary 2*, *Chinese Literature Today*, *Comparative Literature Studies*, *Frontiers of Literary Studies in China*, *Harvard Journal of Asiatic Studies*, *Inter-Asia Cultural Studies*, *Journal of Asian Studies*, *Journal of Contemporary China*, *New Left Review*, *New Literary History*, and *Social Text*. An extensive, periodically updated online English bibliography is the Modern Chinese Literature and Culture Resource Center, maintained by Kirk Denton (http://u.osu.edu/mclc).

7   Peculiarly, English scholarship on modern Chinese literature has consistently bypassed full-length narrative history, so far with only one possible exception (McDougall and Louie 1997), which resembles a reference work.

Sometimes, multi-authored chapters or sections on modern Chinese literature are tagged on toward the end of a general history of Chinese literature (Mair 2001; K. Chang and Owen 2010: 413–714). The good news is that a comprehensive literary history of modern China is finally in production (D. Wang 2016).

8 Two related areas are not represented in this companion: first, literature and translation (Eoyang 1992; Eoyang and Lin 1995; L. Liu 1999; Gamsa 2008; L. Chan 2010; McDougall 2011; St. André and Peng 2012; Tam and Chan 2012; L. Wong 2013; H. Peng and Rabut 2014), which may also include film adaptations of literature (Deppman 2010; H. Peng and Dilley 2014); second, reception of literature, including audience studies, both domestic (Link 2000; S. Kong 2005; K. Hang 2013; Y. Zheng 2013) and overseas (Mair 2001: 1079-104; L. Chan 2003; McDougall 2003; Lovell 2006).

9 This sampling of English books does not include titles in comparative literature that compare a Chinese writer with one or more Western writers in relation to specific genres and issues.

REFERENCES

Alber, Charles J. 2002. *Enduring the Revolution: Ding Ling and the Politics of Literature in Guomindang China*. Westport, CT: Praeger.

Alber, Charles J. 2004. *Embracing the Life: Ding Ling and the Politics of Literature in the PRC*. Westport, CT: Praeger.

Barlow, Tani E. Ed. 1993. *Gender Politics in Modern China: Writing and Feminism*. Durham, NC: Duke University Press.

Barmé, Geremie R. 1999. *In the Red: On Contemporary Chinese Culture*. New York: Columbia University Press.

Berninghausen, John, and Ted Huters. Eds. 1976. *Revolutionary Literature in China: An Anthology*. White Plains, NY: M. E. Sharpe.

Berry, Michael. 2008. *The History of Pain: Trauma in Modern Chinese Literature and Film*. New York: Columbia University Press.

Birch, Cyril. Ed. 1972. *Anthology of Chinese Literature*. 2 vols. New York: Grove Press.

Braester, Yomi. 2003. *Witness against History: Literature, Film and Public Discourse in Twentieth-Century China*. Stanford, CA: Stanford University Press.

Button, Peter. 2009. *Configurations of the Real in Chinese Literary and Aesthetic Modernity*. Leiden: Brill.

Cai, Rong. 2004. *The Subject in Crisis in Contemporary Chinese Literature*. Honolulu: University of Hawaii Press.

Chan, Koonchung. 2011. *The Fat Years: A Novel*. Trans. Michael Duke. Random House, Google eBook.

Chan, Leo Tak-Hung. 2010. *Readers, Reading and Reception of Translated Fiction in Chinese: Novel Encounters*. Manchester, UK: St. Jerome Publications.

Chan, Leo Tak-Hung. Ed. 2003. *One into Many: Translation and the Dissemination of Classical Chinese Literature*. Amsterdam: Rodopi.

Chan, Shelley W. 2011. *A Subversive Voice in China: The Fictional World of Mo Yan*. Amherst, NY: Cambria Press.

Chang, Kang-i Sun, and Stephen Owen. Eds. 2010. *The Cambridge History of Chinese Literature, Volume II: From 1375*. Cambridge, UK: Cambridge University Press.

Chang, Sung-sheng Yvonne. 1993. *Modernism and the Nativist Resistance: Contemporary Chinese Fiction from Taiwan*. Durham, NC: Duke University Press.

Chang, Sung-sheng Yvonne. 2004. *Literary Culture in Taiwan: Martial Law to Market Law*. New York: Columbia University Press.

Chen, Jianguo. 2009. *The Aesthetics of the "Beyond": Phantasm, Nostalgia, and the Literary Practice in Contemporary China*. Newark: University of Delaware Press.

Chen, Lingchei Letty. 2006. *Writing Chinese: Reshaping Chinese Cultural Identity*. New York: Palgrave Macmillan.

Chen, Sihe陳思和and Wang Dewei 王德威. Eds. 2011. *Jiangou Zhongguo wenxue xiandai duoyuan gong-sheng tixi de xin sikao*建構中國現代文學多元共生體系的新思考 (New thoughts on constructing a multivalent and symbiotic system of modern Chinese literature). Shanghai: Fudan daxue chubanshe.

Chen, Xiaomei. 1995. *Occidentalism: A Theory of Counter-discourse in Post-Mao China*. New York: Oxford University Press.

Chen, Xiaomei. 2002a. *Acting the Right Part: Political Theater and Popular Drama in Contemporary China*. Honolulu: University of Hawaii Press.

Chen, Xiaomei. Ed. 2002b. *Reading the Right Text: An Anthology of Contemporary Chinese Drama*. Honolulu: University of Hawaii Press.

Chen, Xiaomei. Ed. 2010. *The Columbia Anthology of Modern Chinese Drama with a Critical Introduction*. New York: Columbia University Press.

Chen, Xiaomei. Forthcoming. *Performing Chinese Revolution: Founding Fathers, Red Classics, and Revisionist Histories of Twentieth-Century China*. New York: Columbia University Press.

Chen, Xiaoming. 2008. *From the May Fourth Movement to the Communist Revolution: Guo Moruo and the Chinese Path to Communism*. Albany: State University of New York Press.

Chen, Yu-Shih. 1986. *Realism and Allegory in the Early Fiction of Mao Tun*. Bloomington: Indiana University Press.

Cheng, Eileen. 2013. *Literary Remains: Death, Trauma, and Lu Xun's Refusal to Mourn*. Honolulu: University of Hawaii Press.

Cheung, Dominic. 1979. *Feng Chih*. Boston: Twayne.

Chiang, Howard, and Ari Larissa Heinrich. Eds. 2013. *Queer Sinophone Cultures*. New York: Routledge.

Chou, Eva Shan. 2012. *Memory, Violence, Queues: Lu Xun Interprets China*. Ann Arbor, MI: Association for Asian Studies.

Chow, Rey. 1991a. "Violence in Other Country: China as Crisis, Spectacle, and Woman." In *Third World Women and the Politics of Feminism*. Edited by Mohanty, Chandra Talpade, Ann Russo, and Lourdes Torres. Bloomington: Indiana University Press. 81–100.

Chow, Rey. 1991b. *Woman and Chinese Modernity: The Politics of Reading between West and East*. Minneapolis: University of Minnesota Press.

Chow, Rey. Ed. 2000. *Modern Chinese Literary and Cultural Studies in the Age of Theory: Reimagining a Field*. Durham, NC: Duke University Press.

Choy, Howard Y. F. Ed. 2008. *Remapping the Past: Fictions of History in Deng's China, 1979–1997*. Leiden: Brill.

Conceison, Claire. 2004. *Significant Other: Staging the American in China*. Honolulu: University of Hawaii Press.

Crespi, John A. 2009. *Voices in Revolution: Poetry and the Auditory Imagination in Modern China*. Honolulu: University of Hawaii Press.

Daruvala, Susan. 2000. *Zhou Zuoren and an Alternative Response to Chinese Modernity*. Cambridge, MA: Harvard University Asia Center.

Davies, Gloria. 2013. *Lu Xun's Revolution: Writing in a Time of Violence*. Cambridge, MA: Harvard University Press.

Davies, Gloria. Ed. 2001. *Voicing Concerns: Contemporary Chinese Critical Inquiry*. Lanham, MD: Rowman and Littlefield.

Denton, Kirk A. 1998. *The Problematic of Self in Modern Chinese Literature: Hu Feng and Lu Ling*. Stanford, CA: Stanford University Press.

Denton, Kirk A Forthcoming. *The Columbia Companion to Modern Chinese Literature*. New York: Columbia University Press.

Denton, Kirk A., and Michel Hockx. Eds. 2008. *Literary Societies of Republican China*. Lanham, MD: Lexington Books.

Deppman, Hsiu-Chuang. 2010. *Adapted for the Screen: The Cultural Politics of Modern Chinese Fiction and Film*. Honolulu: University of Hawaii Press.

Des Forges, Alexander. 2007. *Mediasphere Shanghai: The Aesthetics of Cultural Production*. Honolulu: University of Hawaii Press.

Ding, Yi. 1955. *Zhongguo xiandai wenxue shilüe* (A brief history of modern Chinese literature). Beijing: Zuojia chubanshe.

Dirlik, Arif. 1989. "Postsocialism? Reflections on 'Socialism with Chinese Characteristics.'" In *Marxism and the Chinese Experience*. Edited by Arif Dirlik and Maurice Meisner. Armonk, NY: E. M. Sharpe. 362–384.

Dirlik, Arif, and Xudong Zhang. Eds. 2000. *Postmodernism and China*. Durham, NC: Duke University Press, 2000.

Doleželová-Velingerová, Milena. Ed. 1980. *The Chinese Novel at the Turn of the Century*. Toronto: University of Toronto Press.

Doleželová-Velingerová, Milena. Ed. 1987. *A Selective Guide to Chinese Literature, 1900–1949. Vol. I. The Novel*. Leiden: Brill.

Doleželová-Velingerová, Milena, and Oldřich Král. Eds. 2001. *The Appropriation of Cultural Capital: China's May Fourth Project*. Cambridge, MA: Harvard University Asia Center.

Dooling, Amy. 2005. *Women's Literary Feminism in Twentieth-Century China*. New York: Palgrave.

Duke, Michael S. 1985. *Blooming and Contending: Chinese Literature in the Post-Mao Era*. Bloomington: Indiana University Press.

Duke, Michael S. 1993. "Thoughts on Politics and Critical Paradigms in Modern Chinese Literature Studies." *Modern China*, 19.1: 41–70.

Duke, Michael S. Ed. 1989. *Modern Chinese Women Writers: Critical Appraisals*. Armonk, NY: M. E. Sharpe.

Duran, Angelica, and Yuhan Huang. Eds. 2014. *Mo Yan in Context: Nobel Laureate and Global Storyteller*. West Lafayette, IN: Purdue University Press.

Eagleton, Terry. 1983. *Literary Theory: An Introduction*. Oxford, UK: Basil Blackwell.

Eberstein, Bernd. Ed. 1989. *A Selective Guide to Chinese Literature, 1900–1949. Vol. IV. The Drama*. Leiden: Brill.

Eoyang, Eugene. 1992. *The Transparent Eye: Reflections on Translation, Chinese Literature, and Comparative Poetics*. Honolulu: University of Hawaii Press.

Eoyang, Eugene, and Lin Yao-fu. Eds. 1995. *Translating Chinese Literature*. Bloomington: Indiana University Press.

Farquhar, Mary Ann. 1999. *Children's Literature in China: From Lu Xun to Mao Zedong*. Armonk, NY: M. E. Sharpe.

Faurot, Jeannette L. 1980. *Chinese Fiction from Taiwan: Critical Perspectives*. Bloomington: University of Indiana Press.

Feng, Jin. 2004. *The New Woman in Early Twentieth-Century Chinese Fiction*. West Lafayette, IN: Purdue University Press.

Feng, Jin. 2013. *Romancing the Internet: Producing and Consuming Chinese Web Romance*. Leiden: Brill.

Ferrari, Rossella. 2012. *Pop Goes the Avant-garde: Experimental Theater in Contemporary China*. London: Seagull Books.

Feuerwerker, Yi-tsi Mei. 1982. *Ding Ling's Fiction: Ideology and Narrative in Modern Chinese Literature*. Cambridge, MA: Harvard University Press.

Feuerwerker, Yi-tsi Mei. 1998. *Ideology, Power, Text: Self-Representation and the Peasant "Other" in Modern Chinese Literature*. Stanford, CA: Stanford University Press.

Fitzerald, Carolyn. 2013. *Fragmenting Modernisms: Chinese Wartime Literature, Art, and Film, 1937–49*. Leiden: Brill.

Fokkema, Douwe W. 1965. *Literary Doctrine in China and Soviet Influence, 1956–1960*. The Hague: Mouton.

Foster, Kate. 2013. *Chinese Literature and the Child: Children and Childhood in Late-Twentieth-Century Chinese Fiction*. New York: Palgrave Macmillan.

Foster, Paul B. 2006. *Ah Q Archaeology: Lu Xun, Ah Q, Ah Q Progeny and the National Character Discourse in Twentieth Century China*. Lanham, MD: Lexington Books.

Gálik, Marián. 1969. *Mao Tun and Modern Chinese Literary Criticism*. Wiesbaden: F. Steiner.

Gálik, Marián. 1980. *The Genesis of Modern Chinese Literary Criticism (1917–1930)*. Trans. Peter Tkáč. London: Curzon Press.

Gálik, Marián. 1986. *Milestones in Sino-Western Literary Confrontation, 1898–1979*. Wiesbaden: Harrassowitz.

Gamsa, Mark. 2008. *The Chinese Translation of Russian Literature: Three Studies*. Leiden: Brill.

Gao, Mobo. 2008. *The Battle for China's Past: Mao and the Cultural Revolution*. London: Pluto Press.

Goldblatt, Howard. 1976. *Hsiao Hung*. Boston: Twayne.

Goldman, Merle. 1967. *Literary Dissent in Communist China*. Cambridge, MA: Harvard University Press.

Goldman, Merle. Ed. 1977. *Modern Chinese Literature in the May Fourth Era*. Cambridge, MA: Harvard University Press.

Gong, Haomin. 2012. *Uneven Modernity: Literature, Film, and Intellectual Discourse in Postsocialist China*. Honolulu: University of Hawaii Press.

Grieder, Jerome. 1970. *Hu Shih and the Chinese Renaissance*. Cambridge, MA: Harvard University Press.

Groppe, Alison. 2013. *Sinophone Malaysian Literature: Not Made in China*. Amherst, NY: Cambria Press.

Gunn, Edward M. 1980. *Unwelcome Muse: Chinese Literature in Shanghai and Peking, 1937–1945*. New York: Columbia University Press.

Gunn, Edward M. 1991. *Rewriting Chinese: Style and Innovation in Twentieth-Century Chinese Prose*. Stanford, CA: Stanford University Press.

Gunn, Edward M. 2006. *Rendering the Regional: Local Language in Contemporary Chinese Media*. Honolulu: University of Hawaii Press.

Haft, Lloyd. Ed. 1988. *A Selective Guide to Chinese Literature, 1900–1949. Vol. III. The Poem*. Leiden: Brill.

Hamm, John Christopher. 2005. *Paper Swordsmen: Jin Yong and the Modern Chinese Martial Arts Novel*. Honolulu: University of Hawaii Press.

Hanan, Patrick. 2004. *Chinese Fiction of the Nineteenth and Early Twentieth Centuries: Essays by Patrick Hanan*. New York: Columbia University Press.

Hang, Krista Van Fleit. 2013. *Literature the People Love: Reading Chinese Texts from the Early Maoist Period, 1949–1966*. New York: Palgrave Macmillan.

Hill, Michael Gibbs. 2012. *Lin Shu, Inc. Translation and the Making of Modern Chinese Culture*. Oxford, UK: Oxford University Press.

Hockx, Michel. 1994. *A Snowy Morning: Eight Chinese Poets on the Road to Modernity*. Leiden: Research School CNWS.

Hockx, Michel. Ed. 1999. *The Literary Field in Twentieth-Century China*. Honolulu: University of Hawaii Press.

Hockx, Michel. 2003. *Questions of Style: Literary Societies and Literary Journals in Modern China, 1911–1937*. Leiden: Brill.

Hockx, Michel. 2014. *Internet Literature in China*. New York: Columbia University Press.

Hohendahl, Peter Uwe. 1989. *Building a National Literature: The Case of Germany, 1830–1870*. Trans. Renate Baron Franciscono. Ithaca: Cornell University Press.

Hsia, C. T. 1961. *A History of Modern Chinese Fiction, 1917–1957*. New Haven, CT: Yale University Press.

Hsia, C. T. 1963. "On the 'Scientific' Study of Modern Chinese Literature: A Reply to Professor Průšek." *T'oung Pao* 50.4–5: 428–474.

Hsia, C. T. 1968. *The Classic Chinese Novel: A Critical Introduction*. New York: Columbia University Press.

Hsia, C. T. 1971. *A History of Modern Chinese Fiction*. Second edition. New Haven, CT: Yale University Press.

Hsia, C. T. 夏志清. 1979. *Zhongguo xiandai xiaoshuo shi* 中國現代小説史 (A history of modern Chinese fiction). Trans. Joseph S. M. Lau et al. Hong Kong: Union Press.

Hsia, C. T. 1999. *A History of Modern Chinese Fiction*. Third edition. Bloomington: Indiana University Press.

Hsia, C. T., and Joseph S. M. Lau. Eds. 1971. *Twentieth-Century Chinese Stories*. New York: Columbia University Press.

Hsia, Tsi-an. 1968. *The Gate of Darkness: Studies on the Leftist Literary Movement in China*. Seattle: University of Washington Press.

Hsiung, Yuwen. 2013. *Expressionism and Its Deformation in Contemporary Chinese Theatre*. New York: Peter Lang.

Hsu, Kai-yu. 1980. *Wen I-to*. Boston: Twayne.

Hsu, Kai-yu. Trans. and Ed. 1963. *Twentieth-Century Chinese Poetry: An Anthology*. Garden City, NY: Doubleday.

Hsu, Kai-yu. Ed. 1980. *Literature of the People's Republic of China*. Bloomington: Indiana University Press.

Hu, John Y. H. 1972. *Ts'ao Yü*. New York: Twayne.

Hu, Ying. 2000. *Tales of Translation: Composing the New Woman in China, 1898–1918*. Stanford, CA: Stanford University Press.

Huang, Nicole. 2005. *Women, War, Domesticity: Shanghai Literature and Popular Culture of the 1940s*. Leiden: Brill.

Huang, Yibing. 2007. *Contemporary Chinese Literature: From the Cultural Revolution to the Future*. New York: Palgrave Macmillan.

Hung, Chang-tai. 1985. *Going to the People: Chinese Intellectuals and Folk Literature, 1918–1937*. Cambridge, MA: Harvard Council on East Asian Studies.

Huss, Ann, and Jianmei Liu. Eds. 2007. *The Jin Yong Phenomenon: Chinese Martial Arts Fiction and Modern Chinese Literary History*. Yongstown, NY: Cambria Press.

Huters, Theodore. 1982. *Qian Zhongshu*. Boston: Twayne.

Huters, Theodore. Ed. 1990. *Reading the Modern Chinese Short Story*. Armonk, NY: M. E. Sharpe.

Huters, Theodore. 2005. *Bringing the World Home: Appropriating the West in Late Qing and Early Republican China*. Honolulu: University of Hawaii Press.

Jones, Andrew F. 2011. *Developmental Fairytales: Evolutionary Thinking and Modern Chinese Cultures*. Cambridge, MA: Harvard University Press.

Kaldis, Nicholas. 2014. *The Chinese Prose Poem: A Study of Lu Xun's Wild Grass (Yecao)*. Amherst, NY: Cambria Press.

Kao, Hsin-sheng C. Ed. 1993. *Nativism Overseas: Contemporary Chinese Women Writers*. Albany: State University of New York Press.

Khoo, Tseen, and Kam Louie. Eds. 2005. *Culture, Identity, Commodity: Diasporic Chinese Literatures in English*. Montréal: McGill-Queen's University Press.

King, Richard. 2014. *Milestones on a Golden Road: Writing for Chinese Socialism, 1945–80*. Hong Kong: Hong Kong University Press.

Kinkley, Jeffrey C. 1987. *The Odyssey of Shen Congwen*. Stanford, CA: Stanford University Press.

Kinkley, Jeffrey C. 1994. "The New Chinese Literature: The Mainland and Beyond." *Choice* 31.8: 1249–1265.

Kinkley, Jeffrey C. 2000. *Chinese Justice, the Fiction: Law and Literature in Modern China*. Stanford, CA: Stanford University Press.

Kinkley, Jeffrey C. 2007. *Corruption and Realism in Late Socialist China: The Return of the Political Novel*. Stanford, CA: Stanford University Press.

Kinkley, Jeffrey C. Ed. 1985. *After Mao: Chinese Literature and Society, 1978–1981*. Cambridge, MA: Harvard University Council on East Asian Studies.

Knight, Sabina. 2006. *The Heart of Time: Moral Agency in Twentieth-Century Chinese Fiction*. Cambridge, MA: Harvard University Asia Center.

Kong, Shuyu. 2005. *Consuming Literature: Best Sellers and the Commercialization of Literary Production in Contemporary China*. Stanford, CA: Stanford University Press.

Kong, Shuyu. 2014. *Popular Media, Social Emotion and Public Discourse in Contemporary China*. London: Routledge.

Kowallis, Jon Eugene von. 1996. *The Lyrical Lu Xun: A Study of His Classical-Style Verse*. Honolulu: University of Hawaii Press.

Kubin, Wolfgang, and Rudolf G. Wagner. Eds. 1982. *Essays in Modern Chinese Literature and Literary Criticism*. Bochum, Germany: Brockmeyer.

Kunze, Rui. 2012. *Struggle and Symbiosis: The Canonization of the Poet Haize and Cultural Discourses in Contemporary China*. Bochum: Projekt Verlag.

Kuo, Jason. Ed. 2007. *Visual Culture in Shanghai, 1850–1930*. Washington, D.C.: New Academia Publishing.

Łabędzka, Izabella. 2008. *Gao Xingjian's Idea of Theatre: From the Word to the Image*. Leiden: Brill.

Lancashire, Douglas. 1981. *Li Po-yuan*. Boston: Twayne.

Lang, Olga. 1967. *Pa Chin and His Writings: Chinese Youth Between the Two Revolutions*. Cambridge, MA: Harvard University Press.

Larson, Wendy. 1991. *Literary Authority and the Modern Chinese Writer: Ambivalence and Autobiography*. Durham, NC: Duke University Press.

Larson, Wendy. 1998. *Women and Writing in Modern China*. Stanford, CA: Stanford University Press.

Larson, Wendy, and Anne Wedell-Wedellsborg. Eds. 1993. *Inside Out: Modernism and Postmodernism in Chinese Literary Culture*. Aarhus, Denmark: Aarhus University Press.

Lau, Joseph S. M. 1970. *Ts'ao Yü, the Reluctant Disciple of Chekhov and O'Neill: A Study in Literary Influence*. Hong Kong: Hong Kong University Press.

Lau, Joseph S. M. Ed. 1976. *Chinese Stories from Taiwan, 1960–1970*. Foreword by C. T. Hsia. New York: Columbia University Press.

Lau, Joseph S. M. Ed. 1983. *The Unbroken Chain: An Anthology of Taiwan Fiction since 1926*. Bloomington: Indiana University Press.

Lau, Joseph S. M., C.T. Hsia, and Leo Ou-Fan Lee. Eds. 1981. *Modern Chinese Stories and Novellas, 1919–1949*. New York: Columbia University Press.

Laughlin, Charles A. 2002. *Chinese Reportage: The Aesthetics of Historical Experience*. Durham, NC: Duke University Press.

Laughlin, Charles A. 2008. *The Literature of Leisure and Chinese Modernity*. Honolulu: University of Hawaii Press.

Laughlin, Charles A. Ed. 2005. *Contested Modernities in Chinese Literature*. New York: Palgrave Macmillan.

Lee, Gregory. 1989. *Dai Wangshu: The Life and Poetry of a Chinese Modernist*. Hong Kong: Chinese University Press.

Lee, Haiyan. 2007. *Revolution of the Heart: A Genealogy of Love in China, 1900–1950*. Stanford, CA: Stanford University Press.

Lee, Leo Ou-fan. 1973. *The Romantic Generation of Modern Chinese Writers*. Cambridge, MA: Harvard University Press.

Lee, Leo Ou-fan. 1999b. *Shanghai Modern: The Flowering of a New Urban Culture in China, 1930–1945*. Cambridge, MA: Harvard University Press.

Lee, Leo Ou-fan. Ed. 1985. *Lu Xun and His Legacy*. Berkeley: University of California Press.

Lee, Mabel. 2012. *Gao Xingjian: Aesthetics and Creation*. Amherst, NY: Cambria Press.

Leenhouts, Mark. 2005. *Leaving the World to Enter the World: Han Shaogong and Chinese Root-Seeking Literature*. Leiden: CNWS Publications.

Leung, Laifong. 1994. *Morning Sun: Interviews with Chinese Writers of the Lost Generation*. Armonk, NY: M. E. Sharpe.

Li, Dian. 2006. *The Chinese Poetry of Bei Dao, 1978–2000: Resistance and Exile*. Albany, NY: Edwin Mellen Press.

Li, Hua. 2011. *Contemporary Chinese Fiction by Su Tong and Yu Hua: Coming of Age in Troubled Times*. Leiden: Brill.

Li, Peter. 1980. *Tseng P'u*. Boston: Twayne.

Lieberman, Sally Taylor. 1998. *The Mother and Narrative Politics in Modern China*. Charlottesville: University Press of Virginia.

Lin, Julia C. 1972. *Modern Chinese Poetry: An Introduction*. Seattle: University of Washington Press.

Lin, Julia C. 1985. *Essays on Contemporary Chinese Poetry*. Athens: Ohio University Press.

Link, E. Perry. 1993. "Ideology and Theory in the Study of Modern Chinese Literatrue: An Introduction." *Modern China*, 19.1: 4–12.

Link, E. Perry. 2000. *The Uses of Literature: Life in the Socialist Chinese Literary System*. Princeton, NJ: Princeton University Press.

Liu, Kang. 1993. "Politics, Critical Paradigms: Reflections on Modern Chinese Literature Studies." *Modern China*, 19.1: 13–40.

Liu, Kang. 2000. *Aesthetics and Marxism: Chinese Aesthetic Marxists and Their Western Contemporaries*. Durham, NC: Duke University Press.

Liu, Kang. 2004. *Globalization and Cultural Trends in China*. Honolulu: University of Hawaii Press.

Liu, Kang, and Xiaobing Tang. Eds. 1993. *Politics, Ideology, and Literary Discourse in Modern China: Theoretical Interventions and Cultural Critique*. Durham, NC: Duke University Press.

Liu, Jianmei. 2003. *Revolution Plus Love: Literary History, Women's Bodies, and Thematic Repetition in Twentieth-Century Chinese Fiction*. Honolulu: University of Hawaii Press.

Liu, Jin. 2013. *Signifying the Local: Media Productions Rendered in Local Languages in Mainland China in the New Millennium*. Leiden: Brill.

Liu, Lydia H. 1995. *Translingual Practice: Literature, National Culture, and Translated Modernity—China, 1900–1937*. Stanford, CA: Stanford University Press.

Liu, Lydia H. Ed. 1999. *Tokens of Exchange: The Problem of Translation in Global Circulations*. Durham, NC: Duke University Press.

Liu, Petrus. 2011. *Stateless Subjects: Chinese Martial Arts Literature and Postcolonial History*. Ithaca, NY: Cornell East Asian Program.

Liu, Shousong劉綬松. 1956. *Zhongguo xin wenxue shi chugao* 中國新文學史初稿 (A draft history of Chinese new literature). 2 vols. Beijing: Zuojia chubanshe.

Liu, Ts'un-yan. Ed. 1984. *Chinese Middlebrow Fiction: From the Ch'ing and Early Republican Eras*. Hong Kong: Chinese University Press.

Liu, Wu-chi. 1972. *Su Man-shu*. Boston: Twayne.

Louie, Kam. 2002. *Theorising Chinese Masculinity: Society and Gender in China*. Cambridge, UK: Cambridge University.

Louie, Kam. Ed. 2012. *Eileen Chang: Romancing Languages, Cultures and Genres*. Hong Kong: Hong Kong University Press.

Lovell, Julia. 2006. *The Politics of Cultural Capital: China's Quest for a Nobel Prize in Literature*. Honolulu: University of Hawaii Press.

Lu, Jie. Ed. 2007. *China's Literary and Cultural Scenes at the Turn of the 21st Century*. London: Routledge.

Lu, Sheldon H. 2001. *China, Transnational Visuality, Global Postmodernity*. Stanford, CA: Stanford University Press.

Lu, Sheldon H. 2007. *Chinese Modernity and Global Biopolitics: Studies in Literature and Visual Culture*. Honolulu: University of Hawaii Press.

Lu, Sheldon H. 2008. "Review of Shu-mei Shih, *Visuality and Identity*." *Modern Chinese Literature and Culture* (Jan.). http://mclc.osu.edu/rc/pubs/reviews/lu.htm.

Lu, Sheldon H. 2012. "Notes on Four Major Paradigms in Chinese-Language Film Studies." *Journal of Chinese Cinemas*, 6.1: 15–25.

Lu, Tonglin. 1995. *Misogyny, Cultural Nihilism and Oppositional Politics: Contemporary Chinese Experimental Fiction*. Stanford, CA: Stanford University Press.

Lu, Tonglin. Ed. 1993. *Gender and Sexuality in Twentieth-Century Chinese Literature and Society*. Albany: State University of New York Press.

Luo, Liang. 2014. *The Avant-Garde and the Popular in Modern China: Tian Han and the Intersection of Performance and Politics*. Ann Arbor: University of Michigan Press.

Lyell, William A., Jr. 1976. *Lu Hsün's Vision of Reality*. Berkeley: University of California Press.

Mair, Victor H. Ed. 2001. *The Columbia History of Chinese Literature*. New York: Columbia University Press.

Manfredi, Paul. 2014. *Modern Poetry in Chinese: A Visual Verbal Dynamic*. Amherst, NY: Cambria.

Mao, Nathan K. 1978. *Pa Chin*. Boston: Twayne.

Martin, Fran. 2003. *Situating Sexualities: Queer Representations in Taiwanese Fiction, Film and Public Culture*. Hong Kong: University of Hong Kong Press.

Martin, Helmut, and Jeffrey C. Kinkley. Eds. 1992. *Modern Chinese Writers: Self-Portrayals.* Armonk, NY: M. E. Sharpe.

McClellan, Thomas Michael. 2005. *Zhang Henshui and Popular Chinese Fiction, 1919–1949.* Lewiston, NY: Edwin Mellen Press, 2005.

McDougall, Bonnie S. 1971. *The Introduction of Western Literary Theories into Modern China, 1919–1925.* Tokyo: Centre for East Asian Cultural Studies.

McDougall, Bonnie S. 2002. *Love-Letters and Privacy in Modern China: The Intimate Lives of Lu Xun and Xu Guangping.* Oxford, UK: Oxford University Press.

McDougall, Bonnie S. 2003. *Fictional Authors, Imaginary Audiences: Modern Chinese Literature in the Twentieth Century.* Hong Kong: Chinese University Press.

McDougall, Bonnie S. 2011. *Translation Zones in Modern China: Authoritarian Command versus Gift Exchange.* Amherst, NY: Cambria Press.

McDougall, Bonnie S. Ed. 1984. *Popular Literature and Performing Arts in the People's Republic of China.* Berkeley: University of California Press.

McDougall, Bonnie S., and Kam Louie. 1997. *The Literature of China in the Twentieth Century.* New York: Columbia University Press.

McGrath, Jason. 2008. *Postsocialist Modernity: Chinese Cinema, Literature, and Criticism in the Market Age.* Stanford, CA: Stanford University Press.

Mi, Jiayan. 2004. *Self-Fashioning and Reflexive Modernity in Modern Chinese Poetry.* Lewiston, NY: Edwin Mellen.

Moran, Thomas. Ed. 2006. *Chinese Fiction Writers, 1900–1949.* Columbia, SC: Bruccoli Clark Layman.

Moran, Thomas, and Ye (Dianna) Xu. Eds. 2013. *Chinese Fiction Writers, 1950–2000.* Detroit: Gale Cengage Learning.

Mostow, Joshua. Ed. 2003. *The Columbia Companion to Modern East Asian Literature.* New York: Columbia University Press.

Nieh, Hua-ling. 1972. *Shen Ts'ung-wen.* New York: Twayne.

Nieh, Hua-ling. Ed. 1981. *Literature of the Hundred Flowers.* 2 vols. New York: Columbia University Press.

Owen, Stephen. 1992. *Readings in Chinese Literary Thought.* Cambridge: MA: Harvard University Press.

Peng, Hsiao-yen, and Isabelle Rabut. Eds. 2014. *Modern China and the West: Translation and Cultural Mediation.* Leiden: Brill.

Peng, Hsiao-yen, and Whitney Crothers Dilley. Eds. 2014. *From Eileen Chang to Ang Lee: Lust, Caution.* London: Routledge.

Pickowicz, Paul G. 1981. *Marxist Literary Thought in China: The Influence of Ch'ü Ch'iu-pai.* Berkeley: University of California Press.

Pickowicz, Paul G. 1994. "Huang Jianxin and the Notion of Postsocialism." In *New Chinese Cinemas: Forms, Identities, Politics.* Edited by Browne, Nick, Paul G. Pickowicz, Vivian Sobchack, and Esther Yau. New York: Cambridge University Press. 57–87.

Pickowicz, Paul G., Kuiyi Shen, and Yingjin Zhang. Eds. 2013. *Liangyou, Kaleidoscopic Modernity and the Shanghai Global Metropolis, 1926–1945.* Leiden: Brill.

Pollard, David. 1973. *A Chinese Look at Literature: The Literary Values of Chou Tso-jen in Relation to the Tradition.* Berkeley: University of California Press.

Průšek, Jaroslav. 1961. "Basic Problems of the History of Modern Chinese Literature and C. T. Hsia, *A History of Modern Chinese Fiction.*" *T'oung Pao*, 49.4–5: 357–404.

Průšek, Jaroslav. 1969. *Three Sketches of Chinese Literature.* Prague: Oriental Institute in Academia.

Průšek, Jaroslav. 1980. *The Lyrical and the Epic: Studies of Modern Chinese Literature.* Ed. Leo Ou-fan Lee. Bloomington: Indiana University Press.

Pruyn, Carolyn S. 1988. *Humanism in Modern Chinese Literature: The Case of Dai Houying.* Bochum: Brockmeyer.

Pusey, James Reeves. 1998. *Lu Xun and Evolution*. Albany: State University of New York Press.

Qian, Suoqiao. 2011. *Liberal Cosmopolitan: Lin Yutang and Middling Chinese Modernity*. Leiden: Brill.

Quah, Sy Ren. 2004. *Gao Xingjian and Transcultural Chinese Theater*. Honolulu: University of Hawaii Press.

Rojas, Carlos, and Eileen Cheng-yin Chow, Eds. 2013. *The Oxford Handbook of Chinese Cinemas*. Oxford, UK: Oxford University Press.

Rojas, Carlos, and Andrea Bachner. Eds. 2016. *The Oxford Handbook of Modern Chinese Literatures*. Oxford, UK: Oxford University Press.

Rojas, Carlos, and Eileen Cheng-yin Chow. Eds. 2009. *Rethinking Chinese Popular Culture: Cannibalizations of the Canon*. London: Routledge.

Ross, Timothy. 1974. *Chiang Kuei*. Boston: Twayne.

Roy, David T. 1971. *Kuo Mo-jo: The Early Years*. Cambridge, MA: Harvard University Press.

Sang, Tze-lan D. 2003. *The Emerging Lesbian: Female Same-Sex Desire in Modern China*. Chicago: University of Chicago Press.

Schaffer, Kay, and Xianlin Song. 2013. *Women Writers in Postsocialist China*. London: Routledge.

Shen, Shuang. 2009. *Cosmopolitan Publics: Anglophone Print Culture in Semi-Colonial Shanghai*. Piscataway, NJ: Rutgers University Press.

Shih, Shu-mei. 2001. *The Lure of the Modern: Writing Modernism in Semicolonial China, 1917–1937*. Berkeley: University of California Press.

Shih, Shu-mei. 2007. *Visuality and Identity: Sinophone Articulations across the Pacific*. Berkeley: University of California Press.

Shih, Shu-mei. 2011. "The Concept of the Sinophone." *PMLA*, 126.3: 709–718.

Shih, Shu-mei, Chien-hsin Tsai, and Brian Bernards. Eds. 2013. *Sinophone Studies: A Critical Reader*. New York: Columbia University Press.

Shu, Yunzhong. 2000. *Buglers on the Home Front: The Wartime Practice of the Qiyue School*. Albany: State University of New York Press.

Slupski, Zbigniew. 1966. *The Evolution of a Modern Chinese Writer: An Analysis of Lao She's Fiction with Biographical and Bibliographical Appendices*. Prague: Czechoslavk Academy of Science.

Slupski, Zbigniew. Ed. 1987. *A Selective Guide to Chinese Literature, 1900–1949. Vol. II. The Short Story*. Leiden: Brill.

Song, Binghui W 宋炳輝. 2013. *Wenxue shi shiye zhongde Zhongguo xiandai fanyi wenxue—yi zuojia fanyi wei zhongxin* 文學史視野中的中國現代翻譯文學—以作家翻譯為中心 (Translated literature in modern China). Shanghai: Fudan daxue chubanshe.

St. André, James, and Peng Hsiao-yen. Eds. 2012. *China and Its Others: Knowledge Transfer through Translation, 1829–2010*. New York: Rodopi.

Stuckey, Andrew G. 2010. *Old Stories Retold: Narrative and Vanishing Pasts in Modern China*. Lanham, MD: Lexington Books.

Tam, Kwok-kan, and Terry Siu-han Yip. Eds. 2010. *Gender, Discourse and the Self in Literature: Issues in Mainland China, Taiwan and Hong Kong*. Hong Kong: Chinese University Press.

Tam, Kwok-kan, and Kelly Kar-yue Chan. Eds. 2012. *Culture in Translation: Reception of Chinese Literature in Comparative Perspective*. Hong Kong: Open University of Hong Kong Press.

Tan, E. K. 2013. *Rethinking Chineseness: Translational Sinophone Identities in the Nanyang Literary World*. Amherst, NY: Cambria Press.

Tang, Xiaobing. 2008. *Origins of the Chinese Avant-garde: The Modern Woodcut Movement*. Berkeley, University of California Press.

Teng, Emma Jinhua. 2004. *Taiwan's Imagined Geography: Chinese Colonial Travel Writing and Pictures, 1683–1895*. Cambridge, MA: Harvard University Asia Center.

Tsu, Jing. 2006. *Failure, Nationalism, and Literature: The Making of Modern Chinese Identity, 1895–1937*. Stanford, CA: Stanford University Press.

Tsu, Jing. 2010. "Epilogue: Sinophone Writings and the Chinese Diaspora." In *The Cambridge History of Chinese Literature, Volume II: From*

1375. Edited by Chang, Kang-i Sun, and Stephen Owen. Cambridge, UK: Cambridge University Press. 706–714.

Van Crevel, Maghiel. 1996. *Language Shattered: Contemporary Chinese Poetry and Duoduo*. Leiden: CNWS Publications.

Van Crevel, Maghiel. 2008. *Chinese Poetry in Times of Mind, Mayhem and Money*. Leiden: Brill.

Visser, Robin. 2010. *Cities Surround the Countryside: Urban Aesthetics in Post-socialist China*. Durham: Duke University Press.

Vohra, Ranbir. 1974. *Lao She and the Chinese Revolution*. Cambridge, MA: Harvard University Press.

Wagner, Rudolf. 1990. *The Contemporary Chinese Historical Drama: Four Studies*. Berkeley: University of California Press.

Wagner, Rudolf. 1992. *Inside a Service Trade: Studies in Contemporary Chinese Prose*. Cambridge, MA: Harvard University Press.

Wang, Ban. 1997. *The Sublime Figure of History: Aesthetics and Politics in Twentieth Century China*. Stanford, CA: Stanford University Press.

Wang, Ban. 2004. *Illuminations from the Past: Trauma, Memory, and History in Modern China*. Stanford, CA: Stanford University Press.

Wang, Ban. Ed. 2011. *Words and Their Stories: Essays on the Language of the Chinese Revolution*. Leiden: Brill.

Wang, Ban, and Jie Lu. Eds. 2012. *China and New Left Visions: Political and Cultural Interventions*. Lanham, MD: Lexington Books.

Wang, David Der-wei. 1992. *Fictional Realism in Twentieth-Century China: Mao Dun, Lao She, Shen Congwen*. New York: Columbia University Press.

Wang, David Der-wei. 1997. *Fin-de-siècle Splendor: Repressed Modernities of Late Qing Fiction, 1849–1911*. Stanford, CA: Stanford University Press.

Wang, David Der-wei. 1999. "Introduction." In *A History of Modern Chinese Fiction* by Hsia, C. T. Third edition. Bloomington: Indiana University Press. vii–xxxv.

Wang, David Der-wei. Ed. 2016. *A New Literary History of Modern China*. Cambridge, MA: Harvard University Press.

Wang, David Der-wei, and Carlos Rojas. Eds. 2007. *Writing Taiwan: A New Literary History*. Durham, NC: Duke University Press.

Wang, Hui. 2003. *China's New Order: Society, Politics, and Economy in Transition*. Edited by Theodore Huters. Cambridge, MA: Harvard University Press.

Wang, Hui. 2009. *The End of the Revolution: China and the Limits of Modernity*. London: Verso.

Wang, Hui. 2011. *The Politics of Imagining Asia*. Edited by Theodore Huters. Cambridge, MA: Harvard University Press.

Wang, Jing. 1996. *High Culture Fever: Politics, Aesthetics, and Ideology in Deng's China*. Berkeley: University of California Press.

Wang, Lingzhen. 2004. *Personal Matters: Women's Autobiographical Practice in Twentieth-Century China*. Stanford, CA: Stanford University Press.

Wang, Xiaojue. 2013. *Modernity with a Cold War Face: Reimagining the Nation in Chinese Literature across the 1949 Divide*. Cambridge, MA: Harvard University Asia Center.

Wang, Yao 王瑤. 1953. *Zhongguo xin wenxue shigao*中國新文學史稿: 1919–1950 (A draft history of new Chinese literature). 2 vols. Shanghai: Xin wenyi chubanshe.

Wang, Yiyan. 2006. *Narrating China: Jia Pingwa and His Fictional World*. London: Routledge.

Widmer, Ellen, and David Der-wei Wang. Eds. 1993. *From May Fourth to June Fourth: Fiction and Film in Twentieth-Century China*. Cambridge, MA: Harvard University Press.

Williams, Philip F. 1993. *Village Echoes: The Fiction of Wu Zuxiang*. Boulder: Westerview Press.

Witchard, Anne. 2012. *Lao She in London*. Hong Kong: Hong Kong University Press.

Woesler, Martin. Ed. 2000. *The Modern Chinese Literary Essay: Defining the Chinese Self in the 20th Century*. Bochum: Bochum University Press.

Wolff, Ernst. 1971. *Chou Tso-jen*. New York: Twayne.

Wong, Lawrence Wang-chi. Ed. 2013. *Towards a History of Translating: In Commemoration of the 40th Anniversary of the Research Centre for Translation, CUHK*. 3 vols. Hong Kong: Chinese University Press.

Wong, Lisa Lai-Ming. 2009. *Rays of the Searching Sun: The Transcultural Poetics of Yang Mu*. New York: Peter Lang.

Wong, Wang-chi. 1991. *Politics and Literature in Shanghai: The Chinese League of the Left-Wing Writers, 1930–1936*. Manchester: Manchester University Press.

Yan, Haiping. 2006. *Chinese Women Writers and the Feminist Imagination, 1905–1948*. London: Routledge.

Yang, Xiaobin. 2002. *The Chinese Postmodern: Trauma and Irony in Chinese Avant-Garde Fiction*. Ann Arbor: University of Michigan Press.

Yeh, Michelle (Xi Mi奚密). 1991a. "Chayi de jiaolü: yige huiying" 差異的焦慮: 一個回應 (The anxiety of difference: a rejoinder). *Jintian* 今天 (Today), 1: 94–96.

Yeh, Michelle. 1991b. *Modern Chinese Poetry: Theory and Practice since 1917*. New Haven, CT: Yale University Press.

Yeh, Michelle. 1992. *Anthology of Modern Chinese Poetry*. New Haven, CT: Yale University Press.

Yeh, Michelle. 1999. "Chinese Postmodernism and the Cultural Politics of Modern Chinese Poetry." In *Cross-Cultural Readings of Chinese: Narratives, Images, and Interpretations of the 1990s*. Edited by Yeh, Wen-hsin. Berkeley: University of California, Institute of East Asian Studies. 100–127.

Yeh, Michelle. 2000. "International Theory and the Transnational Critic: China in the Age of Multiculturalism." In *Modern Chinese Literary and Cultural Studies in the Age of Theory: Reimagining a Field*. Edited by Chow, Rey. Durham, NC: Duke University Press. 251–280.

Yeung, Jessica. 2008. *Ink Dances in Limbo: Gao Xingjian's Writing as Cultural Transition*. Hong Kong: Hong Kong University Press.

Ying, Ruocheng, and Claire Conceison. 2008. *Voices Carry: Behind Bars and Backstage during China's Revolution and Reform*. Lanham, MD: Rowman and Littlefield.

Yip, Wai-lim. Ed. and trans. 1970. *Modern Chinese Poetry: Twenty Poets from the Republic of China, 1955–1965*. Iowa City: University of Iowa Press.

Zha, Mingjian 查明建 and Xie Tianzhen 謝天振. 2007. *Zhongguo 20 shiji waiguo wenxue fanyi shi* 中國20世紀外國文學翻譯史 (A history of translated foreign literature in twentieth-century China). 2 vols. Wuhan: Hubei jiaoyu chubanshe.

Zhang, Jeanne Hong. 2004. *The Invention of a Discourse: Women's Poetry from Contemporary China*. Leiden: CNWS Publications.

Zhang, Longxi张隆溪. 1986. *Ershi shiji xifang wenlun pingshu*二十世紀西方文論評述 (Twentieth-century Western literary theory). Beijing: Sanlian shudian.

Zhang, Longxi. 1992a. *The Tao and the Logos: Literary Hermeneutics, East and West*. Durham, NC: Duke University Press.

Zhang, Longxi. 1992b. "Western Theory and Chinese Reality." *Critical Inquiry*, 19: 105–30.

Zhang, Longxi. 1993. "Out of the Cultural Ghetto: Theory, Politics, and the Study of Chinese Literature." *Modern China*, 19.1: 71–101.

Zhang, Longxi. 1998. *Mighty Opposites: From Dichotomies to Differences in the Comparative Study of China*. Stanford, CA: Stanford University Press.

Zhang, Longxi. 2005. *Allegoresis: Reading Canonical Literature East and West*. Ithaca, NY: Cornell.

Zhang, Longxi. 2007. *Unexpected Affinities: Reading across Cultures*. Toronto: University of Toronto Press.

Zhang, Xudong. 1997. *Chinese Modernism in the Era of Reforms: Cultural Fever, Avant-garde Fiction, and the New Chinese Cinema*. Durham, NC: Duke University Press.

Zhang, Xudong. 2008. *Postsocialism and Cultural Politics: China in the Last Decade of the Twentieth Century*. Durham, NC: Duke University Press.

Zhang, Yingjin. 1994. "The Institutionalization of Modern Literary History in China, 1922–1980." *Modern China*, 20.3: 347–377.

Zhang, Yingjin. 1996. *The City in Modern Chinese Literature and Film: Configurations of Space, Time, and Gender*. Stanford, CA: Stanford University Press.

Zhang, Yingjin. 2016. "September 1952: *Literary Gazette* Criticized Wang Yao's History of New Literature." In *A New Literary History of Modern China*. Edited by Wang, David Der-wei. Cambridge, MA: Harvard University Press.

Zhao, Henry Y. H. 1997. "Post-Isms and Chinese New Conservatism." *New Literary History*, 28.1: 31–44.

Zhao, Henry Y. H. 2000. *Towards a Modern Zen Theatre: Gao Xingjian and Chinese Theatre Experimentalism*. London: School of Oriental and African Studies, University of London.

Zhao, Jiabi 趙家璧. Ed. 1935. *Zhongguo xin wenxue daxi* 中國新文學大系 (A compendium to Chinese new literature). 10 vols Shanghai: Liangyou.

Zheng, Yi. 2013. *Contemporary Chinese Print Media: Cultivating Middle Class Taste*. London: Routledge.

Zhong, Xueping. 2000. *Masculinity Besieged? Issues of Modernity and Male Subjectivity in Chinese Literature of the Late Twentieth Century*. Durham, NC: Duke University Press.

Zhong, Xueping, and Ban Wang. Eds. 2014. *Debating the Socialist Legacy and Capitalist Globalization*. New York: Palgrave Macmillan.

Zhou, Gang. 2011. *Placing the Modern Chinese Vernacular in Transnational Literature*. New York: Palgrave Macmillan.

Zhu, Aijun. 2007. *Feminism and Global Chineseness: The Cultural Production of Controversial Women Authors*. Youngstown, NY: Cambria Press.

Part I
History and Geography

2
Literary Modernity in Perspective

Zhang Longxi

Modern Chinese literature is inseparable from the concept of Chinese "modernity" and therefore inseparable from the social and historical conditions at the turn of the nineteenth century to the twentieth, which witnessed unprecedented challenges to traditional Chinese social structure, the collapse of the Qing Empire, and the end of dynastic history. The concept of modernity was self-consciously defined against that old imperial system and the entire traditional apparatus that sustained its political and cultural edifice. However, modernity is by no means a simple concept, and there is much discussion of its problematic nature in recent scholarship because it is a contested concept not only in the discourse of postmodernism, which supposedly supersedes it, but also in the critique of modernity as a normative concept based on European historical experience at the expense of a more expansive view of global history. Since the beginning of the twenty-first century, "multiple modernities" has become a common term in the scholarly discourse in the humanities and social sciences. "One of the most important implications of the term 'multiple modernities' is that modernity and Westernization are not identical. Western patterns of modernity are not the only authentic modernities, though they enjoy historical precedence and continue to be a basic reference point for others" (Sachsenmaier, Riedel, with Eisenstadt 2002: 27). In other words, modernity is now understood as a much broader concept than what an earlier discourse of modernization signified in much of the twentieth century, in which modernity was understood largely on the basis of European history and Western social, political, and cultural patterns.

Not only has the idea of multiple modernities been proposed to accommodate a more expansive view, but the idea of multiple "early modernities" has also been discussed with fruitful results. It is not enough just to recognize that "the modern age, in both its geopolitical aspirations and economic underpinnings, was always already

A Companion to Modern Chinese Literature, First Edition. Edited by Yingjin Zhang.
© 2016 John Wiley & Sons, Ltd. Published 2016 by John Wiley & Sons, Ltd.

global," but it is also necessary to avoid the conventional assertion that "modernity arose solely as a by-product of the Age of Discovery" (Porter 2012: 5). The Western patterns of modernity basically conceptualized world history as determined by the geographical expansion of Europe buttressed by its economic and political development. "To take as the universal benchmark of modernity the sweeping consequences of this expansion," as David Porter argues, "is to relegate to the extra-European a merely facilitating role that, being at once intrinsically primal and forever belated, must remain structurally exterior to any historical conception of the modern." Porter and his colleagues dated the beginning point of "early modernity" not to the conventional 1492 or 1500, but to 1100, with special consideration of the fact that "we can observe features of the late Song dynasty China in the year 1100 that bear resemblances to China in the year 1600 as well as to Italy at roughly the same time" (Porter 2012: 5). Their deliberate change of the date effectively redefined "early modernity" in a global context far beyond European expansion, and the comparative approach they took in conceptualizing "early modernities" proved to be highly productive and stimulating in our understanding of historical transitions and social changes that moved the world into what we recognize as the modern times.

In China, quite a lot of ink was spilt for a long period of time before the 1990s over the question of whether or when China had developed its "buds of capitalism." Though it is no longer debated in those terms, the implicit issue of modernity in the debate is unavoidable, for it tried to identify some basic features of capitalist development, especially in commercial activities and correlative social structure in the counties and prefectures, in the affluent region south of the Yangtze River. That discussion actually has some suggestive similarities with the "early modernities" discussed more recently by Porter and his colleagues. Zhu Weizheng, a distinguished historian, thought of modern Chinese history as a long process of moving "out of the Middle Ages," and he conceptualized this process as "the history of ideas and culture from the late Ming to the late Qing dynasty," roughly from the late sixteenth to the late nineteenth century (Zhu Weizheng 2007: 6). He clearly stated that the so-called "history of budding capitalism" debated by Chinese historians decades ago was in fact "the history of transition from the medieval to the modern times" (Zhu Weizheng 2007: 9). Whereas Porter and colleagues questioned the concept of "early modernity" based on the history of European expansion, Zhu borrowed the European concept of the "Middle Ages" not to map Chinese history onto a European concept, but precisely to challenge the Eurocentric view of world history that marginalized modern China as passively responding to the external impact of European expansion. Therefore, he opposed the conventional view that the Opium Wars in the 1840s marked the beginning of modern history in China. If one "believed that only British cannons could beat China from the wilderness of the Middle Ages into the gate of modern civilization," says Zhu (2007: 6) in a sarcastic vein, one would have to come to the conclusion that "the Chinese were incapable of stepping into modernity, but could only have modernization thrust upon them." His discussion of the late Qing self-reform movement and one of its leading figures, Gong Zizhen, was meant to disprove that "British cannons" or "the salvos of the

October Revolution" had beaten the stagnant and backward China "into the gate of modern civilization." That is to say, China's historical transition from the "Middle Ages" to modernity was a long and arduous process, but it was not and could not be a passive process of "forced modernization."

The idea of change was certainly not "imported," and, in this respect, Gong Zizhen was an important pioneer thinker in the late Qing period. As early as 1814–1815, long before the Opium Wars, he already called for self-reform in the Qing Empire, arguing that the rise of each and every new dynasty was based on reform and change. "Looking back on our ancestors," says Gong Zizhen (1999: 6), "was it not in changing the failure of the previous dynasty that they could rise up? And was it not in changing the failure of their predecessors in turn that the previous dynasty could rise up?" The need to learn from foreign powers for self-strengthening became more widely acknowledged after the Opium Wars, and various proposals were put forward by influential figures from Lin Zexu, Wei Yuan, Feng Guifen, to Xue Fucheng and Zhang Zhidong. Zhang's principle of upholding traditional Chinese learning as the main body (*ti*) to be aided by Western learning as serviceable auxiliaries (*yong*) was most well-known and influential, which was originally meant to open China up for learning from the West, particularly in terms of technological advancement. The doctrine of *ti* and *yong* or the main and the auxiliary, however, has difficulty in adjusting to the quickly evolving social and historical conditions at the time, and its limitations became more and more discernible as reform gradually touched upon the different aspects of Chinese social life and cultural tradition. Some scholars have pointed out that "to insist on formulating a model of cultural combination of China and the West by defining it in terms of the main body and auxiliaries (*ti yong*), roots and twigs (*ben mo*), or the main and the supplementary (*zhu fu*) will inevitably lead to embarrassing inconsistencies and numerous flaws" (W. Ding and Chen 1995: 173). Indeed, Zhang Zhidong's doctrine had the conservative purpose of retaining what he thought to be the foundation of Chinese moral and political system—the three principles (*san gang*) that guarantee the superiority of the monarch over the subjects, father over the son, and husband over his wife. "Once one knows the principle of the monarch over the subjects, then the idea of the rights of the people will not do," he argues; "once one knows the principle of father over the son, then the idea of holding father and son as equal in legal terms and abandoning ancestor worship will not do; and once one knows the principle of husband over wife, then the idea of male–female equality will not do" (Zhang Zhidong 2002: 12). The rights of the people or democracy and the equality of men and women are all major ideas in a modern society, from which Zhang Zhidong evidently tried to distance himself, and thereby also to distance himself from reformists such as Kang Youwei and Liang Qichao and their more radical proposal of a constitutional monarchy.

The failure of the so-called "Hundred Days Reform" in 1898 made it clear that effective fundamental changes were impossible under the declining but rigid structure of the Qing Empire, and more radical social changes were needed to build up anything different and new. Yet, what was new could not come out of the blue, unrelated to what was old and already existent, for "the idea of a new man," as Liang Qichao (1984: 211) famously argued, "does not mean that people of our country must abandon all that is old to follow others. There are two meanings of the word *new*: first, to temper what one originally had and make it new; and second, to take what one did not have and acquire it as new." In other words, whatever was new and modern must arise from the social and cultural environment that necessarily contained the old, which was either to be changed or to be eliminated, and nothing could be completely rootless and afloat without indigenous moorings. History follows a route all its own in each of the world's nations and cultural traditions; so the concept of modernity cannot and should not be narrowly defined on Western patterns only, without proper consideration of historical experiences of other, non-Western cultures and traditions. That is what Zhu Weizheng tried to argue in his historical writings, in which he pioneered the study of Christianity and modern China (a subject forbidden in China before the 1980s), the cultural interrelations between China and Europe during the late Ming and the early Qing dynasties, the unorthodox and more open-minded ideas of Wang Yangming's brand of Confucianism and its influence, the significance of Matteo Ricci and the other Jesuit missionaries, and also the ignorance and xenophobia of conservative elements in traditional Chinese society.

It is with a sense of continuity and transformation that many scholars today are rethinking modern Chinese history, trying to find the intricate trajectory and operations of historical forces, and navigating carefully between a simplistic view of China as passively modernized in response to external impact from the West on the one hand, and, on the other, a totally inward-looking view that refuses to see China in the larger picture of major changes in regional and global history. If modernity in the West was problematically related to nineteenth-century imperialism and colonialism, modernity (and nationalism) in China and the other non-Western countries have a different character—that of resisting the pressure from the West, while at the same time trying to transform the traditional society into a modern one, with such basic and recognizably modern features as industrialization, rational behavior in social transactions, development of trade and market economy, scientific reasoning and education, a sense of individuality and individual rights, women's rights, and a social and political structure in conformity with the ideas of human rights and democracy. As a consequence, the concept of modernity in China is a complicated and difficult one, as it is neither a close copy of Western modernity, nor a concept different from that of the West to such a degree as to violate all the basic features listed earlier, which, as core ideas and values, define what is eminently modern. Multiple modernities make sense, but they must all lead to modernity, not to its opposite or negation.

At the beginning of the twentieth century, however, when the last imperial dynasty was overthrown after being repeatedly defeated at the hands of Western powers and a modernized Japan, and humiliated by several unequal treaties, the situation in China appeared much darker and more precarious than a hundred years later, and many Chinese intellectuals at the time had an acute sense of urgency and anxiety over the fate of China, the anxiety of national survival. Perhaps Chen Yinque, a highly respected scholar and historian in modern China, can be seen as an exemplary spokesman for his generation of intellectuals at the turn of the century. In October 1910, when he was traveling in Europe as a 20-year-old young man and heard the disturbing news of the annexation of Korea by imperial Japan, Chen wrote a poem to lament the fate of Korea and also express his dismay at the fate of China. He was in Berlin at the time, and the poem in part reads (Chen Yinque 1993: 3; trans. Zhang Longxi):

> At times looking toward the East over volumes of clouds,
> I dare not look back in the twilight under the sinking sun;
> Horrified that the land of the ancient sage Jizi had suffered,
> In the last ten years twice being slaughtered and wronged.
> Alas, the king surrendered and left the seal bestowed in vain
> By the Superior Empire, and in a prisoner's cage sadly gone.
> Renamed Changde, he dwelled lower than Fushimi Castle,
> A worse fate than such that lost his country, as Yao's son.
> Tao Qian lived so far after Emperor Fuxi, and I even later
> Than Tao Qian; but the anger now and in days bygone
> Over the loss of our country cries out to heaven
> From my lonely heart a sorrowful song!

Seventeen years later, when his close friend and famous scholar Wang Guowei (aka Mr Guantang) committed suicide by drowning himself in the Kunming Lake of the Summer Palace in Beijing, Chen Yinque wrote a moving tribute to his friend and interpreted Wang's death as a personal sacrifice to the demise of Chinese culture, a sacrifice that carried a deeply symbolic meaning only to be understood in the specific historical circumstances at the time. Chen wrote in the preface (1993: 10):

Some have asked for the reason of Mr Guantang's death, and I offer this as a reply: In recent time people have been talking about Eastern and Western cultures, of which we need not discuss whether the geographical division is appropriate, their differences or similarities, superiority or inferiority; but we may posit a hypothesis. We may hypothesize that at the time when a system of cultural values is in decline, those who are cultivated in that culture must feel the pain, and the more splendidly they manifest that culture, the greater their pain; when the pain reaches to the extreme degree, nothing but suicide can put their heart at ease and fulfill their aspirations.

The core of Chinese culture, Chen continues to argue, is made of the fundamental "three principles and six disciplines," namely the hierarchical relationships of the monarch over subjects, father over son, husband over wife, and the other ethical relationships governing people's social behaviors. In this argument, we may see clearly that Chen inherited from Zhang Zhidong the same understanding of the core of traditional Chinese culture. These basic values and principles were as abstract as Plato's ideas, Chen went on to say, but they were embodied in the social and economic systems of traditional Chinese society. In earlier history, Buddhism from India held views contrary to these basic Chinese principles, but it failed to destabilize the social and economic structure of Chinese society, even though Buddhism had spread in China for many centuries. In the last few decades, however, a totally different and new adversary had come to challenge the foundation of Chinese culture, and the impact of that new adversary, Western culture, was different from any foreign forces encountered previously. Under that impact, says Chen, the core of Chinese culture was disintegrating. He continued in a sorrowful tone (Chen Yinque 1993: 11):

> For today's China is suffering huge calamities and undergoing most unusual changes never seen before in the past thousands of years. As calamities and changes reach to the extreme, how can those who epitomize the spirit of this culture not share its fate and die with it? And that is the reason why Mr. Guantang could not but die and thus made all later generations feel the most profound sorrow and the deepest sense of loss.

In Chen Yinque's interpretation, Wang Guowei's suicide was a consciously made decision to offer his own life as sacrifice to the demise of traditional Chinese culture. The unprecedented changes and huge calamities never encountered before in the long history of China formed the basic framework within which we may understand the radical reactions among Chinese intellectuals, both those such as Wang Guowei, Chen Yinque, and Wu Mi, who lamented the decline of traditional Chinese culture and tried to salvage whatever was possible against the grain in an overall social tendency toward Westernization, and those such as Chen Duxiu, Lu Xun, and Hu Shi, who believed that the only way for China to be rejuvenated and move forward was to get rid of the heavy burden of history and tradition, particularly the Confucian politics and ethics of "the three principles and six disciplines," so that China could be changed and modernized. The latter group of intellectuals became movers and shakers of the May Fourth New Culture Movement and precipitated the social and historical changes in early-twentieth-century China. Though different in their reactions to the impact of modernization and Westernization, both groups of intellectuals were deeply concerned about China's present and future, and both groups were not only rooted in traditional Chinese culture, but had profound knowledge and even personal experience of the foreign—Japan, Europe, or the United States.

Lu Xun (1981: 1: 130), who saw himself as "bearing the heavy burden of tradition and shouldering the floodgate of darkness to let the young escape to a spacious place of light," is perhaps most representative of those radical iconoclastic intellectuals of the May Fourth Movement. Such a self image shows that Lu Xun thought of his own generation as being bogged down in the old tradition, but he was hopeful of the possibilities for China's younger generation to be different and better—which bore a sign of the times, when ideas of Darwinian evolution theory formed a powerful background for understanding the transformation of history and society. Lu Xun (1981: 1: 286) described himself as a fighter turned against his own tradition, in which he was himself deeply embedded, a fighter who, "coming from the old camp and seeing things more clearly, was able to hit the strong enemy lethally by turning the weapon back to strike." One of his most controversial remarks was his reply to a newspaper's enquiry about drawing up a reading list for Chinese youth: "I think it is better to read less—or even no—Chinese books, but read more foreign books" (Lu Xun 1981: 3: 12). Such a remark should be understood in the social conditions in early 1925, when old "Chinese books" were still being read widely and cultural conservatives were advocating reading Confucian classics among school children and young students, while Lu Xun and the other advocates of the New Culture were trying to change the fundamental elements of literary culture, including the very medium of writing from the classical language to *baihua* or the modern vernacular, a fundamental change comparable to that from Latin to modern European languages during the Renaissance. In China, literary modernity manifested itself as writing in the vernacular *vis-à-vis* the classical language, elevating traditionally neglected genres, such as fiction and drama, while importing new genres from the West, such as the Western-style novel and new poetry, and representing a whole set of new ideas and values against the traditional value system, the Confucian orthodoxy in particular.

This is, of course, a familiar story of radical changes during the New Culture movement, a story that puts emphasis on the new and the modern within the general context of a grand narrative of social evolution and development, in which literary and cultural transformations are inextricably bound up, particularly in mainland China after the 1950s, with the political discourse of progress and revolution. It is undeniable that the spirit of the May Fourth Movement was radically anti-traditional, and that the debates at the time were rather heated and fierce, sometimes even virulent, but cultural changes were impossible if there were only breaks, but no continuity or inheritance. Yu Yingshi is certainly right to point out the continuities between the May Fourth and traditional culture by arguing that the iconoclastic tendency of the May Fourth radicals was already adumbrated in the rather arcane debate between the "present-day script school" and the "archaic script school" (*jin gu wen zhi zheng*) in classic studies in the late Qing dynasty. Advocates of New Culture were not only deeply rooted in traditional learning, but they used their knowledge of the tradition to fight against tradition, which was exactly what Lu Xun thought he was doing. "In their fight against tradition and Confucian moral principles," says Yu (1982: 102–103), "they would first go back, wittingly or unwittingly, to the fountainhead of unorthodox or anti-orthodox thoughts within the tradition itself in search of legitimacy. For in comparison these thoughts were what they felt most familiar with. As for the new foreign ideas, as they had neither long experience nor deep understanding of them, those ideas could generate new meanings only by grafting themselves somewhat incongruously onto some concepts and ideas already within the tradition."

Although not all foreign ideas were "incongruously" grafted onto old concepts in the Chinese tradition during the May Fourth period, grafting is actually not a bad metaphor for the process of cultural interaction by means of which cultural elements from a foreign tradition may take root in an indigenous one, integrated with some native ideas and thereby endowing these ideas with new meaning and gradually causing changes in the substance of the whole tradition. This may be said to characterize the general process of cultural integration of any kind, a process that has happened in all traditions in history. That is to say, no tradition is completely pure, just one with itself, for it always contains orthodox ideas that tend to preserve and stabilize what already exist, but also unorthodox ideas that tend to destabilize, change, and be different from the status quo. Therefore, any radical tendency of thought would naturally go back to tradition and try to find unorthodox or anti-orthodox precursors. Since most discussions of the May Fourth Movement focused on its radical anti-traditionalism, it becomes a much-needed corrective and a complementary view to look at the continuities and interrelations between the May Fourth Movement and traditional Chinese culture.

It is thus important to understand modern Chinese literature in its relations with the native classical tradition on the one hand, and the new Western forms of literary expression on the other. What was "modern" and its evaluation were largely determined by the historical circumstances at the time, and they would inevitably change in perceptible degrees as the historical circumstances changed. The literary scene in the early twentieth century was rich, multivalent, and varied. The May Fourth New Literature was radically new, but Lu Xun also drew literary resources in both form and content from classical works, and Hu Shi started experimenting new poetry under the influence of Song *ci* poetry, while other writers continued writing in traditional forms with traditional themes. What is considered new and modern and what is perceived to be the main question of the time are largely determined by the social and historical circumstances of a given time. One hundred years ago, China was weak and its traditional culture was in decline, lamented by those who cherished traditional values and wanted to recuperate those values from demise, but pushed down further by those who thought that these values were the very reason for China's weakness and decline. "Now many people have big fear, so do I," Lu Xun (1981: 1: 307) wrote in an article published in *New Youth* (Xin qingnian) in November 1918; "what many people fear is that 'Chinese' as a name will be wiped out; but what I fear is that Chinese will be nudged out of 'people of the world'." For Lu Xun and many other intellectuals at the time, whether China and the Chinese would be able to survive as a nation and a culture was a real and pressing issue. Similarly, it was still largely felt to be the issue in the 1980s when China had just stepped out of the disastrous self-enclosure and political infighting during the Cultural Revolution.

The situation today is, of course, very different, as China has been on the rise in the last 30 years in the era of reform and opening-up, having grown into the second largest economy in the world, and playing an increasingly more important role economically and politically in world affairs. It is quite unlikely that anyone in China today would have the same kind of fear Lu Xun talked about, and with the change of times and conditions, the concept of modernity and how people think about modern Chinese history would also change. In Western historiography, contemporary scholarship no longer speaks of the "dark" Middle Ages, from which Renaissance used to be understood as a completely different and new period, a sudden and total break; instead, historians now mostly focus on continuities and gradual changes in thinking about historical transitions from the medieval to the modern. Likewise, in Chinese scholarship since the 1990s, there is much rethinking of modern Chinese history since the May Fourth

Movement, a revaluation of tradition, and a revived interest in Confucianism and in traditional culture in general. Literary modernity is also, of necessity, being rethought and reconceptualized.

From the 1950s till the end of the Cultural Revolution in the late 1970s, history and literary criticism were heavily politicized in China, with a predominant official narrative that appropriated the May Fourth New Culture as part of the success story of New China led by the Communist Party and its supreme leader, Chairman Mao. In that official discourse, Lu Xun was deified as a sort of patron saint of the Communist revolution, even though he never joined the Communist Party. "The chief commander of China's Cultural Revolution, he was not only a great man of letters, but a great thinker and revolutionary"—with these words Mao sanctioned Lu Xun's canonization. "On the cultural front, he was the bravest and most correct, the firmest, the most loyal, and the most ardent national hero, a hero without parallel in our history" (Mao 1965: 2: 372). However, Lu Xun's deification also meant the drastic reduction and simplification of this great writer, the erasure of his self-doubts and self-critique, while many of his close friends and followers, such as Hu Feng and Feng Xuefeng, were persecuted and severely criticized in China, even arrested and imprisoned as counter-revolutionary for several decades. The post-Mao era saw some dramatic changes in contemporary Chinese society, and many old and orthodox ideas were put in question. A significant sign of the change was the call to rewrite literary history in the 1980s, and there appeared many efforts as correctives of the stifling official discourse in literary criticism in the previous decades.

In Beijing in the 1980s, Qian Liqun, Huang Ziping, and Chen Pingyuan (2004: 11) proposed to re-envision the history of twentieth-century Chinese literature as the following:

> a process of change and transition, and the final completion of such transition, from ancient Chinese literature to modern Chinese literature, a process in which Chinese literature walks towards and is merged into the general structure of world literature, a process of the formation of modern national consciousness (including aesthetic consciousness) from a literary perspective (alongside political, moral, and many other perspectives) under the circumstances of great cultural encounters and exchanges between the East and the West, and a process in which the rejuvenation and rise of this old Chinese nation, in a time of great transition from the old into the new, are refracted and represented through the art of language.

The salient points made here, particularly the emphasis on the correlation of Chinese literature and world literature and the aesthetic and artistic aspects of literary creation, were evidently new in the specific context of the 1980s and were opposed to the ideological control of literature in the orthodox theory of "revolutionary realism," which insisted on viewing literature as a "reflection" of social reality and, at the same time, a serviceable "tool" in the cause of socialist revolution.

In Shanghai, also in the 1980s, Chen Sihe and Wang Xiaoming led the discussion of rewriting literary history and published a number of articles in a literary magazine. Later, Zhang Peiheng and Chen Sihe, both teaching at Fudan University, led another significant discussion of the history of modern Chinese literature, particularly the issue of periodization. Again, their attempt at new ways of conceptualizing modern literary history was first and foremost a reaction against the official discourse that offered a distorted view of modern Chinese literature as a tool of political struggle. This is clearly indicated by Zhang Peiheng when he identified "a certain authoritative way of periodization" as the root cause of the problem of periodization in the study of modern Chinese literature, namely, the division of Chinese history of the last 150 years into early modern history (*jindai shi*), from the Opium Wars of the 1840s to the May Fourth Movement of 1919, and modern history (*xiandai shi*), from the May Fourth movement of 1919 to the founding of the People's Republic of China (PRC) in 1949. The former or early modern history was thought to be the history of China's "old democratic revolution" led by the bourgeoisie, and the latter was supposed to be the history of a "new democratic revolution" led by the proletariat. "Added to such periodization the idea of literature as an auxiliary to politics," says Zhang Peiheng, "one would arrive at the logical conclusion that literature from the Opium Wars to the May Fourth movement was early modern literature, of which the main trend was a literary embodiment of the demands of bourgeois democracy, while literature starting with the May Fourth Movement was modern literature" (P. Zhang and Chen 2002: 12). No respectable scholar of modern Chinese literature today would endorse such a periodization and its rationale, and the attempt to rewrite literary history became a much needed corrective of the official discourse, an effort to depoliticize literary history that was in itself a significantly political move, which should be understood within the internal politics of Chinese history since the end of the Cultural Revolution and the end of Mao's rule.

And yet, the study of Chinese literature is not just an internal business in China, but one that goes far beyond the borders of the Chinese mainland. In fact, native Chinese scholarship since the 1990s has been increasingly connected with, and influenced by, China studies outside China, particularly in the United States. This is especially true of the attempt at rethinking modern Chinese literature and literary modernity. Generally speaking, if we may characterize native Chinese scholarship in the 1980s and its effort to rewrite literary history as largely responding to internal political changes in the post-Mao era, China studies in the United States, particularly the study of modern Chinese literature, may be seen as responding to a very different intellectual milieu, in which postmodernism, postcolonialism, cultural studies, gender studies, and many other theoretical issues and concerns constitute an overall context for the search of research questions and their interpretations. Redefining literary modernity against the main discourse of modernization represented by the May Fourth New Culture has been the substance of much rethinking of modern Chinese literature in the past few decades. One important aspect of such rethinking is the critical attention paid to what was marginalized in the May Fourth Movement, a revaluation of the late Qing as either anticipating much of what was considered modern in later history, or offering an alternative to what the May Fourth mainstream represented. As early as 1980, Milena Doleželová-Velingerová—and even earlier, a number of her Czech and Russian colleagues—already argued for a critical re-examination of late Qing fiction as a transitional form from the old to the new, thus representing a predecessor of the new novel in twentieth-century China. More recently, David Wang clearly puts forward an argument against the May Fourth mainstream as he declares that "late Qing fiction is not a mere prelude to 'modern' Chinese literature, but a most active stage that precedes its rise. Late Qing fiction would have led to a very different version of the Chinese modern had it not been rejected by high-minded 'modern' Chinese writers as so obviously 'pre-modern'" (1997: 16). Works of late Qing fiction rejected by the May Fourth intellectuals as decadent or "pre-modern" include works of four genres, what Wang (1997: 22) called "depravity romance, chivalric cycles, grotesque exposés, and science fantasy." Wang argues that these late Qing works, often dismissed as low-brow popular fiction by later critics, are "repressed modernities" in Chinese literature, but his argument is not just meant to locate the "origin" of the modern elsewhere, earlier than the May Fourth, or merely to "rehabilitate" those works, but to rethink literary history by imagining an alternative picture of Chinese modernity. The idea of "repressed modernities" refers to a "rethinking of literary history," says Wang (1997: 21):

> I do not see the appearance of the modern in late Qing literature as having followed a singular, inevitable format of evolution or revolution, a view commonly held by literati since the May Fourth. Rather, drawing on theories recently developed in certain social and human sciences, I see the late Qing as a crucial moment in which many incipient modernities competed for fulfillment.

In other words, what we see today as modern might have been something very different, if those "repressed modernities" given expression in late Qing fiction were acknowledged to be legitimately modern, particularly in the framework of "theories recently developed in certain (Western) social and human sciences."

Such radical rethinking of literary modernity has a strong impact on scholarship in China, and it has at least the effect of opening up new prospects in the study of modern Chinese literature. "From adventures in time to erotic fantasies, from visions of transvestitism to tales of horror" (D. Wang 1997: 18), such works become worthy of critical attention, mainly because the themes and innovations in these works have a sort of resonance with the interests and issues that have become prominent in the recent development of Western theories. This is clearly recognized by some Chinese scholars as well. In their comment on Wang's work, for example, Ji Jin and Yu Xiayun cautiously expressed their doubts as well as their appreciation. Drawing on the theoretical works of Michel Foucault, Gilles Deleuze, Fredric Jameson, Mikhail Bakhtin, and Homi Bhabha, Wang's effort to elevate those "repressed modernities" displays, they argue, "greater hermeneutic abilities than knowledge of historical documentation," so much so that some critics have faulted Wang for leaning too much toward "historical imagination," but not enough to make a convincing case for his rehabilitation of late Qing fiction. At the same time, however, they also argue that Wang's "value system and narrative strategy, clearly different from those of the May Fourth, should at least be positively acknowledged and fully understood as offering an alternative way of writing about modern Chinese literature" (S. Chen and Wang 2011: 218).

Perhaps every generation has the impulse and desire to rethink the past and rewrite history in response to its own social and cultural conditions at a specific historical moment. In China, rethinking modern literary history evidently has some bearing on the changed and changing situation in economic, social, and political terms since the 1990s, showing a greater variety of positions and viewpoints than the more unified critical tendency in the 1980s that mainly, and rather consciously, continued the May Fourth legacy. The world is changing, and for China, it seems to be changing to a better condition, a brave new world really, while the West is going through the difficult time of an economic downturn. Rethinking history, however, cannot and should not simply take an opposite or positional stance *vis-à-vis* what an earlier generation took, but should have a healthy dose of sympathetic understanding of our predecessors and the major historical events that existed at the time. One hundred years ago, whether China could survive as a nation seemed to many Chinese intellectuals a real concern, both to traditionalists such as Wang Guowei and Chen Yingque and to anti-traditionalists such as Chen Duxiu and Lu Xun. The last dynasty collapsed, followed by chaotic conflicts among warlords, and, even long afterward, Chinese history was filled with danger, as much of the territories was lost under the aggressive Japanese invasion. Today, all that is past, and national survival is no longer an issue. On the contrary, the rise of China has generated a sense of national pride, and we often hear the optimistic prediction that the twenty-first century will be China's century. That is certainly promising, but for a more sober-minded understanding of the present and the future, informed with historical knowledge, it is perhaps better for us still to listen to what Lu Xun (1981: 1: 359) counseled the Chinese of his generation almost a century ago:

> The race that has many who are not self-content will always move forward and always have hope.

> The race that knows only to blame others without reflecting on itself is rife with imminent danger and disasters!

References

Chen, Sihe 陳思和 and Wang Dewei 王德威. Eds. 2011. *Jiangou Zhongguo wenxue xiandai duoyuan gongsheng tixi de xin sikao* 建構中國現代文學多元共生體系的新思考 (New thoughts on constructing a multivalent and symbiotic system of modern Chinese literature). Shanghai: Fudan daxue chubanshe.

Chen, Yinque 陳寅恪. 1993. *Chen Yinque shiji, fu Tang Yun shicun* 陳寅恪詩集—附唐篔詩存 (Chen Yinke's poems with appended poems by Tang Yun). Beijing: Qinghua daxue chubanshe.

Ding, Weizhi 丁偉志 and Chen Song 陳崧. 1995. *Zhong Xi ti yong zhijian* 中西體用之間 (Between

China and the West, the main and the auxiliary). Beijing: Zhongguo shehui kexue chubanshe.

Gong, Zizhen 龔自珍. 1999. *Gong Zizhen quanji* 龔自珍全集 (Gong Zizhen's complete works). Edited by Wang Peizheng王佩錚. Shanghai: Shanghai guji chubanshe.

Liang, Qichao 梁啓超. 1984. *Liang Qichao xuanji* 梁啓超選集 (*Liang Qichao's selected works*). Edited by Li Huaxing 李興華 and Wu Jiaxun 吳嘉勛. Shanghai: Shanghai renmin chubanshe.

Lu, Xun 魯迅. 1981. *Lu Xun Quanji*魯迅全集 (Complete works of Lu Xun). 16 vols. Beijing: Renmin wenxue chubanshe.

Mao, Zedong. 1965. *Selected Works of Mao Zedong*. 4 vols. Beijing: Foreign Languages Press.

Porter, David. Ed. 2012. *Comparative Early Modernities: 1100–1800*. New York: Palgrave Macmillan.

Qian, Liqun 錢理群, Huang Ziping 黃子平, and Chen Pingyuan 陳平原. 2004. *Ershi shiji Zhongguo wenxue san ren tan—manshuo wenhua* 二十世紀中國文學三人談——漫説文化 (Three-way conversations on twentieth-century Chinese literature—random thoughts on culture). Beijing: Beijing daxue chubanshe.

Sachsenmaier, Dominic, and Jens Riedel, with Shmuel N. Eisenstadt. Eds. 2002. *Reflections on Multiple Modernities: European, Chinese and Other Interpretations*. Leiden: Brill.

Wang, David Der-wei. 1997. *Fin-de-siècle Splendor: Repressed Modernities of Late Qing Fiction, 1849–1911*. Stanford, CA: Stanford University Press.

Yu, Ying-shih 余英時. 1982. *Shixue yu chuantong* 史學與傳統 (Historiography and tradition). Taipei: Shibao.

Zhang, Peiheng章培恒 and Chen Sihe 陳思和. Eds. 2002. *Kaiduan yu zhongjie: xiandai wenxue shi fengqi lunji*開端與終結:現代文學史分期論集 (Beginning and end: essays on the period- ization of modern literature). Shanghai: Fudan daxue chubanshe.

Zhang, Zhidong 張之洞. 2002. *Quanxue pian* 勸學篇 (Exhortation to study). Shanghai: Shanghai shudian.

Zhu, Weizheng朱维铮. 2007. *Zouchu zhong- shiji* 走出中世纪 (Out of the Middle Ages). Expanded edition. Shanghai: Fudan daxue chubanshe.

3
Late Qing Literature, 1890s–1910s

Hu Ying

In conventional history, modern Chinese literature came into being on the heels of the New Culture Movement of 1919. Indeed, in the 1920s, a new literature appeared and, within a couple of decades, dominated the cultural scene. Unlike the past 2,000 years, this literature was written in the vernacular language; its frame of reference was more frequently modern Euro-America rather than the Confucian classics; its protagonist was rarely the traditional literati but a modern individual, either a New Woman (*xin nüxing*) or a modern man, speaking a markedly different language and revealing a psychic landscape quite different from that of the familiar literati. The iconoclastic champions of this modern literature, in their eagerness to proclaim a new beginning, were flamboyant in renunciation of the past, including and especially the period immediately preceding itself, the late Qing.

At first glance, literature of the last decades of the Qing dynasty (1890s–1910s) seems to confirm the modernists' portrayal: writers were largely trained for the literati–official career; they favored classical poetry and prose; even their satirical fiction is reminiscent of novels of late imperial times. Yet, despite appearances, late Qing literature was responding to a distinctly modern set of problems generated by a very turbulent time. Since the Opium Wars of the 1840s, Western imperial powers had made their presence felt. The humiliating defeat of the Qing navy by the recently risen Japan sent a final wakeup call to the literati class as it effectively dashed the hopes of the Self-Strengthening Movement aimed at preserving the Chinese cultural essence while adopting Western technology and warfare. Meanwhile, the wide spread of modern printing made possible the dissemination of national and international news, as the public read daily about Russia's incursion into Northeast China, the partition of Poland, and the Philippines Revolution. In this period of rapid political, social, and

A Companion to Modern Chinese Literature, First Edition. Edited by Yingjin Zhang.
© 2016 John Wiley & Sons, Ltd. Published 2016 by John Wiley & Sons, Ltd.

cultural changes, a new literature arose that gave expression to the tumultuous times and offered creative responses to the onslaught of modernity. Hardly a dark age before the enlightenment era of May 4, the late Qing was a time of culture ferment, characterized by daring experimentations and flourishing creativity.

In the late Qing cultural landscape, one of the most striking features is the promotion of, and indeed frenzy for, the "new." Barely a few decades earlier, the term was associated chiefly with negative connotations: in the 1880s, a Qing diplomat found his ancestral home ransacked and his books banned because he was perceived to be espousing "the new"—that is, foreign and heterodox—ways (Hu Ying 2000). By the turn of the twentieth century, everywhere one looked, something "new" was happening: news stories from around the world were carried in the daily papers; leading reformists called for "making new" the people in 1898; even the Qing court proclaimed its "new policy" in 1902 and abrogated the more than 1,000-year-old system of the civil service examination in 1905. Not only did the term take on a positive connotation, but "newness" in and of itself came to be equated with "goodness," as it became a repository of hope and longing for cultural regeneration.

Correspondingly, there was a growing tide of criticism of the "old." Indeed, in the 1898 call for the new novel, we find bitter criticism of traditional fiction as "teaching nothing but robbery and lechery" (Liang Qichao 1936: 2: 56), and many writers passionately denounced classical poetry—oftentimes voiced within classical poems. And yet, what later modernists called "the old tradition" was not as moribund as we might think: during the late Qing to the early Republican era, ancient-style prose supplied the medium for translating Charles Dickens, and parallel-prose was wildly popular in modern romance. Indeed, traditional cultural practices not only persisted well into the twentieth century but continued to supply a vital resource to the Chinese experience of modernity. With the advantage of hindsight, the image of traditional culture as an ossified monolith appears largely a narrative constructed between the late Qing and the early Republican era, a kind of modernist decision to break from the past. In this context, the commonplace idea of the late Qing as a "transitional period" may also be misleading, as it implicitly assumes a particular direction for history and thus sees in the late Qing only those trends that later became dominant in the modern era. Recent scholarship seeks to discard this restricted view and reveal a widely divergent literary field where experimentation of many kinds flourished.

Late Qing literature presents a kaleidoscope where elements of presumably distant categories exist side by side, their very proximity showcasing the great cultural vibrancy that characterizes the age. Thus, the same author may enthusiastically advocate the vernacular in an essay penned in the classical language; within a poem, the meter may be strictly regulated by tradition going back to the fifth century while the vocabulary was so new-fangled that its contemporary readers might have as hard a time deciphering it as we do today. The resulting literary work is oftentimes a kind of pastiche in which incongruous elements coexist and divergent interests compete for attention, perhaps not always the most polished works but brimming with creative energy, its somewhat ambivalent undertone and often fragmentary structure offering a good mirror for the turbulent times.

In order to understand modern Chinese literature, its origins, as well as its alternatives, we must begin in the late Qing period. This chapter first presents the reformists' call for revolution in literature, and then follows up with the trends and changes in the three major genres—prose essay, poetry, and fiction.

Revolution in Literature

In 1899, the leading reformist Liang Qichao called for "revolution in poetry" and "revolution in prose." Significantly, these calls first came out in his *Travel Journal of Hawaii (Hanman lu*, 1899), giving us a clue about his exposure to foreign literature and the hope that incorporation of it would rejuvenate Chinese literature. In grafting the political term "revolution" (*geming*)—freshly re-introduced into Chinese via Japan— onto literary endeavors, Liang was consciously departing from the many earlier movements to renovate literature, itself a tradition in the history of Chinese literature. In the past, when writers and poets critiqued hackneyed writings and called for renovation, they had generally couched it in the framework of adhering closer to the ancients; this time, however, Liang was turning his gaze not so much back as out, conceptualizing a Chinese literature in the global context. His call for literary revolution signals a kind of utopian hope for a new political and social order, a new historical era. With his rousing rhetoric and affective enthusiasm, Liang had named himself "New Citizen of China," and "Youth of Young China," effectively the spokesman for this new era.

Liang was himself an avid practitioner of the new prose style he championed for, which "interlarded colloquialism, verses, and foreign expressions quite frequently, letting his brush flow freely, and without restraint … the flow of his brush was often full of feeling, exerting a special charm over the readers" (Liang Qichao 1936: 8: 142). In the construction of this new writing style, the function of foreign words (primarily Japanese compounds) was to extend the narrow confines of worn-out Chinese expressions. And in this process, translation was to play a pivotal role: to allow the Chinese language to be powerfully affected by Japanese, and through Japanese, by European languages. Through this grafting together of new and markedly alien elements, the ancient Chinese language would be revitalized. The task that Liang had set for himself, then, was the forging of a new literary medium that would be able to reach a larger audience than the assumed readers of classical literature—that is, literati educated in the classics.

Similar to his championing of the unorthodox style of prose, his 1899 conception of the new poetry did not shrink from an admixture of Chinese and foreign elements: "First there must be a new poetic imagination; then there must be a new language; and then they need to be embodied in poetic styles consistent with the ancients" (Liang Qichao 1936: 7: 76). Note the subtle difference if we compare "revolution in prose" with "revolution in poetry." For prose, Liang appears enthusiastic about the infusion of foreign and colloquial styles, whereas in poetry, he is reluctant to let go of "styles consistent with the ancients." For the rest of the twentieth century up to the present, more than any other traditional genres, poetry in the classical forms continues to attract a sizable group of practitioners, testifying to the continued appeal of traditional prosody and the expressive efficacy of poetry's accumulated cultural stock (see Chapter 9 by Michelle Yeh).

More than his calls for new prose and poetry, Liang's championing of new fiction had the most significant social and cultural impact. If prose and poetry mostly serve as channels for a writer's own expression, then a newly invigorated version of them allows more efficient expression suited to the modern times. In contrast, new fiction is primarily motivated by its effect on the audience—to carry out the mission of transforming the Chinese populace into modern citizens. Because of its ability to move and stimulate the audience, fiction was being imagined as the most appropriate form to reach a wider readership and have a transformative effect on them. Around the turn of the twentieth century, many intellectuals interested in political and cultural reform championed "revolution in fiction." In 1897, the preeminent translator Yan Fu and his friend Xia Zengyou first pointed to the social utility of fiction in the modern world as they set forth the power of fiction to affect the largest possible reading public. Liang Qichao further politicized fiction by explicitly harnessing it unto the cause of national reform: "In order to make new a country's citizens, it is absolutely necessary to make new a country's fiction writing." The urgency of Liang's proclamation may be directly linked to his experience of the failed 1898 reform. Attributing the political failure in part to the lack of popular support, Liang believed that he had found a solution in political fiction by such politician–novelists as Bulwer-Lytton and Benjamin Disraeli, whose works had been translated into Japanese after the Meiji Restoration. Writing "in brush dipped in emotion," as Liang (1936: 8:142) described his own affective prose in 1902, he painted a picture of "great European intellectuals" who turned to the writing of fiction, claiming "it often happened that when a work freshly came off print, a whole nation would change its views on current affairs." Borrowing the term "new fiction" from Japanese, Liang pronounced fiction to be "the highest form of literature." Thus, the Chinese generic hierarchy, in which fiction barely counted as literature in the previous 2,000 years, was turned upside down. Following Liang's lead, progressive intellectuals called for the translation of political fiction from abroad, and many attempted writing new fiction themselves. Typically, these political novels are set in the near future where the protagonists debate at length over the advantage of the parliamentary system or expound on John Stuart Mill's views on the equality of the sexes (see Chapter 14 by Amy Dooling). Even though much of the new fiction turned out to be rather dry political tracts and the narrowly defined "new fiction" itself did not last long on the literary scene, the call for a new fiction could be heard repeated at considerable frequency in the following century.

What makes the late Qing call for cultural renovation particularly modern is the conceptual framework of evolutionary thinking, recently introduced to China and, at the time, believed by many intellectuals to possess extraordinary explanatory power in political, social, and cultural life. A literary genre, for example, was thought to be similar to a live organism, its vitality needing to be stimulated by competition. If it were no longer adaptive to historical progress, it would naturally meet its demise. Despite periodic criticism, this social Darwinist strain held long-lasting consequence for all aspects of modern Chinese culture, including literature. More than ever before, literature would be charged with an explicit social mission of facilitating social progress, and writers were urged to take on the responsibility of ushering in a new world.

The Prose Essay: Debate over the Proper Literary Language

When Liang Qichao (1936: 8:142) described his new style in 1921, he self-consciously positioned it as a rejection of the classical styles, as "the older generation" was "resentful of it and slandered it as heretical." What was at stake was the choice of a proper literary language, which would generate a heated debate for the next few decades and resulted in the meteoric rise of the vernacular, which in turn led to the most significant break with tradition.

The choice of literary language did not constitute a problem in late imperial times, at least not overtly so. What we call today classical Chinese (*gudai hanyu*) was known simply as literary Chinese (*wenyan wen*), a concise and allusive language of the literati and the accepted medium of polite writing. Its key element, *wen*, etymologically means "elegant patterning." While its narrow definition is the composition of fine writing, in connotation, *wen* encompasses everything that is aesthetically refined, including the classics, the histories, as well as literature. Thus, Confucius says: "Words lacking pattern and refinement (*wen*) do not go far." *Wen*, in short, has long been taken to mean the essence of the Chinese cultural tradition. Its mastery signaled culture and learning and paved the way to social advancement, since it was also the medium for the examination essay for the civil service examination.

Over the long history of Chinese literature, there were numerous occasions when writers called for a more "correct" literary language, defining it usually as one that was closer to the ancients, thus more orthodox, and purer than the corrupt and hackneyed current practice. Starting around the eighth century, the centrality of literary Chinese also weathered powerful challenges from Buddhism, which legitimated the use of vernacular, first in Buddhist sermons and translated scriptures, then in popular literature such as fiction and drama. For practical purposes, some form of written vernacular had also been in existence in late imperial China. In the nineteenth century, Western missionaries, similar to the Buddhists before them, also used the vernacular to translate the Bible so as to reach the semi-literate. Still, literary Chinese held sway as the only legitimate medium for respectable literature until the last decade of the nineteenth century.

The question over the literary language first came to a head in the debate over what is the proper language to translate Thomas H. Huxley or Charles Dickens. That translation would ignite this important debate is not surprising if we recall that the late Qing saw the greatest translation boom in Chinese cultural history. At its height— between 1902 and 1907—works of translation exceeded original works (Tarumoto 1998: 39). Interest in translation was first kindled soon after the Opium War, notably by Commissioner Lin Zexu, who himself was made famous by his dramatic strike against the opium trade and his decisive role in the ensuing war with Britain in 1840. He commissioned the translation of several volumes on international law, geopolitical surveys of "the four continents," and various topics on "Western opinions on Chinese affairs" gleaned from Western newspapers, later compiled and circulated among the literati. The 1860s saw the establishment of government-sponsored translation houses such as the College of Languages in the north and Jiangnan Arsenal in the south. With the immense popularity of the newspaper industry beginning in the second half of the nineteenth century, an additional medium came into play in the translation boom. Between 1895 and 1900, more than 30 newspaper houses around the country carried special translation sections in their papers. The translation of Western literature, which was all but absent in the initial phase of the translation boom, burgeoned with the immense success of Lin Shu's translation of Dumas, *fils' La Dame aux camélias* in 1899. In barely a decade between 1899 and 1911, some 400 Western novels and plays were translated (Chen Pingyuan 1989: 28).

For translators in late Qing China, rather than rendering Western languages into one uniform "Chinese," there were several possible choices for the target language: the terse ancient-style prose (*guwen*), the ornate parallel prose (*pianwen*), or the journalistic new style (*xinwenti*) advocated by Liang Qichao (Huters 1989). Each one of the choices carried its specific cultural and historical implications as well as intense personal and emotional investment on the part of individual writers, for these choices not only constituted a writer/translator's own cultural persona as imagined by himself and others, but it was ultimately through these different language choices that the late Qing intellectuals imagined the meanings of tradition and modernity.

The ancient-style prose was championed by the Tongcheng School, which sought to revive the prose styles of the Tang and Song dynasty classicists who in their time had attempted a "Renewal of Antiquity." At its best, Tongcheng members produced socially engaged essays whose styles captured classical simplicity and clarity; at its worst—and this was the subject of frequent caricature by early-twentieth-century iconoclasts—they turned out moralizing essays with obsolete diction. Parallel prose was the preferred medium of the Wenxuan School, which championed a high prose style of composition that requires grammatical and metrical couplets as its basic structure, a style that is highly allusive and displays a rich vocabulary. Clearly removed from the spoken language, it is a style whose practitioners self-consciously distinguished it from the more utilitarian writings.

The foremost translator Yan Fu placed a premium value on the correct language. The evidence of his appeal was clear, in that the youth generation at the time could all recite at least the first paragraph of Huxley's *Evolution and Ethics*, just as though it were a Chinese classic. Arguing against the use of colloquial vernacular, Yan Fu wrote a letter in 1902 in reply to Liang Qichao, who had attempted to persuade him to translate in the vernacular:

> If one were to use popular vernacular so that it would be accessible to ignorant country bumpkins, that to the literary world is not revolution but butchering. My translation is meant for those who have steeped themselves in the classical tradition. For those people whose eyes have never glanced at the ancient pages, and then proceed to criticize my translation, the fault is with the reader, not the translator. (Yan Fu 1986: 3: 513)

Implicit in this concept of fidelity is the understanding that style is what bestows true moral value to a literary work, and, therefore, if the foreign works are to have any moral weight, the orthodox archaic style has to be the medium.

For Yan Fu, the use of ancient-style prose is a very deliberate choice, as its eminence in the Chinese literary tradition is what gives it the power to perform successfully in the new task of introducing Western learning. Yan Fu conceived of his primary aim as the persuasion of the literati class to be receptive to non-Chinese ideas: the ancient-style prose acts as the medium to prevail upon the particular readership he had in mind, those "who have steeped themselves in the classical tradition." Inherent in the rhetorical function that the ancient-style prose is called upon to perform, however, is a paradoxical relation between the telos of the persuasion and the method of achieving it, encompassing both a move toward the foreign other and a contrary move to stick as close to the familiar self as possible. For only when commensurability can be established between the two can there even be hope of approaching the ideal of universalism. Yan Fu was clearly conscious of this paradoxical situation, as is evident in his naming himself "adapter" rather than "translator," and in his warning that "it would be a mistake for latecomers to imitate him," a phrase borrowed from Kumarajiva, the great translator of Buddhist scriptures in the Tang dynasty (Yan Fu 1986: 5: 1321). This self-conception shows a profound understanding that the practice of translation means compromise, a compromise of one's ideals and one's aims, and negotiation between the foreign and the self, negotiation between different facets of the self.

Thus, Yan Fu's repeated appeal to the ideal of universalism, the hallmark of the late Qing generation of literati, is both the cause of his immediate success as well as the reason for his undoing soon afterward. As Theodore Huters (2005: 73) puts it poignantly: "The particular and local practice that any given thinker tried to hold onto as the local base for the application of the universal becomes for the next generation precisely that which delegitimizes him." The all-important "local base," in this case, is ancient-style prose, a particular practice of the late Qing that furnishes an easy target for the May Fourth critique of tradition. Within barely two decades, ancient-style prose became so remote from the practice of modern Chinese writers that it could only be associated with antiquity.

Lin Shu, the most popular translator of Western literature, also used the classical language exclusively in his works. Similar to Yan Fu, he saw a rich reservoir of meanings in the classical language, without which the words became mere words, and no longer the powerful *wen*, the medium that carried the weight of moral philosophy, or *Dao*, the medium that had the power it had because it could be traced to the fountainhead of Chinese civilization. Colloquialism and foreign expressions, to Lin Shu, err in much the same way: neither partakes in the long literary tradition. On the other hand, it is precisely Liang Qichao's advocacy of the novel as a populist vehicle for political reform that allows Lin Shu to justify his own translation of Western literature. In other words, Liang Qichao's highly politicized campaign for new fiction opens the space for Lin Shu's translation by supplying a kind of *Dao*: national salvation becomes the contemporary *Dao*, which then overrides the traditional critique of the genre often voiced by literati otherwise politically closer to Lin Shu.

While ancient-style prose is historically associated with the Tongcheng School of prose writing in eighteenth and nineteenth-century China, at the beginning of the twentieth century, it briefly became the basis of a national written language when Lin Shu's translation was enormously popular. That Lin Shu's publisher was the powerful Commercial Press allowed the possibility for ancient-style prose to transform itself from one among several prestigious writing styles to one that could represent the larger unity of China. Recent scholarship demonstrates that Lin Shu established himself as a master of ancient-style prose only after he had gained national fame as a translator; and that this was at least partially accomplished through his identification with writers such as Washington Irving, whose "modern nostalgia" led to Lin Shu's own formulation of "a modern cultural conservatism" (Hill 2012: 127). Via Irving, Lin Shu's prose joins a "global movement of nostalgia," offering a response to and critique of the violent arrival of modernity that threatened to liquidate traditional community and ways of life. Rejecting the authority of a hermetically sealed original, Lin Shu treats the source language text as open-ended, and the act of translation enters into this open space, establishing a linkage between the text and contemporary politics, in which the translated text then intervenes.

By the second decade of the twentieth century, the May Fourth generation, which grew up on the works of pioneer translators such as Liang Qichao, Yan Fu, and Lin Shu, began to dominate the debate on the choice of literary medium. By that point, the debate was re-framed in terms of *wenyan* (classical language) and *baihua* (plain colloquial language). For their iconoclastic attack on all things traditional, including the classical language, Lin Shu served as the most convenient target—convenient not only because of his immense popularity in translating Western literature but also because of his vehement defense of tradition. Despite Lin Shu's creative efforts in bringing together Western literature and ancient-style prose, the tremendous power that Western literary texts enjoyed in early twentieth century made it impossible for the next generation to imagine the kind of commensurability that Lin Shu strived for. And, for that very reason, Lin Shu as a brand name would meet with an ignominious demise at the new inauguration of Chinese literary modernity in 1918.

Poetry: The Most Tenacious Literary Form

Decades before Liang Qichao called for "revolution in poetry," the poet–diplomat Huang Zunxian had gone considerable distance in his poetic experimentation, incorporating neologism, describing foreign sights and new concepts, reviving marginal sub-genres, and generally pushing the limit of traditional poetry. Indeed, to some extent, Liang's call may be seen as a *post facto* defense of just the sort of experimentation that Huang was engaged in. And yet, Huang did not abandon the traditional forms of poetry; in fact, as he matured as a poet, he realized "that even the most inspired author cannot create great poetry from his inner thoughts without the assistance of tradition, and that, although the universe may be a wonderful symphony of sound, it is impossible to mold the discrete phenomena of the external world into an artistic whole without the discipline of language and form bequeathed to us by earlier authors" (Schmidt 1994: 54). Conventional literary history has usually interpreted Huang's work as a failed attempt at modernizing poetry. More recent scholarship points out, however, that we need to read his innovation in the context of the power and centrality of poetry in early-twentieth-century politics and social life. Both as a response to Western presence and maintaining deep roots with native cultural resources, the poetic practice of Huang, but also of other more obviously traditionalist poets, revisits the very premises of Chinese modernity and the utility of "tradition" in its unfolding. Their works demonstrate that classical poetry, rather than being stagnant to social change, was in fact a dynamic force responding innovatively to the challenges of modernity.

Reading conventional literary history, one would not have realized that classical poetry, similar to ancient-style prose, was flourishing in the early twentieth century. Rather than a few die-hard practitioners holding on to a moribund tradition, this literature continued to have a great many practitioners—even including many of those advocating the vernacular—who formed major literary societies and had abundant publication venues. Writers identified with the old literary tradition drew from it resources to interact dynamically with the contemporary historical moment. Responding to the catastrophic events of 1900—the Boxers Uprising, the flight of the Imperial court, and the occupation of the capital by the allied forces of eight foreign countries—poets such as Wang Pengyun produced an outpouring of poetry as historical witness, the exchange of which created a community of poets with shared mourning and a common mission of cultural transmission during a time characterized by great loss (S. Wu 2013). Wang's life-long practice of poetic composition, similar to that of many literati of his generation, meant more than technical competence and normative cultural literacy. It also signaled his unwillingness to relinquish poetry's historical roots. These roots tapped into a vast intellectual and aesthetic tradition, especially the tradition of the "poet–historian" that had seen a significant revival in Qing poetry (Lo and Schultz 1986).

Another major force of poetry production came from women poets. Although dismissed by those such as Liang Qichao as producers of "a few trifling poems on breeze and moonlight" and made to represent the enfeebled lyrical tradition as a whole, the late Qing is, in fact, a time when women poets further expanded their range of poetic production, a trend that set in by the seventeenth century. By the late nineteenth century, women poets eagerly participated in the rising nationalist sentiments and mobilized available poetic discourses to give voice to a gendered perspective on historical change. A prominent figure in this respect is Qiu Jin, a feminist and revolutionary, beheaded for her involvement in anti-Qing uprisings. Born into a literati family and well-read in traditional literature, Qiu Jin used traditional poetry and drama to express her political engagement and issue impassioned pleas to the women of China to become active participants in the unfolding of history. Her works vividly illustrate how traditional culture served as a rich resource for responding to modernity. When Qiu Jin died, her sworn sisters Wu Zhiying and Xu Zihua braved political persecution to give her a proper burial. In their commemoration of her, Wu and Xu wrote poetry, biography, and even deployed the *Book of Changes* (*Yijing*) to interpret her role while creating powerful voices of their own (Hu Ying 2004). Rather than "lame-duck" inheritors of the literati tradition, these women gave it a brilliant flowering by reinventing it to respond to the modern times.

Fiction: The Politicization of Literature

In the practice of fiction writing, the actual product turned out far more diverse and less instrumental than the reformers would have hoped. Even Liang Qichao, after trying his hand at writing political fiction himself, recognized that turning social theories into entertaining reading was not easy. The majority of fiction produced at the time is not strictly speaking political fiction but rather in the subgenres of social exposé, detective stories, science fiction, and courtesan tales. Underneath the pervasive hope for a new age, an utopian future portrayed in some of the late Qing new fiction, lurked a fundamental ambivalence, engendered by the collective trauma that accompanied the onset of modernity.

A good illustration of the patchwork model of late Qing fiction is perhaps Liu E, the author of *The Travels of Lao Can* (*Lao Can youji*, 1906–1907; English 1990), eclectic in his learning, part traditional literati, part traveling medicine man, and a sometime-entrepreneur particularly known for effective flood control on the Yellow River. His novel is modeled on travelogue, following the footsteps of the protagonist Lao Can, a literati physician who tries to "cure" physical as well as social ills with his many unconventional skills. In its critique of contemporary society, the work shares some characteristics with the typical exposé novel. At the same time, it has been lauded (and sometimes criticized) for its lyrical passages, its allegorical structure, and its experimentation with detective fiction. Unlike many of its contemporary publications, *The Travels of Lao Can* exhibits some of the refined augmentation of the traditional literati novel; the refinement, however, is typically employed to depict folk rather than elite culture. Similarly, the most profound moral philosophy in the novel comes out of the mouth of a courtesan–nun.

One striking characteristic, shared by many late Qing fictional works, is satirical engagement with contemporary society. In *Strange Events Witnessed Over Twenty Years* (*Ershinian mudu zhi guai xianzhuang*, 1906–1910), for example, the author Wu Jianren (aka Wu Woyao) portrays the decaying empire in all its putrid aspects—a world of utter moral squalor full of corrupt officials, degenerate literati, and unscrupulous businessmen. *A Brief History of Enlightenment* (*Wenming xiaoshi*, 1906; English 1996) by Li Boyuan (aka Li Baojia), on the other hand, exposes the pretense of those who espouse the latest trends and newest ideas, a world of fake reformers and phony progressives. Both writers made their careers in Shanghai as newspapermen, and their novels, serialized in popular fiction periodicals, have been described as social exposé, in which all aspects of a corrupt society, whether of the ancient regime or of the new elite, are targets for satirical treatment. This kind of writing was condemned in 1924 by Lu Xun, the preeminent May Fourth critic, for its superficiality, its lack of subtlety, and penchant for exaggeration. This harsh proscription dominated the evaluation of late Qing fiction as a whole until recently, when scholars tried to reverse the verdict by arguing for the thematic and formal complexity of the exposé novel. There are many experiments with narrative techniques, some scholars argue, such as introducing the first-person perspective, which addresses the larger problem of the writing subject, a problem that has continued to plague writers of the following generations too. In addition, what may be described as grotesque realism in exposé novels offers a different model from that of critical realism, which dominated the landscape of Chinese literature for the next decade (D. Wang 1997). Furthermore, Lu Xun's criticism may reflect his own inability to accept the lack of a comprehensive guideline to the world, a grand scheme that writers such as Wu Jianren did not or were not willing to offer (Huters 2005).

Wu Jianren is perhaps the most technically innovative of late Qing fiction writers. In several of his novels—for example, *The New Story of the Stone* (*Xin Shitou ji*, 1908)—the narrative for the most part is focalized through a single, naïve character, a new technique that is particularly well suited to satirical purposes (Hanan 2004). Giving an ironic twist to Liang Qichao's "Youth of Young China," the narrator of *The New Story of the Stone* calls himself "Old Youth" and guides the naïve character, a reincarnated Jia Baoyu from the eighteenth-century novel *Story of the Stone* (aka *Dream of the Red Chamber* or *Honglou meng*), through the utopian Civilized World, but not until the main character has first gone through the Barbarous World, a thinly disguised late Qing dystopia. Combining the original novel's mythical framework of "mending heaven" and a decidedly modern subject of nationalism in a technologically advanced world, *The New Story of the Stone* presents an intriguing science fantasy. *The Sea of Regret* (*Henghai*, 1906; English, 1995), another important novel by Wu Jianren, was perhaps the most popular novel of romance and sentimentality in the late Qing. Set against the backdrop of the tumultuous days of the Boxer Uprising and its aftermath, it portrays a young woman's devotion for a wastrel to whom she has been betrothed since childhood. In its response to the theme of love and marriage in the modern world, the novel exhibits an ambivalent morality. Most striking are the excessiveness of the female protagonist's virtue and the melodramatic manner with which she conforms to the wifely ideals of Confucianism. Thus, a seemingly simple allegory of doomed love and female sacrifice becomes a vehicle to explore the coming modernity, with its rapidly changing relationships between men and women and between parents and children (X. Tang 2000: 48).

At the inception of modernity, the late Qing gives us a window to the complex origins of modern Chinese literature: the tremendous power of the flood of translated Western literature, not just in satisfying the readers' curiosity about the outside world or even in inspiring writers toward hitherto unimagined literary experiments, but in providing a new reference system that would soon become ubiquitous (see Chapter 13 by Zha Mingjian). Still, as scholars have increasingly realized, above and beyond the veneer of references to the West and the new, tradition supplied major cultural resources for responding to modern issues. A fuller understanding of the late Qing, then, offers a possibility of reconceptualizing modernity as well as tradition (see Chapter 2 by Zhang Longxi).

REFERENCES

Chen, Pingyuan 陳平原. 1989. *Ershi shiji Zhongguo xiaoshuo shi, diyijuan 1897–1916* 二十世紀中國小説史, 第一卷 1897–1916 (A history of twentieth-century Chinese fiction, vol. 1, 1897–1916). Beijing: Beijing daxue chubanshe.

Hanan, Patrick. 2004. *Chinese Fiction of the Nineteenth and Early Twentieth Centuries: Essays by Patrick Hanan*. New York: Columbia University Press.

Hill, Michael Gibbs. 2012. *Lin Shu, Inc. Translation and the Making of Modern Chinese Culture*. Oxford, UK: Oxford University Press.

Hu, Ying. 2000. *Tales of Translation: Composing the New Woman in China, 1898–1918*. Stanford, CA: Stanford University Press.

Hu, Ying. 2004. "Writing Qiu Jin's Life: Wu Zhiying and Her Family Learning." *Late Imperial China*, 25.3: 119–160.

Huters, Theodore. 1989. "From Writing to Literature: the Development of Late Qing Theories of Prose." *Harvard Journal of Asiatic Studies*, 7.1: 51–96.

Huters, Theodore. 2005. *Bringing the World Home: Appropriating the West in Late Qing and Early Republican China*. Honolulu: University of Hawaii Press.

Liang, Qichao 梁啓超. 1936. *Zhongguo jinsanbainianxueshushi* 中國近三百年學術史 (A history of Chinese scholarship in past three hundred years). Shanghai: Zhonghua shuju.

Li, Boyuan. 1996. *Modern Times: A Brief History of Enlightenment*. Trans. Douglas Lancashire. Hong Kong: Chinese University Press.

Liu, E (Liu T'ieh-yün). 1990. *The Travels of Lao Ts'an*. Trans. Harold Shadick. New York: Columbia University Press.

Lo, Irving, and William Schultz. Eds. 1986. *Waiting for the Unicorn: Poems and Lyrics of China's Last Dynasty, 1644–1911*. Bloomington: Indiana University Press.

Schmidt, J. D. 1994. *Within the Human Realm: The Poetry of Huang Zunxian, 1848–1905*. Cambridge, UK: Cambridge University Press.

Tang, Xiaobing. 2000. *Chinese Modern: The Heroic and the Quotidian*. Durham, NC: Duke University Press.

Tarumoto, Teruo. 1998. "A Statistical Survey of Translated Fiction 1840–1920." In *Translation and Creation: Readings of Western Literature in Early Modern China, 1840–1918*, ed. David Pollard. Amsterdam: John Benjamins. 37–42.

Wang, David Der-wei. 1997. *Fin-de-siècle Splendor: Repressed Modernities of Late Qing Fiction, 1849–1911*. Stanford, CA: Stanford University Press.

Wu, Jianren. 1995. *The Sea of Regret: Two Turn-of-the-Century Chinese Romantic Novels*. Honolulu: University of Hawaii Press.

Wu, Shengqing. 2013. *Modern Archaics: Continuity and Innovation in the Chinese Lyrical Tradition, 1900–1937*. Cambridge, MA: Harvard University Asian Center.

Yan, Fu 嚴復.1986. *Yan Fu ji* 嚴復集 (Collected works of Yan Fu). 8 vols. Beijing: Zhonghua shuju.

4

War, Revolution, and Urban Transformations: Chinese Literature of the Republican Era, 1920s–1940s

Nicole Huang

War, revolution, and urban transformations were recurrent themes in Chinese literature from the immediate aftermath of the New Culture Movement of 1917 to the violent mid-century transition that ended the Republican era on the mainland in 1949 (although the Republic of China or the ROC has officially continued in Taiwan since then). The three decades of the 1920s–1940s witnessed drastic social, political, and cultural transformations. Yet, the volatile context did not curtail literary creativity, as literary historians have documented tremendous creative output for this period in all four major genres—fiction, poetry, drama, and essay. Literary historians have also established the affinity between Republican-era literature and its immediate predecessor, late Qing literature. Recent scholarship has revised and expanded our understanding of literary modernity in the Chinese context (D. Wang 1997; Hu Ying 2000; Huters 2005). Republican-era Chinese literature is indebted to the advocacy and experimentation of late Qing writers and intellectuals. For instance, a good portion of the Republican-era fiction writing, in particular its vast output of middlebrow fiction, was a continuation of nineteenth-century experimentation with prose genres, styles, and language (see Chapter 3 by Hu Ying).

Chinese literature after 1917 does, however, take on a distinctive identity, marked by a set of fresh voices and fueled by a range of radical discourses. A new breed of foreign-educated writers and intellectuals, who often aligned themselves with their counterparts in the modern Euro-American world, promoted a modern vernacular that was distinctively different from the hybrid language prevalent in previous decades and centuries. Revolution of literary language was pivotal in the minds of Hu Shi and Chen Duxiu, the two leaders of the New Culture Movement. Together, they engineered

A Companion to Modern Chinese Literature, First Edition. Edited by Yingjin Zhang.
© 2016 John Wiley & Sons, Ltd. Published 2016 by John Wiley & Sons, Ltd.

a "literary revolution" (*wenxue geming*), argued for the wholesale rejection of traditional Chinese literature and aesthetics, including the late Qing tradition, and demanded a new national literature that was fit for a revolutionized subject, in tune with everyday experiences and expressions, free of classical associations, and accessible to the masses (Anderson 1990: 26–37).

To many, the short story "Diary of a Madman" ("Kuangren riji," 1918) by the literary giant Lu Xun signals the beginning of this new national literature. The story constitutes a skillful application of the first-person voice and a daring experiment in the diary form as a new fictional subgenre. With his proud eccentricity and sharpened senses, Madman's wholesale rejection of traditional ethics marks him as a generational icon. Written in a highly introspective tone, the story also defines psycho-narration as a crucial feature of modern Chinese fiction (L. Lee 1987: 49–69; L. Liu 1995: 77–102). Introspective narratives mushroomed in the decade following the publication of "Diary of a Madman." The two collections of short fiction by Lu Xun—*Outcry* (*Nahan*, 1923) and *Vacillation* (*Panghuang*, 1926)—were subsequently canonized and revered as a model for all modern fiction to follow. In post-May Fourth China, a generation of younger authors, men and women, depicted personal journeys set against a volatile social and political landscape punctuated by war and revolution.

To be sure, fiction was by no means the only genre that renewed its creative energy and flourished in the early Republican decades, and Lu Xun's brand of short fiction was far from being the dominant mode of writing. Revolutionary potential was generated in other genres as well, but the proclaimed newness was never quite thorough and often appeared complicated by undercurrents of condemned literary traditions. While the New Culture Movement recognized theater as another powerful site capable of effecting social and political transformations, new forms of drama, in particular spoken drama (*huaju*) of the Western stage, coexisted with traditional forms of music theater, such as Peking Opera and Yue Opera, throughout the Republican era. Modern poetry written in the vernacular continued to flourish in the iconoclastic tradition championed by Huang Zunxian and Liang Qichao since the last decades of the nineteenth century, albeit taking on ever-more divergent influences from romanticist, symbolist, modernist, imagist, and other poetic movements of the Euro-American world, leading to a myriad of poetic societies in the 1920s–1930s. Meanwhile, classical elements were never completely ruled out; on the contrary, classical-style poetry, including the regulated verse and the uneven *ci* poetry, continued to be practiced by some major modern writers throughout the period (S. Wu 2013). The modern essay as a major literary genre is often left out of conventional histories of modern Chinese literature. Almost all major modern writers published significant numbers of essays, and being able to stylize a fine essay was still considered a baseline that testified to the maturity of an author. Modern essay writing was as vibrant and diversified as fiction and poetry. Various Euro-American influences as well as classical Chinese prose tradition converged, contributing to a modern Chinese prose culture that was fluid and diverse.

Many literary historians agree that realism (*xieshi zhuyi*) had been the mainstream since the early twentieth century in China. Republican-era writers were drawn to critical realism mainly as a tool for effecting radical social transformations. But how exactly literature intervenes and relates to the social reality—a critical issue plaguing many writers, critics, and intellectuals—often came to mark one literary group from another and sharply divided the literary field into many fragments and camps. The 1920s–1930s were two decades punctuated by frequent and fierce literary debates, charged by political interests and cultural influences from all directions. The outbreak of a full-scale Sino-Japanese war in 1937 temporarily shut down all ongoing literary activities and forced most to set aside their differences. An alliance—the All-China Resistance Association of Writers and Artists (*Zhonghua quanguo wenyijie kangdi xiehui*)—was established in 1937 to galvanize all literary and artistic camps toward the common goal of national salvation. But this united front could hardly shield the sharply divided literary field. Many writers, some already with canonical status, became deeply suspicious of the realist mode of writing, even while they continued to champion literature for social regeneration and actively render war, revolution, and urban transformations in their writings (Anderson 1990). Wartime Chinese literature of the 1930s–1940s appeared even more diverse and heterogeneous than that of the previous decade.

A myriad of voices and styles were presented in the literary field of Republican-era China: writers embarked on politically and culturally divergent paths, and a variety of interests and forces fought over publication channels and resources. During the three decades, various literary schools, societies, and communities formed, regrouped, merged, expanded, or disintegrated, an indication of literary production becoming a hotly contested political battleground where diverse interests, discourses, and ideologies converged and combated with each other. In the rest of this chapter, we first discuss Republican-era literature as a contested field, and then continue to address individual genres, styles, and key authors, with the focus on the divergent paths that modern Chinese writers took in their representations of war, revolution, and urban transformations.

Contestation in Genres and Styles

That the Republican-era literature was a hotly contested field is evident in the mushrooming of literary schools, societies, and communities after the 1910s. A list of some of the more visible groups include writers of butterfly fiction, the Literary Association (*Wenxue yanjiu hui*), the Creation Society (*Chuangzao she*), the Sun Society (*Taiyang she*), the Yusi Society (*Yusi pai*), the Analects Group (*Lunyu pai*), the Southern Society of Drama (*Nanshe*), the Crescent Moon Society of Poetry (*Xinyue she*), the New Sensationalist School of Fiction (*Xin ganjue pai*), the League of Left-Wing Writers (*Zhongguo zuoyi zuojia lianmeng*), and the All-China Resistance Association of Writers and Artists. Writers rarely worked alone; most were associated with clusters of writers, critics, and theorists, mobilized around a set of publication channels. Literary pursuits became increasingly professionalized, with growing dependency on networks of people and resources (Hockx 1999; Denton and Hockx 2008). Mapping this literary field would generate a complex, layered, and dynamic web-like structure, testifying to the fluidity and vibrancy of literary production during these turbulent decades.

Genres, mediums, and styles are one way to demarcate one literary school from another. Fiction writers took center stage in the Literary Research Association, although many were also essayists and poets. Poets took the helm in the Creation Society and the Sun Society, although some members became important critics and theorists. The Yusi and Analects Groups gathered key essayists of the 1920s–1930s, while members of the Crescent Moon Society practiced all four major literary genres, with poetry being the most prominent. Contestation took place between different societies not only along fundamental issues such as the social function of literature and the roles of writers and intellectuals, but also on the very perimeters of specific genres and styles.

The late Qing reformer and intellectual leader Liang Qichao's championing of fiction, highlighting its social function as unmatched by that of other literary genres, might have given fiction the position as the favored child of modern Chinese literature (X. Tang 2000: 11–21) (see Chapter 12 by Yiyan Wang). But battles fought over poetry and prose were just as fierce. The Crescent Moon Society had been the target of criticisms from left-leaning literary groups since its formation in 1928. The fiercest attacks came from poets and theorists in the Creation Society. Lu Xun joined the campaign in late 1929 as he became the spiritual leader of the newly formed League of Left-Wing Writers. When Liang Shiqiu, Luo Longji, and other key members of the Crescent Moon Society defended their pursuits in the name of freedom, they met immediate counterattacks by Feng Naichao and others from the Creation Society. Feng and his associates argued that the Crescent Moon members used literary freedom as a pretense to safeguard their own class privilege; and for literature to be of any value, the correct class consciousness had to be built into any endeavor (L. Wong 2008: 299–305). Left-wing writers and theorists passionately called for a leap from "literary revolution" to "revolutionary literature" (*geming de wenxue*). They distanced themselves from the legacy of the May Fourth Movement and demanded that bourgeois writers part with their old tastes and values and move closer to proletarian needs. Poetic experiments keenly pursued by poets and theorists of the Crescent Moon Society were deemed out of date and even toxic to the collective cause.

Battles fought over the essay genre tell a related but different story; they are a fine example to illustrate the literary community's constant effort at engendering sub-genres, forming subgroups, and drawing different camps. The term "essay" (*sanwen*) was frequently redefined as it could no longer contain an increasingly diversified pool of modern essayists. The subgenre of *xiaopin wen* (informal essay), exemplified by works of Zhou Zuoren and Lin Yutang, is characterized by a light and relaxing tone, simple and elegant diction, political disengagement, wit, a leisurely mood, sheer delight in everyday pleasures, and a highly aestheticized vision of reality. The modern *xiaopin wen* demonstrates much affinity to its premodern precedent, the late Ming informal essay, a landmark of the time-honored literati culture of sixteenth and seventeenth centuries (Daruvala 2000: 113–168; Laughlin 2008). *Zawen* (critical essay) grows out of the *xiaopin wen* tradition as a corrective measure to steer the genre away from its focus on personal and seemingly apolitical matters and toward a socially engaged and politically charged angle. *Zawen* as the revolutionized *xiaopin wen* is personified by Lu Xun and many of his followers, including a group of leftist writers residing in Shanghai during the Orphan Island (*gudao*) era of 1937–1941 (Gunn 1980; L. Lee 1987: 110–129). The *zawen* style emphasizes intellectual sharpness and rhetorical eloquence, advocates active engagement with social reality, and maintains the belief that literary writing should be employed as a powerful tool for social criticism and political intervention (see Chapter 11 by Qian Suoqiao).

Genres and mediums often bleed into each other, while prose styles grow to be a mix of the modern and the archaic. Here, the modern essay provides more fine examples. The most interesting of these is Lu Xun's collection of modernist essays, *Wild Grass* (*Yecao*, 1926), published in the same year as his fiction collection *Vacillation*. These celebrated short pieces are often called "prose poems" (*sanwenshi*), another subgenre of the essay form. Rich in imagery, laden with both Western symbolist and Chinese classical associations, they are good examples of how poetry and prose blend to create a literary hybrid and how traditional poetics holds a strong place for even the most iconoclastic writer of the time (L. Lee 1987: 89–109). As Lu Xun's most personal writings, the pieces in *Wild Grass* are also a good indicator of how contestation takes place within an individual author. By 1926, Lu Xun had already become a literary giant, a leader to a generation of younger writers and intellectuals who looked to him for directions. But his inner torments and constant meditation between hope and despair, combined with an acute sense of genres, mediums, and styles, and an innate desire toward linguistic experimentation, finally found a channel of expressions in *Wild Grass*.

Writing War, Romancing Revolution

Lu Xun's *Wild Grass* reveals a side of him that seems to betray his public persona, but he was no doubt the most influential literary figure who worked to advance a literature of social and political engagement from the 1920s until his death in 1936. Lu Xun's active participation in the left-wing movement during the last years of his life helped steer the movement into the mainstream. From the iconoclastic voices of the May Fourth period to left-wing writings of the 1930s–1940s, a progressive literary tradition thrived against the violent background of urban and rural reforms, civil unrest, mass movements, and wars.

Revolution on various scales was a prevalent theme in Chinese fiction of the 1920s–1930s. A young generation of writers and intellectuals took on revolution as a political gesture, a cultural pursuit, an individual journey, an intellectual inquiry, and a career project. Revolution as a concept and a practice permeated daily life during the three decades (Chen Jianhua 2000; Huang Ziping 1996; D. Wang 2004: 77–116). Ye Shengtao's novel *The School Master Ni Huanzhi* (*Ni Huanzhi*, 1928) depicts a young educator finding himself on the streets of Shanghai in 1925, in the midst of what was called the "Bloody Massacre of the May Thirtieth." This close proximity to proletarian revolution shakes him to the core, reshapes his understanding of mass movements, and propels him to forego prior individual pursuits and join the collective cause. Similarly, the young female protagonist in Mao Dun's novel *Rainbow* (*Hong*, 1929) could very well represent a generation of emancipated women who have left the confines of a traditional home in their discovery of personal liberation, eventually also finding themselves on urban streets, in the midst of revolution, and witnessing exhilarating moments as well as brutal consequences. Similar to many other leftist narratives of the time, *Rainbow* combines political awakening with the female protagonist's sexual emancipation, contributing to a prevalent formula of writing known as "revolution plus love" (J. Liu 2003; D. Wang 2004: 77–116).

When the Chinese League of Left-Wing Writers was formed as an alliance between Lu Xun and the leftist camp in 1930, Mao Dun, Zhou Yang, and Qu Qiubai became the league's most important figures, and Mao Dun was revered as the league's leading novelist. He continued to produce narratives that combined urban sensibilities with a sharpened sense of a divided world and a futuristic vision of revolution on an even larger scale. His novel *Midnight* (*Ziye*, 1933), arguably his most important work, pictures Shanghai as a stratified city on the brink of a major proletarian revolution. He renders vividly the crisis of urban bourgeoisie, the intensifying labor relations, and the impending doom of indigenous capitalism in the face of encroaching national and international forces.

A large-scale war is already looming on the horizon as Mao Dun's *Midnight* draws to a close. Japan's encroachment of Chinese territories, beginning with the occupation of Manchuria (Northeast China) in 1931 and the bombing of Shanghai in 1932, set China into wartime mode and compelled writers and intellectuals to form a united front in a common battle against the foreign invaders. Wartime experiences are featured prominently in Chinese literature of the 1930s–1940s. Individual writers, however, approach such experiences differently. There are direct depictions of Japanese atrocities and Chinese resistance efforts, as in narratives by Northeastern writers Xiao Jun and Duanmu Hongliang, who wrote and published while in exile, far away from their lost homeland. Xiao Jun's *Village in August* (*Bayuede xiangcun*, 1935; English 1944), for instance, depicts how a village is ravaged by Japanese soldiers and how resistance fighters form a militia group on the ruins of the village and fight the Japanese fearlessly (see Chapter 19 by Haili Kong).

When the full-scale war broke out in 1937 and Japan occupied much of Eastern China, many progressive writers and intellectuals joined a massive exodus and retreated to the hinterland. Literature of resistance continued to be produced, albeit scattered in separate regions. Drama and essay took center stage in Shanghai between 1937 and 1941, during the Orphan Island phase, where progressive writers and intellectuals used literature as a tool to directly comment on the ongoing war efforts and mobilize masses in a patriotic campaign. Key figures in this movement included essayists Tang Tao and Ke Ling and dramatists Li Jianwu and Yu Ling (P. Fu 1993). After Mao Zedong's "Talks at the Yan'an Forum on Literature and Art" ("*Zai Yan'an wenyi zuotanhui shang de jianghua,*" 1942; hereafter "Yan'an Talks"), literature produced in Communist-controlled rural areas stepped up war mobilization efforts and anticipated a new literary landscape to evolve after the 1949 transition.

While the literature of resistance is loud and clear, there are many narratives from the period that deal with war and wartime experiences implicitly or figuratively. In Eileen Chang's (Zhang Ailing) short story "Blockade" (Fengsuo, 1943), a male office worker encounters a female college teacher on a streetcar caught in the middle of an air raid when the city of Shanghai comes to a standstill. As the story concludes, the blockade is lifted, the brief "romance" draws to an abrupt end, and the streetcar moves again. Both protagonists resume their original positions, "as if all that occurred during the blockade never happened. The whole of Shanghai had dozed off and dreamed an unfathomable dream" (Zhang Ailing 1946: 387). The interior of a streetcar caught in the middle of a citywide blockade conveniently provides the spatial and temporal frame for the reader to imagine what it is like to live in a war-torn city. As in Chang's other narratives, war is depicted only in a metaphorical sense, functioning more as a literary device to create a sense of temporal and spatial suspension (N. Huang 2005: 22–23).

Arguably the most important narrative that deals with experiences of wartime atrocities is Xiao Hong's *The Field of Life and Death* (*Shengsi chang*, 1935; English 1979). Though canonized in the same leftist context, this novel is different from *Village in August* and other anti-Japanese resistance literature of the time. A Northeastern writer in exile far away from her homeland, Xiao Hong's focus is not on the awakening and revolt of a rural population against foreign invasion. The novel is filled with stark depictions of the animal-like existence of villagers who are stricken by poverty and sickness. The narrative is organized by a cyclical rhythm—daily life flows from summer into autumn, which is followed by a long winter and a spring that arrives gingerly. "Birth, old age, illness, and death" are the natural law that dominates the world inside the novel. In the first two-thirds of novel, time seems to stand still, which renders the sudden invasion of Japanese forces in the last third of the book all the more violent and cruel, and Xiao Hong's narration changes from cyclical to linear with the brutal entry of the Japanese (N. Huang 2006: 241–249). *The Field of Life and Death* is Xiao Hong's effort at locating a voice that is both true to her time and uniquely hers.

Narratives of Urban Transformations

Revolution and war transformed the vast countryside as well as urban regions in the Republican era. To be sure, urban sensibilities in modern Chinese literature cannot be simply understood as experiences developed in major urban centers along coastal China. Rather, the sense of the urban is layered, fluid, and closely intertwined with the ideas of childhood, homeland, villages, towns, travel, displacement, and homecoming (see Chapter 20 by Weijie Song). For instance, few people would consider Shen Congwen as an urban writer. But Shen, a prolific writer known for his enchanting and often gloomy narratives of the mountainous region of West Hunan, was nonetheless writing in major cities and for a predominantly urban readership. He wrote from his memories of growing up away from urban centers, his travels through the often treacherous regions of China's inlands, and his deep sense of nostalgia and displacement in an established literary life (Kinkley 1987; D. Wang 1992). In Shen's short story "Lamp" (Deng, 1929), the young narrator, a budding writer residing in Shanghai, is frequently visited by a young woman at night. She finds an old oil lamp on his desk intriguing and demands to hear stories about it. The narrator willingly turns into a storyteller, producing a narrative that lengthens with each night's visit. At the end of the story, the narrator has built a travelogue of the lamp associated with a distant place and a bygone era (Shen Congwen 1936: 169–195). The self-reflexivity of the story cannot be missed: here, through the medium of a short story, Shen Congwen reflects on the role of an urban storyteller who constructs rural tales for a living, and on the physical as well as imaginary distance that separates the present from the fictional past.

Shen Congwen's narratives set in West Hunan can be seen as a continuation of the tradition first established by Lu Xun. Lu Xun's short story "Hometown" ("Guxiang," 1921) defines a key fictional subgenre called "native soil fiction" (*xiangtu xiaoshuo*), a form of writing that persisted throughout the Republican era. The recurrent image of a returning traveler no longer finding a home in modern narratives can be traced to Lu Xun's early efforts. But Shen has certainly moved a step further by finding a narrative home through repeated and incessant retelling of an unofficial history of a distant time and place.

Further complicating Lu Xun's tradition as well as our understanding of urban narratives of the Republican era is a set of narratives by the stylist Shi Tuo, who championed a small town model with works such as *Chronicle of Orchard Town* (*Guoyuancheng ji*, 1938) and *A Master in a Village of No Hope* (*Wuwangcun guanzhu*, 1941) (Y. Zhang 1996: 38–40). The Chinese small town, the liminal zone caught between a major metropolis and the vast countryside, finds its most skillful manifestation in Xiao Hong's posthumously published *Tales of Hulan River* (*Hulanhe zhuan*, 1942; English 1979). This last novel by Xiao Hong forms an interesting contrast with her first novel. The themes of misery and physical pain that accompany the characters in *The Field of Life and Death* are overshadowed in *Tales of Hulan River* by Xiao Hong's attempt to delve into inner spiritual depression and to achieve a more thorough lyricism, which is skillfully realized in the episodic structure of *Tales of Hulan River*. Similar to Shi Tuo's Orchard Town, the true protagonist of Xiao Hong's novel is a place, a small town called Hulan, and the memories associated with it. Episodic narrative of a gallery of hometown figures is juxtaposed with the childhood reminiscences of a grown-up woman. The novel skillfully weaves personal history with the history of a region.

If Xiao Hong's small town remains timeless and stands still throughout her narratives, a great amount of urban narratives produced in the Republican era have dealt with social transformations on a larger scale. War, revolution, and urban transformations are intertwined in the vast output of popular fiction that appealed to an urban middlebrow readership in Chinese cities and towns throughout the Republican era.

To many, the modern city was a site of sharp contrasts and drastic social, political, and cultural changes. Leftist writers depicted it as a breeding ground of proletarian revolution that would overthrow the old order and give rise to a brave new world. Modernist writers pictured the modern city as an exhilarating labyrinth filled with discoveries as well as traps. For popular fiction writers, however, modernity was rarely an overnight project; modern ways of life gained its ground gradually, over a long course of small steps and minor changes. These writers would choose to represent urban transformations in a more piecemeal fashion. A look at how the modern city was envisioned differently would further testify to the earlier argument on the literary field as a sharply divided territory.

A history of the urban literature of Republican-era China would have to include a substantial discussion of butterfly fiction. This school of popular fiction and the journals that it was associated with never faded from the cultural imagination of urban readers in China throughout the first half of the twentieth century. The school's most glorious days were in the 1910s–1920s, when many of the butterfly writers were themselves entrepreneurs in a burgeoning publishing industry. These individuals were the first group of professional writers who were pushed to the center stage of urban life by the ever-flourishing urban commerce and burgeoning media culture since the late nineteenth century. They and their writings were tied to every facet of the modern urban life (Link 1981; Z. Zhang 2005: 49).

Many veteran butterfly authors are fine examples of writers acting as public intellectuals and entrepreneurs. Zhang Henshui, for instance, edited newspapers during his earlier years before he became a very prolific butterfly writer, with representative works such as *Fate in Tears and Laughter* (*Tixiao yinyuan*, 1930) and *Shanghai Express* (*Ping Hu tongche*, 1935) (see Chapter 15 by Yi Zheng). An even more persuasive example is Zhou Shoujuan, who, between 1920 and 1932, edited the "Unfettered Talk" (*Ziyou tan*) column for the *Shanghai Daily* (*Shenbao*) before the position was taken over by Li Liewen. Li subsequently introduced Lu Xun's fiery critical essays to his readers, a further reminder of how the field of popular print had always been a political battlefield throughout the Republican era (N. Huang 2005: 54–56). Zhou and others were such seasoned editors and publishers that they ensured the success of popular fiction as an urban enterprise.

By the 1930s, the prevalent linked-chapter style of fiction (*zhanghui xiaoshuo*) in butterfly journals began to lose its readership in competition with the Shanghai modernist literature represented by the experiments of a group of French-influenced writers surrounding the journal *Les Contemporains* (*Xiandai*). The rise of literary and artistic modernism in China was concurrent with the height of the leftist movements. Called the "New Sensationalists," this modernist trend, joined by fiction writers, poets, theorists, and visual and performing artists, became popular from the late 1920s to the mid-1930s. Pages of Shanghai's commercial print media were filled with literary and artistic representations of a range of subversive and seductive women, created by modernist writers and artists such as Mu Shiying, Liu Na'ou, Ye Lingfeng, and Guo Jianying. In these verbal and visual representations, male travelers to the city visit hotels, coffee houses, dance halls, neon-lit streets, brilliant shop windows, and, of course, enigmatic women. Trapped in an urban maze, a male protagonist confronts a wide range of emotions that include wonder, fascination, anguish, frustration, confusion, and distress. Emerging from these tumultuous emotions is a pieced-together female image of the Chinese Modern Girl (*modeng nülang*), reminiscent of the *moga* of Taishô Japan (Y. Zhang 1996: 185–231; L. Lee 1999b: 191–231; Shih 2001; N. Huang 2005: 84–85) (see Chapter 25 by Tze-lan Sang).

With the beginning of the Second Sino-Japanese War in 1937, this prominent image of a menacing woman quickly disappeared and was replaced by a focus on national resistance and salvation. A good portion of the wartime literary output in major Chinese cities, however, seemed to deal less with the external context directly and to focus more on personal journeys through a divided map. But even in the least political of these narratives, one can still detect themes of war and revolution lurking in the background. Through much of the violent first half of the twentieth century, urban literature thrived in a flourishing print industry and formed a mutually supportive relationship with an ever-growing reading populace (Reed 2004; W. Yeh 2008).

The butterfly writers and editors played a major role in sustaining cultural life in war-ravaged cities, particularly in Shanghai. By the early 1940s, veteran butterfly writers decided to renew the school's tradition by promoting a younger generation of urban writers, particularly young women authors just out of college. They wanted to appeal to a generation of young urban readers and thereby reclaim the important position that the school and its cultural products had occupied in the leisure life of urban China. The rise of women writers in Shanghai during the war, particularly during the Japanese occupation period, had everything to do with butterfly writers' work in discovering and promoting young women authors, redefining popular literature and reestablishing its importance, sustaining and incorporating previous literary traditions, and maintaining and widening its reading public. The butterfly school played a leadership role in constructing a wartime culture that was primarily centered around practices of reading, writing, and publishing—that is, the sphere of modern print culture—during a period when other forms of modern life were being smashed to pieces (N. Huang 2005: 50–83).

The most important writer to emerge out of this wartime surge of popular print culture is Eileen Chang. Chang began her writing career in the early 1940s in Japanese-occupied Shanghai and went on to become the most prominent author and public intellectual in the besieged city. Many of her early works were collected in two volumes, a collection of short stories and novellas entitled *Romances* (*Chuanqi*, 1944) and a book of prose entitled *Written on Water* (*Liuyan*, 1945). Chang's writing from the period was deeply imprinted with marks of her own time. An alternative wartime narrative was constructed to contradict the grand narratives of national salvation and revolution. In an age punctuated by landmark historical events, Chang highlighted the seemingly irrelevant details of daily life in her stories of ordinary men and women caught in wars, revolutions, and drastic social transformations. In both her wartime fiction and essays, her impressionistic view of the modern era displays colors, lines, shapes, textures, and moods, which are often crystallized in the rapidly changing styles of women's clothes. Chang is at her best when she juxtaposes fragments of an external reality (e.g., air raid, blockade, hunger, death, and scarcity) with the intricacies of a domestic and private life (e.g., love, loss, fantasy, yearning, and artistic creativity). What shines through her highly stylized prose is the entanglement of a personalized inward journey and a persistent—although not always explicit—attempt to come to terms with a tumultuous time.

In Eileen Chang's novella "Love in a Fallen City" ("*Qingcheng zhi lian*," 1943), argu-ably her best work of fiction, the protagonists travel between Hong Kong and Shanghai around the outbreak of the Pacific War. This is one of Chang's many "tales of two cities"—narratives set in Hong Kong and Shanghai, written with Shanghai readers as her target audience. Its title alludes to an ancient Chinese tale in which the beauty of a woman is blamed for the collapse of a kingdom. Chang's modern narrative shares with the ancient legend a sense that war and turbulence are always lurking in the background and will eventually emerge as a substantial force that transforms individ-uals. As the story unfolds, the young and defiant widow Bai Liusu encounters Fan Liuyuan, a wealthy dandy from an overseas Chinese aristocratic family. She decisively leaves the repressive house of her parents and travels to Hong Kong to be with Liuyuan. In Hong Kong, a city depicted as an exotic mirror image of Shanghai, Liusu gradually falls under the spell of Liuyuan's scheme of seduction. She would succumb to the fate of being Liuyuan's mistress if not for the outbreak of the war, which destroys the city but seals marital commitment between the two protagonists: "The demise of Hong Kong completes her. In this inexplicable world, who can say for sure what is the cause and what is the effect? Who knows… Perhaps a metropolis is toppled precisely for the sake of fulfilling her romance" (Zhang Ailing 1946: 190).

If Chang's fiction is of any indication, then agency and creativity of many modern Chinese writers should be defined against a violent context. Wartime Chinese literature displayed such a range of diverse voices and styles precisely because writers chose to exercise their agency and creativity despite external constraints. While many chose to confront such experiences directly, others such as Eileen Chang and Xiao Hong expressed no interest in composing a comprehensive account of war, resistance, or the awakening of individual consciousness. While many would picture a world filled with sharp con-trasts, others would render heroes and villains both absent in their works. Chang herself has explained such absence clearly in one of her own essays in which she discusses "Love in a Fallen City": "Liusu escapes from her decadent family, but the baptism of the Battle of Hong Kong does not mold her into a revolutionary woman" (Zhang Ailing 1945: 18). Similarly, in contrast with many writers who would focus on a world ravaged by massive destruction, Xiao Hong alone chose to paint the still life of a hometown that turns at its own pace. While war, revolution, and urban transformations are indeed recurrent themes in Republican-era Chinese literature, a wide range of choices in how these themes are represented suggest the energy, diversity, and sustaining powers of this literature.

Postwar Departures

The divergent paths that writers took in representing war, revolution, and urban transformations extended into the postwar era. When Japan surrendered on August 15, 1945, the Nationalist government returned to reclaim the previously occupied cities in Eastern China. Writers and intellectuals who had joined the massive exodus to seek refuge in the hinterland returned to coastal cities to rebuild a literary field. While China's war of resistance had ended, conflicts between the Nationalists and Communists over the control of China intensified. Peace was fleeting. As many had foretold in their writing, an even larger destruction was on its way.

The postwar era witnessed a few departures from wartime literary tradition. Most significant was a new surge of literary modernism, particularly in poetry and fiction. In poetry, a group of nine poets, who published in the two journals *Poetry Creation* (*Shi chuangzao*) and *New Poetry of China* (*Zhongguo xinshi*), championed a new brand of modernist poetry that was a synthesis of inward journey and social engagement. Several members of the group studied foreign languages and literatures in college and were brought together by a common interest in Anglo-American modernist poetry. Most active during 1946–1948, the group was later renamed as the Nine Leaves School (*Jiuye pai*) of poetry. Mu Dan, often considered the most complex poet among the group, was himself a survivor of the preceding war. As a volunteer soldier in a Chinese military expedition that fought the Japanese in Burma, he witnessed half of the 50,000 troops perishing in a harsh environment. This unspeakable experience finds its paradoxical manifestations in his poetry where innermost feelings are juxtaposed with a deep distrust of the capacity of language in representing love, loss, and trauma.

This interest in inward journey was shared by members of the most important literary society of the 1940s—the July School (*Qiyue pai*). The July School also produced a number of modernist poets, but fiction represents its highest achievements. The leftist writer and theorist Hu Feng was the school's theorist and spiritual leader. Hu's theories of literature emerged out of the leftist politics of the 1930s, evolved during the war years, and eventually departed from the leftist tradition with an increasing emphasis on writer's individuality and the depth of psycho-narration. The concept of a "world literature" (*shijie wenxue*) appeared in the writings of Hu Feng and his associates. Hu painstakingly situated the progressive literature of China, beginning with the May Fourth tradition, in the global context of a world literature. Resisting the tendency of worshipping the May Fourth literary tradition on a divine pedestal, Hu insisted that the most meaningful way to carry on the May Fourth legacy was to recognize that the enlightenment project was incomplete, and that it ought to be carried forth by a new generation of writers and intellectuals (Denton 1998; Y. Shu 2000).

Hu Feng's ideas of a new literature of enlightenment and psychological depth were best realized by his closest associate, a young novelist named Lu Ling, who came of age in the 1930s and published his debut novel *Hungry Guo Su'e* (*Ji'e de Guo Su'e*, 1943) at age 21 years. Lu's expansive novel *Children of the Rich* (*Caizhu de ernümen*, 1945) presents the physical journeys and psychological odysseys of the younger generation of a gentry family through war and revolution. Lu's fiction in the immediate postwar years focused on the impoverished social classes, particularly the rural population. Destitute farmers in his postwar narratives displayed similar depth in physical and psychological torments as urban intellectual figures. In charging all his main characters with contradictions and vitality, Lu chose a unique angle to render individuals against the violent context of war and revolution.

The July School's championing of subjectivity in literature met increasing criticisms from other members of the leftist literary community, but Lu Ling and others continued their literary activities through the mid-century transition into the early years of the socialist era. The group arrived at its demise in 1955 when it was formally branded as "counter-revolutionary" by the new Communist regime and its members were publicly disgraced and incarcerated, effectively closing an important final chapter in Republican-era Chinese literature.

References

Anderson, Marston. 1990. *The Limits of Realism: Chinese Fiction in the Revolutionary Period.* Berkeley: University of California Press.

Chen Jianhua 陳建華. 2000. *Geming de xiandaixing: zhongguo geming huayu kaolun* 革命的現代性:中國革命話語考論 (The modernity of revolution: a study of Chinese discourses on revolution). Shanghai: Shanghai guji chubanshe.

Daruvala, Susan. 2000. *Zhou Zuoren and an Alternative Response to Chinese Modernity.* Cambridge, MA: Harvard University Asia Center.

Denton, Kirk A. 1998. *The Problematic of Self in Modern Chinese Literature: Hu Feng and Lu Ling.* Stanford, CA: Stanford University Press.

Denton, Kirk A., and Michel Hockx. Eds. 2008. *Literary Societies of Republican China.* Lanham, MD: Lexington Books.

Fu, Poshek. 2000. *Passivity, Resistance, and Collaboration: Intellectuals Choices in Occupied Shanghai, 1937–1945.* Stanford, CA: Stanford University Press.

Gunn, Edward M. 1980. *Unwelcome Muse: Chinese Literature in Shanghai and Peking, 1937–1945.* New York: Columbia University Press.

Hockx, Michel. Ed. 1999. *The Literary Field in Twentieth-Century China.* Honolulu: University of Hawaii Press.

Hu Ying. 2000. *Tales of Translation: Composing the New Woman in China, 1898–1918.* Stanford, CA: Stanford University Press.

Huang, Nicole. 2005. *Women, War, Domesticity: Shanghai Literature and Popular Culture of the 1940s.* Leiden: Brill.

Huang, Nicole. 2006. "Xiao Hong." In *Dictionary of Literary Biography: Chinese Fiction Writers, 1900–1949,* ed. Thomas Moran. New York: Thomson Gale. 241–249.

Huang, Ziping 黃子平. 1996. *Geming, lishi, xiaoshuo* 革命, 歷史, 小説 (Revolution, history, fiction). Hong Kong: Oxford University Press.

Huters, Theodore. 2005. *Bringing the World Home: Appropriating the West in Late Qing and Early Republican China.* Honolulu: University of Hawaii Press.

Kinkley, Jeffrey C. 1987. *The Odyssey of Shen Congwen.* Stanford, CA: Stanford University Press.

Laughlin, Charles A. 2008. *The Literature of Leisure and Chinese Modernity.* Honolulu: University of Hawaii Press.

Lee, Leo Ou-fan. 1987. *Voices from the Iron House: A Study of Lu Xun.* Bloomington: Indiana University Press.

Lee, Leo Ou-fan. 1999b. *Shanghai Modern: The Flowering of a New Urban Culture in China, 1930–1945*. Cambridge, MA: Harvard University Press.

Link, E. Perry. 1981. *Mandarin Ducks and Butterflies: Popular Fiction in Early Twentieth-Century Chinese Cities*. Berkeley: University of California Press.

Liu, Jianmei. 2003. *Revolution Plus Love: Literary History, Women's Bodies, and Thematic Repetition in Twentieth-Century Chinese Fiction*. Honolulu: University of Hawaii Press.

Liu, Lydia H. 1995. *Translingual Practice: Literature, National Culture, and Translated Modernity— China, 1900–1937*. Stanford, CA: Stanford University Press.

Reed, Christopher A. 2004. *Gutenberg in Shanghai: Chinese Print Capitalism, 1876–1937*. Vancouver: University of British Columbia Press.

Shih, Shu-mei. 2001. *The Lure of the Modern: Writing Modernism in Semicolonial China, 1917–1937*. Berkeley: University of California Press.

Shu, Yunzhong. 2000. *Buglers on the Home Front: The Wartime Practice of the Qiyue School*. Albany: State University of New York Press.

Tang, Xiaobing. 2000. *Chinese Modern: The Heroic and the Quotidian*. Durham, NC: Duke University Press.

Wang, David Der-wei. 1992. *Fictional Realism in Twentieth-Century China: Mao Dun, Lao She, Shen Congwen*. New York: Columbia University Press.

Wang, David Der-wei. 1997. *Fin-de-siècle Splendor: Repressed Modernities of Late Qing Fiction, 1849–1911*. Stanford, CA: Stanford University Press.

Wang, David Der-wei. 2004. *The Monster That Is History: History, Violence, and Fictional Writing in Twentieth-Century China*. Berkeley: University of California Press.

Wong, Lawrence Wang-chi. 2008. "Lions and Tigers in Groups: The Crescent Moon School in Modern Chinese Literary History." In *Literary Societies of Republican China*, Edited by Kirk Denton and Michel Hockx. Lanham: Lexington Books. 279–312.

Wu, Shengqing. 2013. *Modern Archaics: Continuity and Innovation in the Chinese Lyrical Tradition, 1900–1937*. Cambridge, MA: Harvard University Asian Center.

Yeh, Wen-hsin. 2008. *Shanghai Splendor: A Cultural History, 1843–1949*. Berkeley: University of California Press.

Zhang, Ailing 張愛玲. 1945. *Liuyan* 流言 (Written on water). Shanghai: Zhongguo kexue gongsi.

Zhang, Ailing 張愛玲. 1946. *Chuanqi zengdingben* 傳奇增訂本 (Romances, expanded Edition). Shanghai: Shanhe tushu gongsi.

Zhang, Zhen. 2005. *An Amorous History of the Silver Screen: Shanghai Cinema, 1896–1937*. Chicago: University of Chicago Press.

Zhang, Yingjin. 1996. *The City in Modern Chinese Literature and Film: Configurations of Space, Time, and Gender*. Stanford, CA: Stanford University Press.

5
Socialist Literature Driven by Radical Modernity, 1950–1980

Chen Xiaoming (translated by Qin Liyan)

In 1949, China established a proletarian state. In retrospect, if we try to understand Chinese history in the last six decades from the perspective of China's inevitable choice of modernity, perhaps we can find a more tolerant attitude toward history. By looking at the literary history of these years as a process of modernity, a necessary path for China to cope with Western challenges, we can see not only the radicality and rationality of history but also its difficulties and passions. Chinese literature in these decades is not outside of world modernity, but it surely has its distinct features.

In spite of ruptures, the history of contemporary Chinese literature has inherent connections with modern Chinese literature before 1949. From the Republican Revolution aimed at overturning monarchy, to the Communist revolution aimed at erasing exploitations, the pressure of time and enthusiastic ideals transformed Chinese modernity quickly. Literature was deeply involved in this process and underwent a series of phases: from the construction of the feelings of a subject, to the propagating of political symbols; from bourgeois enlightenment literature to revolutionary literature, and then to socialist revolutionary literature. Some landmark events, thoughts, and texts provide clues for us to understand this history. Mao Zedong's "Yan'an Talks" is such a milestone, to which a definitive change of direction in contemporary Chinese literature can be traced.

From the campaigns against *The Life of Wu Xun* (*Wuxun zhuan*, directed by Sun Yu, 1950) and "Researches on *Dream of the Red Chamber*" ("*Hongloumeng yanjiu*"), to the campaign to eradicate the residues of Hu Shi's bourgeois thoughts and the Cultural Revolution, Chinese socialist culture tried to blaze a trail outside of modern bourgeois literature. This process was difficult, complex, and costly, but its lessons are not merely

A Companion to Modern Chinese Literature, First Edition. Edited by Yingjin Zhang.
© 2016 John Wiley & Sons, Ltd. Published 2016 by John Wiley & Sons, Ltd.

negative. Judged from its purpose and motivation, socialist revolutionary literature is a "miracle" worthy of reexamination.

After the Cultural Revolution, China entered the New Era (*xin shiqi*). In this period, the Cultural Revolution was interpreted as a deviation from the originally correct historical route, and a return was called for. From this new vantage point, the New Era was linked to the route of realism since the 1950s. In literature, the beginning of the New Era indeed kept some links with the 1950s, and some debated topics (e.g., the typicality of realism, human nature, humanism, and aesthetics) were handed down from the 1950s. However, if "scar literature" (*shanghen wenxue*) and "reform literature" (*gaige wenxue*) still tried to restore realism early on, Chinese literature became more diverse with "Misty Poetry" (*menglong shi*) and subsequent modernism, "roots-searching literature" (*xungen wenxue*), theories of subjectivity, and the emergence of the avant-garde. After the 1990s, diversification quickened. One group after another of young writers came onto the stage with their new experiences of life and literature (see Chapter 6 by Tao Dongfeng). Now, a consumer society has emerged, which not only challenges the art forms that depend on paper, but also calls for new literary experiments. Chinese literature in the last six decades incorporates experiences that are not available to any other national literature. It is difficult, if not impossible, to understand and interpret Chinese literature with one fixed standard or paradigm.

The Direction of Revolutionary Literature and the Construction of the Subject

There are obviously ruptures between modern enlightenment literature and the proletariat revolutionary, which account for the complexity of Chinese modernity and the history of contemporary Chinese literature. Although there are many links between May Fourth literature, revolutionary literature, and socialist literature, the turn to socialist literature is surely sharp. Here, the most important rupture lies in that a proletarian worldview replaced the enlightenment worldview cultivated by the May Fourth proponents. Li Zehou's "variations of the two themes of enlightenment (*qimeng*) and national salvation (*jiuwang*)" provides an effective means of explaining the change in modern Chinese thoughts. Through "variations" we find a tendency toward increasing radicality, which culminated in the dominance of national salvation; thus, as alternative modernity, radical revolution could not be accommodated with enlightenment (Li Zehou 1987: 7–49).

After 1949, Chinese literature embarked on a long road of socialism. Indeed, before that, in the liberated area of Yan'an, socialist literature and art had already begun. In May 1942, Mao's "Yan'an Talks" established the theoretical foundation for revolutionary literature, dictating its nature, tasks, and direction. The paramount issue in the "Yan'an Talks" is that of standpoints, attitudes, and worldviews. Here, the crucial difference between revolutionary literature and May Fourth literature is that writers are asked to give up their standpoints based on individual freedom, which was formed in line with bourgeois enlightenment thoughts. As a further clarification for the change of worldview, the "Yan'an Talks" set "the direction of workers, peasants, and soldiers" for socialist literature. Mao put forth the question of factionalism: "for whom does one work?" The "factions," referencing literary societies formed according to May Fourth enlightenment thoughts and liberal ideas of individualism (see Chapter 4 by Nicole Huang), are deemed the fortresses of bourgeois "modernity" and thus the obstacles to achieving a unified leadership in literature. The methods of "popularization" (*puji*) and "enhancement" (*tigao*) are put on the agenda. "Popularization" means two things. First, the intellectuals' position as the subjects of enlightenment is changed; now their task is to serve the people and produce works that are welcomed by them. Second, "popularization" means to unify and educate the people and attack the enemies. "Unification" (*tuanjie*) and "education" (*jiaoyu*) are not individualistic expressions of the intellectuals, but are the projects of spiritual/aesthetic mobilization under the Party leadership and in the name of the proletariat. The "Yan'an Talks" laid down the foundation of Chinese Marxist literature, specifying that art comes from life, and clarifying methods of artistic creation and standards of art. Since then, revolutionary literature became the mainstream of Chinese literature, which not only reflects the process and ambitions of the revolution, but also constructs its own grand, yet difficult history.

Ding Ling's *The Sun Shines over the Sanggan River* (*Taiyang zhaozai Sangganhe shang*, 1948) is one of the most important novels published in the liberated areas after the "Yan'an Talks," and is a direct, vivid reflection of Mao's thoughts. The novel represents the dramatic land reform in terms of class struggles, and portrays the fates of different characters. Its repeated urge—"do not lag behind the masses, and do not forget where one comes from"—is a classic slogan of the land reform and also a characteristic expression of the increasing radicality of the Chinese Revolution. The novel reveals the landlords' despairs and fears and the poor peasants' sense of vengeance and their eagerness to become new masters. The radicalized revolutionary masses (*qunzhong*) that was created in imaginative fiction would become the engine of the absolute radicalization of revolution.

Similar to Ding Ling's novel, Zhou Libo's *The Hurricane* (*Baofeng zhouyu*, 1948) is another typical example of the classic works in the liberated areas. Works like Ding's and Zhou's hinted at the following rules of socialist realist literature that would come into being in New China:

1   Class struggle determines the features of the characters.
2   Class hatred replaces enlightenment "love" or "compassion" and becomes the paramount emotion.
3   The pleasure principle of revolutionary violence: in the novel, scenes of struggles are represented as the climax and success of revolution, and are the earliest symbolic rituals of carnivalesque class struggles.

Guided by Mao's "Yan'an Talks," literature thrived in the liberated areas and many important works emerged. They created a series of new peasant characters who are awakened in class struggles and become the principal force of the revolution. In addition to popularizing revolutionary ideals, these works greatly encouraged the masses.

In this phase of early revolutionary literature, Zhao Shuli, with his originality, spontaneity, and simplicity, became a "flag." If revolutionary literature before him was in the shadow of May Fourth and was still the revolutionary myth enacted in the city, the spiritual home of bourgeois enlightenment, then with Zhao, revolutionary literature acquired, for the first time, an authentic origin in the poorest rural areas. Although the origin of revolutionary literature is a dubious and shifting point, Zhao is the symbol of a certain period. Cutting off the link with the intellectual tradition, he was a proof to Mao's axiom that "art and literature originated in life." Chinese literature turned from the urban bourgeoisie center to the countryside, and revolutionary literature acquired a brand-new time–space, simultaneously subverting and reconstructing the world literature of modernity.

Revolutionary literature produces aesthetic effects in two drastically different ways: one is to represent the *Zeitgeist* (*shidai jingshen*), express the concepts of revolution, and reveal the direction of historical development; the other is to go back to life itself, to lived situations that seem to have no ideological significance. That artistic forms should be "welcomed by the people" is not only a way of producing art, but is the aesthetic ideology of revolution. However, being "welcomed by the people" calls for a return to life and may make people forget revolution. Between revolutionary ideas and ordinary life, does revolutionary literature sew them together seamlessly, or does it reveal a fundamental gap?

The Institutionalization of Literature and Cultural Leadership

On July 2, 1949, the first PRC national congress of writers and artists took place, setting the stage for the beginning of literature in New China. Mao was present and Zhou Enlai delivered a speech. On July 4, Mao Dun delivered a report about revolutionary literature struggling in areas controlled by the Nationalists in the 1940s. In this report, the origin of revolutionary literature was confirmed to be the liberated areas centered in Yan'an. Revolutionary literature in areas under the Nationalists must realign with this origin by identifying with the "Yan'an Talks" in spirit. On July 5, Zhou Yang presented "New Literature and Art of the People" and delineated a history of revolutionary literature in China: with Mao's "Yan'an Talks," literature and art in the liberated areas are new creations in both content and form and are truly the new literature and art of the people.

The congress was a ritual at a historic juncture. In 1949, history was traced back and 1942 was sanctioned as the origin of revolutionary literature and art. The congress also set up basic institutions and rules, recognizing Mao's thoughts as the leading principles of literature. In a creative way, it also laid down the condition for the fundamental difference between socialist and bourgeois literature: whereas bourgeois artists are free and scattered individuals, and the capitalist market provide their living space, socialist literature and art not only call for the transformation of the artists' worldview, but will facilitate their wholesale transformation through institutionalization.

The first congress set up rules so that revolutionary literature could be closely linked with Party-organized activities and would effectively become cogs of the proletariat machinery. With the establishment of various national associations of writers and artists and important newspapers and journals, such as *People's Literature* (*Renmin wenxue*), the Party's leadership in literature was institutionalized, and socialist literature began to unfold its increasingly radical practices. The experiences of literature in the early PRC showed that institutionalization and individual passions were closely interacted in their radicality. For artists in New China, revolutionary literature and art pointed to a new future.

After the inauguration ceremony of the new government, He Qifang, a poet, enthusiastically wrote "Our Greatest Festival" ("*Women zui weida de jieri*") to praise Mao. Hu Feng's long poem "Time Now Begins" ("*Shijian kaishi le*") first appeared in the *People's Daily* on November 20, 1949. However, Shen Congwen had expressed depression, anxiety, and fear in his diary on May 30, 1949. This private text, invested with more psychological than literary values, is a record of helplessness, reflecting the intellectuals' anguish at being rejected by revolution and collectivity. The distinct feature of socialist cultural leadership—its powerful institutional basis—made Shen feel that he had no part in anything, which caused pains and terrors. Obviously, the historical practices of literature, in the form of institutionalization, far exceeded, in its radicality, Gramsci's conception of cultural hegemony. In numerous campaigns after 1949, with the gradual consolidation of socialist cultural leadership, Shen Congwen and Hu Feng became the first unlucky targets, and neither their public praise nor their private writing could help them resist the historical force of creating a new era.

In 1950, Xiao Yemu's short story "Between Husband and Wife" ("*Women fufu zhijian*," 1950) was severely criticized by Ding Ling and others, leading to criticisms against works with similar tendencies. Revolutionary literature developed through campaigns. The fact that Feng Xuefeng wrote under the pseudonym of a common reader and attacked Xiao Yemu shows that artists now thought and wrote in the name of the imagined people, so as to incorporate individual actions into collectivity and history.

On May 20, 1951, an editorial was published in the *People's Daily* that set the stage for the campaign against the film *The Life of Wu Xun*. Heavily revised by Mao himself, the editorial expressed his vision of history and socialist art. First, class struggle is the principle; second, artistic questions are political questions; third, a long-term task for artists is to transform their petty bourgeois thoughts. After that, Mao launched an attack on "Researches on *Dream of the Red Chamber.*" Li Xifan and Lan Ling interpreted the classic novel with realist theories and criticized Yu Pingbo's subjective tendency and empiricist scholarship. Since the two young scholars applied the concepts of class struggles in historical materialism, concepts that are urgently needed for the construction of socialist literature, Mao saw in them the possibility to eradicate bourgeois residues and establish socialist theories. A more direct reason might be that Mao saw in the debate the shadow of Hu Shi's influence in the new era, even though Mao had already labeled the May Fourth Movement, through his interpretation of Lu Xun, as belonging to the "revolution of new democracy" (*xin minzhu zhuyi geming*).

The collision between Hu Feng and revolutionary art was inevitable: Hu had been engaged in revolution through arts (i.e., the politicization of arts), but the nature of revolutionary art is to do arts through revolution (i.e., politics becomes art). In 1953, Lin Mohan and He Qifang began publishing articles critical of Hu Feng. In 1954, Hu Feng wrote his "Letter of 300,000 Words" and argued that the two articles by Lin and He exposed the five theoretical knives—a Communist worldview; life of a worker, peasant or soldier; transformation of thoughts; a national form; the subject—that had long been planted on the heads of the reader and the writer, and behind these knives was "factionalism" (*zongpai zhuyi*). Mao was not pleased, and labeled Hu's thoughts as "bourgeois idealism, thoughts against the Party and the people." On May 13, 1955, the *People's Daily* published an article denouncing Hu Feng's "anti-Party clique"—"a reactionary faction hidden in the revolutionary camp, an independent underground kingdom," "with the purpose of overthrowing the PRC and restoring the rule of imperialism and the Nationalists." On May 25, 1955, Hu Feng was stripped of all his positions. Opinions sympathetic with Hu Feng were all judged to be reactionary, and a national purge ensued.

Revolution and Pleasure: The Literary Picture of Class Struggles in the Countryside

Revolutionary literature was no doubt trapped in a paradoxical situation between the expressing subject and the expressed/receiving subject, in which the latter is always silent, imagined, elusive, and yet to be realized. How literature would represent peasants, make them the subject of a historical revolution, and merge them in a historical narrative, presented a great challenge. China's peasant revolution took place in the context of modernity and was the early product of the encounter between Marxism and Chinese reality. It can be traced to Marxism politically, but culturally it could not find resources in world modernity and thus had to turn to China's national tradition. From the perspective of China's revolution, to break away from tradition in thoughts was the inevitable choice, but revolution brought great anxieties, which needed literature and art to provide artistic images that were understandable and tangible. In this sense, revolutionary literature not only depicts and constructs the violence of revolution, but also has the correlated task of healing and soothing over the traces of violence. Mao had sought the national form and style of revolutionary art, so that it could be more acceptable locally. Even under political pressure, localized revolutionary literature still keeps some aesthetic significance.

Writers such as Zhao Shuli, who retained folk memory and entered the revolution with their simple rural experiences and original local colors, are a rare breed. However, even Zhao could not avoid depicting changes that were taking place in the countryside. Thus, in *The Village Sanliwan* (*Sanliwan*, 1955), he represented the struggle between capitalism and socialism in the process of rural collectivization. Indeed, for peasants of that time, the violence of struggles between different lines was abstract. Zhao was not a passionate adherent of ideologies, but he had to go along with the political tide and confront lived experiences and facts. Exaggerated conflicts in history and between classes seem to be superficial problems that Zhao addressed. What he devoted great efforts to was the inherent conflicts in the rural society, such as family problems. In socialist literary narrative, we can often see this gap: on the one hand, the urge to understand historical developments politically, to represent the thinking of peasants from the vantage point of socialist ideology, and to describe their progressiveness and backwardness accordingly; on the other hand, once back to everyday life and ethics of peasants in rural China, a simple life begins to emerge. The strong rural color is the mediator between class struggles and changing rural realities, with the former giving literature a foothold in the socialist era, and the latter retaining what makes literature count as literature.

In 1953, Li Zhun published "We Cannot Go That Way" ("*Buneng zou natiaolu*"), a story of the peasants' changing their minds collectively, and the timely revelation of a widespread problem in the countryside: the peasants were still enamored of the land and dreamt of going back to the route of "getting rich" in traditional society. In 1960, Li Zhun again captured a hot topic in "A Little Biography of Li Shuangshuang" ("*Li Shuangshuang xiaozhuan*"), which was quickly adapted into a film. The story tells of how a rural woman is eager to set up a canteen, and it glorifies the Great Leap Forward by showing the new collective spirit of rural women. As a political intervention, the story's lesson was soon proved wrong by history; however, as a literary text, it is not just an illustration of the outdated ideology because, even read today, the story still retains some of its affective power back then.

Seen through the perspective of modernity, it is precisely the rupture of revolution that brought great social pains to rural China, needing popular artistic forms to heal, and traditional folk artistic resources provide some aesthetic compensation in this regard. Zhou Libo's novel *Great Changes in a Mountain Village* (*Shanxiang jubian*, 1958) captures the profound changes and the new spiritual state brought by rural cooperatives. However, the author devoted less space to class struggle than to the "middle characters" and the "right-leaning characters," which arguably better reflects the reality at the time. Zhou believes in Mao's thoughts on literature, but he was writing about the changes taking place in the countryside based on his experiences. Seen from this angle, the novel's copious portrayals of natural landscapes and beautiful lyricism seem to be incongruent with the tumultuous revolution: is all this meant to be opposition, compensation, replacement, or simply nostalgia?

Liu Qing's *The Builders* (*Chuangye shi*, 1960) can be seen as the highest achievement of socialist realist literature. First, as a literary text, it consciously aims to answer two urgent questions in reality: why socialist revolution takes place in rural China and how the revolution is conducted. Second, socialist realist literature consciously portrays heroes that incorporate reality and imagination. Third, this kind of literature can also present authentic figures and everyday life in the countryside, especially the relationship between revolution and family ethics. Revolution tries to reshape family ethics but it fails to revolutionize the family. Thus, realistic plots and details are presented in the conflicts of family. Fourth, the socialist realist novel can be rich in its narration. Liu's novel is very successful in exploring the psychology of not only the protagonist but also minor characters.

All in all, the fundamental requirement of socialist revolutionary literature is to structure its plot around class struggle, a requirement that doubles as the reflection of radical politics in Chinese modernity. China's radical modernity requires its reflection in literature, while socialist literature provides ample examples and necessary solaces for such radical imagination.

Grand Construction: The Unfolding of the Narrative of Revolutionary History

Through political campaigns, historical practices of New China's literature were incorporated into the socialist political structure, and their connotations and strategies obviously carried the features of the nation state. A basic task of socialist literature was to reshape history and merge history with reality. The literary expression of modernity in China was seen in its wish to construct grand historical narratives, so as to show the revolutionary identity of the nation state and to construct a history progressing to a new stage that transcends all previous history and prefigures a new historical era. In literature with historical narratives, both the narrator and the fact of narration become hidden, although some literary qualities can still be glimpsed.

Du Pengcheng's *Defending Yan'an* (*Baowei Yan'an*, 1954) portrays the heroic story of the Communists' triumph after difficult battles. The novel reveals that realist art was already mature by then. The plot is suspenseful and dramatic; the characters are shown through their actions in a tense atmosphere of war; violence is, for the first time, realistically documented. Literature is not only a reflection of the *Zeitgeist*, but it shapes the *Zeitgeist*. In the 1950s, China was faced with great challenges in revolution and construction in an inhospitable international situation, and people needed war novels to re-experience exhilarating battles, ecstasies, and triumphs. Wu Qiang's novel *The Red Sun* (*Hongri*, 1957) represents war in different scenarios, the Communist soldiers' bravery, and the historical inevitability of the people's triumph over reactionary forces.

The 1950s was a period passionate for miracles, and socialist revolutionary literature affirms that the winners' history must become sublime. Qu Bo's *Tracks in the Snowy Forest* (*Linhai xueyuan*, 1957) shows that socialist literature reached its limits quite early, as the novelist demonstrated the inevitable victory, heroism, and pleasure of revolution as well as nuanced psychological descriptions. In Liang Bin's *Genealogy of the Red Flag* (*Hongqi pu*, 1957), the concepts of revolutionary history, along with its narration and aesthetic tastes, mark the maturity of socialist literature.

However, can we find any trace of the writing subject in revolutionary writing? How should we understand the position and function of such a subject, as well as the possibilities suggested by words and rhetorical devices? It is on this level that radical revolutionary writing is linked to literary tradition and can be recognized as literature. On the one hand, while keeping their references to reality, words lead to rhetorical devices and connotations in literature. On the other hand, personal memory is the basis for the creative nature of literary works. In *Genealogy of the Red Flag*, a complete revolutionary history is established on the basis of incomplete personal memory. When Liang Bin talked about the novel, he often repeated emotional fragments and episodes about rural China. Reconstructed "memories" of his hometown, with no fundamental connection to revolutionary history, indeed become the flesh and blood of the novel, giving "revolution" a concrete image, an existence that can be felt and experienced. Perfect and complete revolutionary literature is difficult to find, but we can find good literature that combines concepts of revolution and memories of the writer.

Personal Sentiments outside History

In January 1956, Zhou Enlai delivered a speech whereby he tried to give intellectuals a status equal to the working classes and called for the intellectuals to dedicate themselves to Communist revolution and socialist construction. On May 2, 1956, the platform of letting "a hundred flowers blossom" (*baihua qifang*) and "a hundred schools contend" (*baijia zhengming*) was formally launched, and it gave much stimulus to literature. Many young writers responded with a sense of mission and wrote poignant works to intervene in reality and expose problems. Wang Meng's "The Young Newcomer in the Organization Department" ("*Zuzhibu xinlai de nianqingren*," 1956) is centered on the experience of 22-year-old Lin Zhen, an idealistic elementary school teacher. He has long been upset by doubts and disappointments with bureaucracy but finally he stands up to fight. The story was passionately received precisely because of its exposure of the dark side of the government. Individual consciousness, inherited from the May Fourth but suspended in revolutionary literature, again finds its voice here. It would be a worthy project to examine the connection between the intellectual in this story and in May Fourth literature. Although socialist literature takes the rural as its origin and refuses to represent the petty bourgeoisie, the writing subject can always give us a glimpse of the subject's inner feelings. The campaigns after 1949 effectively eradicated "residues of bourgeois thoughts," but the laws of literary writing made it impossible for proletarian ideology to completely wipe out all traces of literary expressions.

Theoretical debates on realism, typicality, human nature, and thinking through imagery reached a climax in the first half of 1957. These issues hinted at the possibility of breaking away from the principle of class struggles and the abstract, formulaic mode, toward a new kind of socialist art that would be both artistic and welcomed by common people. Regrettably, in reality, these issues only resulted in the further radicalization of literature, and would not reappear until the early 1980s.

In the mid-1950s, some literary works paid attention to the complex psychology of characters beneath "classes" and "Party lines." Such texts include Lu Ling's "Battle on the Lowlands" ("*Wadi shang de 'zhanyi'*," 1954), which portrays the frustrated romance between a Chinese soldier and a Korean girl; and Zong Pu's "Red Beans" ("*Hongdou*," 1957), which tells the hesitation of a college girl choosing between love and revolution. In Ru Zhijuan's "Lilies" ("*Baihehua*," 1958), a rural bride donates her bridal quilt embroidered with lilies to wounded Communist soldiers. The vivid episode of a soldier borrowing the quilt to wrap himself and the subtle psychology of the bride make the story impressive. The beautiful story is linked with the era because, in the Great Leap Forward, people were asked to donate their household pots and bowls. A hidden link might be that Ru Zhijuan was doubtful and fearful of the war-like mobilization, and turned her attention to innocent lives lost in war, thereby generating a profound sadness wrapped with beauty.

In "The Prehistory of Tiemu" ("*Tiemu qianzhuan*," 1956), Sun Li continued to focus on the impact of the advent of the new society on interpersonal relationships in the countryside. In an age of change, Liu'er and Man'er, who are resistant to change, exhibit a sense of beauty and tragedy and an unconquerable tone of rural romance. It is striking that the two are backward, but this does not bring pains. Although they cannot be quickly incorporated into the new life, in a lucid and slightly sentimental atmosphere, they are straightforward rural figures rarely seen in China's revolutionary literature.

Among works on city life, Zhou Erfu's *Morning in Shanghai* (*Shanghai de zaochen*, 1958) unravels the complexities in the first half of the 1950s when the Party engineered a socialist transformation of capitalist industries and commerce. It is noteworthy that this novel, enormous in scale and profound in thought, has not been given recognition it deserves.

Individuals in History: Making Revolutionary History Concrete and Legendary

In the 1950s, socialist revolutionary literature began to construct grand historical narratives, which, told by omniscient narrators, are collective in nature and lack individuality. How to make total history concrete was the challenge to revolutionary literature required by both revolutionary mission and artistic creation. Here, historical narrative faces three difficulties: first, how to make historical concepts assume the features of individual experiences; second, how to incorporate the subject expressing history into the history so expressed; and third, which is the crux of the problem, how to combine the individuality of intellectuals with the objective nature of revolutionary history. The last problem is successfully dealt with through the stories of the personal growth of intellectuals.

To change the hero in the historical narrative to the intellectual is a surreptitious substitution. Behind the literary narrative is the myth of the intellectual's growth, in which the revolutionary intellectual goes along with revolutionary history, a subject expressing himself/herself, a narrator narrating his/her gaining subjectivity, instead of being just a narrator outside revolutionary history.

Yang Mo's *The Song of Youth* (*Qingchun zhige*, 1958) tells the story of how an educated young woman, after upheavals in her personal life, dedicates herself to revolution. As Hong Zicheng (1999: 119) points out, this novel illustrates through the "growth" of the heroine that "growth" is the only way out for intellectuals. Under the Party leadership, after difficult transformation from individualism to collectivism, from fantasies of individual heroism to the collective struggles of class liberation, individual life can acquire value only after merging itself with workers and peasants as the true subjects of the revolutionary cause. Surprisingly, revolution and desire become intertwined in the novel, and the tension between the two pushes the story forward.

Another representative text is Ouyang Shan's novel *Three-Family Lane* (*Sanjiaxiang*, 1959), which tells how, in Guangzhou of the 1920s, traditional relationships of families and neighbors were impacted in the tumultuous years of revolution. The novel is vividly written, with a flowing narrative, a vast historical picture and lifelike characters, presenting a strong color of life in South China. The author integrates class concepts into characterization and constructs a historical narrative of the working class becoming the leader of Chinese revolution. However, irrepressible kinship and individual features still brim over in the text. The novel represents revolutionary history through the personal history of the protagonist, and personal sentiments are palpable so that the historical narrative becomes individualized.

Luo Guangbin and Yang Yiyan's *The Red Crag* (*Hongyan*, 1961) deals with how, right before 1949, imprisoned Communists endured suffering and tortures but remained strong and steadfast. In the novel, characters are heroic, their faith is absolute, and the plot legendary. The revolutionaries acquire their legitimacy through a full display of tortures and violence. From *Defending Yan'an* and *The Red Sun* to *The Red Crag*, the display of violence is vested with revolutionary fervor: sublimated by the predetermined future victory, violence is often accompanied by ecstasy and satisfaction.

Superego and the Small Self: The Lyrical Subject of the Republic

The establishment of the PRC needed praises and affirmations. Eulogies provided not only a way for history to affirm itself and acquire outside recognition, but a way for the subject to express himself/herself. The poets not only sang praises of the Party and the leaders, but more often the new life of all people after the liberation. The poets became the mouthpieces of the new age, the singing voices of the superego of the Party, the people, and the state.

Zang Kejia's poem "Some People" ("*Youde ren*," 1949), which commemorates Lu Xun and compares two sets of values, is almost a declaration of war by collectivism against individualism. It expresses the eagerness of the new age and enhances its need for "superego" poetry. The most outstanding eulogy poet was certainly He Jingzhi, who excels not only in his deep feelings but also in the best ways of expressing eulogies to the PRC: first, to construct an absolutely ideal image of the country; second, to construct a lyrical subject; third, to express sublime, strong passions; fourth, to create a sense of vastness; and fifth, to embody "truth."

After exuberant eulogies, it was difficult for poets to replace poetic qualities with socialist events, as Guo Moruo had done. In the face of new things in New China, the emotional nature and the rhetorical requirements of language called for poets to return to their individual experiences. The difficulty faced by poets was to transcend history and find appropriate signifying strategies between abstract history and real experiences of the self. He Qifang's "The Answer" ("*Huida*," 1954) expresses doubts and depressions in which personal reflection cannot be erased: the poet feels anxious for the possibility of his artistic expressions in the new age. Wen Jie's poems emphasize emotions and often focus on labor and love, or love in labor, with unique lyricism. Guo Xiaochuan, through an independent lyrical subject, articulates thinking, feelings, memories, and political ideas with distinct personal colors. Of course, there were poets, such as Ai Qing and Tian Jian, who did not find equilibrium between the superego of the age and the artistic self.

The Extreme of Historicization: Literature during the Cultural Revolution

The decade between May 1966 and August 1976 is often called the Cultural Revolution. Its prelude took place in November 1965, when Yao Wenyuan published an article criticizing Wu Han's historical play *Hai Rui Dismissed from Office* (*Hai Rui baguan*). In February 1966, Lin Biao collaborated with Jiang Qing to draw up "The Main Points of the Conference for Literature and Art Work in the Military" ("*Budui wenyi gongzuo zuotanhui jiyao*") and put forth the idea of "a dictatorship of the black line in literature and art," with which they criticized all achievements in the 17 years after 1949. They dictated that "the basic task of socialist literature and art … is to create heroic images of workers, peasants, and soldiers," which became the basis for the abstract nature of literature during the Cultural Revolution.

With a few exceptions, most literary works produced in the previous years were reclassified as "poisonous weeds" (*ducao*), and eight operas restaged under Jiang Qing's supervision were designated as "model theater" (*yangban xi*). For lack of other works, the eight pieces of model theater became extremely popular because, with spectacular singing and performance, they provided a limited aesthetic space for people to enjoy. Created on the abstract rules of sublime and perfect heroism, these plays are still significant today as examples of the modern expression of Peking opera.

The majority of veteran writers suffered political persecution during the Cultural Revolution, and literary production reached a low point. Among a few acceptable novels were Hao Ran's *Bright Sunny Skies* (*Yanyang tian*, 1965) and *The Golden Road* (*Jinguang dadao*, 1972). *Bright Sunny Skies* makes class struggle and struggles of political lines completely explicit and structures its narrative around rules affirmed by ultra-leftist politics. The struggles generate intense and suspenseful conflicts between a protagonist who represents the direction of socialism and an antagonist who represents the reactionary forces.

At the same time, "underground literature" (*dixia wenxue*) was going on quietly. Many inaugurators of new poetry and Misty poets were active in the underground art saloon presided by Zhao Yifan. The representative pieces of underground poetry included Shi Zhi's "Beijing at 4:08" ("*Zheshi sidian lingbafen de Beijing*," 1968) and "Believe in the Future" ("*Xiangxin weilai*," 1969), both expressing deep feelings and firm beliefs of the youth in the revolutionary period. The most influential underground poetic society was the "Bai Yangdian school" (*Baiyangdian shipai*), which embodied the unconquerable spirit and freedom of poetry in the age of political repression.

Display of Scars: Historical Reflections after the Cultural Revolution

On September 9, 1976, Mao Zedong died, and on October 6, the ultra-leftist "Gang of Four" (including Jiang Qing and Yao Wenyuan) was arrested, thus marking the end of the Cultural Revolution. With great passion, literature of the New Era criticized the radical leftism that had dominated China for a long time. The restoration of human nature, the thriving of realism, and the self-awareness of the writers' subjectivity combined to make this period one of the new discoveries.

Scar literature, which immediately followed Misty Poetry, was the origin of mainstream literature in the era. Guided by the *Zeitgeist* of "dismissing the chaos and restoring the correct road" (*boluan fanzheng*), scar literature tried to heal wounds and construct a new historical totality by providing a new structure of feeling for the time. On the one hand, its historical narrative singled out the Gang of Four as the instigators of the decade-long havoc wreaked on Chinese society during the Cultural Revolution; on the other hand, it reestablished the subject of history and a history of the subjects, whose theoretical significance has long been neglected in much of subsequent research.

As the representative piece of scar literature, Liu Xinwu's "The Class Monitor" ("*Banzhuren*," 1977) examines from the perspective of a teacher the spiritual state of some students after the crackdown on the Gang of Four and reveals the vicious influence of cultural despotism on the young generation. Lu Xinhua's "The Scar" ("*Shanghen*," 1978), from which scar literature received its name, also reveals in a striking way that the titular scar applies not only to the parents' generation but to the hearts of the younger generation as well. The way sufferings are retold in scar literature indicates that, on the one hand, it seeks recognition from the historical mainstream, and, on the other hand, it seeks to take part in the construction of a new dominant culture, so that each person can acquire his or her new significance of existence.

Thus, retelling the history of the Cultural Revolution is more than simply displaying scars, for it also expresses the character of those persecuted old cadres and intellectuals who kept their loyalty to the Party and their faith in the revolutionary cause. Such retelling reestablishes the history of the historical subject of the new era, so that the sufferers gain a historical continuity in their existence. Lu Yanzhou's *Legend of the Tianyun Mountain* (*Tianyunshan chuanqi*, 1979) tells how the hero, wrongly condemned as a Rightist, endures the sufferings and remains loyal to the Party. The significance of the work lies in that historical reflection is turned into a narration of the self by the intellectual, and the passive, persecuted individual is turned into a subject of history who has always been faithful to the Party. Likewise, Cong Weixi's "literature behind the walls" (*daqiang wenxue*), so called because he often featured incarcerated old cadres, tried to retell history comprehensively so that the history of the subject becomes a total history. Scar literature is not merely about wounds, for it addresses healing; more importantly, it proves not the wounds themselves but the strong will that endures and thus transcends wounds.

For Zhang Xianliang, retelling the history of the Cultural Revolution is to represent not simply sufferings, but the beauty that comes out of scars. His works—"The Soul and the Flesh" ("*Ling yu rou*," 1980), "Mimosa" ("*Lühua shu*," 1984), and "Half of Man is Woman" ("*Nanren de yiban shi nüren*," 1985; English 1987)—are masterly in their treatment of the opposition and the unity of the soul and the flesh. With the erasure of the sufferings and scars of the subject, the irrationality and illegitimacy of history are also erased. The subject, with whatever suffering, can experience love and beauty. Far from being alienated by history, the subject is united with history in a special historical situation.

Wang Meng kept some distance from the mainstream of scar literature. His works explore possible aberrations when the post-traumatic individual tries to enter the new historical phase, and he refuses the concept of a rational and continuous history. Stories such as "Bolshevik Salute" ("*Buli*," 1979) pay attention to the inner world of the characters and show the gaps between those in power and the people, which persisted after the Cultural Revolution. His novel *The Man with Movable Parts* (*Huodong bianrenxing*, 1987) explores the dilemmas of an old-fashioned Chinese intellectual in both new and old societies. Educated in traditional Chinese and modern Western cultures, Ni Wucheng is a typical figure in the May Fourth style and thus makes the novel resemble a symbolic trial of "the father." Doubtful that enlightenment after the May Fourth could have saved China, Wang Meng believes instead that the Chinese intellectuals must be rooted in Chinese soil after accepting the ideas of a Communist revolution. In his efforts to cover his intellectual doubts with artistic devices, Wang unexpectedly employs the technique of stream of consciousness, and is the first to combine historical narration and personal introspection at the same time. Thus, with its deliberation on the fate of the historical subject and the nation/state/people, this novel is raised to a higher level of artistry, although these issues remain unresolved in his stream-of-conscious narration.

Scar literature's explanation of history is simple, as it believes that the renewed emphasis on human nature and humanism is the way to avoid or correct historical tragedies. Zhang Jie's "Love Must Not Be Forgotten" ("*Ai, shi buneng wangji de*," 1979; English in Link 1984: 245–260), with a feminine sensitivity, reveals people's yearning for love, in correspondence to the new *Zeitgeist* that is eager for the freedom of feelings and for a true human nature. Zhang Xian's *The Corner Forgotten by Love* (*Bei aiqing yiwang de jiaoluo*, 1980) makes a similar plea but turns its gaze to the impoverished countryside. In these works, personal emotional appeals strongly reflect the turmoil of history and politics, and the call for human nature can be connected to the unfinished work dating back to early-twentieth-century China.

Misty Poetry: From Being Underground to Becoming a Bugle of the New Era

In its nascent stage, Misty Poetry embodied doubts and resistance to mainstream ideas, and its poets became the most powerful avant-garde of literature in the New Era. During the Cultural Revolution, secret writings and exchanges made "Bai Yangdian," a place where many educated young people from Beijing were concentrated, the sacred origin of China's poetic new wave. These poets, with their rebellious "pure art," were completely opposite to the political atmosphere of the time. Poetry-writing was not only their passion but also a direct means for them to rethink reality. This shaped their dual style, which was drastically different from the mainstream: on the one hand, their poems carried sincere personal emotions; on the other, with heavy use of metaphors, they expressed thoughts and feelings in a circuitous way.

With the expansion of the circle, the school's center was moved to Beijing. The various reading materials that circulated within the inner circles and foreign literary works that were not confiscated facilitated their reflection on reality and made a yearning for spiritual freedom the soul of their poetry. In December 1978, *Today* (*Jintian*), edited by Bei Dao and others, began to circulate among friends as manuscripts, and was later mimeographed. By 1980, *Today* had published nine issues. In addition to newly written poems, the journal also carries translated poems, fictional works, and critical pieces, and most of those who wrote for the journal became the pillars of Misty Poetry. The development from "Bai Yangdian" to the "*Today* school" indicates that a profound revolution in poetry was happening in China.

Bei Dao's poetry, characterized by its distinct sense of doubt/negation and refusal/transcendent form of critique, expresses the wishes of a generation of Chinese youths walking out of the shadow of radical leftism in the Cultural Revolution. Bei Dao was among the first to describe the human: "In this age without heroes/ I only want to be a human being" ("Declaration" ["*Xuangao*"], 1980). At the same time, strong emotions, an irrepressible spirit, and a tragic consciousness give Bei Dao's poetry an inner force of reasoning. Shu Ting's poetry is characterized by its nuanced feelings and lucidity, and is intent on expressing personal emotions while employing subtle rhetorical devices. Her poetry differs from mainstream poetry's revolutionary features and has the effect of opening up people's hearts. Gu Cheng's poetry has the quality of surprising passions, childlike innocence, and direct, simple ideas: "Dark night gives me dark eyes/ with which I seek light" ("A Generation" ["*Yidai ren*"], 1980). Dedicated to seeking truth for his generation, Gu Cheng exists only in his personal world and is happy to be one who refuses to grow up.

At its birth, Misty Poetry was adopted by a new movement of liberating ideas, and when gaining legitimacy, it became the expression of a collective wish. While refusing to be the mouthpiece of the *Zeitgeist*, it quickly became the bugle of the New Era. Indeed, based on their experiences of the Cultural Revolution, Misty poets were deeply divided in their missions: Bei Dao and Ouyang Jianghe blew the horns for the age, while Shu Ting and Gu Cheng provided affective solaces to their readers.

Idealism in Reconstructing the Subject: Reform Literature and Literature of Sent-Down Youths

Some writers took up the subject of economic reform, and expressed the historical urge in a heroic mode. Jiang Zilong's *Manager Qiao Assumes Office* (*Qiao changzhang shangren ji*, 1979) was the first work of reform literature. The novel features a reformer who takes up office in a time of crisis, a hero who leads people toward modernization and reconstruction of a new utopia. Some novels during this period addressed changes in the countryside after the de-collectivization. Gao Xiaosheng's "Li Shunda Builds a House" ("*Li Shunda zaowu*," 1979) deals with the absurd fate of the peasants in a series of political campaigns, and his series "Chen Huansheng's Adventure in Town" ("*Chen Huansheng jincheng*," 1980) captures the happiness of peasants after they become owners of their lands.

After the Cultural Revolution, many sent-down youths who returned to the city or entered college began to write, and their works are called "literature of sent-down youths" (*zhiqing wenxue*). The nostalgia for the youthful time, a profound love of the land, and a preference for natural landscape in the countryside combine to turn the experiences of sent-down youths into the song of youth, at once melancholy and beautiful. As this generation obtained more opportunities in the society, the tone of their literature changed from low key to high key. This type of literature also constructs sent-down youths as a subject of history. Kong Jiesheng's "On the Other Side of the Stream" ("*Zai xiaohe nabian*," 1979; English in Link 1984: 172–173) tells the love story of two sent-down youths who are attracted to each other and become interdependent for life, and the story does not hide the regret for wasted youth. Ye Xin's *Eventful Years* (*Cuotuo suiyue*, 1980) confers a tone of the sublime and the tragic to such literature. The novel features a sent-down youth who is hardworking but comes from an unlucky family; yet, in spite of obstacles and adversities, he keeps striving forward and upward. Upon publication, the novel was instantly welcomed by readers of the same generation.

All in all, in the late 1970s, Misty Poetry, scar literature, reform literature, and literature of sent-down youths—although these categories overlap to some degrees—reflected on the traumas of the Cultural Revolution, looked for lost youth, condemned the evil doings of the Gang of Four, and explored the road of change for China. Literature at the beginning of the New Era is characterized by its deeply felt pains and by a new consciousness of history, which can easily turn into an inspiring passion. The generation of sent-down youths represents the mainstream of the era. The radical modernity sanctified earlier was now replaced by an emerging self-awareness of the subject. In this sense, Misty Poetry was especially representative of the transition phase. Chinese literature in this phase may appear to be passionate or urgent, but its uplifting spirit, expansive scale, and historical vision are unprecedented and unparalleled in its subsequent developments.

REFERENCES

Hong, Zicheng 洪子誠. 1999. *Zhongguo dangdai wenxueshi* 中國當代文學史 (A history of contemporary Chinese Literature). Beijing: Beijing daxue chubanshe.

Li, Zehou 李泽厚. 1987. *Zhongguo xiandai sixiangshi lun* 中国现代思想史论 (On modern Chinese intellectual history). Beijing: Dongfang chubanshe.

Link, E. Perry. Ed. 1984. *Roses and Thorns: The Second Blooming of the Hundred Flowers in Chinese Fiction, 1979–1980.* Berkeley: University of California Press.

Wang, Meng. 1989. *Bolshevik Salute: A Modernist Chinese Novel.* Trans. with introduction and critical essay by Wendy Larson. Seattle: University of Washington Press.

Zhang, Xianliang. 1987. *Half of Man Is Woman.* Trans. Martha Avery. New York: Viking.

6
Thirty Years of New Era Literature: From Elitization to De-Elitization

Tao Dongfeng (translated by Angie Chau)

The Elitization of Literature, 1970s–1980s

New Era literature began by distancing itself from Maoist totalitarian literary ideology, which denied literary art through the official direction of workers, peasants, and soldiers as best represented by revolutionary model theater (see Chapter 5 by Chen Xiaoming). The New Era's negation of "using class struggle as the guiding principle" was a response to the previous anti-intellectual, populist ideology, and such negation involved a reevaluation of "seventeen-year literature" (1949–1966), which included writers (e.g., Ai Qing, Liu Binyan, and Wang Meng) who had been denounced as the Rightists in the late 1950s but were now rehabilitated. This chapter starts with the elitization of literature in the first decade of the New Era (1976–1989) when the government worked to "bring order out of chaos," and then discusses the trend of de-elitization in subsequent decades (Chen Sihe 1999; Z. Xu and Ding 2002; Hong Zicheng 2007; D. Tao and He 2008; Chen Xiaoming 2009).

Although populism (*mincui zhuyi*) has been variously interpreted around the world, the consensus is that anti-elitism is its shared fundamental characteristic. In order to understand populist thought, one must establish the central relationship between the elite social class and the common masses. Populism places the masses at its foundation and plays down the elite. It does not trust modern organizations (e.g., state apparatuses, universities, financial institutions) or elite individuals, and believes that the masses possess real morality, and only their politics and wisdom are legitimate (Lin Hong 2007: 7–8).

A Companion to Modern Chinese Literature, First Edition. Edited by Yingjin Zhang.
© 2016 John Wiley & Sons, Ltd. Published 2016 by John Wiley & Sons, Ltd.

In much of the twentieth century, Chinese literature operated clearly under this conception of populism, and examples include the movement of "going to the people" (*dao minjian qu*) in the 1920s–1930s, proletarian literature of the 1940s, and the post-1949 reeducation of intellectuals. In socialist China, this populism occupied an increasingly dominant position and culminated in the Cultural Revolution when the entire population accepted slogans such as "studying is useless" and "workers rule schools." Mao Zedong's maxims—for instance, "The masses are the real heroes" and "The lowly are the most intelligent, the elite are the most ignorant"—are typical expressions of such populist discourse, which worked to depreciate the intelligentsia and promote literary productions by the masses, resulting in official policies such as the "popularization of literature and art" (*wenyi dazhonghua*).

When New Era literature began to critique populist ideology, the elitization of literature was not an isolated occurrence but part of the widespread "liberation of thoughts" (*sixiang jiefang*) across the country. "Respect knowledge, respect talent" now replaced "the more knowledge, the more reactionary" and became one of the eye-catching slogans of the reform period. When Deng Xiaoping (1994: 51) issued the order to "rehabilitate the intelligentsia," it is clear that the elitization of literature affirmed the new reform policy, "to the point that it served as a vanguard of liberation ideology" (Zhang Xianliang 2009). In bidding farewell to populism, the intellectual class was in unanimous agreement with the government: both used the negation of Mao's populism to achieve self-legitimacy, although this shared interest lasted merely a decade.

The Two Stages of Elitization: Reform Literature and Pure Literature

The elitization of New Era literature can be divided into two stages: "enlightenment literature" (*qimeng wenxue*) and "pure literature" (*chun wenxue*). In the first stage, enlightenment literature encompassed "scar literature," "reflective literature" (*fansi wenxue*), and "reform literature" from the late 1970s to the late 1980s. The term "scar literature" came into circulation with the publication of Lu Xinhua's story "The Scar" (1978), but its origin is generally attributed to Liu Xinwu's "The Class Monitor" (1977). Scar literature's defining characteristic is the spiritual trauma that the Cultural Revolution inflicted on individuals, and its leading figures are the intelligentsia. Reflective literature, including Lu Yanzhou's *Legend of Tianyun Mountain* (1979), Wang Meng's "The Butterfly" ("*Hudie*," 1980; English 1983), Chen Rong's "At Middle Age" ("*Ren dao zhongnian*," 1980), and Gu Hua's *Hibiscus Town* ("*Furong zhen*," 1981), appeared slightly later than scar literature, and its aim was to rethink the Cultural Revolution. But the boundaries between scar literature and reflective literature are by no means distinct. The surge of reform literature occurred nearly simultaneously with the peak of reflective literature. Jiang Zilong's *Manager Qiao Assumes Office* (1979) was the first to open up a new road in reform literature by focusing on industrial workers. At the same time, literature that addressed rural reform appeared in great numbers, such as Gao Xiaosheng's series of "Chen Huansheng's Adventure in Town." Many writers of this period were passionate in depicting their characters, emphasizing their personalities and inner worlds, and this resulted in a legendary and heroic quality.

The literature of this time was aligned with the dominant mode of cultural thinking, which was enveloped in elitist intellectual critique, emphasizing an enlightenment spirit reminiscent of the May Fourth (especially Lu Xun) and the values of establishing a free democratic society and culture.[1] Literary works possessed an intensely elitist mentality, an enlightenment complex, and a sense of social responsibility. The Cultural Revolution had firmly reversed the relationship between the intellectual class and the masses: intellectuals were the students of the masses, in need of reeducation, and the masses were their teachers. The New Era first saw a complete redress: intellectuals were the leaders of the masses, and the masses their students, in need of enlightenment.

The "new" in this period was preoccupied with rethinking political standpoints and revising cultural concepts (e.g., calling for freedom and humanism). With the exception of Misty Poetry and modernist writers such as Gao Xingjian, the first few years of New Era literature were still constrained by socialist realism. In Hong Zicheng's judgment (2007: 201): "The materials and themes of this literary stage were mainly directed toward the sociopolitical level, and for the most part shared a quality of sociopolitical intervention… In terms of aesthetics and its methods, deeper transformations had not yet received close attention." Indeed, literature in the political service of smashing the Gang of Four was the defining feature of the early phase. Ji Hongzhen (2006: 123) states, "Thematic politicization was the common attribute of all of the works from the Cultural Revolution, so the fact that New Era literature used political critique as its starting point is not surprising at all." As a harbinger, scar literature pioneered the genre of "social problem fiction" (*shehui wenti xiaoshuo*) and briefly gained popularity in the late 1970s. Its distinctive quality was a weak literary sensibility complemented by a strong political consciousness. In the early 1980s, although enlightenment literature became profound and matured aesthetically, it nonetheless remained on the surface level of political critique. Literature's primary task was still enlightenment, and literary experimentation on the whole had not yet taken shape.

In the second stage of elitization, pure literature—also known as "experimental literature" (*shiyan wenxue*)—appeared in the mid-1980s. Modernism, roots-searching literature, along with experimental and "avant-garde literature" (*xianfeng wenxue*), became leaders in literary movements. Beginning from around 1985, under the influence of Western modernism (due to a surge of translations in the early 1980s), combined with the strong creative impulse of 1980s enlightenment literature, some writers and critics paid increasing attention to questions of "how to write" (i.e., language, form, style) as opposed to "what to write" (i.e., subject, content, theme).[2] This obvious shift represents the foray of elitization into the formal realm.

With the appearance of novelists such as Ge Fei, Ma Yuan, Sun Ganlu, Yu Hua, and critics such as Li Tuo, new ideas such as the "carnival of the signifier" (*nengzhi de kuanghuan*) became fashionable in critical discourse, and this group became known as the avant-garde.[3] From the start, avant-garde fiction attached great importance to experimental form and emphasized its fictional nature by revolting against the conventional narrative method. Its primary influence came from Western modernism, in particular French *nouveau roman* (*xin xiaoshuo*) and Latin American magical realism (e.g., Jorge Luis Borges, Gabriel García Márquez), along with the American "anti-novel" (*fan xiaoshuo*) of the 1960s–1970s.

In an unprecedented breakthrough in China, avant-garde fiction turned narrative into a mystery. Narrative itself was viewed as an object of aesthetic beauty, and much of avant-garde fiction targeted the act of narration. Avant-garde writers employed different experimental methods, explored various kinds of narrative possibilities, and often incorporated these explorations in their fiction. In their efforts to criticize traditional realism for fabricating a seemingly real delusion and to proclaim their mission to reveal the act of narration, they made narrative into a mystery so opaque that "I can't understand" became the most common reaction from readers. Ma Yuan, whose "The Goddess of the Lhasa River" ("*Lasahe de nüshen*," 1984) is considered the harbinger of experimental fiction, is fond of reminding his readers of his role as storyteller: "I am the Chinese man named Ma Yuan." From the reader's perspective, such a self-explanatory act of revealing oneself actually would increase the story's obscurity and confusion, but Ma Yuan could not care less. His "Fabrication" ("*Xugou*") uses the process of writing fiction itself as the story's content, so the story becomes, in effect, fiction about fiction. In this way, avant-garde fiction strictly maintained its distance from reality, refusing to give readers any interpretations concerning actual events related to politics, society, ethics, or human nature.

Judging from the avant-garde criteria, enlightenment literature was not "pure" or "new," nor was it sufficiently "elitist." Li Tuo (2001) observes, "The scar literature of the beginning of New Era literature" was "essentially a form of old literature." And Cai Xiang (2002) agrees: "the traditional realist mode of coding as a literary concept in the 1970s–80s still possessed a certain influence and furthermore directly gave birth to scar literature, the reform novel, and 'problem literature' (*wenti wenxue*). It was precisely amidst this particular historical context that the notion of pure literature was introduced, corresponding to an intense sense of revolutionary spirit." Although pure literature operated as a negation of enlightenment literature, it did not challenge the Cultural Revolution's "revolutionary literature." When pure literature appeared, the negation of the Cultural Revolution had already been accomplished by the rehabilitation of the intelligentsia and by the new form of elite literature— enlightenment literature. If writers of enlightenment literature were known as masters of consciousness, then avant-garde writers were the wizards of language, and their strategy of elitization did not serve the agenda of enlightenment but instead made a puzzle out of language by way of worshipping literary form. If enlightenment writers saw the masses as students of their ideas, then avant-garde writers used the masses as students of artistic forms. The latter's "labyrinthine language" (*yuyan migong*) rejected easy decoding from the masses, hence ensuring its mystery and its special cultural capital.

Despite the aforementioned differences between enlightenment literature and pure literature, both nonetheless belong to elitist literature and therefore pursue one aim: literary autonomy. But their interpretation of autonomy differs in a number of ways. The autonomy of enlightenment literature emphasizes literature of an independent nature, and the defining feature of independent autonomy was writers' critical consciousness vis-à-vis society and politics. The autonomy of pure literature emphasizes the distance between linguistic form and everyday life, advocating "art for art's sake" rather than "art for politics' sake" or "art for wealth's sake."

The De-Elitization of Literature, 1990 to the Present

From the beginning, elitist literature faced a tremendous crisis, as hegemonic discourse established during the New Era was quickly assaulted by a new trend of vulgarization. Starting from 1992, due to the decreased political participation, the rise of the marketplace, the spread of popular culture and consumer values, along with the introduction of new forms of mass media, especially the Internet, a strong tendency of de-elitization emerged in China's literary world. Simultaneously challenging enlightenment literature and pure literature and threatening any literary autonomy, the de-elitization has rejected elitist culture's concern with enlightenment and the myth of autonomy, thereby dragging literature down from its previous peak of glory.

If the elitization of the 1980s moved from top to bottom, to a large extent championed by the intelligentsia, then the de-elitization since the 1990s has proceeded from bottom to top, commercially driven and immensely popular. Its immediate impetus came from the marketization of cultural activities, the popularity of new technologies of dissemination, and the rise of popular consumer culture. Cultural phenomena such as "The Super Girl" (*Chaoji nüsheng*) television competition, the Internet celebrity Sister Lotus (*Furong Jiejie*),[4] and "body writing" (*shenti xiezuo*) authors each enjoyed brief moments of popularity, and a massive quantity of Internet literature and cell phone text message writing, the trend of "consuming classics" (*jingdian xiaofei*, i.e., parodying and vandalizing classical works), the outgrowth of "literariness" (*wenxue xing*), and the aestheticization of everyday life were all representative of the connection between popular culture, commerce, and the de-elitization.

When the de-elitization trend spread in the early 1990s, it encountered intense resistance and condemnation from the elite. A series of articles debating the "humanist spirit" (*renwen jingshen*) from 1993 to 1995 rejected the "ruins of wasteland" and "Internet trash" and called upon the elite to join forces and "resist surrender."[5] By the end of the 1990s, popular culture firmly established its dominant position, which continues to the present, where it has accomplished in making Internet literature— increasingly the primary reading material for the younger generation—an integral part of popular culture.

All this did not happen without a fight. Those in defense of humanist literature criticized vulgarization in popular culture, with the intention of protecting social classes firmly established in the 1980s and upholding the sacred position of the intelligentsia in literature and culture. In their earnest protection of pure literature, the elite attacked popular culture from two angles—aestheticism and morality. In terms of aesthetics, they believed that popular culture was insufficient, based on imitation and lacking in imaginative power; in terms of morality, they criticized popular culture for ethical degeneracy and indulgence in desires.

The elite's criticism of popular culture may appear rational, but their analytical and critical language requires closer investigation. In methodological terms, their discourse operates on the abstract level of aesthetic and moral criticism but not the concrete level of sociopolitical criticism. It fails to uncover political functions of popular culture in sociopolitical theory and therefore misses the essence of popular culture. The true threat of popular consumerism is not due to a shortage of abstract "idealism" or "sublimation," but rather the freedom of choice in entertainment. Moreover, the freedom of consumption has replaced political freedom, as the prosperous sphere of entertainment conceals a decline of the public sphere, and the consumerist fervor now serves as a substitute for political apathy.

The origins of de-elitization: Hooligan literature and body writing

With the advent of de-elitization, literature is no longer measured solely by its mission to address solemn sociopolitical issues or by its experiment with labyrinthine literary forms. The de-elitization of literature quickly moved to dethrone "authors" (*zuojia*) and replaced them with "scripters" (*xieshou*, literally "writing hand"), to the extent that "literature" (*wenxue*) would become mere "words" (*wenzi*).

The origins of de-elitization can be traced to Wang Shuo, who became known as a "hooligan" (*pizi*) writer.[6] Wang was the first to employ the hyperbole for the "disenchantment" (*qumei*) of elite literature and the intelligentsia. He dethroned literature from its lofty spiritual heights to the mediocrity of the material world, or even below ground. Typical of Wang's cynicism, writers who make a living through writing become "wordsmen" (*mazi gong*). In "The Troubleshooters" ("*Wanzhu*," 1987) and its sequel "Pure Nonsense" ("*Yidian zhengjing meiyou*,' 1989), Wang blasphemed literature in more ways than one: "The key is to make sure you fuck literature and don't let literature fuck you" (Wang Shuo 1989: 125); "there are a hundred ways to commit suicide, and one of those is to marry a writer" (Wang Shuo 1987: 51). In such an unprecedented use of derogatory words, Wang denies the professional dignity recently reclaimed by Chinese writers. Sure, Wang's nihilist gesture may be his self-mockery as a writer, but he puts into practice what he preaches in "The Troubleshooters": "I'm a hooligan, so whom am I afraid of?" (Wang Shuo 1989: 127). While the narrator may not be equated entirely with the author himself, it is evident that at least part of the "I" here echoes Wang's cynical views.

As a pioneer of de-elitization literature, Wang was still lonely in the late 1980s, as Chinese literature on the whole had not yet encountered the onslaught of de-elitization. After a period of tremendous growth on the Internet, vulgarization in consumer culture became intensified and produced countless writers such as Wang Shuo. When "body writing" arrived in 1990s China, the desecration of literature shifted from a conceptual game (as in Wang Shuo's case) to an embodied practice. Originally a Western feminist concept, "body writing," as delivered by Mian Mian, Muzi Mei, and Wei Hui, moved beyond hooligan literature and unabashedly indulged in sexual desires and bodily pleasures, thereby hyping its commercial values through media controversies. Not surprisingly, Wang Shuo came to Mian Mian's defense: "The body can achieve so much more than the mind... Having a body is luckier than having a brain" (*"Dongfang xinwen,"* 2000). The trend of anti-intellectualism seemed to be all the rage in popular culture.

The Internet and De-elitization in Literature

Obviously, the Internet has played a crucial role in polarizing China's cultural landscape between popular and unpopular since the 1990s. The de-elitization was the result of numerous factors, among which the most important was the termination of the intelligentsia's monopoly in literary production. In pre-modern China, the readership was extremely limited due to low literacy rates. After the modern popularization of education, literacy rates finally grew and thus undermined the monopoly of the elite. Nevertheless, even though the spread of education drastically improved modern society, the number of those who could publish literature—excluding works written for one's own enjoyment at home, namely "desk-drawer literature" (*chouti wenxue*)—remained rather limited, since mass media was monopolized by the elite until the end of the twentieth century.

The growth of mass communications, in particular the Internet, has made it impossible for the elite to monopolize the media anymore, and the Internet becomes a site for the masses, especially for the web-savvy young generation who takes full advantage of its convenience. Writing and publishing activities can be pursued with unprecedented freedom, and any individual can participate in the popularization movement. The Internet is the easiest to access: there is no copy editor, no approval process, and the barrier to publication is almost nonexistent. Nearly anyone's work, written at any time, can be published on the Internet. Once publishing venues are opened up, writing also becomes freer; people can write whatever they want, and it does not matter if it is complete nonsense. Internet writers and "Internet vagabonds" (*wangluo youmin*) may not be writers by profession, but they are often more popular and influential than their professional counterparts nowadays.

All this has exerted a serious impact on the formerly elite cultural system. As the celebrated Internet writer Li Xunhuan explains, "In the old cultural system, literature belonged to writers of the field, and to editors and critics. They wrote, published, and critiqued with gusto, but unknowingly and increasingly distanced themselves from ordinary people... Now that we have the Internet, there's no need to stay up writing until midnight, mail it to the editor, and wait for a reply to revise... All you have to do is turn on your computer and type, then send it, and that's it." Li Xunhuan believes that Internet literature's essence is freedom ("Not only can anyone write, but anyone can write freely") and equality ("The Internet doesn't believe in authority, and authority doesn't exist; everyone has an equal right to express himself"). He asserts, "Internet literature's true contribution to literature is returning literature to the people." According to Li Xunhuan, if the May Fourth Movement resolved the issue of "linguistic barrier" between literature and the masses by promoting the vernacular, then Internet literature resolved the "passage barrier" issue by providing virtually unrestricted access. Zhu Weilian (2000), the editor of the website *Under the Banyan Tree* (*Rongshu xia*), concurs: "The Internet's infinite reach created a fertile soil, and the open space of the popularization of creative freedom made this expanse even broader."

All this has resulted in a literary carnival that everyone can celebrate, and the subsequent de-elitization of literature is inevitable. Popular phenomena such as the "Super Girl" and Sister Lotus would not have been possible without the Internet, which guarantees low costs, efficient transmission, and a non-elite, convenient mode of participation. Ordinary people's desire for self-expression has been greatly aroused, and the Super Girl's philosophy—"Sing if you want to sing"—is the most emphatic manifestation of this kind of passion and aspiration.

The most dramatic de-elitization impact of the Internet is the change of status for the writer as scholar. Historically, the notion of the author's independent talent—which Pierre Bourdieu calls the authorial myth of charisma—is a cultural construct inextricably tied to German Romanticism. In reaction against rationalism and universalism valued by the Enlightenment, German Romanticism upheld individual personality, individuality, creativity, and self-realization in the highest esteem (Lukes 2001: 15). This concept of the individual genius who possesses charisma and embodies *Zeitgeist* foregrounds the magical creativity of a select few and deifies both the author and his work.

In China as in the West, the period during which this concept of the author was prevalent occurred simultaneously with the strong reinforcement of the belief in the privileged position of elite writers. The mythology of the author's charisma was also fashionable in 1980s China, especially within the community of the intelligentsia. However, due to the popularization of mass media, literature's front door is now open to practically everyone, and professional authors are no longer an elite group. The mysterious enchantment surrounding the title "author" has vanished, and writers have become non-professionalized: the popular Internet writers Jin Hezai and Lin Changzhi are not even "professional" writers. At the same time that a few professional writers fell, thousands and thousands of new writers have emerged. Once the process of writing is demystified, people no longer have to go through the checkpoints of autonomy, inspiration, psychoanalysis, and the subconscious in order to earn their admission to the literary world.

One positive aspect of Internet culture is its democratizing effect, but along with this comes its negative impact—so-called "Internet waste." Because anyone can enter the literary world without an admission ticket, a large amount of irresponsible writing—writing in poor taste, without any sense of duty, intended for self-amusement and self-pleasure—has been generated and disseminated. The Internet's playful nature has resulted in the return of the repressed and the forbidden, and it has furnished plenty of opportunities for bad taste and behavior.

The aestheticization of everyday life and the outgrowth of literariness

In literary form, the impact of anti-elitism has resulted in the marginalization of pure literature, the outgrowth of literariness, and the aestheticization of everyday life. In the new century, the literary landscape consists of the decline of serious literature, elite literature, and pure literature on the one hand and the rampant outgrowth of literariness on the other. The outgrowth of literariness can be understood from two perspectives. First, the outgrowth of literariness in everyday life is due to the emergence of social media and consumer culture's inroads in everyday symbolization and visualization. Second, literariness has permeated into social sciences and other fields outside the realm of literature (Yu Hong 2002). I focus on the first perspective and discuss the practices of both "disenchantment" and "pro-enchantment" (*humei*) (Tao Dongfeng 2004).

Due to the upsurge of the service industry and the culture industry, the economization of culture has occurred, and the boundaries between literature and anti-literature, art and anti-art, aestheticism and anti-aestheticism have become blurred. Compared to the agricultural and heavy industries, the service industry and the culture industry had a more prominent cultural content, and its rise has increased the role of materialism, especially in lifestyle consumption. At the same time, the growth of productivity has led to an increase in people's leisure time, which has caused a shift in their demands. In addition to material consumption, other symbolic forms of aesthetic consumption have appeared, including the creative industry (the "gold collar" class), the entertainment industry, the beauty industry, the body industry, and the spiritual economy. The rise of mass media and screen culture has dramatically increased the ubiquity of different symbols and images of everyday life, and people start assigning symbolic values to material goods. The phenomenon of brand name consumer goods is particularly prominent in fashion merchandise, which is visible everywhere in China's metropolises.

Ironically, the decline of pure literature and the inundation of art occurred simultaneously with the outgrowth of literariness. The commercialization of art, along with the aestheticization of commodity, develops side by side: besieged by works of art and non-art, the boundaries between aesthetic experience and non-aesthetic experience become increasingly blurred. The distance between the realm of life and aesthetic space is narrowing to the extent that it may have completely disappeared by now. Shopping malls, supermarkets, and vacation resorts are new primary sites for aesthetic experience, and the difference between these places and the specialized sites of concert halls and art galleries are almost non-existent. In short, the far-reaching outgrowth of literariness forms the most important material base of de-elitization in contemporary culture.

The diffusion of literariness into commercialization has worked against autonomous art and represents one of the most significant expressions of de-elitization. We should recall that autonomous or pure literature is a modern construct. In China as in the West, "literature" in ancient theory refers to works that served a material purpose and belongs to the category of "miscellaneous literature" (*zawenxue*). Passing through a series of inclusions and exclusions, literature eventually identifies itself as distinct from its other: non-literature. The principle that Bourdieu calls "distinction" refers to division, the act of drawing boundaries, which is actually a form of elitist literature, an act of "reenchant-ment" (*fumei*). Literature, especially pure literature, originally passes through a series of eliminations and divisions in order to preserve its autonomy; after achieving a certain degree of scarcity, mysticism becomes the "enchantment" of literature, but the outgrowth of literariness has coincidentally destroyed the aforementioned divisions and thus has dealt a fatal blow to literature and art, especially pure literature.

Consuming classics, parodying literature

Literary classics have been praised as cultural exemplars, and the elite often serve as the protector of the classics due to their investment in literature and art and their culture's confidence in their specialized knowledge. Nonetheless, this is not to say that the elite always unconditionally defend the classics but rather that they are unable to imagine an alternative without classics. In reality, the elite's attitude toward the classics is fre-quently divided between conservatism and radicalism, as evident in the May Fourth polarizing approaches toward the Confucian canon. Guided by tradition in premodern China, the literati's reverence for the classics endowed the canon with sacred authority, and this act of "reenchantment" reflected an absolute faith in the original text. As a time-honored technique, recitation played a fundamental role in education in ancient China and was elite culture's basic strategy of "pro-enchantment," although as such it was also an important method of regulating cultural authority. In response, the new intelligentsia's rebellion against tradition started with the assault on the classics by way of disenchantment. Kang Youwei went through archival verification to expose many sanctified classical works as inauthentic. Gu Jiegang's aim in critiquing ancient history was to challenge the classics in order to overthrow tradition. The madman's awakening in Lu Xun's "Diary of a Madman" occurs unexpectedly with the decoding of two characters between the lines of the classics: "eat humans" (or cannibalism). All these examples represent the practice of disenchantment.

In today's consumer era, the "disenchantment" of classics takes place when the clas-sics are consumed like fast food. The approach of May Fourth enlightenment intellec-tuals in attacking the classics was certainly extreme, but their intention initially was a sincere desire for change and an urgent sense of mission, which prevented a slide toward nihilism and cynicism. By contrast, the 1990s trend of consuming classics was promoted and controlled by the postmodern culture industry in China and catered to popular consumer needs for generating financial profits. Through modern technologies of sound and image, the classics now are remade into a game of fragmentation and rewriting, rich with sensory stimulation and commercial signifiers, until its original enchantment is all dispelled. For instance, Beethoven's *Symphony No. 5* is used as the opening score in a commercial for acoustic equipment, and huge replicas of the *Mona Lisa* are used as advertisement for tiles along the streets of Beijing. All sorts of films and television shows recklessly play with history and rewrite the classics.

The disenchantment of the classics has prompted an impressive cultural trend of parody, resulting in the emergence of "parody literature" (*dahua wenxue*). Inspired by *A Chinese Odyssey* (*Dahua xiyou*, 1995) from Hong Kong director Stephen Chow (Zhou Xingchi), and popularized by Lin Changzhi's *Q Reader* (*Q ban yuwen*, 2004), the tide of parody art and literature has swept over nearly all literary classics from around the world.[7] Among these are *Dream of the Red Chamber*, *Journey to the West* (*Xiyou ji*), as well as "red classics" such as the socialist novel *Tracks in the Snowy Forest* and the revolutionary model theater *The Red Detachment of Women* (*Hongse niangzi jun*).

Parody literature embodies the troubled relationship between the disenchantment of classics and the endorsement of consumerism in the 1990s, and it problematizes the destiny of literary classics and cultural authority in the age of consumerism. The fundamental trait of parody literature is its use of caricature, collage, and bricolage, to play with or even subvert the existing order of classical discourse, as well as the aesthetic, moral, and cultural hierarchy. Manipulated by parody literature, the classics not only lose their prestige as a sacred object of worship but are victimized by surprise attacks of embezzlement.

As a consequence of such disenchantment, classical authors and works, along with their celebrated textual meanings and interpretations established by a time-honored tradition, are thoroughly overturned. For instance, Lin Changzhi resorts to outrageous distortions when playing with the classics, and his acts of disenchantment are performed in nearly every aspect of the text—from characters and plots to time–space relations and discursive modes. After Sima Guang cracked open the ceramic vat, out came the Seven Dwarves, Bugs Bunny, Doraemon, and Mashimaro, along with Li Yapeng. The old father in Zhu Ziqing's "Silhouette" ("*Beiying*," 1925) danced in a freestyle rap, and the narrator in Zhu's "Moonlight at the Lotus Pond" ("*Hetang yuese*," 1919) became a peeping Tom. Parody literature makes fun of cultural consciousness, breaks through the confines of time, place, and culture, and haphazardly combines ancient phrases with contemporary words and slangs. Santa Claus, Liu Laogen, and Melon Boy come together to dismantle the barrier that used to divide elite culture from popular culture. Snow White now wears a high-cut bathing suit to go hunting; the Little Match Girl becomes a fashionable salesgirl; Gu Baoyu unexpectedly tells Gu Zheng, "Don't follow me, I'm going online." Specialized expressions from the "new humans" (*xin xinrenlei*), such as "shuang" (awesome), "ku" (cool), "MM," "dongdong," and "886," became ubiquitous on the Internet (see Chapter 23 by Jing Feng).

Parody literature appeals to the younger generations and reaffirms the tenet of youth culture that nothing is sacred in this world anymore: there is no authority, and role models no longer exist; everything can be made into a joke and overturned. In a manner more radical than its May Fourth counterparts, parody literature effects disenchantment of not only traditional culture but also of modern elite culture and revolutionary culture. The targets of *Q Reader*'s humorous parody includes modern classics such as Lu Xun's "Kong Yiji" (1919), Western classics such as Hans Christian Anderson's "The Little Match Girl," as well as revolutionary classics such as Mao's "The Foolish Old Man Who Removed the Mountains" (*"Yugong yi shan,"* 1945).

Admittedly, the thrust of disenchantment—its suspicious, rebellious energy—has a positive impact in that it discourages any blind following and worship of authority. But without any alternatives, "play on words" (*xishuo*) is a double-edged sword: on the one hand, it dispels all modern myths of power, and on the other hand its adaptation of postmodern self-deconstruction lacks sustained values and ideals. Consequently, it borders on cynicism or nihilism. Cynics can be richly imaginative and intelligent, but at the same time never believe in any lofty ideal worth dedication and devotion. Brave enough to challenge cultural authority, cynicism fails to address sensitive issues of reality in its careful evasion of actual power and oppressive forces. History has proven that cynics and nihilists have been unable to resist authority (Tao Dongfeng 2005).

Elite Literature during the De-elitization Era

In spite of the rise of popular culture and the de-elitization of literature during a far-reaching transformation of sociocultural conditions since the early 1990s, elite writers have continuously adjusted their tactics and produced noteworthy new works. Among other things, they have shown growing concerns for the fast-changing reality and have ventured creatively into formal explorations.

Growing concerns for reality and formal explorations

After 1992, market reform has produced a sweeping development in China, which is gradually integrated into the world economy after China joined the World Trade Organization (WTO) in the late 1990s. Since then, global consumerism and popular culture have expanded even more rapidly. Whether intervening in social problems as in enlightenment literature, or pursuing formal experimentation as in avant-garde literature, elite literature now has lost its ability to create a sensational effect. Instead, sensationism has become a defining characteristic in the production and consumption of popular literature, as exemplified by Guo Jingming's works and his popular magazine *Top Fiction* (*Zui xiaoshuo*). Due to the marketization of culture and literature, a new social group consisting of non-professional writers and self-employed professionals has emerged, and the changing status of the writer took another step in disenchantment.

The literary trend is defined not only by de-elitization but also by anti-spiritualization and vulgarization. Under this circumstance, elitization has declined on the whole, and its influence has diminished, thus clearing the way for Internet literature to flourish.

Nevertheless, elite writers have forged ahead with serious writing in the new century, and they share two main tendencies. First, they continue to carry out formal experimentation, albeit more grounded in Chinese context than in catching up with the West, as what happened in the 1980s. Second, whereas avant-garde writers of the 1980s distanced themselves from social reality and participated in de-politicization, elite writers since the 1990s have started to address sociopolitical problems again and have demonstrated growing concerns for contemporary and historical issues. Obviously, China's reform has been hijacked by interest groups, and countless new problems have surfaced, such as massive layoffs of formerly state-employed workers, hundreds of millions of migrant workers in large cities, the uneven distribution of wealth, and the widening of income gaps.

Post-1990s elite literature is difficult to categorize, and literary works have become increasingly individualized. In general, elite writers are self-conscious with their formal experimentation; but, in contrast to the 1980s, this time around it is integral to their serious meditation on reality and history.[8] Formal exploration is carried out with a new level of sophistication, and modernist technique is now part of a seamless Chinese narrative. For instance, Jia Pingwa's *Ancient Kiln* (*Gulu*, 2011) contains elements of roots-searching literature, and Yan Lianke's *Little Pleasures* (*Shouhuo*, 2003; English as *Lenin's Kisses*, 2012) is reminiscent of magical realism. As illustrated by Mo Yan, elite literature in the new century is both rooted in Chinese reality and has international resonance and recognition.

Mo Yan and his generation of elite writers

Since the 1990s, the majority of active elite writers are those born in the 1950s (e.g., Han Shaogong, Jia Pingwa, Li Rui, Mo Yan, Wang Anyi, Yan Lianke, and Zhang Wei) or in the early 1960s (e.g., Su Tong and Yu Hua), and their creativity has outlasted those writers born in the 1930s–1940s and has far surpassed those born in the 1970s and later. Not only is their work superior in technique, their thoughts have also grown increasingly profound. These elite writers share a respect for literature's solemn mission, and they have protected literature from becoming a merely profit- and pleasure-driven enterprise. Significantly, these writers now prefer the novel, and most settings of their novels are socialist China, with a few exceptions such as Ge Fei's *Peach Blossom Beauty* (*Renmian taohua*, 2004), Liu Xinglong's *The Shengtianmen Gate* (*Shengtian menkou*, 2005), and Tie Ning's *Stupid Flower* (*Benhua*, 2006). To a certain extent, New China is no longer new, for the PRC is more than 60 years old, and the New Era has lasted over 30 years. Crucial historical events from socialist China—the land reform, the Anti-Rightists Campaign, the Great Leap Forward, the people's communes, the Cultural Revolution, and the economic reform—have all found their way into elite writers' new novels. These writers have personally experienced many of these events, so they are their ideal narrators.

Given the space limitations, I will offer only a brief discussion of Mo Yan in this concluding section. After winning the 2012 Nobel Prize in Literature, Mo Yan has renewed the myth of elite literature in China. In his 1990s works, Mo Yan carried on and further developed his subjects, themes, and basic styles from the 1980s, as in his "The Transparent Carrot" (*Touming de hongluobo*, 1985), and continued to enrich the magical literary world of his hometown "Gaomi county," which is comparable to well-known fictional places such as Lu Xun's "Lu Town," Shen Congwen's "West Hunan," William Faulkner's "Yoknapatawpha county," and Márquez's "Macondo." Apart from Western modernist traditions, the creation of Gaomi has also drawn from traditional Chinese folk literature such as Pu Songling's stories. Yet, Mao Yan's work is characterized by his unique individual charm, rich visuality, and vibrant language. His expansive literary world is permeated with strong smells of alcohols, bloods, and unbridled passions, and his characters move in and out of a fantastic landscape of wildness.

As with all writers, Mo Yan has his distractors. Some have criticized his eccentric imagination, excessive narrative details, and sinister exaggeration of corrupt officials, while others have reproached him for his Communist Party membership and his vice-presidency in the China Writers Association. Either way, it is true that Mo Yan's fiction conveys abundant political messages, and his imaginative world does not evade Chinese reality and history. Instead, he consistently directs attention to peasants' sufferings inflicted by Chinese revolutions and narrates their fates in extraordinary, hyperbolic, and magical ways—all these features shared by his fellow writers such as Yan Lianke. Mo Yan's celebrated novels such as *Big Breasts and Wide Hips* (*Fengru feitun*, 1995; English 2004) and *Life and Death Are Wearing Me Out* (*Shengsi pilao*, 2006; English 2008) cover the tortuous, traumatic history of the twentieth century. Gaomi's peasants are depicted as having no control of various inhuman social systems and brutal political forces. In *Frogs and Babies* (*Wa*, 2009), his novel on China's controversial policy on birth control, both local peasants and family planning workers become victims of the political institution. In *The Republic of Wine* (*Jiuguo*, 1992; English 2000), the motif of cannibalism is elaborated in hilarious scenes of extravagant banquets and moral degradation in an effort to satirize the dark side of corrupt officialdom.

Mo Yan's fiction consists of tales of suffering in his hometown Gaomi, with an emphasis on hunger and poverty. His characters often have an empty stomach and a craving for sex, but against all odds they manage to make the best of it: eating, drinking, fighting, humiliating each other, sleeping around, giving births, and burying their dead. Such scenes, along with those of ordinary people's daily lives, are inextricably interwoven with fantastical imagination. He employs magical and peculiar methods of expressing everyday lives—not only "bizarre realism" (*guaidan xianshi zhuyi*) but also "brutal realism" (*canku xianshi zhuyi*)—and out of such methods a series of blood-drenched landscape, brutal reality, and historical memory have emerged. In *Life and Death Are Wearing Me Out*, Ximen Nao refuses to drink a soup called "goddess of the wind" that would cause someone to forget, but rather prefers to be transformed into a donkey, a cow, a pig, a dog, in a countless round of reincarnations. The plot is surely ludicrous, but the novel is replete with bloody historical memories.

It is difficult to categorize Mo Yan's protagonists as socialist heroes. In his earlier novel *Red Sorghum* (*Hong gaoliang jiazu*, 1987; English 1993), the portrayal of the male protagonist Yu Zhan'ao fundamentally subverts the image of the anti-Japanese resistance hero previously established by socialist literature, for it abandons the binary opposition between good and evil deeply engrained in official culture. Yu is not a hero possessing the outstanding morals of a Party member but a blood-thirsty bandit chief who disregards any existing social laws and moral order and who is portrayed as a macho character. Similarly, the female protagonist in the novel, the narrator's grandmother, is a countrywoman who flouts traditional feminine virtues in pursuit of her own happiness, a figure who would be denounced under either feudal or Communist society for moral transgression.

Mo Yan's stories combine avant-garde experimentation with strong Chinese nativism, and they are alive with ghosts, myths, and legends from rural folk culture. He emphasizes the significance of the body in all its materiality and immediacy, which is reflected in his honest attention to natural instincts and biological needs (e.g., eating, drinking, and defecating). In many of his stories, a recurrent theme is hunger, and eating appears again and again as a dominant motif. The image of excrement also appears frequently in his stories, along with other descriptions of the lower half of the body. In sharp contrast to rampant voyeurism surrounding the materialistic body of consumer culture and body writing, in Mo Yan's fiction the body is a regenerative force inseparable from production and reproduction. All of these features endow his works with utterly different qualities from those found in dominant elite intellectual culture and consumer culture.

In conclusion, Mo Yan's unique contribution to New Era literature of the last 30 years demonstrates that elite literature is still alive and well in the tug of war between elitization and de-elitization. After all the hype of disenchantment, Mo Yan shows to the world that enchantment can still be found in the best of literature.

NOTES

1   The 1980s intellectual tendency was to classify the Cultural Revolution, along with feudalism and autocracy, as "premodern," and modern enlightenment is thus distinguished from premodern feudalism in China. No one back then would accept the recent New Left contention that socialism was "another modernity project" (Tao Dongfeng 1999).

2   The year 1985 is significant in Chinese literary history because a large number of literary works published that year are characterized by formal experiments, and they defy conventional realism: Can Xue's "The Hut on the Mountain" ("*Shanshang de xiaowu*"), Han Shaogong's "*Bababa*," Liu Suola's "You Have No Other Choice" ("*Ni biewu xuanze*"), Ma Yuan's "The Temptation of the Gangdisi" ("*Gangdisi de youhuo*"), and Wang Anyi's *Baotown* ("*Xiaobaozhuang*"; English 1989).

3   Since the mid-1980s, writers such as A Cheng, Mo Yan, Li Rui, and Wang Zengqi have all engaged in literary experiments, although they are rarely classified as avant-garde writers.

4   "The Super Girl" was an annual singing contest for female vocalists launched by Hunan
Satellite Television in 2004, and its grassroots,
popular-style operation subverted the rules of
traditional artistic contests. It soon became the
highest rated entertainment program in China,
and the term "*chaonü*" became synonymous
with the younger generation's fantasy of using
mass media to achieve fame overnight. Sister
Lotus (born Shi Hengxia) was a college graduate hailing from an ordinary worker household
in Shaanxi province, but due to her daily posting of her photographs online, she became the
most famous anti-idol Internet celebrity in
2005.

5   The humanist spirit was a widely debated issue
in 1990s China. Citing the vulgarization of
literary works, Wang Xiaoming (1993a) discusses the crisis involving the entire humanities.

6   *Pizi* is a local hooligan who lives in the margins
of society and whose lifestyle and values deviate
from the mainstream. In his fictional work
Playing for Thrills (*Wande jiu shi xintiao*, 1989;
English 1997), Wang Shuo stages the subcul-
ture's rebellion against the intelligentsia
through mockery.

7   A huge box office success in Hong Kong,
A Chinese Odyssey gained popularity on college
campuses in mainland China after 1999, in
part due to its clever dialogue and postmodern
style. *Q Reader* playfully transforms 31 well-
known Chinese school texts into hilarious non-
sensical tales, and their humorous content,
fantastical plot, and witty dialogue became the
most famous work of "nonsense literature"
(*wulitou wenxue*).

8   Most representative of this integration is Yu
Hua, an avant-garde writer who published a
series of novels, such as *To Live* (*Huozhe*, 1992;
English 2003b) and *Chronicle of a Blood
Merchant* (*Xu Sanguan maixue ji*, 1995; English
2003a), that mark his shift toward realism,
although he has continued to pay close
attention to form and style.

References

Cai, Xiang 蔡翔. 2002. "Hewei wenxue benshen"
何謂文學本身 (The meaning of literature
itself). *Dangdai zuojia pinglun* 當代作家評論
(Contemporary writers review), 6: 31–42.

Can, Xue. 2007. "The Hut on the Mountain." In
*The Columbia Anthology of Modern Chinese
Literature*. Edited by Lau, Joseph S. M., and
Howard Goldblatt. Second edition. New York:
Columbia University Press. 325–328.

Chen, Sihe 陳思和. Ed. 1999. *Zhongguo dangdai
wenxue shijiaocheng* 中國當代文學史教程 (A
textbook history of contemporary Chinese literature). Shanghai: Fudan daxue chubanshe.

Chen, Xiaoming 陳曉明. 2009. *Zhongguo dangdai
wenxue zhuchao* 中國當代文學主潮 (Major
trends in contemporary Chinese literature).
Beijing: Beijing daxue chubanshe.

Deng, Xiaoping 鄧小平. 1994. *Deng Xiaoping
wenxuan* (1975–1982) 鄧小平文選 (1975–
1982) (The selected works of Deng Xiaoping,
1975–1982). Beijing: Renmin chubanshe.

Dongfang xinwen 東方新聞. 2000. "Wang Shuo
ping 'Yong shenti xiezuo' de Mian Mian he *Tang*"
王朔評"用身體寫作"的棉棉和《糖》(Wang
Shuo criticizes body writer Mian Mian and *Candy*)
(June 7). Accessed 10 July 2014. http://news.
eastday.com/epublish/gb/paper7/20000607/
class000700002/hwz56239.htm.

Hong, Zicheng 洪子誠. 2007. *Zhongguo dangdai
wenxueshi* 中國當代文學史 (A history of contemporary Chinese literature). Beijing: Beijing
daxue chubanshe.

Ji, Hongzhen 季紅真. 2006. "Lun xinshiqi
xiaoshuo de jiben zhuti" 論新時期小說的基本

主題 (A discussion of the main themes in New Era literature). In *Bashi niandai de wenhua yishi* 八十年代的文化意識 (Cultural Consciousness of the 80s), Edited by Gan Yang 甘阳. Shanghai: Shanghai renmin chubanshe. 1–23.

Li, Tuo 李陀. 2001. "Manshuo chun wenxue" 漫説 "純文學" (On "pure literature"). *Shanghai wenxue*, 3: 4–15.

Li, Xunhuan 李尋歡. "Wode wangluo wenxueguan" 我的網絡文學觀 (My view on internet literature). http://dept.cyu.edu.cn/zwx/jiaoxueziliao/wdewangluowenxueguan.htm.

Lin, Changzhi 林長治. 2004. *Qban yuwen* Q版語文 (Q Reader). Kunming: Yunnan renmin chubanshe.

Lin, Hong 林紅. 2007. *Mincuizhuyi* 民粹主義 (Populism). Beijing: Zhongyang bianyi chubanshe.

Lukes, Steven (史蒂文·盧克斯). 2001. *Individualism* (個人主義). Trans. Yan Kewen 閻克文. Nanjing: Jiangsu renmin chubanshe.

Mo, Yan. 1993. *Red Sorghum: A Novel of China*. Trans. Howard Goldblatt. New York : Viking.

Mo, Yan. 2000. *The Republic of Wine: A Novel*. Trans. Howard Goldblatt. New York: Arcade Publishing.

Mo, Yan. 2004. *Big Breasts and Wide Hips: A Novel*. Trans. Howard Goldblatt. New York: Arcade Publishing.

Mo, Yan. 2008. *Life and Death Are Wearing Me Out: A Novel*. Trans. Howard Goldblatt. New York: Arcade Publishing.

Rongshu, xia (*Under the banyan rree*), http://www.rongshuxia.com.

Tao, Dongfeng 陶東風. 1999. "Cong huhuan xiandaihua dao fansi xiandaihua xing" 從呼喚現代化到反思現代化性 (From cheering for modernization to rethinking the nature of modernization). *Wenyi lilun* 文藝理論 (Literary theory), 7: 116–126.

Tao, Dongfeng 陶東風. 2004. "Richang shenghuo de shenmeihua yu wenyi shehuixue de chongjian" 日常生活的審美化與文藝社會學的重建 (The aestheticization of everyday life and the reconstruction of literary sociology). *Wenyi yanjiu*, 1: 15–19.

Tao, Dongfeng 陶東風. 2005. Dahua wenxue yu dangdai zhongguo de quanruzhuyi 大話文學與當代中國的犬儒主義 (Parody literature and cynicism in contemporary China). *Tianjin shehui kexue* 天津社會科學 (Tianjin social sciences), 3: 89–94.

Tao, Dongfeng 陶東風 and He Lei 和磊. 2008. *Xinshiqi wenxue sanshi nian* 新時期文學三十年 (Thirty years of New Era literature). Beijing: Zhongguo shehui kexue chubanshe.

Wang, Anyi. 1989. *Baotown*. Trans. Martha Avery. New York: Viking.

Wang, Meng. 1983. *The Butterfly and Other Stories*. Beijing: Chinese Literature.

Wang, Shuo 王朔. 1987. "Wanzhu" 頑主 (The troubleshooters). *Shouhuo* 收穫 (Harvest), 6: 24–54.

Wang, Shuo 王朔. 1989. "'Wanzhu' xupian: Yi-dian zhengjing meiyou" 《頑主》續篇:一點正經沒有 (Pure nonsense). *Zhongguo zuojia* 中國作家 (Chinese writers), 4: 110–140.

Wang, Shuo. 1997. *Playing for Thrills: A Mystery*. Trans. Howard Goldblatt. New York: William Morrow and Company.

Wang, Xiaoming 王曉明. 1993a. "Kuangye shang de feixu—wenxue he renwen jingshen de weiji" 曠野上的廢墟-文學和人文精神的危機 (Ruins on the wasteland—the crisis of literature and the humanities spirit). *Shanghai wenxue* 上海文學 (Shanghai literature), 6: 63–68.

Xu, Zhiying 許志英 and Ding Fan 丁帆. Eds. 2002. *Zhongguo xinshiqi xiaoshuo zhuchao* 中國新時期小説主潮 (Trends in Chinese New Era fiction). Beijing: Renmin wenxue chubanshe.

Yan, Lianke. 2012. *Lenin's Kisses*. Trans. Carlos Rojas. New York: Grove Press.

Yu, Hong 余虹. 2002. "Wenxue de zhongjie yu wenxue xing manyan: jiantan houxiandai wenxue yanjiu de renwu" 文學的終結與文學性蔓延:兼談後現代文學研究的任務 (The end of literature and the spread of literariness: discussing the task of research on postmodern literature). *Wenyi yanjiu*, 6: 15–24.

Yu, Hua. 2003a. *Chronicle of a Blood Merchant*. Trans. Andrew F. Jones. New York: Pantheon Books.

Yu, Hua. 2003b. *To Live: A Novel*. Trans. with an afterword by Michael Berry. New York: Anchor Books.

Zhang, Xianliang 張賢亮. 2009. *Women zheyidai zuojia* 我們這一代作家 (Our generation of writers). *Wenxuebao* (Sept. 17): 2.

Zhu, Weilian 朱威廉. 2000. "Wenxue fazhan de feiwo turang" 文學發展的肥沃土壤 (The fertile soil of literary growth). *Wenxue bao* (Feb. 27).

7

Building a Modern Institution of Literature: The Case of Taiwan

Sung-sheng Yvonne Chang

Taiwan was a Japanese colony between 1895 and 1945, and since 1949 has constituted the main sovereign territory of the Republic of China (ROC). After the lifting of martial law in 1987, Taiwan emerged as a new democracy in East Asia. On the one hand, literary history in modern Taiwan shares key features with its East Asian neighbors: drastic shifts in its literary culture as a result of war, revolution, and regime change; ubiquitous state control that tends to escalate into totalitarian mobilization of writers in times of emergency; and recurring eruptions of left-versus-right aesthetic contentions wedded to internecine political struggles. On the other hand, the trajectory along which a modern literary institution has developed in Taiwan exhibits such distinctive features that as a case it both challenges and potentially illuminates existing analytical paradigms.

In the mid-1920s, when Taiwanese intellectuals, inspired by the May Fourth Movement in mainland China, advocated a "new literature" using a modern vernacular, they were primarily concerned with pushing their society past the threshold of modernity. However, the focus of their contention shifted shortly thereafter. Which modern vernacular, Chinese or Taiwanese, should they promote? Heated debates ensued. In the end, however, neither agenda prevailed: by the time the next generation of colonial Taiwanese writers came of age in the late 1930s and early 1940s, Japanese, their colonizer's language, clearly dominated. These writers acquired their apprenticeship either in Tokyo or through colonial institutions in Taiwan and produced sophisticated "modern" literary works; many became self-identified as Japanese, notwithstanding their sensitivity to the discriminatory social order in the colony. Career aspirations harbored by this generation of Taiwanese writers were entirely different from those of their predecessors.

A Companion to Modern Chinese Literature, First Edition. Edited by Yingjin Zhang.
© 2016 John Wiley & Sons, Ltd. Published 2016 by John Wiley & Sons, Ltd.

Before long, the wheels of history turned again, swiftly and abruptly. Taiwan was retroceded to the ROC at the end of World War II. After its mass retreat in 1949, the Nationalist regime earnestly pursued re-Sinicization on the island, transplanting cultural institutions from China's Republican era (1911–1949). The classical Chinese tradition was extolled. Cold War alliances with the United States further facilitated the transmission and fervent reception of modernist aesthetics from the West, giving rise to an impressive literary renaissance. Not everyone nurtured by this cultural importation subscribed to the Cold War liberal ideology, though. Protesting against the right-wing mainstream, a socialistically informed "nativist literary movement" (*xiangtu wenxue yundong*) erupted in the 1970s. While short-lived, the counter-hegemonic energy it unleashed was era-breaking. In the following decade, while a middle-class Sinocentric literature flourished in the pages of the *fukan* (newspaper literary supplements), a robust "Localist trend" (*bentuhua chaoliu*) also gathered momentum. This trend openly challenged the Nationalist-endorsed dominant culture, exalted identification with the land and history of Taiwan, and began to resurrect the then-stigmatized colonial heritage. From 1987 onward, receiving a boost from post-martial law liberalization, the Localist trend has significantly altered the cultural outlook of Taiwan's residents in general and has led to a complete overhaul of Taiwan literature studies in particular.

The end of martial law ushered in an open society virtually overnight. Since then, cultural production in Taiwan has increasingly resembled that of advanced capitalist societies, where literature's turf continues to dwindle, frequently turning into a specialized commodity. More recently, Taiwan has witnessed the coming of age of a digital generation of writers who not only partake in the global reshaping of the category "literature" but also act as a vanguard in promulgating a progressive ethos and in exploring alternative forms of identity. In so doing, they continue to play an essential part in the society's dynamic transformation in the globalized age.

In the literary history of modern Taiwan, there have been moments of glory, despite flagrant ruptures and fragmented genealogies ultimately attributable to regional and global political conflicts. This chapter intends to explore some specific aspects of this phenomenon within the broader regional context of East Asia. Section I discusses the motives, strategies, and unique challenges of two competing vernacular movements—the "Mandarin movement" (*baihuawen yundong*) and the "written Taiwanese movement" (*Taiwan huawen yundong*)—that Taiwanese intellectuals vigorously launched during the Japanese colonial period in an effort to build a locally based "modern" literary institution. A scandalous fact entailed by the premature abortion of both movements under the tightened "national language" (monolingual Japanese) policy that followed the outbreak of the Sino-Japanese War was that, in a sense, modern Taiwanese literature reached its first maturation in works written in Japanese. The two aborted vernacular movements in colonial Taiwan, notwithstanding their brevity and atrophied forms, were properly *modernist* projects generated by the same historical impulses as those behind similar cultural processes in other parts of East Asia.

Section II of this chapter first highlights some theoretically meaningful structural affinities between these movements and their more full-fledged counterparts in modern Japan and Republican China. Special emphasis is placed on the evident disparities among these evolutionary trajectories—looming large behind them are different types of historically wrought disjuncture. It then recounts the Republican legacy in post-1949 Taiwan's literary production. Out of the political turmoil in the mid-century associated with World War II, the Chinese civil war, and the global-scale Cold War, an unexpected fruit was borne, in the sense that Taiwan's cultural field was made a depository of several rich cultural traditions, including, significantly, a major strand of modern Chinese vernacular literature that had evolved during the Republican period on the mainland but was subsequently denounced there during the first decades of socialism. The chapter concludes by postulating some methodological implications of studying Taiwan's modern literature as a locally based institution.

Trajectories of Vernacular Movements in Colonial Taiwan

"Taiwan over the past century provides *a textbook case* that illustrates how political motivations can far outweigh linguistic factors in the design and implementation of *policy on a standard language* for the community"—this remark by sociolinguist Ping Chen (2001b: 108; added emphases) may be easily extended to encompass the entire cultural realm in twentieth-century Taiwan. Politically enforced monolingual policies, first featuring Japanese and then in mid-century abruptly shifting to Mandarin Chinese, undoubtedly constitute the overarching factor that shaped the trajectory along which the modern institution of literature has developed in Taiwan. Our inquiry naturally begins with the closely intertwined vernacular movements in language and literature in 1920s Taiwan, triggered by the advent of modernity.

Two competing vernacular movements

As Ann Heylen succinctly sums up, the literary component in the Mandarin *baihuawen* movement, inspired by the May Fourth Movement in Republican China, was prominent:[1]

> Mandarin *baihuawen* as a language reform movement was introduced as a literary movement in Taiwan. It made available a range of new ideas through literature, often translated from Western and Japanese works. Among these "literary imports" were "proletarian literature" and "nativist literature." Even though the distribution of Chinese literature was on a small scale, it instilled a new pride in the Chinese cultural heritage. It re-instituted Mandarin *baihuawen* in the perpetuation of a Chinese literature responding to modernization in its own right. This facilitated the formation of a "Chinese language reading middle class" in Taiwan. (Heylen 2012: 196)

Differing from many existing accounts, a subtext of the preceding passage is the suggestion that, by the mid-1920s, Taiwan had already been sufficiently alienated from its ancestral land that a sense of pride in its Chinese cultural heritage had to be *rekindled*. Another noteworthy point is her emphasis on the middle class.

Taiwan's educated middle class, an emergent social formation predisposed to new ideas and instrumental in spearheading the society's modernization process, eventually swung from the Chinese cultural sphere to the Japanese one as time went by. According to official statistics collected by Fujii Shōzō (1998: 35), "less than one half of one percent of the Taiwanese population could understand Japanese in 1905 but by 1941 fifty-seven percent of the population could." Whereas historian Zhou Wanyao (2002: 10) points out that the latter might be an inflated figure, as it could have included people who had merely attended short-term language workshops during the *kominka* campaign, she nonetheless also asserts that members of the educated class, especially writers, who had received a complete education in Japanese, were likely to have a high command of the language. In any event, it is important to recognize tensions and intricate negotiations among several cultural matrixes in colonial Taiwan during this transition: between Chinese loyalism, pragmatic efforts to lift Taiwan out from under "China," and, what became most prevalent in the last years of the colonial period, inserting oneself into the colonizer's narratives and thus entering the triangulated relationship featuring Chinese/Taiwanese, Japanese, and the Westerners.

Those among the first generation of colonial Taiwanese writers who advocated Mandarin *baihuawen* most likely had attended *shufang*, private tutorial classes for Chinese gentry-class children geared toward preparing for the civil service examination of imperial China, before the latter were abolished in 1905 in the wake of the establishment of popular education. As enlightened members of the gentry class, and inspired by the May Fourth Movement in China, these writers attacked the worldview and cultural practices of Taiwan's conservative literary sector, traditional literati whose activities revolved around *shishe* (classical-style Chinese poetry clubs), and they blamed the difficulty that ordinary people had in becoming competent in the classical language for obstructing Taiwan's modernization. The anti-colonial motives were unmistakable, evidenced by the significant overlap between the Mandarin *baihuawen* advocates and the membership of the Taiwan Culture Association (*Taiwan wenhua xiehui*), a local intellectual organization founded in 1921 that contested the colonial authorities and fought for the right to steer Taiwan's future.

Literature's inherently mimetic nature inevitably foregrounded the disparity between Mandarin *baihuawen*, based primarily on Northern Chinese dialects, and the vernacular forms actually used in Taiwan, namely Southern Fukienese (*Minnan yu*, aka *Hoklo* or *Heluo hua*) and Hakka (*Kejia hua*). A written Taiwanese movement thus arose in the 1930s that proposed the creation of a new writing system based on Southern Fukienese (*Taiwan huawen* or written Taiwanese), to be used as the medium for a "nativist literature."

You are a Taiwanese standing under Taiwanese sky and on Taiwanese earth. Your eyes witness Taiwanese things and your ears hear Taiwanese news. You experience Taiwanese time and speak the Taiwanese tongue. Therefore, your pen of sharp articulation, your pen of colorful creation, should write Taiwanese literature.[2]

The preceding quotation is a routinely cited passage from the movement's earliest advocate Huang Shihui, a left-leaning intellectual. Resorting to an inviolable nativity as a rallying point became a hallmark of the leftist literary culture in the coming decades, which even survived the generational shift as a potent animating force for writers of the 1940s with a different artistic orientation.

As conventional wisdom has it, contention between advocates of Mandarin *baihuawen* and written Taiwanese was the precursor of later struggles between Chinese and Taiwanese nationalisms. This idea is in fact unwarranted, likely an anachronistic projection of contemporary problems onto the past. The next section, therefore, adopts a more properly literary approach and focuses on the divergent textual models espoused by the two groups.

Visions of textuality: the modernist project, the primacy of sound, layers of meaning

The boundaries of "literature" as a category have been increasingly challenged in the digital age. The foreign origin and relatively recent history of the term—dated to nineteenth-century Europe—has also raised doubts about the appropriateness of applying it to non-Western traditions. It may be useful to introduce the notion of textuality, which highlights the openness of the "text" to different manners of concretization into a meaningful "work." In a nutshell, writers in colonial Taiwan were denied the opportunity to fully carry out their quests for textual models that met the formal and ideological requirements of a pre-conceived category, namely, a locally based institution of "modern literature." Rather, in the end, the Japanese textual vision, influenced by the modern Western one, prevailed.

The literary output produced by both the Mandarin *baihuawen* and the written Taiwanese movements was scanty, to say the least. Both movements suffered serious setbacks with the official abolition of Chinese-language newspaper columns in 1937. Nonetheless, the associated polemic gathered so much momentum in the first half of the 1930s that it became a public forum for local intellectuals to articulate various practical and ideological concerns. For our purposes, the exceptionally vibrant intellectual exchanges between advocates of these two movements allow us to examine their underlying assumptions about textuality, assumptions pointing to core issues similarly encountered in vernacular literary movements elsewhere in East Asia.

The "new" versus "old" literary debate in 1924, the harbinger of the Mandarin *baihuawen* movement, was spurred by two articles by Zhang Wojun, a Taiwanese attending university in Beijing. Zhang's views echoed closely the principle of the "eight don'ts" proposed by Hu Shi for the May Fourth Movement (see Chapter 9 by Michelle Yeh), and featured a normative conception of modern vernacular literature that privileged a simple and direct relationship between the text and the reality it purportedly represented. Whereas Hu warned against excessive formal embellishment and a "lack of substance," Zhang explicitly treated superfluous stylistic traits as symptomatic of the "decadent" and reactionary lifestyles and worldviews of Taiwan's traditional literati class and faulted the traditionalists for obstructing Taiwan's social progress.

Briefly, the ideal textual models envisioned at this time were often associated with the Western-imported term "realism," and they implied suitability for capturing the everyday realities of modern life, thus possessing democratic potential. Insofar as the model favored the paring down of thick layers of compositional maneuvering to ensure precision and transparency in literary representation, it resonated with the animating spirit of *genbun'itchi*, literally meaning "consistency between written and spoken languages," which originated in late-nineteenth-century Japan and became a universal guiding principle for the vernacular movement in the Sinosphere. Both Western "realism" and Japanese *genbun'itchi* seemed to hold sway over proponents of the Taiwanese vernacular movements. While there is little indication of serious theoretical interest in the concept, there appeared to be an intuitive subscription to the seemingly self-evident implications of *genbun'itchi*. This ultimately brought proponents of both movements of Mandarin *baihuawen* and written Taiwanese to a similar quandary, namely, subscribing to a naïve belief in the possibility of eliminating the inherent gap between the spoken, colloquial language and the written, literary language.

Reductive as it may appear, some snapshots of the life of Lai He, the "father of modern Taiwanese literature," illustrate well that, in its essence, the dilemma went beyond the contention between usage of either Mandarin *baihuawen* or written Taiwanese as a literary medium. Relatively extensive exposure to traditional Chinese learning and a brief sojourn in Xiamen as a medical doctor gave Lai a certain advantage over his peers in writing literature in Mandarin *baihuawen*. Yet, he was also among the few at this time who actually tried their hand at creating written Taiwanese fiction, although he later abandoned the experiment due to unsatisfactory results. In the last years of his life, however, especially after being released from a short prison term, despondent and in declining health, Lai reverted to classical Chinese poetry as a means of artistic self-expression. No one can overlook the irony of this, given Lai's pioneering role in Taiwan's modern vernacular movement. Classical Chinese poetry, stigmatized as obsolete and degenerate by that movement, turned out to be the only textual model capable of providing an aesthetic frame mature enough to fulfill his intimate expressivist needs.

Most scholars do not put Guo Qiusheng and Lian Heng (Lian Yatang) side by side, most likely because they belonged to different intellectual cohorts and social strata. However, from today's vantage point, their shared passions for, and markedly divergent approaches to, the construction of a new Taiwanese script system represented two polarized visions of textual models and the related issues pertaining to aesthetic resources.

Guo Qiusheng published articles with meticulous blueprints for the new written Taiwanese script system. As Bert Scruggs points out, Guo's scheme often privileged conformity between speech and sound, a value that was apparently aimed at maximizing the system's utility for the less educated, and concomitantly at resisting the encroachment of Japanese into the sphere of Taiwanese daily life (Scruggs 2015: 14–15). Fighting illiteracy was at the very top of the agenda for Taiwanese intellectual activists in the 1930s, who were deeply concerned about the long-term implications of the inadequacy of language education in public schools, where Japanese was poorly taught while, at the same time, the hours of Chinese lessons were reduced.

Lian Heng, a member of the older literati and author of the well-known *A General History of Taiwan* (*Taiwan tongshi*, 1908–1918), had a firm conviction about the unique merits of the Taiwanese language, traceable to its origins in classical Chinese. Between 1929 and 1933, Lian conducted extensive archival research on the etymology of contemporary Taiwanese and compiled a dictionary, which was partially serialized in the *Three-Six-Nine Little Gazette* (*San liu jiu xiaobao*) with a preface written in classical Chinese.[3] Lian's approach, which treated texts as deposits of layers of meaning accrued over long periods of history, echoes views embraced by traditionalists everywhere.

Whereas Lian's dictionary temporally overlapped with the written Taiwanese debates, the two exerted impact in different discursive spaces, not an uncommon phenomenon: the traditionalists and "new" intellectuals in the transitional period occupied different positions in the cultural field and were often segregated to a greater or lesser extent. For our purposes, both efforts of Guo's Taiwanese script and Lian's Taiwanese dictionary represent the coexistence of opposite views regarding language and desirable textual models, and the closely related issue of aesthetic resources critical to the establishment of the modern institution of literature.

Whether to draw aesthetic resources from the classical tradition or to give priority to the demands of a modernizing society is a battle that must be fought out over the longer course of the evolution of a modern vernacular literature. During this process, people must come to terms with the sociolinguistic phenomenon of "diglossia," to overcome or displace problems it has presented to literary composition and representation. In colonial Taiwan, as in Republican China, classical Chinese obviously was the "high language" in the diglossia, a "highly codified (often grammatically more complex) superposed variety, the vehicle of a large and respected body of written literature, either of an earlier period or in another speech community, which is learned largely by formal education and is used for most written and formal spoken purposes but is not used by any section of the community for ordinary conversation" (Ferguson 1959: 336).[4] The task at hand, therefore, was to transform either Mandarin *baihuawen* or spoken Taiwanese or both in such a way that they could simultaneously perform these higher and quotidian functions, and would "transcend the daily vernacular in terms of sophistication and richness in grammar, lexicon, and style, and be sufficiently equipped to suit a whole range of purposes in literature" (Ping Chen 2001a: 53).

This leads to another unique situation in colonial Taiwan, which has developed its own subsets of diglossia over a couple of centuries, thanks to Taiwan's geographical remoteness from the center of the Chinese Empire. As generations of gentry-class Han settlers attended *shufang* to prepare for a bureaucratic career, a whole set of pronunciations evolved for reading classical Chinese texts (*Hanwen*) that were different from both the Mandarin (*guanhua*, the basis for *baihuawen*) and the spoken Taiwanese. This premodern legacy created a situation in Taiwan that could probably be compared to early Meiji Japan, when multiple ways of matching the sound and script of the language coexisted. This inevitably further compounded the task faced by the promoters of written Taiwanese: aside from overcoming the limitations of everyday speech, they must also reconcile spoken Taiwanese with literary *Hanwen* readings and their vocabulary of a more formal diction, as well as with the newly incorporated Japanese elements.[5]

The colonial government's intensification of its monolingual policy in 1937 barred both movements of Mandarin *baihuawen* and written Taiwanese from venturing beyond the early phases of development. Japanese, the sanctified "national language," became the officially designated vehicle for literary activities by younger and supposedly all future generations of Taiwanese writers. True enough, works written in Mandarin *baihuawen* still claimed a large number of readers in Taiwan, and one Chinese-language popular literature magazine, *Moonlit Wind* (Fengyue bao), did survive the ban. Yet, from the desperate tone in which Liao Hanchen (Yu Wen), a leading literary figure, pleaded to his readers—"insist on writing in the vernacular and promote the objectives of New Literature" (Chang, Yeh, and Fan 2014: 12), one cannot fail to discern a justified pessimism that this might very well be a losing battle. In sum, the 8 years between 1937 and 1945 witnessed a structural transformation in Taiwan's literary field. Most significantly, the textual models pursued by Taiwanese writers switched again, this time to predominantly Western-originated literary concepts and conventions mediated by the Japanese.

Hybridity as the emerging cultural order

The last phase of Taiwan's Japanese period saw the emergence of a full-fledged colonial society, with mounting pressures from Japan's imperialist warfare. Many scholars have noted that the war intensified such aggressive assimilation programs as the *kominka* movement and the national-language family program. Of no less relevance were sociological factors. The coming-of-age of a generation of Taiwanese educated under the Japanese public school system, established island-wide around 1918–1919, meant that, by the mid-1930s, a Japanese-reading middle class had come into existence, overlapping and even threatening to supplant the Chinese-reading one. The full implications of this transition for literary history are seen in the critical ways in which Japanese-educated writers diverged from their predecessors. These differences encompassed two crucial aspects of the institution of literature, namely, the channels through which writers received their literary apprenticeship and developed their vocational vision, and the textual models they used.

Lai He's generation may be appropriately considered as reformist intellectuals that appeared toward the tail-end of the declining premodern era, whose writings were still fraught with traces of traditional Chinese narrative conventions and worldviews, as well as gentry-class sociocultural self-expectations, even while they were poignantly critical of the feudalist past. By contrast, the next generation, those born around

1905–1915, who began occupying center stage in the literary field in the mid-1930s, received their literary orientations either in Japan or through Japanese institutions established in the colony. Despite the fact that the colonizer's language was forcibly imposed, serious members of this generation of writers were well-positioned to take advantage of the aesthetic resources it made abundantly accessible to them—not least of which were sophisticated, Western-imported literary concepts and textual models. In the more mature phase of their literary careers, such writers as Lü Heruo, Zhang Wenhuan, Long Yingzong, and Weng Nao unquestionably exhibited artistic convictions and visions of textuality entailing complex structures of meaning and an immanent fullness characteristic of prevalent modern Western literary conceptions, and their best works were mostly of a higher artistic caliber than those of their older contemporaries writing in Mandarin *baihuawen*.

As more fully constituted colonial subjects, this generation of Taiwanese writers had an inherently ambivalent relationship with the colonizers. While tacitly accepting the discriminatory social order as a reality, their spirited fights for the right to define legitimate discourse in the literary field they shared with the colonizers, best exemplified by a 1943 confrontation over "*kuso* realism" between two literary journals—one led by Nishikawa Mitsuru and the other by Zhang Wenhuan and his associates— evinced a sense of entitlement as equal players, which Lai He and his peers did not possess. The root cause for this change in self-positioning was that the literary field they found themselves in was much more integrated than before. As Taiwan entered the fifth decade of Japanese reign, there existed more complex patterns of personal alignment and structural mutual dependency between the colonizer and the colonized in various social spheres. A literary history of colonial Taiwan would not be complete without judicious accounts of all of its sectors, including Japanese literary agents (in the broad sense) who actively participated in the field (Chang, Yeh, and Fan 2014; Y. Huang 2006; Kleeman 2003; Nakajima 2003; Scruggs 2015). At the same time, it is indisputable that, due to the structurally determined privileges enjoyed by the colonizing class, the greater prominence of the Japanese element in the hybrid constitution of colonial Taiwan's literary institutions necessarily impinged upon the cultural space formerly available to the vernacular movements, a situation that contributed to their premature atrophy before the colonial era ended abruptly in 1945.

Comparative Perspectives: Meiji Japan, Republican China, and post-1949 Taiwan

By the early 1940s, the prospects of Taiwan's locally launched vernacular literature movements appeared to be extremely grim, given that the practice of Mandarin *baihuawen* literature—a variety inflected with Taiwanese vocabulary and expressions— was confined to the older generation, and since a properly codified script system for written Taiwanese did not yet exist. History, however, presents many surprises. The retrocession of Taiwan to the ROC in 1945 unexpectedly heralded a triumphant comeback of Mandarin *baihuawen*. In the decades that followed, Chinese vernacular, or the version of Mandarin *baihuawen* developed in mainland China, replaced Japanese as the only legitimate linguistic medium for literary writing. While literature thrived along with other vigorous sociocultural developments in contemporary Taiwan in the second half of the twentieth century, the snappy mid-century transition claimed as innocent casualties an entire generation of Japanese-educated Taiwanese writers by virtually forcing them out of the literary field. Meanwhile, the written Taiwanese movement was effectively suppressed by Nationalist re-Sinicization policies before it resurged with a vengeance in the post-martial law period. The assembly of a standard-ized script system under the auspices of the Ministry of Education during the Democratic Progressive Party (*Minjin dang*) administration (2000–2008) in Taiwan has energized written Taiwanese literature activists and attracted new supporters, especially among the younger generation. At the same time, that movement's significant symbolic value inevitably makes it a prize in the ongoing contention between Taiwanese and Chinese nationalisms, as endorsed by the Pan-Green (*fanlü*) and the Pan-Blue (*fanlan*) coalitions, respectively.

What insights, after all, could we derive from this unusually convoluted literary history, in which political agendas collude with tensions and negotiations between cultural matrixes, and individual literary agents juggle with imperatives from ethnic identification, ideological commitment, and aesthetic quests? Whereas plenty of scholarly works have dealt with these struggles, this chapter draws attention to certain structural factors through which historical and geocultural forces play out and exert their impact on the trajectory of modern Taiwanese litera-ture, as it comes into existence, thrives and matures, or declines and atrophies. More specifically, this section uses the temporal duration, sequential order, and patterns of intertwinement between the symbiotic vernacular language and vernacular liter-ature movements as benchmarks for reaching a comparative perspective, ultimately aiming to better comprehend the processes by which the institution of modern literature, essentially a Western importation, has evolved in various modern East Asian societies.

The Japan case

Vernacular language and literature movements in early modern Japan not only enjoyed longer and more continuous cycles of evolution than in Taiwan but the trajectories of the two movements, while intertwining, were sufficiently separate from each other as to maintain relatively distinct identities. Nanette Twine (1991: 162) observes how one movement benefited the other:

> The new novel [realistic fiction] could not have succeeded without the colloquial style so suited to its objectives; and the progress of acceptance of colloquial style outside literary circles was significantly aided by its modeling in the novel. The first of these assertions is undeniably true; the second is more difficult to substantiate … but given the role of

literature in modeling what so frequently transmutes from the avant-garde to the subsequently accepted norm, it seems a reasonable assumption that the one helped the other.

Literature's comparatively high degree of distinction in the Japanese vernacular movement, as opposed to its position in Taiwan and China, was evident even in the earliest attempts at creating colloquial-style fiction in these societies. Modernizing the society of Taiwan and resistance to Japanese colonialism were the conspicuous themes of the first two vernacular stories by Lai He written in the mid-1920s, whereas antitraditionalism and a plea for cultural regeneration centrally informed "Diary of a Madman" by Lu Xun. By contrast, Futabatei Shimei, who published the first Japanese colloquial novel *The Drifting Clouds* (*Fuyun*) between 1887 and 1889, was a student of nineteenth-century Russian literature and a follower of Tsubouchi Shōyō, author of *The Essence of the Novel* (1885), which introduced modern Western literary concepts to Japan. Futabatei's colloquial experiment was likely motivated by its suitability for a psychological realism that captured the mundane realities of modern life, whereas the next novelist of colloquial-style Japanese, Yamada Bimyō, is said to have been so aesthetically self-conscious that his stylistic innovation substantially hindered the popular reception of his work. It is fair to say, therefore, that compared to their Taiwanese and Chinese counterparts, these early endeavors at creating a vernacular Japanese literature bore a closer and more direct relationship with forces internal to the modern institution of literature.

Undoubtedly, such properly "literary" concepts as realism, the key to the modernization of the East Asian literary institution in the twentieth century, also flooded the cultural space in modern China and Taiwan at the time when their vernacular movements burst out as part of an overarching cultural regeneration. And yet, the revolutionary ethos created a literary culture patently overladen with extra-literary elements, which in turn set the basic tenor for the movements' ensuing development. By contrast, while the evolution of vernacular Japanese literature was also deeply affected by political factors, it followed a rather different pattern. According to Twine, the vernacular literary trend set off by Futabatei and Yamada suffered a setback in the early 1890s, as a result of the reaction to Meiji Westernization endeavors and popular sentiments calling for a return to "things Japanese." Mori Ogai, for instance, wrote his first short story "The Dancing Girl" (1890) in the traditional style. The dynamics of an oscillation between modernity and tradition must account for the resumption of efforts to modernize through Western-inspired notions in the late 1890s. One factor was the boost to the Japanese national sense of self-confidence engendered by their victory in the 1895 Sino-Japanese war. These efforts culminated in 1902, when German-trained linguist Ueda Kazutoshi launched the *kokugo* movement under the auspices of the Ministry of Education, followed by programs aimed at "disseminating colloquial style based on the Tokyo dialect as the standard form of written expression through the classrooms of Japan" (Twine 1991: 165, 258).

Twine suggests that "the modern colloquial style reached perfection as a literary medium" in the hands of the elitist-bent Shirakaba (White Birch) writers in the 1910s–1920s, and she proceeds to sketch the intertwining trajectories of the evolution of vernacular/colloquial-style language and literature in modern Japan:

Although [the colloquial style] was not to displace traditional styles outside of the literary world until 1946, from this time on it held unchallenged supremacy in the novel, successive authors molding it to their individual patterns. The stages of its progress in literature may be simplistically but succinctly summed up by saying that Futabatei introduced it, Bimyo spread it, Koyo polished it, Naturalism established it, and the Shirakaba writers perfected and individualized it. (Twine 1991: 161)

Risking over-generalization, one may observe that there was an interval of nearly 60 years between the first colloquial novel *The Drifting Clouds*, published between 1887 and 1889, and the general adoption of the written vernacular in post-war Japan. As we know, the script–speech relationship was unusually complex in Meiji Japan, when multiple writing and reading systems coexisted, compounded by rigidly codified systems of diglossia. The 1902 language standardization, backed by the powers of the state, with such modern institutions as education and the press at its disposal, must have contributed significantly to leveling the field for writers to explore new textual models on a relatively stable linguistic basis.

One could stress that the *genbun'itchi* principle, built on a false presumption of the potential of transparency of the medium, powerfully steered the quests for textual models from the convention-driven "thickness" of compositional complexity to compositional simplicity and directness. Literary texts, however, privilege openness in interpretation and a linguistic medium "supple enough to support impressionistic prose, expressionistic poetry" (Heylen 2012: 193). These concepts underpin the fact that the creative innovation of literary writing helps to expand the lexicon of the vernacular, refine its linguistic features, and elevate its status—all important for transforming a "vernacular" into a more sophisticated "language." The lengthy cycle of evolution that Japanese vernacular literature enjoyed was apparently a great advantage. Above all, it allowed successive generations of writers to experiment with different types of textual models, in accordance with the internal requirements of the particular institution of modern literature. This included a lengthy struggle with the notion of "realism" (*genbun'itchi*) as well as shifts in the epistemological and cognitive modes that accompanied the transition from the premodern to the modern. Karatani Kojin's (1993) argument that the "birth" of modern Japanese literature followed in concert with the establishment of other types of modern social and political institutions in the third decade of Meiji (i.e., the 1890s) is enlightening, in that it sees a correlation among the processes in which various types of modern institutions are entrenched in indigenous soil.

Republican China

Whereas vernacular language reform in China began in the late nineteenth century, and official efforts toward language standardization were made in the early years of the ROC, it was the May Fourth Movement in the late 1910s and early 1920s that gave reform a solid boost. Ping Chen attributes its sweeping success to the strategic design of Hu Shi's calling for "literature in the national language" (*guoyu de wenxue*) and "a literary national language" (*wenxuede guoyu*):

> By the former, Hu Shi proposed that the literary language should be based on a national language accepted and used by the whole population, and by the latter he suggested that the national language should transcend the daily vernacular in terms of sophistication and richness in grammar, lexicon, and style, and be sufficiently equipped to suit a whole range of purposes in literature. Hu Shi's proposals turned out to be an essential constituent of the guiding principle in language planning on the development and standardization of Modern Chinese in the decades to follow. (P. Chen 2001a: 53)

Hu Shi may be credited for another successful psychological manipulation: the evocation of the European Renaissance as a model for the Chinese vernacular movement. By comparing classical Chinese with Latin, Hu both associates it with China's past glory and simultaneously condemns it as a "dead" language that hinders the country's social progress in the modern age. This uplifting narrative of civilizational regeneration, seen alongside the poignant and deeply self-critical discourse put forth by Lu Xun, nicely conjures up a vision of the cultural fabric of the time and anticipates the subsequent deeper "liberal–humanist versus radical–socialist" divide.

The explosive power generated by the convergence of activities in multiple social spheres explains the relatively brief interval between the first literary attempt in the modern vernacular and the society-wide adoption of it, resulting in the popular perception of these changes as "revolutions." One incident illustrates the power and mechanisms through which forces of the revolution came to shape an individual writer's choices among available textual models: an eloquent essay by Zhou Zuoren in an early issue (February 1918) of *New Youth* (*La Jeunesse, Xin qingnian*) possessed such persuasive power that it caused Liu Bannong to abandon his original plans, and he "switched to translating and writing poetry in the rhymeless vernacular" (Hockx 2003: 183).

As a rule, revolution generates totalizing dynamics: as it tends to facilitate arbitrary choices, it also effectively suppresses previously viable alternatives. As Edward Gunn (1991) points out, multiple writing styles coexisted on the eve of the May Fourth Movement. A letter from Zhu Jingnong to Hu Shi in 1918 gave several alternatives for the soon-to-be-launched grand campaign:

> These days there are four kinds of positions regarding the literary revolution: (first) reform classical Chinese, rather than abolishing classical Chinese; (second) discard classical Chinese, and reform the vernacular; (third) preserve the vernacular, and adopt a phonetic system to replace the character script; (fourth) abolish both classical Chinese and the vernacular, and adopt an alphabetic language as the national language. (G. Zhou 2011: 36)

This was a moment with multiple possibilities. Out of the four scenarios that Zhu presented then, the first and second resonate well with the proposals made by Lian Heng and Guo Qiusheng in the written Taiwanese movement. While the second option is sanctioned in most East Asian societies—except for Korea—it is nonetheless critical to bear in mind that hegemony never means complete monopoly: the suppressed traditions almost always play determinant roles in the language's longer process of evolution. What is more, certain alternatives suppressed by the revolutionary euphoria might enjoy a comeback when the ruling regime finds political utility in them. This was certainly the case in the elevation of the classical tradition in post-1949 Taiwan, which can be clearly traced back to Republican China.

The last 15 years or so have seen a number of revisionist works on Republican China that challenge the established narrative of an overarching May Fourth hegemony. Here are some examples immediately relevant to our discussion: Michel Hockx's emphasis (2003) on the persistent prevalence of traditionalist Chinese literary culture and networking styles in literary associations and journals; Gang Zhou's critique (2011) of the "vernacular only" writing mode; and, in particular, Ping Chen's summary (2001a), from a sociolinguistic viewpoint, of the major sources from which the Chinese vernacular movement received enrichment: (1) non-Mandarin dialects, especially those of the Wu region, where many literary figures of the May Fourth movement originated, (2) classical Chinese, and (3) foreign languages.

The Republican legacy in post-1949 Taiwan

Highlighting the multifarious nature of the evolution of Chinese vernacular in China's Republican period and calling attention to the previously downplayed traditionalist strand helps to better characterize the legacies passed on to Taiwan's post-1949 era. Behind the Nationalist regime's wholesale transplantation of the Republican period's cultural institutions were specific political needs. Simply put, in the early Cold War period, the ROC deployed neo-traditionalism to reinforce its status as an internationally recognized "Chinese" government. The liberally inclined intellectuals who followed Chiang Kai-shek (Jiang Jieshi) to Taiwan were predisposed to denounce the radical anti-traditionalism taken to extremes by the ultra-leftist policies of the Mao era. Combined with other factors, this peculiar circumstance has extended the evolutionary cycle of certain strands of the modern Chinese vernacular movement, giving them a second life of sorts.

As the Nationalists pursued the "road not taken," they also significantly re-wrote the May Fourth tradition, shifting focus from the revolutionary ethos to the more refined cultural reform, as evidenced by the designation of the May 4 as a national holiday of "literature and the arts." In his provocative appeal to "Lower the Flag to Half-Mast for May Fourth" ("*Xia Wusi de banqi*," 1964), Yu Guangzhong took issue with the unimaginative, hollow, and anemic style prevailing in contemporary literary prose—in his view a legacy of the "May Fourth *baihuawen* movement"—and proclaimed that, whereas the May Fourth succeeded as a vernacular *language* movement, it failed as a *literary* revolution by the standards of the European Renaissance. The perception that the modern Chinese literary revolution was somehow "incomplete," a project yet to be brought to fruition, was a common conviction among the modernist generation in post-1949 Taiwan, especially its academic sector, a situation that had far-reaching ramifications. In a sense, refining modern Chinese *as an artistic medium*, fully exploiting its extraordinarily rich, inherent aesthetic resources, has been an animating vision behind the literary careers of such important writers as Wang Wenxing, Li Yongping, Zhu Tianwen, and Wu He.

As dictated by a powerful generational logic, whereas writers educated in the colonial period became victims of the mid-century regime change, the next couple of generations of "Taiwanese" (*Taiwan ren* or *bensheng ren*) writers, having received a complete education under the Nationalists, were coauthors, alongside the "Mainlanders" (*dalu ren* or *waisheng ren*), of a literary renaissance in the 1960s–1970s that was deeply entrenched in a Sinocentric ethos. Significantly, contemporary Taiwanese writers have continued to dedicate themselves to a highly conscious exploration of the potential of the Chinese vernacular, aiming to bring it to maturation as a literary medium through a synthesis of the classical and Western traditions. What they have managed to achieve is particularly meaningful in view of the fact that Chinese writers on the mainland pursued the socialist model of literary creation, with radically different aesthetic assumptions and institutional determinants. As these achievements attest, there are alternative ways to carry on the evolution of the modern Chinese vernacular literary reform inherited from the first half of the twentieth century.

Conclusion: Understanding Modern Literature in Taiwan as a Locally Based Institution

Insofar as a modern literary institution is constituted by both a material dimension (the publishing industry, associations, journals, literary prizes, etc.) and a conceptual one (textual models, aesthetic conventions, etc.), it is by definition locally based, irrespective of literary agents' self-identifications, or the foreignness of its constitutive elements (Bürger 1992; Hohendahl 1989), or even the linguistic medium used in literary creation. Political factors aside, Taiwan's off-shore location, sizable population, cohesive social structure, and dynamic cultural sectors all contribute to the distinctively *local* form of the modern literary institution developed there.

Some distinctive local features of Taiwan's modern literary institution, however, have been routinely misconceived. For instance, the periods from the late 1930s to mid-1940s and from the late 1950s to the 1970s clearly stand out in the literary history of modern Taiwan, as they witnessed the artistic maturation of, respectively, the second generation of Taiwan's colonial writers and the postwar modernists, both symptomatic of the consolidation of a locally based modern literary institution. And yet, scholars accustomed to a China-centric approach often feel ambivalent about the former group, whose works were written in Japanese, whereas at the height of Taiwan's Localist trend, the latter group was often stigmatized as accomplices to the Nationalists' cultural repression. These are clear examples of the drawbacks inherent in understanding literary history primarily through the lenses of sociopolitical histories, understandings that can easily be inflected by preset notions about ethnic–national–cultural identifications, political–territorial disputes, or other ideological issues.

This chapter adopts a different entry point and zeroes in on such structural factors as evolutionary trajectory and the temporal duration of the processes by which the modern institution of literature was initially entrenched in different East Asian localities. At the same time, it uses the patterns of variation thus discerned as yard-sticks to better understand the suppressed, concealed, or latent and undeveloped trends that are underrepresented or misunderstood by literary historians. Viewed from this perspective, the longer evolutionary cycle of the vernacular language and literature movements in modern Japan offered relatively ample space for both movements to develop according to their own internal dynamics. In China, by contrast, the greater convergence of the two movements in the late 1910s and early 1920s pointed to a more explosive, revolutionary model. And yet, the paradigmatic split—socialist revolution versus Republican continuity—that occurred subsequently suggests the coexistence of evolutionary and revolutionary elements in such movements. Similarly, this approach allows us to put into perspective the complex relations between the disruption of locally motivated vernacular movements in Taiwan and the unusual trajectory of its development of a modern literary institution, marked by impressive accomplishments nourished by "borrowed" aesthetic resources.

To the extent that the literary history of modern Taiwan complicates and compounds the notions of linguistic nativity and cultural authenticity, it enables us to gauge more precisely the usefulness of critical paradigms commonly adopted by researchers these days. The notion of Sinophone literature (see Chapter 8 by Ping-hui Liao), for instance, appears to speak powerfully to the Taiwan situation, as it pries open the untenable monolithic assumption of "Chinese" literature. Yet, one cannot deny that, when dealing with the sophisticated artistic output of Taiwan in the 1940s, we are forced to take into consideration the no less complex "Japanophone" phenomenon in the mid-century. Postcolonialist theorists' penetrating insights undoubtedly benefit studies of periods of modern Taiwan under non-native political governance, and yet since the imprints of colonial conditions under Western imperialism in South Asia and the Middle East remain deep in these theories, potentially confounding mismatches are inevitable. Of particular concern are inadequacies coming from the disparate lengths of the colonial rules and the different civilizational relationships between the colonizers and the colonized in the premodern era. Conversely, other critical concepts may also be employed to shed light on some aspects of Taiwanese literary production. For example, while the adoption under duress of a non-indigenous language and literary tradition in Taiwanese society as a whole in the 1940s and the 1960s evidently differs from the individual choices made by such diasporic writers as Joseph Conrad, Vladimir Nabokov, and Ha Jin, affinities may yet be found between these writers and the post-1949 mainlander writers in terms of their relationship with the "homeland." Even Gilles Deleuze's notion of "minor literature" may be applied fruitfully to high-light some features of the status of the literary output of Taiwanese writers in the pre-war and post-war periods vis-à-vis that of Japanese and mainland Chinese writers.

The ultimate goal of this chapter is to explore new taxonomies of East Asian comparative literature. All things considered, the ostensible "anomalies" in modern Taiwan's literary development, shaped as they were by epochal forces and geopolitical realities shared across East Asia, exemplify a salient feature of the region's "compressed modernity"—the frequently interrupted evolutionary cycle of various modern institutions that local intellectuals strove to adopt and develop. Shifting focus from the political circumstances, often traumatic, that caused the disruption to structural factors that mediated their impact on the development of particular institutions, the proposed approach aims to provide new frameworks for the study of cultural processes in modern East Asia from a comparative perspective.[6] I also hope that this chapter has succeeded in demonstrating that, as a locus of intricate patterns of political conflict and complex forms of cultural convergence, and with the benefit of its moderate size, Taiwan offers excellent material for studies that could potentially re-orient our research in more fruitful directions.

NOTES

1   By comparison, literature played a much less prominent, mainly indirect, role in the slightly later, locally initiated written Taiwanese movement. That was even more the case with a third language reform program, the Romanization (*Romaji*) movement, launched almost single-handedly by Cai Peihuo.

2   Original in *Five People News* (August 16–September 1, 1930); reprinted in Nakajima 2003: 7–52.

3   The dictionary was published posthumously in its entirety in 1957 by his son, Lian Zhendong, a high-ranking Nationalist official and the father of Lian Zhan.

4   Gang Zhou (2011) argues that *wenyan* (classical Chinese) and *baihua* coexisted for centuries in Chinese society, performing different social and class functions, and that the users were good at switching from one system to the other.

5   What further aggravated the situation was the fact that Chinese characters were also part of the Japanese language (*kanji*), in which they are for the most part pronounced differently. In public school education in colonial Taiwan, the Chinese language was often taught using Japanese pronunciations. Traces of this practice are still discernible in language use in contemporary Taiwan.

6   An example par excellence is the study of the pervasive cultural impact of mid-twentieth-century political upheavals and the Cold War world order in East Asia, emphasizing the structural factors, currently a popular topic of interest.

REFERENCES

Bürger, Peter. 1992. *The Institutions of Art*. Lincoln: University of Nebraska Press.

Chang, Sung-sheng Yvonne, Michelle Yeh, and Ming-ju Fan. Eds. 2014. *Columbia Sourcebook of Literary Taiwan*. New York: Columbia University Press.

Chen, Ping. 2001a. "Development and Standardization of Lexicon in Modern Written Chinese." In *Language Planning and Language Policy: East Asian Perspectives*. Edited by Gottlieb, Nanette, and Ping Chen. Richmond: Curzon. 49–73.

Chen, Ping. 2001b. "Policy on the Selection and Implementation of a Standard Language as a Source of Conflict in Taiwan." In *Language Planning and Language Policy: East Asian Perspectives*. Edited by Gottlieb, Nanette, and Ping Chen. Richmond: Curzon. 95–110.

Ferguson, Charles A. 1959. "Diglossia." *Word*, 15: 325–340.

Fujii Shozo. 1998. *Taiwan bungaku konohyakunen* (One hundred years of Taiwanese literature). Tokyo: Tohoshoten.

Heylen, Ann. 2012. *Japanese Models, Chinese Culture and the Dilemma of Taiwanese Language Reform*. Wiesbaden, Germany: Harrassowitz Verlag.

Hockx, Michel. 2003. *Questions of Style: Literary Societies and Literary Journals in Modern China, 1911–1937*. Leiden: Brill.

Hohendahl, Peter Uwe. 1989. *Building a National Literature: The Case of Germany, 1830–1870*. Trans. Renate Baron Franciscono. Ithaca: Cornell University Press.

Huang, Yingzhe 黃英哲. Ed. 2006. *Rizhishiqi Taiwan wenyi pinglunji* 日治時期臺灣文藝評論集 (Literary criticism in Taiwan under Japanese rule). Tainan: National Museum of Taiwan Literature.

Karatani, Kojin. 1993. *Origins of Modern Japanese Literature*. Durham, NC: Duke University Press.

Kleeman, Faye Yuan. 2003. *Under an Imperial Sun: Japanese Colonial Literature of Taiwan and the South*. Honolulu: University of Hawai'i Press.

Nakajima, Toshio 中島利郎. 2003. *1930 niandai Taiwan xiangtu wenxue lunzhan ziliao huibian* 1930 年代臺灣鄉土文學論戰資料彙編 (Sourcebook of the 1930s debate over nativist literature in Taiwan). Gaoxiong: Chunhui.

Scruggs, Bert. 2015. *Translingual Narration: Colonial and Postcolonial Taiwanese Fiction and Film*. Honolulu: University of Hawaii Press.

Twine, Nanette.1991. *Language and the Modern State: The Reform of Written Japanese*. London: Routledge.

Yu, Guangzhong. 1964. "Lower the Flag to Half-Mast for May Fourth!" *Literary Star*, 79 (April 15); reprinted in *Carefree Wandering* (Taipei: Jiuge, 2000). 13–17.

Zhou, Wanyao 周婉窈. 2002. "Rizhi moqi 'guoge shaonian' de tongzhi shenhua ji qi shidai beijing" 日治末期 "國歌少年" 的統治神話及其時代背景 (The political myth of the "national-anthem boy" during the last period of the Japanese rule and its historical context). *Haixingxi de niandai: Riben zhimin tongzhi moqi Taiwan shilunji* 海行兮的年代: 日本殖民統治末期臺灣史論集 (The era of the song "Sailing to the Ocean": essays on Taiwanese history of the last period of the Japanese colonial rule). Taipei: Yunchen. 1–12.

Zhou, Gang. 2011. *Placing the Modern Chinese Vernacular in Transnational Literature*. New York: Palgrave Macmillan.

8

Sinophone Literature

Ping-hui Liao

Sinophone literature calls attention to alternative genealogies and histories of literary production in Chinese communities all over the world. Its expanding corpus includes works by writers with diverse backgrounds, ranging from the global Chinese diaspora to ethnic minorities within China, so as to highlight heterogeneity and multilingualism in response to the "Middle Kingdom" hegemony, particularly now with the rise of China as a global superpower. A main concern in Sinophone studies is the ways in which these writers draw on multicultural heritage to develop new visions of being Chinese along the direction of linguistic innovation and geopolitical imagination. Often, questions are raised over theoretically problematic but politically volatile conceptual frameworks—such as center versus periphery, origin versus derivatives, standard language versus local dialects, national versus ethnic self-identification, and less versus more than Chinese—on top of other ideas such as imaginary homeland, flexible citizenships, and many other critical issues.

Rey Chow, for instance, suggests that Hong Kong writers such as Leung Ping-kwan (Liang Bingjun, pen name Ye Si) find it necessary to define their literary works in relation to a sense of inadequacy or lack, in constructing images of the former British colony as both minus (marginal, inauthentic, or impure) and plus (multilingual, hybrid, and cosmopolitan). To many Chinese, Hong Kong is neither Chinese nor British. It is a colonial (and hence degenerate, inferior) port city severed from its fatherland, with residents speaking Cantonese dialect and seemingly solely preoccupied with "the material economic culture" (R. Chow 2013: 214). To give voice to Hong Kong culture and highlight its relatively unique positionality in between China and Britain, Chow (2013: 214) observes, Leung "makes the 'origin' of Hong Kong— origins that are economic and colonial—part of the process of his writing." According to Chow (2013: 214), Leung himself "has described his poetry as 'homeless'." However,

A Companion to Modern Chinese Literature, First Edition. Edited by Yingjin Zhang.
© 2016 John Wiley & Sons, Ltd. Published 2016 by John Wiley & Sons, Ltd.

Leung's poems not only articulate a space "between English and Chinese, between standard Chinese and Cantonese," constituting an interesting case of "minor literature written in a major language," but depict the material world in light of the political economy of movement and of transition, thus producing a "poetry of wandering, traveling, observing, and talking with people from different places and cultures" (Chow 2013: 215). In subtle ways, Leung tries to interweave things Chinese and foreign, to invent words as a means of bricolage—"a bricolage of sensations as well as of practices—in which things are put together in small, detailed, varied angles that produce new relations" (Chow 2013: 217).

All this is most evident in one of Leung's poems (quoted in Chow 2013: 223):

> I know that you don't believe in flags or fireworks.
> I will give you fragmented words rather than "realistic" portrayals,
> (showing that you are) not a center surrounded by magnificent buildings
> But simply a (circular) pond
> Of ripples, where moving signs come and go.

In this poem, flags and fireworks operate as national symbols. Apparently, the protagonist ("You") does not want to entertain such sentiments of cultural belonging. Instead, he is only offered fragmented words, so as to deconstruct the centralist ideology, through conjuring up an uncanny image of unfathomable water with ripple effect (or affect) that would emerge and disappear. It is to reveal the unstable parameter of Chinese or British identity.

Sinophone Hong Kong writers such as Xi Xi, Liu Yichang, Wong Bik-wan (Huang Biyun), Dung Kai-cheung (Dong Qizhang), and several others join Leung in viewing Hong Kong identity as arbitrary, contrived, and ephemeral—as "moving signs that come and go." Xi Xi, for example, depicts Hong Kong as a mysterious city floating in the air, while Liu Yichang's fictional characters are often *flâneurs* or wanderers in transit to some strange, duplicitous worlds. For these Sinophone Hong Kong writers, the solid ground underneath one's feet frequently gives way or transforms itself into something no longer easily recognizable.

In many respects, Singapore and Malaysia resemble Hong Kong, as they are both former British colonies whose residents are prominently of Chinese descend—more than 90% in Singapore, whereas in Malaysia up to 25%. In Malaysia, components made up of language, culture, and religion are far more complex, with Malay primordialism, Muslim fundamentalism, racial discrimination, and so on at work to undermine Chinese political representation and cultural reproduction. Philip Kuhn (2008) has traced the formation of Chinese communities in Southeast Asia, especially in terms of the migrants' corridors, niches, and struggles in times of social discrimination and ethnic cleansing. He has also teased out the warring forces of language difference and variant ecologies across communities. It is small wonder that quite a few Malaysian Chinese and Sinophone writers re-emigrated to other countries such as the United States and Taiwan. Remarkably, these writers develop layered, nuanced textual strategies in response to the perils and rewards of multilingual and postcolonial encounters back home.

Li Yongping is in this regard very different from Zhang Guixing, his younger colleague who also decided to leave Malaysia and find a new home in Taiwan. As a proto-modernist, Li confesses that his desire is to "purify" his mother tongue: "I cannot bear the kind of Chinese that has been aggressively Westernized"; and he goes on (Tsu 2010: 708): "I later wrote *Retribution: The Jiling Chronicles*. For eight years, on and off, I painstakingly worked on it so as to build a pure, Chinese literary form." Li's Sinophone project is to reinvent his literary identity "through the purification of the Chinese language … to purify the language brought from one's native land, to de-nativize, and to get rid of the impure sediments from one's native home" (Tsu 2010: 708). As a result, his narrative is in a reconstructed, idealized vernacular style reminiscent of the traditional novel *Water Margin* (*Shuihu zhuan*) and does not in any way correspond to the colloquialism of any Malaysian or Taiwanese locality. On the other hand, Zhang Guixing celebrates linguistic creolization and frequently evokes the rainforests of his native Borneo as a crucial (albeit entangled) site in which aboriginal, Chinese, Malay, and other local dialects intersect. Zhang draws on tropical flora and fauna to call for a neo-primitivism, so that all sorts of violence done by native inhabitants, European and Japanese colonial officers, and Chinese settler migrants can be brought together to illuminate each other, to criticize them from within, and to reconsider the uncontrollable mix of racial heritages and languages in light of their residue, survival, and decay. Zhang's novels such as *My South Seas Sleeping Beauty* (*Wo sinian de changmian zhongde nanguo gongzhu*, 2001), *Herd of Elephants* (*Qunxiang*, 1998), and *Monkey Cups* (*Houbei*, 2000) stage crucial scenes of ethical reawakening in the jungle or tropical garden.

Many Sinophone Malaysian writers fall between the extremes of Li and Zhang. Ng Kim Chew (Huang Jinshu) treats Sinoscript as if it were dead—or at least antiquarian—national souls or specters; he remains the most vehement critic of Chinese nationalism even though he attempts to make the Chinese language more descriptive and precise. Wang Runhua and several Sinophone Malaysian writers of the older generation provide nostalgic narrative accounts of their home country, while Pan Yu-tong, Chan Tah-Wei (Chen Dawei), Choong Yee Voon (Zhong Yiwen), Li Zishu, and Wen Ruian write about diaspora experience, travel, and transnationality, blending modernist and magic realist traditions. Kim Tong Tee, a Malaysian writer–critic currently teaching at Taiwan's National Sun Yat-sen University, has offered an overview of Sinophone Malaysian literature since 1919 and discussed the legacy of "Nayang local color literature" and of more globalized modernist or postmodernist fictions as inspired by contemporary Latin American and Chinese writers such as Jorge Luis Borges, Márquez, Su Tong, Wang Anyi, and Zhang Dachun (Chang Ta-chun). Tee mentions quite a few artists as Sinophone writers who stay in Malaysia and actively engage in local cultural politics, among them Wan Kok Seng (Wen Xiangying), Tan Kee Keat (Xiao Hei), and Ng Neoh Leng (Song Ziheng).

However, many Sinophone Malaysian writers publish their works and live in Taiwan after they finish college degrees there as "overseas Chinese" (*huaqiao*) students. As a hub of Sinophone literature in its publication and dissemination, Taiwan in fact holds a special place in not only attracting a rich diversity of Sinophone writers, such as Bai Xianyong, Gao Xingjian, Xi Xi, Eileen Chang, and many others, to publish their works there or even to stay on as artists in residence, but also in producing prominent Sinophone scholar–critics such as David Wang, Jing Tsu, Chien-hsin Tsai (Cai Jianxin), and Shu-mei Shih, who were either born or, in Shih's case, received college education on the island.

According to Shu-mei Shih, a majority of Taiwanese writers may be qualified as Sinophone, especially those who write to complicate our thinking about the relationship between "roots" (Chineseness) and "routes" (Taiwaneseness). In her seminal book (Shih 2007) and her follow-up work (Shih, Tsai, and Bernards 2013), Shih outlines the Sinophone as literary expressions in response to "China proper" and its continuing continental and settler colonialism. In her vision of Sinophone articulations, Taiwan, Hong Kong, Tibet, Mongolia, Xinjiang, and other ethnic minority territories represent different voices against Han Chinese nationalism (see Chapter 16 by Mark Bender). She advocates that "Sinophone studies has as one of its objects the culture, history, and society of minority peoples who have acquired or are forced to acquire the standard Sinitic language of Mandarin, often at the expense of their native language" (Shih, Tsai, and Bernards 2013: 3). This would apply to Taiwanese writers under both the Japanese rule (1895–1945) and, immediately after that, the Nationalist regime (since 1945), although it would not apply to Sinophone Malaysian writers who voluntarily pick up the Chinese language and culture as ethnic heritage to combat Malay nationalism. However, in her discussion of Taiwan literature and film, Shih often turns to works by diasporic, feminist, or aboriginal artists. And, in terms of the principle of selection and significance, Jing Tsu and David Wang (2010) seem to be more oriented toward the Chinese diaspora and the so-called "post-loyalists"—political refugees who try to keep the memory of an imaginary homeland or imagined community alive while in diaspora. Bai Xianyong and Luo Yijun are among David Wang's favorite subjects for literary analysis, whereas Jing Tsu would often draw on works by Zhang Guixing, Lin Yutang, Zhang Wojun, or Chen Jitong to make her point. On the other hand, Chien-hsin Tsai, David Wang's former student at Harvard and one of the co-editors with Shih, tends to focus on Hakka literature, particularly fictions by Chung Lihe (Zhong Lihe) and Lung Yingzhong.

If we follow David Wang, Sinophone Taiwanese writings can be said to have begun with Shen Guangwen (1612–1688), who fled to the island in the mid-seventeenth century with Koxinga (Guoxingye, or Zheng Chenggong, 1624–1662), a "post-loyalist" sea captain who defeated the Dutch and attempted to use Taiwan as a bastion to restore the Ming dynasty in defiance against the Qing reign. Shen mourned the homeland long lost and wrote about his diaspora experience on the small island, revealing his local knowledge of the aboriginal, tropical flora, climate, geography, and so on. Shen dedicated himself to educating students and initiated a poet society in Taiwan. Shen was among the first Chinese émigrés who decided to take root in the island and to write in classical Chinese about his traumatic memories that developed between the two worlds—Ming China that was then under the Manchu rule, and the new home in Taiwan that was, in many ways, "uncivilized" as well as strange and uncanny (un-homely). A few decades before the publication of Shen's poems, Taiwan was co-colonized by the Dutch (in the southern part of the island), the Spanish (in the north), and Chinese migrant workers mostly from Fujian province of China. Several types of writing systems and local dialects—aboriginal and Fukianese—in fact prevailed. The Dutch missionaries, for example, had transliterated tribal oral narratives and stories of the Bible, trying to negotiate between European and Austronesian languages. Koxinga himself was born in Nagasaki as a child of interracial marriage—his father was Fukianese and his mother Japanese. The multilingual and multiracial situations rendered Shen's writing and its reception peculiarly complex and revealing as he employed classical Chinese to articulate and interrelate his literary expressions of the old and new worlds—the former on the verge disappearance and the latter entangled in battles between European and Chinese empires, between the aborigines and the Han settlers, between official language (Mandarin) and local dialects (or mother tongue).

Shen Guangwen's choice of classical Chinese is significant as the written scripts are shared among Chinese-speaking communities in spite of the difference in their dialects and speech deliveries. However, Shen also provides new content to Mandarin Chinese in terms of its capacity to expand expressivity. He lives in Taiwan and writes about native people as if they were partially mythological figures recorded in ancient texts—having differential features not to be seen in China proper. Shen's "nativist" approach and his semantic innovation thus help constitute an alternative genealogy of Sinophone literature and differentiate Taiwanese literature from mainstream Chinese literary texts. And these two aspects in relation to Sinitic scripts are further complicated as Taiwan encounters Japanese colonialism, the Nationalist government's re-Sinification project, and, later on, global (especially American) popular culture. During the Japanese period, Taiwanese were forced to use Japanese as the official language. Writers such as Wu Chuo-liu (Wu Zhuoliu) published their works in Japanese and often had to struggle to find a voice in relation to censorship and racial discrimination. Wu in fact elaborates on the trope of "Asia's Orphan" to depict Taiwanese as neither Japanese nor Chinese (see Chapter 7 by Sung-sheng Chang).

However, the Japanese colonial government also reinforced its policy of sharing the "same written scripts" and "same racial heritage" to facilitate the assimilation processes. Colonial administrators such as Gotō Shinpei or educators such as Ishikawa Kin'ichirō, who were trained in the early Meiji period, would show off their Chinese poetry and calligraphy to impress and convert the local elites. As a consequence, Sinophone Taiwanese writers both in classical and vernacular traditions would frequently need to develop a double awareness of the Chinese scripts both enabling and disabling—on the one hand, as a shared means of intercultural communication, providing a common platform for conveying their ideas to the general reading public (including even the colonizers), but on the other hand as an inferior language that is being marginalized or looked upon as premodern, if not antiquarian.

Experienced by a famous Japanese writer who traveled to the colony, the following encounter reveals multiple levels of irony and mixed responses, expressing a sense of wonder beneath cultural superiority. Satō Haruo, a distinguished writer in post-Meiji Japan, made a 3-month visit to Taiwan in 1920. He compared the customs and discursive practices between the Japanese and the Taiwanese, in addition to being fascinated by the aborigine's tall tales. Satō showed keen interest in meeting a poet in Taiwan, who, he had heard, was capable of doing all sorts of experiments with classical Chinese. After expressing this requirement to his Taiwanese guide several times, he eventually manages to acquire four volumes of the poetry in question. While this might in part have been triggered by curiosity or the desire to show off his knowledge of classical Chinese, Satō's eagerness to appreciate local expressive culture appears to have been sincere and persistent. He even went on to transcribe a poem that seemed both archaic and relevant, though he found most of the poems very difficult to read, some of them dealing with the aborigine's deer hunt, the new middle class's collection of phonographs, earthquakes in Jiayi, and even the lament over the national treasure stolen during the Opium Wars. Satō (2002: 293) writes, "I was immediately taken by the extraordinarily novel and place-based lyric subjects" and "I cannot help becoming more intrigued by a rich diversity of unusually lively expressions."

Satō (2002: 294) quotes the section of a regulated verse on the unsuccessful attempt to quit smoking opium, as follows:

> Half of my life devoted to alchemy,
> Only to realize my body rotten and decaying,
> I flee and escape into practicing Zen Buddhism.
> As ancient hermits drown their sorrows in wines,
> So I indulge in eating opium,
> To sermon what is left and to blow out the smoke,
> The pipe contains and relieves my youth and ambition,
> As if I were lord of the rosy castle,
> Or master poet of the famous hall,
> With no exit or any outlet in view,
> Puffing airs that fill the cosmos,
> Lying on a small bed, surrounded by hundreds of books,
> With a pillow as my sole companion in a tiny urn.
> (translated by Ping-hui Liao)

Satō associates the poem with Charles Baudelaire's *Fleurs du mal*, suggesting that the Taiwanese poet Hung Qisheng deploys the Chinese language in such an innovative fashion that it sounded very French and modern. Satō (2002: 295) considers this episode a climactic moment charged with "inexhaustible poetic thrills—even though accompanied by excruciating pains of extreme indigestion." The way Satō praises the poet in terms of literary modernism and nativism, highlighting the aesthetic value of strangeness and obscurity while savoring the humor and cynical reason embedded in the poem, puts him totally apart from many of his Japanese colleagues who tend to be condescending and even in denial vis-à-vis Taiwan. Because of such a "Sinophone" reading encounter, Satō developed sympathetic affinity with local cultural dynamics to such an extent that he found Taiwan's tropical heat and humidity actually refreshing. He even concluded his travels to the colony by predicting that Taiwanese would endure and might eventually outdo Japanese with their diligence and capacity to survive the harsh weather.

It is in the innovative synthesis of literary modernism and nativism that Taiwan's Sinophone writers of the 1960s and 1980s—such as Huang Chun-ming, Wang Chen-ho (Wang Zhenhe), Chen Yingzhen, Wang Wenxing, and Li Ang, among others—would carry on the tradition set by Hung Qisheng. Set against the background of the US-led Cold War, these "nativist" (*xiangtu*) writers touch upon Taiwan's ambivalent roles in the era of industrialization, trans-Pacific segregation (South Korea versus North Korea; Free China versus Communist China), and global market economy by incorporating local dialects and pidgin English into their Sinophone expressions, so as to assert Taiwan's identity as distinct from China. They explore everyday life in Taiwan, with specific references to local social settings and landscapes. Mainly using traditional Chinese written characters, but occasionally drawing on Indo-European languages, these "native" sons and daughters try to capture their mother tongues' idiomatic expressions and syntactic structures.

Apart from the nativist group, overseas Sinophone writers such as Bai Xianyong, Chen Ruoxi, Zhang Xiguo, Hua-ling Nieh (Nie Hualing), and many others who studied and lived in the United States, together with Malaysian Chinese artists from elsewhere, have published their works in Taiwan since the 1960s, making Taiwan a hub of Sinophone literary and cultural articulations, especially with its emphasis on traditional Chinese written characters and on refined ways of life. From the 1980s on, social movements triggered by the new demands of democratic representation, gender equality, human rights, gay discourse, fair distribution, class mobility, multicultur-alism, local community reconstruction, and so forth have helped push Taiwan farther away from China. Writers in these categories tend to appropriate postmodernism and magical realism from such diverse sources as Japanese, French, German, Eastern European, and Latin American literature, and they consider themselves to be no longer just Chinese. Even in terms of syntactic structure, their sentences drag on in the manner fashioned by James Joyce or Borges. Wang Wenxing, Wu He, and Qiu Miaojin are most notable examples. Their use of the Chinese language also differs from Chinese writers who tend to draw on colloquialism and everyday speech. When she visited Malaysia, the Shanghai-based writer Wang Anyi commented on the style of Sinophone writers as "archaic," almost similar to the characters found in classical Chinese novels.

The "archaic" nature of Sinophone literary expressions may have to do with the time lag between the motherland and the new home, between the imaginary (or idealized, as in the case of Li Yongping) community and the foreign land. Nowhere is such archaic articulation more prevalent than in Angel Island poetry. In the field of US literary history, overseas Chinese literature has long been doubly minoritized, first by the main-stream American society, then by Asian American literary critics who tend to focus solely on writings in English. The fate changes with the introduction of Sinophone discourse that expands the horizon of reception and interpretation of global literature in Chinese. Literary scholars such as Shan Te-hsin take us back not only to overseas Chinese student literature but also to poems, letters, and graphics inscribed on the prison walls of Angel Island that gave vent to many Chinese immigrants' hopes and fears as they anxiously waited at the gateway to their dreamland—*Meiguo* (literally, the "beautiful country")—for weeks and even years. The Angel Island poems were originally written by immigrants from China detained in the Immigration Station just outside of San Francisco during the period from 1910 to 1940, when the majority of 175,000 immigrants used this site as their port of entry into the United States. First written down and then carved on the wooden walls by the immigrants, these poems almost vanished when the immigration station was destroyed in a fire in 1940. In 1970, park ranger Alexander Weiss accidentally discovered the archives, but it was not until 1976, through the concerted effort of the Asian American community, that the building was reconstructed and preserved as a living monument in the history of Asian American immigrants. "As a result, these poems have become the textual evidence of one of the saddest chapters in the history of American immigration" (T. Shan 2013: 385).

The poems, totaling 135, are mostly written in the style of regulated verse, with more than half of them (73) in seven-character quatrain. The writers are hardly famous poets, but they make revealing allusions not only to classical Chinese narratives of hostages or captives who would later on become heroes (e.g., King Wen of Zhou dynasty and Su Wu of Han dynasty), but also to modern Western political figures such as Napoleon Bonaparte, whose name in Chinese transliteration suggests "breaking the island" or "conquering the hill"—a reference to the Gold Mountain that is San Francisco (and by implication, California, or the United States). They hope to build new careers in the United States and seek recognition or even revenge, so as to surprise or surpass their American hosts. While a number of them committed suicide, the majority were admitted into the United States. According to the website put up later (and still well maintained), these Chinese immigrants and their descendants have done quite well. Shan and the poetry anthology editors highlight gloomy scenes of frustration and despair, but on the website there are interviews and memoires that show the brighter sides of the detainees' diaspora experience on Angel Island. One detainee, for example, said that he found almonds on the Island to be the juiciest, and that he made good friends there, even learning a lot of American things from the guards. But overall, these Angel Island poems lament over the weakness of China as a political entity, while expressing confidence and even pride in being Chinese as distinct from Western "barbarians," whose history is short and whose culture shallow.

In fact, this sort of double rhetoric, seeking shelter in America but retaining Chinese cultural identity, is also noticeable in Bai Xianyong's "Winter Night" (*Dongye*, 1970), in which a Chinese American history professor confesses to a dual, ambivalent role of being a "plain deserter." To those who stayed to educate Chinese people, "how could I have mustered enough self-respect to stand up and speak for the May Fourth Movement?" he asks. "That's why, too, in all my expatriate days, I've never talked about the history of the Republican period," he continues. "That time at the University of California I saw how excited the students were in the middle of their movement, so I mentioned the May Fourth only to humor them—it was no more than a joke." But Professor Wu is still proud of being Chinese, especially in relation to ancient China: "The glories of the past are easy to talk about. I don't feel ashamed when I tell my students, 'The Tang dynasty created what must have been the most powerful, and culturally the most brilliant, empire in the world at that period in history'" (X. Bai 2007: 217).

As if to rid the guilt of being a "plain deserter," Chen Ruoxi and her husband decided, similar to quite a few other overseas Chinese and Chinese Americans, to go back to China during the Cultural Revolution. Chen's "homecoming" journey ended in tumult. Her despairs and frustrations found expressions in a series of Sinophone magical realist tales that zoom in on scenes of betrayal and brutality, state violence and collective evil. She describes the malicious ways in which neighbors, friends, and family members in rural China suddenly turn against each other, just to protect their own self-interest. On the other hand, Chen also writes about the miseries of the Chinese diaspora in America. The position of always remaining a stranger, never at home, renders her characters nostalgic but eventually critical of the nation-state. As James Clifford (1997: 251) argues, "diaspora discourse articulates, or bends together, both roots *and* routes to construct … alternate public spheres, forms of community con-sciousness and solidarity that maintain identification outside the national time/space in order to live inside, with a difference." Chen's Sinophone writings reveal ways to stay and be different, to be Chinese but also American, to be constantly tormented by a sense of living on the borderline as neither an insider nor an outsider.

Eileen Chang is another intriguing case of Sinophone articulation on the borderline where the Sinophone and Anglophone literary traditions intersect. It is well known that Eileen Chang won recognition from US-based scholars such as C. T. Hsia, Leo Lee, and Joseph Lau (Liu Shaoming), who have praised her since the 1960s as the most tal-ented woman writer in modern China. However, Chang's fame in the Sinophone world might have owed more to the wide circulation of her work as promoted by Taiwan's Huangguan (Crown), a major publishing company that made available romance novels and popular fictions by leading women writers in the 1970s–1980s. Chang came to California from Hong Kong in 1955 as arranged by the US Information Service Agency, so that she could write about the corruptions in Communist China to endorse America's interventions across the Pacific in terms of freedom and human rights during the Cold War period. However, Chang's English novels were not well received in the United States. Many scholars have tried to explain Chang's years in the United States in terms of American Orientalism or her self-translation project. Her English-language ethno-graphic articulation of Chinese peasant consciousness in *Rice-Sprout Song* (*Yangge*, 1955), for example, is looked upon as traces not only suggestive of a new global order established by the US defeat of precedent colonial powers, but also reminiscent of colo-nial cartography and Orientalist desires. As David Wang (1998: vii) points out, Chang wrote three novels in English: *Rice-Sprout Song* and *Naked Earth* (*Chidi zhilian*, 1957) were written during her sojourn in Hong Kong from 1952 to 1955, as "part of an anti-Communist literary campaign sponsored by the United States Information Service," while *The Rouge of the North* (*Yuannü*, 1967) was a result of Chang's long period of work toward launching her career as a writer of English fiction after coming to United States in 1955. To David Wang, the two supposedly "anti-Communist" novels by Eileen Chang "flaunt politics in ways Chang would not have chosen," and even *Rouge of the North* is "a novel not of national politics but about politics as a daily practice of life," not only probing the reactionary meaning of "Chinese obsessiveness" (1998: vii) but also "a last imaginary refuge after [Chang] had taken political asylum in the US" (1998: xxviii), in a new country where Chang found that "fictional experience had infiltrated lived experience, and that she herself might finally have become the embittered woman" (1998: xxix). Wang considers Chang's English fiction as part of her translation (and transgression) project, so that the novelist can reinvent early stories and characters, renegotiate the "fates of Chinese women," rethink the significance of remembrance and repetition (1998: xxvii–xxviii). "Shifting back and forth on linguistic, cultural, gender, and temporal territories," Wang (1998: xxviii) suggests, Chang is able to find that "between memory and reality an awkward disharmony frequently arises, and because of this a disruption—at once heavy and light—and a struggle—serious, yet still nameless—are produced."

In fact, during her stay in the United States, Eileen Chang was attracted to the new environments, especially Hollywood's screwball comedy. She developed a "late style" to start her diaspora project to re-link with Hong Kong and Shanghai by rewriting or re-translating some of her early novels. How do we come to terms with all these conflicting interpretations, particularly now with more and more posthumous materials by Chang coming to light and calling for renewed critical inquiries regarding her late years in the United States? The correspondences between Chang and Stephen Soong (Song Qi), memoirs from William Tay (Zheng Shusen), commentaries by Chen Zishan, on top of Yingjin Zhang's illuminating work (2011) on Chang's use of Hollywood screwball comedies, not to mention some of Chang's late novels and journals, help shed a different light on Chang's post-Cold War years in the United States. In this regard, Chang's late work is not just about "reminiscence" or about Shanghai or even China, as David Wang and Leo Lee correctly noted; rather, it is also her multilingual and polyphonic project aiming to piece together the broken glass in a new home where a Sinophone writer attempts to reach out to the Anglophone world in spite of a profound sense of being deserted and estranged. Therefore, she tries her hand on new genres and media, writing film scripts, appropriating Hollywood comedy and musical, and readjusting her textual strategies in response to the demands of Hong Kong's film industry. To paraphrase Theodore Adorno (2009: 18), who was speaking of Beethoven then, we may well say that Chang's late works are processes in which extremes and catastrophes are forced together, to produce moments of friction and dissonance.

Along this line of interpretation, we should not even consider the works of Ha Jin and Gao Xinjian to be exclusively about trauma and memory, as simply remembrances of things back in China. Ha Jin (who takes his pen name "Ha" from his favorite multilingual city "Harbin") migrated to the United States and decided to write in English in a mode of self-exile and self-emancipation. Whereas, in Ha Jin's work, the Sinophone meets the Anglophone, in Gao Xingjian's work the Sinophone is brought into contact with the Francophone. Evoking literary giants and predecessors such as Joseph Brodsky, Vladimir Nabokov, and Joseph Conrad, Ha Jin (2013: 120) indicates that, in the choice of English as medium, he differs from Lin Yutang, who "served as a 'cultural ambassador' and who spoke to the West about China and to the Chinese about the West." Rather than depending on China for literary existence, Ha Jin opts for a model set by Conrad and Nabokov, "who didn't represent their native countries and instead found their places in English." Even though the bulk of his fiction is often set in China, Ha Jin has been accused by Chinese authorities of "betraying" his native country and "uglifying" the Chinese to please the West (Ha Jin 2013: 122). Indeed, Ha Jin (2013: 123) finds nationalist and patriotic sentiments to be problematic, if not self-serving: "What if your country has become a fascist state? What if your country invades another country or commits genocide? What if your country bullies its own people and robs them of their voices? What if your country makes your life miserable and insufferable?" As a migrant and a writer, Ha Jin thus employs English as a mode of communication and expression to "speak truth to power."

In the same way, the Nobel laureate Gao Xinjian has also turned to French writers such as Marguerite Duras for inspiration. He calls his own writing "cold literature," as detached in every way possible from political, moral, and social concerns. According to Gao (2005: 6), "Chinese literature, exhausted by almost a century of having to be politically and ethically correct, has now fallen into a morass of isms, ideologies and debates on creative methodology that have little to do with literature but from which it cannot extricate itself." "It is only by being an unwavering solitary individual without attachments to some political group or movement that the writer is able to win a thoroughgoing freedom," Gao (2005: 6) concludes. Ha Jin and many other Sinophone writers would certainly agree.

It is not only Chinese diasporic writers such as Gao Xingjian who contribute to Sinophone literature, but also people such as minority writers living inside China (e.g., Lao She, Alai, and Syman Rapongan); Chinese immigrants residing in New Zealand (e.g., Gu Cheng and Yang Lian) or in Europe (Bei Dao as he was once in Sweden, Chen Jitong in France, Hong Ying in the United Kingdom, among others); and Chinese American and Latin American writers who have ties to Chinese ancestry. Lao She is an intriguing case of a mainstream Manchu intellectual turned a minority writer during the Republican era after the Qing Empire was overturned in 1911. His 1966 "suicide" still remains a puzzle in modern Chinese literary history. However, it is clear that his Manchu identity (understood to be a bad element attributing to the ancient "feudal" system) got him into trouble. The Red Guards and the masses tried every way to punish and torture him when the Cultural Revolution was launched in May 1966. Lao She had been attempting to conceal his Manchu origin but was apparently tormented by a sense of split identity during the time of turmoil. As if to negotiate the identity crisis, a number of his stories are about the problematic transitions from the old to the new world order. In "An Old and Established Name" ("*Laozi hao*,"

1936), for example, the gentlemanly, honest, and civilized manager Qian is forced to quit when a new, vulgar (but popular) businessman takes over the Fortune Silk Store. The new manager Zhou cheats on his customers, but he gives them the impression that they are receiving bargains. Rather than stick to the "established name," Zhou puts everything on sale and transforms the shop into "something akin to a carnival sideshow" (Lao She 2007: 75). To the dismay of the narrator, a senior apprentice who actually prefers and endorses the traditional ways, Zhou succeeds in winning customers over and eventually defeating the old shop. In telling stories such as this in Chinese—a new and "common" language—Lao She might have been tormented by a profound feeling of malcontent and even betrayal. After all, to write in the victor's language in suppression of his ethnic heritage is very much like murdering the "old and established" heritage.

Similar to Lao She who find articulating a voice in the other's language and to the new world very unsettling, minority writers such as Alai and Syman Rapongan struggle with more pains and internal conflict to come to terms with such labels as "traitor" or the in-between "comprador," especially now with many Tibetan and aboriginal artists promoting writing in native tongues as a way of seeking cultural autonomy and political sovereignty. Alai is a Tibetan Muslim who mixes with Han Chinese writers but tries to find a unique voice on the margins of Tibetanness and Chineseness, whereas Syman, a Yami (Yamei) writer living in Orchid Island, at the edge of Taiwan, writes about fish, canoes, lives of the aborigines, and their disappearing worlds. Alai and Syman are by no means the only representative cases in Sinophone minority writings. According to Lopez-Calvo (2013), we cannot ignore the contribution of Sinophone writers from Latin America and the Caribbean who use Spanish to redefine their Chineseness in terms of diaspora and family genealogies. In fact, several of these Sinophone Cuban and Caribbean writers have moved on to places such as Florida and have become Chinese American writers, to such an extent that they fit uncomfortably into our map of Sinophone literature.

With such a vast spectrum and diverse repertoire, Sinophone literature shares little in common except its varying attempts to de-nationalize, to debunk "China proper," and to think beyond "Chineseness." The term "Sinophone" is not without problems though. Long established traditions such as "Anglophone" or "Francophone" refer to the literature of the Commonwealth or former French colonies, respectively, but in the case of Malaysia or Hong Kong, British (rather than Chinese) colonialism was the main dominating force, and in the case of Taiwan, it was the Japanese colonial rule. Chinese written scripts had, for centuries, been used throughout Japan, Korea, and Vietnam up until these countries developed their own national language and scripts to resist Chinese hegemony. As a way to reinforce cultural identity, the South Korean government, for example, refuses to acknowledge premodern Sinophone writings by Korean intellectuals as part of its national literature. "Sinophone" literature and "Sinitic" language therefore have varying cultural connotations and political consequences throughout Asia. This may be why Jing Tsu and David Wang (2010) opt for "global" or "world" literature in Chinese, even though Tsu (2010a) herself would tie the "Sinophone" with the Chinese diaspora. Yet, Shu-mei Shih does not endorse the concept of "diaspora" as such. She is against the use of diaspora and suggests that diaspora should have "an end date," because Chinese communities are linguistic communities of "change" and are open to the new demands of the local (Shih, Tsai, and Bernards 2013: 37).

Would a Sinitic script system then contribute to the Han Chinese hegemony as a main source of literary expression and everyday speech? Victor Mair has advocated over the years an alternate notion of Chinese "topolects" as a way to deconstruct the single source of language formation. Mair (2001: 25) suggests that scholars have continued to embrace the wrong idea that "all Sinitic expressions, when written down, represent the same linguistic entity." He argues with solid evidence that "Han-yu is not a single language" because the "Sinitic is a group of languages," and many of them are "mutually unintelligible" (Mair 2001: 25). Jing Tsu in fact raises issues over the discrepancies between sound and script in the Chinese language, especially with linguistic communities open to translingual neologism, creolization, decay, and transformation. Jin Liu (2013) similarly provides us details about films and television programs in China that are constantly dubbed in local dialects, so that the audiences can make sense of what is being shown on screen. How about the de-nationalization project intended by Sinophone discourse? Arif Dirlik (2013) has recently indicated that the term "Sinophone" is now being aggressively appropriated by China's leading scholars as a way to broaden the horizon of Chinese studies and to disseminate Chineseness in the name of global Chinese literature. Wang Ning (2012: xxi) of Tsinghua University in Beijing, for one, has this to say: "we will appreciate all the more the great efforts made by Chinese American writers who have helped promote Chinese culture and literature worldwide, pushing it closer and closer to the mainstream of world literature." It would be an irony if Sinophone literature were soon to be taught at the Confucius Institutes worldwide as an integral part of mainstream Chinese literature.

References

Adorno, Theodor W. 2009. "Beethoven's Late Style." *Night Music: Essays on Music 1928–1962*. Trans. Wieland Hoban. New York: Seagull. 11–18.

Bai, Xianyong. 2007. "Winter Nights." In. *The Columbia Anthology of Modern Chinese Literature*. Second edition. Edited by Lau, Joseph S. M., and Howard Goldblatt. New York: Columbia University Press. 210–223.

Chow, Rey. 2013. "Things, Common/Places, Passages of the Port City: On Hong Kong and Hong Kong Author Leung Ping-kwan."

In *Sinophone Studies: A Critical Reader*. Edited by Shih, Shu-mei, Chien-hsin Tsai, and Brian Bernards. New York: Columbia University Press. 207–226.

Clifford, James. 1997. *Routes: Travel and Translation in the Late Twentieth Century*. Cambridge, MA: Harvard University Press.

Dirlik, Arif. 2013. "Literary Identity/Cultural Identity: Being Chinese in the Contemporary World." MCLC Resource Center Publication (Sept.). Accessed 15 Nov. 2013. http://mclc.osu.edu/rc/pubs/dirlik.htm.

Gao, Xingjian. 2005. *Cold Literature: Selected Works by Gao Xingjian*. Trans. Gilbert C. F. Fong and Mabel Lee. Hong Kong: Chinese University Press.

Ha Jin. 2013. "Exiled to English." In *Sinophone Studies: A Critical Reader*. Edited by Shih, Shu-mei, Chien-hsin Tsai, and Brian Bernards. New York: Columbia University Press. 117–124.

Kuhn, Philip A. 2008. *Chinese among Others: Emigration in Modern Times*. Lanham, MD: Rowman and Littlefield.

Lao She. 2007. "An Old and Established Name." In *The Columbia Anthology of Modern Chinese Literature*. Second edition. Edited by Lau, Joseph S. M., and Howard Goldblatt. New York: Columbia University Press. 74–81.

Liu, Jin. 2013. *Signifying the Local: Media Productions Rendered in Local Languages in Mainland China in the New Millennium*. Leiden: Brill.

Lopez-Calvo, Ignacio. 2013. "Latin America and the Caribbean in a Sinophone Studies Reader?" In *Sinophone Studies: A Critical Reader*. Edited by Shih, Shu-mei, Chien-hsin Tsai, and Brian Bernards. New York: Columbia University Press. 409–424.

Mair, Victor H. Ed. 2001. *The Columbia History of Chinese Literature*. New York: Columbia University Press.

Satō, Haruo 佐藤春夫. 2002. *Zhimindi zhilu* 殖民地之旅 (Travels in the Colony). Trans. Chiu Ruosan 邱若山. Taipei: Caogen.

Shan, Te-hsin. 2013. "At the Threshold of the Gold Mountain: Reading Angel Island Poetry." In *Sinophone Studies: A Critical Reader*. Edited by Shih, Shu-mei, Chien-hsin Tsai, and Brian Bernards. New York: Columbia University Press. 385–396.

Shih, Shu-mei. 2007. *Visuality and Identity: Sinophone Articulations across the Pacific*. Berkeley: University of California Press.

Shih, Shu-mei, Chien-hsin Tsai, and Brian Bernards. Eds. 2013. *Sinophone Studies: A Critical Reader*. New York: Columbia University Press.

Tee, Kim Tong. 2013. "Sinophone Malaysian Literature: An Overview." In *Sinophone Studies: A Critical Reader*. Edited by Shih, Shu-mei, Chien-hsin Tsai, and Brian Bernards. New York: Columbia University Press. 304–314.

Tsu, Jing. 2010. "Epilogue: Sinophone Writings and the Chinese Diaspora." In *The Cambridge History of Chinese Literature, Volume II: From 1375*. Edited by Chang, Kang-i Sun, and Stephen Owen. Cambridge, UK: Cambridge University Press. 706–714.

Tsu, Jing, and David Der-wei Wang. Eds. 2010. *Global Chinese Literature: Critical Essays*. Leiden: Brill.

Wang, David Der-wei. 1998. "Foreword." In *Rouge of the North* by Eileen Chang. Berkeley: University of California Press. vii–xxx.

Wang, Ning. 2012. "(Re)Considering Chinese American Literature: Toward Rewriting Literary History in a Global Age." *Amerasia Journal*, 38.2: xv–xxii.

Zhang, Yingjin. 2011. "Gender, Genre, and the Performance in Eileen Chang's Films." In *Chinese Women's Cinema: Transnational Contexts*, Edited by Wang, Lingzhen. New York: Columbia University Press. 55–73.

Part II
Genres and Types

9
Modern Poetry in Chinese: Challenges and Contingencies

Michelle Yeh

Modern poetry written in Chinese was initially known as New Poetry (*xinshi*) or vernacular poetry (*baihuashi*), in contradistinction from classical poetry or Old Poetry (*jiushi*). It arose in the 1910s as a self-proclaimed iconoclast in the "literary revolution" (*wenxue geming*) led by young intellectuals. By that time, classical poetry had a tradition of almost 3,000 years, going back to *The Book of Songs* (*Shijing*), the first collection of Chinese poetry compiled in the sixth century BCE, and Confucius is considered its editor. Classical poetry not only boasted of unbroken continuity—arguably the longest in the world—but also enjoyed a privileged position in Chinese society and culture.

Beginning with Confucius, poetry was regarded as essential to foundational education and moral cultivation. In the second century BCE, Confucianism was adopted as the state ideology under Emperor Wu of the Han dynasty, with *The Book of Songs* topping the list of Confucian canonical texts. These texts formed the core curriculum at the first academy in China, established in 124 BCE under the same emperor. From this point on, poetry not only served an important moral and educational function but also began to take on a political role. This role became more prominent as poetry was incorporated into the institution of the civil service examination from the early seventh century to 1905, when it was abolished by the Qing court in response to the increasingly vocal calls for political reform that could no longer be ignored.

Finally, notwithstanding the fact that poetry was primarily written by and for members of the elite, from emperors to scholar–officials, it was highly visible, if not ubiquitous, in public space. Poetry was inscribed and engraved in myriad forms and venues: tablets and columns, boulders and walls, temples and shrines. Its presentations were often inseparable from calligraphy on the one hand, and paintings on the other.

A Companion to Modern Chinese Literature, First Edition. Edited by Yingjin Zhang.
© 2016 John Wiley & Sons, Ltd. Published 2016 by John Wiley & Sons, Ltd.

It is no exaggeration to say that poetry occupied a uniquely privileged position in traditional Chinese society in general, and was a preeminent representative of high culture in particular.

This situation changed drastically as China entered the twentieth century. In the political arena, the Qing dynasty was overthrown in the Republican Revolution of 1911 and replaced by the Republic of China (ROC). In the educational sphere, as part of the ongoing national project of modernization, China adopted the Western model of education, including a new system of categorizing, producing, and disseminating knowledge. In the cultural and intellectual realm, the May Fourth Movement of 1919—often dubbed the Chinese Enlightenment or the Chinese Renaissance— represented a wholesale effort to rid China of its "feudal" concepts and practices derived from the Confucian orthodoxy and folk religions. In their place, such Western ideas as democracy, scientism, and nationalism were introduced and promoted with the aid of the modern mass media. Finally, no less important than the abovementioned structural changes, the everyday life of the Chinese people was increasingly modernized and Westernized: from print culture to the entertainment industry, from fashion to trans- portation, from cityscapes to social etiquettes. In short, by the time modern poetry arrived on the scene in 1917, China had been rapidly undergoing seismic changes in almost every respect.

Modern poetry was not simply a response, however; it both contributed to and epitomized those epochal transitions. As an effort to "revolutionize" Chinese poetry, pioneers of modern poetry promulgated an agenda that was more radical than modern fiction but somewhat similar to modern drama. To wit, modern poetry replaces the classical Chinese language with the contemporary vernacular; it no longer conforms to any traditional Chinese poetic forms but favors free verse or other imported forms from Europe and Japan, such as the sonnet, haiku, and concrete poetry. Other differences between modern and classical poetry are more intangible, which have to do with literary conventions in terms of theme and imagery as well as structures of feeling and worldview. The challenges to modern poetry are thus twofold: structural and aesthetic. I will discuss them briefly in what follows.

Marginalization of Poetry

The "seismic changes" outlined in the preceding text led to what I have called the marginalization of poetry in the twentieth century and beyond (M. Yeh 1992: xxiii–l). Poetry no longer plays the myriad roles or serves the multiple functions that it did for centuries in traditional China. Concomitantly, it has lost the importance and prestige it once enjoyed. Even in the literary domain, late Qing reformers touted fiction as a major tool for social reform and nation building; fiction was replacing poetry as the privileged genre. More generally, fiction has been the most popular genre in Chinese society as it is also closely related to such modern forms of entertainment as film and television.

This does not mean that poetry has never taken on a broader, public role in modern times. During the Sino-Japanese War of 1937–1945, for example, poets joined other writers to create uplifting works to promote unity of the people and resistance against the invaders. Poetry was recited and performed literally at street corners or pasted on billboards and city walls as patriotic slogans. Another example comes from the People's Republic of China (PRC) in the late 1950s, when the state sponsored a folksong campaign as part of the Great Leap Forward, which literally produced billions of poems by the masses across the country. It was Mao Zedong who finally called an end to the craze. Both examples are motivated by specific political needs. Historically speaking, they are the exception rather than the rule. Moreover, very little of the populist poetry has survived the test of time.

Poetry in Search of Readers

In "The Motive of the Magazine" published in the inaugural issue of *Poetry*, Harriet Monroe, who founded the avant-garde magazine in Chicago in October 1912, registers a complaint on behalf of poetry:

> Painting, sculpture, music are housed in palaces in the great cities of the world; and every week or two a new periodical is born to speak for one or the other of them, and tenderly nursed at some guardian's expense. Architecture, responding to commercial and social demands, is whipped into shape by the rough and tumble of life and fostered, willy-nilly, by men's material needs. Poetry alone, of all the fine arts, has been left to shift for herself in a world unaware of its immediate and desperate need of her, a world whose great deeds, whose triumphs over matter, over the wilderness, over racial enmities and distances, require her eve-living voice to give them glory and glamour.
>
> Poetry has been left to herself and blamed for inefficiency, a process as unreasonable as blaming the desert for barrenness. This art, like every other, is not a miracle of direct creation, but a reciprocal relation between the artist and his public. The people must do their part if the poet is to tell their story to the future; they must cultivate and irrigate the soil if the desert is to blossom as the rose.

I quoted the passage at length because it is equally applicable to modern Chinese poetry. Clearly, the marginalization of poetry was not unique to China. In the United States, during the 1910s, poetry was marginalized because it was perceived as unable to respond adequately to "economic and social demands." The Chinese case, I submit, is far more daunting because poetry's "fall from grace" was worse than its American counterpart, since it used to be held in such high esteem in traditional society and culture.

Monroe's image of cultivating the desert so flowers can grow also sheds light on the historical conditions surrounding modern Chinese poetry. As the political, educational, social, and cultural structures underwent epochal changes, the new poetry needed to cultivate a new readership against three formidable, interrelated, and mutually reinforcing challenges, to which we now turn.

The classical paradigm

I have compared the relation between New Poetry and classical poetry to David and Goliath (M. Yeh 2001: 3). The formidable challenge came from the enormous influence of classical poetry throughout the millennia. Chinese people take pride in classical poetry and, to this day, still refer to China as a "nation of poets." Classical poetry is venerated as a national treasure not only because of its extraordinary artistry or because it is part of the standard curriculum at schools, but, more importantly, because it has helped shape the Chinese language. Much as Shakespeare has a lasting influence on the English language, famous verses and memorable images from classical poetry, going all the way back to *The Book of Songs*, are extensively and deeply "sedimented" in the Chinese language. They have been used for so long that speakers and writers of Chinese may not even be aware of their origins. To give a couple of examples, even though most modern readers would have a hard time understanding *The Book of Songs* without annotations, they can assuredly recite these lines about courtship from the opening poem: "A quiet girl is a good match for a gentleman," or these about longing from poem no. 72: "One day not seeing you / feels like three autumns."

Concomitant with the sedimentation of classical poetry in the Chinese language, the aesthetic paradigm embodied in classical poetry is also deeply ingrained in Chinese readers' perception and reading of poetry. When it comes to poetry, native speakers, whether they are well educated or not, tend to turn to the classical paradigm as the standard-bearer and sole criterion for poetry, wittingly or unwittingly. We can imagine the shock that Chinese readers must have felt when they first encountered modern poetry, which was incongruous with their idea of poetry in almost every way, whether it is language, form, imagery, or ideas and feelings. From the beginning, the "foreignness" of modern poetry has generated much doubt about its identity and validity in a dual sense: as "poetry" *and* as "Chinese" poetry. Such doubt has underlined many criticisms, debates, and controversies in the history of modern Chinese poetry, from its inception in the 1910s to the early twenty-first century. Ironically, even as modern poetry has become more and more accessible to general readers, it is often those intellectuals and scholars who are most knowledgeable about, and appreciative of, classical poetry that are most reluctant to accept modern poetry.

The expansion and dilution of readership

Paradoxically, the second challenge facing modern Chinese poetry stems from the marked rise of literacy among the population in the modern period. Even as education became more available and literacy, at least in modern Chinese, became widespread, the potential readership of modern poetry has been both vastly expanded and, at the same time, greatly "diluted": expanded because modern poetry is written in the contemporary vernacular, so at least in theory all literate Chinese can understand it. Unlike classical poetry, the writing and reading of modern poetry is no longer limited to the elite. However, even as the reading population has grown exponentially since the early twentieth century, there is no guarantee that more people are reading poetry. Unlike classical poetry, which enjoyed a community of readers with similar—if not identical— educational background, cultural competency, and hermeneutic horizons, modern poetry no longer has that luxury. When the situation is compounded by the prevalence of classical poetry in the Chinese language on the one hand, and the radical formal and aesthetic reform represented by modern poetry on the other, it is understandable why it has taken decades for modern poetry to be accepted by the general population. Alongside classical poetry, which has continued to be written by educated Chinese and circulated in multimedia to this day, modern poetry has finally established itself as a valid and respected form of Chinese poetry.

The shackles of freedom

At its inception, modern Chinese poetry boldly proclaimed itself as an iconoclast. Having rejected the aesthetic paradigm of classical poetry with all its conventions and criteria, modern poetry started out with a clean slate, a blank canvas, on which poets could freely experiment. What this means for modern poetry is more than a radical reform of language and form, important as that is; it also compels poets to engage in a rethinking of poetry as represented by these fundamental questions: "What is poetry?"; "To whom do poets speak?"; and "Why poetry?" The first question refers to the very identity of poetry. When one writes a poem in the classical style, one can follow the rules governing form, which include prosody, parallelism, and so on, to produce a poem. Readers may consider a classical poem mediocre or good, but they cannot deny that it is poetry. However, when it comes to modern poetry, there are no set rules and no universal standards; a modern poem may not exhibit any familiar, recognizable features of poetry, whether in language or in form. Much of the doubt about modern Chinese poetry since the 1910s has come from its shocking foreignness: Is this poetry when it looks no different from prose? Is this poetry when it sounds just like everyday speech? Is this poetry when there are no rhymes and no "poetic" images?

Paradoxically, the newfound freedom is both a boon and a curse for modern Chinese poets. On the positive side, poets are free to experiment with language and form in the most diverse and creative ways; they are also free to theorize poetry from new perspectives. Collectively, modern poets have created a new aesthetic paradigm that stands parallel to and distinct from classical poetry. On the other hand, the emancipatory discourse that underlies modern poetry from the beginning has become a source of enormous pressure on the poets that hardly existed in classical poetry. It is not that originality and innovation are not valued in the Chinese poetic tradition, but those criteria exist within clearly defined parameters, which no longer exist for modern poetry. The ideal of "Make it new"—which, ironically, Ezra Pound borrowed from Confucianism—demands a constant quest for newness.

A Survey of Modern Chinese Poetry

Having contextualized the rise of modern Chinese poetry historically, structurally, and aesthetically, I will provide in this section an overview of its development and milestones. Rather than cataloging numerous poets and movements (J. C. Lin 1972; M. Yeh 1991b; Hockx 1994), I will succinctly delineate the historical trajectory of modern poetry by introducing some of the landmark achievements in each phase of its development.

The formative period, 1910s–1920s

Modern Chinese poetry was born in January 1917, when Hu Shi, an overseas graduate student of philosophy at Columbia University, published "A Preliminary Proposal for Literary Reform" ("*Wenxue gailiang chuyi*") in the progressive journal *New Youth*, founded and edited by Chen Duxiu, the newly appointed Dean of Humanities at Peking University. In the essay, Hu proposed the "Eight Don'ts" (*babu*), eight principles that would guide the new poetry he envisioned:

1 Make sure there is substance.
2 Do not imitate the ancients.
3 Abide by grammar.
4 Do not groan if you are not sick.
5 Get rid of clichés and formulaic expressions.
6 Do not use allusions.
7 Do not abide by parallelism.
8 Do not avoid colloquial words and expressions.

As if to illustrate these tenets, in the following month Hu published eight original poems in the same journal. They represented the earliest effort to create a new poetry in contradistinction from its traditional counterpart. Hu went on to publish a slim collection of poems in 1920, aptly titled *Experiments* (*Changshi ji*). The call for New Poetry or Vernacular Poetry won enthusiastic support among young intellectuals, many of who experimented with the new genre with varying degrees of success.

Although *Experiments* bears clear traces of classical poetry in its diction, regular forms, and use of end rhymes, a few elements stand out as new. For example, "Dream and Poetry" ("*Meng yu shi*") emphasizes the uniqueness of personal experience, which in turn serves as the basis for poetry rather than emulation of masters of the past. The last two lines of the poem summarize what Hu called his "poetic empiricism": "You cannot write my poems, / Just as I cannot dream your dreams."

Some scholars have argued that Hu Shi borrowed his "Eight Don'ts" from American Imagism in that there are some similarities to Pound's "A Few Don'ts by an Imagiste," originally published in *Poetry* in 1913. While Hu did read a book review of Imagism in a newspaper and saved a clipping, there was no other mention of Imagism in his diaries. Moreover, when we pore through the dairies he kept as a student in the United States in the 1910s, it is demonstrable that he was far more interested in, and knowledgeable about, Victorian and Edwardian poetry than the avant-garde movement of Imagism. Moreover, "A Few Don'ts by an Imagiste" and "Eight Don'ts" are similar only in a superficial way. Hu Shi's "Eight Don'ts" makes no claim about the specific qualities of imagery and musicality that are essential to Pound's Imagism. What they have in common is their rebellions against respective poetic conventions. After all, to challenge the mainstream is the *raison d'être* of all new movements. Second, from a historical point of view, many literary movements also advocate the use of the living language or common speech of the time, whether it be William Wordsworth or Pound. Should it be a surprise that both Hu and Pound advance the same?

Hu Shi readily admitted that his early efforts were overshadowed by classical poetry, especially the song lyrics (*ci*), and were therefore far from successful. In witty self-deprecation, he referred to his experiments as "bound feet unbound," a metaphor drawn from the longstanding practice in traditional China of binding women's feet into tiny "golden lotuses." While studying in the United States, Hu took classes in Western poetry, such as Shakespeare and Robert Browning, and discussed his burgeoning idea of poetry reform with other students from China. According to his own account, Hu owed his more mature works to his experience in the translation of Anglo-American poetry into Chinese; the one translation he singled out was "Over the Roofs" by the American poet Sarah Teasdale. "Over the Roofs" is selected from a sequence of four poems published in *Poetry* in March 1914:

> I said, "I have shut my heart
> As one shuts an open door,
> That Love may starve therein
> And trouble me no more."
>
> But over the roofs there came
> The wet new wind of May,
> And a tune blew up from the curb
> Where the street-pianos play.
>
> My room was white with the sun
> And Love cried out to me,
> "I am strong, I will break your heart
> Unless you set me free."

In his translation, Hu changed the title of the poem to "Cannot Hold It In" ("*Guanbuzhule*"). This is consistent with his principle of "Do not avoid colloquial words and expressions." Moreover, although personification and dramatization are not uncommon in classical Chinese poetry, the personification of love as someone impatient and eager to break out of the speaker's heart to pursue love freely is novel.

The bold voice and the dynamic image are clearly distinguished from classical Chinese poetry, in which longing for love is typically expressed in a wistful tone and cloaked in such familiar images as spring breeze and mandarin ducks.

Hu Shi is a game-changer in Chinese history because his proposal provided the originary theory, and his poems its earliest experiments, of modern poetry. More broadly, he embodied important historical forces at work in early modern China. Similar to Hu, many young men and women had studied abroad. As early as the 1870s, the Qing court had begun to send youngsters overseas to study in the West. The numbers went up in 1909–1929 when the Boxer Indemnity Scholarship Program sponsored approximately 1,300 Chinese students, including Hu Shi, to study in Britain, France, Germany, Japan, and the United States. Also similar to Hu Shi, many returned students became leaders and active players in the May Fourth Movement. The rebellion against the revered classical poetry was part and parcel of the May Fourth's general critique of traditional values and practices. Finally, Hu and his generation were avid translators who served as a conduit of Western learning (see Chapter 13 by Zha Mingjian).

The first translation bureau in China was established in 1862 by the Qing court. Translations of world literature thrived in the late nineteenth and early twentieth centuries; many exerted formative influences on Chinese writers. While the selections of source texts were sometimes haphazard or indiscriminate, they introduced a broad range of literary styles and movements, from romanticism to symbolism, from Greek tragedies to naturalist fiction, from Johann Wolfgang von Goethe to Ibsen. Similar to Hu Shi, many pioneers of modern Chinese poetry were translators as well, a phenomenon unseen, certainly not on the same scale and of the same import, in the tradition of classical poetry. In fact, the phenomenon of poet–translators has continued to this day.

"Translation is likewise good training, if you find that your original matter 'wobbles' when you try to rewrite it. The meaning of the poem to be translated cannot 'wobble'"—these words from "A Retrospect" by Pound (1962: 108) aptly describe the symbiosis between translation and creative writing throughout the history of modern Chinese poetry. In the formative period, Guo Moruo, who studied medicine in Japan, and Xu Zhimo, who studied economics and political science in the United States and Britain, embraced European romanticism. While Guo Moruo took a left turn from romanticism toward "revolutionary literature" in the mid-1920s, Xu became the Chinese romanticist *par excellence* with his writings as well as his legendary life. His poetry pays tribute to the pursuit of love and freedom, the innocence of the child, and the unity between human beings and nature. Among other pioneers, Li Jinfa and Dai Wangshu both studied in France and considered themselves disciples of the French symbolists. Ai Qing, who was a poor art student in Paris, sang of Arthur Rimbaud and Guillaume Apollinaire. Feng Zhi, who studied literature and philosophy in Germany, found inspiration in Rainer Maria Rilke. Bian Zhilin, though he did not visit Britain until the 1940s, was already translating W. B. Yeats and T. S. Eliot in the 1920s–1930s. Numerous

Chinese poets found in Western literature new resources for developing their own poetic theories and practices.

The war years, 1937–1945

Poetic experimentation did not come to an end with Japan's all-out invasion of China and the outbreak of what is known to the Chinese as the War of Resistance in July 1937. On the contrary, while public recitations of poetry to raise morale were popular among the masses, new poetry found fertile ground at Southwest Associated University (*Xi'nan lianda*), the wartime conglomerate of three leading universities—Peking, Tsinghua, and Nankai—relocated from North China to the southwestern city of Kunming in 1938. Many established poets such as Wen Yiduo, Zhu Ziqing, Feng Zhi, and Li Guangtian taught there. They were joined by William Empson, a preeminent literary critic and poet from Britain who had accepted a position of visiting professor at Peking University at the start of the war. Under their tutelage, a new generation of poets were exposed to the major figures of British High Modernists, including Eliot, Yeats, and, above all, W. H. Auden, who visited China with Christopher Isherwood in 1938 and published *Journey to a War* in the following year. Nine representative poets from the younger generation would be grouped together retroactively as the "Nine Leaves School" in the 1980s. Among them, four were students at Southwest Associated University: Du Yunxie, Mu Dan, Yuan Kejia, and Zheng Min, while the other five were active in postwar Shanghai in association with two journals, *Poetry Creation* and *New Poetry of China*: Chen Jingrong, Tang Qi, Tang Shi, Xin Di, and Cao Xinzhi. Among the "Nine Leaves," Mu Dan, who was an English major at Southwest Associated University, stands out with his profound contemplations of youth, love, and life, especially the painful contradiction between impermanent love and cool-headed reason.

The fact is that, despite the massive relocations of institutions and writers during the war, poets continued to create first-rate works in different parts of China. Ai Qing, who moved to Yan'an in 1941, won national fame with his powerful renditions of the war-torn country, best represented by "Snow Is Falling on the Land of China" ("*Xue luozai Zhongguo de tudi shang*"). Feng Zhi in Kunming wrote a collection of twenty-seven sonnets in 1941–1942, which combined vignettes of wartime life with Rilkean musings. In Shanghai, the "Orphan Island" occupied by the Japanese, Louis (Luyishi), pen name of Lu Yu who was trained in Western painting, emerged as a fresh voice of defiant individualism and whimsical surrealism. Still other poets landed in Hong Kong, which fell to the Japanese in December 1941. Dai Wangshu, the erstwhile co-founder and editor of the modernist journal *Les Contemporains*, was jailed and tortured by the Japanese. "With My Maimed Hand" ("*Wo yong cansun de shouzhang*") and "Inscribed on the Prison Wall" ("*Yu zhong tibi*") are moving testimonials to the suffering of the people during the war. Finally, in the Communist base in Northwest China, poetry was modeled after local folksongs in distinct forms and rhymes to sing of the downfall of corrupt Nationalist officials, greedy landlords, and ruthless invaders.

Modernism in postwar Taiwan and Hong Kong

In 1949, as the civil war between the Communists and the Nationalists was winding down, the PRC was founded in Beijing on October 1. Hu Feng composed a long poem of more than 4,600 lines, appropriately titled "Time Now Begins," to pay tribute to New China. In retrospect, it also portended the beginning of decades of subjugation and persecution of writers and intellectuals throughout a series of political campaigns. Hu Feng himself was arrested in 1955 as the alleged leader of a "counter-revolutionary clique," which implicated many fellow poets; he was jailed until 1978, when he was rehabilitated. In the Anti-Rightist Campaign of 1957–1958, Ai Qing was purged and banished to the borderlands to do hard labor, first in Heilongjiang and then in Xinjiang.

Although not everyone suffered as harshly as Hu Feng and Ai Qing did in the 1950s, most poets who had been active before 1949 stopped writing in view of the stifling state policy that literature must serve workers, peasants, and soldiers exclusively (see Chapter 5 by Chen Xiaoming). Instead, they devoted themselves to translation and scholarship. For example, Mu Dan became a prominent translator of Russian and English romantic poetry; Chen Jingrong's translation of Baudelaire was to exert a significant influence on an entire generation of young poets in post-Mao China. As the political climate grew worse and culminated in the Cultural Revolution in 1966–1976, literature was virtually decimated; the only works that were openly circulated during the decade were eight pieces of model theater and a few politically correct novels approved by Jiang Qing, Mao Zedong's powerful wife. To write was to risk imprisonment, exile, or even death. It was not until the late 1970s, when China adopted an open door policy under Deng Xiaoping, that a modicum of creative freedom returned.

In contrast, Taiwan across the strait and British-ruled Hong Kong witnessed a golden age of modern Chinese poetry, characterized by an original brand of modernism. Taiwan had been ruled by Japan for fifty years, from 1895 to 1945. In 1949, the Nationalist government retreated from the mainland to the island, and with it came more than a million émigrés. As the curtains were raised on the Cold War in 1953 at the end of the Korea War, Taiwan became a close ally to the United States against the Communist bloc. The cultural influence that came with the political alliance and American economic aid was enormous. Internally, in anticipation of the imminent retreat from the mainland, the Nationalist regime imposed martial law in May 1949, two years after the February 28 Incident of 1947, in which local Taiwanese revolted against the new regime. Into the 1950s, intermittent military conflicts between the Communists and the Nationalists continued on a smaller scale. For fear of "Communist infiltration," Taiwan cut off all communication with the mainland, a situation that continued until 1987.

Although political control was not as tight, and political persecution not as pervasive, as Mao's China, postwar Taiwan underwent a repressive period known as White Terror; civil liberties were curtailed and censorship was imposed on the press and mass media. In the cultural sphere, the state promoted "anti-Communist and counter-Soviet literature" and encouraged writers to contribute by offering generous prizes and publication opportunities. Surprisingly, the bleak postwar scene did not stop Ji Xian, previously writing under the pen name "Louis" in wartime Shanghai, from launching a "second revolution" of modern poetry. Rebelling against the then-popular sentimental lyrics in regular forms derived from Xu Zhimo and other Crescent Moon poets in the 1920s–1930s, Ji Xian looked to the avant-garde in the West and Japan for alternative models. He single-handedly founded the quarterly *Modern Poetry* (*Xiandaishi*) in 1953 and the Modernist School (*Xiandaipai*) in 1956. Echoing Hu Shi's "Eight Don'ts," Ji Xian (1956: 4) advanced the "Six Tenets" of the Modernist School:

1   We are a group of modernists who selectively incorporate the spirit and key elements of all new poetry schools since Baudelaire.
2   Thus, the new poetry is a horizontal transplant rather than a vertical successor.
3   Explore the new continent of poetry and cultivate the virgin land of poetry.
4   Emphasize intellect.
5   Pursue the purity of poetry.
6   Uphold patriotism and anti-communism, freedom and democracy.

The second tenet of the Modernist School stirred up much controversy in the conservative postwar society. However, the journal and the school were a cradle for young poets, most of whom were students and servicemen. Some of them went on to form their own poetry groups and launched their own journals. Most notably, three young officers in the navy—Luo Fu, Zhang Mo, and Ya Xian—founded the Epoch Poetry Society (*Chuangshiji*) in 1954; the same year also saw the founding of Blue Star (*Lanxing*) under the leadership of Qin Zihao and Zhong Dingwen. Blue Star preferred a lyricism that blended French symbolism and classical Chinese poetry, while Epoch became a fervent advocate of French surrealism after the initial phase. Regardless of their different positions and occasional debates, memberships in these poetry groups overlapped somewhat. Together, they brought about the golden age of modernism in Chinese poetry.

Modernism flourished in the 1950s–1960s despite government censorship and disparagement from the conservative cultural mainstream. It changed the literary scene by introducing new poetic models and establishing new theories and practices. Among its best representatives are: Shang Qing, the greatest prose poet and surrealist poet in the history of modern Chinese poetry; Yu Guangzhong, whose moving expressions of nostalgia for lost China has made him the most popular poet in postwar Taiwan as well as in contemporary China; Ya Xian, who wrote about alienation in a dual sense, both as a modern man and as an exile from China; Zheng Chouyu, who created a unique lyrical mode that is both Chinese and modernist; and Yang Mu, whose journey through romanticism and modernism has established him as one of the finest craftsmen in modern poetry in the Chinese language. All of these poets helped shape Chinese literary history and exerted a lasting influence on the poets of Taiwan and Hong Kong for generations to come.

In nearby Hong Kong, where the British authority imposed few ideological restrictions on the Chinese population, poets enjoyed virtually complete freedom to engage in artistic experimentation. Easy access also resulted in wide exposure to literary trends and works in the Anglophone world and continental Europe. In 1956, Ma Lang founded *New Trends in Literature and Arts* (*Wenyi xinchao*). In 1963, Kun Nan founded *Cape Good Hope* (*Haowangjiao*). Both promoted modernism across multiple genres, not only in poetry but also in fiction and film. Hong Kong poets found kindred spirits in the modernist poets in Taiwan. The two groups engaged in frequent collaborations on journals and anthologies. The momentum was carried into the 1970s when younger poets launched new journals with a cosmopolitan outlook. Liang Bingjun (Leung Ping-kwan) emerged on the scene and went on to become arguably the greatest poet in Hong Kong, as well as a major fiction writer, scholar, and culture critic. Before his untimely death in 2013, he was in effect the most eloquent spokesperson for Hong Kong on the international literary scene.

As a movement born in Europe and America in the early twentieth century, with roots going back at least to the first half of the nineteenth century, modernism was a reaction to modernization in the West, which had begun with the Industrial Revolution. If modernism was astutely critical vis-à-vis social reality, it was emphatically experimental when it came to literary creation. Both the critical and experimental dimensions found powerful expressions in modernist poetry in Taiwan and Hong Kong in the 1950s–1960s. Moreover, the modernist spirit has continued to play an important role among younger generations despite new developments in poetry.

Nativism in Taiwan and Hong Kong

Taiwan witnessed a marked shift from modernism to nativism in the 1970s–1980s. Setbacks in the international political arena in the early 1970s included the loss of the seat in the United Nations to the PRC and the severing of diplomatic relations with the United States and Japan. This led to a legitimation crisis and triggered a wave of self-reflection among Taiwan's intellectuals and writers. Modernism came under scathing attack for its alleged solipsism, over-Westernization, and indifference to social reality. In contrast, many critics and poets, especially of the younger generation, called for a return to the Chinese cultural roots and a renewed sense of social responsibility grounded in Taiwanese reality. The nativist turn in modern poetry was a forerunner of the full-fledged nativist literature movement in fiction in the second half of the 1970s. By the end of the decade, the nativist trend on the literary scene merged with the escalating political opposition movement, which culminated in the lifting of martial law in 1987 and ushered in an era of full democratization. Throughout the 1980s–1990s, poets broke political taboos by dealing with the February 28 Incident and White Terror; they also sought to recover the long-repressed history of Taiwan's past and call attention to contemporary social malaise, from indigenous peoples' plight and child prostitution to gender discrimination and environmental devastation.

If the poetry that addressed social and political themes was often marred by explicit didacticism and emotional outpour, some works succeeded in both contents and artistry. For example, Liu Kexiang (Liu Ka-shiang) was a pioneer in two types of themes, political and environmental. His political poems meditate on the vicissitudes of Taiwanese history as the island lived through centuries of colonization—Portuguese, Dutch, Japanese, and Chinese. Better known today as a nature writer in prose, Liu initiated new nature poetry in the 1980s that was closely tied to local ecology: the birds and plants of Taiwan.

Nativism also found expressions in poetry written in Taiwanese (Hokkien or Minnan hua) and Hakka, two dialects spoken by two of the four major ethnic groups that constitute Taiwan's population (the other two being the indigenous peoples and the émigrés from mainland China around 1949). The poetry tends to add a strong local color and renders vivid the everyday life of the two ethnic groups.

New subject matters and artistic experimentation were by no means mutually exclusive. The modernist approach to the poem as a self-contained, organically constructed artifact remained influential among younger poets, who also drew on postmodernism for inspiration. In Taiwan in the 1980s–1990s, the postmodern subversion of poetic conventions in language, form, and sensibility was not so much a radical questioning of the modernist ideology, the way it was in the West, as a new creative possibility and an enlargement of the modernist canon. The most successful poets across the modernist–postmodernist divide are Xia Yu (Hsia Yü) and Chen Li.

Both Chen and Xia were born in the mid-1950s and baptized in postwar modernism. In the early 1980s, Xia Yu published her first poetry collection titled *Memoranda* (*Beiwanglu*), which created an instant sensation on the poetry scene. It stood out for several reasons. First, although self-publishing was not uncommon when it came to books of poetry, *Memoranda* was unique in its design—the small square shape of the book, the texture and color of the paper, the poet's childlike handwriting and cartoonish illustrations—as well as its contents. For the first time in the history of modern Chinese poetry, such pedestrian images as pimples and eating the white part of an egg appear in love poems. More importantly, in this and subsequent poetry collections, Xia Yu has successfully created a memorable persona of the urban modern woman. She is both childlike and highly sexualized: childlike in her vulnerability in love but sexualized as she casually talks about promiscuity and masturbation. She yearns for love but is, at the same time, jaded and fatigued. Above all, the persona in Xia Yu's poetry is a writer who is tireless in experimenting with the visual and aural attributes of the Chinese language, a woman who lives through her words.

No less experimental in language and form than Xia Yu, Chen Li consciously explores local–historical themes, from erotic myths of indigenous tribes to everyday life in his hometown Hualian, a small city on the eastern coast of Taiwan. Chen's poetry is filled with witty puns and unexpected associations in dealing with serious themes. For example, "The Refusal to Curl the Tongue Movement" (*Bu juanshe yundong*) is fantastic in its title and content: comparing curling the tongue when speaking to wearing a bowtie, citing a tongue twister that tells an elaborate story using one pronunciation. However, behind these images is the message that Taiwanese Mandarin with little curling of the tongue is the natural result of historical development; it should not be forced to conform to the mainland Chinese standard. Chen's concrete poem "The War Symphony" (*"Zhanzheng jiaoxiangqu"*) is a masterful combination of the visual and aural elements of four simple Chinese characters to express anti-war sentiments.

Underground poetry in the PRC, 1960s–1980s

The 1970s marked a dramatic turning point in the PRC. With the death of Mao Zedong and the arrest of the Gang of Four in 1976, Deng Xiaoping opened China to the "free world" after three decades of little communication. He also launched the national project of "four modernizations" (in economy, science, agriculture, and national defense) and ushered in the New Era (see Chapter 6 by Tao Dongfeng). For the first time since the founding of the PRC, underground journals mushroomed across China in late 1978 and early 1979, such as *Explorations* (*Tansuo*) founded by Wei Jingsheng, *Enlightenment* (*Qimeng*) by Huang Xiang, and *Today* (*Jintian*) by Bei Dao and Mang Ke. This period of revived freedom of expression was known as "Beijing Spring" (*"Beijing zhichun"*), but it came to an abrupt end in March 1979 with the arrest of Wei Jingsheng, who was convicted of conspiracy to subvert the government. All underground journals were shut down.

Unlike Mao's China, however, this time poetry could no longer be stifled. A renaissance in literature and art took place in the liberalizing climate, pioneered by underground poetry. *Today* was the first underground journal devoted exclusively to literature in post-Mao China, but it was not the first in PRC history. Already in the 1960s a few underground journals had existed in Beijing and elsewhere, but they were short-lived and never distributed outside a small coterie of friends. During the Cultural Revolution, underground poetry was widely circulated mainly because, unlike fiction or drama, poetry was typically short and rhythmic, therefore easily memorized and hand-copied. Some of the underground poetry found popularity among millions of the "sent-down youth"—urban young men and women who were sent to the countryside for reeducation. The best-known case was Shi Zhi (literally "Index Finger"), pen name of Guo Lusheng. His poems in the late 1960s were lyrical and personal, at times painfully confessional, a refreshing departure from the revolutionary romanticism that characterized mainstream poetry. "Beijing at 4:08" depicts the heart-wrenching scene of sent-down youths leaving Beijing by train. "Believe in the Future" expresses optimism in the midst of bleak reality; it was inspired by an underground poet whom Shi Zhi knew before he escaped arrest by the authorities.

Underground poetry, or "unofficial poetry," played an important, highly visible role in the cultural field in post-Mao China. As in the May Fourth period and postwar Taiwan, poetry was not only a barometer of the time but in fact spearheaded new trends in literature and art. Likewise, underground poetry both reflected and contributed to the larger enlightenment movement known as "culture fever" (*wen-huare*) in China in the 1980s. Immensely popular, especially among intellectuals and students, most of the unofficial poetry may be seen as part of the scar literature that emerged in the late 1970s. Gu Cheng's "Ending" ("*Jieshu*") mourns the lives lost in the violence of the Cultural Revolution; his "A Generation" ("*Yidai ren*") expresses persistent optimism despite the manmade catastrophe and is, in essence, a manifesto of the entire generation: "Dark night gave me dark eyes, / But I use them to look for light." The new poetry was dense in language and figurative imagery, and its tone personal, at times somber, at times fantastic.

Predictably, the new poetry's departure from the official mode of writing also made it a target of attack by the establishment. Its perceived foreignness was criticized as too obscure and Westernized, hence the derogatory label "Misty Poetry." In fact, in the political campaigns in the 1980s, including the Anti-Spiritual Pollution (*Fan jingshen wuran*) and the Anti-Liberalization (*Fan ziyouhua*) Campaigns, the new poetry was singled out for criticism, along with other undesirable works of fiction, drama, and film.

As the first post-Mao generation of underground poets, the Misty poets were canonized in a short few years. In the mid-1980s, the next generation burst on the scene. Compared with their predecessors, the younger generation was larger in number and more diverse in writing style and subject matter. However, they all shared an acute sense of belatedness; coming after the groundbreaking Misty poets, they sought to distinguish themselves from their haloed predecessors. Instead of somber reflections on the Cultural Revolution, the new generation turned their attention to mundane experiences. Instead of the elegiac and the sublime often found in Misty poetry, the new generation preferred an ironic, self-deprecating tone. Instead of the predominantly male perspectives (with notable exceptions of Shu Ting and Wang Xiaoni), the new generation boasted a large group of women poets who expressed the female psyche and created a new discourse of women's poetry. Instead of the romantic–nostalgic approach to nature, the new generation delved into the primal and mystical aspects of the natural world. Throughout the 1980s, underground poets founded many journals and collaborated closely with one another. Although the authorities could shut down their journals, the poets would simply move on and start new journals, playing a cat-and-mouse game with the police.

The golden age of underground poetry was disrupted in June 1989 when the government brutally cracked down on the student-led democracy movement in Beijing. For many poets, the Tiananmen Incident marked the end of an era—and along with it, the youthful idealism of the 1980s. The sense of disillusionment was compounded by China's rapid economic transformation into a market economy or capitalism with "socialist characteristics." Into the 1990s, as the society became more and more affluent, poetry lost its erstwhile halo and became more and more marginalized. Many poets stopped writing and joined the trend of "jumping into the sea" (*xiahai*) of the business world. In the new century, those who became successful would become patrons of poetry, funding poetry festivals, prizes, publications, and even institutes.

Although restrictions on publication still exist in China today, underground poetry is a thing of the past. Even the line between "official" and "unofficial" poetry is blurred. Some poets are appointed professors at universities, some are members of the state-funded Chinese Writers Association, and some are editors at official presses. These structural changes have shaped the ecology of the poetry scene in contemporary China, which is in many ways similar to the poetry scenes in Taiwan and Hong Kong (Van Crevel 1996; Van Crevel 2008; J. H. Zhang 2004; Kunze 2012). Moreover, as the Internet is widely used, geopolitical and cultural boundaries no longer play a decisive role in the circulation and reception of poetry.

In conclusion, modern poetry in the Chinese language has come a long way. Since the 1910s, it has weathered debates and controversies, wars and exodus, censorship and political persecutions. Despite all that, it has produced many fine poets and truly original works. Literary history is a process of naturalization and acculturation; it is also a cyclical process of defamiliarization and familiarization. What started out as strange and novel in New Poetry has been transformed into the natural and "normal." After nearly a century, the new paradigm that modern poetry represents has finally, albeit gradually, been integrated into the educational system and accepted by general readers. Just as classical poetry has shaped how Chinese people speak and write, so modern poetry is slowly finding its way into the spoken and written language. That, in the final analysis, is the measure of the greatness of poetry.

References

Hockx, Michel. 1994. *A Snowy Morning: Eight Chinese Poets on the Road to Modernity*. Leiden: Research School CNWS.

Ji, Xian. 1956. "Explicating the Six Tenets of the Modernist School," *Modern Poetry* 13 (Feb. 1): 4.

Kunze, Rui. 2012. *Struggle and Symbiosis: The Canonization of the Poet Haize and Cultural Discourses in Contemporary China*. Bochum: Projekt Verlag.

Lin, Julia C. 1972. *Modern Chinese Poetry: An Introduction*. Seattle: University of Washington Press.

Pound, Ezra. 1962. "A Retrospect." In *Prose Keys to Modern Poetry*. Edited by Karl Shapiro. New York: Harper & Row. 104–112.

Van Crevel, Maghiel. 1996. *Language Shattered: Contemporary Chinese Poetry and Duoduo*. Leiden: CNWS Publications.

Van Crevel, Maghiel. 2008. *Chinese Poetry in Times of Mind, Mayhem and Money*. Leiden: Brill.

Yeh, Michelle. 1991b. *Modern Chinese Poetry: Theory and Practice since 1917*. New Haven, CT: Yale University Press.

Yeh, Michelle. 1992. *Anthology of Modern Chinese Poetry*. New Haven, CT: Yale University Press.

Yeh, Michelle. 2001. "Introduction." In *Frontier Taiwan: An Anthology of Modern Chinese Poetry*. Edited by Michelle Yeh and N. G. D. Malmqvist. New York: Columbia University Press. 1–53.

Zhang, Jeanne Hong. 2004. *The Invention of a Discourse: Women's Poetry from Contemporary China*. Leiden: CNWS Publications.

10

Modern Chinese Theater Study and its Century-Long History

Xiaomei Chen

When we speak of "modern Chinese drama," we are referring mostly to spoken drama (*huaju*), which was introduced from the West at the turn of the twentieth century in the tradition of Shakespeare, Chekhov, Ibsen, and others as a modern alternative to traditional Chinese operatic theater (*xiqu*). Several major figures of the May Fourth Movement advocated spoken drama as a powerful critique of the so-called immoral conservative tradition that had existed for a thousand years without social significance and literary values. Hu Shi, for example, introduced Ibsen in 1919 as a realist playwright who had examined social ills through their manifestations in family drama, as seen in his *A Doll's House* and *Ghosts*, and in his social problem plays such as *Pillars of Society* and *An Enemy of the People* (Ge Yihong 1990: 44–46). Hu's promotion of Ibsen's spirit of individualism and his imitation of *A Doll's House* in his own scripting of an early spoken drama, entitled *The Main Event in One's Life* (*Zhongshen dashi*, 1919), established realist theater and social problem plays as an important trend in May Fourth drama, which combined Western-style drama's social functions with modern aesthetic tastes (W. Wang, Song, and Zhang 1998: 28–30).

Other critics such as Zhang Houzai and Song Chunfang, however, attempted to rescue traditional Chinese opera by pointing to its humanistic essence and aesthetic traditions. Having traveled to France, Germany, Italy, and the United States to survey Western theaters, Song introduced to China the global phenomenon of modernist theater as practiced by Gordon Craig, Max Reinhardt, Maurice Maeterlinck, J. M. Synge, and others, as well as various performance schools such as "experimental theater" (*xiao juchang yundong*), "expressionist theater" (*biaoxian zhuyi xiju*), and "symbolist theater" (B. Chen and Dong 1989: 375–376). Song argued for the coexistence of spoken drama

A Companion to Modern Chinese Literature, First Edition. Edited by Yingjin Zhang.
© 2016 John Wiley & Sons, Ltd. Published 2016 by John Wiley & Sons, Ltd.

with Chinese traditional opera, whose rich artistic traditions had in fact also inspired Western symbolist theater (Song Baozhen 2002: 66). In his farsighted but lonely defense of Chinese opera, Song proved to be ahead of his time when attacks on the remnants of traditional culture had been carried out as the main task of the May Fourth Movement.

Indeed, the subsequent history of modern Chinese theater has shown a gradual acceptance of reformed traditional opera as an equally important genre both in aesthetic form and in social function, as seen in the successful use of opera for wartime mobilization performances, to name just one example. In the period of the PRC (1949 to present), state-sponsored Peking opera reform succeeded in establishing revolutionary model theater during the Cultural Revolution (1966–1976) as the dominant artistic genre, at a time when almost all other literary and artistic works had been discarded as having reflected "feudalist, bourgeois, and revisionist ideologies" (*feng zi xiu wenyi*). Five "revolutionary and modern model Peking operas," for example, were celebrated by the official press as having presented exemplary "proletariat arts" for the sole purpose of serving the interests of workers, peasants, and soldiers in socialist China. In theatrical forms, model Peking operas such as *Taking Tiger Mountain by Strategy* (*Zhiqu Weihushan*) skillfully introduced Western-style orchestras that played together with traditional Chinese instruments, and combined certain features of time-honored character roles such as *laosheng* (the old man), *wusheng* (the acrobat/military man), and *xiaosheng* (the young male) in creating Communist heroes. This Peking opera, for example, dramatizes the legendary character Yang Zirong, who led his Communist troops to defeat their Nationalist enemies during the civil war (1945–1949). Several decades later, Yang's well-known aria from this Cultural Revolutionary–era opera continued to be popular even in the post-Mao (i.e., post-1976), postsocialist period when the Maoist revolutionary spirit was waning. The artistic and nostalgic appeal of the model Peking operas has prevailed because these operas remind contemporary Chinese people of positive emotions and values of the past.

In the post-Mao period, moreover, the theatrical concepts, techniques, and aesthetics of Chinese opera likewise found their way into the experimental performances of spoken drama and inspired the initial trend toward avant-garde theater. The innovative production of Gao Xingjian and Liu Huiyuan's *Absolute Signal* (*Juedui xinhao*, 1982), for example, has been celebrated as having returned to the symbolist conventions of Chinese opera, which had inspired Bertolt Brecht's concept of the "alienation effect" in the first place. Gao Xingjian's other experimental pieces, such as *Wildman* (*Yeren*, 1985), embraced at once Western modernist and Chinese operatic traditions (X. Chen 1995: 119–32), and were therefore viewed as the beginning of neo-realist theater in the New Era (Hu Xingliang 2000: 184). In the twenty-first century, both operatic theater and spoken drama are equally present in university curricula, institutional establishments, scholarly research, and stage performance; by the same token, they have suffered from a declining audience base because of fierce competition with commercial culture, television shows, and touring Western theater troupes.

Three Founding Fathers in Spoken Drama and in Opera Reform

The history of modern Chinese drama has credited Tian Han, Hong Shen, and Ouyang Yuqian as "the three founders of spoken drama" in recognition of their crowning achievements in scriptwriting, directing, and theater performances in the 1920s–1930s. Tian Han, for example, successfully initiated one of the most active, independent theater movements (*zaiye de xiju*) in his formation and management of the Southern Drama Society (Nanguo she) in the 1920s. His 1930 theater manifesto, "My Self-Criticism" (*"Women de ziji pipan"*), has been interpreted in modern Chinese theater history as his left-turning/socialist-leaning moment when he began to shift from his earlier beliefs in both "art for art's sake" and "art for life's sake" (under the influence of Western realist and modernist theater) to his later devotion to the social significance of theater art (under the influence of Japanese and Soviet socialist artists and especially Marxist theories of literature and art). Tian's contributions to left-wing theater performances and his subsequent appointment as the first president of the China Drama Association (Zhongguo xijujia xiehui) in the PRC have testified to his significant contributions to the development of spoken drama.

I want to emphasize, however, the lesser-known fact that all three founding fathers of spoken drama were also at the same time pioneers in Chinese opera reform. Tian Han, for example, scripted not only 63 modern spoken dramas but also 27 traditional operas (including Peking, Hunan, and Henan operas), two Western-style operas (*geju*), 12 movie scripts, a substantial body of literary criticism, and translated plays by Shakespeare, Oscar Wilde, and Kikuchi Kan, among others. The first drama script Tian wrote, at the age of 15, was indeed a new opera, entitled *The New Story of Educating a Son (Xin Jiaozi)*, in which the widowed Sanniang educates her son about his father's heroic deeds in the Republican revolution against the die-hards of the Qing court in Hunan, in order to encourage him to realize his father's dream of unifying China (X. Chen 2006: 186–96). Tian's appointment as the director of the Bureau of Chinese Opera Reform right after 1949 demonstrated his prominent role in leading operatic reform and his extensive social networks with fellow folk artists before and after the founding of the PRC (Liu Ping 1998: 590–4).

Indeed, Tian's leadership in traditional opera reform was significant in paving the way for the creation of revolutionary model theater during the Cultural Revolution. Ironically, even though Tian was the first to try his hand at adapting an early version of the revolutionary Peking opera *The Red Detachment of Women (Hongse niangzijun)* from the original film, the legend goes that Jiang Qing, Mao Zedong's wife, who had been in charge of promoting model theater, did not like Tian's script (Liu Ping 1998: 692). Tian subsequently died in detention by the Red Guards, who had accused him of being a representative of the anti-Party clique against socialist and proletariat art, which, paradoxically, Tian had pioneered in the Republican era (1921–1949) through his achievements in promoting both spoken drama and opera reform.

By the same token, scholarly accounts of Hong Shen, the second founding father of spoken drama, have also emphasized his seminal role in this Western-imported genre.

Modern drama histories indicate that, unlike Tian, who only *read* about Western drama while studying in Japan from 1916 to 1922, Hong benefited directly from Western culture as the first Chinese overseas graduate student to enroll in theater in the West; as a student in Professor George Pierce Baker's famous drama class at Harvard University, known as "Workshop 47," Hong went through the same rigorous training that produced Eugene O'Neill, George Abbott, and Maurine Dallas Watkins in different classes. During his time in the United States, from 1916 to 1922, Hong wrote English-language spoken dramas about the Chinese people's way of life and worked in Boston and New York theaters to familiarize himself with theater management, from makeup to advertising, ticket sales, accounting, ushering, and cloak room service (Hong Shen 1936: 478–86; X. Chen 2014: 226–7).

Upon his return to Shanghai, Hong wrote his first modernist play, *Yama Zhao* (*Zhao yanwang*, 1922), in imitation of the expressionist style of Eugene O'Neill's *Emperor Jones*. Influenced by O'Neill's use of episodic structure, stream of consciousness, and psychological drama, Hong depicted the title protagonist as a depressed soldier who hallucinates about talking to various characters in his past and present life while escaping from his captors. Hong directed the play and passionately performed the role of the protagonist, only to a lukewarm reception. Hong finally won over his Shanghai audience 2 years later in 1924 with his successful adaptation of Wilde's *Lady Windermere's Fan* (*Shao Nainai de Shanzi*), which transposed the English comedy into the milieu of the upper class in Shanghai and established him as a new authority in scripting, directing, and managing Western-style spoken drama (M. Chen and Song 1996: 87–95).

Similar to Tian's scripting of traditional operas, in his scholarly writing of theater history, Hong took into account the parallel developments of Chinese operatic theater and spoken drama. In his canonical survey of wartime drama from 1937 to 1947 (Hong Shen 1948), Hong characterized the war period as a golden age for spoken drama, when theater troupes traveled to the war front and to the interior areas with innovative scripts, stage design, makeup, and music. At the same time, he acknowledged the war period as a perfect opportunity to modernize traditional Chinese opera and mine its rich aesthetic potential. Hong illustrated how the artists in Guangdong opera (*Yueju*), Hebei opera (*Pingju*), and Hubei opera (*Chuju*) revised the old tales of patriotic heroes to rally the masses against foreign invaders.

Ouyang Yuqian, the third founding father of spoken drama, began his spoken drama career in Japan, where he participated in the Chinese student performance of *The Black Slave Cries Out to Heaven* (*Heinu yutian lu*, 1907), a dramatic adaptation of Harriet Beecher Stowe's novel *Uncle Tom's Cabin*, staged by the Spring Willow Society (*Chunliu she*). In the first two decades of the twentieth century, Ouyang became known for his early spoken drama scripts, such as *After Returning Home* (*Huijia yihou*, 1922), still regarded as one of the key canonical texts of the May Fourth period (X. Chen 2010: 7–8). Faulting the then popular May Fourth belief that China must learn from the West how to build a strong nation through science and democracy, *After Returning Home* pointed to the negative American influences on

Chinese intellectuals and, by extension, on Chinese society and traditions at large. The sad, backward "prison house" in rural China in other well-known plays of the period is transformed, in Ouyang's play, into an idyllic landscape where the Western-bound traveler finds love, tranquility, understanding, and forgiveness in an arranged marriage, one of the most venerable traditional practices attacked by the May Fourth generation. It was therefore understandable that Hong Shen, in his introduction to the first anthology of modern Chinese drama, published in 1935, would point out that, if produced carelessly, the play could easily have been interpreted as a "shallow" piece that expressed a reaction against "the overseas students" and, by extension, Hong implied, against the progressive, iconoclastic agendas of the May Fourth Movement (Hong Shen 1935: 70).

More so than Tian and Hong, Ouyang was well versed in Western dramaturgy and Peking opera, the latter being his stronger suit and setting him apart from his two peers. In fact, his claim to mastery of the art was almost equal to that of Mei Lanfang; whereas he was the master performer of Peking opera in the south, Mei dominated the opera stage of the north, as attested to by the then popular phrase "*nan Ou bei Mei*," that is, "famous Ouyang in the South and renounced Mei in the North." In 1927, Ouyang joined Tian Han's Southern Drama Society, for which he scripted, directed, and played the female title role of *Pan Jinlian* in the style of Peking opera. In this typical May Fourth play, the heroine of the title, portrayed as an adulteress and murderess in the traditional novel *Water Margin*, is transformed into a brave modern woman who rebels against the patriarchal society and its arranged marital system by openly declaring her passion for Wu Song, the younger brother of her husband, whom she has murdered. Whereas the script was written as a spoken drama, the familiar storyline from *Water Margin* in the traditional theater made the play a perfect candidate to be performed using the acting conventions of Peking opera, highlighted by Ouyang's supreme singing, dancing, and acting skills as a Peking opera star. Ouyang's *Pan Jinlian* therefore seamlessly combined the best dramaturgy of both spoken drama and Chinese opera, both the modern and the traditional.

Equally influential in theater history, Ouyang devoted his talents and vision to theater education. In 1918, Ouyang funded the Opera Workers Training School (Linggong xueshe) in Nantong, Jiangxi province, one of the first drama schools to train opera and spoken drama performers and new orchestras. In 1929, he established the Guangdong Theater Research Institute, which consisted of a drama school and a music school; published the *Drama Journal* (*Xiju*); and scripted several influential spoken dramas. He successfully directed Mikhailovich Tretyakov's so-called anti–Western imperialist spoken drama entitled *Roar China!* in 1930, directed a sound film entitled *New Peach Blossom Fan* (*Xin Taohua shan*) in 1934, and scripted and directed a new Gui opera (*Guiju*) entitled *Liang Hongyu*. Ouyang's pioneering efforts in reforming a minor subgenre of Guangxi opera culminated in 1939, during the war period, in his funding of a Gui opera school in Guilin, while at the same time retaining his leadership role in scripting and directing spoken dramas in collaboration with Tian Han and other artists.

Ouyang's creative energies were celebrated half a century later in 2009 when the Guangxi Gui Opera Troupe staged a Gui opera entitled *Ouyang Yuqian*, which recounted his ingenious success in rescuing Gui opera from extinction and his passionate support for, and professional training of, young opera actresses. Could this single opera from 2009, some audiences and critics asked, really revive Gui opera and prevent it from extinction, in the now highly commercialized contemporary theater scene, in the same way Ouyang's contemporaries had wondered in the late 1930s? Even though it might be hard to justify a positive answer to the fate of this small, regional opera, scholars have noted that, thanks to his record of success in the Republican period, Ouyang was appointed president of the China Central Drama Academy in 1950, which originally included professional training in spoken drama, Western-style opera, and dance, and in 1952 began to specialize in spoken drama only (J. Dong and Hu 2008: 10).

Around that time, in the budding years of the newly founded PRC, the theater circle witnessed a historically unprecedented great unity, when artists who had worked either in the Nationalist-occupied areas or in the Communist-occupied areas, either in traditional operas or in spoken drama, joined forces in building a national theater system, which included state-sponsored professional training schools, professional and semi-professional theaters, and amateur performing troupes at all branches and levels of the government, from the municipal and the provincial all the way to the national level. One estimate listed about 3,000 troupes that had officially registered with the government in the early 1950s (J. Dong and Hu 2008: 11). Perhaps unparalleled in any other national theater history, a large majority of previously starving artists, struggling private theater troupes, and unemployed script writers, actors, and actresses had now been assigned salaried jobs, on government payrolls, with guaranteed "rice-bowls" with health and retirement benefits and, most important, social prestige. State sponsorship led to the rapid development of theater as an important cultural institution in promoting a new state ideology, which all three founding fathers of modern theater had embraced, and they have remained as visionary leaders after 1949 through their administrative posts. Their collaborations before 1949 had also helped construct the blueprints for socialist realism, a dominant trend in the Maoist period.

Irreconcilable Dramatic Conflicts: "Class Struggle" or Greek Theater Recreated?

Modern drama histories credit three founding fathers as having pioneered and promoted the social function of theater, with the task of transforming Chinese audiences into modern and enlightened citizens through the dramatic arts. They all supposedly spoke for average citizens and spoke against their sufferings in an unjust society of class exploitation and oppression. A struggling playwright himself in search of a theater, Tian Han, for example, depicted the sorrows and struggles of the artist in his early writings, such as *Violin and Rose* (*Fan'elin yu qiangwei*, 1920), and he continued in this vein in his major plays, written and performed at the peak of the Southern

Drama Society movement. In his more mature plays of the 1930s, Tian scripted a series of spoken dramas on the everyday struggles of the working class, as seen in his most successful play, *The Raining Season (Meiyu,* 1931) (B. Chen and Dong 1989: 260–263).

Against such a dominant political reading of the Maoist period, scholars in the post-Mao period naturally criticized the strict censorship that had controlled literary production and reception. In the process, they singled out "class struggle" as a favored theme at the expense of artistic innovations—especially during the Cultural Revolution, when carrying out a fierce class struggle between the proletariat and the bourgeoisie and other reactionary forces became the overarching storyline of some of the model theater productions. According to the same logic, the best plays in the post-Mao period have finally returned to the May Fourth spirit of humanism, enlightenment, freedom, and individuality. The movement to "depoliticize theater" has therefore brought about a new renaissance of realist and experimental theater, according to several recent drama histories.

Either emphasized as an indispensable theme, which had created "great" theater in the Maoist period, or blamed as the reason why brilliant playwrights such as Cao Yu had failed to produce "masterpieces" after 1949, class struggle has been singled out as key dramatic conflict, for better or worse. However, I argue, in the second part of this chapter, that Chinese dramatists have in fact ingeniously "put new wine into an old bottle" (*jiuping zhuang xinjiu*): they juxtaposed key Western dramatic concepts, such as oppositional forces in the universe, with "class struggle" by structuring irreconcilable dramatic conflicts, therefore combining the social theories of Marxism, Leninism, and Mao Zedong Thought with Western dramaturgy. By so doing, they skillfully blended content with form, socialist proletariat spirit with capitalist bourgeois art, the East with the West, the modern with the traditional, and ideological function with aesthetic pursuits.

Tian Han's most accomplished play, *The Death of a Famous Actor (Mingyou zhisi,* 1927), for example, has been interpreted as "an excellent realist work that had illustrated social problems and hence reflected Tian's revolutionary thought," with "a theme of exposing the dark, semi-colonial and semi-feudalist Chinese society through a dramatization of the tragic life of an artist" (B. Chen and Dong 1989: 253–254). Partially basing his play on the true story of the tragic death of a brilliant Peking opera actor who had also excelled in spoken drama performance, Tian created the character of Master Liu in "a play within a play"—that is, an inner play in which Liu performs his operatic dramatic role onstage, and an outer play in which his real-life struggle to survive is revealed in the form of spoken drama.

At the play's outset, Master Liu is upset with his apprentice Liu Fengxian, because, after becoming a star, she no longer bothers practicing her art. She has lapsed into a materialistic lifestyle, going out with Master Yang, a rich man who passes his time seeking out beautiful women backstage. Crestfallen at seeing the shattering of his dream of training "talented" and "loyal apprentices," Master Liu collapses onstage in reaction to some people in the audience, who have been provoked by Master Yang into heckling him. He leaves behind a grief-stricken Liu Fengxian, now painfully aware that she would give anything to bring back her dear master and surrogate father by whom she was raised and transformed from orphan to opera star.

Despite the play's somber ending, however, Tian attributed to one of the characters—a progressive friend of Master Liu—his own optimistic view that society in the future would appreciate artists. Sooner or later, this friend assures Master Liu, this world will have to change for the better. Opera singers will have a new life in which they can sing to their hearts' content onstage and rest comfortably when they are not performing. Liu's friend likewise expresses Tian's own bitterness at the unjust treatment of performers: "Why does the life of the most famous actor of an entire generation end with such a tragic death!" (Tian Han 1927: 356–357).

While not erasing this possible reading in terms of class conflict, one could also interpret Master Liu's fate as sharing similar features with Yeats's concept of examining a tragic hero's opposing will, which forces him "to the ultimate confrontation with self and reality that leads both to the tragic defeat and unification with the higher sphere" (Carlson 1984: 306). Seen in this light, Master Liu's tragic fall—on stage and in real life—can be perceived as an artist's utter failure in his life's journey: having excelled in theatrical arts, he still fails to capture his audiences, and hence succumbs to the powerful force of the universe that exhausts an artist; the irreconcilable forces between the higher realm of art and an artist's limited ability to combat it parallel neatly the theme of class conflict. The opposing force in this play could be at once the ills of an oppressive society and the unforeseeable forces in the universe. The universal theme of "the individual versus society," therefore, cuts both ways in a social–political reading and an aesthetic rendering, which stresses the essence of dramatic conflicts in Western dramaturgy.

Seen in this light, we can better appreciate the complex reception history of Cao Yu's *Thunderstorm* (*Leiyu*, 1934), one of the best Chinese spoken dramas of the twentieth century by most critics' accounts. At age 24, upon the play's publication, Cao enjoyed almost immediate recognition, something none of his predecessors had known. Indeed, *Thunderstorm* heralded the arrival of Chinese drama's golden age in which the best of Western drama melded with equally compelling Chinese situations and characters. Its premiere in Tokyo in 1935, however, fashioned an ideological reading of *Thunderstorm* that defined the history of its subsequent reception for the rest of the twentieth century. The critics interpreted the point of the love triangles and incest stories to be the exposure of an evil, bourgeois family shaken by a "thunderstorm" that forecast its eventual downfall. Similarly, the initial Chinese production of *Thunderstorm*, prompted by the same political reading, interpreted the play as a critique of Chinese society's unhealthy marital and ethical system (Feng Jiao 1935) and as a clear indication of the arrival of a great new era (Bai Mei 1935).

Confronted with these leftist readings, Cao defended himself by claiming that *Thunderstorm* was not a social problem play; it was, rather, driven by his desire to express certain surging, primitive, and irresistible emotions that could not be rationally explained. Cao would have agreed with an earlier twentieth-century

Western call for drama's engagement with its public through "emotional tension" resulting from "the struggle of will against will" (Carlson 1984: 333). Seeing the play in this light, one can argue that every character in *Thunderstorm* is engaged with internal conflicts against his/her opposing desires, even in the case of Zhou Puyuan, the so-called antagonist who victimizes the women in his life and their sons in "a big, evil family." Zhou, for example, repents having deserted Lu Shipin, his first love, 30 years ago, by preserving her old furniture. In the preface and the epilogue, a sad, lonely Zhou had turned the Zhou mansion into a Catholic mental hospital in order to take care of the two insane women he had mistreated, to whom Zhou paid frequent visits so that he could redeem himself. Cao's complaint about the preface and the epilogue of his play being elided in the play's premiere in Tokyo did not prevent them from being similarly dropped from subsequent performances and anthologies; the exclusion of them could more easily render a leftist reading of the play as revealing a theme of "class struggle" between Lu Dahua, Zhou's son, who participates in a workers' strike against his father, a capitalist who now has no redeeming qualities without the context of the preface and epilogue.

Perhaps thanks to the rich potential for diverse interpretations, Cao's amazing play enjoyed a long history of frequent performances, accompanied by continued justifications of its political readings. So much was this the case that, after the founding of the PRC in 1949, Cao himself fully embraced the leftist, anti-feudalist theme, which, he claimed, had only later become clear to him after critics had pointed it out. He regretted having hewed to his "fatalist approach" to explain entangled family relationships and failing to portray Zhou Puyuan as an evil member of the declining bourgeois class (Cao Yu 1996). Yet, during the Cultural Revolution, *Thunderstorm* was singled out as a "reactionary attack" on the working class because of its weak characterization of Lu Dahai (Tian Benxiang 1988: 424). In post-Mao China, after the Cultural Revolution radicals were ousted in 1976, *Thunderstorm* was staged again to celebrate the end of the 10-year disaster and the beginning of a new era of renaissance, and it has since been adapted into several regional traditional operas, as well as ballet and folk dance dramas. The post-Mao drama history, nevertheless, still clings to a political reading that celebrates the play's ingenious plot and characters *and* its timely theme of a workers' strike against a heartless capitalist, therefore reflecting "struggles between two confrontational classes" (B. Chen and Dong 1989: 398). The best of the spoken dramas, critics and scholars seem to agree, are those timeless masterpieces that seamlessly combine artistic innovations with a pertinent message advocating for social change.

More so than that of Cao Yu and Tian Han, the legacy of Hong Shen in postsocialist China continues to be that of a pioneer of a realist theater most useful for political propaganda. In the twenty-first century, for example, Hong is blamed for having initiated and promoted a "utilitarian concept of theater" that used to dominate the stage and eventually led to the ultra-leftist model theater of the Cultural Revolution (Song Baozhen 2002: 243). Hong's rural trilogy, written in the 1930s, has likewise been celebrated for its depictions of a poverty-stricken rural China where poor peasants confronted rich landlords who had exploited them in the Republican period. Such a political reading—in part thanks to Hong's own writing of drama history—runs contrary to the internal contradictions embodied in Hong's best plays.

In fact, Hong's rich and multifaceted theater defies easy classification either in terms of "isms" or "schools" and cannot be simply interpreted as either politically or artistically oriented. In the first play in Hong's rural trilogy, *Wukui Bridge* (*Wukui qiao*), a confrontation between rich gentry and poor peasants provides a dramatic conflict between two powerful oppositional forces that defy reconciliation. This is similar to the spirit of the Greek tragedy *Antigone*, in which Antigone's determination to bury her brother Polyneices, to fulfill her duty as a sister, is matched by the equally persuasive resolve of Creon, the king of the land, to observe the law of the state rather than honor a traitor (Polyneices). By the same token, in *Wukui Bridge,* a group of poor villagers are determined to demolish the bridge to clear the way for a boat carrying a Western-made pump that will provide desperately needed water for their rice fields during a severe drought. They are met with stubborn obstruction from Mr. Zhou, a rich member of the gentry whose ancestors had built the bridge, in an effort to protect the "geomantic elements" (*fengshui*) of his land and the local community. Here, Hong ingeniously combined his pursuit of an aesthetic theater with his newly discovered concept of class struggle in structuring dramatic conflicts into a "well-made play" (*jiagou ju*) (X. Chen 2014: 228–230).

Hong's overarching interest in structuring irreconcilable dramatic conflicts prompted some left-wing critics to attack the last play in his trilogy, entitled *Qinglong Pond* (*Qinglong tan*), for its confused depiction of Sha Xiaoda, a young peasant who insists on building a new road by cutting down cherry trees—the source of the villagers' livelihood—in a year of severe drought. After the drought gets worse, older peasants in the village finally give in to Sha's idea of building a road in exchange for a foreign-made pump to bring water to the distressed fields. The pump, however, comes too late to save the crops; worse still, Sha now frenziedly throws himself into the praying-for-rain rituals, against which he had originally fought. Hong's insights into the peasants' ignorance, superstition, and selfishness prompted left-wing critics to point to Hong's "narrow-minded realism" that kept him at a distance from the peasants without a real understanding of them (M. Chen and Song 1996: 146). From the point of view of scriptwriting, however, one could emphasize Hong's skill in structuring a rapidly developing dramatic crisis, which sees the essence of drama through "the art of crisis" in "destiny or circumstance" in "clearly furthering the ultimate event," as explained by William Archer, an early-twentieth-century Western theater critic (Carlson 1984: 309). Hong's interest in uncompromising conflicts *within* individuals, and with his peers and his environment, challenges a one-dimensional theme of class struggle, while leaving room for those who choose to pursue this line of political reading. His so-called failed attempt in critical realist theater, nevertheless, in part points to the rich potential of multiple meanings beyond a particular school or approach.

Similar examples can be found in the first 17 years (1949–1966) of the PRC, when socialist realist theater dominated the stage. The official ideology promoted three kinds of plays—the workers play, the peasants play, and the soldiers play—in order to portray the new life of the masses in socialist China as a contrast to their "sufferings" in the "old society" of the Republican period. A "fourth kind of theater" (*disizhong xiju*), however, emerged briefly to test this boundary, as seen in the reception of a controversial play entitled *Joys and Sorrows* (*Tonggan gongku*, 1956), written by Yue Ye. The play features Meng Shijing, a high-ranking Party official who is torn between his desire for his ex-wife and his love for his current wife, with whom he "fell in love" during the revolutionary war period. He is confused, however, when his ex-wife, Liu Fangwen from the countryside, pays a visit with their child in his city home, and she impresses him as a new woman who has transformed herself from a victim of an arranged marriage in the old society into a dynamic Party leader in the collective farming movement in her home village.

The love triangle in this play was indeed a breath of fresh air in 1950s theater, which, similar to other genres in literature and arts, rarely depicted romantic stories in order to promote loyalty to the Party, the people, and the new socialist nation. In its plot, *Joys and Sorrows* strongly resembles Ouyang Yuqian's *After Returning Home* (discussed earlier): Liu reminds us of Wu Zifang in the latter play, as the virtuous and formidable wife from the countryside. The problem arises, however, with the regime change from the Nationalist rule in the Republican era to the Communist "new society": when Lu Zhiping, an American-educated man, returns home to "embrace" his rural wife through arranged marriage in *After Returning Home*, he challenges his Western education and its embedded values, as a result revealing the confusion of a modern man in pre-1949 society. *Joys and Sorrows*, however, allows a high-ranking Party official to repeat the dilemma of a May Fourth man, therefore rejecting the progress of history in the socialist experience, by pairing a Party leader with his liberal counterpart before the liberation.

Most significantly, Liu's transformation into an emancipated Party leader illustrates the gain of women's liberation in socialist China, where they now "hold half of the sky," with equal pay and equal rights. On the other hand, however, her dual image of being at once *traditional* (with a soft voice and total acceptance of her man) and *revolutionary* (with sophisticated knowledge of the socialist experience in her village) paradoxically critiques her ex, the very image of the Party official, whose changing taste in women disqualifies him as an exemplary representative who is thus expected to be faithful to his wife. Yet, as shown in the most ingenious part of the plot, Meng's dramatic action fits the very profile of a good Party official: his position as the deputy director of the Department of Agriculture in a provincial Party committee makes it natural for him to feel drawn to Liu, whose enthusiasm for bringing change to her home village provides him with new visions for his own leadership role.

Their common interests and rural roots—a theme that would have been desirable in a "peasants play" under normal circumstances without a complex triangular relationship—nevertheless did not prevent the play from being criticized, during the Anti-Rightist Campaign of 1957, as a "Rightist play" for its "attack on the Party and its officials," in spite of its popular productions by many theater troupes across the country. At the heart of the matter, however, we see a typical case of "new wine in an old bottle": a socialist realist theater reflecting the great changes in the country, and in celebration of women's liberation, provides the new context of the play; the old bottle, however, still holds a time-honored love story, in which a male protagonist struggles with his opposing desires for two types of woman. Their binary opposites intensify his emotional experience in a universal struggle in search of true love, which is all the more alluring when no longer available. When a new socialist man becomes equally confused by his choices in women, as his predecessor did in the 1920s, the play implicitly speaks against the still-male-dominated new era when a Party leader continues to be troubled by the "true" value of women and their "proper" place in history.

It is thus no wonder that post-Mao and postsocialist theater history has singled out *Joys and Sorrows* as one of the few exceptional plays produced in the first 17 years of the PRC, which had briefly pushed the boundaries of the ultra-leftist, dogmatic approach to theater (J. Dong and Hu 2008: 13–14). Against the norms of the high Mao period, moreover, *Joys and Sorrows* did not depict any of its characters as either positive or negative, critics argued, but explored instead their "inner world" and "complex emotional experience" in their personal relationships at the time of social changes, while exposing the emerging problems among the Communist leaders in an increasingly bureaucratic and authoritarian society (J. Dong and Hu 2008: 65–66). Here, we see once again how the "old bottle" shared similar traits in Hong Shen's well-made play in terms of dramatic conflicts; the "new wine" now relates to the specific, emotional experience of the Chinese people around 1956 in the context of social changes in early Maoist China. In the postsocialist period, drama historians once again "refill" the old bottle with its own "new wine," which has finally restored the play to its original place in theater history, in praise of its dramaturgy.

The same can be argued for post-Mao theater in the 1980s–1990s, when experimental theater coexisted with realist theater, and traditional Chinese operas in their various regional forms shared the spotlight with modern spoken drama, borrowing from each other's techniques and conventions to enrich their aesthetic appeals. In realist theater, Yang Limin's *Geologists* (*Dizhi shi*, 1997) examined the "afterlife" of the revolutionary legacy of the Maoist era, and its impact on the lives of young scientists in the next three decades. *Geologists* has four acts, set in 1961, 1964, 1977, and 1994, respectively, covering high Mao culture, the early post-Mao life, and the Deng reform period with its rapid modernization and globalization. The play takes pains to address questions: What inspired and frustrated them as dedicated geologists working in the remote and desolate region? Do they have any regrets? These issues ultimately speak to the values, pitfalls, and sorrows of idealism, socialism, utopianism, postsocialism, capitalism, modernism, and globalization in contemporary Chinese life. *Geologists* evokes the nostalgia, compassion, frustration, and forgiveness of an entire generation of Chinese scientists, who long for some sort of spiritual strength comparable to what they experienced during the Mao era, and this longing, still unmarred by their experience during the Cultural Revolution, becomes the only memory worth holding on to.

The play apparently related to the contemporary audience in its social content, but this "new wine" of a postsocialist reflection on socialist experience is still housed in the old bottle of a triangle love story: Lu Jing longs for the unavailable Luo Ming, but she cannot be united with him, since Luo Ming does not want her to follow him to work in the remote area; he feels she does not deserve the harsh life. Lu is stuck in her unhappy marriage to Luo Dasheng, a geologist who was transferred back to Beijing, an initially lucky break that has unfortunately brought him a mediocre career as a bureaucrat with no academic success to boast of. At the end of the play, when the three college classmates reunite in Lu's apartment in Beijing three decades later, Luo Ming breaks into tears, mourning the loss of his love in spite of his newly found international fame as a top geologist. The universal love story dramatizes the deep pathos and despair of the protagonists and their contradictory desires—to pursue career or love, to venture afar or stay home-bound, to be true to one's own self or to conform to social norms.

Here, we see another instance in which the new wine of postsocialist critiques of the Maoist experience works perfectly well with the old bottle of irreconcilable dramatic conflicts within oneself and with one's peers in the universe. The popular reception of *Geologists* also marked the success story of a key genre known as "main melody drama" (*zhuxuanlü xiju*), which promotes the official ideology of socialist culture (J. Dong and Hu 2008: 280). By the 1990s, dramatists' attempts to overcome the "drama crisis" had resulted in the parallel development of three genres: (1) "main melody" or mainstream plays, sponsored by state initiatives and financial support; (2) experimental or avant-garde theater, which pushed the boundaries in theatrical innovations and realist traditions while imitating various schools of Western modernist theater; and (3) commercial theater, operated by private theater producers, which gestured toward an emergent "independent theater" (*minjian xiju*) and a theater market, thereby providing a new challenge to the mainstream theater practices and their official culture (J. Dong and Hu 2008: 280–282). Coexisting with these three trends in spoken drama, traditional operas from numerous regions also flourished, especially in the ancient-costume genre (*guzhuang xi*), which has revived classical stories while making them relevant to contemporary life in terms of thematic concerns and dramatic conflicts. By the same token, performances in contemporary-costume genres (*shizhuang xi*) also shared spoken drama's concern with social problems, such as the corruption and bureaucracy of the Party, and its representations of revolutionary war heroes, in order to remind the ruling powers never to forget the Chinese people who had sacrificed their lives to put them in power. Realist, experimental, commercial, or otherwise, both spoken drama and operatic theater have attempted to relate to contemporary audiences in order to carve out a meaningful, albeit increasingly limited, space of their own.

References

Bai, Mei 白梅. 1935. "*Leiyu* de piban" 《雷雨》 的批判 (The critique of *Thunderstorm*). *Dagongbao* 大公報 (Dagong news) (Aug. 20–23).

Cao, Yu 曹禺. 1996. "Wo dui jinhou chuangzuo de chubu renshi" 我對今後創作的初步認識 (Preliminary thoughts on how to proceed with my writing in the future). In *Cao Yu quanji* 曹禺全集 (Complete works of Cao Yu). Vol. 5. Beijing: Huashan wenyi chubanshe. 44–48.

Carlson, Marvin. 1984. *Theories of the Theatre*. Ithaca, NY: Cornell University Press.

Chen, Baichen 陳白塵, and Dong Jian 董健. 1989. *Zhongguo xiandai xiju shigao* 中國現代戲劇史稿 (A draft history of modern Chinese drama). Beijing: Zhongguo xiju chubanshe.

Chen, Meiying 陳美英, and Song Baozhen 宋寶珍.1996. *Hong Shen zhuan* 洪深傳 (A biography of Hong Shen). Beijing: Wenhuayishu chubanshe.

Chen, Xiaomei. 1995. *Occidentalism: A Theory of Counter-discourse in Post-Mao China*. New York: Oxford University Press.

Chen, Xiaomei. 2014. "Mapping a 'New' Dramatic Canon: Rewriting the Legacy of Hong Shen." In *Modern China and the West: Translation and Cultural Mediation*. Edited by Peng Hsiao-yen and Isabelle Rabur. Leiden: Brill. 224–245.

Chen, Xiaomei. Ed. 2010. *The Columbia Anthology of Modern Chinese Drama with a Critical Introduction*. New York: Columbia University Press.

Chen, Xiaomei. 2006. "Reflections on the Legacy of Tian Han: 'Proletarian Modernism' and its Traditional Roots." *Modern Chinese Literature and Culture*, 18.1: 155–215.

Dong, Jian 董健, and Hu Xingliang 胡星亮. 2008. *Zhongguo dangdai xiju shigao* 中國當代戲劇史稿 (A draft history of contemporary Chinese drama). Beijing: Zhongguo xiju chubanshe.

Feng, Jiao 馮椒. 1935. "*Leiyu* de yuyan" 《雷雨》的預演 (The preview of *Thunderstorm*). *Dagongbao* (Aug. 17–18).

Ge, Yihong 葛一虹. 1990. *Zhongguo huaju tongshi* 中國話劇通史 (A history of modern Chinese drama). Beijing: Wenhua yishu chubanshe.

Hong, Shen 洪深. 1935. "Daoyan" 導言 (Introduction). In *Zhongguo xin wenxue daxi: xijuji* 中國新文學大係:戲劇集 (Compendium of new Chinese literature, drama volume), Edited by Hong Shen. Shanghai: Liangyou. 1–10.

Hong, Shen 洪深. 1936. "Xiju de rensheng" 戲劇的人生 (A life of drama). In *Hong Shen wenji* 洪深文集 (Selected works of Hong Shen). Vol. 1. Beijing: Zhongguo xiju chubanshe, 1957. 474–488.

Hong, Shen 洪深. 1948. "Kangzhan shinian lai Zhongguo de xiju yundong yu jiaoyu" 抗戰十年來中國的戲劇運動與教育 (Chinese theater movement and education during the ten-years of war of resistance against Japan). In *Hong Shen wenji*. Vol. 4. Beijing: Zhongguo xiju chubanshe, 1957. 121–261.

Hu, Xingliang 胡星亮. 2000. *Zhongguo xiquyu Zhongguo huaju* 中國戲曲與中國話劇 (Chinese opera and Chinese spoken drama). Shanghai: Xuelin chubanshe.

Liu, Ping 劉平. 1998. *Xijuhun: Tian Han ping zhuan* 戲劇魂—田漢評傳 (The soul of drama: Tian Han). Beijing: Zhongyangwenxian chubanshe.

Song, Baozhen 宋寶珍. 2002. *Canque de xiju chibang* 殘缺的戲劇翅膀 (*The injured wings oftheater*). Beijing: Beijing guangbo xueyuan chubanshe.

Tian, Benxiang 田本相. 1988. *Cao Yu zhuan* 曹禺傳 (A biography of Cao Yu). Beijing: Shiyue wenyi chubanshe.

Tian, Han 田漢. 1927. *Minyou zhisi* 名優之死 (*The Death of a Famous Actor*). In *Tian Han quanji* 田漢全集 (Complete works of Tian Han). Shijiazhuang: Huashan wenyi chubanshe, 2000. Vol. 1: 321–357.

Wang, Weiguo 王衛國, Song Baozhen 宋寶珍, and Zhang Yaojie 張耀杰. 1998. *Zhongguo huaju shi* 中國話劇史 (A history of modern Chinese theater). Beijing: Wenhuayishu chubanshe.

11

Literariness (*Wen*) and Character (*Zhi*): From *Baihua* to *Yuluti* and *Dazhongyu*

Qian Suoqiao

The Triumph of the Vernacular *Baihua*

Ithaca, New York. A group of Chinese students had happened to gather here for the summer of 1915. They included Hu Shi, Zhao Yuanren, Mei Guangdi, Ren Hongjun, Yang Quan, and Tang Yue. Over their summer conversations, a literary revolution began brooding. In fact, it was not going to be merely a "literary revolution" but rather a "cultural revolution" that would usher Chinese culture irreversibly into modernity. The topic of their discussion, or debate, was the Chinese language, or the modernity of the Chinese language. Hu Shi, against the objection of most of his fellow students, claimed that the Chinese language was dead! Or, the Chinese written language, *wenyan*, which had been in practice for several thousand years and in which all respectable Chinese literature was composed, was a dead language, or at least half-dead. Instead, Hu Shi said, the vernacular Chinese, or *baihua*, should be upgraded as an interim national language, to be replaced eventually by a phonetic system of writing based on the Chinese vernacular. Hu Shi's call for a "literary revolution" to proclaim the death of the classical Chinese among his fellow students was basically ignored and ridiculed.

The summer passed, but the debate lingered on. As Hu Shi (1998: 1: 140–163) recounts in "Forced to the Path of Revolution" ("*Bishang liangshan*," 1934), it was precisely the objections from his fellow students that enabled him to formulate his ideas for a "literary revolution" more clearly and firmly. Since Hu Shi could only find unsympathetic resistance from his fellow students in the United States, he tried to seek allies elsewhere—from a group of revolution-minded returned students from Japan. Chen Duxiu had already launched *New Youth* in Shanghai in 1915, which was to become the

A Companion to Modern Chinese Literature, First Edition. Edited by Yingjin Zhang.

signature journal for the New Culture Movement. Hu Shi wrote to Chen with his ideas for a literary revolution and got Chen's immediate enthusiastic support. Hu's essay "A Preliminary Proposal for Literary Reform" was published on *New Youth* (Vol. 3, No. 1, March 1917), which ignited the literary revolution and consequently an entire epistemic change of Chinese culture. Chen's unrelenting support on the key issue of the literary revolution, namely, proclaiming the death of the written classical Chinese and the rebirth of *baihua*, was not only forceful but dogmatic, as Chen (1917: n.p.) put it in his reply to Hu Shi:

> The call for the literary reform has already been made and heard in the country, supporters and opponents are half and half. Your idea is to allow different opinions for free discussion, which is of course a sound principle for academic development. However, in terms of reforming Chinese literature and affirming the vernacular as the canonical literature, what is right and what is wrong is already self-evident. We must not allow any room for discussion with our opponents. We must uphold our claims as absolutely correct and must not allow any rectification by our opponents.

The definitive accomplishment of the New Culture Movement was the triumph of *baihua*: by the early 1920s, merely a few years after Hu Shi's 1917 essay, *baihua* had become the dominant "national language" used in journals and newspapers nationwide.

This dramatic change in the medium of Chinese writing was quite surprising. The Chinese written language, *wenyan*, had been in use for several thousand years since the beginning of Chinese civilization, and was being widely practiced and recognized as the literary language. Hu Shi's opponents such as Mei Guangdi was certainly right in ridiculing Hu's statement that *wenyan* was dead or half-dead, since you cannot possibly claim a living medium of expression dead or half-dead merely because certain phrases had more colloquial means of expression. Indeed, it was a hilarious accusation that denied the complex contours of development of *wenyan* over different dynastic cycles, which carried very much the finest oeuvres of Chinese literature.

However, that was precisely the point. *Wenyan* was *proclaimed* dead. In other words, Hu Shi and other New Culturalists wanted it to be dead, and successfully achieved their goal in a matter of several years. In addition to the radical push of the New Culturalists, this success was possible thanks to both internal and external factors. Internally, *baihua* writing had in fact been in existence for a thousand years ever since the translation of Buddhism began. In Song dynasty, influenced by Buddhist translations, Neo-Confucianists were recording their philosophy in vernacular *yuluti*, not to mention the flourishing of the vernacular drama in Yuan and *xiaoshuo* or fiction in Ming and Qing dynasties. Yet, the development of Chinese writing had its own logic, and the existence and relevance of these vernacular writings did not even constitute part of its discursive concern, that is, not until Hu Shi and other New Culturalists pointed this out. And their inspiration definitely came from Western influences. Using European literary and cultural history as their frame of reference, Hu Shi saw that the advance of European vernacular languages to replace the classical Latin was at the core of the European Renaissance. And it was believed that the vernacular and phonetic nature of European languages were key factors that enabled the educational and cultural superiority of Europe. By the 1910s, Chinese intellectuals' confidence in the self-sufficiency of the Confucian politico-cultural system had already been shattered over China's disastrous defeat in the First Sino-Japanese War of 1895, which signaled the bankruptcy of the Self-Strengthening Movement of the earlier period. The establishment of the ROC in 1912 did not help much to boost such confidence. Rather, the focus of Chinese self-reflection was shifting to the alleged cultural defects of Chinese tradition. The notion that the Chinese written language was inadequate or incompatible with modernity had already emerged. This is partly due to the great enterprise of translating all kinds of Western documents, literary or non-literary, into classical *wenyan* (ironically!). Western missionaries had also long begun to translate the Bible into local dialect phonetic scripts. Indeed, compared to the more radical call to annihilate all Chinese characters and transcribe Chinese into a phonetic script system, which a large group of modern Chinese intellectuals were convinced must happen, the vernacular revolution seemed a much more sensible and practical interim solution.

Of course, the phonetic replacement of Chinese characters did not happen, but *baihua* has become the standard "modern Chinese," constituting a defining feature of Chinese cultural modernity. This is of course not merely a matter of the change of the writing medium. It is a literary and cultural revolution, out of which the Chinese literary tradition was re-evaluated and re-canonized. And, indeed, new concepts of "literature" were born, and literary writings were grouped into four major genres—poetry, fiction, drama, and prose—in line with modern Western conventions. The modernity of mapping Chinese literature along such categorization of the four genres was readily recognized and pointed out by literary historians (Chen Pingyuan 2005). Nevertheless, contemporary literary historians are more inclined to producing grand narratives of a "history" of Chinese poetry or fiction. To investigate and identify key *problematiques* of modern Chinese prose, it would be more useful to highlight ruptures and re-connections between tradition and modernity. It is from such ruptures and re-connections that we can see the birth pangs of modern Chinese prose that are still very much with us today.

Until the literary revolution of the 1910s, Chinese literary writings can be broadly grouped into two genres: *shi* (poetry) and *wen* (literary writings or prose). Chinese culture is a poetic one, and the importance and prestige of poetry in Chinese culture perhaps surpasses that in any other culture. Ever since *The Book of Songs*, which is one of the canonical classics, Chinese poetry has followed its own contour of development with sub-genres such as *fu* in Han dynasty and *ci* in Song dynasty. Besides poetry, the rest of Chinese literary writings, *wenzhang*, can all be called prose, which also had its own features of development with many more sub-genres and its own contentions in different dynastic periods. Broadly speaking, since the boom of Chinese writing in the Classical Period during the Spring and Autumn and Warring States times, Chinese prose evolved into a form of rhythmic prose, or *pianwen*, through the later Han and Six

Dynasties, in which extravagant literary embellishment characterized by parallelism and ornateness were cherished features. As a reaction to such "literariness" (*wen*), Tang and Song dynasties produced great prose writers—the so-called Great Eight Prose Writers (*Tang Song ba dajia*)—out of the Classical Movement (*guwen yundong*), which calls for a "return" to the Classical style of writing that emphasizes "substance" and "character" (*dao* or *zhi*) rather than literary embellishment (*wen*). And in Ming and Qing, there was another Classical Movement whose representatives from the Tongcheng School were precisely the authoritative and prestigious literary figures against whom the New Culturist revolutionaries targeted and rebelled.

During this long and complicated debate in the history of Chinese prose, vernacular writings did not even come into the discourse, since they were considered to be vulgar and marginal for low-class popular entertainment consumption. However, for Hu Shi, who also characterized the history of Chinese writing in terms of the *problematique* of *wen* (literariness, embellishment) and *zhi* (substance, character), all Chinese writings in classical *wenyan*, and particularly those from Tongcheng School of writers, were too "literary" and lacking real substance. And, to remedy that, you need to look in the hitherto neglected vernacular writings. However, Hu's opponents were rather scornful of Hu's assessment of the vernacular: Chinese literature as literature, whether poetry or prose, relies first of all on literati's cultivation of language. If the raw speech of street vendors were all works of literature, what is a writer for and what is literature? Hu Shi's answer was: it is up to you and me—modern enlightened intellectuals—to create and bring forth vernacular writings worthy of literature for our modern times.

Since the vernacular became the standard "national language," modern Chinese writing was liberated in terms of its production. If we follow the traditional categorization of literature into *shi* (poetry or rhymed works) and *wen* (prose or all non-rhymed writings), modern Chinese prose achieved unprecedented development and accomplishments in terms of its quantity and expansion of new horizons. There emerged many new types of expository writings, such as political treatise, philosophical essays, scientific treatise, popular scientific writings, not to mention journalistic writings, reportage, and so on. Hu Shi alone produced voluminous writings of many kinds, including academic treatises, biographies, and political and cultural commentaries. Hu Shi's prose follows a distinctive style: clear, succinct, no literary allusions, easy to understand, just as the way you speak, which is precisely what *baihua* should be like as he advocated. One can hardly find any effort in "cultivating" the language as such.

While I personally believe Hu's prose should occupy an important place in modern Chinese prose precisely because of that style, most literary historians would not even count Hu's prose as "literature." There we find the paradoxical dilemma of modern Chinese prose: in reference to the traditional notion, it had been significantly enriched with new horizons and new territories, but when categorized into one of the four literary genres of fiction, poetry, drama, and prose, it has achieved least importance with marginal literary status. As Chen Pingyuan (2005: 9) put it: "Before the literary revolution, literature means first of all prose (*wenzhang*), and then poetry, whereas fiction and drama don't really count; afterward, it is completely overturned: fiction and drama achieved primary status while the prestige of prose shrunk considerably." That is mainly because modern prose has been suffering from an identity crisis: the majority of its production does not really count as literature as such. Then what is really "literary" prose?

Zhou Zuoren's *Meiwen* and Lu Xun's *Zawen*

In 1923, Hu Shi assessed the accomplishments of the literary revolution in the first 5 years: compared to poetry, drama, and fiction (both short stories and novels), the vernacular prose made the most remarkable progress. In addition to *yilun wen* (critical commentaries), the most notable achievement was in *xiaopin sanwen* (little-taste essays), promoted and practiced by Zhou Zuoren, which "totally smashed the myth that '*baihua* cannot produce *meiwen* (elegant essays)'" (Hu Shi 1998: 3: 263). Hu's comments were surely farsighted, as Zhou's essay writings were merely getting started and had not attracted much attention when Hu made the high praise. It was not until 10 years later when Lin Yutang launched the literary periodicals *Lunyu* (Analects), *Renjianshi* (This human world), and *Yuzhou feng* (Cosmic wind) successively that *xiaopin* essays flourished and became a dominant force in the literary scene (Laughlin 2008).

The reason why Hu Shi called Zhou's essays *meiwen* and was elated about it was because now we could find "literary" essays written in *baihua* by contemporary writers worthy of the name "literature," therefore proving his opponents wrong in their scorn of the uncouth vernacular. Zhou Zuoren and his better-known elder brother Lu Xun (Zhou Shuren) are generally regarded as leading essayists in modern Chinese literature, the former for *xiaopin sanwen* and the latter for *zawen* (miscellaneous essays). Both leaders of the literary revolution, Lu Xun was credited with producing the first short story in *baihua*, while Zhou Zuoren was credited with developing a distinctive style of prose in *baihua*: the little-taste essay. The term "*meiwen*" was the title of one of Zhou's essays written in 1921, which Zhou claims as referring to the essay form in English literature, yet still not being practiced in China. The narrative essay, whether descriptive or lyrical, is artistic (therefore the term "*meiwen*"), and can serve as a bridge between poetry and fiction. When certain thoughts are ill-fitted to be expressed in either poetry or fiction, the artistic essay may be the best vehicle, and Zhou calls upon Chinese writers to "open up a new territory for New Literature" (Zhou 1991: 14).

Zhou was, of course, a leading New Culturalist rebel against the classical literary tradition, and he was fully aware of the cultivated style of classical prose. The distinctive style of Zhou's *baihua* prose seems intent on being stripped of "literariness": its compact size has no set structure; its narration can jump from one topic to another rather freely; and the topics are wide-ranging—particularly recurring are casual things or events at hand, as well as commentaries on his erudite readings from various (usually marginal) historical sources, domestic or foreign. His *baihua* style strives for simplicity and clarity, as if his writing came directly from plain speech between friends' conversations. And of course, Zhou's prose definitely does not "carry the Dao" (*zaidao*), as each essay does not seem to have any particular objective except for what it is. Yet, Zhou's essays are appreciated as "elegant," as they denote a distinctive aesthetics whose principles are precisely against the perceived "literariness." However, Zhou's aesthetics in fact inherits the quintessential Chinese cultural and literary tradition—the Daoist aesthetics, in which "simplicity" is appreciated as a highly cultivated principle of art. The keyword for such aesthetics is *dan*, as in *qingdan*, *pingdan*, or *chongdan*, which Ernst Wolff and Lin Yutang explain respectively as follows:

> [*Dan*] denotes the purity of a liquid that has not been adulterated, spiced, or excessively flavored. *Ch'ing-tan* [*qingdan*] then seems to emphasize mildness and purity, freedom from adulterations, admixtures, or heavy one-sided flavoring. The term "p'ing-tan" [*pingdan*] has added in *p'ing* [*ping*] a vision of an unruffled expanse of water, while the "ch'ung" [*chong*] in *ch'ung-tan* [*chongdan*] conveys the idea of rinsing out all hard and harsh colors to leave behind only shades of pastel lightness. (Wollf 1971: 26)

> *tan* [*dan*]: mild, pale in color, as of a misty lake. Probably the quality in a painting or writing that gives the greatest pleasure to a man of mature taste is *ch'ingtan* [*qingdan*] (lucid and mild), *p'ingtan* [*pingdan*] ("even and mild," the natural aroma of simple writing), or *tanyuan* [*danyuan*] (... mild-toned and "distant" in perspective, either in painting or in style of thought). A man of a retiring mild temperament is *t'ientan* [*tiandan*] (quiet and easily contented, or loving simple joys); he adopts an attitude toward money and fame described as *tanpo* [*danbo*] (mild and thin). (Lin Yutang 1937: 442)

In Zhou's little-taste essay "Wild Vegetables from Hometown" ("*Guxiang de yecai*," 1924), for instance, we have a taste of such *dan* aesthetics. When his wife bought some wild vegetables from the street markets in Beijing, as Zhou writes, that brought him to thoughts of wild vegetables in his hometown in the South. He then goes on to describe several kinds of wild vegetables common to his native hometown area. Readers will get a taste of some aspects of the authentic folk culture associated with these wild vegetables in their daily lives. Readers will also get a taste of Zhou's broad knowledge as he cites cultural and botanical annotations of these wild vegetables from both Chinese and Japanese sources. But one would hardly get a taste of any warm nostalgic feeling toward one's hometown customs and lifestyles from one's childhood memories. At the very beginning of the essay, before it touches on the topic of wild vegetables, Zhou already warns the reader that he does not have a "hometown" as such, as he had lived in many places (in both China and Japan) in his life, and he treats all the places he has lived in as his hometowns. That is certainly cool and detached. When Zhou describes the folk scenes associated with the wild vegetables in his hometown, we see images of children singing a folk song about certain wild vegetable, but we see more images of funeral ceremonies when people wear these wild vegetables as wild flowers. The essay ends with a boat scene where riders wear certain wild vegetables, which serve as a definite sign that this boat is specifically sending people to sweep tombs. This is certainly not a rosy picture, and indeed, underneath Zhou's light description, one cannot help noticing a rather chilling tone.

It would be far-fetched to infer from one essay that Zhou's aesthetics is underlined by a deep nihilistic undertone. If we look at Zhou's essays as a whole, together with his life practices, however, it is not that difficult to see the serious defect: lack of character, or in Chinese literary terminology, lack of *"fenggu."* Literary historians more or less refuse to relate Zhou's essays with his life. However, one should not forget that, in modern Chinese intellectual history, Zhou offered one of the most deplorable examples of how an intellectual loses his character and kowtows to the powers that be. This is not merely referring to his collaboration with Japanese invaders and active participation in the activities of the puppet regime, but also his subsequent kneeling under the Communist regime to beg for a bowl of rice, so to speak (Ni Moyan 2003). One important aspect of Zhou's literary aesthetics is that one should write truthfully what one observes and reflect and be reflected as such. The Chinese phrase *"wenru qiren"* (one's writing ultimately reflects one's personality) would not be a far-fetched comment on Zhou's literary practices (Daruvala 2000).

Exactly opposite to Zhou's image of a "willowy" weakling, his elder brother Lu Xun was eulogized for his "hard-bone" (*ying gutou*) spirit, as reflected particularly in his *zawen*. The Zhou brothers were both literary leaders of the New Culture Movement, and they used to live under one family house until 1923, when a quarrel associated with Zhou Zuoren's Japanese wife broke out and the brothers would never speak to each other again. They still collaborated on literary projects. For instance, both were main contributors to the *Yusi* literary periodical, though they avoided each other at the monthly gatherings of the *Yusi* group of prose writers. Their personal break-up is also symbolic of their diametrically opposed essay styles. Lu Xun treats his *zawen* as daggers (*bishou*) thrashing at his polemical enemies, real or imagined. As such, Lu Xun left us with a notoriously long list of his various enemies, and yet Lu Xun has been exalted precisely for his relentless polemical knack. His *zawen* were certainly powerful with its sharp and sarcastic tone, knowing exactly where to attack, so much so that each of his essays is "bloody," just as the dagger of an effective and skilled warrior is supposed to be. One of Lu Xun's most well-known masterpieces is his dagger directed to Liang Shiqiu (Shao Jian 2008: 298–331), entitled "'Homeless' 'Poor Running Dog of the Capitalists'" ("*Sangjia de*' '*zibenjia de fa zougou*'," 1930), which has been a standard selection in all school textbooks in the PRC (Lu Xun 1981:4: 246–249). Lu Xun's fighting spirit was so determined and unbending that, even at his death bed, in referring to his long list of polemical enemies, his last words were: "I will not forgive any single one of them" (Lu Xun 1981: 6: 612). This is indeed some character.

One wonders, though, what it is good for. We know Lu Xun's fighting spirit was exalted to be the "banner" for the Communist revolutionary cause, and indeed, for Mao Zedong's ideological control of intellectuals under the proletariat dictatorship. Most Lu Xun critics brush this aside as merely crude political appropriation of Lu Xun and therefore not reflecting his true face. The point is: it must be usable to be appropriated. Lu Xun critics are inclined to emphasize his "modernist" sophistication or his relentless aura of "fighting against despair." Lu Xun (1974: 3) likes to compare himself to "wild grass," as it "strikes no deep roots, has no beautiful flowers and leaves, yet it imbibes dew, water and the blood and flesh of the dead, although all try to rob it of life. As long as it lives it is trampled upon and mown down, until it dies and decays." He sees his fighting the "wild-grass-style" as very much an endless cyclical struggle between living and being trampled down, decay and sucking blood for rebirth. In other words, it is endless fighting for the sake of fighting, a very much nihilistic fight. Perhaps, the Zhou brothers were not that quite apart after all. The two pillars of modern Chinese prose were actually two sides of the same coin. No wonder that, even after they broke up, they still followed each other's works very closely.

Lin Yutang, *Yuluti*, and *Dazhongyu*

In categorizing and summarizing various types of modern Chinese prose, Yang Mu identifies Zhou Zuoren as the leader of *xiaopin*, Lu Xun as the leader of *zawen*, Hu Shi as the leader of *shuoli* (expository), and Lin Yutang as the leader of *yilun* (critical commentaries). Yang points out that Lin's critical essays have developed a distinctive style, familiar yet forceful, witty and humorous, most resembling the quintessential features of the Western essay. However, Lin's brand is difficult to follow, and hardly anyone could match the rigor of Lin's essays in the ensuing development of modern Chinese prose (Yang Mu 1981: 5–7).

Lin Yutang was quite unique among modern Chinese writers, in that his first published works were his short stories and essays written in English in *Echo*, the student journal of St. John's University in Shanghai (S. Qian 2012: 1–19). As an English instructor at Qinghua College in Beijing at the height of the New Culture Movement, Lin went through a self-unlearning process, namely, to unlearn his Christian missionary education and reground himself in the Chinese cultural soil, which in turn gave him a unique perspective on Chinese culture and the literary revolution. His ensuing graduate study at Harvard University, where he engaged in a debate with a group of Chinese disciples of Irving Babbitt, further strengthened his take on the prospects of the literary revolution.

On the one hand, Lin was quite attracted to the cosmopolitan appeal of the literary revolution. He was surprised to find at Harvard that most Chinese students there, influenced by Babbitt's teachings, were rather negative toward the literary revolution going on heatedly back home. Except for their contempt of *baihua* literature as barren and slovenly, they objected to the literary revolution on patriotic grounds, because they believed the abandonment of classical Chinese would mean an incredible loss to Chinese culture, since its literary tradition was really its flower and crown achievement. Lin countered that there were two kinds of patriotism: the conservative and the liberal. The former put emphasis on preserving what one had already achieved, while the latter emphasized on achieving what one might accomplish through realizing one's potential. Most importantly, Lin argued that the opponents of the literary revolution missed the point that the key to the literary revolution was to propose an entirely new concept of literature from the West in which literary embellishment was no longer the principal criteria:

We have seen a new conception of literature as criticism of life that towers far above the paltriness of the mere stylist's ideal. We are met with the new conception that the aim of all great literature is to see life steadily and see life whole, that literature is to play for us the part of the interpreter of life, that insight into human nature, a penetrating sense of the tragedy of human life, and a clear, close vision of the enigmatic face of the great being called the universe, are the first qualifications of a great writer. (Lin Yutang 1920a: 28)

On the opponents' accusation of the inadequacies and immaturity of *baihua*, however, Lin was much more concessionary. Calling upon Western literary history as point of reference, Lin pointed out that vernacular writing itself need not necessarily be barren and slovenly. On the contrary, it could demonstrate logical coherence of thought, sensible structure and form, and rhetorical beauty. There was no reason why the Chinese vernacular could not do the same. The promotion of *baihua* was then precisely "to create in literature a greater beauty of logical thought, imagination and culture" (Lin Yutang 1920b: 41). However, Lin acknowledged that the maturity of modern Chinese prose in *baihua* would require stylistic and aesthetic cultivation, and *baihua* literature should not mean to write exactly the way one spoke. Unlike Hu Shi, who prioritized a discursive emphasis on the plainness of *baihua*, Lin saw the risk of *baihua* becoming "a housewife's rattle"—talkative, long-winding, and pointless. Instead, Lin (1918: 367) recommended that *baihua* should pay particular attention to its stylistic cultivation and strive for "lucidity, perspicuity, cogency of thought, truth and appropriateness of expression" as commonly found in Western literature. Lin's qualified support to the *baihua* movement was a distinctive voice that appeared on *New Youth* in 1918 in the heat of the New Culture Movement, and it anticipated his promotion of *yuluti* style prose in the 1930s.

Modern Chinese prose reached its height in the 1930s thanks to Lin Yutang's promotion of *xiaopin* essays through launching a series of essay journals such as *Lunyu, Renjianshi*, and *Yuzhou feng*, which attracted both *Haipai* (Shanghai-style) and *Jingpai* (Beijing-style) writers with left, right, and middle political inclinations. It is not surprising that it is in this boom period that the development of *baihua* was under questioning and challenge. Considering themselves as the most progressive inheritors of the May Fourth and New Culturalist spirit, leftist writers now took *baihua* as lagging behind the tide of historical progress, and proposed to replace *baihua* with what they call *dazhongyu* (mass language). As a policy decision of the League of Left-wing Writers, the proposal of *dazhongyu* was first discussed in the league journal *Mass Literature and Arts* (*Dazhong wenyi*) and was later debated in various journals and newspapers around the country. *Dazhongyu* was apparently a neologism and its connotation is better understood in terms of its opponents. For Hu Yuzhi (1935: 57), the progressiveness of *dazhongyu* was diametrically opposed to the regressive turn to *wenyan* in four contemporary trends: first, the revival of *wenyan* itself, as it was not totally dead; second, the employment of *baihua* to express "feudal" literary consciousness as in the Saturday (*libailiu*) school of writers; third, impure use of *baihua* by some writers who somehow "sneaked" into the world of vernacular literature; and fourth, the promotion of *yuluti* in the name of *fenggu* and *xingling*, which was roguishly appealing but ultimately regressive.

It is clear from Hu Yuzhi's exposition that *dazhongyu* was an ideological construct designed to highlight the proletariat class consciousness. On the one hand, this "mass language" was supposed to be more *bai* (plainer) than *baihua*—in other words, similar to the "street vendor's speech." Since "street vendors" were now deemed as belonging to the "proletariat," their speech was extolled as superior to, and more progressive than, the kind of *baihua* advocated by the New Culturalists. On the other hand, to be "plain" did not guarantee that it was *dazhongyu* at all; the primordial criteria for this ideological construct was its ideological line—all those outside its camp, whether the Saturday (or butterfly) writers practicing excellent *baihua* or those who "sneaked" into the world of vernacular literature, were deemed as "regressive" and was to be overcome. Moreover, so long as it was in conformity with Marxist ideology, even though the style deviated from the "mass language" as such, it would be tolerable and acceptable, which explains the widespread practice by leftist writers of a Europeanized, long-winding style of translating German and Russian philosophical and literary works.

Although the debates on *dazhongyu* in the 1930s literary world were inconclusive, in that the leftist ideological construct was not able to prevail over other literary practices, the former did become the dominant mode of practice in the ensuing development of modern Chinese prose after Mao's "Yan'an Talks" in 1942 and the establishment of the PRC in 1949, all the way to the late 1970s. During the reform era and even today, this tight ideological grip on modern Chinese prose is still far from being shaken off. When we look back on the 1930s then, alternative practices deemed as "regressive" and "reactionary" by the ideological vanguards of *dazhongyu* appear quite refreshing and enlightening, particularly Lin Yutang's "promotion of *yuluti* in the name of *fenggu* and *xingling*."

In his promotion of "little-taste essays" by launching a series of essay journals, Lin Yutang was also dissatisfied with certain trends in the latest development of *baihua*. What Lin saw as the danger of *baihua* development was not so much its becoming a "housewife's rattle" but rather the emergence of an Europeanized style of Chinese with convoluted sentences, vague diction, and incredible redundancy as a result of Chinese translation of Western literary and philosophical works. This might not be confined to the practices of leftist writers, but theirs was certainly exemplary and influential. For Lin, this translational style seriously deviated from the original practices and vision of *baihua*, and constituted a neo-dogma in the name of Westernization. In a series of essays such as "Disgusting Dogmatic *Baihua*" ("*Kezeng de baihua siliu*," 1933a), "On the Use of *Yuluti*" ("*Lun yuluti zhi yong*," 1933b), and "A Talk With Mr. Xu on *Baihua* and *Wenyan*" ("*Yu Xujun lun baihua wenyan shu*," 1935), Lin condemned such practice of translational style as *siyang buhua* (ill digestion of Western modernity) and promoted the use of *yuluti*—the vernacular style employed by writers in Ming and Qing dynasties—as an alternative model for contemporary *baihua*.

From a Hegelian/Marxist historical perspective, the use of *yuluti* seems a rather "regressive" move. In terms of understanding Western culture or its translation, however, Lin was unparalleled among modern Chinese intellectuals. He insisted that the development of modern Chinese prose be modeled upon the "familiar style" of

English essays. However, to translate the "familiar style" of English essays does not mean to Europeanize the Chinese language linguistically and stylistically. Rather, the modernization and vernacularization of Chinese must be based and rooted in the history of the Chinese language itself. To promote the practice of *yuluti* in the 1930s, Lin was pointing to a realistic and cross-cultural path for the "literary cultivation" of vernacular modern Chinese based in the historical context of vernacular Chinese while borrowing "familiar essays" from English as a point of reference, yet not enslaved by Europeanized translational style. His bilingual essays in English and Chinese are examples *par excellence* in this respect (S. Qian 2012). These bilingual essays, mostly written in the 1930s, in English first and then "translated" into Chinese, constitute a unique literary phenomenon not only in modern Chinese literature but perhaps in world literature at large. With a number of stylistic maneuvers, Lin's "translation" makes sure that his *yuluti* Chinese version of these bilingual essays read as smoothly and naturally as if they are written for Chinese readers originally, rather than translations as such.

What is difficult to follow in Lin's brand of essays is not so much his style of writing in *yuluti* as such, as it is also implicitly related to his promotion of the quintessential Chinese aesthetic notions of *fenggu* or *xingling*, best translated into English as "character." It is precisely such unique cross-cultural integration of Chinese *fenggu* and English "character" that is the essence of the aesthetic principles behind Lin's translating "humor" into Chinese culture and reviving Yuan Zhonglang and *Gong'an* school of writers in terms of "leisure" (*xianshi*) and "personality" (*xingling*). And it is such cross-cultural combinations that differentiate Lin's "character" from either Lu Xun or Zhou Zuoren's (Qian 2011).

Contemporary Prose: *Wen* (Literariness) and *Zhi* (Character)

Recently, the German Sinologist Wolfgang Kubin (Gu Bin) lamented about what he called a world literary phenomenon: when we talk about literature nowadays, it means novels, novels, and novels (2013). Literary works in other genres such as poetry, drama, and prose are little read and seldom mentioned. In terms of prose, few people in the United States or Germany read them, whereas it still has considerable readership in China. My wager is that there will always be sizable readership in China for poetry and prose. Compared to the long-held prestige of poetry and prose in Chinese cultural life, Chinese modernity dates only about a hundred years, and is still evolving and changing. Radical forms of Westernization, whether as Marxist ideology or crude evolutionary logic, are losing their attraction, if not already lost. Chinese prose, or Chinese culture for that matter, will find means of reconnecting to its historical legacy.

Nevertheless, the devastating impact of the *dazhongyu* ideology under the Maoist regime of the 1950s–1970s—sometimes called the "Mao-style" (*Mao wenti*)—cannot be underestimated. Even after three decades of reform, it is still practiced in official and semi-official discourse, and its reach and impact on the cultural consciousness is quite noticeable. Under Mao, the healthier development of modern vernacular prose was sustained overseas, and since the reform era, this thread converged with a new generation of prose writers in mainland China. The contemporary scene of modern Chinese prose is one of both stigma and possibilities. One of the major problems is the lack of critical prowess, which is closely associated with the critical reflection of Chinese cultural modernity as a whole.

As I have been arguing here, the key *problematique* of modern Chinese prose is very much associated with the birth pangs of modern prose in elevating *baihua* as the norm, and concerned with modern appropriation and re-invention of *wen* (literariness, embellishment) and *zhi* (substance, character) as its constituent qualities. The Confucian term *"wen zhi binbin"* could perhaps still serve as guidelines for modern prose. Unfortunately, this term in current usage has deteriorated to being merely "scholarly and refined," perhaps even suggesting an image of a weakling scholar. What is originally meant, however, is that an ideal gentleman should possess the qualities combining both cultivation (*wen*) as well as raw, wild, and unrelenting character (*zhi*). I will cite three contemporary essays here that embody such gentlemanly quality.

"Enemy of the State: the Complicated Life of an Idealist" by Zha Jianying appeared in *The New Yorker* on April 23, 2007. Yes, I am citing an English-language essay here, precisely to make the point that "modern Chinese prose" does not necessarily have to be in Chinese,[1] just as Hu Shi's and Lin Yutang's English essays should be part of our critical landscape. Zha's essay is exemplary not so much in her excellent English exposition, as in her skillful command of the familiar style for powerful execution. The essay is concerned with a most politically sensitive subject: the imprisonment of the author's half-brother Zha Jianguo for his democracy activism in China. Instead of an outcry and indictment for the government's violation of human rights, the essay is infused with a moving personal touch characterized by a sense of ease and poise, balanced perspectives, and even a sense of humor. What is presented is not a heroic democracy fighter as such, but rather an "ordinary" elder brother with a "complicated life" not that uncommon to the generation he grew up with, and with a simple and idealistic character imbued with a strong sense of loyalty and justice. It is precisely the "literariness" of the essay that brings alive not only the character of the protagonist but also the drab and ultimately unjust imprisonment of such a character. Zha Jianguo has now been released from prison after serving his sentence, and is still very active in advocating democracy for China. He may or may not agree with his sister's portrayal of him in the essay, but I wager that the "literary image" of a political dissident will go down in history even if his political cause were to fail.

"That Blue Khata" ("*Natiao lanse de hada*," 2009) by Su Wei tells the story of a seemingly "joyful" experience: the author leads a team of his Chinese-language students from Yale University to participate in the "Chinese Olympic" Debating Contest organized by CCTV in Beijing, and after his students win the top prize in the competition, they present him with a blue *khata* (a traditional Tibetan ceremonial scarf) in appreciation of their Chinese-language teacher. To Su Wei, a diasporic writer exiled after the Tiananmen Incident of 1989 and "fortunate" enough to be a Chinese-language instructor at Yale, this was by no means a "heroic return." Rather, the "blue *khata*," hanging in his studio at Yale, represents an exiled Chinese scholar's deep-felt "pain and pride" for his diasporic existential bearing. In refined contemporary *baihua* Chinese and with three traditional-style poems inserted in the short essay, Su's prose achieves a poetic loftiness in terms of both literary cultivation and personal forbearing. The global experience of modern Chinese writers, among which Su belongs to the group from post-Mao mainland China, offers a brand-new horizon for Chinese literature. Su's essay demonstrates the possibility of a sophisticated artistic horizon for modern Chinese prose.

Finally, I believe that Li Chengpeng's "A Melon Farmer's Chinese Dream" ("*Yige guanong de Zhongguo meng*") can stand on par with, if not outshine, any piece of prose by modern Chinese literary giants, whether Lu Xun, Zhou Zuoren, or Lin Yutang. It is in the best *yilun wen* tradition of modern Chinese prose, with its pungent wit, critical audacity, and eloquent language. The fact that Li's critical barb directly targets the most current ideological jargon ("Chinese Dream") put forward by the Party Secretary and he is not put into prison for it shows that China now is no longer like Mao's paranoia times, but more like the 1930s when writers could keep testing the limits of the authoritarian rule, albeit with great risk. What affords Li's essay with stunning power is not only its blunt yet witty critical prowess, but also its terse and elastic style of expression. It does not avoid, for instance, various allusions to traditional or Communist classics, which certainly add to its literary effect.

From this group of essays, I see hope for modern Chinese prose from a new generation of writers free from the shackles of the *dazhongyu* ideology. For modern Chinese prose to reset—back to the 1930s—we have important historical hindsight to our advantage, gained through a critical examination of the development of modern Chinese prose from *baihua* to *yuluti* and *dazhongyu*.

NOTE

1 For a subsequent Chinese version, see Zha Jianying (2014). Apparently, the Chinese essay is still not publishable in mainland China.

REFERENCES

Chen, Duxiu 陳獨秀. 1917. "Dashu" 答書 (Reply to Hu Shi). *Xin qingnian* 新青年 (New youth), 3.3 (May 1).

Chen, Pingyuan 陳平原. 2005. *Zhongguo sanwen xiaoshuo shi* 中国散文小说史 (A history of Chinese prose and fiction). Taipei: Eryu wenhua.

Daruvala, Susan. 2000. *Zhou Zuoren and an Alternative Response to Chinese Modernity.* Cambridge, MA: Harvard University Asia Center.

Hu, Shi 胡適. 1998. *Hu Shi wenji* 胡適文集 (Collection of Hu Shi's works). Edited by Ouyang zhesheng 歐陽哲生. Vols. 1–2. Beijing: Beijing daxue chubanshe.

Hu, Yuzhi 胡愈之. 1935. *Dazhong yuwen lunzhan* 大眾語文論戰 (*Debate on dazhongyu*), ed. Xuan

Haoping 宣浩平. Shanghai: Shanghai qizhi shuju.

Kubin, Wolfgang 顧彬. 2013. "Mo Yan, Gao Xingjian yu wenxue weiji" 莫言, 高行健與文學危機 (Mo Yan, Gao Xingjian and literary crisis). *Ming Pao Monthly*, 8: 53–56.

Laughlin, Charles A. 2008. *The Literature of Leisure and Chinese Modernity*. Honolulu: University of Hawaii Press.

Li, Chengpeng 李承鵬. 2013. "Yige guanong de Zhongguo meng" 一個瓜農的中國夢 (A melon farmer's Chinese dream). Accessed 27 April 2014. http://bbs.tianya.cn/post-free-3498797-1.shtml.

Lin, Yutang 林語堂 (林玉堂). 1918. "Lun Hanzi suoyin zhi ji xiyang wenxue" (論漢字索引制及西洋文學). *Xin qingnian*, 4.4.

Lin, Yutang. 1920a. "The Literary Revolution and What Is Literature." *The Chinese Students' Monthly*, 15.4 (Feb.).

Lin, Yutang. 1920b. "Literary Revolution, Patriotism, and the Democratic Bias." *The Chinese Students' Monthly*, 15.8 (June).

Lin, Yutang林語堂. 1933a. "Kezeng de baihua siliu" 可憎的白話四六 (Disgusting dogmatic baihua). *Lunyu* 論語 (Analects), 26 (Oct. 1): 84–85.

Lin, Yutang 林語堂. 1933b. "Lun yuluti zhi yong" 論語錄體之用 (On the use of yuluti). *Lunyu*, 26 (Oct.): 82–84.

Lin, Yutang 林語堂. 1935. "Yu Xujun lun baihua wenyan shu" 與徐君論白話文言書 (A talk with Mr. Xu on baihua and wenyan). *Lunyu*, 63 (April 16): 722–725.

Lin, Yutang. 1937. *The Importance of Living*. New York: John Day Co.

Lu, Xun (Lu Hsun). 1974. *Wild Grass*. Peking: Foreign Languages Press.

Lu, Xun 魯迅. 1981. *Lu Xun Quanji* 魯迅全集 (Complete works of Lu Xun). 16 vols. Beijing: Renmin wenxue chubanshe.

Ni, Moyan 倪墨炎. 2003. *Kuyuzhai zhuren Zhou Zuoren* 苦雨齋主人周作人 (Zhou Zuoren: master of the bitter-rain studio). Shanghai: Shanghai renmin chubanshe.

Qian, Suoqiao 錢鎖橋. 2011. *Liberal Cosmopolitan: Lin Yutang and Middling Chinese Modernity*. Leiden: Brill.

Qian, Suoqiao 錢鎖橋. Ed. 2012. *Little Critic: The Bilingual Essays of Lin Yutang* 小評論:林語堂雙語文集. Beijing: Jiuzhou chubanshe.

Shao, Jian 邵建. 2008. *Hu Shi yu Lu Xun: 20 shiji de liangge zhishifenzi* 胡適与魯迅:20世纪的两个知识分子 (Hu Shi and Lu Xun: two twentieth-century intellectuals). Beijing: Guangming ribao chubanshe.

Su, Wei 蘇煒. 2009. *Zou jin Yelu* 走進耶魯 (Entering Yale). Beijing: Fenghuang chubanshe.

Wolff, Ernst. 1971. *Chou Tso-jen*. New York: Twayne.

Yang, Mu 楊牧. Ed. 1981. *Xiandai Zhongguo sanwen xue I* 現代中國散文選 I (A selection of modern Chinese prose I). Taipei: Hongfan.

Zha, Jianying. 2007. "Enemy of the State: The Complicated Life of an Idealist." *The New Yorker* (April 23). Accessed 27 April 2014. http://www.newyorker.com/reporting/2007/04/23/070423fa_fact_zha?currentPage=all.

Zha, Jianying 查建英. 2014. *Nonchaoer: Zhongguo jueji zhongde xingdongzhen he tuidongzhe* 弄潮兒:中國崛起中的行動者和推動者 (Tide players: the movers and shakers of a rising China). Hong Kong: Oxford University Press.

Zhou, Shoujuan 周瘦鵑. 1921. "Ziyou tan zhi ziyou tan" 自由談之自由談 (Free talk within free talk). *Shenbao* 申報 (Shanghai daily) (March 27): 14.

Zhou, Zuoren 周作人. 1991. *Zhitang xiaopin* 知堂小品 (Essays of Zhou Zuoren), ed. Liu Yingzheng 劉應爭. Xi'an: Shaanxi renmin chubanshe.

12

Fiction in Modern China: Modernity through Storytelling

Yiyan Wang

Fiction as a Beacon of Social Modernity

Although fiction writing began roughly around the seventh century in China, it was considered an inferior art form, especially in comparison with poetry and essay. As it was primarily produced for popular entertainment and its major audience was common people without much education, fiction was marginalized by elite Confucian scholars who disapproved of such subjects as fantasies, reinvented histories, or love or erotic stories. The Chinese term for fiction, "*xiaoshuo*" (meaning "small talk"), confirms its genetic make-up and low social standing. However, from the start of the twentieth century, *xiaoshuo* quickly overtook poetry, essay, and drama to become the dominant genre in modern Chinese literature.

Among the many factors for this change of status were the development of the printing industry and the reform of the educational system. Late Qing years had already seen newspapers enter ordinary households. Wider access to education had enabled more people, especially women and working-class men, to take up reading when they moved to large cities. Works of fiction were mostly serialized first, in newspapers and periodicals, before they were published as books. Serialization meant both larger audiences and extra incomes for writers.

Late Qing readers were exposed to a large number of translated works from other countries. Although early translations were still done in classical Chinese and in conformity with formal conventions of the traditional Chinese novel, such as the linked-chapter structure and poetic lines mingled in narratives, they introduced different ways of storytelling, different emotions, and different goals in life. Most

A Companion to Modern Chinese Literature, First Edition. Edited by Yingjin Zhang.
© 2016 John Wiley & Sons, Ltd. Published 2016 by John Wiley & Sons, Ltd.

striking for Chinese readers and writers at the time was that fiction could be written realistically to express individual concerns, family matters, and social problems. Exposure to writings from other cultural traditions changed the attitude of the Chinese cultural elite, and they began to connect fiction to nation building. In addition to popular entertainment, late Qing fiction articulated political ideology, exposed official corruption, represented ideas for a new nation, and expressed personal aspirations. The rise of the printing media and the mass consumption of fiction were indicative of the arrival of China's social modernity, as newspapers and magazines were part of the emerging public sphere (L. Lee 2001). The function of fiction as a platform for social commentary led to a sharp increase in the numbers of authors and readers. By 1911, it was estimated that the number of published works of fiction amounted to at least 1,000, including 120 Chinese novels and 400 translated novels (A Ying 1996: 1).

Storytelling as Social Commentary: Fiction in the 1900s

The earliest signs of fiction as a vehicle for social change were *qianze xiaoshuo* (fiction of indictment), which included *Travels of Lao Can* (1903–1904) by Liu E; *The Bureaucrats: A Revelation* (*Guanchang xianxing ji*, 1903–1905) and *A Brief History of Enlightenment* (1903) by Li Boyuan; *Strange Events Witnessed Over Twenty Years* (1905) by Wu Jianren; and *A Flower in the Sea of Sins* (*Niehai hua*, 1905) by Zeng Pu. These novels started the trend of popular social criticism based on the authors' observations, and they were the first to expose political corruption for social betterment. On the one hand, their social engagement was new in Chinese fiction and their quasi-realism was modern, without the fantastical and supernatural elements prevalent in premodern Chinese fiction. On the other hand, their structure and narrative modes resembled traditional Chinese novels, and their focus was the development of plot and events. Still, these were the first novels to benefit from the development of mass media. Li Boyuan and Wu Jianren were editors of newspapers and magazines themselves, and their novels appeared in the periodicals to reach a wider audience, which in turn helped spread the message of social criticism. As with Li and Wu, Han Bangqing had serialized his novel, *The Sing-Song Girls of Shanghai* (*Haishang hua liezhuan*, 1892; English 2005), in his literary journal. This novel about Shanghai courtesans was narrated in local Shanghainese and was the first to emphasize regional characteristics in fiction.

Before Han's novel, there was a long tradition of Chinese love stories between "the talented scholar and the beauty" (*caizi jiaren*), although their plot variation and characterization were rather limited. Love stories from foreign cultures broadened the horizons of Chinese writers, who in turn created a new style of story that explored the emotional depths of characters. The earliest works in this direction include Wu Jianren's *The Sea of Regret* (1905) and Su Manshu's *The Lone Swan* (*Duanhong lingyan ji*, 1911) and *The Burnt Sword* (*Fenjian ji*, 1912). Su Manshu is often left out of modern Chinese literary history partly because he wrote in semi-classical language and partly because he was a prolific writer of classical poetry. However, his novels contained new characteristics such as psychological tension and confessional narrative, which would influence subsequent writers.

As a result of the increased output, new terms emerged to group fictional works by themes: *yanqing xiaoshuo* on emotional matters, *seqing xiaoshuo* on sexual seduction, *shiqing xiaoshuo* on social mores, *qianze xiaoshuo* on social evils, *fengci xiaoshuo* on satirical human weaknesses, and *lishi xiaoshuo* on historical events. Those terms were commonly used until after the founding of the PRC when public discourse on literature changed drastically. Whereas some categories are still applied to certain subgenres of fiction, such as *huangse xiaoshuo* for pornography, subgenres in fiction emerged newly after the mid-1970s would be classified as types of *wenxue* (literature), although, strictly speaking, *wenxue* covers all literary genres. In the past 50 years, common fiction subgenres are *shanghen wenxue* (scar literature), *xungen wenxue* (roots-searching literature), *zhiqing wenxue* (literature of sent-down youths), *liuxuesheng wenxue* (literature about students overseas), *xiangtu wenxue* (native-soil literature), *chengshi wenxue* (urban literature), *qingchun wenxue* (youth literature), and *nüxing wenxue* (women's literature). That *wenxue* now replaces *xiaoshuo* in categorizing fiction subgenres is an indication of the increased significance of fiction in the Chinese literary hierarchy.

Enlightenment versus Entertainment: Fiction in the 1910s

In 1911, the Republican Revolution overthrew the Manchu Qing monarchy, and the ROC was established in 1912 by the Nationalist Party led by Sun Yat-sen (Sun Zhongshan). Despite the volatile political situation, modern Chinese fiction and translated fiction continued to flourish. The 1910s saw the emergence of some new subgenres. In 1912, Xu Zhenya published *Jade Pear Spirit* (*Yuli hun*, 1912), which won instant popularity and became the representative of emotional fiction (*yanqing xiaoshuo*). This subgenre gained popularity in the 1920s and developed into "butterfly literature," a derogatory term used by critics who believed that fiction should serve political causes such as national salvation rather than self-indulgence (Link 1981).

The 1910s also saw hundreds of Chinese students traveling overseas to acquire Western knowledge (*xixue*). Xiang Kairan's *Stories of Chinese Students in Japan* (*Liudong waishi*, 1916) inaugurated the literature about students overseas, and he went on to create another important genre in modern Chinese literature a few years later—the martial arts novel. Nonetheless, Xu Zhenya and Xiang Kairan are two modern writers who have been overlooked in literary history.

In contrast, Lu Xun is given a monumental status, and his "Diary of a Madman" (1918) is credited as being the most effective in creating fiction for social enlightenment. The madman in the story suffers from paranoia regarding Confucian norms and calls for social change. Before Lu Xun, Liang Qichao was best known for his argument that the creation of new fiction might help with the formation of a new nation, although this idea had been previously voiced by Yan Fu and Xia Suiqing before Liang (A Ying

1996: 2). Different from his late Qing predecessors, Lu Xun belonged to the May Fourth Movement, which advocated national salvation through cultural renovation. One of the most celebrated May Fourth achievements was the invention of modern vernacular Chinese, which would soon become the standard language in administration and education throughout China and the preferred language for fiction.

Short Stories in New Literature: Fiction in the 1920s

In the 1920s, the first cohort of students who had studied in Japan, Europe, and North America started to return. There were also large numbers of domestic graduates from colleges and high schools that taught Western knowledge. Consequently, when members from this generation became fictional writers, they wrote differently from their predecessors. Many believed that New Literature was vital to a new China and that Chinese storytelling should be transformed for that purpose. Writers of all political persuasions fashioned their storytelling on European or Japanese models. Significantly, the majority of fiction published in the 1920s was short stories.

Chinese literary historiography has consistently focused on writers more in tune with the May Fourth agendas, such as women's liberation, personal freedom, and nationalist and other social concerns. Authors such as Lu Xun, Ba Jin, Yu Dafu, Mao Dun, Hu Yepin, Jiang Guangci, Xu Dishan, and Wang Tongzhao are considered significant. In the 1920s, all of them wrote short stories, although Ba Jin and Mao Dun would become major novelists. The central concern of these writers was how to awaken the masses by exposing social evils. Their national consciousness was a strong indication of literary modernity in the service of nation building. The 1920s was the most productive decade for Lu Xun as a fiction writer, and his short stories revealed social evils and captured the pathetic mentality of Chinese people as a whole. His novella, "The True Story of Ah Q" ("*Ah Q zhengzhuan*," 1921), was at the forefront of a national debate on the Chinese national character.

A more ambivalent kind of literary modernity was articulated in short stories written by women about women, with a focus on their emotions and their dissatisfaction with society. Feng Yuanjun, Lu Yin, Bing Xin, Ling Shuhua, and Ding Ling were their representatives. In Chinese history, there have always been women writers and artists from elite families, but what was new in the 1920s was that women writers reached a wide readership through publication. Their writing was their means of social participation, through which they voiced opinions on matters concerning them. Fiction became a form of self-expression and identity construction for them, as part of the creation of the modern self (Dooling and Torgeson 1998: 1–31). Although not directly demanding women's liberation, their stories of women's educational and domestic lives portrayed a significant aspect of Chinese modernity embedded in changes that occurred in their everyday life.

Ding Ling's "Diary of Miss Sophie" ("*Shafei nüshi de riji*," 1928) adopted the diary form to express the inner turmoil of Miss Sophie, a college student in Beijing. The female student (*nü xuesheng*) was a significant symbol of Chinese modernity in 1920s stories written by male writers, but her images were projected from a distance, as was Zijun in Lu Xun's "Remembrances of the Past" (*"Shangshi,"* 1925). The frank portrait of Miss Sophie's sexual desires in the voice of the young woman herself sent a shock wave through the literary circles and established Ding Ling's literary fame. Ling Shuhua, however, wrote mostly about female students after they graduated from college. Her "Boredom" (*"Wuliao,"* 1928) captured the side effects of "being modern," in that the enlightened female subject realizes she is having "an experience without quality" and her intellectual capacity for reflection leads to melancholy and ennui (Goodstein 2005: 4).

In the late 1910s, Lu Xun had introduced the concept of "children's literature" (*ertong wenxue*) with his translation of stories for children from Germany and Russia. Soon, similar works from other cultures also entered China. Again, there had always being writings for children in Chinese history, but these were primarily intended to indoctrinate Confucian values. Chinese intellectuals began to see the need for children's stories to convey modern values to children. In 1921, Ye Shengtao started writing stories for children, and, in 1923, his first collection, *The Scarecrow (Daocao ren)*, was published. Bing Xin's *To the Young Readers (Ji xiao duzhe)* appeared in the literary supplement of *The Morning Post (Chenbao,* 1923–1926). Ye Shengtao is now remembered as the founder of modern Chinese children's literature, although he was one of the earliest modern novelists and was also known for *The School Master Ni Huanzhi* (1928).

The butterfly romance genre continued to attract large readership. Toward the end of the decade, Zhang Henshui's novels were most popular, especially *Fate in Tears and Laughter (Tixiao yinyuan,* 1929–1930). When it was serialized in *The News (Xinwen bao)*, this Shanghai newspaper's daily circulation reached 150,000. However, popular writers such as Zhang were under fierce attack by intellectuals, and the derogatory label "butterfly" stuck with them. These once-popular books disappeared from mainland China between the 1950s and the 1980s.

Shanghai had developed into a publishing hub in the 1920s, and it was possible for people to become professional writers and make a living on creative writing. This possibility attracted many writers to Shanghai, where Chinese fiction would experience another growth spurt.

The Maturation of the Novel: Fiction in the 1930s

Short stories popular in the 1920s had prepared writers for returning to the novel by experimenting with new narrative techniques. This was certainly the case for Mao Dun and Ba Jin, two major novelists of the 1930s. Mao Dun began his career as an apprentice at the Commercial Press (*Shangwu yinshu guan*) and became the editor of its prestigious journal, *Short Story Monthly (Xiaoshuo yuebao)*. His early short stories were about villagers near Shanghai where he originally came from, and they were collected in the "Eclipse" trilogy (*Shi,* 1927–1928). His *Midnight (Ziye,* 1933), which met with immediate critical acclaim, is an ambitious novel intending to capture the complexity of China's experience with early industrial development through the lens of Marxism. Set in Shanghai, *Midnight* places the "nationalist" industrialist Wu Sunfu in conflict with financial dealers supported by international (read imperialist) capital on the one hand and the demand for better employment conditions from the workers aroused by Communist ideas on the other. Wu's factory eventually falls to imperialist powers. Mao Dun's realist fiction in the 1920s–1930s and his Marxist perspective would secure him a leadership role in the PRC literary establishment, and his legacy is assured in the Mao Dun prize, a top national literary award offered every 4 years since 1982.

Ba Jin's "Torrents" ("*Jiliu*") trilogy—*Family* (*Jia*, 1933), *Spring* (*Chun*, 1938), and *Autumn* (*Qiu*, 1944)—is set in Chengdu, his hometown in Southwest China, and describes how different generations of a traditional gentry family respond to sweeping social changes. The central characters are students with both traditional and modern education, who struggle to reconcile the competing demands of tradition and modernity. Also affiliated with Chengdu, Li Jieren published a trilogy to capture social changes—*Ripples on Dead Water* (*Sishui weilan*, 1936), *Before the Tempest* (*Baofengyu qian*, 1937), and *The Great Wave* (*Dabo* 1938). Li Jieren's approach to urban life differs greatly from that of either Ba Jin or Mao Dun, in that his major characters are "petty city dwellers" (*xiao shimin*), whose primary interest is to pursue a good life. Strongly influenced by French Naturalists such as Émile Zola, some of whom he studied and translated from French, Li Jieren is fascinated as much with the tapestry of local life as with the significance of social events. Interestingly, the destiny of these three novelists and their receptions could not have been more different: in contrast to Mao Dun and Ba Jin, who enjoyed prestige before and after 1949, Li Jieren has been ignored until recently.

Lao She began his writing career in the late 1920s when he was a teacher of Chinese in London, and his early works include *The Philosophy of Lao Zhang* (*Lao Zhang de zhexue*, 1926) and *Ma and Son* (*Er Ma*, 1926). His best-known novel is *Rickshaw Boy* (*Luotuo Xiangzi*, 1936; English 1979), which tells the tragic life story of a young rickshaw puller in Beijing. A passionate spokesman for the poor, Lao She was the first novelist to depict the struggles of the urban lower classes. His writings stood out also because he was the first to use Beijing local expressions in fiction.

In sharp contrast to Lao She's engagement with impoverished urban dwellers in Beijing, a group of modernist writers in Shanghai known as "New Sensationalists" depicted cosmopolitan Shanghai as viewed through aesthetic and psychological sensitivities. Shi Zhecun's "One Rainy Evening in Spring" ("*Meiyu zhixi*," 1929) describes how a young man observes the city while wandering in the rain in search of aesthetic pleasures. Shi Zhecun, together with Liu Na'ou and Mu Shiying, published the journal *Les Contemporains* from 1932 to 1935 and showcased their modernist writings and contemporary literary trends around the world. The group's writings were removed from public view from the 1950s to the 1980s, but have since attracted much scholarly attention.

The 1920s–1930s were the period when Beijing and Shanghai attracted young talent. In 1922, Shen Congwen moved to Beijing and started publishing short stories about his native West Hunan, an area where people of different ethnicities live in close proximity, and of which he had fond memories. Shen's nativist stories benefited from his lyrical rendering of simple-minded people living with minimum Confucian restrictions. He produced dozens of excellent works, including "Border Town" ("*Biancheng*," 1934) and "A Girl from Hunan" ("*Xiaoxiao*," 1934), but he stopped creative writing for political reasons after 1949.

The bustling literary scene was interrupted by the Japanese invasion in 1937. Many writers fled with the Nationalist government to Southwest China, although some chose to stay in occupied areas. In the meantime, the Communists managed to establish their base area in Northen Shaanxi with its headquarters in a small town called Yan'an, and subsequently attracted many left-leaning writers to move there. From the late 1930s, Chinese fiction developed differently in three political systems—the Japanese occupied regions (including Hong Kong and Taiwan), the Communist area, and the areas under the Nationalist government. In Nationalist-controlled areas, patriotism became a uniting force, and disputes among writers calmed down considerably. There was discussion on the most effective literary genre to mobilize the people and resist the Japanese. To this end, many writers switched to producing theatre and organizing performances on the streets in order to reach a wider audience.

Slightly earlier, two writers had come to prominence in connection with patriotic writings. Xiao Jun and Xiao Hong, a couple from Northeast China (then labeled "Manchuria" under Japanese rule), had arrived in Shanghai after the Japanese invaded their homeland in 1931. *Village in August* (1935; English 1944) by Xiao Jun was the first novel about Chinese resistance against the Japanese, and *The Field of Life and Death* (1935; English 1979) by Xiao Hong described the harsh life of village women in Manchuria. Duanmu Hongliang, their fellow Manchurian, also wrote about guerrilla war against the Japanese invasion. After Japan occupied Shanghai, Xiao Hong moved to Hong Kong and produced an autobiographical novel, *Tales of Hulan River* (*Hulanhe zhuan*, 1944; English 1979) (see Chapter 19 by Haili Kong).

The Wars and Warring Ideologies: Fiction in the 1940s

After the initial impact of the Japanese invasion, Chinese fiction revived slowly, and writers repositioned themselves intellectually. Mao Zedong's "Yan'an Talks" in 1942 demanded that literature and art must create heroic characters of the masses in order to serve the people and ultimately the Communist goals. A few years earlier, Ding Ling had relocated to Yan'an and was appointed editor of the literature and arts supplement of *Liberation Daily*, after her rescue by the Communists from a Nationalist prison in Shanghai. She tried to tune in with the Party while retaining focus on women's issues. "When I Was in Xia Village" ("*Wo zai Xiacun de shihou*," 1941) tells the story how an outcast young woman is distained by her community after she has sacrificed herself by serving Japanese soldiers in order to save the village. Ding Ling was severely criticized by the Communist establishment for her ambivalent portrayal of villagers, and subsequently switched her focus to class struggle. Her novel *The Sun Shines over the Sanggan River* (1948) is about the land reform instigated in the Communist areas and portrays the Communists as central heroes.

Mao's call for writers to produce revolutionary literature for the masses saw fruition in Zhao Shuli, whose stories of village life under the Communist rule are told in a traditional style, especially *kuaiban* (a clapper tale narrated in fast-rhyming couplets). Although not a peasant himself, Zhao Shuli has been regarded as a peasant writer primarily due to his familiarity with village life in Shanxi, which enabled him to create credible peasant characters who speak the local language and practice indigenous customs. His two novels published in 1943, *The Marriage of the Young Blacky* (*Xiaoerhei jiehun*) and *The Rhymes of Li Youcai* (*Li Youcai banhua*), were popular in the Communist area and were adapted into stage performances.

Sun Li, educated at Lu Xun College in Yan'an, published "Lotus Lake" ("*Hehua dian*," 1947) and "Reed Flowers Lake" ("*Luhua dang*," 1949), depicting the guerrilla warfare against the Japanese and highlighting village women as wives of the Communist soldiers. Sun Li's stories are mostly set in his hometown region in Hebei, known for beautiful waterways, and the merging of storytelling with his depiction of natural beauty created a new narrative style. Projecting oneself through nature had long been a Chinese literary tradition, so it is not a surprise that Sun Li's lyrical storytelling would subsequently enter school textbooks and influence writers such as Wang Zengqi and Jia Pingwa in the 1980s.

In Japanese-occupied Shanghai, popular magazines continued to publish fiction. Xu Xu, a young man recently returned from France, was stranded in Shanghai and began publishing love stories with traditional plots. His *In Love with Ghost* (*Guilian*, 1937) and *The Rustling Wind* (*Feng xiaoxiao*, 1943) were widely read at the time. Eileen Chang wrote disenchanting stories about women from families with declining wealth and prestige, and the most famous include "Love in a Fallen City" (1943) and "The Golden Cangue" ("*Jinsuo ji*," 1944). Chang's tales focus on women's struggles for a better life against all odds. Despite her sympathy toward them, her women characters tend to be flawed as their unfortunate life inevitably distorts their personalities. Chang continued to write after she immigrated to the United States in the 1950s, but her writings became more introspective, as in "Lust, Caution" ("*Se, Jie*," 1973), which is about a woman's difficult choice between love and politics during the Japanese occupation. She published two novels while staying in Hong Kong in the 1950s, *The Rice-Sprout Song* and *Naked Earth*. Both are about the brutality of the Communist rule and have attracted little attention. Her posthumous works published in recent years continue to circulate widely in the Chinese-speaking world.

In 1940s Shanghai, Su Qing shared a reputation similar to that of Eileen Chang, with her popular fiction works, published in magazines, portraying urban women's domestic lives. Her best-known novel, *Ten Years of Marriage* (*Jiehun shinian*, 1943–1944), is an autobiographic tale about a wife's struggle from her wedding day to her divorce after she discovers that her lawyer husband has an affair. Another brilliant writer of the 1940s whose writing shared Eileen Chang's grudge about family and marriage was the academic novelist Qian Zhongshu. Qian had studied at Oxford and in Paris and returned to China to teach at Southwest Associated University in Kunming. Although he also wrote interesting short stories, it is his novel *Fortress Besieged* (*Weicheng*, 1944) that made his reputation in literary history. "Fortress" is intended as a metaphor for marriage as a trap, and the novel is a witty satire on the pretentiousness of the educated, especially those who studied overseas only briefly but were fond of showing off their superficial knowledge.

Socialist Realism and the Red Classics: Fiction in the 1950s and Beyond

The Communists' victory over the Nationalists in 1949 has profound ramifications for Chinese literature. Chinese fiction continued to develop along different directions already set in motion during the war. The regime change perpetuated the division of China into the mainland, Taiwan, Hong Kong, and the Chinese diaspora around the world. Between 1895 and 1945, Taiwan was a Japanese colony, and literature was largely written in Japanese. The Nationalist government attempted in the late 1940s to "re-Sinify" Taiwan and suppressed subversive local voices. In the following decades, Taiwan would produce fiction very different from that in mainland China. Some Chinese writers would later move to the United States, and Chinese diasporic fiction would emerge there and elsewhere (see Chapter 8 by Ping-hui Liao). In Hong Kong, martial arts novels became the most successful genre, both in terms of popular appeal and narrative sophistication. As an indigenous genre in Chinese literary tradition, martial arts novels can be linked to classical novels such as *Journey to the West* and *Water Margin*. Liang Yusheng and Jin Yong in Hong Kong—as well as Gu Long in Taiwan— were immensely popular, and their readership has been both transgenerational and transnational in the Chinese-speaking world.

In mainland China, all writers were required to follow the Communist ideology, and the Maoist approach to literature dictated that central figures of literature be workers, soldiers, or peasants. Faced with strict political demands, many established writers such as Shen Congwen, Qian Zhongshu, Mao Dun, and Zhang Ziping stopped producing fiction. Many writers of love stories and other popular genres also stopped writing, and their previous works were removed from public circulation.

In the 1950s, the Communists completed two major tasks—land reform in rural areas and the nationalization of industry and commerce in urban areas. The first law implemented in the PRC was the marriage law, which banned polygamy and arranged marriage. Fiction of the 1950s addressed these subject matters. In 1955, Zhao Shuli published *The Village Sanliwan* and depicted how the villagers responded to changes brought about by the land reform and the new marriage law. Zhou Libo's two novels, *The Hurricane* (1948) and *Great Changes in a Mountain Village* (1958), became part of what was later called "red classics." Interested in capturing the scope and depth of social changes brought about by the Communist revolution, Zhou addressed issues of the land reform in *The Hurricane* and the rural collectivization in *Great Changes in a Mountain Village*. Many novels dealing with rural changes appeared in the 1950s–1960s, such as Li Zhun's *Li Shuangshuang* (1960) and Liu Qing's *The Builders* (1960). As for urban literature, Zhou Erfu's *Morning in Shanghai* (1958) portrayed the nationalization process in the early 1950s. Following Mao Dun's *Midnight* in 1933, this novel also illustrated class struggle but was a rare example of urban fiction that attempted to represent socialist industrialization.

Given the limited subject matter allowed at the time, many writers turned to the Communist revolution and produced a new subgenre, "new revolutionary legend" (*geming xin chuanqi*), by utilizing techniques and styles of traditional historical fiction. These novels include Zhi Xia's *Guerrilla Fighters along the Railway* (*Tiedao youjidui*, 1954), Gao Yunlan's *Spring and Autumn in a Small Town* (*Xiaocheng chunqiu*, 1956), Yang Mo's *The Song of Youth* (1958), Li Yingru's *Revolutionary Tales in an Ancient City* (*Yehuo chunfeng dou gucheng*, 1958), Feng Deying's *Bitter Vegetable Flowers* (*Kucaihua*, 1958), Ouyang Shan's *Three-Family Lane* (1959), and *Red Crag* (1961) by Luo Guangbin and Yang Yiyan. Many of them were popular, and were adapted to films in the 1960s. As titles of "red classics," some have been recently readapted into television series to popular acclaim.

The establishment of new literary journals in the PRC encouraged the production of short stories. Wang Meng's "The Young Newcomer in the Organization Department" (1956) appeared in *People's Literature* (*Renmin wenxue*). Although his mild criticism of the Party bureaucracy won him recognition, Wang was classified as a Rightist in 1957 and banished to Xinjiang for reform through labor until 1986.

The Cultural Revolution: Fiction as Political Victim in the 1960s–1970s

The relative prosperity of the literature of the 17 years (1949–1966) came to an abrupt end when Mao launched the Cultural Revolution (1966–1976). The ensuing extreme political repression destroyed literary expression and persecuted most writers. Only a handful of novels produced during the decade were accepted by the ultra-leftist authorities for their application of socialist realism and socialist romanticism. Hao Ran's *Bright Sunny Skies* (1964, 1966, 1971) and *The Golden Road* (1972–1974) portray rural social structure and class conflicts and show how family life has been transformed by the Communist revolution. These novels illustrate how literature can blindly follow political indoctrination. Another novel endorsed by the authorities was Yao Xueyin's three-volume historical novel *Li Zicheng* (1963, 1976, 1981). Li Zicheng's peasant rebellion near the end of the Ming Dynasty fitted perfectly with the Communist campaign at the time that aimed to prove "only people are true historical heroes."

The repressive political climate pushed many writers underground. In the 1970s, a number of hand-copied fiction works (*shouchaoben xiaoshuo*) enjoyed immense popularity: *One Embroidered Shoe* (*Yizhi xiuhua xie*) by Zhang Baorui, *The Second Handshake*

(*Di'er ci woshou*) by Zhang Yang, *The Open Love Letters* (*Gongkaide qingshu*) by Jin Fan, *Giant Waves* (*Jiuji lang*) by Bi Ruxie, *Waves* (*Bodong*) by Bei Dao, and *When the Twilight Disappeared* (*Wanxia xiaoshide shihou*) by Li Ping. Many of these titles were formally published when the political climate changed in the late 1970s.

Renaissance and Experimentation: Fiction in the 1980s

Mao's death in 1976 ended the horrendous Cultural Revolution, and draconian political repression eased gradually. Writers woke up to newly given intellectual freedom and started reassessing both their personal experiences and China's recent political history. In the early 1980s, a large number of writers were actively engaged in writing, and literary journals resurfaced and provided ample opportunities for publication.

Many writers' initial response was to reflect on their suffering in the previous years. The trend began with Liu Xinwu's "The Class Monitor" (1977), but it was Lu Xinhua's "The Scar" (1978) that brought the pains to the national consciousness. Soon, a large number of writings on the sufferings during the Cultural Revolution or those of earlier political periods appeared, and the most influential included Zheng Yi's *Maple* (*Feng*, 1979), Zhang Xianliang's *The Soul and the Flesh* (1980), and Gu Hua's *Hibiscus Town* (1981).

In the 1980s, writers were respected as the intelligentsia and considered responsible for solving social problems. Discussions on the Cultural Revolution led to the questioning of personal responsibility and Chinese tradition. Reflective literature started with Ru Zhijuan's "The Story Mistakenly Edited" ("*Jianji cuole de gushi*," 1979), and was followed by Zhang Jie's "Love Must Not Be forgotten" (1979) and Chen Rong's *At Middle Age* (1980). Wang Meng returned to Beijing and questioned the fundamental cultural inertia of Chinese society in stories such as "The Butterfly" (1979) and "Bolshevik Salute" (1979). His work was also ahead of its time by experimenting with new techniques such as the stream of consciousness and psychological realism.

Another issue that interested writers in the mid-1980s was the connection between fiction and cultural traditions in narrative style and subject matter. Dubbed "roots-searching literature," this trend shifted attention to current social conditions and cultural traditions, and it included writers such as A Cheng, Han Shaogong, Jia Pingwa, Wang Anyi, and Wang Zengqi. Wang Zengqi's "The Love Story of a Young Monk" ("*Shoujie*," 1980) and "A Tale of the Big Nur" ("*Danao jishi*," 1981) were early examples, and Jia Pingwa's *Three Records of Shangzhou* (*Shangzhou sanlu*, 1983–1984) further developed storytelling through lyrical prose. Exploration of cultural traditions also directed attention to urban traditions. Deng Youmei's "Snuff-Bottles" ("*Yanhu*," 1984) deals with the object fetish among the Manchu dilettantes in Beijing. Set in Tianjin, Feng Jicai's *The Three-Inch Golden Lotus* (*Sancun jinlian*, 1986; English 1994) details the practice of foot binding and reveals its cultural logic in objectifying women as sexual objects.

The 1980s also witnessed a new sense of urgency to catch up with world literature. Works by writers such as Márquez, Milan Kundera, and Duras overwhelmed Chinese writers with new perspectives and narrative styles. Magical realism, for instance, subverted the conventional Chinese understanding of literary modernity after the May Fourth Movement, and compelled Chinese writers to explore their own literary traditions to find magical realist elements.

In the mid-1980s, avant-garde literature arrived with the claim that "how to write" was more important than "what to write." The earliest such output included short stories with an unreliable narrator or multiple narrators, a disoriented sense of space and time, and other narrative devices intended to undo the Maoist discourse. Ma Yuan, Can Xue, Chen Cun, Hong Feng, Ge Fei, Sun Ganlu, Yu Hua, and Su Tong were among the pioneers. "The Goddess of the Lhasa River" (1984) by Ma Yuan and "The Hut on the Mountain" (1985) by Can Xue both abandoned a cohesive plot line and a "normal" sense of temporal progression. Experimentation with different narrative styles and techniques became a common feature among the avant-garde writers, and through their focus on narrative devices the writers subverted both social conventions and Communist orthodoxy.

In the late 1980s, Yu Hua, Mo Yan, and Su Tong took the avant-garde to a new height of subversion, as their plots usually involved violence and cruelty, but their stories were told either in a dispassionate voice or with primitive passions. Striking examples include Yu Hua's "Mistakes by the River" ("*Hebiande cuowu*," 1988) and "One Kind of Reality" ("*Xianshi yizhong*," 1988), Su Tong's *The Opium Family* (*Yingsu zhijia*, 1986) and *Wives and Concubines* (*Qiqie chengqun*, 1989), both collected in *Raise the Red Lantern* (Su Tong, 1993), as well as Mo Yan's *Red Sorghum* (1987).

Many writers became attracted to "neo-realism," a new style of storytelling toward the end of the 1980s, namely to narrate straightforwardly with no emotional involvement or value judgment. They wrote stories of the past, set in a village or a small town involving insignificant characters who spend all their energies on the basics of survival, and such deadpan descriptions of crude lives of people at the bottom of society became the trademark of neo-realism. Examples include Chi Li's "The Troubled Life" ("*Fannao rensheng*," 1987), Liu Heng's "Dog Shit Food" ("*Gouride liangshi*," 1988), Li Rui's *Solid Land* (*Houtu*, 1988), and Fang Fang's "The Floating Clouds and the Flowing Water" ("*Xingyun liushui*," 1991). Through a total removal of sentimentalism, romanticism, and idealism, neo-realist fiction forced Chinese readers, for the first time, to confront the meaninglessness of the everyday as opposed to admiring the hyperbolized grandeur in socialist realism or the grotesque miniatures elaborated by the avant-garde.

The 1980s concluded with the so-called Wang Shuo phenomenon. With outrageous works such as *The Trouble Shooters* (1987), *Playing for Thrills* (1989; English 1997), and *I Am Your Papa* (*Wo shi ni baba*, 1992), Wang shocked the public by mocking all socio-cultural norms of the time. Wang Shuo's image as a rebellious youth was also built on his open criticism of Lu Xun and his welcome of the commercialization of literary production (see Chapter 6 by Tao Dongfeng).

Commercialization and Diversification in Storytelling: Fiction in the 1990s

China's economic reform went into full swing in the 1990s and commercialization of the publishing sector quickly changed the production and distribution of literary works. The changes also affected the status of the writers: from their prestigious position previously as "engineers of the soul of the people" with salaries guaranteed by the state, by the 1990s they were reduced to being mere producers of cultural products for consumption. With or without political significance, their writings must have market value. Although political censorship still applied, writers became subjected to the market demand. The relationships between writers, readers, publishers and the authorities have irreversibly changed. If the central question for writers in the 1980s was how to write as opposed to what to write, in the 1990s the question became whether to aim at commercial success. In other words, commercialization of the publishing industry entailed both the possibility and, to some degree, the necessity to entertain readers. It contributed to the renaissance of fiction but also diversified what and how to write.

In 1993, two novels by two writers residing in Xi'an attracted national attention: *The Defunct Capital* (*Feidu*) by Jia Pingwa and *White Deer Plain* (*Bailu yuan*) by Chen Zhongshi. *Defunct Capital* deals with the impact of the sociocultural change on the writer, on how he writes, how the market values his writing, how the state awards his literary success with political status, but more significantly, how all this results in his loss of the self. The narrator details the problems with his sexuality and his daily life as a significant cultural and political figure in a provincial capital. The narrative style is a return to the classical vernacular fiction with emphasis on the natural flow of narrative events. The narrative is enriched by classical expressions and poems in the traditional style. The book was very popular and sold over a million copies before the government decided to ban it. In 2011, the ban was lifted after the author agreed to remove one particular narrative device—small boxes used to indicate omitted words of erotic content.

White Deer Plain is intended as an epic that begins with the Republican overthrowing of the Manchu monarchy and ends with the Communists taking over China in 1949. The novel intertwines the story of two rural families with China's modern history and details the process of how the Nationalists and the Communists diverged from a common goal of building a strong China. The most interesting aspect of the story is how the children of the families choose to join either the Nationalists or the Communists and end up being antagonists to each other.

The 1990s also produced a group of women writers, including Chen Ran, Lin Bai, and Hai Nan, whose writings focus on psychological and personal issues particularly relevant to contemporary women. "Sunshine Between the Lips" ("*Zuichun lide yangguang*," 1992) by Chen Ran tells of how a female patient's acceptance of a male dentist's love relies upon her overcoming the psychological disturbance in her childhood. Because their writings deal with issues fundamentally individual rather than social or collective, characters created by this new group differ from those by their predecessors in the 1920s (e.g., Ling Shuhua and Ding Ling) or in the 1980s (e.g., Wang Anyi's "love trilogy" [Sanlian]).

Tang Haoming's *Zeng Guofan* (1992) signaled the emergence of "new historical fiction," a trend that would continue into the new century with many novels devoted to court intrigues and personalities in the Qing dynasty, which in turn would become the materials for popular television series. Moving in another direction, Zhang Chengzhi declared his Islamic faith in the 1990s and began publishing on Chinese Muslims in Northwest China. *History of the Spirit* (*Xinling shi*, 1992) and *Black Steed* (*Hei junma*, 1994) are based on original tales of oral history from Muslim communities. Zhang's writing was a new development of literature about ethnic minorities written in Chinese by ethnic writers, which began with Tashi Dawa's short stories on Tibet in the late 1980s (see Chapter 16 by Mark Bender).

Liu Zhenyun's "Chicken Feathers Everywhere" ("*Yidi jimao*," 1991) and *Yellow Flowers in the Hometown* (*Guxiang, tianxia, huanghua*, 1991) are regarded as representative works of neo-realism. These works display sharp observations of sociocultural changes that affect people living at the bottom of society. Liu later moved from Henan province to Beijing and has collaborated with Feng Xiaogang, China's most commercially successful director, who has adapted Liu's works such as *Cell Phone* (*Shouji*, 1993) and *Back to 1942* (*1942*, 2010). Liu's recent novels, *One Sentence Worth Ten Thousand* (*Yiju ding yiwanju*, 2009) and *I Am Not Pan Jinlian* (*Wo bushi Pan Jinlian*, 2012), demonstrate his profound insight into conflicts between the authorities and ordinary people in contemporary Chinese society.

As with Liu Zhenyun, Yan Lianke lives in Beijing but comes from a poor village in Henan. Yan's novels likewise show a deep concern for people struggling for survival, but he differs from Liu in that his narratives often go to the grotesque extreme in an attempt to show how poverty drives people to desperate measures, such as selling blood and skin for an income. Yan's best-known novels include *The Flow of Time* (*Riguang liunian*, 1998), *Hard as Water* (*Jianying rushui*, 2001), *Little Pleasures* (2004), and *Dream of Ding Village* (*Dingzhuang meng*, 2006). In particular, his *Serve the People!* (*Wei renmin fuwu*, 2004) delivers a scathing satire of the hierarchy and hypocrisy within People's Liberation Army, and it was banned soon after its publication.

The 1990s was a golden decade for the Chinese novel when many top writers published their representative works, such as Mo Yan's *Big Breasts, Wide Hips* (1995), Yu Hua's *To Live* (1992; English 2003b) and *Chronicle of a Blood Merchant* (1998; English 2003a), Wang Anyi's *The Song of Everlasting Sorrow* (*Changhen ge*, 1995; English 2008), Shi Tiesheng's *The Temple of Earth and Me* (*Wo yu Ditan*, 1993), and Han Shaogong's *Dictionary of Maqiao* (*Maqiao cidian*, 1996). While established writers dealt with China's traditions and heavy burdens of the past, a group of young writers turned their gaze to China's newly emerging urban scenes, including middle-class lifestyles and workplace culture of transnational companies. These works include Qiu Huadong's *Tie Me Up* (*Ba wo kunzhu*, 1996) and Zhu Wen's *I Love Dollars* (*Wo ai meiyuan*, 1995; English 2007).

The Past in the Present: Fiction in the Twenty-First Century

Globalization in the twenty-first century has brought the Chinese-speaking world closer, and Chinese writers are increasingly read overseas. Gao Xingjian won the Nobel Prize for Literature in 2000, and his *Soul Mountain* (*Lingshan*, 1990) received glowing praises. The 2012 Nobel Prize went to Mo Yan and once more confirmed the importance of Chinese fiction in world literature. Meanwhile, digital technology and the Internet have transformed how Chinese authors tell stories and how readers consume them.

Similar to what the printing press did a century ago, the Internet has enabled many aspirational writers to publish their works, and online discussions have influenced the creative process and outcome. Popular Internet writers are often approached by publishers to have their works published in book form, and notable titles include Murong Xuecun's *Leave Me Alone: A Novel of Chengdu* (*Chengdu, jinye qing jiangwo yiwang*, 2003; English, 2009), Anni Baobei's collection of short stories, *The Remains of August* (*Bayue weiyang*, 2001), and Liu Lianzi's historical fiction on the Manchu court life, *A Biography of the Imperial Concubine, Zhenhuan* (*Hougong Zhenhuan zhuan*, 2007) (see Chapter 23 by Jin Feng).

As Internet writing spread in the country, "scripters"—as distinguishable from "writers"—have entered the scene. Some writers, especially those born in the 1980s (or the "post-1980"), prefer the term "scripters" as they consider writing to be a pastime activity instead of a serious profession. Indeed, there has been a group of youngish best-seller writers whose writings have not received much critical assessment but have been very popular. Most of them are not accepted by the writers association despite their market success.

When the term "the post-1980" was coined in the 1990s, it was associated with youth and the first one-child generation coming of age. As youth literature, their writing is about high-school student life, love, computer games, and fantasies. The expected resistance to parental pressure and, by extension, to state ideology, is manifested through their relentless pursuit of materialism and proclaimed disinterest in "big" issues, whether political, social, or cultural. Han Han established his fame with *The Triple Gates* (*Sanchong men*, 2000), a realist novel of high school life that sold over 2 million copies. Guo Jingming topped the list of China's richest authors several times, first with *The City of Fantasies* (*Huancheng*, 2003), then with *Hide and Seek* (*Micang*, 2005), an attempt to incorporate pop songs into fiction, and recently with *Cry Me a Sad River* (*Beishang niliu chenghe*, 2007). He also edits a popular youth magazine, *Top Fiction* (*Zui xiaoshuo*), which addresses trendy urban youth topics with illustrations resembling Japanese comic books. Guo Jingming directed *Tiny Times I–II* (*Xiao shidai*, 2013), two widely popular films that prove his generation to be interested only in fashion and style.

However, writers committed to serious literature remain a formidable social presence. Alai is ethnic Tibetan but writes in Chinese, his second language. He has published three novels set in Tibetan communities around his hometown Aba in northwest Sichuan. His *Dust Settles* (*Chen'ai luoding*, 1998; English as *Red Poppies*, 2002) deals with the changes that happen in a Tibetan region in the first half of the twentieth century when the Chinese state first came into contact with Tibetan villages. Whether the intervention was from the Nationalists or later the Communists, Tibetan life and the local social fabric were seriously damaged. His three-volume *Empty Mountains* (*Kongshan*, 2005–2007) tackles the process of social transformation instigated by the state from the 1950s onward, and ends on a bleak destruction of local environments where mountain forests are lost to commercial logging. His third novel is a rewriting of the Tibetan epic, *King Gesar* (*Gesaer Wang*, 2009), as part of the Canongate Books project of rewriting mythology.

Chi Zijian attracted attention with novels dealing with China's northeast border regions with Russia. After her three-volume novel *The Puppet Manchukuo* (*Wei Manzhouguo*, 2000–2004), she documented the historical transition of ethnic tribal communities in the forests in *The Right Bank of the Argun River* (*E'erguna he you'an*, 2005; English as *The Last Quarter of the Moon*, 2013). Jia Pingwa won both the Mao Dun Prize and the Dream of the Red Chamber Prize for his tenth novel, *Shaanxi Opera* (*Qinqiang*, 2005). His other notable recent novels include *King of Trash* (*Gaoxing*, 2007), *Ancient Kiln* (2011), and *The Woman Cadre Daideng* (*Daideng*, 2013). Jia's ambition is to keep alive Chinese cultural traditions endangered by urbanization and to portray villagers who can no longer make a living by tilling their land.

In his Nobel Prize acceptance speech, Mo Yan calls himself a "storyteller," and indeed he has been innovative with narrative voices in polishing his "hallucinatory realism." Deeply rooted in his native Shandong, all his stories can be seen as a literary ethnography of the local region. His recent novels include *Sandalwood Death* (*Tanxiang xing*, 2001), *41 Guns* (*41 pao*, 2003), *Life and Death Are Wearing Me Out* (2005; English 2008), and *Frogs and Babies* (2009). Su Tong's contribution to the project of rewriting mythology initiated by Canongate Books is a work of historical fiction, *Binu and the Great Wall* (*Binu*, 2006; English 2007). His novel *The Boat to Redemption* (*He'an*, 2009; English 2010) revisits the harsh years of Maoism. Still set in "Acacia Street" in an imaginary town on the lower stretch of the Yangtze River, *The Boat to Redemption* reveals the horrors and absurdities of life when ideological repression goes to the extreme. The novel won the Man-Booker Asia Prize for fiction in 2009. Similar international reputation is given to Yu Hua as he has been writing a regular column for *The New York Times* in recent years. A major achievement in contemporary Chinese fiction, Yu's *Brothers* (*Xiongdi*, 2005; English 2009) presents a surrealistic view of the violence and inhumanity of the Maoist years to today's rampant commercialism.

Wang Anyi has remained prolific. *The Era of Enlightenment* (*Qimeng shidai*, 2007) is her reassessment of the sent-down youth in the troubled years of the 1960s. Her *Heavenly Fragrance* (*Tianxiang*, 2011) is the story of a traditional business of Suzhou-style embroidery in the late Ming dynasty before Shanghai became an international port city. An influential writer in the new century, Yan Geling was not recognized as a significant figure until she published *Auntie Tatsuru* (*Xiaoyi Duohe*, 2008), although she has a dozen novels, collections of short stories, and screenplays under her name after the mid-1980s. *Auntie Tatsuru* deals with the survival of a Japanese woman in a Manchurian village after World War II. Yan's other major novels include *The Ninth Widow* (*Dijiuge guafu*, 2009) and *Criminal Lu Yanshi* (*Lufan Yanshi*, 2011). The latter revisits China's recent political history through the family tragedy of Lu Yanshi, an intellectual persecuted repeatedly by the authorities. The novel was adapted by Zhang Yimou into a film, *Coming Home* (*Guilai*, 2014), which became a box-office hit in the PRC.

Concluding Remarks

The past 150 years have witnessed enormous growth in all aspects of Chinese fiction, a growth closely connected with the social, political, economic, and technological changes that have taken place in China and around the world. When fiction writing began narrating the nation, it became the dominant literary genre in modern China and has remained so until today. The broadening of the purposes of storytelling from entertainment to social criticism enhanced the status of fiction, and the higher status of fiction led to a higher status for writers. Throughout the twentieth century, writers who took social engagement seriously were respected as intellectuals, and many fiction writers have become influential. For this reason, writers were both privileged and disciplined, depending on the political climate of a given time. Fear of their power of public influence is the major reason for continuous censorship in the PRC.

The adoption of the vernacular in storytelling is an early sign of modernity in Chinese fiction. The vernacular enabled fiction to reach a larger audience because more people were able to read it. Furthermore, the vernacular bridged the gaps between fiction and ordinary people's lives. When storytelling facilitated the reader's identification with fictional characters, a solid foundation for popular readership was built. Another sign of modernity is the influence from foreign cultures, which has enriched Chinese fiction. Appropriated to criticize the national character or to voice individual aspirations, many "isms" have come and gone, but creative trends continue to change. Although Chinese fiction remains plot-driven and event-focused, there have been dynamic developments in stories of bildungsroman, and more Chinese fiction has engaged in exploring characters' inner worlds.

Focus on local cultures is another sign of modernity in Chinese storytelling. There are at least two reasons why telling local stories signals literary modernity: first, national aspirations need to be constructed locally; second, local stories tend to be ethnographic, and local ethnography is modern in the very sense that a local community is being created through literary imagination.

Politics of story-telling aside, the role of entertainment remains central to the vitality of fiction. There have been many popular subgenres in modern China— butterfly romance, martial art novels, historical fiction, and youth literature on fashion and lifestyle, to name but a few—all of which have attracted large readerships. Moreover, these readerships are not only socially heterogeneous but also transnational and transgenerational.

In the twenty-first century, China is one of the superpowers in the production and consumption of fiction. It has the largest number of literary magazines where emerging and established writers often have their fiction published first before issuing it in book form. Each year, more than 1,000 novels are produced, in addition to a greater number of short stories in conventional print media. There are also a large number of Web publications generated by the online communities of readers and writers. Diversity characterizes contemporary Chinese fiction. Although government censorship still applies, commercialization of the publishing industry since the 1990s has created market incentives for the production of fiction in large quantity and variety. New technology and multiplicity in publishing venues entail that stories are increasingly created by writers from diverse social, ethnic, and age groups.

Chinese fiction keeps its immediate kinship with the screen. Chinese television and film industries still rely on published fiction as sources of their plots, and they also provide the most effective means for stories to reach the widest possible audiences. Whether new or old, stories retain their presence through their reincarnations on screens big and small. While radio broadcast and audio books help stories reach more readers in the Chinese-speaking world, there has been a sharp increase in the number of translators who specialize in translating Chinese fiction into other languages, ensuring that a good proportion of Chinese fiction reaches the international readership.

References

Alai. 2002. *Red Poppies*. Trans. Howard Goldblatt and Sylvia Li-chun Lin. Boston: Houghton Mifflin.

A Ying 阿英. 1996. *Wan Qing xiaoshuo shi* 晚清小説史 (A history of late Qing fiction). Beijing: Dongfang chubanshe.

Chi, Zijian. 2013. *The Last Quarter of the Moon*. Trans. Bruce Hume. London: Harvill Secher.

Feng, Jicai. 1994. *The Three-Inch Golden Lotus*. Trans. David Wakefield. Honolulu: University of Hawaii Press.

Goodstein, Elizabeth S. 2005. *Experience without Qualities: Boredom and Modernity*. Stanford, CA: Stanford University Press.

Lao, She. 1979. *Rickshaw: The Novel of Lo-t'o Hsiang Tzu*. Trans. Jean James. Honolulu: University of Hawaii Press.

Lee, Leo Ou-fan. 2001. "Incomplete Modernity: Rethinking the May Fourth Intellectual Project." In Doleželová-Velingerová, Milena, and Oldřich Král. Eds. 2001. *The Appropriation of Cultural Capital: China's May Fourth Project*. Cambridge, MA: Harvard University Asia Center, 31–65.

Link, E. Perry. 1981. *Mandarin Ducks and Butterflies: Popular Fiction in Early Twentieth-Century Chinese Cities*. Berkeley: University of California Press.

Mo, Yan. 2008. *Life and Death Are Wearing Me Out: A Novel*. Trans. Howard Goldblatt. New York: Arcade Publishing.

Murong, Xuecun. 2009. *Leave Me Alone: A Novel of Chengdu*. Trans. Harvey Thomlinson. Crows Nest, NSW: Allen & Unwin.

Su, Tong. 1993. *Raise the Red Lantern: Three Novellas*. Trans. Michael Duke. New York: William Morrow.

Su, Tong. 2007. *Binu and the Great Wall*. Trans. Howard Goldblatt. Edinburgh, UK: Canongate.

Su, Tong. 2010. *The Boat to Redemption*. Trans. Howard Goldblatt. London: Doubleday.

Yu, Hua. 2003a. *Chronicle of a Blood Merchant*. Trans. Andrew F. Jones. New York: Pantheon Books.

Yu, Hua. 2003b. *To Live: A Novel*. Trans. with an afterword by Michael Berry. New York: Anchor Books.

Wang, Shuo 王朔. 1987. "Wanzhu" 頑主 (The troubleshooters). *Shouhuo* 收穫 (Harvest), 6: 24–54.

Wang, Shuo. 1997. *Playing for Thrills: A Mystery*. Trans. Howard Goldblatt. New York: William Morrow and Company.

Xiao, Hong. 1979. *The Field of Life and Death and Tales of Hulan River: Two Novels*. Trans. Howard Goldblatt. Bloomington: Indiana University Press.

Xiao, 1944. *Village in August*. Trans. Edgar Snow. New York: World Publishing Co.

Yu, Hua. 2009. *Brothers*. Trans. Eileen Cheng-yin Chow and Carlos Rojas. New York: Pantheon Books.

13

Modern China's Translated Literature

Zha Mingjian

Translated literature in modern China has contributed to the modernization of Chinese literature and made a significant impact on modern Chinese society and culture. Literary translation is not just a simple conversion between languages independent from China's literary system; rather, it is closely related to China's literature and culture of specific historical periods. All concerns regarding translation's aim, selection, strategies, and reception are under the influence of China's politics, ideology, and literary culture in any given time.

Literary translation is accomplished in the polysystem of the target culture, and it is under the constraint of the coexisting polysystems of ideology, politics, economy, language, and other spheres in the target culture, including its literature's internal system. André Lefevere (1992: 1–40) observes that ideology, poetics, and patronage are three major forces that manipulate literary translation. In modern China, two major influences on literary translation are ideology and poetics. Ideology (especially political ideology) and poetics (especially concepts of literary value) in different historical periods are the determinants of translation's selection and norms, thus influencing features and values of literary translations in different periods.

The reason why the requirement of ideology and the pursuit of literary values could hardly coordinate with each other in most cases of China's literary translation is that not all the texts could satisfy both the specific ideological demand and the literary pursuit of a given time. Hence, the selection for literary translation in modern China is usually faced with a dilemma: either to satisfy the ideological requirement for literature, or to pursue the aesthetic ideal of literature. Modern Chinese literature, since its beginning, has taken on an extremely strong feature of political utilitarianism. Reformists and revolutionists mostly take literature as a means of political improvement and social transformation. Liang Qichao, for instance, clearly embodies

A Companion to Modern Chinese Literature, First Edition. Edited by Yingjin Zhang.
© 2016 John Wiley & Sons, Ltd. Published 2016 by John Wiley & Sons, Ltd.

the ideology of utilitarianism. In 1898, he exaggerated the effects of political fiction on social reform:

> At the beginning of the reform in European countries, great masters and erudite scholars usually committed to their novels what they had experienced and desired in political ideas… Once a book was published, it would become the topic of conversation. In countries like the United States, Britain, Germany, France, Austria, Italy, and Japan, their political systems are well developed for the reason that their political novels have made the biggest contributions. (P. Chen and Xia 1989: 21–22)

Liang's emphasis actually foreshadowed the politically oriented literary practices in modern Chinese literature. For the most part, modern China suffered from the invasion of foreign enemies, civil wars, and frequent political movements. Against such a backdrop, the pursuit of aesthetics in the selection of literary translation usually gave way to the demand of political concerns of the given times and the requirement of the dominant ideology. Such a literary orientation toward political utilitarianism has become a basic characteristic of modern Chinese literature and has likewise determined the main features of translated literature in modern China.

Translated Literature in Late Qing and Early Republican Periods

Translated literature in modern China can be traced back to late Qing literary translation. In his 1898 "Preface to the Translation" ("*Yi liyan*") in Huxley's *Evolution and Ethics* (*Tianyan lun*), Yan Fu elaborated "three difficulties in translation: faithfulness (*xin*), expressiveness (*da*), and elegance (*ya*)," and these three concepts have since been considered the standards of translation in China. In 1899, *La Dame aux camellias* (*Bali chahuanü yishi*), translated by Lin Shu, was published, and it enjoyed immediate popularity. In a sense, translated novels aroused great interest in the late Qing intellectual circles. The beginning of the twentieth century witnessed a proliferation of literary journals, such as *Illustrated Fiction* (*Xiuxiang xiaoshuo*, 1903), *New New Fiction* (*Xin xin xiaoshuo*, 1904), *All-Story Monthly* (*Yueyue xiaoshuo*, 1906), *The Grove of Fiction* (*Xiaoshuo lin*, 1907), *The Fiction Times* (*Xiaoshuo shibao*, 1909), and *Short Story Monthly* (*Xiaoshuo yuebao*, 1910), and, in these journals, translated fiction usually took up almost half of each volume. Publishers such as the Commercial Press and the Press of Fiction Grove also relied on translated literature and contributed to its popularity. Literary translation became a new trend in the world of letters, and many fiction writers of late Qing and early Republican China participated in translation with full enthusiasm. As a result, the number of translated fiction works increased year by year, and its total soon equaled or exceeded that of original fiction writing.

Under the influence of Liang Qichao, who himself both wrote and translated political fiction, the translation of political novels became a highlight in the late Qing period. Although Liang originally meant to take advantage of fiction to promote political reform and saw translated works as the most convenient tool of social enlightenment, his criticism of traditional Chinese fiction and his promotion of Western political novels undoubtedly opened up an ample space for subsequent literary translation in China.

In the late Qing and early Republican periods, fiction translation played a leading role, whereas poetry and drama translations were limited in numbers. Political novels directly appealed to political ideals and were largely devoid of entertainment values, so very soon other types of fiction emerged, such as detective and romance, and political novels lost much of their readership. To measure by countries, British literature was translated most frequently into Chinese and added up to nearly 300 titles, far exceeding works from other countries. Ranking after the Great Britain are France, Japan, the United States, and Russia. To measure by genres and authors, the most frequently translated are detective fiction, romance, and science fiction, from Arthur Conan Doyle, Henry Rider Haggard, Jules Verne, Alexandre Dumas *fils*, and Oshikawa Shunrō. The attractions of their works include exciting suspense, extraordinary imagination, and sentimental moods. But the seeming irrelevance of such fiction to politics does not mean that the value orientation of literary translation has switched to aesthetics. As a matter of fact, regardless of genres, the translators usually emphasized the social function and political significance of their translated works in their prefaces or postscripts. For example, in the "Postscript" to *Complete Stories of Sherlock Holmes* (*Fuermosi zhentan an quanji*, 1916), Liu Bannong highlighted the educational significance of detective stories: "Such books are indispensable to the society ... only by means of changing the way ... could [we] enlighten the people"; and he continued, "such is the original objective of Conan Doyle" (P. Chen and Xia 1989: 519–520).

In the late Qing and early Republican periods, Lin Shu's influence topped that of all others. He worked together with Wei Yi and Wang Shouchang in translating more than 180 foreign literary works, including those by Shakespeare, Daniel Defoe, Henry Fielding, Dickens, Jonathan Swift, Sir Walter Scott, and Victor Hugo. Translated by Su Manshu and Chen Duxiu, respectively, Hugo's *Les Miserables* (*Can shijie*, 1904) and *Collection of Byron's Poems* (*Bailun shixuan*, 1908) were quite influential at the time. Ma Junwu adopted the Chinese chanting style in his translation of foreign poetry, for instance, Lord Byron's *The Isles of Greece* (*Ai Xila*, 1905), and his translations captured Byron's classic elegance and were thus highly valued and widely circulated. Alexandre Dumas's *The Three Musketeers* (*Xiayin ji*, 1907), translated by Wu Guangjian, is one of the earliest works translated into vernacular Chinese in the history of Chinese translated literature. In the early twentieth century, there were many popular translated works, such as: *A Collection of Foreign Fictions* (*Yuwai xiaoshuo ji*, 1909) translated by the Zhou brothers (Lu Xun and Zhou Zuoren); Hugo's novels translated by Zeng Pu; and Russian works by Alexander Pushkin, Mikhail Lermontov, Anton Chekhov, and Maxim Gorky translated by Wu Tao, Ji Yihui, and Chen Gu, respectively.

As they engaged more and more with foreign literature, Chinese translators came to appreciate the exquisite narrative art of foreign works and realize deficiencies in Chinese fiction. The significance of fiction translated by Lin Shu is precisely his introduction of world literature to Chinese writers and his broadening of Chinese readers' literary horizons. Lin Shu (1907; 1908) compared Dickens's *The Old Curiosity Shop* (*Xiaonü naier zhuan*, 1907) and *David Copperfield* (*Kuairou yusheng shu*, 1908) with two Chinese classic novels, *Dream of the Red Chamber* and *Water Margin*, and located the deficiencies of these Chinese novels in subject matter, narrative structure, and characterization. Similarly, translators such as Zhou Guisheng and Xu Nianci would "consciously identify the artistic value of foreign works and take them as examples of Chinese fiction writing" (Chen Pingyuan 1989: 29).

Late Qing Chinese translators did not have a full picture of world literature and, for the most part, selected works according to the market demand or their own interests. Such arbitrariness resulted in the coexistence of good and bad translated works. What were translated then were mostly third-rate foreign works, while masterpieces were often neglected. Given Chinese readers' taste and their moral preference, the majority of translated works suffered too many additions and deletions, because the prevailing translation practices at the time were free translation and paraphrased translation. Nonetheless, translated literature in late Qing and early Republican China contributed a great deal to enlighten readers and cultivate a new generation of writers. It assisted in the timely transition of traditional Chinese literature to modern Chinese literature and paved the way for May Fourth New Literature.

Translated Literature from the May Fourth Period to the 1940s

The publication of *New Youth* in 1915 marked another upsurge of literary translation in modern China. From 1915 to 1921, *New Youth* published translated literary works from such countries as Russia, Britain, France, the United States, Japan, Norway, and India, and these translated works came from Ivan Turgenev, Anton Chekhov, Guy de Maupassant, Henrik Ibsen, Henryk Sienkiewicz, Hans Christian Andersen, Maxim Gorky, Mikhail Artsybashev, Mushanokōji Saneatsu, and Oscar Wilde, among others. *New Youth* gave priority, in its earlier stages, to the translation of European realist and aestheticist literature, and in its later stages to the translation of Russian and Japanese literature and the literature of small nations. Its "Ibsen Issue" (Vol. 4, 1918) was quite influential, for it corresponded with the core ideas of the New Culture Movement, which included "science," "democracy," "women's emancipation," and "individualism."

In 1917, Zhou Shoujuan published his translated collection of short stories by European and American masters, which contained 47 works by writers, from 14 countries, all of them readily recognized by Chinese intellectuals at the time. Lu Xun complimented this book as "a sparkle in the night" (Zhou Shoujuan 1987: 1). The purposeful selection of works written by "masters" represents the awakening of a "literary" translation consciousness, and the labeling of "masters" also marks a better understanding of world literature in China. The year 1917 is thus an important turning point in the history of literary translation in modern China and links the late Qing with the period of New Literature.

New literature developed quickly from 1917 to 1937, during which "literature for enlightenment" (*qimeng de wenxue*) was transformed into the "enlightenment of literature" (*wenxue de qimeng*), with the former favoring political utilitarianism and the latter seeking the enrichment of literature itself. A variety of new trends of literature were introduced, and the literary circles showed diversified aesthetic selections in literary translation. As a result, an aesthetically oriented trend became conspicuous. These two decades represented the height of literary translation and displayed the broadest vision in the first half of the twentieth century, as they witnessed the translation of diversified literary works, from ancient Greek literature to modern literature of various countries and schools.

Literary societies played a positive role in the promotion of literary translation in the 1920s. Their core members were passionately engaged in the translation of foreign literature, as much as they were occupied with literary creation. Literary societies with distinctive aesthetic orientations also showed distinctive tendencies in the selection of what was to be translated. The Literary Association preferred realist works from Russia, France, and Northern and Eastern Europe, and kept abreast of the latest trends in foreign literature. The Creation Society focused on the translation of romantic literature and Japanese literature, and the introduction of various literary theories. The Unnamed Society (*Weiming she*) organized by Lu Xun emphasized Russian literature. Other associations also made great contributions to the prosperity of translated literature in this period, such as the translation of foreign folk literature and humor literature by the Yusi Society; the translation of Romain Rolland, Oscar Wilde, and Friedrich Nietzsche by the Bell Society (*Chenzhong she*); and the translation of Shakespeare and Katherine Mansfield by the Crescent Moon Society.

In this period, Russian literature became the favorite of literary translation, and famous writers translated included Ivan Turgenev, Leo Tolstoy, Fyodor Dostoevsky, Anton Chekhov, Maxim Gorky, Leonid Andreev, Mikhail Artsybashev, Nikolai Gogol, Alexander Pushkin, and Alexander Fadeyev. Another highlight of translation then was French literature, involving celebrated writers such as Molière, Romain Rolland, Victor Hugo, Guy de Maupassant, Anatole France, Alphonse Daudet, Émile Zola, Gustave Flaubert, and Voltaire. For Japanese literature, the most often translated were the representatives of the school of Shirakaba: Mushanokōji Saneatsu, Shiga Naoya, Takeo Arishima, and Kikuchi Kan. In the late 1920s, works by Natsume Sōseki and Akutagawa Ryūnosuke were also translated. Other translated works came from Greece, the United States, Denmark, Italy, Poland, Spain, Belgium, India, and Sweden. Translations from this period covered celebrated writers such as Homer, Dante Alighieri, Giovanni Boccaccio, Gabriele D'Annuzio, Hans Christian Andersen, Sinclair Lewis, Jack London, Nathaniel Hawthorne, Henryk Sienkiewicz, Maurice Maeterlinck, and Rabindranath Tagore.

In the 1930s, China's realist literature prospered greatly, which stimulated the translation of its foreign counterparts, especially critical realism from Europe and the United States, and socialist realism from the Soviet Union. In terms of their influence on Chinese literature, critical realism from Europe and the United States did better than socialist realism from the Soviet Union. Another development during this period was the flourishing of Western modernist literature, which inspired numerous Chinese modernist works, such as New Sensationist fiction by Shi Zhecun, Liu Na'ou, and Mu Shiying, or modernist poetry by Dai Wangshu and Bian Zhilin. *Les Contemporains*, a journal edited by Shi Zhecun, published a large number of modernist poems and introduced many modernist writers from Europe and the United States, and it carried special issues such as "Modern American Literature" (vol. 5, no. 6, 1935). Though the translation of modernist literature was still on the margins of the literary translation system, it undoubtedly enriched translated literature in the 1930s and provided references for promising young writers.

The 1930s also saw a boom of the translation of foreign dramas, and as many as 206 plays were translated and published from 1930 to 1937, an equivalent to the total of the previous 22 years (Z. Guo and Li 1998: 398). The genres of translated dramas covered tragedies and comedies of ancient Greece and Rome translated by Yang Hui, Luo Niansheng, and Shi Pu; Shakespeare's plays by Liang Shiqiu and Cao Weifeng; Henrik Ibsen's realist dramas by Pan Jiaxun; Moliere's comedies by Zhao Shaohou; Johann Wolfgang von Goethe's and Friedrich Schiller's enlightenment dramas by Guo Moruo and Zhou Xuepu; Oscar Wilde's aestheticist dramas by Wang Hongsheng and Lin Chaozhen; Bernard Shaw's realist dramas by Lin Yutang and Yao Ke; and modernist dramas of Eugene O'Neill, Maurice Maeterlinck, and Luigi Pirandello by Gu Youcheng, Gu Zhongyi, Xiao Shijun, and Xu Xiacun.

After 1937, China's sociopolitical environment underwent a significant change, and literary themes of the times changed accordingly. A growing number of writers and translators were devoted to national salvation. The Second Sino-Japanese War further intensified Chinese intellectuals' political consciousness, and more translators identified with the mainstream ideology and changed or modified their aesthetic dispositions. Therefore, the translation of war literature and anti-fascist works was highlighted, and so was the translation of Russian literature.

During the May Fourth period, literary translation was mainly produced by men of letters rather than professional translators. When it came to the 1930s–1940s, a community of professional translators came into being, and such professionals as Zhu Shenghao, Fu Donghua, Fu Lei, Ge Baoquan, and Geng Jizhi were specialized in the study and translation of foreign literature. In spite of wartime complications, Zhu Shenghao translated a total of 31 Shakespearean plays, and his work's style and elegance won him a great reputation for decades to come.

In the first half of the twentieth century, the ideal objective of literary translation should both meet the ideological demand of "literature for enlightenment" and benefit from the construction of new literary norms for the "enlightenment of literature." Since few works could simultaneously satisfy both requirements, political demand and aesthetic pursuit in literary translation usually formed two conflicting forces, and only one of them could be taken into consideration. Literary translation would thus swing back and forth between the two forces, and political demand was usually the first consideration because translators believed that "the ideological level of the foreign literary works is a key condition as to whether they should be translated or not"

(Bian Zhilin et al. 1959: 42). In their translation of works from Ivan Turgenev, Leo Tolstoy, Fyodor Dostoevsky, and Anton Chekhov, Chinese translators tended to concentrate on their perceived social significance and to use "literature for life's sake" as their interpretive frame. Burdened by the historical mission of literature, any defense of "literature for literature's sake" and any individual aesthetic experiment deviating from the *Zeitgeist* was deemed dangerous by the mainstream ideology. As far as literary translation is concerned, Qu Qiubai's rhetorical questions said it all: "Who could assert that this is something personal??! Who?!" (1985: 504).

Translated Literature from the 1950s to the 1970s

After 1949, a new socialist ideology based on the theory of Marxism and Leninism was quickly established, and political ideology dominated the Chinese cultural polysystem. Literary translation activities were largely ideologically motivated during this period as socialist realism was imposed on literature and arts. Imported from the Soviet Union as early as the 1930s, socialist realism was exalted to be the highest principle for literature and arts, which should glorify Communist ideals. However, as a creative method, socialist realism was never clearly defined. In the 1950s, Chinese theorists integrated the principle of socialist realism with Mao Zedong's concept of proletarian literature and his criterion that political considerations should override artistic ones, a criterion Mao put forward at his "Yan'an Talks" in the early 1940s. Socialist realism and Mao's literary thoughts were theorized together as a kind of political poetics and became the guide for literature and arts. Needless to say, it was out of political considerations that socialist China would highly praise socialist realist literature and proletarian literature as the most "progressive" and "advanced" kinds in the world. Literary translation was closely regulated and controlled under such a political poetics and used as a tool to produce the required ideological effects.

In the early 1950s, during the socialist transformation of capitalist enterprises, most private publishers were transferred to joint state–private ownership and eventually became state enterprises. It was stipulated that only a few newly established presses had the privilege to publish translations of foreign literature, and they included People's Literature Press and China's Drama Press. This way the state effectively controlled literary translation and managed its three major components: ideology, poetics, and patronage. Literary translation was institutionalized and no longer fell in the sphere of private activities, as it was the case in the first half of the twentieth century.

Although there were no well-defined translation policies and selection criteria, literary translation in the 1950s–1960s was subject to the dominant political ideology. As Lawrence Venuti (1998: 68) indicates, "a calculated choice of foreign text and translation strategy can change or consolidate literary canons, conceptual paradigms, research methodologies, clinical techniques, and commercial practices in the domestic culture." According to China's propaganda orders of that time, it was only under the category of "excellence" (*youxiu*) or "progressiveness" (*jinbu*) that a foreign literary work was permitted for translation into Chinese. Consequently, an inventory of translated literature was established to align with mainstream values. However, without a clear and consistent definition, "excellence" and "progressiveness" were subject to different political interpretations. For instance, Western literary masterpieces such as *Jane Eyre*, *Wuthering Heights*, *Tess of the d'Urbervilles*, *Le Rouge et le Noir*, and *Jean-Christophe* were recognized as "excellent" and "progressive" in the early 1950s, but they all fell into disfavor in the 1960s when ultra-leftism prevailed (Ye Shuifu 2001: 54–55). In general, a work that could be universally acknowledged as "excellent" or "progressive" by China's political ideology of the 1950s had to strictly correspond to socialism and Communism in its theme and style, preferably exemplifying critical realism.

Conditioned by ideological considerations, a new repertoire of translated literature was constructed. As Itamar Even-Zohar (1990: 49) observes, "As a system, translated literature is itself stratified. While one section of translated literature may assume a primary position, another may remain secondary." The works on the primary position were most likely exalted to a canonical position. Even-Zohar (1990: 19) divides canons into two categories, static and dynamic, the former "referring to the level of texts" and the latter "to the level of models." The canonicity of static canons lies in their literary reputation in world literature, but they claim neither productiveness nor influence and efficiency within a literary system. In other words, static canons "are canonized in the sense that they are largely recognized and their prestige acknowledged, yet they are not central in the sense that they do not meet contemporary prevailing literary norms nor serve as active models for producing new texts" (Sheffy 1990: 517). In contrast to static canons, dynamic canons provide productivity for the literary system and deserve attention because a literary model established by dynamic canons "is the most crucial for the system's dynamics" (Even-Zohar 1990: 19).

In the early 1950s, China followed the Soviet policies and theories of literature and arts, and gradually established a set of concepts for literary stratification. According to this new hierarchy, general realist and romantic literature was ranked higher than other types of literature, but lower than critical realist and positive romantic literature, and socialist realist literature and proletarian literature were superior to all other types (Hong Zicheng 1999: 21). Located at the top of this literary pyramid, socialist realist literature and proletarian literature were highly praised to be dynamic canons because they would not only enrich and enforce the ideological discourse but also provide a model for producing desired ideological effects. Typical strategies in cannon formation were to praise given works intended to be canonized as "masterpieces," to recommend them to readers and writers as important references, to compile them into an anthology of literary works, and to include them in Chinese textbooks. The propaganda machinery made every effort in the popularization of socialist and proletarian literature by praising them as the most advanced literature in the world, and therefore the best examples for Chinese writers to follow (Zhou Yang 1953). As a result, the works by Maxim Gorky, Vladimir Mayakovsky, Alexander Ostrovsky, Alexander Fadeyev, Semen Petrovich Babaevsky, Ethel Lilian Voynich, and Kobayashi Takiji soon became part of modern dynamic canons in the new Chinese literary system.

In this socialist period, the translation of Western literature focused more on classical writers such as Shakespeare, Miguel de Cervantes, François Rabelais, Honoré de Balzac, Victor Hugo, Stendhal, Émile Zola, Charles Dickens, Thomas Hardy, and Heinrich Heine, and most of their works, under the category of critical inheritance, were either retranslated or reprinted based on their previous translations. They were granted political legitimacy this time partly due to their praise by Karl Marx and Friedrich Von Engels, their exemplary techniques of realist writing, their "progressiveness in anti-feudalism," or their exposure of the corruption and cruelty of capitalism. However, they were generally underestimated and treated simply as static canons.

However, a few exceptional modern Western literary works were categorized as "excellent" or "progressive." In the early 1950s, a minority of authors from capitalist countries were qualified for translation, and they included George Bernard Shaw, John Galsworthy, Romain Rolland, Louis Aragon, Henri Barbusse, Paul Éluard, Ann Steele, Thomas Mann, Stefan Heym, Martin Andersen Nexø, Hans Kirk, Theodore Dreiser, John Steinbeck, Jack London, Howard Fast, Albert Maltz, Langston Hughes, Kobayashi Takiji, Tokunaga Sunao, and MiyamotoYuriko. Some of them were proletarian or Communist writers with their guaranteed political qualification for translation, such as Louis Aragon, Henri Barbusse, Kobayashi Takiji, Tokunaga Sunao, Miyamoto Yuriko, Howard Fast, and Martin Andersen Nexø. Others were recognized as "progressive" because their works unveiled the corruption of capitalism or depicted the miserable life of the working classes.

Nevertheless, an array of eminent modern Western novelists and poets had been deliberately ignored, or even denounced as reactionary or decadent writers—Franz Kafka, T. S. Eliot, W. B. Yeats, James Joyce, D. H. Lawrence, Jean-Paul Sartre, Albert Camus, Hermann Hesse, F. Scott Fitzgerald, and Eugene O'Neill—because their works came in conflict with socialist ideology or vastly differed from realist poetics. Among these writers, D. H. Lawrence, the son of a coal miner, should have been qualified for translation, given his family background. However, his works were kept from Chinese readers due to "the tendency towards degeneration and corruption," and he was denounced as "a traitor to his working-class background" (Yuan Kejia 1963). Jean-Paul Sartre was a friend of China and travelled there in 1955. In his essay "My Observations of the New China" published on *People's Daily*, he highly praised the development of new China: "With regard to this great forward-looking nation and her miserable past, the feeling the French people share is friendship" (Sartre 1955). However, his existentialist plays were inconsistent with China's dominant ideology and mainstream poetics at that time. Therefore, his translated works were allowed only for internal circulation.

Since the late 1950s, when the relationship between China and the Soviet Union became deeply strained, the translation of Soviet literature had gradually decreased in volumes. Meanwhile, as ultra-leftist ideology became increasingly evident, American and European literary canons were also restricted for translation. From the late 1950s to the Cultural Revolution, literary works by Vietnamese, North Korean, Egyptian, Iraqi, Cuban, and Chilean writers became popular for translation. Those translations had been regarded as political activators, rather than mere literary pursuits, to strengthen relations between China and its allies, which in return enhanced the discursive system of political ideology and reinforced the legitimacy and power of China's political regime.

During the Cultural Revolution, foreign literature was forbidden, and newly published translated works were nowhere to be found. Even *World Literature* (*Shijie wenxue*), China's most influential literary magazine for translating foreign literature, was suspended for publication. In the late period of the Cultural Revolution, only 30 titles by "revolutionary" and "progressive" writers, such as Maxim Gorky, Alexander Ostrovsky, Alexander Fadeyev, and Takiji Kobayashi, were allowed to be published. Meanwhile, more than 40 works of modern literature from the Soviet Union, the United States, and Japan were also published, but only for internal circulation. These publications were used for internal criticism or for domestic and international political struggles rather than for literary appreciation. Nevertheless, those internal publications in fact would become a source of the latest information on contemporary foreign literature for Chinese readers and lay a foundation for literary reflection in the New Era.

Translated Literature from the 1980s to the 1990s

The cultural transition in post-Mao China led to reflection on the alienation of humanity and literature in the Cultural Revolution. The idea that "literature is about and for human beings" (*wenxue shi renxue*) regained its acceptance in China's literary circles in two aspects. First, humanity and humanitarianism were highlighted, and a series of new literary developments such as "scar literature" and "reflective literature" strengthened the subjectivity of literature. Second, the nature of literature itself was reconsidered as Chinese writers attempted to abandon old literary concepts and devices and surmount the barrier of ultra-leftism, pseudo-realism, and pseudo-romanticism. Since the late 1970s, literary translation had started its new journey to another peak in the twentieth century, this time with a special focus on modern and contemporary literature. For Even-Zohar (1990: 45–51), as the dynamics within the polysystem creates turning points when the established models are no longer tenable, translated literature may assume a central position. The late 1970s to the early 1980s is precisely the historical moment for such a change in Chinese literature.

In 1977, *World Literature* resumed publication. A wide range of literary publications were launched to introduce foreign literature, including *Foreign Literature and Art* (*Waiguo wenyi*), *Foreign Literature Studies* (*Waiguo wenxue yanjiu*), *Chunfeng Collection of Translated Literature* (*Chunfeng yicong*), *Contemporary Foreign Literature* (*Dangdai waiguo wenxue*), *Contemporary Soviet Literature* (*Dangdai Sulian wenxue*), and *Soviet Literature* (*Sulian wenxue*). These literary magazines, along with a wide array of translated literary works, all contributed to the golden age of translated literature in China.

Literary translation began to regain its vigor and vitality, and lots of foreign literary classics were reprinted, especially those by Russian, European, and American realist and romantic writers. Many modern and contemporary European and American literary works were translated and published in magazines of foreign literature, filling the blank of translated literature after 1949. Modernist literature was recognized by literary magazines such as *Foreign Literature and Art* and *World Literature*, with an array of translated works of black humor, existentialism, *nouveau roman*, and magical realism. By the mid-1980s, translated literature had covered nearly all major foreign writers, and there were several retranslations of some of their works. The Foreign Literature Press and the Shanghai Translation Press initiated a joint translation project to translate 200 top works in world literature. Contemporary Latin American literature became popular through translation, particularly after the mid-1980s. Works of major Latin American writers, such as Gabriel García Márquez, Vargas Llosa, Miguel Ángel Asturias, and Jorge Luis Borges, were translated into Chinese, some available in different versions.

Since 1987, literary translation has entered a phase of development, the concept of *foreign literature* based on their diverse Chinese translations has been established, and a panorama of world literature has emerged. Owing to the shift within China's ideology and poetics after the 1980s, a new canonized repertoire with advanced translation standards was created. In this new polysystem of translated literature, modern and contemporary Western literature rose to the center stage, while socialist and proletarian literature—including literature of socialist countries such as Vietnam and North Korea—assumed a peripheral position. Many writers highly regarded in the 1950s–1960s were no longer popular now, whereas the works of Oscar Wilde, James Joyce, T. S. Eliot, and D. H. Lawrence, all previously criticized as negative examples, assumed a prominent position. Many eminent writers previously limited or ignored were now placed under spotlight in the 1980s–1990s, and they included Virginia Woolf, Ernest Hemingway, Eugene O'Neill, William Faulkner, Saul Bellow, Joseph Heller, Charles Baudelaire, Marcel Proust, Jean-Paul Sartre, Albert Camus, Thomas Mann, Boris Pasternak, S. A. Yesenin, Anna Akhmatova, Jorge Luis Borges, Miguel Ángel Asturias, Kawabata Yasunari, as well as post-1960 writers such as Chinghiz Aitmatov, Yuri Bondarev, Kurt Vonnegut, Isaac Singer, John Cheever, Alain Robbe-Grillet, Gabriel García Márquez, and Vargas Llosa. Some of their works even had several translated versions and would become the "dynamic canon" of translated literature in the 1980s, such as *Metamorphosis* (*Die Verwandlung*), *Death without a Tomb* (*Mort sans sépulture*), *The Stranger* (*L'Étranger*), *Waiting for Godot* (*En attendant Godot*), *The Old Man and the Sea*, *For Whom the Bell Tolls*, *The Sound and the Fury*, *Mrs. Dalloway*, *In Search of Lost Time* (*À la recherche du temps perdu*), *Ulysses*, *Catch-22*, *One Hundred Years of Solitude* (*Cien años de soledad*), and *The Garden of Forking Paths* (*El Jardín de senderos que se bifurcan*).

Although modernism was a controversial topic in the late 1970s and the early 1980s, literary translation was less influenced by political ideology and more measured by artistic values of the works to be translated. A special focus now was the modernity of world literature and its related modernist and postmodernist writings. In the 1980s, literary translation became directly linked to creative writing in China, and together they promoted the conceptual reform of Chinese literature. In the first half of the twentieth century, translated literature influenced creative writing by bringing in new literary subjects such as women's liberation. When it comes to the 1980s, it played an important role in shaping new literary concepts and techniques. Moreover, translated literature related to Jean-Paul Sartre's existentialism generated a series of enlightening concepts on humanity, such as humanitarianism, freedom, individualism, dignity, existence, alienation, and the value of life, and all these were in conflict with mainstream ideology and therefore facilitated conceptual transformation.

With regard to reception, in Russian and Soviet literature, Fyodor Dostoevsky, Chinghiz Aitmatov, and Boris Pasternak ranked higher than Leo Tolstoy and Maxim Gorky. In British literature, D. H. Lawrence, Virginia Woolf, and James Joyce were more significant than realist writers such as Charles Dickens, William M. Thackeray, and Charlotte Brontë. In American literature, Mark Twain, Theodore Dreiser, John Steinbeck, and Jack London gave way to Ernest Hemingway, William Faulkner, Saul Bellow, and Joseph Heller. Among Germanic and French writers, Franz Kafka, Hermann Hesse, Heinrich Böll, Marcel Proust, Jean-Paul Sartre, Albert Camus, Marguerite Duras, and other *nouveau roman* writers enjoyed a greater literary reputation than Johann Wolfgang von Goethe, Honoré de Balzac, Victor Hugo, Stendhal, and Romain Rolland. As for Asian, African, and Latin American literatures, Kawabata Yasunari, Akutagawa Ryūnosuke, Ōe Kenzaburō, Gabriel García Márquez, Vargas Llosa, and Jorge Luis Borges took the place of Kobayashi Takiji, Tokunaga Sunao, Miyamoto Yuriko, Pablo Neruda, José Martí, Nicolás Guillén, and Jorge Amado. These changes show a shift in literary concepts, which owes much to the influence of literary translation. Nearly all Chinese writers of the 1980s have been influenced by translated literature. For example, Nobel Laureate Mo Yan (1986: 298–299) has acknowledged his debt to Gabriel García Márquez and William Faulkner.

The translation of Western modernist literature offered a unique reference for Chinese writers as they adapted modernist techniques in their own creative writing. In the early 1980s, writings of stream of consciousness, psychological realism, expressionism, and other modernist works were widely translated, from which Chinese writers would borrow narrative tropes such as absurdity, symbolism, emotional association, and interior monologue. In the mid-1980s, with the expansion of translation selection, an increasing number of modernist and postmodernist works were translated. Magic, metaphors, fables, shifts in narrative angles, indirect speeches, and other avant-garde literary devices were all adopted into Chinese creative writing, and it was not uncommon to see an integrated style of modernism and postmodernism in a Chinese novel.

As James McFarlane (Bradbury and McFarlane 1978: 79) points out, "One of the more striking features of Modernism is its wide geographical spread, its multiple nationality… Yet each of the contributing countries has its own cultural inheritance and its own social and political tensions, which impose distinctively national emphasis upon Modernism and leave an account which relies on a single national perspective misleadingly partial." In this respect, Chinese modernist writings in the 1980s offered a new model for the transmission and transformation of modernism around the world, illustrating a new pattern of this literary genre under the dominance of national ideology and poetics. Together with modernist works of other countries, Chinese modernism has not only enriched the literary repertoire of the world's poly-system of modernism, but has also modified the definition and nature of modernist and postmodernist literature.

The interaction between translation and creative writing after the mid-1980s has not been as active as that in the early 1980s. After filling the blank, the main task for literary translation is to construct a vista of world literature in synchrony with its development. In this way, Chinese writers would feel the presence of world literature. With more and more global ingredients combined into its own literary writing, Chinese literature has finally joined in the mainstream of world literature.

Conclusion

In view of the history of translated literature in modern China, we can conclude that its development is closely related to its various social contexts, political ideologies, and cultural poetics. Foreign literature subject to translation is no longer foreign literature on its original soil, for it has become part of the target culture's literature and has influenced the cultural quality of specific eras in modern China. Translated literature has enriched and expanded modern China's literary creation and reception, forming the relations of heterogeneous isomorphism with creative literature and becoming an integral part of China's literary polysystem.

REFERENCES

Bian Zhilin 卞之琳, Ye Shuifu 葉水夫, Yuan Kejia 袁可嘉, and Chen Shen 陳燊. 1959. "Shinian lai de waiguo wenxue fanyi he yanjiu gongzuo" 十年來的外國文學翻譯和研究工作 (Translation and research of foreign literature in the recent decade). *Wenxue pinglun* 文學評論 (Literature review), 5: 41–77.

Bradbury, Malcolm, and James McFarlane. 1978. *Modernism: A Guide to European Literature 1890–1930*. London: Penguin Books.

Chen, Pingyuan 陳平原, and Xia Xiaohong 夏曉虹, eds. 1989. *Ershi shiji Zhongguo xiaoshuo lilun ziliao (di yi juan) 1897–1916* 二十世紀中國小說理論資料 (第一卷) *1897–1916* (Theoretical materials for Chinese fiction of the twentieth century, vol. 1, 1897–1916). Beijing: Beijing daxue chubanshe.

Chen, Pingyuan 陳平原. 1989. *Ershi shiji Zhongguo xiaoshuo shi, diyijuan 1897–1916* 二十世紀中國小說史, 第一卷 *1897–1916* (A history of twentieth-century Chinese fiction, vol. 1, 1897–1916). Beijing: Beijing daxue chubanshe.

Even-Zohar, Itamar. 1990. "The Position of Translated Literature within the Literary Polysystem." *Poetics Today*, 11: 45–51.

Guo, Zhigang 郭志剛, and Li Xiu 李岫, eds. 1998. *Zhongguo sanshi niandai wenxue fazhan shi* 中國三十年代文學發展史 (A history of the development of 1930s Chinese literature). Changsha: Hunan jiaoyu chubanshe.

Hong, Zicheng 洪子誠. 1999. *Zhongguo dangdai wenxueshi* 中國當代文學史 (A history of contemporary Chinese Literature). Beijing: Beijing daxue chubanshe.

Lefevere, André. 1992. *Translation, Rewriting and the Manipulation of Literary Fame*. London: Routledge.

Lin, Shu 林紓. 1907. "Xu" 序 (Preface). In *Xiaonv naier zhuan* 孝女耐兒傳 (The Old Curiosity Shop). Trans. Lin Shu 林紓 and Wei Yi 魏易. Beijing: Shangwu yinshu guan.

Lin, Shu 林紓. 1908. "Qianbian xu" 前編序 (Preface). In *Kuairou yusheng shu* 塊肉餘生述 (David Copperfield). Trans. Lin Shu 林紓, and Wei Yi 魏易. Beijing: Shangwu yinshu guan.

Liu, Bannong 劉半農. 1916. "Ba" 跋 (Postscript). In *Fuermosi zhentan an quanji* 福爾摩斯偵探案全集 (Complete stories of Sherlock Holmes). Trans. Cheng Xiaoqing 程小青 et al. Shanghai: Zhonghua shuju.

Mo, Yan 莫言. 1986. "Liangzuo zhuore de gaolu—Jiaxiya Maerkesi he Fukena" 兩座灼熱的高爐—加西亞.馬爾克斯和福克納 (Two blasting furnaces: García Márquez and William Faulkner). *Shijie wenxue* 世界文學 (World literature), 3: 298–299.

Qu, Qiubai 瞿秋白. 1985. "Lun fanyi—gei Lu Xun de xin" 論翻譯—給魯迅的信 (On translation—letters to Lu Xun). In *Qu Qiubai wenji wenxue bian, diyi juan* 瞿秋白文集.文學編, 第一卷 (Collected works of Qu Qiubai: literature series, vol. 1). Beijing: Renmin wenxue chubanshe.

Sartre, Jean-Paul 薩特. 1955. "Wo dui xin Zhongguo de guangan" 我对新中國的觀感 (My observations of the new China). *Renmin ribao* 人民日報 (People's daily) (Nov. 2).

Sheffy, Rakefet. 1990. "The Concept of Canonicity in Polysystem Theory." *Poetics Today*, 11.3: 511–522.

Venuti, Lawrence. 1998. *The Scandals of Translation: Towards an Ethics of Difference*. London: Routledge.

Ye, Shuifu 葉水夫. 2001. "Woguo wenxue mingzhu fanyi zhong de yixiang dianjixing gongcheng" 我國文學名著翻譯中的一項奠基性工程 (A foundation project for the translation of world's classics in China). *Zhongguo fanyi* 中國翻譯 (Chinese translators), 1: 54–55.

Yuan, Kejia 袁可嘉. 1963. "Lüelun Mei Ying 'xiandaipai' shige" 略論美英"現代派"詩歌 (A short account of American and British "Modernist" poetry). *Wenxue pinglun*, 3: 64–85.

Zhou, Shoujuan 周瘦鵑, trans. 1987. *Ou Mei mingjia duanpian xiaoshuo* 歐美名家短篇小說 (Short stories by European and American masters). Changsha: Yuelu. First edition 1917.

Zhou, Yang 周揚. 1953. "Shehui zhuyi xianshi zhuyi—Zhongguo wenxue de daolu" 社會主義現實主義—中國文學的道路 (Socialist realism: future road for Chinese literature). *Renmin ribao* (Nov. 1).

14

Writing Chinese Feminism(s)

Amy Dooling

Near the end of the twentieth century, Li Xiaojiang, a prominent feminist scholar often credited with pioneering the field of women's studies in the PRC, lamented (1993: 15):

> It's really not surprising that women don't care for history. They don't know how many of their commendable heroic accomplishments there are in history, and they don't know how to locate themselves in a history that has submerged women. It's as though women's history has been artificially severed, in history books, in museums, and in people's minds.

Such a view is emblematic of a new gender discourse in the contemporary reform era that critiques the modernity projects of the twentieth century, including Maoist state feminism, for having subsumed female agency, rendering women mere symbols of male-centered discourses or, at best, passive objects of a bestowed liberation. Only in the present moment, Li contends, have Chinese women begun to emerge as true subjects in their own right, capable of self-consciousness and self-representation and thus writing themselves into history.

Efforts to reclaim women's history in recent decades—as evident in the extraordinary corpus of scholarship that has emerged—register this new consciousness on the part of the PRC-based academic feminists. Comprised of various approaches, including oral histories, ethnographies, and studies of women's lives, past and present, a central characteristic of this scholarship has been its insistent privileging of female experiences, perspectives, and voices. It has also, in its convergence with a dynamic transnational field of interdisciplinary work by China scholars abroad, enabled a rethinking of

A Companion to Modern Chinese Literature, First Edition. Edited by Yingjin Zhang.
© 2016 John Wiley & Sons, Ltd. Published 2016 by John Wiley & Sons, Ltd.

women's participation in the historical development of Chinese feminism(s) that contextualizes and complicates Li's claim in intriguing ways. If Li's efforts have played a crucial strategic role at this particular juncture in Chinese feminism by "help[ing] to dislodge Maoist class analysis and enabl[ing] the emergence of 'woman' as a legitimate subject of research" (Hershatter and Wang 2008: 1416), the interpretive spaces that new scholarship has helped open up also reveal not just the erasures that have occurred but significant resistances and interventions that, similar to Li herself, Chinese feminists have been making all along.

As many have observed (Hershatter and Wang 2008; Wang 2007), feminist theory has played an undeniable (albeit not uncontested) role in the recent transformation of Chinese and English scholarship on Chinese women. Of equal importance is the return to the archive to seek out new source materials and retrieve past textual records, including the writings of women themselves. In literary studies, newly resurrected volumes of poetry, drama, fiction, reportage, histories, novels, autobiographies, and love-letter collections, as well as a fascinating body of periodical texts dating from as far back as the 1890s, have fundamentally altered conceptions of women's writing, revealing not only legacies of female literary expression that extend well before the advent of the twentieth century, but also a rich record of cultural activity on the part of modern women invisible in standard historiography. Meng Yue and Dai Jinhua's *Emerging on the Horizon of History* (1989), an early example of the PRC scholarship, marks a stunning breakthrough in the study of Chinese women's literary history, both in terms of the exhilarating range of source materials the authors consider and the feminist theoretical perspective they bring to bear on the subject.

Today, canonical figures such as Ding Ling, long considered the quintessential modern female/feminist author and example *par excellence* of the possibilities and constraints of writing as a woman in a modern revolutionary context, appear less representative, as multiple and often discordant voices of writers of the past century are once again made available, via reprints, newly compiled anthologies, biographies, and translations of their work. To give one example of the large-scale endeavors launched in the 1990s to recover Chinese women's literature, Shanghai Guji Publishing House's Hongying series showcased Republican-era writers as stylistically and ideologically diverse as Yang Gang, Luo Hong, Chen Hengzhe, Shi Jimei, Feng Yuanjun, Chen Ying, Su Xuelin, Lin Huiyin, Mei Niang, Lu Yin, Guan Lu, Luo Shu, Ling Shuhua, and Zhang Ailing (Eileen Chang). The collected works of Chen Xuezhao, Shi Pingmei, Yang Jiang, Xie Bingying, and Zong Pu, among many others, also began appearing in rapid succession in the 1990s. While this publishing phenomenon or "frenzy" (S. Kong 2005) has been fueled by the rapid rise of a consumer-oriented literary market that threatens to contain the subversive potential of female literary voices (through marketing strategies that fortify narrow stereotypes of femininity and female sexuality or that reinforce highly essentialized conceptions of female writing), the very availability of the wide-ranging creative output of modern female authors makes possible for it to be re-read and critically analyzed as part of Chinese cultural history and, simultaneously, to recast that history from fresh perspectives. The field is arguably still in the initial stages of sorting through, interpreting, and evaluating the significance of China's long overlooked female authors. But one thing such writing has unequivocally established is that literary women participated in far more inventive and polemical ways than has previously been assumed in the various projects of Chinese feminism.

We now know that the seemingly unprecedented burst of textual activity by radical women at the *fin-de-siècle* had historical roots in the literary (and editorial) practices and new modes of political consciousness of learned elite women of late imperial times; if the "writing woman" would soon be appropriated as a key trope of modernity by twentieth-century intellectuals and artists, there was in fact nothing inherently novel about women writers. Meanwhile, recently unearthed examples such as Lü Bicheng, an accomplished *ci* poet who continued to compose in the classical style into the 1920s–1930s but who embodied and expressed an undeniable modernity in her writing and life choices, suggest hitherto unacknowledged continuities and ambiguities that revise the conventional May Fourth genealogy of twentieth-century women's writing (Fong 2004). Still, most scholars would agree that the confluence of particular sociohistorical forces in the late nineteenth and early twentieth centuries—among them, expanding opportunities for women to pursue higher education and professional careers, access to the global arena through translations and travel, the rise of the urban periodical press along with new literary and visual media forms, and heady intellectual trends that disrupted Confucian social norms—also shaped a *new style* of female literary intellectual who participated in public culture along with a burgeoning modern discourse on women's writing itself.

Neither the shifting roles of women in the literary sphere during this eventful era nor the shifting notions of the female author can be disentangled from the development of progressive ideas and ideals that constituted early feminist thought. This is not to say, of course, that female-authored texts of this era necessarily constituted feminist writing. At a time of sweeping yet profoundly uneven sociopolitical transformations, the creative practices of twentieth-century literary women (and, for that matter, their male counterparts) have encompassed wide-ranging styles, genres, forms, thematic foci, and aesthetic and political agendas, only some of which addressed feminist concerns and perspectives. In fact, in the first half of the twentieth century, among those most critically attuned to the status of women were progressive male intellectual elites who not only took young female authors under their wings as protégés but actively (and often rather vociferously) explored and promoted ideologies of gender equality in their own writing. The motivations and, more crucially, the lasting implications of the central engagement of male elites in Chinese feminist projects have become the focal point of much current revisionist scholarship. Contemporary critics have investigated a persistent paternalism underlying much of the writing on women that undermines its ostensible critique of male power and privilege. But to conclude that feminist literary expressions of this era amounted to little more than a façade behind which lurked unreformed male chauvinism is overly reductive. One area that warrants further attention is the ways in which feminists (male and female) of earlier eras posed pertinent and sometimes contentious questions about the practices and politics of representing women, and engaged shifting articulations of the problem of female self-representation itself. If, as some contemporary academic feminists posit, the profound alienation that Chinese women experience vis-à-vis modern history is (at least in part) a function of masculinist historiography, tracing these moments of discursive struggle is as relevant as teasing out examples of patriarchy's stubborn tenacity.

This chapter concerns the voices of Chinese feminists writing in the first decade of the twentieth century for whom, it turns out, locating women in history as active makers of their own fates was also of paramount concern. Yet, unlike post-Mao feminists who call for a revisiting of the past to inscribe women anew, for late Qing women writers it was the prospect of an as-yet unwritten history of the future from which they drew inspiration. The fictions they crafted about revolutions-on-the-horizon engaged a vital process of carving out imaginative space from which, it was hoped, a new female subject would emerge. In this project, they placed particular emphasis on the transformative power of texts.

Back to the Future: Reading Utopian Imaginaries in Late Qing Feminist Fiction

Late Qing feminist fiction abounds with exuberant, idealized representations of newspapers, manifestos, political treatises, novels, and translations of foreign books, all part of a modern print culture imagined as crucial to the revolutionary processes they narrate. As a key conduit for political ideas and information, written texts are depicted as profoundly altering the way (elite) women envisage their place in the world and their roles in creating new (personal and national) futures. Indeed, it is frequently an encounter with a printed text that sets in motion the female protagonist's quest, causing her to undergo a spectacular shift in self-identity, while subsequent engagements with reading and writing are depicted as significant public/political acts that advance the social justice causes she pursues. Modern texts are also represented as radically reshaping female characters' relationships to other women and to the public domain in general—we find fictional heroines in many stories reading about each other in the new-style press; they cite, promote, and transmit each other's written words; and they actively circulate their own texts to influence and rouse readers to action, creating an ever-widening literate female public (*qun*). The inclusion of such self-reflexive gestures registers the palpable sense of possibility afforded by the various new paradigms of female literacy being discussed and debated in late Qing China. But, above all, it suggests a conscious desire to write women into the story of revolution itself, not as merely symbolic figures of historical change but as empowered agents capable of transforming the world.

Such textual self-reflexivity registers momentous cultural and political developments unfolding in China at the turn of the twentieth century, a time of acutely perceived national crisis and intellectual ferment. Aside from widespread debates about the meaning(s) of female learning that unfolded in this context, this period also saw the rapid influx of translations (often via Japanese sources) whose strategic appropriation disrupted established textual and intellectual traditions underpinning gender norms, while the rise of the political press and new journalistic ideals afforded elite literate women access to a powerful venue of public discourse (Y. Ma 2010). The years leading up to the Xinhai Revolution in 1911 were marked by the proliferation of newspapers and periodicals targeting female audiences, some two dozen or so launched by activist women with feminist leanings such as Chen Xiefen, Luo Yanbin, He-Yin Zhen, and Qiu Jin. Even though most of these publications were short-lived and none achieved a broad circulation, confidence in the potential of the modern press to edify and mobilize the general public is abundantly apparent. In an editorial statement for her magazine, Qiu Jin (1907) proclaims:

> Who is responsible for controlling the force of public opinion and taking charge of guiding the citizens of the nation if not the press? Today, this magazine will unite our two hundred million women by circulating our news and serving as our general head-quarters. It will enliven the *nüjie* and arouse their spirits.

Rhetorical flourishes notwithstanding, modern print culture helped in beginning to construct, consolidate, and disseminate alternative notions of female gender roles and identities in this period, both through the imported lexicon it popularized as well as its unorthodox content, which included articles addressing women's rights, entitlements, and interests, news accounts of current events in "the women's world" (*nüjie*), both at home and abroad, practical information, as well as literary works in various genres. It is no coincidence that among the new-style female exemplars whose biographies were often featured in the reform press were nineteenth-century women journalists themselves: Margaret Fuller Ossoli, Mary Livermore, and Juliette Adam were among those introduced to late Qing readers, while Lü Bicheng, one of the pioneer female journalists in China at the time, also garnered significant media attention herself. More so than other role models being proposed and circulated in print at the time, the female journalist embodied an alternative gendered public identity that melded together disparate ideals about writing, women's emancipation, civic participation, political transformation, physical mobility, and global modernity. Indeed, the new-style female journalist had accrued so much cultural capital at the time that male literati began adopting feminine pennames (Volz 2007).

Political fiction produced in the last decade of the Qing dynasty also thematized such ideals, not just by figuring women as journalists, but by enlisting representations of modern print forms as a rich and productive site for exploring links between gender and revolution, between female literacy and social justice. Here, I draw from four key examples: Wang Miaoru's *Flowers in the Female Prison* (*Nüyuhua*, 1904), Yi Suo's *Huang Xiuqiu* (1905), Qiu Jin's *Stones of the Jingwei Bird* (*Jingwei shi*, 1907), and *Women's Rights* (*Nüziquan*, 1907) by Siqi Zhai (penname of Zhan Kai). I emphasize the pivotal role played by texts in the heroines' revolutionary journey, a recurring motif that projects a vision of female liberation as entailing more than overcoming corporal limitations or relocating bodies from private to public spaces. The unbinding of feet and physical departure from the inner chambers are often salient features of the fictional narrative of female transformation in this period as well, but crucially it is the mental and imaginative shift produced by the reading of new texts that is depicted as the genesis of a new storyline.

A prime example of this occurs in *Huang Xiuqiu*, one of the better known works of late Qing feminist fiction, in which the eponymous protagonist experiences political "enlightenment" after the French revolutionary Madame Roland appears to her in a dream vision and bestows upon her three volumes—a translation of Plutarch's *Parallel Lives*, a book of world geography, and Roland's own memoir. The fact that Roland, and a number other historical Western women whose life stories had been introduced to Chinese readers in the political press, make their way into late Qing novels, provides further testimony of how fiction is imprinted by new-style journalism. The encounter is said to "hit her at the bottom of her heart" (Yi Suo 1988: 183) and instantly transforms her relationship to language itself: overcoming her rudimentary knowledge of foreign languages, she now devours the contents of these books and suddenly becomes capable of "reading ten lines at glance" (Yi Suo 1988: 191):

> It was her emotions that spawned the dream and the dream that spawned wisdom. The books discussed by the lady in the dream opened a train of thought and gave her new ideas. It was as though she had been taught by the immortal Buddha, as though she had been instantly enlightened.

In these and other similar fictional scenarios, exposure to new texts transforms the meaning of previous feminine experience. Although the description may strike the reader as unsubtle today, what is conceptualized here is that gender emancipation is in part a matter of consciousness; that the subjective realm of the imagination is as urgently in need of transformation as the realms of politics and society. In Qiu Jin's *tanci* narrative, *Stones of the Jingwei Bird*, the moment of "awakening" entails a pivotal shift from feminine lament to feminist resistance. The author sets the scene by staging an emotional dialogue in which a group of young learned women (*cainü*) air their grievances over the myriad restrictions associated with orthodox gender roles. The perspective is clearly intended to convey that of the educated, elite boudoir woman (*guixiu*), and it is significant that Qiu Jin has her characters voice the intense frustration and despair borne of stifled intellectual aspirations as part of their broad-ranging critique of female sufferings—which includes lifelong economic dependency on men; imposed physical frailty; arranged marriage; concubinage; polygamy; the physical and mental paralysis resulting from enforced idleness; the debilitating mindlessness of embroidery and other conventional feminine arts; restrictions on public mobility; and more.

Significantly, references to soaring ambitions, multifaceted talents, and great wisdom that remain painfully unfulfilled under the conditions of Confucian domesticity articulate a view quite distinct from the disparaging image of *cainü* put forth by prominent political reformers such as Liang Qichao at the time, for whom the cloistered woman was the embodiment of the obstacles to China's national progress.[1] Rather than blame *cainü* for society's contemporary malaise, Qiu Jin condemns society for denying women endowed with intellectual, moral, and artistic capacities the proper outlets to realize their full potential.[2] Yet, the author goes on to use the scene to critique the limits of *guixiu* consciousness: just as the chapter reaches an emotional crescendo, the young ladies are depicted as dissolving into a flood of tears (and poetry), apparently unable to imagine new horizons beyond their predetermined domestic destinies (Qiu Jin 1998: 63): "[They] were all depressed too, dreading what awaited them in the future. The women's world is so cruel, but who can avoid it?"

This is the precise point at which the plot turns to the arrival of the heroine Huang Jurui, whose stirring oral transmission of foreign texts (surreptitiously supplied by her tutor) enables the girls to grasp the possibility of a transgressive future. The message has a heady nationalistic ring to it: citing the (alleged) freedoms and rights enjoyed by Western women, Huang invokes the familiar late Qing formulation that "[t]he strength of a nation and a race hinges entirely on women" (Qiu Jin 1998: 71). But given the narrative focus on the specific conditions of feminine suffering, the characters' embrace of alternative ideals seem predicated on grounds other than purely national well-being. What strikes a chord is the promise of personal autonomy and fulfillment, not the prospect of becoming modern wives and mothers capable of running efficient households or rearing citizen–sons to serve the project of nation-building. Indeed, no sooner has the protagonist invoked examples of Western women leading self-determined public lives than the group resolves to throw off their domestic shackles and pursue modern studies and personal independence in Japan. The author ends the scene by conjuring up a sanguine vision of female self-initiative, as the newly formed sisterhood collectively formulates a plan to secure sufficient funds for their venture, plots an escape route, and agrees upon the necessity of unbinding their feet. We do not have the complete text of *Stones of the Jingwei Bird* (left unfinished at the time of the author's execution for sedition in 1907), but the extant table of contents indicates that Qiu Jin intended to trace the eventual political mobilization of the rebellious sorority: having made their way abroad, the projected plotline appears to follow the characters as they swear political oaths, demonstrate in public rallies, build factories, go through military training, and eventually take part in the revolutionary movement to restore Chinese/Han sovereignty and found a Republic.

Feminist practitioners of the "political novel" also imagined women's new political identities and allegiances in plots that featured characters who bonded through public expression of ideas and opinion and, in some cases, formed collaborative relationships through journalism.[3] Books and newspapers are able to infiltrate the inner quarters to galvanize *cainü* (as in *Stones of the Jingwei Bird*), but are also envisioned as decisive in mobilizing the new breed of female students inhabiting modern schools. The protagonist of *Women's Rights*, for instance, is catapulted to fame after publishing an article in a major daily newspaper. Inspired by the character's personal experience of thwarted romance, the article examines the root causes of female subordination and calls for the restoration of women's rights through education and the development of professional occupations. Typical of the overt pedagogical thrust of such fiction in this era, a brief summary of the argument appears in the narrative itself. But again, what is interesting is how print media is imagined as instrumental in bringing together individual women and female students across the land into political unity (Siqi Zhai 1907: 23):

> At this time, the rail system in China was very efficient, and the *Tianjin Daily* had a daily circulation of over 100,000 copies. So when the essay appeared, within a day Zhenniang's name was known far and wide. By the next day, the essay had been widely reprinted in other papers. As a result, there was not a female student anywhere who was not talking about Zhenniang, a Chinese female gallant promoting women's rights. After a while, the academic world hailed her as the female Spencer.

Not unlike actual turn-of-the-century periodicals comprising the emergent women's press, which trumpeted a sense of vast geographic reach through the self-conscious display of far-flung locations of distribution (stretching from Beijing and Shanghai to Guangdong and Sichuan, but also to Japan, Europe, and the United States), here too we are presented with the vision of an expansive network of female readers whose consciousness has been aroused through texts and thereby linked to a common public cause. Modern print culture, in short, is attributed as being instrumental in constituting *qun*—both in terms of reshaping relationships/modes of solidarity between women, and creating communities anchored not in kinship but in intellectual affinities and shared commitment to civic causes.

Perhaps the more significant point is how the figure of the journalist herself serves as a way for the author to imagine and explore a newly constructed ideal of modern Chinese womanhood. Implicitly challenging both established paradigms of female selfhood and emergent nationalist ideals of *xianqi liangmu* (virtuous wives and kind mothers), the journalist embodies (through her writing) a distinctly public identity, distinguished by her ability to traverse geographic barriers, to communicate with a broad audience, and to deploy her public voice to shape and influence political and social affairs, including most importantly issues pertinent to women themselves. Thus, in contrast to the competing late Qing image of benighted womanhood in dire need of being liberated by enlightened male saviors, we see here an attempt to envisage the modern woman herself in the role of feminist advocate.

Notably, the depiction of print media in these examples portrays Chinese women as members of a global arena, who are invested emotionally and politically in the lives and experiences not just of their compatriots but of female counterparts the world over. Thus, in *Women's Rights*, the press coverage of the legislative victories of the American suffragettes or the struggles of female labor unions in Russia not only brings great emotional satisfaction to the heroine when she reads of them in the newspaper but further inspires her to forge on with her own crusade for women's rights in China. In *Flowers in the Female Prison*, coverage of a feminist insurrection in China in the French press also conjures up a vision of a transnational movement for equality in which the struggles of Chinese women are deemed a relevant part. Not unlike the "news" or "current events" columns in actual late Qing women's periodicals,[4] which often deliberately juxtaposed reports about contemporary activities of women in China alongside those of international women, fictive representations of the modern press articulate a vision that seems to go beyond a purely nationalist concept of citizenship and identifies 'the modern woman' as belonging to a global modernity.

Finally, we find in these works exuberant representations of the role of print media in social and political transformation. A particularly self-reflexive instance occurs in *Women's Rights,* in which the central heroine launches a daily newspaper, *The Woman Citizen (Nü guomin)*, aimed at a female readership to promulgate educational reform and professional vocations for women. As if to underscore the collective nature of the enterprise, the protagonist instructs her classmates to collaboratively formulate the editorial policies that will guide the newspaper. Notably, the resulting 10 regulations (on everything from format, content, and proper balance between classical and vernacular linguistic registers, to hiring and advertising policies) are recorded in full within the text itself (Siqi Zhai 1907: 25–26). Much of the episode, moreover, is devoted to outlining step-by-step the concrete process whereby the newspaper gets off the ground: raising capital, attracting shareholders, electing an editorial board, renting office space, and so forth. Needless to say, the venture proves a great success: at the end of the chapter, we learn that *The Woman Citizen* immediately achieves a wide circulation (even capturing attention abroad) and spurs the rapid growth of schools and factories throughout the land. The chapter itself reads much like a how-to manual for publishing a newspaper. The details do little to either further the plot or develop characters; instead, their function is to equip the reader with the practical knowledge needed in order to pursue the course of action the novel calls for.[5]

Yet, the fictional representation of modern texts emphasizes more than their utilitarian function in the delivery and circulation of vital news, facts, and information. Embedded in these and other examples is the notion that new writing resists and transforms the gendered status quo by disrupting entrenched linguistic habits and investing the lexicon with new meanings that reflect anti-patriarchal values and assumptions. In other words, it is not simply that the female reader needs greater awareness of the world from which she has hitherto been denied access; she needs different awareness of the world she already inhabits. A prime instance of this occurs in *Flowers in the Female Prison*, which presents a bold feminist tract entitled *The Book of Enmity (Choushu)*, authored by the formidable Sha Xuemei for the newspaper run by her and her colleagues. As a character who advocates the use of physical violence as a revolutionary tactic, Sha symbolizes an extremist position in the political spectrum from which the author distances herself by having the character meet a spectacular demise. The text Sha leaves behind, interestingly, is endorsed by the novel's other central protagonist, the moderate reformer Pingquan, who summarizes its content in the stirring speech she delivers at the inauguration of her newly founded school. In one example, she notes thus (Wang Miaoru 1994: 59):

> The book has a chapter on all sorts of feminine adornments: for instance, to wear earrings means to puncture the ear as punishment; to wear bracelets is to be handcuffed; to bind one's feet is tantamount to being be-footed; to apply rouge and powder is to paint one's face with a brush dipped in shit and lie prostrate awaiting punishment.

By re-labeling common beauty practices as cruel modes of corporal punishment, the (fictional) author subverts the valence of such terms, pushing the reader to apprehend them anew in terms of the harm they inflict on the female body and to associate their practice with a misogynistic exercise of male power. Pingquan deems the radical language excessive but nevertheless confirms the valuable shift in perspective achieved through the author's rhetorical violence.

Qiu Jin also accentuates the connection between the practices that reinforce female subordination and discursive power: in the allegorical story that frames her *tanci* narrative, she describes the origins of conventional gender doctrines codified in traditional texts in terms of fictions of female inferiority: thus, the age-old maxim "*nüzi wucai bianshi de*" (for women, lack of literary talent is a virtue) is said to be a phrase concocted for the purpose of "keeping women from learning and making them completely ignorant" (Qiu Jin 1960: 126). The manipulations and falsifications enacted through patriarchal language are what, for Qiu Jin, have bred the debilitating habits of thought/imagination that bind women to narrow modes of female conduct and morality (Qiu Jin 1960: 126):[6]

> Who knew that men and women alike are born with four limbs and five sense organs, and that their abilities, wisdom, courage and strength are all identical. Their duties and rights are also identical. But because women could not read, were deprived of experience outside of the home, and could not engage in activities in public, but instead spent their entire lives inside, they threw away every bit of talent and allowed men to occupy the superior position, who in turn thought up one way after another to oppress women.

So again, we see the notion that a break from traditional gender boundaries requires fundamental reconfiguration of the discursive realm.

It is worth noting that hyperbolic rhetorical maneuvers of this kind are found throughout other genres of feminist writing at the time—an indication, perhaps, of the fact that, for this generation, Confucian texts were still "living texts" (Ko 2009). In her impassioned political tract "On the Revenge of Women" ("*Nüzi fuchou lun,*" 1907), the anarcho-feminist theorist He-Yin Zhen offers an extended critique of the ways in which gender inequalities are inscribed in the Chinese language, and marshals copious evidence in an effort to denaturalize the semantic connotations of common terms and inflect them anew. To cite just a couple of her voluminous examples, cloistering is renamed as a form of imprisonment, while rites and propriety are in fact humiliation. Even the long-venerated Confucian scholar Ban Zhao is bestowed with the new appellation Banzei (Traitor Ban), to expose her complicity in crafting the "scholarship" that has yoked and injured women. What makes He-Yin Zhen especially prescient for her time was her critique of the feminist neologisms that were gaining currency within late Qing political discourse—as her tract argues, appropriating new rhetoric alone would not guarantee new gender relations; rather, it might become a new impediment to revolution in merely creating the mere veneer of change. Not unlike Sha Xuemei's fictional *Book of Enmity*, He-Yin Zhen's historical text underscores how words can exert violent discursive power by twisting and distorting the realities of the gender hierarchy and ultimately subordinating the female mind itself.

Back to History: Textual Legacies of Late Qing Feminists

The texts I have briefly addressed in the preceding section expand the notion of how revolution itself was imagined and conceived by feminist-leaning intellectuals at the time—they used fiction (and other textual forms) to call for changes in social and political institutions, but they were equally passionate about the need for transformation of the imagination itself, a process that would necessarily involve new forms of texts and language as new and vital arenas of interaction. Each one of these texts reveals a trenchant understanding not just of the predicaments of Chinese women at the time but the importance of literary and journalistic culture in moving beyond them.

In the decades following 1911, the gendered transformations imagined in these future-looking novels were no longer confined primarily to a fictional landscape but became increasingly tangible as part of social reality. Certainly, while the revolution itself never fully materialized, considerable strides were made over the course of the early twentieth century in terms of expanding women's access to higher education and professional employment, choice in marriage, and of course the political realm— all pressing areas on which the first-wave of late Qing feminist thinkers and writers had turned a critical gaze. Feminist campaigns for formal political rights would not come to fruition until 1947, but the suffrage struggle itself flourished as a vibrant and vocal movement, at least for elite urban women, throughout the Republican era. Activists with more radical convictions were drawn to the labor movement and Marxist organizations—including the Chinese Communist Party—to address the status of women in relation to more fundamental structures underpinning social and economic inequalities.

Yet, at least at first glance, it would appear that beginning with the "new" Republic of China, Chinese feminist activists and writers, no matter where they located themselves on the political spectrum, drew little inspiration from the legacies of their late Qing predecessors. There is of course one well-known exception: Ding Ling's novel *Mother* (*Muqin*, 1933), which depicts the political awakening of elite women of her mother's generation at the turn of the century, marks an attempt to situate women's liberation within wider processes of historical change, a shift in narrative practice prompted by the author's growing commitments to Marxism. Critics at the time, and later, have condemned the work as a failure. For the most part, however, feminist imaginings in the 1920s–1930s seldom seem to glance back in this way, preoccupied instead with locating the story of the birth of the "new" Chinese woman in the present moment. Turning to scholarly accounts published in the 1920s–1930s that addressed the historic rise of the Chinese women's movement confirms this impression, with their striking tendency to present the momentous years leading up to the Revolution of 1911 as a mere prelude to what is deemed the "real" story of change. This is true not only of influential studies by scholars such as Chen Dongyuan (1928) but also of some works authored by feminists who inscribed this history from a more personal vantage point. Veteran suffrage campaigner Liu-Wang Liming, for instance, reduces the political ferment at the turn-of-the-century to a few short lines that portray women's participation in terms of patriotic duty and self-sacrifice:

> Ever since *Nüjiezhong* advocated that women ought to take up the duty of saving the nation, there were women who were awakened, throwing themselves into the revolution and even passionately conspiring with men to overthrow the Manchu Qing government. After the news of Qiu Jin's demise spread, even more joined the revolution. During the Wuchang uprising, women joined in militant activities, and later many joined the Red Cross to tend to wounded soldiers. In the first year of the Republic the parliament was established, women started to struggle for political rights and from that period until now, even though this movement has occasionally fallen silent, in fact women have never ceased struggling in this direction. (Liu-Wang Liming 1934: 18)

For all its brevity, one can spot in this passage the key hallmarks that have (until relatively recently) dominated discourses of Chinese modernity: the enlightened male intellectual who champions women's emancipation; the awakening of female patriots; and the virtuous acts of feminine self-sacrifice for the cause for national salvation. The reference to Qiu Jin is especially predictable, given the symbolic status she had accrued by this time as a nationalist "female hero" and an embodiment of revolutionary idealism. That Qiu Jin was an accomplished writer—a poet, essayist, fiction writer, and journal editor—who sought to change women's place in the world through her words seems to have been long forgotten.

The power of this gendered narrative cannot be underestimated. Even now, with compelling critical paradigms that problematize the invented May Fourth story (Ko 1994) or explore the repressed modernities of the late Qing (D. Wang 1997), it is not uncommon to find descriptions (in academic as well as popular accounts) of fin-de-siècle feminism that adhere to this basic formation. Yet, the interpretative space emerging in the present moment as a result of archival recuperations also enables the possibility of reading beyond May Fourth discourses of national modernity to examine late Qing feminism anew (N. Qian, Fong, and Smith 2008), not just by investigating the long-overlooked textual and political practices of that generation of writers themselves but by taking a fresh look at its historical legacies in the May Fourth and post–May Fourth periods.

Here is one example that comes into view when we shift the lens of analysis: the real-life feminist journalist Tan Sheying. A graduate from a women's normal school, Tan's biography bears a striking resemblance to the new-style fictional protagonists who populate the emancipatory fantasies examined in the preceding text. Not only was her life trajectory radically reshaped by expanding opportunities for women in the realms of higher education and public life, but she combined political activism with a career in journalism. In addition to her own freelance writing, she edited numerous newspapers and periodicals in the 1920s–1930s, including the short-lived magazine *The Woman Citizen* while becoming increasingly involved in the organized women's movement. What is crucially different is that she exhibits a political consciousness that was clearly shaped and nurtured by the knowledge of feminist activism in the recent past and the pride of belonging to a new historical trajectory. Her comprehensive history of the Chinese women's movement (Tan Sheying 1936) reflects an extraordinary—and, given prevailing assumptions, surprising—effort to preserve the record of feminist activities at the turn of the century and claim a place for these foremothers in history.

Compiled amid an increasingly vocal leftist critique of the Chinese women's movement as a narrow bourgeois enterprise, Tan Sheying gives little credence to the low opinion of commentators but nevertheless evinces deep anxieties in her preface about the erasure of the movement's legacies. In her view, contemporary scholarship is itself to blame for this loss: "In fact, most texts focusing on women privilege commentary and ignore the facts; they emphasize present conditions and pay little attention to the past; for these reasons, even though works discussing women increase with each passing day, very rarely do they contain anything substantive about the women's movement" (Tan Sheying 1936: 2). To make up for this lacuna, and to ensure the past would not be forgotten, Tan presents an extensive chronicle of feminist activism in the years leading up to the founding of the ROC. She highlights, in particular, women's journalistic activities at the turn of the twentieth century (referring to more than a dozen magazines by name); organizations formed by Chinese female students in Japan; women's groups engaged in promoting educational reform; and efforts of educators to found women's schools. Women's participation in the dramatic events of 1911 is also described at length (in a chapter of its own) with details about their militant actions, intelligence gathering, medical relief efforts, and fundraising campaigns. Throughout, the emphasis is on tracing women's own voices in calling for gender emancipation from the late nineteenth century on, a goal she accomplishes thanks in no small measure to the textual records from which she draws and copiously cites; from editorial prefaces of progressive and radical women's journals of the period; poetry and political manifestos; and even the published proclamations and bylaws of the organizations formed by this pioneer generation of activists. The result is a densely *textured* account of the great variety of women's political activism in the years leading up to the toppling of the Qing dynasty, an account that brings to life the multitude of voices and rich gendered political imaginary that this generation helped craft. The shift in focus is significant: rather than the stock images of martyred feminine bodies and male saviors, what emerges is a narrative centered on independent women engaged in rethinking and rewriting womanhood for themselves. Rereading works such as Tan's history— which, similar to so many other hitherto marginalized examples of feminist cultural work done by novelists, poets, translators, theorists, historians, and journalists from the late Qing and Republican eras, has now been reissued or reexamined—is not merely a recuperative gesture; rather, it provides a crucially different vantage point from which to rethink the rise of early Chinese feminism, and the struggles of women to remain a central part of its narrative.

Laying claim to history has persisted as an important strand within the Chinese feminist imagination throughout the modern era, albeit manifesting in myriad different ways in response to changing circumstances. Tan Sheying's contemporaries Bai Wei and Xie Bingying both defied prevailing revolutionary aesthetic modes by enlisting their own life histories to affirm the continuing relevance of female subjectivity to processes of historical transformation. In *A Tragic Life (Beiju shengya*, 1936), Bai Wei details her embodied experience of psychosexual trauma and disease not just to represent the sociocultural impediments to women's political commitment, but to substantiate her provocative claim that her autobiography is not merely the story of "I" but the record of women's subaltern status. In the post-1949 era, confronted with the consolidation of the official history and its mythologization of women's liberation as a gift bestowed from above, veteran writers such as Yang Gang and Wang Ying wrote narratives of female self-discovery that trace the roots of the modern female intellectual's revolutionary consciousness in May Fourth feminism. In the contemporary period, critically acclaimed voices of young writers such as Zhao Mei turned their gaze to ancient dynastic history to examine the very notion of female historical agency. Her trilogy of Tang women's biographies, *Princess Gaoyang (Gaoyang gongzhu*, 1996), *Wu Zetian* (1998), and *Shangguan Wan'er* (2000), combine historical evidence and fictional license to reconstruct her subjects but also to offer a self-consciously feminist critique of scholarly interpretations that have vilified powerful public women in China's past (Schaffer and Song 2013: 118–130).

Writing the history of literary feminism in modern China remains an ongoing and politically relevant project. Early efforts have focused on the recuperation of formerly marginalized authors and investigations of formal literary practice. Promising new avenues of inquiry have also begun to open up: these include how Chinese feminists have engaged the visual and performing arts to challenge and change patriarchal culture; the unique forms that PRC feminist cultural production has assumed in the contemporary moment to tackle new and resurgent gender inequities amidst postsocialist reform, market expansion, and rapid globalization; and consideration of Sinophone feminist aesthetic practices as they have emerged in response to the specific circumstances in Taiwan, Hong Kong, and the global Chinese diaspora.

Notes

1 In his essay "On Women's Schooling" (*Lun nüxue*, 1897), Liang Qichao famously mocked the image of *cainü* as one who merely "teased the wind and fondled the moon, plucked flowers and caressed the grass, and then toyed with ditties mourning the passing of spring and sad farewells in order to compile volumes of poetry" (Bailey 2007: 17).

2 Qiu Jin's view was shared by other female advocates of gender reform at the time. Xue Shaohui, best known for her biographies of eminent Western women, published a rebuttal to Liang Qichao's essay in note 1 (N. Qian 2004).

3 Again, empirical evidence suggests that, historically, print media played an important role in bringing together like-minded educated women. Qiu Jin, for instance, sought out Lü Bicheng, after the latter began publishing her poetry and essays in *Dagongbao*. Later, *Dagongbao* carried news of Qiu Jin's intent to study abroad and eventually even printed the letters she sent to Lü Bicheng. These more or less served as public announcements about educational opportunities for Chinese women in Japan (G. Fong 2004).

4 What qualified as "news" in late Qing women's periodicals encompasses a broad and often eclectic range of topics and stories, from those with more obvious social and political relevance (e.g., coverage of the British suffragettes) to those with more tabloid quality (e.g., reports on a German woman who became a bullfighter or a lawsuit by a Russian woman whose teeth were broken in a train accident).

5 At a moment when women activists faced tremendous obstacles in sustaining and broadening their print media enterprises to reach a larger audience, this may strike as a rather fanciful representation. Yet, the example registers the impact of modern media in another way: namely, the ways in which fiction itself begins to bear the imprint of journalism as a genre distinguished by attention to factual information.

6 An abundance of tropes (e.g., captivity, blindness, servility, slavery, slumber, and darkness) are deployed throughout the feminist writing of this period to capture this last notion.

References

Bailey, Paul. 2007. *Gender and Education in China: Gender Discourses and Women's Schooling in the Early Twentieth Century*. London: Routledge.

Chen, Dongyuan 陳東原. 1928. *Zhongguo funü shenghuo shi.* 中國婦女生活史 (History of Chinese women's lives). Shanghai: Shangwu yinshuguan.

Fong, Grace S. 2004. "Alternative Modernities, or a Classical Woman of Modern China: The Challenging Trajectory of Lü Bicheng's (1883–1943) Life and Song Lyrics." *Nan Nü: Men, Women, and Gender in China*, 6.1 (2004): 12–59.

Hershatter, Gail, and Wang Zheng. 2008. "Chinese History: A Useful Category of Gender Analysis." *American Historical Review*, 113.5: 1404–1421.

Ko, Dorothy. 1994. *Teachers of the Inner Chambers: Women and Culture in Seventeenth-Century China*. Stanford, CA: Stanford University Press.

Ko, Dorothy. 2009. Presentation at "Translated Feminisms: China and Elsewhere: An International Workshop." Columbia University, New York, October.

Kong, Shuyu. 2005. *Consuming Literature: Best Sellers and the Commercialization of Literary*

Production in Contemporary China. Stanford, CA: Stanford University Press.

Li, Xiaojiang 李小江. 1993. *Zouxiang nüren* 走向女人 (Toward women). Hong Kong: Qingwen.

Liu-Wang Liming 劉王立明. 1934. *Zhongguo funü yundong* 中國婦女運動史 (Women's movement in China). Shanghai: Shanghai Commercial Press.

Ma, Yuxin. 2010. *Women Journalists and Feminism in China, 1898–1937*. Amherst, NY: Cambria Press.

Meng, Yue 孟悦, and Dai Jinhua 戴錦華. 1989. *Fuchu lishi dibiao* 浮出歷史地表:中國現代女性文學研究 (Emerging on the horizon of history: studies in Chinese women's literature). Zhengzhou: Henan renmin chubanshe.

Qian, Nanxiu. 2004. "Borrowing Foreign Mirrors and Candles to Illuminate Chinese Civilization: Xue Shaohui's Moral Vision in *Biographies of Foreign Women*." In *Beyond Tradition and Modernity: Gender, Genre, and Cosmopolitanism in Late Qing China*, eds. Grace S. Fong, Qian, Nanxiu, and Harriet Zurndorfer. Leiden: Brill. 60–101.

Qian, Nanxiu, Grace S. Fong, and Richard J. Smith. Eds. 2008. *Different Worlds of Discourse: Transformations of Gender and Genre in Late Qing and Early Republican China*. Leiden: Brill.

Qiu, Jin 秋瑾. 1907. "Fakanci" 發刊詞 (Inaugural address). *Zhongguo nübao* 中國女報 (Chinese women's magazine), no.1.

Qiu, Jin 秋瑾. 1960 (1907). *Jingwei shi* 精衛石 (Stones of the Jingwei bird). In *Qiu Jin ji* 秋瑾集 (Collected works of Qiu Jin). Shanghai: Shanghai guji chubanshe. 121–165.

Qiu, Jin. 1998. *Stones of the Jingwei Bird*. Trans. Amy Dooling. In *Writing Women in Modern China: An Anthology of Women's Literature from the Early Twentieth Century*. Edited by Amy Dooling and Kristina M. Torgeson. New York: Columbia University Press. 43–78.

Schaffer, Kay, and Xianlin Song. 2013. *Women Writers in Postsocialist China*. London: Routledge.

Siqi Zhai 思绮斋 (Zhan Kai 詹塏). 1907. *Nüziquan* 女子權 (Women's rights). Shanghai: Zuoxinshe.

Tan, Sheying 談社英 1936. *Zhongguo funü yundong tongshi* 中國婦女運動通史 (A comprehensive history of the Chinese women's movement). Shanghai: Funü gongming she.

Volz, Yong. 2007. "Going Public Through Writing: Women Journalists and Gendered Journalistic Space in China, 1890s–1920s." *Media, Culture & Society*, 29.3: 461–481.

Wang, Miaoru 王妙汝. 1994 (1904). *Nüyuhua* 女獄花 (Flowers in the female prison). Photo reprint in *Zhongguo jindai xiaoshuo daxi* 中國近代小説大系 (Modern Chinese fiction series). Nanchang: Baihuazhou wenyi chubanshe.

Wang, David Der-wei. 1997. *Fin-de-siècle Splendor: Repressed Modernities of Late Qing Fiction, 1849–1911*. Stanford, CA: Stanford University Press.

Wang, Dewei 王德威. 2007. *Hou yimin xiezuo: Shijian yu jiyi de zhengzhi xue* 後遺民寫作:時間與記憶的政治學 (Post-loyalist writing: The politics of time and memory). Taipei: Maitian.

Yi, Suo 頤瑣. 1988 (1905). *Huang Xiuqiu* 黃繡球. Reprinted in *Zhongguo jindai xiaoshuo daxi* 中國近代小説大系 (Modern Chinse fiction series). Nanchang: Jiangxi renmin chubanshe.

15

The World of Twentieth-Century Chinese Popular Fiction: From *Shanghai Express* to *Rivers and Lakes of Knights-Errant*

Yi Zheng

The origins of modern Chinese popular fiction can be traced to vernacular narrative traditions that flourished in "transformation" (*bianwen*) narratives and chantefables of Tang (618–907), "records" (*zhi*) of Song (960–1279), "drama" (*zaju*) of Yuan (1271– 1368), "popular tale" (*pinghua*) of Yuan and Ming (1368–1644), and "novels" (*xiaoshuo*) of Ming and Qing (1644–1911) periods. These narratives retained a close relationship with the oral and folkloric as well as the classical and literary (*wenyan*) traditions (Hanan 1981: 1–11). The development of popular fiction in modern China is also credited to the copious translations of Western novels at the turn of the twentieth century, which spurred stylistic innovations and incipient modernities that had been in full swing (Hanan 2004; D. Wang 1997; Chen Pingyuan 2010). Moreover, translation also contributed to the formation of the vernacular as a formal narrative medium (Hanan 1981: 6) (see Chapter 13 by Zha Mingjian).

Recent attention to the unprecedented experimentation in fiction writing from the mid-nineteenth to the early twentieth century established the late Qing (1849–1911) era as a pivotal moment in modern Chinese fiction in its transformation from the traditional to the modern. This heightened interest in late Qing fiction demonstrates a revisionist effort to recover repressed modernities from the monolithic, linear history that champions the May Fourth culture, calling attention instead to the historical *longue durée* and complexity of formal as well as affective changes in modern Chinese culture. This shift also highlights the importance of genre novels, in which the popular and the political interchange. The new account now challenges the history of modern Chinese fiction that progressively links such monuments as Liang Qichao's call for "revolution in fiction" as part of a political reform (see Chapter 3 by Ying Hu) to the May Fourth radical

A Companion to Modern Chinese Literature, First Edition. Edited by Yingjin Zhang.
© 2016 John Wiley & Sons, Ltd. Published 2016 by John Wiley & Sons, Ltd.

disassociation with tradition, allowing the inclusion of social transformation with its cultural and affective consequences at different levels of Chinese society during a particularly turbulent time. Besides the political and intellectual reformers (often doubled as the New Novelists), and the cultural avant-gardes who aimed at total revolution in aesthetic and social realms, the heroes of the historical transformation of modern Chinese fiction now include the self-transforming literati (*wenren*) who competed to shape the cultural makeup of the populace through vernacular narratives. In this respect, the significance of the modern experimentation of genre fiction becomes obvious.

Genre novels are the mainstay of modern Chinese popular fiction. They are usually categorized into prototypes such as romances (*yanqing*), social scandals (*shehui heimu*), court cases (*gong'an*), and knights-errant or martial arts (*haoxia*). Their development is divided into different stages in correspondence to modern Chinese history: before 1949, the most popular and developed genres were romances, social scandals, detective stories, knights-errant, and martial arts, some publicized at the time as the butterfly or "Saturday" school of fiction. In mainland China from 1949 to 1966, these forms metamorphosed into inadvertent elements of thrilling, comic, romantic, or tragically cathartic relief for socialist realist fiction, making the didactic and ideological familiar and palatable to a public hankering for diversion. Meanwhile, in other Sinophone regions, especially Hong Kong and Taiwan, these genre forms continued to evolve, with the knights-errant and martial arts becoming one of the most popular leisure readings. By the end of the twentieth-century, genre novels have revived in mainland China and remain prosperous elsewhere.

Since late Qing novels have been the subject of significant recent scholarship, either as vanguard of the new novelistic experimentation or precursor to modern Chinese popular fiction, this chapter devotes attention to the early Republican (pre–World War II) butterfly genres and the mid-century émigré knights-errant and martial arts fiction.[1] Continuing late Qing experiments in modern vernacular literature, these genre forms embodied thematic, formal, and affective transformations that correlate to dramatic changes in modern China. This embodiment and recreation of a sociocultural world as the carnivalesque (Bakhtin 1984) mirror image of modern China is one of the most significant points of interest in these popular genres, as it allows insights into the affective transformation and cultural aspiration of a *minjian* (folk) society that is the field of production, consumption, and vision of these narrative forms.

Of *Jianghu* and *Minjian* in Popular Fiction

The spatial is essential in the embodiment and transformation of social visions. While butterfly fiction is known for its urbanity (Link 1981), knights-errant and martial arts novels are celebrated for their inimitable spatial imagination, fantastic journey motifs and configurations of a modern world of *jianghu* (literary "river and lake"). As there are also genre mixtures in both narratives, the urban and *jianghu* worlds they delineate supplement each other in projecting the phantasmagoria of a fast-changing China.

This chapter examines the configuration of a modern *jianghu* as affective supplement to new urban spaces and argues that the spatial imagination and structural underpinning—from the social to the topographical—of modern Chinese popular fiction is closely related to the dislocation of culture and home as an overriding modern Chinese experience. The traumatic transformation of sociocultural spaces in twentieth-century China—as a consequence of ongoing revolutions, reforms, and wars—grounds the affective orientation of writers and readers. The changed role of the Chinese literati and urbanization are two most immediate transformations in modern Chinese socioeconomic life and spatial arrangements that directly impacted the flourishing of popular fiction in the first half of the twentieth century. While the former accounts for the dramatic increase in the number of fiction writers, the latter predicates the formation of these genres' vast readership and the structure of their sentiments, which in turn cultivates their reading habits. These are augmented by the massive dislocation of populations. In these contexts, to account for the exotic and outlawed world of knights-errant amongst the untamed *jianghu*, or the folkloric in the metropolis, is to understand the modern configuration of Chinese city space and the affective structure of urban readers.

Jianghu and *minjian* are explored here as crucial concepts and spaces that make up the affective and cultural map of modern Chinese genre fiction. They are figured as rivers and lakes, faraway mountains and untamed waters, as well as train carriages, courtyards, city parks and streets. Admittedly, the history of *jianghu* is not confined to modern Chinese fiction. Though its origin has been the subject of much debate, its continuous employment has made it clear that it is a social-spatial concept despite the varied and shifting references. Many accept that "river" and "lake" originally refer to the three rivers and five lakes of the mid-to-lower Yangtze region, and the reference became generalized in the transitional period between Qin and Han (207–200 BC). *The Book of Han* (*Hanshu*, 111 AD) specifies it as unorthodox societies outside the capital. After Song and Yuan (960–1368), with the increase of migrant populations, the nature of *jianghu* societies began to change, and in Ming and Qing (1368–1911) they often metamorphosed into highly organized underground societies in opposition to the imperial court (Han Yunbo 2003). In its long transmutation, *jianghu* acquires a specific reference and connotes not only a world in nature for heroes to roam and conquer, but also a space at the margins of society in uneasy—if not always oppositional—relations with state institutions and elite traditions. What modern genre fiction came to inherit and renew is this historically particularized cultural space. In the early 1920s, when knights-errant fiction became martial arts novels, writers often evoked *jianghu* directly in their titles.[2] Through *jianghu*, popular fiction writers projected their fascination with a cultural tradition as latecomers attempting to capture rampant activities of a volatile modern society, as Zheng Zhengyin did in his "paper *jianghu*" (Han Yunbo 2003: 88).

This sense of the pan-jianghuization of a *fin-de-siècle* world is also what grounds David Wang's reinterpretation (1997) of the late Qing as conjoining conventions of the court case and the knight-errant (*youxia*) into one mixed genre. In Wang's understanding, the necessity to combine magisterial authority, traditionally seen resting in the able hands of upright court officials, which is the implicit affective resolution of the court case genre, with the lawless and willful abandon of knights-errant in carrying out justice for heaven, which is the spiritual underpinning of martial arts fiction, reflects a sense of deepening social crisis. This unlikely marriage of two distinct realms of popular imagination—one for the triumph of orthodoxies and institutional justice, the other for extreme individual moral and physical excess—is for Wang a contemporary compromise of aesthetic tastes that reveals the irredeemable political turmoil and official corruption in late Qing society (D. Wang 2003: 2). Letting *jianghu* serve the court is thus a reflection of a desperate turn in public imagination. In late Qing popular novels such as Shi Yukun's *Three Heroes and Five Gallants* (*Sanxia wuyi*, 1879) and Liu E.'s *The Travels of Lao Can* (1907), beliefs in both the sanctity of reliable state power and in the tradition of the uncompromised knight-errant spirit are abandoned (D. Wang 2003: 4). The unbridled expansion of *jianghu* in public imagination is thus linked to affective disillusionment during troubled times.

The expanded *jianghu* in modern Chinese fiction can be understood in terms of Chen Sihe's conceptualization of *minjian* (2003: 257) as an unorthodox, marginal society. Chen bases his formulation on an extended notion of the folkloric, carrying with it the sense of sociocultural forms traditionally practiced by rural societies and handed down through oral traditions, and connoting perseverance of old ways over change. Chen, however, stresses its oppositional status as a cultural space vis-à-vis the political. He differentiates this space from Jürgen Habermas's civil society and public sphere: whereas civil societies and public spheres are political–spatial understandings grounded in an emerging European bourgeois urban society, *minjian* is mainly a cultural configuration of folk traditions of an agrarian China. In fact, Chen's *minjian* is restricted to the cultural forms of Chinese peasantry, periodically appropriated by the intelligentsia for reformist or oppositional agendas. In this sense, *minjian* is analogous to civil society in one respect but differs in others. The similarity that Chen perceives is the self-organization of a society outside the realm of state power. The Habermasian public sphere presupposes rational democratic participation, whereas *minjian* resonates with the carnivalesque polyphony of the marginal (Bakhtin 1984).

While the self-regulating *minjian* at the margins of the state can be borrowed as a descriptor of modern *jianghu*, Chen's *minjian* overemphasizes the boundary between political and cultural worlds, and the opposition between them. The idea that *minjian* is the conceptual opposite of the state, and that its cultural forms operate outside the state's control, overlooks the historical and structural supplementarity of these social–spatial constructions. Understanding *jianghu* in modern Chinese fiction through *minjian* highlights the latter's phantasmagoric nature vis-à-vis the elite center of power: rather than a natural place of opposition (such as the unchanging countryside forever preserving an external agrarian past), *jianghu* is a mirror image of the perilous modern China where changes are unpredictable and uninterrupted.

However, to predicate the idea of *minjian* and its assertion on the Yan'an debate on "national form" (*minzu xingshi*) in the 1930s–1940s (Chen Sihe 2003: 257) limits the concept's historical valence. The Yan'an debate was initiated by Mao Zedong to signal the emergence of a Marxist political discourse with Chinese ambition. The "national form" is hence a cultural parameter instituted from one of the competing political centers in modern China and has served as a hegemonic framework since then. It is difficult to equate such political employment of the popular with the reassertion of marginal, unsettling cultural forms that *minjian* seeks to elucidate. Moreover, as Chen himself demonstrates, this kind of rediscovery of elements of folk culture at moments of historical crisis by the modernizing Chinese intelligentsia, who otherwise consider such cultures anathema to modern progress in literature and culture since the May Fourth, bespeaks the ambiguity of their choices of modern paths (Chen Sihe 2003: 258).

Robert Redfield's anthropological division of the culture of a given society into "great" and "little" traditions (Calhoun 2002: 72) is appropriate for a structural understanding of *minjian* as a spatial concept. The distinction here is between the elite cultural institutions and orthodoxies of the ruling intelligentsia, orchestrated by the state and its mechanisms of control, and those informal, popular cultural practices whose realms of activity are at the margins of the direct authority of the state and its institutions of power. The latter, as divergent cultural practices, often transcend the political ideological status quo and represent life at the lower end of society, expressing and championing the psycho-ethical and aesthetic cultures of the under-represented. Through Yu Yingshi's reformulation of Redfield's cultural division for the Chinese case, Chen Sihe (2003: 258–259) sees the "great" tradition historically in court-authorized classics, the civil service examination, and Confucian ethics buttressed by its institutions of education, while locating the "little" tradition almost exclusively in oral traditions of the peasantry. *Minjian* is then what coheres around the agrarian: it is authentic but residual, primitive but unrestricted.

Though insisting on the residual nature of *minjian*, Chen Sihe (2003: 258–259) attends to its modern history. For him, it is part of a tripartite structure that underpins the intellectual formation in modern China: it is separate from, but at the same time cuts through, the other two spaces, which he calls the "temple" (*miaotang*) and the "square" (*guangchang*). Unlike *minjian*, the other two represent the places where modern Chinese intelligentsia strive for power, status, and prestige either directly as establishment intellectuals serving the state or as harbingers of new (often transgressive) ideas in the public space. Over the course of the twentieth century, the tripartite spaces are mutually delimiting and penetrating, but for modern Chinese intellectuals, *minjian* is always at best a hidden source for the primitive and raw. The vernacular revolution in Chinese literature is an example.

Hence, an important feature of *minjian* is that it is a place of non-discrimination, tolerance, and conservation, *cangwu nagou*—collecting grime and containing wreckage (Chen Sihe 2003: 269). Historically, *minjian* has indeed always offered a place for cultural elites who were banished or retreated from political life. Thus, one can take Chen's charting of its early-twentieth-century formation at three levels but alter the point and level of emphasis. While Chen (2003: 259) sees it primarily as persevering the cultural traditions of an agrarian China, an argument can be made for *minjian*'s twentieth-century transformation, in structure and function, into the main container of residual traditional cultural institutions and forms banished from the modernizing center, and its articulation in an emerging urban popular culture created by the new commercial market and city space.

Indeed, *minjian* became the retreat of literati who chose to uphold traditional cultural forms in opposition to new culture of the times. But *minjian* also offered chances for those who embraced modernity differently. Thus, it is treated in this chapter not merely as a depository of the residual and agrarian, but as a *seminal* concept with which to approach the *jianghu* world represented in modern Chinese popular fiction. This includes Zhang Henshui's butterfly romances that delineate an urban topography in the turbulent first half of the twentieth century, as well as the mid-century émigré martial arts novels by Jin Yong, whose spatial imagination articulates the longings of millions displaced by a peculiar Chinese geopolitical formation of *liang an san di* (the triangulation of mainland China, Taiwan, and Hong Kong into three separated territories across the Taiwan Strait). While Zhang's realist romances depict the human vicissitudes of a world of sweeping changes, which is the modern equivalent of the unruly *jianghu* for his plebeian, middleclass urban readers, as much as for fictional characters inhabiting his works, Jin Yong's *jianghu* presents forbidden palaces and exotic wilderness of the long ago and far away, and conjures up a different *minjian* vision of a displaced modern China.

From Old Beijing to Shanghai Express: Modern Love in Zhang Henshui's Butterfly Romances

Zhang Henshui is regarded as a major butterfly writer because his vernacular episodic novels are almost exclusively love stories, and they remind readers of traditional scholar-meets-beauty romance (Liu Yangti 1997: 4). However, Zhang's love stories seldom end happily in the turbulent world of modern China, and true love is not always rewarded. In fact, modern-day romances in Zhang's voluminous corpus often become nightmarish adventures for his heroes and heroines, in which the traditional and the modern conspire against them. That is why some scholars (Zhang Zhongliang 2011) classify his romances (often published in newspaper installments) as realist portraits of social customs, conventions, and mentalities of an unruly and often war-torn society. Commenting on his motivation in writing *Flower of Peace* (*Taiping hua*, 1931), Zhang Henshui (1993: 62; 55) asserts that what he set out to capture is the pain of homelessness and displacement that haunt millions of his fellow citizens, including himself (for he had traveled the length and width of China because of war and for career opportunities). His long career as a newspaper journalist allowed him access to all levels of society and provided him the chance to practice and master the wherewithal of capturing and shaping them through writing.

The stress on Zhang as a socially aware realist novelist, however, concentrates mostly on his painstaking exposure of the society both high and low. The social is understood, in this case, as a critical consciousness akin to social realism, although Zhang is often blamed for hijacking his own realist cause due to his undue sentimentalism or mercenary concerns (Liu Yangti 1997: 200–234). Perry Link, on the other hand, defines the social in this case as representations of modern social and spatial formations. The emergence of the class and class culture of "petty city dwellers" (or petite urbanites) is a process that is significantly spatial, for it depends on and generates concurrent urban cultural institutions and practices (Link 1981: 4–6). The city as a spatial organization is essential for the development of popular fiction.

Zhang Henshui's romances take place more often in the older-style Beijing than in modern Shanghai, but his Beijing-based *Fate in Tears and Laughter* (1930; hereafter *Fate*) "establishes the 'modern popular' character" of urban fiction in modern China (Link 1981: 13). This novel became part of the modern urban entertainment institutions soon after its publication: it was serialized in a popular newspaper; "two movies, several stage plays and many comic book versions were all in circulation at once; a serialization in popular storytelling form was done for radio; the author was suing for his copyright" (Link 1981: 13). The social as spatial in Zhang's popular fiction is dependent on his status as a popular writer and the popularity of his writing as genre fiction.

Zhang's novels reveal a worldview that is unmistakably *minjian* in its values. His fictional world is delineated as the space in which protagonists experience the joys and treacheries of love; as the frame of their physical, mental, and affective existence; and as the grid of their movements and actions. His depiction of urban spaces also highlights a field of vision, a repertoire of knowledge, a complex of desires and aspirations, all of them constantly changing and therefore full of surprises. All this is illustrated in Zhang's description of urban topographies of the ancient capital Beijing, the modern metropolis Shanghai, and the wartime capital Chongqing—as the physical stage upon which his characters act, as the demarcation of social formations and life-worlds, as well as the location of these cities' historical memories. Categories such as the "ancient capital" and "modern metropolis" are cultural tropes in modern Chinese literature, which structure cultural imagination, giving a spatial register to changes that are usually perceived as a temporal progression (Y. Zhang 1996: 28–29).

Zhang Henshui's Beijing is often taken to be ethnographic as his interest in recounting the layout and minutiae of life therewith far exceeds what is necessary for the background of the story. Places, architecture, and sights such as the Bridge of Heaven (Tianqiao) and different kinds of square courtyards (*siheyuan*) are given such appreciative detailing (seen through the admiring eyes of the protagonists) that one can almost read them as items from a city guidebook. Zhang's description of urban life in both high and low societies is so systematically miniscule and elegiac that one suspects that even then he was documenting a disappearing folkloric Beijing culture.

However, Zhang's Beijing is more than a folkloric entity that offers the reader and the protagonist affective reassurance in age-old comfort. His protagonists sojourn in and out of the city, occasionally triumph over but are more often swallowed up by the twists and turns of this exhilarating and at times perilous urban world. In Zhang's depiction, early-twentieth-century Beijing is a *bona fide* modern *jianghu*, where life is rough and ready, exciting yet menacing, lived with its conflicting lore and logic. This fictional *jianghu* might have offset the tedium of daily modern urban existence, bringing a legendary and distant life close at hand. But more significantly, it represents the *minjian* view on modernity as it is played out in the changing cityscape.

The close relationship between journalism and early-twentieth-century Chinese fiction is crucial here, as journalist–writers tended to assume the role of an experienced guide taking readers through cities of their real as well as fictional world (Y. Zhang 1996: 302). Besides a journalist, Zhang Henshui (2009: 3–54) was also a noted contributor to the literati genre of familiar place essays, especially those on Beijing and Nanjing, two ancient capitals, all written during the war (1944–1945) as nostalgia pieces for himself and his readers in Chongqing. Sure, Zhang's taste in these essays, as well as in scenes and places in his novels, is a continuation of typical literati jottings of landscapes and places. Similar to most of his predecessors, he eulogized winds, flowers, snows, and the moon. However, he was keener on the life of the plebeian—on markets, teahouses, alleyways, and city parks. With palpable pleasures in enumerating the sights, sounds, smells, and tastes of street lives, he came across to his readers as a cityscape portrait artist and a poetic ethnographer. However, Zhang's ancient capitals are not spatial congealment of passing old times. They comprise also of things new and modern: city parks, train carriages, and car rides are commonplace urban scenes and activities as much as traditional teahouses and drum singings. Moreover, Zhang's world is always contemporaneous with the present, and he is a self-conscious *minjian* writer who notes the social and historical of his times from the margins (Zhang Henshui 2009: 196).

Zhang's *Fate* lays out the urban topography of old Beijing for its protagonist Fan Jiashu, a novice modern student enjoying his first taste of free city life. Fan comes from an official–gentry family from Hangzhou, a garden-like city near modern Shanghai. The first time he looks around upon his arrival, Fan finds the courtyard belonging to his diplomat uncle charming in a way different from his two-storied new-style house back home. The old-style Beijing architecture conjures up a world he used to read about in classical poetry (Zhang Henshui 1997b: 1–2). Here, Beijing fascinates Fan as the material and emotional embodiment of a split life-world, and he becomes absorbed heart and soul in the city.

The social as spatial thus structures the novel, and *Fate* unfolds as an adventure story in which Fan traverses social and affective spaces as he goes around the city, encountering distinct prototypes and forms of urban China. Critics have argued for the modernity of Zhang's episodic novels: unlike traditional episodic narratives, they are moved not by the plot but by the characterization (Wen Fengqiao 2005). This means that Fan is the main observer through whom other characters' lives and feelings are filtered through to the reader. His venture into different worlds of Beijing and his responses to people and events he encounters unite and move the narrative along.

Fan's romances with three young women are therefore as much a conventional love triangle as his encounters with three different types of modern Chinese women who represent the sociocultural worlds of Beijing. Shen Fengxi is Fan's primary love object, and their relationship resembles the traditional scholar-meet-beauty type. However,

Shen is not the beautiful, cultivated woman that scholars dream of meeting in spring gardens; rather, she is a pretty drum-singer whom Fan runs into on one of his sojourns into the underbelly of the old capital. Fan's encounter with her thus resembles the act of "slumming" in modern cities by upper-class urban dwellers (Koven 2004). Fengxi's pitiful demeanor and status, plus her comely appearance, unleashes the Eros and altruism in Fan and sets the tone for their relationship. Though Fan tries to save Fengxi from her demi-monde fate by making her a modern girl student, the way it is arranged—clandestinely paying for her fees and her family's upkeep—is too similar to the age-old institution of concubinage to accord Fan the complete satisfaction that theirs is genuine new-style love. Moreover, he cannot fathom the depth of her world and helplessly watches as she becomes prey to the arch-villain warlord General Liu. This is in part her own doing, as she and her family cannot resist the allure of material wealth. She is thus neither loyal nor chaste according to the accepted *jianghu* rules of the game. The perils of the world of the urban poor and the unmediated brutality of warlords and rogue generals are simply beyond the scope of Fan the modern student.

If Fan fails in new-style romance, he is compensated for by a friendship based on *jianghu* principles, which lends the novel its awaited poetic justice. Fan's induction into the modern *jianghu* of Beijing is immediately rewarded by his camaraderie with martial arts master Guan Shoufeng and his daughter Xiugu. While Fan also helps them financially, it is founded on the principle of mutual admiration and genuine altruism. To Fan's delight, Shoufeng and Xiugu are real knights-errant in hiding. Memories of heroic *jianghu* deeds on horsebacks are still vivid on the Guans' mind, and they await their chance to carry out justice: Xiugu avenges Fengxi by killing General Liu. In its old town, Beijing looks like a modern version of *jianghu*, where the only heroes are the old-style knights-errant, and justice is kept by their lawlessness.

Just as late Qing fiction fuses court case and knight-errant novels, Zhang Henshui mixes genre elements and let the Guans embody the just and good in modern *jianghu* and bring plot resolution in *Fate*. Being Fan's second love interest, Xiugu plays a more active part, although the genre convention prevents her from uniting with Fan—a *jianghu* heroine would be of no use once she married a scholar. According to this logic, *Fate* ends with Fan's possible union with He Lina, Fan's third love interest, a new-style socialite from one of Beijing's richest and most powerful families, who brings Fan back to his own social environment. Interestingly, both Fan and He keep close ties with the Guans and appreciate their *jianghu* exploits. *Fate* is thus both a triangular romance and a knight-errant story. Its development is centered on Fan's emotional and physical adventure into the plebeian bastion of aesthetic and social codes, although his quest ends with both disillusionments and triumphs. Modern scholars with traditional ties like Fan are protected by *minjian* society and share its sentiments, and Zhang Henshui offers a case in which "great traditions" of the literati in exile are preserved in the "little traditions" of urban plebeians in modern China.

In *Shanghai Express* (1935), Zhang's vision of modern urban space and traditional *jianghu* is conjoined cogently, if cynically. In this story of lust and deceit, Zhang develops his narrative in the limited space of one train ride from Beijing to Shanghai.

The drama is staged mostly in one first-class carriage and the deluxe dining car, while characters traverse to the second and third classes and station platforms occasionally. It becomes clear that, for both Zhang and his readers, the moving train is more than a mode of transportation: it is a symbol of modern life in 1930s China. The train represents a delimited space for urban dwellers who can afford it, separating their life from the vast surrounding country (Zhang Henshui 1997a: 5).

As it turns out, the spatial sense of protection is deceptive, as dangers also lurk within. Train carriages are conveniently used to represent microcosms of different social worlds—segregated but open to movement and transgression. As a spatial structure, the moving train becomes the best vehicle for Zhang's narration that allows him to concentrate on the social as spatial. The social formation and distinction in 1930s China is unmistakably reflected in the separately priced carriages and kinds of passengers traveling in them. While passengers do venture into other carriages, these occasions for mixing prove perilous. As it happens, it is through her alleged high-school classmates who had socially declined and thus had to ride in the third-class carriage that enchantress Liu Xichu conspires to seduce and rob wealthy banker Hu Ziyun. In fact, her scheme begins with a transgression, through deceit and seduction, into Hu's first-class carriage. So Hu's forays into lower-class carriages actually leads to his downfall. Sure, Hu does not go slumming on the Shanghai Express, but he desires a femme fatale who claims to belong to his world. Although they find each other modern, there is no romance this time. In the enclosed space of the Shanghai Express, the new-style high society mixes with the underworld in a rough *jianghu* fashion—urban lust meets organized crime. The train in this sense is a modern *jianghu* at its lowest—traditional *jianghu* survives here as underground crime organizations, and the modern liberated woman is actually in an age-old profession, a demi-monde swindler. There is no knight-errant to save the hero: in its delimited space, without old-fashioned knights-errant as the only modern redeemers of universal justice, all is rough and ruined. This un-principled modern *jianghu* is not only deprived of romance, but it precipitates the latter's perils.

Zhang Henshui (1993: 62: 103) repeatedly asserts that he writes for "ordinary men and women," which means his genre fiction works on the emotions of urban dwellers, providing them relief and amusement. This is why his butterfly romances, conjoining genres and conventions such as knights-errant, are predicated on a *minjian* vision of modern Chinese life. It concentrates on the phantasmagoria of the urban everyday, an equivalent of modern *jianghu* where new perils and old lore compete and conflict, where traditions persist in plebeian forms and heroic adventures are undertaken by the marginal who redress modern wrongs by ancient deeds. But this is also a world that metamorphosizes in its conventionality, in which ordinary men and women learn to accept urban modernity in and through distrust and suspicion. This fictional *jianghu* with its perils and lore is not only Zhang's consolation to his readers who are weary of the urban mundane, and who are avid for the extraordinary as well as comfortingly familiar, but it also preserves for modern vernacular Chinese fiction a *minjian* place. It keeps vernacular fiction writing in *minjian*, where it originates and continues to flourish.

Across Beautiful, Yet Perilous Mountains and Waters

Jin Yong has been credited for constructing an original, massive *jianghu* in his corpus of martial arts fiction. The world of his knights-errant consists of countless characters from diverse social and cultural backgrounds, different historical periods, and vast landscapes beyond mainland China. Inhabiting snowy mountains or far-off islands and crossing immense lakes and plains, his protagonists fight in palace grounds, invade the walled compounds, wander along streets and grasslands, and fly over rooftops and mountain cliffs. They belong to various schools of martial arts and secret societies, and pledge loyalty to all manners of hermit masters, clandestine Christian groups, and rebel armies.

With his modern recreation of traditional lore and expansive spatial imagination, Jin's novels contribute to the construction of a "cultural China" appealing to complex and conflicting sentiments in the Chinese-speaking world across national and geopolitical divisions. His debut in the mid-twentieth century signals a new development of the vernacular and *minjian* as a counter-tradition: when the course for literature and culture in mainland China was expressly anti-traditionalist, his novels propagated the polyphony of traditional cultural forms and feelings. Written in the British Colony of Hong Kong from the 1950s to the 1970s, these novels attracted myriad readers around the world and became a de facto symbol of a Chinese culture centered at the margins.

However, rather than a popular pan-Chinese continuation of nation building as some mainland critics would have it (Kong Qingdong 2004: 1), Jin's cultural China is figured exclusively from the *minjian* imagination. Both in its scope and conception, it is a non-national space, a palimpsest of bygone but expansive empires sheltering all grime and wreckage, in which political and elite cultural centers are known to be hostile and utopias always displaced to far-off islands or deserts. And, in terms of form, Jin's new-style martial arts fiction is indebted to a modern vernacular genre—knights-errant stories since the late Qing—that continues to capture the popular imagination but nonetheless remains outside the canon of modern Chinese culture. Similar to Zhang Henshui's romances for urban dwellers, Jin's novels are a carnivalesque transformation of both "great" and "little" cultural traditions in compensatory imagination. This supplementary urban imagination is similarly catered to ordinary readers who inhabit wider yet more confined geographical spaces either by volition or force, and who demand consolation or forms of transgression, or simply the pleasure of trespassing. It is by no means surprising that the narrative structure and imaginative trajectory of Jin's novels are spatial—flights of fancy were one of the few ways to traverse the insurmountable physical as well as geopolitical borders between mainland China, Hong Kong, Taiwan, and other parts of the world during the Cold War (1950s–1980s).

Jin's cultural China is notable for its panoramic grandeur as well as its geographically specific topography. His characters traverse realms of both the fantastic and the mundane. As popular leisure reading, his novels are unusually ambitious: they attempt to capture all the aspects of recognizable Chinese traditions—from Confucianism to Taoism and Buddhism, encompassing the everyday, the folkloric, and the foreign—to varying degrees of success. Unlike Zhang Henshui's ancient capitals and modern metropolis, Jin's cultural geographies are less a showcase for exhaustive ethnographic knowledge than a phantasmagoria of a mosaic map of China. This geographically differentiated cultural China underwrites an imaginative topography that serves as the grid for his readers' affective identification, evoking their memories of a historical and physical home, or embodying their longings for cross-generational ancestral spiritual origins. Regardless of how these novels work on their readers' structure of feelings, it is obvious that they offer a counter-realm of cultural historical experience. Through flights of fancy in time and space, his readers are enticed to forget the political and geographical confines of the warring nation-states.

The expansive spatial terrain and diverse geocultural topography of Jin's *jianghu* reminds his diaspora readers—and subsequently postsocialist mainland readers—of the territorial and spiritual splendor of China's imperial past, which stands in stark contrast to the historical trauma of the modern nation-state with all that it forbids and dislocates. Jin's map in this sense not only embodies nostalgia. It can be understood as the playful third space of imaginative freedom produced by popular Chinese fiction, especially martial arts novels and films, in which fantasy conjoins the real and history is transcended by individual choice (Y. Zhang 2011). Jin's imaginative cultural mapping of an alternative historical China is nonetheless a transformative continuation of the twentieth-century vernacular and *minjian* tradition generically. It relocates *minjian* as the site of cultural production to the diaspora.

Spatial movement is the key structure of Jin's new-style martial arts fiction. In this, they are true to type, though they also contain other genre elements such as the picaresque and romance. In the traditional knight-errant genre, traversal of space and distance (*you*) is as important as seeking justice with martial prowess (*xia*). Jin's contribution to modern Chinese vernacular fiction can be said to reside mainly in his extension of the spatial imagination of the knights-errant genre, especially *you*—the journey as motif and structure. Reliance on the spatial is also a recognized feature of traditional Chinese vernacular historical novels and heroic romance. The Fourteenth- and Sixteenth-century novels *Romance of Three Kingdoms* (*Sanguo yanyi*) and *Water Margin* are famous for their expansive battle scenes. While the former depicts sweeping panoramas of warfare where mountains, plains, and rivers are at the foreground, the latter does not limit its actions to the water margins of Mount Liang, spanning instead its terrain across Shandong to Bianliang in picaresque episodes of its multiple individual heroes. The spatial register in the narrative structure of these novels is meant for presenting vistas, which are featured mainly in scenes rather than movements, even though their characters traverse considerably. A closer prototype for Jin's knight-errant adventures is the mid-sixteenth-century *Journey to the West*, where the rogue heroic adventures of the Monkey King and his fellow travelers string along fantastic geocultural locations and exotic peoples and customs.

Spatial movement has always been a notable feature that distinguishes modern martial arts novels from the May Fourth fiction, as the latter prefers layered description of single scenes or frequent alteration between scenes. Lu Xun, for example, is most adept at emphatic single scene description, whereas Mao Dun is celebrated for his panoramic portrayal of background events and urban settings. But swift spatial

movement is regarded as a significant element of modern martial arts fiction that came
to the fore in the 1920s, an element predicated on the concept of *you* as journeying. In
knights-errant novels of the 1920s–1930s from writers such as Pingjiang Buxiao
Sheng, Zhao Huanting, and Gu Mingdao, *jianghu* is the depth, length, and width of
space in which the hero roams. This signifies an important moment in the development
of modern-genre fiction, when the martial arts genre separates itself from the court
case fiction, and knights-errant become free and mobile again. In modern knights-
errant stories, characterization and plot develop along with the spatial movement,
through which readers not only appreciate the valence and emotions of the heroes but
also marvel at local scenes and customs along the way. This kind of spatial inflection is
largely absent from new literature of the day, which is preoccupied instead with the
vagaries of time in formal and thematic terms.

When Jin Yong and his colleague Liang Yusheng began serializing their émigré
martial arts stories in influential Hong Kong newspapers, the journey home (for some)
or simple scenic tours (for others) became a yearning for what was beyond the horizon
in the Chinese-speaking world, and all this took on a dream quality when faced with
insurmountable borders. It is not surprising that journeying became a requisite element
of martial arts fiction in the second half of the twentieth century. Significantly in this
context, the realm of Jin's novels is not confined to the landmass of China. The protagonist of *The Heaven Sword and the Dragon Sabre* (*Yitian tulong ji*, 1961) is born on the Ice
and Fire Island near the North Pole, fights his enemies from Wudang Mountain to
the Shaolin Temple, leads anti-Yuan rebels across the central north regions, and defeats
the alien missionaries from Persia on the ocean. This kind of sweeping moves across
vast territories is even more frequent in Jin's later works. His last martial novel, *The
Deer and the Cauldron* (*Luding ji*, 1969; *Deer* hereafter), pushes the journey motif to the
extreme, sending its hero Wei Xiaobao to travel all over China and even to visit Yaksa
and Moscow, before he disappears in the vast *jianghu*.

In *The Legend of the Condor Heroes* (*Shediao yingxiong zhuan*, 1957; English 1994a,
Legend hereafter), the *jianghu* world is as much an unorthodox battleground beyond the
political regimes as a fantastic realm of scenic grandeur and cultural phantasm. Its
protagonists Guo Jing and Huang Rong, in a sense, serve as tour guides for Jin's
readers of the Cold War era and bring them along a journey of historical recollection
and cultural homage amidst contemporary traumas inflicted by contending nations,
territories, and ideologies. Unlike Zhang Henshui's modern *jianghu*, which fuses the
increasingly new with the reassuringly familiar, the topography of *Legend* covers areas
outside the familiar centers of political and cultural authority. Jin, as well as his heroes,
appreciates neither the emperors and their capitals nor the cities of the central plain.
For the traveling knights, these urban centers are perilous grounds of evil intrigue.
Guo Jing and Huang Rong, for instance, are often trapped in towns on their way, even
though Huang is well versed in the elite culture. In contrast, the untamed rivers and
lakes are places for *jianghu* heroes to rest and rejuvenate. Guo Jing is sheltered in the
Mongolian pastures when he runs into dangers (he was raised by the Mongolians), and
Huang practices her "Chinese" arts freely only on her father's distant island.

Jin's cultural China is envisioned as a *minjian* world, albeit extended, exoticized, and enlarged. It is for modern urban readers of the Chinese vernacular but can no longer rely on established cities of political or cultural authority as sites for their fantasy or consolation. His *jianghu*, as the mid-century *minjian* for the Chinese-speaking world, must be spatially expansive and psychologically fantastic to alternate as a different realm beyond the margins of the Cold War political regimes. Similar to his outlawed heroes, the reader must be bewildered enough to suspend disbelief and take on a constant journey across sweeping and exotic wilderness.

In Jin's *jianghu*, the world gets better as the radius of power pans out. The places beyond the elite and orthodox political and cultural horizons may not be ideal, for oftentimes they are also beyond the demands of civilization, but they are a less menacing habitat for ordinary local residents as well as for those accustomed to exile. John Hamm (2005: 80) points out that, throughout Jin Yong's martial arts novels, there is a dialectic transformation in his depiction of the movement from the center to the margins: from the scene of exile in his early novels to the consciousness of diaspora in his later ones, which Yingjin Zhang (2011: 9) further elaborates as a movement from loss of home and nation to individual reflections on and alternative practices of home and nation.

This sense of the diaspora as new *minjian*, however, is also present in Jin's earlier martial arts fiction. It is already predicated in the historical development of modern Chinese genre fiction in its carnivalesque relation to Chinese cultural tradition. Jin's new diaspora *minjian* is a spatial expansion as well as logical continuation of the previous tradition. The new *minjian* of *liang an san di* can only be centered in the diaspora as the latter is one of the few remaining margins of cultural possibility vis-à-vis the increasing encroachment of totalitarian and authoritarian regimes. It became the mid-century container of grime and wreckage: a haven for the exiled residuals and a new incubating space for the relocated and expanded vernacular Chinese *minjian* culture. Jin's debut in this sense is more telling than his later novels.

Similar to Jin himself, the hero of the *Romance of the Book and the Sword* (*Shujian enchou lu*, 1955; English 1994b, hereafter *Romance*) is a fallen literatus stranded in *minjian*, a remainder of the older elite culture and an observer of new cultures in the wildness. But, unlike Fan Jiashu in Zhang Henshui's old Beijing, Jin's residual literati are also martial heroes—they sometimes become leaders in the *minjian* world. Chen Jialuo is a talented scholar from Jiangnan, the traditional center of late imperial culture. However, even though he was born into the most illustrious local gentry family, he becomes the head of the largest secret society in Qing China and lives in exile. He studies martial arts in Tianshan Mountain at the empire's far western regions and works with the underground Red Flower Society whose members hail from all walks of life from Central, Northeast, and South China.

As a knight-errant hero, Chen Jialuo is a mixture of prototypes, since the novel also has elements of the butterfly romance. He is the fallen scholar but also a martial artist. Torn between his commitments to love and the cause of justice, Chen is burdened with all that is undesirable in a scholar hero—he sticks to residual literati values and acts like a stereotype: he is alternately too impulsive or too hesitant. And as a result loses all he loves and harms his chosen cause. But he remains loyal to his underground society, whose cause of justice is appreciated by the marginal. Even though Jin still differentiates the Han Chinese from its others, such differentiation is not always in favor of the Han Chinese (Wang Yichuan 2007: 277). Chen's habitat is, from the outset, the perilous *jianghu* made up of a multiethnic cast of heroes and villains. Though the novel begins with the Red Flower brothers' expedition to the political and cultural centers, and their ill-fated cause of changing history at the center, it ends with their tragic failure and retreat back to China's Turkic west. The westward journey is an exile for the ex-literati, ex-central plain martial masters, but it is also a homeward passage for them as they become marginal *minjian* heroes.

In Jin's spatial–martial adventure narratives, the protagonists' displacement from the political and cultural center is an absolute necessity, and theirs are typically journeys of no return. In the course of his long writing career, Jin has become less interested in fallen scholars than in knights-errant of mixed and marginal origins. The heroes of his later fiction, such as Guo Jing of *Legend* and Wei Xiaobao of *Deer*, come directly from the geographical backwater or social underground of the imperial centers and are notably unlearned in elite orthodoxies and cultural arts. The places they inhabit—rivers and lakes, mountain tops and grasslands, far off villages and plebian urban establishments— look less like places of exile but more like their natural habitat or adopted homes. One may conclude that there are significant changes in Jin's depiction of the movement from the center to the periphery and, with it, the emergence of a diaspora consciousness.

Indeed, Jin's mid-to-late-century martial *jianghu* is underwritten and complicated by such defining modern experiences as mass migration, displacement, and fragmentation inasmuch as spaces of the nation-state is concerned. But one should also note that the transformative figuration of such *jinghu* in martial arts fiction as a *minjian* genre is predicated on the transformation and relocation of *minjian* as concept and space in twentieth-century China. Jin re-centers his *jianghu* and his vision of *minjian* as the truly marginal cultural space at the diaspora, just as Zhang Henshui relocated his to the modern Chinese city in the early twentieth century. These relocations sustain *minjian*'s capacity as a cultural space of preservation and recreation, interlocking with but always receding from the contending centers of political and cultural authority. They also re-invigorate modern Chinese popular genre fiction and enable its miraculous flourish in a century of frequent social disruption and austere political and cultural regimes.

NOTES

1   The metamorphosis of popular genre fiction in mainland China since 1949 is a subject that merits separate attention. Its entanglement with the mandate of socialist and revolutionary literature is particularly interesting.

2   Pingjiang Buxiao Sheng, the first notable modern Chinese martial arts novelist, used the word "*jianghu*" in the names of quite a few of his novels, including *The Knight Extraordinaire of the River and Lakes* (*Jianghu qixia zhuan*, 1923).

REFERENCES

Bakhtin, Mikhail M. 1984. *Rabelais and His World*. Bloomington: Indiana University Press.

Calhoun, Craig. 2002. *Dictionary of the Social Sciences*. Oxford, UK: Oxford University Press.

Chen, Pingyuan 陳平原. 2010. *Zhongguo xiaoshuo xushi moshi de zhuanbian* 中國小説敘事模式的轉變 (The evolution of the narrative mode in Chinese fiction). Beijing: Beijing daxue chubanshe.

Chen, Sihe 陳思和. 2003. "Minjian de fuchen: dui kangzhan dao wenge wenxueshi de yige changshixing jieshi" 民間的浮沉:對抗戰到文革文學史的一個嘗試性解釋 (The surfacing and submersion of minjian: A tentative explanation of modern Chinese literary history from the war of resistance to the Cultural Revolution). In *Ershi shiji Zhongguo wenxue shilun* 二十世紀中國文學史論 (On twentieth-century Chinese literary history). Edited by Wang Xiaoming 王曉明. Shanghai: Dongfang chuban zhongxin, 257–264.

Hamm, John Christopher. 2005. *Paper Swordsmen: Jin Yong and the Modern Chinese Martial Arts Novel*. Honolulu: University of Hawaii Press.

Han, Yunbo 韓雲波. 2003. "Minsu fanshi yu ershi shiji Zhongguo wuxia xiaoshuo" 民俗範式與 20 世紀中國武俠小説 (The folklore paradigm in twentieth-century Chinese martial arts fiction). *Wuhan daxue xuebao* 武漢大學學報 (Journal of Wuhan University), 1: 86–91.

Hanan, Patrick. 1981. *The Chinese Vernacular Story*. Cambridge, MA: Harvard University Press.

Hanan, Patrick. 2004. *Chinese Fiction of the Nineteenth and Early Twentieth Centuries: Essays by Patrick Hanan*. New York: Columbia University Press.

Jin Yong 金庸. 1994a. *Shediao yingxiong zhuan* 射鵰英雄傳 (The legend of condor heroes). Beijing: Sanlian shudian.

Jin Yong 金庸. 1994b. *Shujian enchou lu* 書劍恩仇錄 (Romance of the book and the sword). Beijing: Sanlian shudian.

Kong Qingdong 孔慶東. 2004. "Jin Yong yu guomin wenxue" 金庸與國民文學 (Jin Yong

and national literature). Accessed 28 Feb. 2014. http://www.aisixiang.com/data/23633.html.

Koven, Seth. 2004. *Slumming: Sexual and Social Politics in Victorian London*. Princeton, NJ: Princeton University Press.

Link, E. Perry. 1981. *Mandarin Ducks and Butterflies: Popular Fiction in Early Twentieth-century Chinese Cities*. Berkeley: University of California Press.

Liu, Yangti 劉揚體. 1997. *Liubian zhongde liupai: yuanyang hudie pai xinlun* 流變中的流派:鴛鴦蝴蝶派新論 (The changing trends: a new understanding of the mandarin ducks and butterflies school). Beijing: Zhongguo wenlian chubanshe.

Wang, David Der-wei. 1997. *Fin-de-siècle Splendor: Repressed Modernities of Late Qing Fiction, 1849–1911*. Stanford, CA: Stanford University Press.

Wang, Dewei 王德威. 2003. *Xiandai Zhongguo xiaoshuo shijiang* 現代中國小説十講 (Ten lectures on the modern Chinese fiction). Shanghai: Fudan daxue chubanshe.

Wang, Yichuan 王一川. 2007. "Wenhua xugenxing shiqi de xiangxiangxing rentong 文化虛根性時期的想像性認同-金庸的現代性意義 (Imaginative Identification in an Age of Cultural Nihilism—the Modernity of Jin Yong's Novels". In *Jin Yong Pingshuo Wushinian* 金庸評說五十年 (Fifty Years of Jin Yong). Edited by Ge Tao 葛濤. Beijing: Wenhuayishu chubanshe.

Wen, Fengqiao 温奉橋. 2005. *Xiandaixing shiye zhongde Zhang Henshui xiaoshuo* 現代視野中的張恨水小説 (Zhang Henshui's novels in the perspective of modernity). Qingdao: Zhongguo haiyang daxue chubanshe.

Zhang, Henshui 張恨水. 1993. *Zhang Henshui quanji* 張恨水全集 (Complete works of Zhang Henshui). Edited by Xie Zhongyi 谢中一. Taiyuan: Beiyue wenyi chubanshe.

Zhang, Henshui. 1997a. *Shanghai Express*. Trans. William A. Lyell. Honolulu: University of Hawaii Press.

Zhang, Henshui 張恨水. 1997b. *Tixiao yinyuan* 啼笑因緣 (Fate in tears and laughter). In *Zhongguo xiandai wenxue baijia* 中國現代文學百家:張恨水 (A hundred masterpieces in modern Chinese literature: Zhang Henhsui). Edited by Yu Runqi 於潤奇. Beijing: Huaxia chubanshe.

Zhang, Henshui 張恨水. 2009. *Duhe yu fei* 獨鶴與飛 (Flight of a lonely crane). Xi'an: Shaanxi renmin chubanshe.

Zhang, Yingjin. 1996. *The City in Modern Chinese Literature and Film: Configurations of Space, Time, and Gender.* Stanford, CA: Stanford University Press.

Zhang, Yingjin. 2011. "*Youxi yu lishi zhiwai: disankongjian de lilun yu Jin Yong xiaoshuo de yiyi* 游戲於歷史之外:第三空間理論與金庸武俠小說的意義 (Play beyond History: Theory of the Third Space and Jin Yong's Martial Arts Novels." In *Jin Yong yu Hanyu Xinwenxue* 金庸與漢語新文學 (Jin Yong and New Chinese Literature). Edited by Zhu Shoutong 朱壽桐. Macau: University of Macau Publication Center. 73–87.

Zhang, Zhongliang 張中良. 2011. *Zhang Zhongliang jiang xiandaixiashuo* 張中良講現代小説 (Zhang Zhongliang on modern Chinese fiction). Changsha: Hunan jiaoyu chubanshe.

16
Ethnic Minority Literature

Mark Bender

Introduction

Since 1949, the PRC has recognized the existence of minority groups in China, inspired by the ethnic minority model of the former Soviet Union (Mullaney 2010). The criteria for recognition as an ethnic minority group are a combination of characteristics that include a common history, language, customs, area of inhabitation, and livelihood. These *shaoshu minzu* (variously translated as "national minorities," "minority nationalities," and, more recently, "ethnic minority groups") each has an official Chinese name and possibly several other names in native tongues or even foreign languages. *Menggu zu*, for instance, is the official designation of the Mongol ethnic minority group in China. The official groups number 55 at present and range in size from many millions to a few thousand. Making up about 9% of the PRC's population, most minority groups are located in China's extensive borderlands.

The literary traditions of the groups vary significantly. All of the groups have traditions of oral literature, some have traditions of written literature dating back centuries, and writers in many groups have, within the last few decades, employed standard Chinese (the official language of the PRC) as their medium of expression. Since the 1980s, a significant amount of literature in the form of poetry, short stories, novels, and dramas has been produced by a growing number of ethnic minority authors.

Contemporary ethnic minority authors write in a range of voices, from the subjective voice of the individual to voices speaking more as that of a collective ethnic group. Many works, often in a somewhat ethnographic fashion, utilize the imagery of local

A Companion to Modern Chinese Literature, First Edition. Edited by Yingjin Zhang.
© 2016 John Wiley & Sons, Ltd. Published 2016 by John Wiley & Sons, Ltd.

customs, rituals, material culture, and traditional expressive oral forms, as well as the regional environment. This contemporary literature can be divided into what has been called "Sinophone" writing—which uses standard Chinese as the vehicle of expression— and works written in "native tongues." The Chinese Minority Writers Association (Zhongguo shaoshu minzu zuojia xiehui) was founded in 1985 in Beijing and presently has 2,000 members. Moreover, over 1,000 ethnic minority writers have also been members of the Chinese Writers Association, and many more participate in local organizations such as the Xinjiang Writers Association and the Inner Mongolian Writers Association. Besides members of these official organizations, many other ethnic minority writers around the country publish their works in a wide variety of print and online outlets.

The native tongue literature may appear in traditional writing systems of a particular group or in romanized scripts created since 1949. Many ethnic authors find themselves caught between two cultural worlds, and the shaping of an ethnic identity is problematic for some. This is especially so for those with backgrounds removed from more traditional ethnic communities (often located in rural areas). Although relatively few minority writers have attained national and international acclaim, many have strong local and regional followings, especially in the Uygur (Weiwuer zu) communities of Northwest China, Inner Mongolia, the Tibetan (Zang zu) areas of Western China, and the highly diverse Southwest. This chapter will provide a brief background on the oral and traditional literary heritages, and present an overview of the situation since the 1980s, stressing both national trends and local situations.

Ethnicity and Ethnic Writers

In the May Fourth Movement of the 1920s–1930s, several ethnic minority writers joined the ranks of the emerging Chinese modern literati. Most prominent among these were the fiction writer Shen Congwen, famous for his "Border Town," concerning his home area in the Miao and Tujia regions of west Hunan, and Lao She, of Manchu (*Man zu*) heritage, whose novels included *Rickshaw Boy*. Many other younger writers, who would rise to prominence in the post-1949 era, grew up under the influence of modernist writing of the period. Once the PRC was established in 1949, the position of ethnic minorities in the new state underwent a process of review, as did the literature produced by ethnic minority writers. In the early 1950s, during the formative phase of a modern Chinese ethnic minority literature, certain questions were raised that are still the subject of debate, which include: What is ethnic minority literature? What is an ethnic minority writer? What purpose does ethnic minority literature serve? (Zhao Zhizhong 2005: 2–5).

In China, ethnic minority writing is either traditional or modern literature (oral or written) composed by ethnic minorities. The premier research journal *Studies of Ethnic Literature* (*Minzu wenxue yanjiu*), published by the Chinese Academy of Social Sciences (CASS), typically features a mix of articles on traditional oral and written literature as well as modern writing. For contemporary written literature, the official criterion is that ethnic literature must be written by a person registered as an ethnic minority. This criteria, however, also has its complications. For example, a number of writers are of mixed heritage. Many do not speak their ethnic languages or were not raised in ethnic communities where traditions are strongest. Some have earlier in life been registered as Han (often children of mixed marriages), but later assumed minority identity. Individuals have even been encouraged by publishing houses to seek out their minority roots as a means to promote their profile as writers.

While for decades the subject matter of ethnic minority writing was assumed to be on ethnic minority topics, by the early 1980s some authors were writing on themes not immediately apparent as ethnic. Such non-ethnic themes have raised questions about how to categorize such literature. Although most highly recognized works by minority authors do tend to draw heavily on traditional culture, it is not uncommon for post-1980 writers, such as Yi poet Jimu Langge of Chengdu, author of several poetry collections, including *The Silent Revolver* (*Jingqiaoqiao de zuolun*, 2002), to devote a large portion of their writing to less ethnic-centered themes, such as facets of life in China's dynamic urban centers (Dayton 2006). With these conditions in mind, some critics have suggested that ethnic minority writing can encompass non-ethnic subject matter since, regardless of the subject, the authors ultimately write from ethnic minority perspectives (Zhao Zhizhong 2005: 4–5).

An important related question is the position of Han writers who write on ethnic minority themes. A recent example of such writing is Han novelist Jiang Rong's *Wolf Totem* (*Lang tuteng*, 2004; English 2008). The book generated some controversy among Mongol minority authors and critics regarding the representation of certain Mongol customs, but others have accepted it as an alternative view of Mongol life. Chi Zijian's *The Right Bank of the Argun River* (2005) is about the vanishing Evenki (Ewenke zu) reindeer culture of northeast China. The work was actually based in large part on oral interviews of an aged Evenki matron. Nevertheless, while such works are on the subject matter of ethnic minority cultures, they are ultimately written from the perspectives of non-minority writers and cannot be considered the product of ethnic minorities. Works by Han authors are thus not considered as ethnic minority writing. Similar logic prevails in cases of writing by one ethnic minority group about another.

As for the purpose of ethnic minority literature, in the early phases of development, ethnic literature, similar to mainstream Han literature, was meant to serve a social function in the mold of Mao's 1943 "Yan'an Talks," and the traditions of socialist realism borrowed from the former Soviet Union. In the post-1980 era, more works by ethnic minority authors emerged that would enter a more tolerant and diverse body of contemporary Chinese literature. As noted, an increasing number of ethnic minority authors have been admitted to the elite Chinese Writers Association. For instance, Yi poet Jidi Majia was a temporary president of the association in the early 2000s. A special literary award known as the Golden Horse Award (*Junma jiang*) was established in 1981, and is presented every 3 years. Writings in both standard Chinese and minority languages have been recognized on its award lists, which now number several hundred recipients.

Oral Literature

While all ethnic minority groups in China have oral traditions, until recent decades only a few had writing systems. Present-day ethnic minority groups whose antecedents had writing systems and produced extensive bodies of written literature include Uygur, Tibetans, Mongolians, Manchus, Dai, ethnic Koreans (Chaoxian zu), and Yi. Works of literature in these traditions include religious texts, histories, genealogies, political and business documents, astrological and technical information, poetry, essays, and various forms of narratives that may include epics, myths, folk stories, and romances. Of these written traditions, only traditional Yi writing (for which there is still not a universal standardized script) is wholly native to China. In the case of the Mongols, several scripts have been in use historically, the earliest based on a twelfth-century Uygur script. Other local scripts, such as the "pictographic" Naxi script from Yunnan province, had only limited use in conjunction with rituals and astrology. Romanization systems for most ethnic minority languages were created after 1949. Some, such as the romanization systems for several Miao (Hmong) dialects, were based on earlier ones devised by Western missionaries such as Samuel Pollard (Zhou Minglang 2003: 316–317). These systems have seen limited local usage for official documents and, in some cases, short stories, essays, and poems.

Records of oral folk literature were collected from every official ethnic minority group in China today in several mass collecting efforts made by government agencies in the 1950s, 1980s, and again in the 2000s as part of Intangible Cultural Heritage (ICH) projects. These items, which collectively number in the millions, include folk tales, folk songs, epics, local dramas, proverbs and sayings, jokes, and other verbal art (X. Ma, Liang, and Zhang 1992; Mair and Bender 2011). Large numbers of these items have been published in scholarly and more popular formats. Some of these traditions date back hundreds or even thousands of years. With the exception of epic poetry, such traditions are also well represented among local cultures of the Han, China's largest ethnic group.

Two especially prominent genres represented in the repertoires of many ethnic minority groups are styles of antiphonal singing (in a call and response format) that often involve numerous participants, and epic poetry. Although the antiphonal songs are primarily oral, a number of published collections have become popular as written literature. These include several volumes of love songs (*qingge*) published in the Guangxi Zhuang Autonomous Region in the 1980s that are associated with ancient singing traditions evoking the legendary folk singer Third Sister Liu (Liu Sanjie). Folksongs and legends have become a part of ethnic tourist ventures in many parts of China (Schein 2000; Notar 2006).

Although there are many long prosimetric poems in the majority Han local traditions of oral narrative, such as the love stories of the Suzhou *tanci* story-singing style, the term "epic" (*shishi*, literally "poems of history") is usually applied by Chinese scholars to long poems of varying formats in ethnic minority traditions. In some traditions, these long poems are only performed orally, while in others they exist in both oral and written versions. The epics are often categorized either as heroic epics or as epics of creation or origins. Heroic epics tend to be products of northern groups. Outstanding examples are *Jangar* of the Mongols, *King Gesar/Geser Khan* of the Tibetans and Mongols, and *Manas* of the Kirghiz and Kazakhs.

Creation and origin epics—such as *Book of Origins* (*Le'e teyi*), *Meige*, and *Chamu* of various Yi groups; *Sigangli* of the Wa; *Miluotuo* of the Yao; *Buluotuo* of the Zhuang; *Miao Ancient Songs* (*Miao zu guge*) of the Miao; *Creation Story* (*Chuangshiji*) of the Naxi; and many others—have been identified in the folk traditions of the diverse ethnic groups in the mountains of South and Southwest China. While epics such as *King Gesar* have been known to European, Russian, and Chinese scholars since the nineteenth century, most of the epic traditions in the Southwest have only been identified since the 1940s–1950s. The epic tradition called *King of Yalu* (*Yalu Wang*) of the Miao of Ziyun county, in Guizhou province, was only "discovered" by folklorists by about 2007 (Zhongguo minjian wenyi xiehui 2011).

Since the 1980s, the minority epics have received great attention in China, and by the early 2000s became a major focus of ICH projects. Many national and local conferences are held each year for the study of these epics and other ICH traditions. This interest has a certain nationalistic factor, expressed both nationally and locally. Both the epic of *King Gesar* and the Kirghiz epic *Manas* are claimed to be the longest epics in the world. The Mongol epic *Jangar* was claimed by the governments of China and Mongolia through UNESCO as a world heritage ICH item (though the epic is now officially a jointly recognized item). As with other folk traditions, local communities see possible economic gain in the recognition of their local epic traditions. In at least one Mongol community in Xinjiang, government boosters have set up *Jangar* learning classes among schoolchildren in an attempt to carry on an epic singing tradition that is endangered due to lack of tradition bearers.

Traditional epics and other folk literature are also sources of material for modern authors, dramatists, and filmmakers, both minority and Han. Literary examples include Alai's novel *King Gesar* (*Gesaer Wang*, 2009), which draws to some extent on the Tibetan traditions represented in the epic. Many Yi poets have utilized imagery from epics, bridal laments, and ritual chants in their contemporary works. The Yi bridal lament from southern Sichuan about the "run-away bride" Gamo Anyo was studied by a team of choreographers and producers from Beijing and made into a short-lived eponymous dance drama that was performed in the capital city in 2007 (Bender 2007: 215). In some cases, such as the Yao creation epic *Miluotou*, contemporary poets have cast the oral work in written idiom. Many epics have been translated and published in Chinese, along with numerous collections of other types of folk literature. Collectively, these works constitute a new genre of Chinese literature, that of ethnic minority folk literature in standard Chinese translation.

Contemporary Ethnic Minority Writing

Uygur, Mongolian, Korean, and Tibetan are the most widely used written minority scripts today in China. Modern-style novels, short stories, and poems have been written and published in these languages since the early to mid-twentieth century, and the number of publications in each of the languages has grown since the early 1980s. Literature is also produced in several other scripts, such as Yi and Dai and a number of romanized scripts. Readerships for these native tongue literatures are confined to those literate in the respective writing systems, and most audiences are regional. Some works are translated into standard Chinese, but much of this writing remains in the native scripts. The majority of ethnic writing that reaches a national audience is composed and published in standard Chinese.

Although policies have sometimes wavered, since 1949 the Chinese government has specifically recognized the rights of ethnic minority groups to speak and write their own languages. The use of what Yi poet Aku Wuwu has called "native tongues" has a long history among several groups, particularly the Uygur, Mongols, and Tibetans. Romanization systems have been created for virtually all of the official minority languages, though most of these mediums are used only by scholars. At various moments, such minority scripts have been officially promoted at local levels, and stories, poems, newspapers, and government documents have been issued. One example is the Zhuang romanization system used in some counties in Guangxi alongside standard Chinese materials. Although there may be small local followings for the romanized scripts, when used by creative writers they tend to appear in bilingual versions, such as the poems by the Hani poet of Yunnan province, Mo Du.

Although prodigious amounts of literature are written in Uygur, Mongolian, Korean, and Tibetan each year, only a small percentage of that writing appears in Chinese (or other translations). According to Hartley and Schiafinni-Vedani (2008: xxv), many of the works written in Tibetan are in small press runs, often under private sponsorship. In many cases, readers of native tongue literature are writers themselves and a small coterie of students, scholars, other intellectuals, and sometimes monks. Thus, audiences for these writings are limited. On the other hand, although the majority of ethnic minority by authors from other ethnic groups is written in standard Chinese in some regions, there has been movement to reclaim or revisit the use of native tongues to produce contemporary literature.

A number of writers in Southwest China, particularly among the Yi ethnic group, have been promoting native tongue writing since the mid-1980s. The most vocal proponent is the aforementioned Aku Wuwu, who has published poetry collections entirely in the Nuosu dialect of Yi and others in standard Chinese. Using his Han Chinese name Luo Qingchun (2001), he explores issues of "second tongue" and "mother tongue" literature and "cultural hybridism." His work has encouraged young poets of the Yi and other regional ethnic groups such as the Qiang to write in their native tongues. Aside from publications, public poetry readings in minority languages have been held in recent years in bookstores, universities, and other forums in Chengdu, the capital of Sichuan province and home to mainstream poetry movements such as the Not-Not (*feifei*) poets of the 1980s, which included the Yi poet Jimu Langge and the Miao poet He Xiaozhu.

In a majority of cases, minority writers choose to use standard Chinese because of its potential for reaching large audiences and for greater publication opportunities. Many ethnic writers from urban and/or ethnically mixed backgrounds lack the proficiency to write in "native" languages. Also, texts written in Chinese since the May Fourth era have served as models, along with translations into Chinese, of expressive formats such as modernist poetry, short stories, and the novel. In dealing with Tibetans such as Tashi Dawa (Zhaxi Dawa) who utilize standard Chinese for their creative writing, Hartley has employed the term "Sinophone" (Hartley and Schiafinni-Vedani 2008). As noted, this term could be extended to writers of other ethnic groups in China as well.

Uygur and Hui Historical Novels

Written literature has a long tradition among the Uygurs, a Turkish people of Northwest China who adopted Islam by the eighth century and whose writing system was embraced as one of the several scripts historically used by the Mongols. Modern Uygur literature begins in the early twentieth century when Western innovations in style were adopted by numerous writers. In the post-1949 period, Uygur novelists do not come to the fore until the post-1980 period. During the 1980s, publishing houses and literary journals devoted to Uygur literature increased markedly over earlier decades. The first novel to appear was written by Abdullah Talip and entitled *Crest of the Whirlpool* (*Xuanwo langhua*, 1981), which concerns a heroic revolutionary poet of the 1940s. Other works that appeared in the 1980s and garnered national attention were the historical novels—Abdurahim Otkur's *Traces* (*Zuji*) and Seyfeddin Aziz's eponymous *Satuk Bugra Khan* (*Sutuke Bugela Han*). The former is also based on actual historical figures engaged in struggles against oppression in the early twentieth century (Kasgarli 1993: 581–582). Memtimin Hoshur, an editor and novelist who began writing in 1965 and who holds many leading positions in Xinjiang literary societies, has published a series of historical novels, including *The Ancient City Buried in Sand* (*Bei shamo yanmai de chengshi*, 1996) and numerous short story collections.

The Hui are an ethnic group defined by their long-term engagement with Islam. Hui communities are centered in the northern Ningxia Hui Autonomous Region, though Hui communities are found all over China. Zhang Chengzhi is the best-known Hui writer whose works include an intense historical novel set in the late Qing dynasty and early decades of the twentieth century up to the May Fourth Movement. Entitled *History of Soul* (*Xing ling shi*), the work depicts violent cultural conflicts between the Qing dynasty authorities and Sufi (Jahriyya) communities in northern China. The plot of the novel is interwoven with the author's personal spiritual crisis in the 1980s (Garnaut

2006; Leung 1994). Zhang's 1991 work subsequently became controversial. A revised version of the novel, which emphasized unity among ethnic groups in China and with intensified focus on the actions of Red Guards in the Cultural Revolution, was published in China in 2012.

Another Hui novelist, Huo Da, won the 1991 Mao Dun prize in literature for her novel *Muslim Funeral Rites* (*Musilin de zangli*, 1991; English as *The Jade King: History of a Chinese Muslim Family*, 1992). The lengthy saga probes several generations of Hui and Han interaction, from the early twentieth century through the Second Sino-Japanese War and culminating in the early 1980s. A persistent theme is the funerals of characters of several social backgrounds, the first being that of an aged jade worker who died after working on a model of the famous Hui sea explorer Zheng He, who sailed to the coast of Africa in the Ming dynasty. An especially compelling subplot is that of the daughter of a Hui intellectual who attends a university in Beijing and is involved in a love affair with a Han professor. After the young woman becomes sick and dies, her family arranges that her devoted lover be allowed to attend the funeral in disguise.

Mongol Grasslands Literature

One of the first ethnic minority writers to rise to prominence after 1949 was the Mongol author Malaqinfu, a novelist who, in 1951, published the first work of "grasslands literature" about life of nomads on the northern steppes (Sedaoerji 1980). Similar to many of the best-known works by Mongol authors in China, the novel was written in standard Chinese. Much of his early work, similar to that of other writers in new China, was written in praise of the Party and socialist construction of the 1950s. His masterwork, *The Flourishing Grasslands* (*Mangmang de caoyuan*, 1957), still in the socialist realist mold, is a relatively sophisticated work employing varied narrative techniques and featuring vivid portrayals of 20 characters, ranging from electrical technicians, doctors, herders, and storytellers. His portrayal of the life of Mongol nomads set within the sublime vastness of the steppes would influence the style and tone of many subsequent authors of various ethnic backgrounds. Other Mongol authors who began their careers in the 1950s and revived them in the late 1970s include novelists A. Aodesi'er and Zhalagahu, and dramatists Yun Zhaoguang and Chaoketunaren.

More contemporary authors include Guo Xuebo, whose short story collection *Desert Wolf* (*Shalang*, 1996) has been translated into English, French, and Japanese. His *Desert Fox* (*Shahu*, 1985), an award-winning short story collection, was selected for publication and distribution by the United Nations (Dai Qin 2010). Some of his works have been made into films. A younger author, Bao Liying, who authored *Genghis Khan* (*Chengjisi Han*, 2007) and several other Mongol-related historical novels released in the last decade, is actually a 36th-generation granddaughter of the historic Khan.

A'ertai is one of many contemporary Mongol ethnic poets. He writes personal poems that often evoke scenes of the steppe, such as the poem "Mongolian Horse" (*Menggu ma*, 1993), which contains the lines:

> Mongolian horse—
> Let joy and sorrow
> Never be shaped by
> An agate hammer.
> Let youthful hearts
> Be lit without
> Flint and steel.
> (translated by Mark Bender)

Other poets of the post-1980 era are Baoyinhexige, whose poems include "Horsehead Fiddle" (*Matou qin*, 2009); literary critic and poet Chen Ganglong at Beijing University; and Ha Shen, one of the younger women poets, who writes in both standard Chinese and Mongolian.

Ethnic Korean Literature

Ethnic Koreans migrated to Northeast China in the late nineteenth and early twentieth centuries. Korean is still a viable language in the Yanbian autonomous prefecture in Jilin province, and a number of ethnic Korean authors have produced a body of short stories, novels, and poems in Korean, as well as writings in Chinese. A few authors have extended their readership outside China. Among the novelists is Ri Geunjeon (Lee Kun-jun), whose novels *Time of Hardship* (*Kunan shidai*) and *Chronicle of Hardship* (*Kunan niandai*, 1982) were originally written in Chinese and then translated into Korean and marketed in South Korea.

Other notable novels include *Tearful Tumen River* (*Leishui dashile Tumenjiang*, 1999) by Choe Hongil and *Rootless Flower* (*Wugen hua*, 1996) by Xu Lianshun (Heo Ryoensun). Jin Wenxue is fluent in Korean, Chinese, and Japanese, having studied in Japan for several years in the 1990s. His numerous works include the novel *Koreans Become Bastards* (*Choulou de Hanguo ren*, 2011), which concerns Koreans living in Japan and attempting, through incarnations as tigers and insects, to come to terms with the social position of ethnic Koreans in the modern world.

Tibetan Literature and Magical Realism

Historically, most literature in Tibetan was religious texts, though some creative works of poetry and prose were produced. It was not until the 1980s that modern-style novels, short stories, and free-verse poetry became established (Hartley and

Schiaffini-Vedani 2008: xvi–xxv). Throughout that decade, modern writing and literature in both Tibetan and Chinese increased in the Xizang Tibetan Autonomous Region and other Tibetan areas in the Qinghai, Gansu, Sichuan, and Yunnan provinces in Western China. By the 1990s, over 100 Tibetan language journals had ben published by a variety of government and private publishers. The most popular among these is *Tibetan Art and Literature* (*Zang zu wenyi*).

While the early historical novels in the 1980s were in the socialist realist mode, since the 1980s a number of Tibetan authors writing in Chinese have produced novels and short stories in a style that have been labeled "magical realism." Among the first to use these techniques associated with South American writers such as Gabriel García Márquez and Pablo Neruda is Tashi Dawa, of mixed Tibetan and Han background. As a youngster, Tashi was raised in urban environments in East China and did not embrace his Tibetan heritage until his early twenties. His short stories, all written in standard Chinese, include dreamy, ethnographically thick descriptions of nomadic life and life-and-death struggles against the harsh environment of the mountain borderlands. In his story "Tibet, the Spirit Tied in a Knotted Leather Rope" (*Xizang, jizai pisheng jieshang de hun*, 1985), Tashi makes use of multiple viewpoints, shifts in chronological order, imagery of ancient ritual, and a computerized modernity to create mesmerizing, unworldly effects as he forecasts what a modern Tibet would be like in the year 2000 (Batt 2001).

The novelist Alai, of mixed Tibetan and Hui background, has written a series of novels drawing heavily on local lore, Tibetan history, and techniques of multiple narrative points of view and magical realism. His best-known work is the novel *Dust Settles* (Chen'ai luoding), which chronicles events in the pre-1949 Tibetan areas of southwest Sichuan province and features a vivid cast of characters in rival clans who engage in plays of power, greed, and passion, set within local social hierarchies. The technique of magical realism seems suited to the opaque expression of Tibetan identity in narratives set in the thin air and overarching landscapes of the Eastern Himalayas.

Two prominent young Tibetan woman writers are Yangzhen (Yangdron), who wrote *God Without Gender* (*Wu xingbie de shen*, 1994), and Meizhuo (Medron), who penned *Clan of the Sun* (*Taiyang buluo*, 1998). Both novels "humanize and demystify pre-communist Tibet's past to reinforce the importance of Tibetan culture, ways of life and tradition" (Hartley and Schiaffini-Vedani 2008: xxi).

Cosmographic Literature of the Southwest

Since the early 1980s, the imagery of traditional culture, often interlaced with themes of the environment, has been common in both ethnic minority prose and poetry. Beginning with the Great Leap Forward of the late 1950s, the forests, mountains, and rivers of the border areas have been exploited for their resources. Modernization programs of recent decades have increased pressure on scarce natural resources by aggressive timbering and mineral extraction, along with the extensive damming of river systems. Since the late 1990s, the western regions of China have been targeted for increased development, which has included the rapid building of cities, airports, and golf courses. Along with physical changes to the landscape, great social changes have occurred as well. Large numbers of young minority people have become part of China's "floating population" and spend much of their lives away from native villages and out of contact with traditional ways. Many prefer modern lifestyles to traditional ones and develop values and priorities that may conflict with family elders. The ills of contemporary society, including alcoholism and drug addiction, have also put pressure on the integrity of some minority communities (Liu Shao-hua 2010).

In Southwest China, themes of cultural and environmental change have been broached in differing ways by poets of several ethnic groups. Some of these include thick ethnographic writing about the diverse cultures of the southwest and what eco-critic Joni Adamson (2012: 35) calls a "cosmographic" attention to detail and content, reflecting human interaction with the animal and plant communities in the diverse landscapes and bio-regions of the area (Bender 2012a).

Jidi Majia emerged as one of the first minority poets to gain mainstream recognition in the transitional era of the early 1980s (Bender 2009: 127–133; Jidi 2010). A member of the Nuosu branch of the Yi ethnic group, Jidi spent much of his early life in the county seat of Butuo county in the Liangshan Yi Autonomous Prefecture in southern Sichuan. He was influenced by international writers as varied as Pablo Neruda, Gabriela Mistral, and Walt Whitman. After holding several distinguished positions in the Chinese Writers Association, Jidi was appointed to high government positions in the Qinghai province beginning in 2006. An excellent lyricist, Jidi's work has a sonorous feel and is rich in traditional imagery. A recurrent technique in his work is the use of traditional imagery to reaffirm the traditional lore of singing, folk costume, and hunting, while acknowledging the passing of a way of life in the face of modernization.

His Chinese-language poem titled "The Final Summons" (*Zuihou de zhaohuan*, 1992) mourns the loss of a charismatic hunter of leopards (a threatened species in China) who once charmed the mountain women with his folksongs: "Whether at dawn or dusk he always went to the hills / to hunt leopards, to hunt for the ancestor's greatest glory." In "Water Deer Call" (*Zhang shao*, 1992), Jidi again uses the imagery of a hunter who has mixed emotions over the taking of a water deer to evoke feelings of estrangement from some aspects of traditional culture, which no longer have relevance in a swiftly changing modern world. Some of his poems extend beyond the themes of Yi culture and engage his travels in Europe, interaction with foreign cultures, and personal growth. A number of his works have been translated in foreign languages, including Italian and English (Jidi 2014). Utilizing his position in the provincial government, Jidi has sponsored several international poetry gatherings in Qinghai, which included readings by many Chinese ethnic minority poets.

Aku Wuwu, who began writing somewhat later in the 1980s, is known for his Nuosu language poems and prose poems that are rich in cosmographic detail and often have a dream-like dimension that borders on shamanic vision (Aku and Bender 2006; Bender and Aku 2011). As dean of Yi studies at the Southwest University for

Nationalities in Chengdu, Aku has used his position and poetic talents to promote education among the rural Yi and, similar to Jidi Majia, gain an international stage for Yi poetry. His most famous poem, "Calling Back the Soul of Zhyge Alu" (*Zhaohun*, 1994), was inspired by the ancient *Songs of the South* (*Chuci*) written by the poet Qu Yuan in the third century BC, and by the rituals for calling back the wandering souls of ill people that are still conducted by Yi ritualists (Bender 2005). The poem is at once a cry for the recognition of the Yi as a viable ethnic group as well as a warning that the Yi are responsible for their fates in the contemporary world. As a performance poet, Aku energetically declaims his poems in live contexts that include urban opera houses, university auditoriums, bookstores, and rural ethnic minority schools. Growing up deep in the mountains of Liangshan, Aku learned Chinese at age 7 when he began attending a rural school miles from his home near the Yalu River. The theme of rivers looms large in Aku's poetry, and he has created a body of poems in Chinese based on his experiences in the Mississippi and Columbia river systems in the United States, which included his contact with Native American writers.

Other "Liangshan poets" include Luowu Laqie, Asu Yue'er, Ma Deqing, and Sha Ma (Bender 2009). Bamo Qubumo and Lu Juan are among the most accomplished Yi women associated with the Liangshan movement. Bamo holds a high position among Yi intellectuals, and is a director of the esteemed CASS Institute of Ethnic Literature. Her poems draw heavily on traditional Yi epic narratives from Yi groups throughout the Southwest. In a series of poems from her collection *The Origins of Patterns* (*Tu an de laiyuan shi*, 1981), she mixes images from myth, nature, and folk life into poems to create unique perspectives on issues of Yi as an ethnic minority. She has also authored an important study on the poetics of Yi traditional poetry, epics, and literary criticism, all of which was written in poetic form (Bamo 2001). Lu Juan's most adventurous poem "Mute Slave" (*Ya nu*, 2006) is filled with the imagery of ancient Yi texts, mythic figures, plant and animal lore, ancient migrations, personal reverie, and sexuality that call into question traditional women's roles and agency.

Burao Yilu is one of a handful of Wa writers to gain admission to the Chinese Writers Association. Related to an influential nineteenth-century Wa headman, her roots are in the mountains of the western Yunnan province near the border of Myanmar. Although best known as an investigative journalist writing on minority women and their issues, she has produced volumes of prose and poetry. Poems such as "Moon Mountain" (*Yueliang shan*, 2002) and "What the Silver Pheasant Said" (*Baixian zai sushuo shenme*, 2005) touch on issues of cultural viability, the environment, and issues of ethnic identity and stigma, for the Wa are still regarded as the "last head-hunters" in China, though the practice ended in the 1950s (Bender 2011; Bender 2012b). Mo Du, of the Hani ethnic group, is an example of a local writer working in near obscurity, utilizing one of the recently constructed romanization systems to create poetry in Hani, which he publishes in bilingual Hani and standard Chinese editions. Similar to Burao, his work draws on local traditions, but often from the viewpoint of a returnee from the outside world.

In the wake of the great Sichuan earthquake of 2008, a number of poets of the Qiang ethnic group became active in an urgent search for ethnic survival. A large percentage of the small Qiang group was lost in the earthquake, and several Qiang poets and essayists, such as Yang Zi and Qiangren Liu, have created works calling for cultural revival in a new era of radical social change hastened by the catastrophic events and the subsequent move of many Qiang people to modern housing complexes.

Huang Yibing (Mai Mang), a poet of the Tujia ethnic group of Southwest China, is a graduate of Beijing University and among the new-generation poets who emerged in the late 1980s after the Misty Poets of the immediate post-Mao era (Manfredi 2005). Huang took up residence in the United States in 1993 where he holds a professorship of Chinese literature. Among his works is a bilingual Chinese and English collection titled *Stone Turtle Poems: 1987–2000* (2005).

Critical Works and the Generation of Change

Ethnic minority scholars have added critical voices to the study of Chinese ethnic minority literature. Literary histories have been compiled on the traditional and contemporary literatures of writers of several groups, such as the two-volume *History of Yi Literature* (*Yi zu wenxue shi*) (Zuo et al. 2006). Li Hongran (2004), a Hui scholar, has written the most thorough overview of mainstream Chinese ethnic minority literature to date. Chao Gejin, director of the Institute of Ethnic Literature in Beijing, published a groundbreaking study of the oral version of the Mongol *Janggar* epic, employing crucial strategies from Western performance folkloristics (Chao Gejin 2000).

Younger ethnic minority writers already face a literary world in which first-hand traditional resources and languages are disappearing at an accelerated rate. Upcoming generations may have to find new ways of expression beyond the use of traditional ethnographic imagery, since many writers are now urban-based and thus disconnected from rural traditions (which are also changing). The Internet as a medium for ethnic minority writing offers new possibilities (Ming Jiang 2011). The CASS Institute of Ethnic Literature posts information on both traditional and contemporary ethnic minority literature and the Archive of Chinese Ethnic Minority Literature (1949–1999) has a home at www.chinawriter.com.cn/zp/jpwk.

There are blogs devoted to several minority groups (Tibetan, Yi, Dong) that include contemporary poems and short stories, and many minority writers from groups including Tibetan, Hui, Manchu, Mongol, Miao, Yi, Tujia, Yao, Zhuang, Qiang, and others publish their own blogs in Chinese. In 2011, Bruce Hume created a blog that alerts English-language readers to developments in ethnic minority writing in China. Since 2009, *Asian Highlands Perspectives*, an online publishing venture based in Qinghai province and founded by Kevin Stuart and Gerard Roche, has issued a long series of novels in English translation on life in West China. Works by Tibetan and Mongghul authors include Limusishiden's autobiographical *Mongghul Memories and Lives* and Li Dechun (Limusishiden's Chinese name) and Lu Wanfang's *Passions and Colored Sleeves: Mongghul Lives in Eastern Tibet*, which chronicles several generations of members of the Mongghul, a subgroup of the Tu ethnic group.

The study of the growing body of ethnic minority oral and authored literature is still in its infancy. Due to the diverse number of literary traditions within the general category of Chinese ethnic minority literature, scholars are faced with the prospect of dealing with languages other than Chinese if research extends beyond Sinophone writing. As China develops throughout the twenty-first century, it is likely that ethnic minority policy will evolve as well, producing new situations for the creation and study of the literature of the ethnic minority groups living within China's borders.

* Mark Bender thanks Fu Haihong, Graham Zhao, and Elise Marie Anderson.

References

Adamson, Joni. 2012. "Whale as Cosmos: Multi-species Ethnography and Contemporary Indigenous Cosmopolitics." *Revista de Estudios Ingleses*, 64: 29–45.

Aku, Wuwu 阿庫烏霧, and Mark Bender. Eds. 2006. *Tiger Traces: Selected Nuosu and Chinese Poetry of Aku Wuwu*. Columbus, OH: Foreign Language Publications and Services.

Bamo, Qubumo 巴莫曲布嫫. 2001. *Yingling yu shihun: Yizu gudai jingji shixue yanjiu* 鷹靈與詩魂:彝族古代經籍詩學研究 (Golden eagle spirit and poetic soul: a study of Yi nationality poetics). Beijing: Zhongguo shehui kexueyuan chubanshe.

Bao, Liying 包麗英. 2007. *Chengjisihan* 成吉思汗 (Chinggis Khan). Hefei: Anhui wenyi chubanshe.

Batt, Herbert J. Ed. 2001. *Tales of Tibet: Sky Burials, Prayer Wheels, Wind Horses*. Boulder, CO: Rowman and Littlefield.

Bender, Mark. 2005. "The Spirit of Zhyge Alu: The Nuosu Poetry of Aku Wuwu." *Manoa*, 17: 113–130. Special issue entitled *Blood Ties: Writing Across Chinese Borders*.

Bender, Mark. 2007. "Ashima and Gamo Anyo: Aspects of Two 'Yi' Narrative Poems." *Chinoperl Papers*, 27: 209–242.

Bender, Mark. 2009. "Dying Hunters, Poison Plants, and Mute Slaves: Nature and Tradition in Contemporary Nuosu Yi Poetry." *Asian Highlands Perspectives*, 1: 117–158.

Bender, Mark. 2011. "Echoes from Si Gang Lih: Burao Yilu's 'Moon Mountain.'" *Asian Highlands Perspectives*, 10: 99–128.

Bender, Mark. 2012a. "Ethnographic Poetry in North-East India and Southwest China." *Rocky Mountain Review* (Special issue): 106–129.

Bender, Mark. 2012b. "The Cry of the Silver Pheasant: Contemporary Ethnic Poetry in Sichuan and Yunnan." *Chinese Literature Today*, 2.2: 68–74.

Bender, Mark, and Aku Wuwu. 2011. "Four Trees and Three Seas." *Cha: An Asian Literary Journal* (July). Accessed 12 Jan. 2014. http://www.asiancha.com/content/view/890/299/.

Chao, Gejin 朝戈金. 2000. *Kochuan shishi xue: Ranpile "Jiangge'er" chengxu jufa yanjiu* 口傳史詩詩學:冉皮勒《江格爾》程序句法研究 (Oral poetics: formulaic diction of Arimpil's *Jangar Singing*). Nanning: Guangxi renmin chubanshe.

Dai, Qin 岱欽. 2010. "Da mo zhi zi: Guo Xuebo" 大漠之子: 郭雪波 (Son of the desert: Guo Xuebo). *Beifang xinbao*, 3.26: 40.

Dayton, D. 2006. *Big Country, Subtle Voices: Three Ethnic Poets from China's Southwest*. M.A. Thesis, University of Sydney, Sydney, Australia. Accessed 14 Aug. 2007. http://ses.library.usyd.edu.au/handle/2123/1630.

Garnaut, A. 2006. "Pen of the Jahriyya: A Commentary on *The History of the Soul* by Zhang Chengzhi." *Inner Asia*, 8.1: 29–50.

Hartley, Lauran R., and Patricia Schiafinni-Vedani. Eds. 2008. *Modern Tibetan Literature and Social Change*. Durham, NC: Duke University Press.

Huo, Da. 1992. *Jade King: A History of a Chinese Muslim Family*. Trans. Guan Yuehua. Beijing: Panda Books.

Jiang, Rong. 2008. *Wolf Totem*. Trans. Howard Goldblatt. New York: Penguin Press.

Jidi, Majia 吉狄馬加. 2010. *Jidi Majia de shi* 吉狄馬加的詩 (Poems of Jidi Majia). Chengdu: Sichuan wenyi chubanshe.

Jidia, Majia. 2014. *Rhapsody in Black, Poems*. Trans. Denis Mair. Norman: University of Oklahoma.

Kasgarli, Sultan Mahmut. 1993. "The Formation of Modern Uighur Literature and Current Developments." *Central Asian Survey*, 12.4: 577–583.

Leung, Laifong. 1994. *Morning Sun: Interviews with Chinese Writers of the Lost Generation*. Armonk, NY: M. E. Sharpe.

Li, Hongran 李鴻然. 2004. *Zhongguo dangdai shaoshu minzu wenxue shilun* 中國當代少數民族文學史論 (Discussions of the history of contemporary Chinese ethnic minority literature). 2 vols. Kunming: Yunnan jiaoyu chubanshe.

Liu, Shao-hua. 2010. *Passage to Manhood: Youth Migration, Heroin, and AIDS in Southwest China*. Stanford, CA: Stanford University Press.

Luo, Qingchun 羅慶春. 2001. *Ling yu ling de duihua: Zhongguo shaoshu minzu Hanyu shilun* 靈與靈的對話:中國少數民族漢語詩論 (Dialogues between spirits: contemporary ethnic minority poetry in Chinese). Hong Kong: Tianma.

Ma, Xueliang 馬學良, Liang Tingwang 梁庭望, and Zhang Gongjin 張公瑾. 1992. *Zhongguo shaoshu minzu wenxue shi* 中國少數民族文學史 (A history of ethnic minority literature in China). 2 vols. Beijing: Zhongyang minzu xueyuan chubanshe.

Mair, Victor, and Mark Bender. Eds. 2011. *The Columbia Anthology of Chinese Folk and Popular Literature*. New York: Columbia University Press.

Manfredi, Paul. 2005. "Review of Mai Mang's *Stone Turtle: Poems, 1987–2000*." MCLC Resource Center. Accessed 10 Jan. 2014. http://mclc.osu.edu/rc/pubs/reviews/manfredi.htm.

Ming, Jiang 明江. 2011. "Shaoshu minzu wenxue chuangzuo yijing buru le wangluo shidai?" 少數民族文學創作已經步入了網路時代? (Has ethnic minority literature already entered the internet age?). *Wenyi bao: shaoshu minzu wenyi zhuankan*, 5 (13 June): n.p.

Mullaney, Thomas S. 2010. *Coming to Terms with the Nation: Ethnic Classification in Modern China*. Berkeley: University of California Press.

Notar, Beth E. 2006. *Displacing Desire: Travel and Popular Culture in China*. Honolulu: University of Hawaii Press.

Schein, Louisa. 2000. *Minority Rules: The Miao and the Feminine in China*. Durham, NC: Duke University Press.

Sedaoerji 色道爾吉. 1980. Menguzu wenxue gaikuang 蒙古族文學概況 (An overview of Mongol ethnic minority literature). *Neimenggu shehui kexue* 內蒙古社會科學 (Inner Mongolia social sciences), 4: 109–113.

Zhao, Zhizhong 趙志忠. 2005. *Minzu wenxue lungao* 民族文學論稿 (Studies of ethnic literature). Liaoning: Liaoning minzu chubanshe.

Zhongguo minjian wenyi xiehui 中國民間文藝協會 (China folk arts society). Ed. 2011. *Yalu Wang: Han Miao duizhao* 雅魯王:漢苗對照 (King of Yalu: Han and Miao bilingual text). Beijing: Zhonghua shuju.

Zhou, Minglang. 2003. *Multilingualism in China: The Politics of Writing Reforms for Minority Languages 1949–2002*. Berlin: Mouton de Gruyter.

Zuo, Yutang 左玉堂, Guo Sijiu 郭思九, Rui Zengrui 芮增瑞, and Tao Xueliang 陶學良. 2006. *Yizu wenxue shi* 彝族文學史 (A history of Yi literature). 2 vols. Kunming: Yunnan minzu chubanshe.

Part III
Cultures and Media

17

Use in Uselessness: How Western Aesthetics Made Chinese Literature More Political

Ban Wang

Aesthetic Discourse and Literature

A cursory look at critical works of modern Chinese literature gives the impression that the term "aesthetics" (*meixue* or *shenmei*) is used profusely. It seems self-evident that aesthetics discourse has played a critical role in shaping the ways in which Chinese critics in modern times have thought about literature. Aesthetics not only offers guidelines on how literary works are judged but also on how literature should be written and for what purposes. Aesthetic thought has provided motivations for writers to pursue certain aesthetic effects or qualities, which are encapsulated in the related idea of literariness. Indeed, the notion of literariness, integral to aesthetic judgments and assessments of literary texts, gives high priority to the close scrutiny of literature's beautiful, sublime, emotional, formal, or textual elements. Often used synonymously with the aesthetic, literariness isolates and valorizes a set of inner qualities or certain linguistic, generic, emotional, or structural features of a literary work. Self-referential and independent, these literary features are said to embody autonomy and purity. In celebrating such values as being intrinsic, proponents of literariness privilege an abstract concept of aesthetics over context on the presumption that aesthetic works are unconcerned with and free from all murky waters of history, morality, and politics.

While aesthetics is a Western import in China, the intrinsic approach to literature reflects a modernist, truncated concept of aesthetics, which has dominated how critics have thought about the relationship between aesthetics and literature. C. T Hsia's influential work may be a convenient case to clarify this point. In an article that focuses on Yan Fu and Liang Qichao, Hsia (2004) takes issues with the two writers' calls for a

A Companion to Modern Chinese Literature, First Edition. Edited by Yingjin Zhang.
© 2016 John Wiley & Sons, Ltd. Published 2016 by John Wiley & Sons, Ltd.

new type of fiction that would renovate the morality of readers and lift their spirit. Referring to Liang's celebrated essay "Fiction's Relationship to the Governance of Society" (*Lun xiaoshuo yu qunzhi zhi guanxi*, 1902), Hsia complains that, by investing New Fiction with a didactic mission of moral education and by treating it as a means for political purposes, Liang and Yan are treading on the familiar ground of the traditional conception of writing. Embodied in the doctrine "writing must carry the *Dao*" (*wen yi zaidao*), Liang is consumed by the nationalist obsession with China—a stance that frames and limits his understanding of aesthetic values unique to fiction. While he acknowledges the aesthetic power of traditional popular fiction, Liang denigrates its contents for propagating immoralities such as robbery and lust and accuses the vulgar genre for selling outdated, pernicious beliefs that had led to the moral degeneration of Chinese. New Fiction, on the other hand, should take advantage of the genre's aesthetic, emotional, and literary potentials but recycle them to serve nobler political and moral purposes—of building a new society and forging a new morality. This view of fiction provokes Hsia's ire and flies in the face of his aesthetic and literary taste. Hsia dismisses Liang's theory as utilitarian, traditional, ideological, and overly political. In short, it is unaesthetic.

To posit a counter-example, Hsia invokes Huang Moxi, a prominent literary critic and writer who founded the literary magazine *The Grove of Fiction* (*Xiaoshuo lin*) in 1907. Referencing a modern Japanese concept that deems fiction as an art form in its own right, Hsia appraises Huang's staunch defense of literariness premised on aesthetic principles. Deploring the fact that critics overvalued the novel as a means of promoting politics and morality Huang cautioned that the novel would lose its artistic value when pressed into the service of "the statues of the state, the scriptures of a religion, the textbooks to be used in school, and the moral norms of nation and society" (C. T. Hsia 2004: 241). As an art form, fiction should be "aesthetically satisfying" (C. T. Hsia 2004: 241), rather than a panacea for social and political problems. Hsia goes on to place a higher premium on the aesthetic statements in Huang's manifesto over political and social claims by Yan Fu and Liang Qichao in their own manifesto-style essays. Invoking Wang Guowei as the most representative figure in China's embrace of Western aesthetics and as a paramount thinker of literature, Hsia argues that, contrary to Liang Qichao's utilitarian notion of fiction, Wang Guowei upheld the sacred value of aesthetics in Cao Xueqin's novel titled *Dream of the Red Chamber*.

Under the aegis of aesthetics, Hsia projects a horizon of literature presumably broader and richer beyond the utilitarian concerns with political, social, and moral issues. Hsia's notion of aesthetics, however, is mortgaged to romanticism as a movement and discourse in the West, and to the various art-for-art's-sake discourses in nineteenth-century Europe and to early modernism. This concept was resurrected in New Criticism in the United States with its intrinsic approach to literature and its vaunted literariness of the late twentieth century. Hsia wrote the essay in 1978, when New Criticism was still very much in vogue. Hsia's thrust is to uphold aesthetics as an inviolable, inward realm of pleasurable contemplation and as a cultivated taste to savor forms removed from content, airily floating apart from history, society, and politics. In order to show the link between aesthetics and literature, I contend that Hsia's aesthetics is not a broad enough concept. On the contrary, it narrows down the scope of literature that aesthetic discourse is well equipped to engage. By sequestering aesthetics from political, social, and moral contexts, and by upholding literariness be a supreme value, his notion strips aesthetics off its multiple ties with social and political practices in the modern world and reduces this analytical discourse to a fetish.

Rather than making literature more autonomous, I attempt to show that the introduction of aesthetic discourse into the Chinese literary scene at the turn of the twentieth century and its appropriations afterward entangles literature deeper and more intensely into the historical and political contexts. This politically driven aesthetics entails the truth of humans as aesthetic beings and political actors engaged in constant practice to make and remake the sensuous life-world. It is in this sense that aesthetics intertwines with politics. "Politics," the most misunderstood term in this regard, calls for redefinition. Instead of denoting administration, government policy, power struggle in high places, or coercive policing, Jacques Rancière (2004: 10) defines politics as "the embodiment of collective wills and interests and the enactment of collective ideas." In this view, individuals and groups become active political subjects joining a movement in sharing and remaking a common world. This enactment of politics also wields cultural symbols and images and hence is aesthetically driven: political subjects bring a cluster of perceptions and practices into the enactment of collective wills, and politics becomes "a way of framing, among sensory data, a specific sphere of experience" (Rancière 2004: 10). The politics of literature lies in the practice of redistributing what is sensible and sayable by redrawing the boundaries of experience, perceptions, symbols, and meanings. The politics of world-making is aesthetic because it is an "intertwining of ways of being, ways of doing and ways of speaking (Ranciére 2004: 10).

In this connection, literature does not simply envision a fanciful world but acts on those visions in changing the mind, the body, pleasure, moral outlooks, social conditions, and even institutions. Rooted in cultural resources and sensuous experience, literature fulfills a function for achieving the political goal of world-making. I will now consider three Chinese aesthetic thinkers and see how they bring aesthetics into literature in this political, aesthetic way.

Aesthetic Search by Way of Morality: Wang Guowei and Huang Moxi

Raymond Williams (1976: 27) reminds us of aesthetic discourse's initial emphasis on subjective sense activity and on the specialized human creativity of art, as manifest in the works of Alexander Baumgarten and Immanuel Kant. From the outset, aesthetics discourse was marked by a narrow focus on art, on visual appearance, and the category of the beautiful. This subjectivist concept isolates inner sense perception as the basis of art and beauty, distinct and independent from social and cultural concerns. Stemming from "the divided modern consciousness" (Williams 1976: 28) that separates culture from society, aesthetics may express a humanistic, romantic impulse against the dominant ideologies of utilitarianism and materialism of the bourgeois society. Although this romantic, sensuous revolt against instrument rationality is valid, the isolation can be damaging, "for there is something irresistibly displaced and marginal about the now common and limiting phrase 'aesthetic considerations', especially when contrasted with practical or utilitarian considerations, which are the elements of the same basic division" (Williams 1976: 28).

The modern divided consciousness severs art from life, culture from society, the mind from the body. The division of labor compartmentalizes organic, interconnected human activity on the model of commodity production and specialization. From a historical materialist perspective, Williams shows the bourgeois market society and commodity production to be the material basis for the emergence of the narrow concept of aesthetics. Williams' student Eagleton built on his teacher's critique and sought to bring aesthetics out of its subjectivist closet and return it to the contested, interlocking social and political fields where aesthetics engages and clashes with various political, moral, and social issues. In *The Ideology of the Aesthetic*, Eagleton (1990) shows that the crux of aesthetics is the human body, animated and driven by feelings, impulses, drives, and sensations. Instead of the biological body, the aesthetic is concerned with the body's sensible and sensuous access to the world of practice. In its earlier formulation, the aesthetic (in the adjective form in reference to a quality or experience rather than to a thing, institution, or discipline) refers to "the whole region of human perception and sensation" (Eagleton 1990: 13), in contrast to conceptual thought and instrumental rationality. Far from elevating art from life, the aesthetic concerns what is bound up with humans' creaturely life or how art is part and parcel of life itself. Aesthetics engages in "the business of affections and aversions, of how the world strikes the body on its sensory surfaces, of that which take root in the gaze and the guts and all that arises from most banal, biological insertion into the world" (Eagleton 1990: 13). As a "science" that attends to the free particulars of the body, both individual and collective, aesthetics discourse arose in eighteenth-century Germany to address the ways in which bodily experience and sensations may be groomed and educated to fit into a new bourgeois social order. Linking the cultivation of the body to the new formation of modernity, aesthetics took on an elevated significance for political and social power. Political hegemony could not allow the body's freewheeling, anarchistic particulars and its collective discontents to roam freely. To sustain social order, the political powers must rein in minds and bodies by informing, educating, and forging docile subjects from within and by working on and regulating their emotion, taste, and sensibility. In this way, aesthetics emerged as a solution to problems of politics. As Schiller (2004: 27) famously claimed, "it is through beauty that we arrive at freedom."

On the other hand, if hegemonic power resorts to aesthetics to inscribe social norms and authority on the sensuous strata of the embodied subject by winning and transforming its heart and mind, aesthetics, by giving allowance to sensations and feelings, can also become emancipatory. Aesthetics gives vent to sensuous gratification and delivers what may be called the "right to aesthetic freedom." This emancipatory dimension resonates with Rancière's vision of political aesthetics: re-drawing and redistribution of the sensible is a political act of pushing the envelope. Aesthetic experience emancipates individuals from the narrow, divided consciousness and from alienated labor to exercise bodily and intellectual freedom from the externally imposed rules of production and governance. A new, affectively rich subject emerges to perform this self-rule and embarks on a trajectory of modernity by virtue of an educational *Bildung* toward a republic of free personalities, where individuals or a community may author and write their collective rules, "obeying no laws but those which they gave to themselves" (Eagleton 1990: 19). This indicates the function of aesthetics as containing a politically constructive potential, a cultural way of shoring up a body politic. This is the major reason why Chinese thinkers, disheartened by the disintegration of the Qing Empire, were drawn to the political promises of aesthetics.

In their reception of aesthetics, Chinese aesthetic thinkers were indebted to the classic notion of "writing must carry the *Dao*." While the *Dao* may mean the transcendental, cosmic Way beyond the sensory realm, the concept is also rooted in social, moral, and political practice. Instead of rising above daily living, the principles of the *Dao* are immanent in everyday rituals and social relations (Yu and Huters 2004: 3). This mindset allowed the thinkers to find, in Western aesthetics, a cultural key to political reform and to see literary imaginaries as a means to reforming structures of feeling. Instead of cutting it off from the horizon of sociohistorical circumstances, Chinese writers showed a propensity to bring aesthetics deeper into an organic discourse, integrating classic tenets, morality, and character formation.

Aesthetics as the animating spirit for politics is most evident in Cai Yuanpei's arguments for aesthetic education in order to build up the character of the citizen and to foster civic virtue. In the drive to replace the traditional, religious values and beliefs, Cai was the first visionary figure in modern education to put aesthetics on a par with physical, intellectual, and ethical programs on the national education agenda. A well-trained scholar in German aesthetics in his overseas study from 1908 to 1911 in Leipzig, Germany, Cai showed no signs of the "modern divided consciousness" that Williams critiques and betrayed no interest in the depoliticized, art-for-art approach to aesthetics. To him, aesthetics is to cultivate secular, humanist standards and to foster the affective and rational personality of a citizen. These qualities are prerequisite for citizenship and integral to the new republic of the Chinese nation (Cai Yuanpei 1983: 71). Given Cai's position as the minister of education in the first Chinese Republic, it would seem natural that he applied aesthetics to the national project of cultural rejuvenation, civic virtue, and the formation of modern ethics. And Cai's vision of aesthetics continued Liang Qichao's political investment in New Fiction.

In contrast to the visions of Liang and Cai, C. T. Hsia's celebration of Wang Guowei and Huang Moxi reveals a concept of aesthetics as an intrinsic, disinterested value, detached from social and political concerns while prioritizing literature's formal features. Although Hsia stakes his argument on Wang and Huang, a closer look at the two writers tells us that, as inheritors of the morally driven political tradition, the two defenders of aesthetics are as much concerned with social and political issues as those critics of utilitarian literature. The *Dao* of literature was never far from their focus on the apparently "aesthetic" features of literature.

For more than a whole century, Wang Guowei has been regarded as the first literary theorist who read literature from an aesthetic perspective. In his reading of *Dream of the Red Chamber*, Wang uses Arthur Schopenhauer's aesthetic notion of desire and the Kantian aesthetics of the sublime to produce an aesthetically informed analysis. But by engaging social, political issues in the new intellectual landscape, Wang Guowei's discussion of aesthetic qualities of *Dream of the Red Chamber* unravels in many ways beyond the disinterested, intrinsic notion of aesthetics. Although he often presents aesthetics to be a supreme value, Wang's reading is nevertheless anchored to social, philosophical context. The Daoist, escapist moment in *Dream of the Red Chamber*, for instance, is not a mere withdrawal from the practical issues of the day: it is a utopian, active reflection on the historical trauma of Wang's times. Rather than an aesthetic indulgence, it comes as a proactive response to the crisis of Chinese civilization and the collapse of its ethico-political system. As such, Wang's theory is a politically charged aesthetics (Ban Wang 1997: 17–54).

Wang Guowei's essay "Incidental Remarks on Literature" (*Wenxue xiaoyan*, 1906) offers a more striking illustration of the moral understanding of aesthetics. In it, Wang defines literature as equal in value and legitimacy to philosophy, yielding to no power structure, doctrine, or orthodoxy. Similar to philosophy, literature defies the reigning social norms, declares its independence, and displays its originality. So literature that serves the utilitarian purposes of eating and drinking and of gainful interest is false literature (Wang Guowei 1987: 24). Genuine literature, on the other hand, stems from the uninterested, free exercise of a sovereign spirit, which comes into play by releasing energy in generating cognitive apprehension and compelling representations. If these remarks sound like an affirmation of literature's autonomy, Wang turns around in the next few passages to claim that, while the works of poetic giants such as Qu Yan, Tao Yuanming, and Du Fu are of timeless value, the aesthetic value is to be attributed not to the poets' extraordinary verses and poetic genus. Their greatness comes rather from the "noble, magnificent personalities" (*gaoshang weida zhi renge*). Hence, what appears to be poetic is superseded by moral quality and the poet's content of character.

This moral turn is also found in Wang's analysis of *Romance of Three Kingdoms*. In Wang's opinion, the novel does not live up to the standard of genuine literature, though it contains moments of greatness that deserve the honor of great literature. The episode when Guan Yu releases Cao Cao as the latter's entourage is ambushed is one such moment of literary brilliance worthy of a great writer. This "writerly" greatness, how-ever, is not formal and literary. It is a sign of a morally uplifting, exemplary conduct and broadmindedness. While other parts of the novel may be pedestrian and unaesthetic, the image of Guan Yu unconcerned with his own personal welfare commands boundless admiration and provokes imagination in the reader. Wang recalls Kant's maxim that practical reason, which is integrity in moral reasoning, is the ultimate foundation for life and the universe. Thus, Wang (1987: 27) gives priority to morality as the basis for the evaluation of literary works.

If the preceding essay converts aesthetic autonomy into moral exemplariness in a form of an aestheticized morality, another essay titled "Qu Yuan's Spirit of Literature" (*Quzi wenxue zhi jingshen*, 1906) strikes a balance. Linking morality to politics this essay projects an aesthetic image of moral ethos for a good society. Wang first distinguishes two strands of moral–political thought in ancient China. One is imperial (*diwang de*), committed to the maintenance of the dynastic order; the other is plebian, individual-istic, and reclusive. The politically committed school corresponds to the North School of poetics, which makes for "the *Dao* of poetry" *shi zhi wei dao* (Wang Guowei 1987: 31). Taking the moral fabric and political order as a whole, this school is interested in representing life in general—not isolated, individual life but one embedded in "the family, the state, and society" (Wang Guowei 1987: 31). The mainstream of Confucian poetics, this school invariably addresses the moral space between emperor and subjects, father and son, husband and wife. These cardinal relations inform the major thematic content of poetry. In contrast, the Southern school of poetics, represented by Daoist-spirited poets with reclusive bent, tends to be more imaginative, more spontaneous, and less committed. As in the lively, fanciful expressions of a child, the Southern poets are less constrained by conventions and norms. More enjoyable and refined in poetical sentiment and imagery, the works of the Southern school seems to fit the bill of aesthetic quality.

In our present context, these two schools seem to represent the political and aesthetic poles, only to be reconciled in Wang's concluding remarks about Qu Yan. The Northern school worked within the political order and harbored the goal of "changing the old society" (Wang Guowei 1987: 31). This political stance does not mean that the poets are complicit with the status quo or are merely establishment writers patronized by the powerful officials and noblemen. They possessed a strong will and courage, Wang notes, and, keeping faith with their passion for moral ideals, they combated the society even though they met with hostility and rejection. On the other hand, the Southern poets did not simply indulge in poetic fantasy and rhetoric perfection. Their poetic values also depended on the broader function of literature in the political order. While they worked outside the system and appeared politically nonchalant, the Southern poets were still trying to envision and to create a new social world. Barred from access to the political power, the Southern school expressed its ideals and found solace in the utopian enclaves of nature and reclusive refuges. This imaginative and aesthetic gesture, however, does not rule out its underlying politics of literature: projecting a vision of society in image rather than in realty (Wang Guowei 1987: 31).

Instead of separating aesthetics from sociopolitical concerns, Wang claims that both schools have social, reformist motivations and indeed harbor the ardent yearning to correct or reform a degenerate, unjust, or moribund sociopolitical order. The North strives to realize political ideals in practice, engaging or negotiating and often compro-mising with the system; the South withdraws and drops out of the system to elaborate its dreams and visions on the sidelines—roaming the wilderness of mountains and rivers. In sum, the Northern school is more political and the Southern more poetic, but great poetry must come from the former's political obligation buttressed by moral character and conviction. And the greatest poetry will result from a weaving together of the North and the South.

Now, in this scheme with two poles, Qu Yuan comes to the fore as a figure that interweaves these two strands of poetics, combining political commitment with aesthetic accomplishment. Although Qu Yuan was from the South, he imbibed the ideas and poetics of the North and admired the sage king as the moral, political exemplar in the Confucian tradition. Qu Yan's poetic personality could be captured by his self-styled moral profile in terms of *lian* and *zhen*. *Lian* means clean, upright, having integrity, and *zhen* means loyalty, obligation, and commitment. *Lian* characterizes the Southern poets' inner spirit of detachment and integrity, and *zhen* describes the Northerners' unwavering loyalty. After all, Qu Yan was an establishment poet during the good part of his career, an official with a voice in political affairs, and was highly regarded by the king in the Chu court. For all his injuries and exile, he still kept his faith and commitment to an ideal vision of political order. And this order is not to be equated with the existing power relations. On the other hand, Qu Yan's poetry not only exhibits all the poetic flourishes and imaginativeness unique to the Southern poets, but also exhibits his own new poetic patterns and aesthetics. Wang's portrayal of Qu Yuan shows that, while the essence of poetry lies in genuine expressions of feelings coupled with imagination, the moral qualities of sincerity and duty turn out to be more fundamental. In expounding sincerity and duty, we again have moral qualities that are grounds for defining poetic qualities. These had a strong political overtone: loyalty and commitments are not to an actual figure in power but to an ideal political order. The moral personality is the source of the greatness of the Northern and Southern schools and has given us poetic luminaries such as Tao Yuanming and Du Fu.

Apparently, Wang Guowei's younger contemporary Huang Moxi also looked for aesthetic aspects intrinsic to literature, only to extend aesthetics into the historical circumstances of his times—a force field fraught with moral and political debates and polemics. As mentioned earlier, Hsia cites Huang as a counter-example to refute Liang Qichao's utilitarian and "unaesthetic" notion of fiction. As a traditional literatus and the founder of a literary magazine, Huang has received little attention, and existing scholarship perpetuates the impression that he was a staunch defender of aesthetics in literature. A significant figure in promoting Chinese vernacular fiction from its traditional mode to the modern form, Huang was indeed inspired by Western aesthetics and used aesthetic terms in his critical works. In his manifesto-style essay in the first issue of *The Grove of Fiction*, a fiction magazine he founded, Huang (2000: 258) deplores the fact that, in the past, fiction had been denigrated as being of low taste and immoral, whereas contemporary critics elevated fiction to be a panacea for social malaises and political disorder and an instrument for enlightening and educating the population.

Against this utilitarian trend, Huang calls for an enquiry into the essential nature of fiction. The novel, he claims, is a form of literature intimately associated with aesthetic concerns and should be compared to visual art, music, and performance (Huang 2000: 258). Critics should not devalue fiction's sensuous appeals and formal attributes. Thus, rather than focusing on fiction as an illustration of private interests versus public, common good, or as a test between morally positive or negative values, Huang urges critics and readers to pay attention to the aspects of fiction that cultivate *shenmei qingchao*—refined and aesthetic feelings. These feelings are as admirable and noble as understandings of morality and truth. On the other hand, this does not mean that the novel is to engage in the unbridled release of feelings, desire, and sensuality. While a work of fiction should abstain from preaching the scriptural words and pronouncing the truth, this does not give license to the novelist to manufacture sensuous pleasure or emotional effect for its own sake. By painting the most lurid pictures and selling decadent episodes, Huang cautions, the novelist may hasten the decline and breakdown of morality and manners. Thus, while Huang's manifesto purports to herald a new, aesthetically attuned fiction and a reading public capable of aesthetic appreciation, in spelling out ostensibly aesthetic standards, Huang is resorting to moral standards: enlightenment, emotional cultivation, and moral refinement are grounds for justifying aesthetic considerations.

This shift from aesthetics to the moral and political is quite characteristic of a large number of aesthetic thinkers in modern China. Huang's best-known essay, "Incidental Words about Fiction" (*Xiaoshuo xiaohua*, 1907) illustrates this turn dramatically. Decoupling novelistic and narrative techniques from discursive preaching, Huang makes a case for the novel's accessibility and appeal to the educated and uneducated alike and for its attraction to women and children by holding up a mirror to their own everyday lives (Huang 2000: 271). Although the novel is removed from the prevalent discourse of statecraft or civil examination essays, it nevertheless creates a composite, multi-faceted vernacular that incorporates public moral discourses, mixing into literary language folklores, vulgar street talks, gossip in women's quarters, woodcutters' songs, and sayings—all these together serve as "sumptuous material for the palate" (Huang 2000: 272).

So much for the aesthetic perspective: sensory pleasure and sensuous plurality are credited to novelistic techniques, which prevent the work from making unconvincing, idealized portrayals of characters. Yet, the question of fictional characterization—what kinds of characters to create—remains and entails the question of morality. Unlike Wang Guowei's celebrated aesthetic approach to *Dream of the Red Chamber*, Huang spends much more ink on *Water Margin*. While viewing this novel to be a good read, Huang (2000: 273) focuses on its political implications by claiming that it is "purely socialist spirited" (*chunshi shehui zhuyi*). To gather 108 warriors to form and run a small society in an egalitarian spirit is quite unique and unprecedented in Chinese history. Mount Liang is a utopian society governed by socialist principles, where each and every talent has its place and every skill is properly employed. From our present perspective, the Loyalty and Righteousness Hall (*zhongyi tang*), the "town hall" of the outlaw community, seems anything but socialist: it appears archaic, backward, patriarchal, and contrary to the Marxist or Maoist idea of socialism. But to Huang, the hall embodies an ideal set of virtues intrinsic to the fabric of a just community. Exerting oneself to the utmost for social good is called *zhong* (loyalty) and putting this virtue into practice is called *yi* (righteousness). But this form of self-sacrifice is not blind submission to authority, nor the servile behavior and mindset that Shi Xiu, a character of the novel, bemoans. The slogan of the outlaw community is "carry out the *Dao* of Heaven" (*titian xingdao*), which exhorts the warriors to uphold the principle of justice without fears of self-sacrifice. The warriors try to meet the needs and wants of society and communities, and attack what common people hate and despise. They target official corruption, predatory officials, wealthy, exploitative estates, and the pillaging of people by the powerful. Loyalty to Heaven is not pledged to a person, to a specific Son of Heaven, but denotes a firm commitment to social justice and to people's well-being, which is the real meaning of Heaven (2000: 273).

In the history of criticism on *Water Margin*, such prominent figures as Lu Xun and Mao Zedong weighed in on the issue of loyalty: loyalty to Heaven or to the emperor, "the son of Heaven." If the former, then the bandits are really self-seeking, egoistic opportunists who drop out of the system in revolt only to collude with the system in the end. Their rebellious acts are not moral and political. They fight only the corrupt officials, but never oppose the imperial system, as Mao puts it. But another line of reading sees the novel as advocating an anarcho-socialist thought: the bandits of Mount Liang band together in an equalitarian spirit, form a family of brotherhood, and combat injustices suffered by the common folk. This outlaw organization is built on mutual help, care, and commitment. Pearl Buck linked Edgar Snow's *Red Star over China* to this classic "Robin Hood" novel, in which a brotherhood of "good bandits helped the poor and despoiled the rich" (Thomas 1996: 173). Bernard Thomas (1996: 172) remarked that Snow's book of Communist revolutionaries read very much similar to "a modern morality play of good against evil that transcended its immediate Chinese setting."

One of the first to read the novel in terms of anarcho-socialist thought—a widespread intellectual and social force at the turn of the twentieth century in China, Huang deploys political and moral messages to justify the aesthetic appeal of the characters. Song Jiang, the leader of the outlaw community, is a *daxia*, a grand knight-errant, who rises to the heroic pedestal from a humble beginning. An ugly swarthy fellow of short stature, homeless, penniless, and on the run, Song has none of the signs of your regular noble, magnificent heroes. Yet, the warriors and ordinary people flock to him and are ready to die for the cause. Song is able to win the hearts and minds of his followers by displaying wisdom and virtues much superior to those in high places of government. He is much more qualified to lead and govern the social order than the emperor and his ministers and local officials. Identifying Song Jiang's image as derived from Sima Qian's account of the classical knight-errant Guo Jie, whose virtuous conduct deserves the accolades worthy of Confucius, Huang sees in the outlaws' rebellion a defense of and an affirmation of human rights and a rejection of tyranny (*zhong renquan, yi zhuanzhi*). The term "human rights" reflects Huang's modern understanding of the rights of the powerless and disadvantaged against oppression by the powerful. From this perspective, Huang distinguishes two kinds of aesthetically exciting episodes. That Wu Song, with his physical raw power, kills a tiger is dramatically compelling. But it is not as compelling and extraordinary as when he tries to kill a dog unleashed by the local bullies. Lu Zhishen, the monk and a wild character in the novel, displays his superb martial arts skills in many combative scenarios. But none of his feats is as compelling as when he scrambles for food in a temple against other monks who deny him food and bully powerless people. The aesthetic portrayal of these characters depends as much on the appeal of virtue as on the unheroic yet legitimate pursuit of equal rights to food, fairness, and personal dignity.

The Politics of Aesthetics in Lu Xun

In Wang Guowei's discussion, Qu Yuan is a politically ambiguous figure. Given his official position in the political order, Qu Yuan's poems may be complicit with the ruling regime and expresses loyalty, duty, and values crucial to the maintenance of the established power. On the other hand, his Southern-flavored, poetic accomplishment points to a style akin to that of poetry-for-poetry's sake—a perfecting of poetic patterns and aesthetic qualities. In Chinese theories of poetics, the notion of poetry as the vehicle for moral improvement and political order is well known. The "Great Preface" to the *Book of Songs* defines poetry's function in terms of *feng* (influence), which is a poetic instruction whereby the cardinal moral ties between husband and wife, father and son, emperors and subjects are instilled and relationships from small communities to the state are regulated. But matching this top-down influence, whereby "those above transform those below," is a more critical version of *feng* (criticism), where "those below criticize those above." Critical minds, though nestled within the sociopolitical order, enjoy the license to admonish: it is not culpable to speak one's mind and give one's opinion. The critical *feng* is a moral, political voice of critique, admonition, and counsel working within the political system (Owen 1992: 38, 46).

Between these two versions of *feng*, it is very difficult to distinguish a critical poet outside the system from a politically engaged insider. Wang Guowei was drawn to Qu Yuan precisely for this ambiguity. The truncated aesthetics we have noted earlier in C. T. Hsia's critique separates literature from politics and morality and severs the poet's linkage to society and community. It sees literature's ties to morality in terms of an unholy alliance between blind personal allegiance and the system of domination and repression. The moral norms are denigrated as rhetoric of power: they are regulatory and hegemonic, deployed as top-down control of the population and propagating official ideology. Literature imbued with moral teachings invariably carries a negative ring, harbors a cynical agenda, and stands condemned as unaesthetic and utilitarian. Politically charged works are either official propaganda or bottom-up ingenious attempts to slip through the net of censorship. In this view, a notion of artistic propaganda, the utopian image of participatory politics *à la* Rancière, imbued with a public moral ethos and aesthetically articulated, is inconceivable. It is unthinkable to entertain the possibility of a politically engaged, morally inspirational, and aesthetically compelling work of literature. Yet, we have seen how Wang Guowei floats the possibility of this win-win scenario in his short sketch of Qu Yuan. The separation of literature from morality and politics ignores the critical notion in the bottom-up, critical, and reformist function of *feng*. Although the *feng* from below may utter grievances and express spontaneous, multifaceted feelings worthy of aesthetic refinements, it is by no means premised on the poet's disengagement from politics and morality. On the contrary, the critical voice stems from an intense engagement by means of admonition and criticism aimed at moral corruption or political decay. This critical gesture is a short step toward the morally constructive function famously assigned to literature by Liang Qichao. In this literature, writers hold up a mirror image from the past or future to critique and transcend the status quo. In modern Chinese history, this gesture was time and again re-incarnated in a Maoist tradition of rectification, *zhengfeng*—the reform program directed at corrupt morality, orthodoxies, dogma, and governmental politics by means of aesthetic and political re-education.

Lu Xun's discussion of aesthetics illustrates well this constructive *feng*. In his influential essay titled "On the Power of Mara Poetry" (*Moluo shili shuo*, 1907), Lu Xun celebrates the demonic, romantic spirit of Mara poets such as Byron, Shelley, Keats, and others. Mara poets are moral vanguards breaking away from the prevailing moral orthodoxy. They hold on to an ideal of morality in the radical literary movement to break through the conventions that shackle the rebellious body and control the population. Lu Xun mobilizes this iconoclastic energy to combat China's mainstream poetics, which defines morality as the rhetoric of constraint and control. The essence of the 300 classical poems, for example, was to promote thoughts without immoralities, and their social function was to restrain men's emotions and hold spontaneous feelings in check. Yet, the Chinese tradition of poetics also claims that poetry is meant to give vent to feelings and sensations, which contradicts the moral regulatory claim. To insist that poetry is never to step outside the bounds of propriety runs counter to poetry's alleged function as spontaneous, imagistic, and evocative expressions of innermost thoughts and feelings. Chinese poetry is thus split into a school that praises the masters and the powerful, and the other kind that expresses solitary lamentation and pleasures. This second tradition is well articulated by Qu Yuan's poems (Lu Xun 1980: 68).

Echoing Wang Guowei's view, Lu Xun (1980: 69; Kowallis n.d.) recognizes Qu Yuan's aesthetic strength in his exile and near-death experience: "Only Qu Yuan, on the brink of death, when his mind churned with the fury of the waves, could pace by the shores of the Miluo River, looking back upon the mountains of his homeland and lamenting his feelings of isolation in poignant, melancholic lines that depicted his sorrow and wrath." The aesthetic value is joined with moral and political criticism. All constraints off, Qu Yuan, as Lu Xun (1980: 69; Kowallis n.d.) sees it,

> … could at last voice his rancor at the imbecility of the world and the crassness of society. He was free to sing of his own wasted talent and unappreciated learning, and to question with an unprecedented skepticism and in unabashed detail everything from the most basic myths and legends to creation down to the minutiae of history and all life forms with a fearlessness of tone which none before him dared assume.

However, Qu Yuan's legacy throughout centuries has shaded into a realm of the aesthetic and stylistic. Stripped off moral substance, emotional impact, and political will, the beautiful pathos of his poems were not motivated by "a will to fight back"

(Lu Xun 1980: 69). In the theorist Liu Xie's insightful summary, the generations of poets have only emulated the boldness of Qu Yuan's artistic designs and conceits. The mediocre, untalented versifiers seized upon the beauty of his diction; "aficionados savor his images of mountain and rivers, and novices imitate his use of fragrant flora and fauna" (Lu Xun 1980: 69). Deploring this "tragic" loss of meaningful issues in the pursuit of stylistic refinement, Lu Xun calls for radical voices such as that of Mara poets, who employ their talents to create verses powerful enough to remold people's character and elevate their thoughts.

Lu Xun's analysis of Qu Yuan affirms the positive, engaged relation between morality and literature. Exposed to the modern notion of aesthetics from the West, Lu Xun was quite familiar with the intrinsic concept of art as an object in its own right and enshrined in useless autonomy free from utilitarian purposes. Defining the nature of art as "the power of appeal" to readers by means of inspiration or delight, Lu Xun (1980: 71) sets literature off from industrial, commercial, and political enterprises: "By virtue of selfsame property," literature has little to do with the preservation of individual life and the survival of the state; it is purged of practical purposes and utilitarian considerations. In comparison with history as a depository of wisdom and with moral discourse with its tenets and precepts, literature seems rather inferior. Literature does not generate wealth as surely as commerce and industry, nor can it earn social recognition equal to that of an industrialist.

Countering this notion of uselessness in the same breath with a broader, humanist argument, Lu Xun attempts to reclaim literature's social and ethical function. For all its uselessness, literature has the power to launch humanity on the way to fulfillment and completion. Citing the British critic Dowden, he deploys a language of bodily exercise, rigorous training, and physical and spiritual energy. The empowering pleasure of literature is likened to the energizing effect experienced by a swimmer in the ocean. Seeing a "boundless horizon open before him," the swimmer, in Lu Xun's description (1980: 71; Kowallis n.d.),

> ... breasts the waves, and comes forth at the end of the swim feeling physically and spiritually rejuvenated. Though the sea is but a mass of surging wave and churning water, devoid of emotion, which has never uttered a maxim or a moral pronouncement, nevertheless, the physical and mental well-being of the swimmer has been immediately enhanced by it.

In practical matters of self-preservation, human activity splits into a field of industry, endeavor, and improvement, on the one hand, and an experience of hedonistic self-indulgence devoid of a sense of self and future, on the other. Torn between these two extremes, humans are truncated and incomplete. Lu Xun is referring to the split of mind from body—the acute problem of modernity, which embodies a systematic disjunction between instrumental rationality at the heart of material civilization and the spiritual, aesthetic realm now marginalized. Literature steps forward and provides an answer. Literature is able to nurture the imagination, animate the body with spirit, and restore a positive morality. Though inferior to science in the power of investigating nature, literature has an edge in its ability to reveal the subtler truths and human meanings that elude scientific logic. Evoking Mathew Arnold's argument of culture as the key to political order and as a living criticism of life, Lu Xun reconsiders literature as a service provider, and a didactic one at that. Literature offers instructions beneficial to human life, and gives articulation to vital moral qualities, such as self-awareness, courage, and enterprising development (*zijue, yongmeng, fayang, jingjin*). It is instructive to note that Lu Xun uses the word "*jiao*," which could mean teachings of religious significance or moral canons. Religious instruction is to supply moral visions to political order by rendering literature into the service of social and political rejuvenation. An inspirational morality, he adds, is what a weak and declining nation urgently needs.

From the swimming body in its robust exercise to spiritual and ethical revival, Lu Xun envisions a trajectory marked by the tempering of the physical body along with a new form of subjectivity. Propelled by an urgent need to repair the broken fabric of society, this body discourse seeks to forge ethical bonds by integrating fragmented individual bodies into a robust social and political body. Though adjacent to practical matters of survival, writes Lu Xun (1980: 71; Kowallis n.d.), "literature in human affairs is no less important than clothing, housing, religion, or moral teaching."

It would be helpful to distinguish the concept of morality in its conservative inertia from its emancipatory radicalism. Citing a sociological definition of literature, Lu Xun shows that literature is grounded in authentic ideas and feelings. Poeticized ideas and feelings "should accord with universal concepts of humanity" (Lu Xun 1980: 72; Kowallis n.d.). Morality, in this sense, is constituted by universally acceptable human thoughts and notions, which allow poetry to have enduring life and to travel across borders. This universal morality, however, is mistakenly equated with *qunfa*, the law and mores of a particular historical group or society. It is often observed that literature that defies and contradicts the *qunfa* will not last long. Countering this, Lu Xun cites a host of radical poets inspired by the French Revolution and those involved in the national independence movements in Germany, Italy, and Greece. The poets in the Byronic mode transgress "the old limitations and give direct voice to his convictions: his every work resounded with defiant strength and iconoclastic challenge" (Lu Xun, 1980: 73; Kowallis n.d.). While applauding their radical acts and courage in defying and breaking through the convention and morality, Lu Xun does not jettison their moral and political claims. To the contrary, by breaking out the moral containment, the poets project the vision of an inspirational image of society that accords genuinely with universal morality, which he designates as freedom and the law of humanity, *rendao* (1980: 79).

The emotional effect of poetry is related to an image of innate but public morality, which accords with the sharing of moral teachings and enlightenment, in Lu Xun's opinion (1980: 68; Kowallis n.d.):

> Poets are indeed the disrupters of men's hearts. For every human heart contains poetry within it, and when a poet has written a poem, it does not belong to him exclusively, but to whoever can understand it in their heart. If there is no poetry in their heart to begin with, how could they arrive at an understanding? This is only possible because they

themselves have had similar feelings but could not put them into words. Poets say these things for them. As when a musician plucks a note, a response comes immediately from the heart strings of the audience, and the note reverberates throughout the caverns of the soul, causing all men of feeling to look up, inspired as though they were gazing at some new dawn ablaze with light that has the power to strengthen, ennoble, and enlighten.

The power to "strengthen, ennoble, and enlighten" has everything to do with morality. Rather than supplying physical strength and thrill of excitement, poetry energizes and uplifts readers with moral sentiment and strength.

In such a relation to a socio-moral community, literature is by no means a hand-maiden at the bidding of the established moral, political orthodoxy and a vehicle for maintaining the status quo. The narrow concept of aesthetics has had a negative impact and contributed to the rise of intrinsic criticism in Chinese literature. It separates the productive, versatile category of aesthetics from historical context and multileveled engagement with social, moral, and political problems. By considering Huang Moxi, Wang Guowei, and Lu Xun's appropriations of aesthetics, I have attempted to show that, rather than isolating literature as an autonomous, disinterested discourse, the Chinese critics entangled and pushed literature further and deeper into the contextual matrix of social, moral, and political issues. These contextual elements are both external and internal to aesthetic discourse and literature. Huang stakes the claim of fiction's aesthetic appeal on an assessment of moral characters. Wang Quowei posits a symmetrical combination of the Northern and Southern schools of poetry—an ideal of a politically engaged stance combined with poetic innovation. By portraying the poetic power of Mara poets to break through the shackles of established moral conventions, Lu Xun does not disengage moral concerns from literature, but proposes that literature should work toward the nurturing of noble moral sentiments and enlightenment so as to accomplish the political rejuvenation of the Chinese people.

REFERENCES

Cai, Yuanpei 蔡元培. 1983. *Cai Yuanpei meixue wenlun* 蔡元培美學文論 (Selected essays on aesthetics by Cai Yuanpei). Beijing: Beijing daxue chubanshe.

Eagleton, Terry. 1990. *The Ideology of the Aesthetic.* Oxford, UK: Blackwell.

Hsia, C. T. 2004. *C. T. Hsia on Chinese Literature.* New York: Columbia University Press.

Huang, Moxi 黃摩西. 2000. "Huang Moxi wenlu" 黃摩西文錄 (Selected writings by Huang Moxi). In Wang Yongjian 王永健, *Suzhou qiren Wang Moxi pingzhuan* 蘇州奇人黃摩西評傳

(Biography of the extraordinary literati figure Huang Moxi of Suzhou). Suzhou: Suzhou daxue chubanshe. 257–308.

Kowallis, Jon Eugene von. n.d. English translation of "Moluo shili shuo" by Lu Xun. Unpublished manuscript.

Lu, Xun 魯迅. 1980. *Lu Xun quanji* 魯迅全集 (Complete works of Lu Xun). Vol. 1. Beijing: Renmin wenxue chubanshe.

Owen, Stephen. 1992. *Readings in Chinese Literary Thought.* Cambridge: MA: Harvard University Press.

Rancière, Jacques. 2004. "The Politics of Literature." *Substance*, 33.1: 10–24.

Schiller, Friedrich. 2004. *On the Aesthetic Education of Man*. New York: Dover.

Thomas, S. Bernard. 1996. *Season of High Adventure: Edgar Snow in China*. Berkeley: University of California Press.

Wang, Ban. 1997. *The Sublime Figure of History: Aesthetics and Politics in Twentieth Century China*. Stanford, CA: Stanford University Press.

Wang, Guowei 王國維. 1987. *Wang Guowei wenxue meixue lunzhu ji* 王國維文學美學論著集 (Collected essays on literature and aesthetics by Wang Guowei). Taiyuan: Beiyue wenyi chubanshe.

Williams, Raymond. 1976. *Keywords*. Oxford, UK: Oxford University Press.

Yu, Pauline, and Theodor Huters. 2004. "The Imaginative Universe of Chinese Literature." In *Chinese Aesthetics and Literature*. Edited by Dale, Corinne. Albany: State University of New York Press. 1–13.

18

The Linguistic Turns and Literary Fields in Twentieth-Century China

Jianhua Chen

Introduction

Regarding the issue of language and literature in modern China, we first of all have to address the "linguistic turn," a myth created by both the new Republican state and May Fourth intellectuals in the early 1920s: in the name of "language reform" (*yuyan gaige*), the vernacular language (*baihua*) was officially established as the "national language" (*guoyu*), so that the classical language (*wenyan*) lost its legitimacy grounded in a millennia-long literary tradition. Perhaps as one of the most fundamental projects for Chinese modernization (Seybolt and Chiang 1979: 18–19), the language reform was charged with nationalist ethos and intellectual radicalism, and sustained its drive for the task of national salvation and mass enlightenment in the subsequent decades. Despite debates among writers and resistance from those who held on to the literary tradition, the literary field was more or less overshadowed by the ideology of *baihua*, which was further legitimized when the national crisis deepened during the war. Even after 1949, the language reform served the Communist politics with its widespread effects on educational system, ideological campaigns, and literary writings. In the official history of modern Chinese literature published in the early 1960s, those who had deviated from the May Fourth canon, or more precisely from Mao Zedong's "Yan'an Talks," were criticized or excluded. Yet, since the 1980s, the century-long linguistic momentum has gradually faded away when China switched to a new policy in global competition.

Rather than a general survey, this chapter is a reflection on the May Fourth linguistic turn from the perspective of 1990s China. I focus on the polemics of literary language in three historical moments: first, to trace the origins of language reform and the Han

A Companion to Modern Chinese Literature, First Edition. Edited by Yingjin Zhang.
© 2016 John Wiley & Sons, Ltd. Published 2016 by John Wiley & Sons, Ltd.

language (*Hanyu*) as national essence from the late Qing to the early Republican era; second, to review the debate between the old and new literary camps in the early 1920s when the vernacular was officially legitimized as the "national language"; third, to describe the reaction against the linguistic turn in the late twentieth century. These polemics intersected with sociopolitical changes and discursive practices involving major writers and literary groups, and engaged with issues of tradition and modernity, politics and aesthetics, revolution and reformation, nationalism, cosmopolitanism, and print capitalism.

Although emphasizing historical contextualization, this chapter traces the relationship between *wenyan* and *baihua* through a century of vicissitudes. Obviously, there are other cases, such as the controversy between *The Critical Review* (*Xueheng*) and *New Youth* in the early 1920s, in which *wenyan* and *baihua*, as the central subject of their debate, might take this chapter to another direction.[1] Likewise, the issue of the "mass language" (*dazhongyu*) raised by Qu Qiubai in the early 1930s provoked discussions and arguments among the left-wing writers (Goldman, 1962: 85–101; Liu Xiaoqing 2004: 165–173), articulating the canon formation of revolutionary literature and even the Communist literary and art policy in the ensuing decades (Seybolt and Chiang 1979: 4–5). Due to limited space, these cases are not discussed in this chapter (see Chapter 11 by Qian Suoqiao).

Language Reform and the National Essence

Language reform was initiated by Western missionaries such as W. R. P. Martin (1827–1916), Richard Timothy (1845–1919), and others in the late nineteenth century. Unlike their predecessor Matteo Ricci (1552–1610), who respectfully studied Chinese language and culture for his religious activities, these Protestant missionaries regarded Chinese culture as lagging behind the West and felt obliged to help China modernize. They complained about the "defects" of Chinese language, such as countless characters, monosyllabic nature, and, more specifically, the discrepancy between speech and writing as the major reason for a high illiteracy rate.[2] Referring to a Chinese pupil's book, Martin (1881: 64) states, "for in every part of the Empire the style of literary composition is so far removed from that of the vernacular speech that books, and the sounds of their characters convey absolutely no meaning to the mind of a beginner." Martin apparently targeted the classical language as a "dead language." Intending to modernize the Chinese language system, they worked with Chinese reformers and proposed new schemes based on romanized or phonetic characters.

Their discursive practices became more influential after the 1894 Sino-Japanese War, when Chinese intellectuals, led by Kang Youwei and Liang Qichao, launched a nationwide reform movement. During the Hundred Days Reform in 1898, they actively participated in policy-making at the imperial court and in educating the populace through local institutions. It was no accident that, under the influence of language reform, Liang advocated the theory of "uniting speech and writing" (*yanwen heyi*) in order to promote mass education. After the abortive reform of 1898, Liang was exiled to Japan, where he carried on his reformist agenda; in spreading Western theories of humanities borrowed from Japanese translations, he developed a "new-style prose," using moderate classical language mixed with Western grammar, effectively arousing the reader's patriotic emotions. As literature was more engaged with his reform movement, Liang demanded a revolution in poetry in his *Travel Journal of Hawaii*, a diary of his ocean voyage from Yokohama to Honolulu in December 1899. In his critique of those parrot-like poets satisfying themselves with imitating literary masters of the past, he proclaimed that the Chinese future relied on her "poetic destiny," which could be saved from doom only by accepting the modern challenge and breaking with the past. In the aspect of poetic language, Liang extolled Huang Zunxian, who emphasized oral speech in poetic writing, and was well known a decade ago for his poetic motto, "Just put down what my mouth utters." Both Huang and Liang stressed the importance of using the vernacular in poetry so as to empower literary functions in a sociopolitical movement (Chen Jianhua 2003).

In 1902, Liang Qichao further proclaimed the revolution in fiction, by which he aimed to forge a new national soul embodying the "new citizenship" in his "imagined community," and he blandished "old fiction," such as *Water Margin* and *Dream of the Red Chamber*, for enticing youths to be rebellious and lustful. In response to Liang's call, fiction magazines mushroomed in the 1910s, assimilating new ideas from the West and, at the same time, satirically criticizing all sorts of official corruption, people's foolishness, and the imperial system's weaknesses.

In many ways, Liang's works inspired the May Fourth generation. Hu Shi praised the poetry revolution for its practical and populist vein, and especially for its role in transforming poetic language from the classical to the vernacular, which directly contributed to the May Fourth literary revolution. According to Lu Xun, it was the idea of using fiction to construct a new national soul that had made him choose literature as his lifelong career (X. Tang 2002: 256–257).

The 1910s witnessed different linguistic ideas that contested each other in China (Kaske 2008). Aside from literary revolutions undertaken by Liang and his reformists, heated debates on the future of the Chinese language occurred among anti-Manchu revolutionaries. In 1907, a group of Chinese students in Paris published the newspaper *The New Century* (*Xin shiji*), in which Wu Jingheng and some anarchists asserted that Chinese written characters were no more than a backward linguistic system and should be entirely discarded, and that China should adopt Esperanto as her national language, which would make learning and universal communication easier. They received strong objections from Zhang Binglin and his national essence fellows (Luo Zhitian 2001). As Zhang Binglin (1985) argued, although the written system has shortcomings, it is in these characters that all historical and cultural texts are recorded; refuting Chinese characters therefore means refuting China's past. Critical of those who took language merely as a tool of communication, Zhang held that every nation in the world has its own language bearing its people's habits, mentality, and lifestyle. It is absurd to adopt

Esperanto, which is totally alien to Chinese people. In other words, Chinese characters represent Chinese identity as well as her cultural essence.

Zhang Binglin's linguistic stance was embedded in his philosophy of "restoring antiquity" (*fugu*), implying that the "national essence" lies in the culture of pre-Qin period (Hon 2013: 53–68). By using this rebuilt tradition inscribed with modern ideas of freedom and democracy, Zhang aimed to strengthen the Han identity as an ethnic weapon against the Qing Manchu regime. In line of the *fugu* theory, he favored most the literary classics in the period of Six-Dynasties, characteristic of a refined elite style. Interestingly, when Zhang defended the cultural past, he accused the anarchists of taking away the common people's pleasure in their reading of the novels *Water Margin* and *The Scholars* (*Rulin waishi*), which are part and parcel of the national essence. This mention of popular literature seemed to predict the impetus of *fugu* ideology and literary sentimentalism in the following decade, to whose significance literary historians so far have not paid enough attention.

For the revolution in fiction, Liang Qichao's claim that "fiction is the crowning glory of literature" (Denton 1996: 76) succeeded in encouraging a prolific production of fictional works emphasizing social functions, but, in reality, as a literary genre, fiction remained inferior to poetry and prose in traditional literary hierarchy. In the climate of "restoring antiquity," writing fiction in the classical language opened a new trend in the late Qing literary field, and consequently raised fiction's status. A direct influence was evidenced in *An Anthology of Foreign Short Stories* (*Yuwai xiaoshuo ji*, 1909), translated by Lu Xun and his brother Zhou Zuoren during their stay in Japan, where they both became Zhang Binglin's disciples. As Lu Xun acknowledged later, at the time he was indulged in the idea of *fugu*; indeed, the stories were translated in the antique style of the classical language, perhaps too difficult for today's readers to understand.

When the French novel *La Dame aux camélias* was translated into Chinese and published in 1899, it became an immediate hit and aroused sentiments among young readers. Regarded as the first foreign novel to be introduced in China, it was translated by Lin Shu, who had never learnt English; based on his friend's oral account, he wrote the novel in an exquisite classical style. Since then, aided by oral interpreters, Lin translated numerous Western novels. He proudly attributed the classical language he used to the prestigious Tongcheng style, so as to establish himself as a stylist rather than a novelist. As a pioneer of modern Chinese literature, Lin translated dozens of novels on love; in rendering these works, he often admired the Western heroines' independent personality, and he linguistically expanded the traditional rhetoric of depicting women in love. Given the popularity of translated novels such as Lin Shu's, fiction quickly moved to the center of national life.

In a time of national trauma, failed revolutions, and repressed desires, literary sentimentalism came to the fore and was theorized by Wang Guowei in aesthetic terms. In *Criticism of Dream of the Red Chamber* (*Honglou meng pinglun*, 1904), Wang praised this eighteenth-century Chinese novel as a world masterpiece, which he justified through his interpretation of Schopenhauer's philosophy of human tragedy. After 1909, the literary field was mostly occupied by the newly established Southern Society

(Nanshe), a literary anti-Manchu group headed by Liu Yazi. Initially based in Shanghai, it grew fast into a nationwide organization. With revolutionary passions, its members produced countless poems embodying the spirit of national essence.

In the early Republican era, many Nanshe members turned to popular printing enterprises in pursuit of urbanism and mass enlightenment, and consequently their literary products shifted from poetry to fiction. A new wave of classical fiction came from a number of female writers, exemplified by Gao Jianhua, editor of the literary magazine *Eyebrow Talk* (*Meiyu*). The magazine adopted a paradoxical approach to women's subjectivity, holding conservative domesticity as women's proper role in their imagined modern society on the one hand, and on the other hand cherishing the Western idea of free love and challenging the traditional sexual code by publishing pictures of female nudes on its covers. The antique style was extravagantly exhibited by Xu Zhenya's *Jade Pear Spirit*, serialized in the newspaper *The People's Rights* (*Minquan bao*), and published in 1913 in book form. The novel tells of a love affair between a widow and a young scholar, who are both constrained by traditional ethics, and yet they suffer from a burning passion for each other. Finally, the widow dies in despair. A rare gem recognized by later literary scholars (C. T. Hsia 1984), the novel proved to be a commercial success despite its conservative attitude toward women and its obsolete style of parallel prose, as it was reprinted time and again in later decades. In hindsight, *Jade Pear Spirit* seemed to have resolved the anxiety about the novel as a possible form of high art, and elevated fiction as the noblest literary genre in modern China. Probably more than that, the novel provided, politically and aesthetically, a new paradigm with a conservative agenda, which most Nanshe members had followed, showing how to maintain the national essence and embrace literary modernity at the same time. It inherited the "great tradition" of lyrical literature running from *Songs of the South* to *Dream of the Red Chamber*, full of expressions in parallel prose, poetic allusions, and classical cliché, and yet it implicitly mingled with advanced techniques from the West—epistolary style, tragic narrative, and visual description of the protagonists against the natural scenery.

The Linguistic Turn and Literary Debates

The term "May Fourth" implies a duet dance of politics and literature, as it simultaneously denotes the student movement in 1919 and refers to twin essays by Hu Shi and Chen Duxiu published by *New Youth* in 1917. Both literary and political events had been canonized as the origins of an anti-feudal and anti-imperial movement in modern China. After publishing Hu Shi's famous essay (Denton 1996: 123–139), Chen Duxiu, editor of *New Youth*, intended to move beyond Hu Shi's "reform," which meant gradual evolution, by calling for a "literary revolution" (Denton 1996: 140–145), which implied a radical rejection of not only literary but cultural traditions through political violence. It was in line with this revolutionary outcry that the May Fourth iconoclasm was formed.

For Hu and Chen, language was the core issue. They both attributed the literary tradition to its evil root in the classical language, which should be eradicated, and they argued that New Literature should adopt *baihua*, which was used by common people. Yet, ironically, *New Youth* did not use *baihua* until its publication of Lu Xun's "Diary of a Madman" in 1918. With this story, Lu Xun fleshed out the idea of "total rejection" of traditional culture, as he depicts a madman condemning Confucian doctrines as "cannibalistic" in Chinese history. In his other stories, Lu Xun explored how the national soul confined in an "iron house" was unconsciously tortured and murdered by the old culture, namely Confucianism. Usually set in towns and villages, Lu Xun's characters are emotionally and spiritually diseased and oppressed by evil forces such as corrupted politics, social networks, family ethics, the examination system, and religious superstition. By representing these victimized souls, Lu Xun showed his deep sympathy for the poor oppressed by the hierarchical social order.

However, the madman's cry of "saving the children" suggests a dilemma. The "children" as a metaphor for a pure body immune from the epidemic culture implies a utopian ideal as well as a critical criterion, by which he not only condemned the tradition but also the developing capitalism in China. Nevertheless, the madman realizes that he is also a cannibal in the "iron house," and is therefore ineligible as a savior. Lu Xun's writings are often shrouded with this type of self-suspicion, which distinguishes him from his "revolutionary" peers who optimistically believed in a bright future brought about by science and democracy.

In order to promote the new literary movement, Hu Shi, Qian Xuantong, and others actively joined the Education Bureau to push the national language movement forward. As a prominent linguist, Qian was devoted to adopting *baihua* as the national language; his famous slogan "If Han characters were not terminated, China would surely die!" (*Hanzi bu mie, Zhongguo bi wang!*) was widely shared by many new writers. Lu Xun, for example, repeated this slogan on several occasions. At the same time, the *New Youth* members frequently fired at contemporary feudal "demons" in their eyes. Intended to draw public attention, Qian Xuantong and Liu Fu played a notorious duet in *New Youth*: Qian wrote a fake letter by someone named Wang Jingxuan with offensive expressions against New Literature, and then Liu Fu replied with sharp and irritating remarks. On another occasion, Hu Shi picked some examples from Lin Shu's translation of Shakespeare and mocked at Lin's bad translation to "shame" Lin as a literary master. The debate became heated in early 1919 when Lin Shu publicized his opposition to New Literature, and more rage and fury ensued from the *New Youth* camp after Lin published two stories in *Shenbao*, a major newspaper in Shanghai, in which the devilish characters could be easily identified as Chen Duxiu and Hu Shi.

The target soon moved to Shanghai, where literary production managed by the Nanshe members had prospered since the mid-1910s. In 1919, Zhou Zuoren and Qian Xuantong assaulted the "black curtain fiction" (*heimu xiaoshuo*) for its amoral and filthy contents; they also accused *Jade Pear Spirit* of politically allying with Yuan Shikai's conspiracy of restoring the Confucian and imperial past. They labeled this novel

"Mandarin Ducks and Butterflies," and this "butterfly" label was gradually imposed on all popular writers in the Republican period.

The national language movement was also connected to the literary field in Shanghai, though with a different logic and consequences. In 1917, Bao Tianxiao launched *The Pictorial Story Magazine* (*Xiaoshuo huabao*), and declared that "principally fiction uses the vernacular language," and that this new magazine would only publish vernacular works. This idea, states Bao, came from one of his friends working on language reform in the Education Bureau in Beijing. And writing in the vernacular aims at filling the gap between speech and writing, facilitating literacy, and keeping abreast with historical evolution. Given such reasons similar to those of the May Fourth literary revolution, Bao had no ambition to attach the vernacular with a master narrative to radically change Chinese culture, nor did he want to see the literary field entirely taken over by the vernacular.

Affiliated with Nanshe, Bao was a pioneer in mass education via urban print business, as evidenced by *Women's Eastern Times* (*Funü shibao*), which he launched in 1911. Intended to "enhance old morals and disseminate new knowledge," this women's magazine carried with it a local agenda of "virtuous wife and good mother," accompanied with abundant materials about women's daily life translated from the West (Judge 2012). To Bao, both the vernacular and classical languages equally suit his old-and-new cultural politics, and more importantly, he needed both to reach a wider readership for educational and commercial purposes. In fact, when he started the *Pictorial Story Magazine*, he continued to edit *The Grand Magazine* (*Xiaoshuo daguan*), in which most works were written in the classical language.[3] Noticeably earlier than Bao, vernacular stories were encouraged by other literary magazines, such as the *Short Story Monthly*, a flagship of the Commercial Press started in 1910 and edited by Wang Yunzhang, who also belonged to Nanshe. Its opening issue asked for either *wenyan* or *baihua* writings to fulfill its goal to "tell old stories, import new knowledge, and promote the common sense."

We might be surprised that the first response to the May Fourth literary revolution was from *New World Daily* (*Xin shijie*), a tabloid newspaper in Shanghai, edited by Zheng Zhengqiu, a pioneer of Chinese cinema. Its April 1919 issue carried Zhong Xiu's eclectic comments on the dispute between the *New Youth* and Lin Shu: while criticizing Lin's stubborn traditionalism against the tide, the author mocked at those "big shots of the literary revolution" because their new vernacular works were uncompetitive with the *Water Margin* and *Dream of the Red Chamber*.

It is well known that New Literature won the ideological battle in the name of national salvation and progressive history. In 1921, Mao Dun became the editor of *Short Story Monthly* and immediately turned it into a citadel of the Literary Association, thus speeding up the New Culture movement. As Wang Xiaoming (1999: 28) pointed out, the association revealed its ambition to build the magazine into an aggressive institution and used discursive practices of world literature to control the national literary field. Indeed, predicated on the universal concept of literature (*wenxue*), literary discourse was systematically constituted by the interrelated fields of creative writing, translation, literary criticism, and literary history. At the time, Mao Dun was obsessed with European naturalism, which for him embodied the "scientific spirit" distinctive from subjective romanticism and thus signified the newest development of European literature. He stated: "Unavoidably modern literature was baptized by Naturalism; therefore, according to the progressive history of literature, new Chinese literature must follow up this course" (Mao Dun 1921: 3). Following his use of European grammar in translation, Mao Dun even proposed to create a "Europeanized language" (*Ouhua yu*) for the Chinese literary language.

Worries grew among the Nanshe writers. In fear that New Literature would advance, Yuan Hanyun, the leading writer of *The Crystal* (*Jingbao*), a major tabloid in Shanghai, satirized the reformed *Short Story Monthly* for its poor artistic quality, accusing it of promoting Western-style writing at the expense of *wenyan*, the essence of Chinese literary culture. Also in 1921, Zhou Shoujuan, known as the "king of sad love story" at the time, started a "Special Issue of Fiction" (*Xiaoshuo tekan*) in the "Free Talk" (*Ziyou tan*) page in *Shenbao* and published 30 issues, which introduced more than 20 foreign writers, including Balzac, Zola, Conrad, Gorky, and Edgar Allan Poe. However, Zhou's intention to take the lead of literary publication soon involved him in literary polemics with prominent May Fourth figures.

Critical of Mao Dun's "new tide," Zhou and his colleagues asserted that the distinction between the new and the old is determined not by form, but rather by content. For them, using new theory and terms from the West was not necessarily with the best of "newness," whereas using classical Chinese could also express modern feelings. In opposition to Mao Dun's advocacy of European grammar, Zhou praised Lin Shu for his beautiful language in translation. Holding that literary works by those new writers are too high-minded to be accessible to wide readership, Zhou (1921: 14) showed his faith in a *laisser-faire* policy: "Which type is more authentic? So far there is no conclusion. In my opinion, it is best to let the new writer pursue the new, and the old pursue the old. Each may do as he likes, and let the reader choose. If suspicion grows out of jealousy, or attacks are actually launched in the name of criticism, it shows small-mindedness." Here, we see that Zhou and his fellow writers were complacent with their commercial success but fearful of New Literature as a threat to the literary market under their domination.

The debates became increasingly heated and extended to other popular journals such as *The Sunday* (*Xingqi*), edited by Bao Tianxiao; *The Crystal*, edited by Yu Daxiong; and *The Smallest* (*Zuixiao*), edited by Zhang Zhenlü. The new camp was further supported by *The Literary Thrice-Monthly* (*Wenxue xunkan*) under Zheng Zhenduo and *Creation Weekly* (*Chuangzao zhoubao*) under Cheng Fangwu. Zheng Zhenduo, an ardent advocate of "literature of blood and tears" (*xue yu lei de wenxue*), asserted that literature should speak for the oppressed and exploited people in defiance of dark forces. In condemning old literature as aspiring merely to amuse the petty bourgeois for the sake of money and lacking humanist compassion, he even called old-styled writers "literary beggars" (*wengai*) and "literary prostitutes."

In 1922, the controversy had a dramatic twist, as the government ordered the national education system to adopt *baihua* as the "national language." Much indebted to this official enforcement, the literary revolution progressed in full swing; conse-quently, old-styled writers lost their linguistic ground. Historically, this debate had special significance in modern China (J. Chen 2009). Since then, the banal concepts of "new" (*xin*) and "old" (*jiu*) were ideologically coded: the former means historical necessity with a promise of a bright future, and the latter means backward, decadent, and escapist. In the 1930s, left-wing writers continually attacked old literature and further dismissed it as "butterfly," representative of "feudal petty urbanites." Despite the pressure, nonetheless, popular old-styled writers kept their business well, flexibly using both the vernacular and classical languages in their writings. After the war broke out in 1937, their business halted, but in the mid-1940s it came back. In 1943, Zhou Shoujuan renewed *The Violet* (*Ziluolan*) magazine and published literary works in the vernacular and classical languages alike. It was well known that Eileen Chang published her first short story in this magazine and began her illustrious literary career (see Chapter 4 by Nicole Huang).

Recent Reactions against the Linguistic Turn

Since the 1980s, the Chinese government has executed the open-door policy to embrace the global economic order, and meanwhile has preserved "socialism with Chinese char-acteristics." In a social climate of "farewell to revolution," reflections on issues of canon formation, human destiny, and the past and future of national culture have spread over all areas of humanities. Among others, the issue of language was debated by writers and scholars, who almost unanimously critiqued the linguistic turn of the early twentieth century. The new discourse rejected the May Fourth iconoclasm and tried to revive the Chinese cultural tradition. The new concept of *Hanyu* emerged to recover the splendid culture of the past,[4] the passion and responsibility to rebuild the tradition, and the new consciousness of national identity facing the challenge brought by globalization. The term "*Hanyu*" reminded us of the ideal of the national essence amidst the crisis of Chinese identity at the turn of the twentieth century. In defiance of the revolutionary canon, the term envisioned a cultural politics that would develop the national language in plural approaches and would contest the free market.

One conspicuous scene of 1990s China was the proliferation of Western theories, which resulted in a mirage of "post-isms" (*houxue*), in Henry Zhao's opinion. As Zhao (1997) argued, in the West, the theories of poststructuralism, postmodernism, and postcolonialism have been regarded as radical criticism of Eurocentrism or post-capitalist ideology, but in China the post-isms have revealed their "conservative" politics, exemplified by the intellectual denial of May Fourth iconoclasm. Indeed, while showcasing Western theories, it is not difficult to find what is really inferred to in Chinese reality. In the 1990s, young intellectuals talked more often about the "linguistic turn," a term from the famous anthology edited by Richard Rorty in 1967 (Xu Youyu 1999: 4–5; Wang Yichuan 1994), with awareness that the issue of language was at the core of Western humanist discourses in the twentieth century.

It was in this international context that *Hanyu* discourse pursued their historical reflections, mixing local agenda with various theories from the West.

In 1980, Wang Zengqi's "The Love Story of a Young Monk" became a surprise to the literary field and brought a veteran writer back from oblivion. An allegory of pure language, the story depicts an affectionate relationship between a young monk and a girl in the countryside, recalling the lyrical style of the Beijing School in the 1930s represented, in part, by Shen Congwen. Interestingly, as noted by the author, this story was a record of Wang's dream from 43 years ago, suggestive of his unchangeable faith in beautiful human nature despite all hardships through the decades. Wang studied at Southwest Associated University, where Shen was his mentor. Wang wrote many essays about lyrical language and fictional techniques, often linked to aesthetic theories in classical literature; time and again, he wrote about Shen Congwen, and, in praise of artistic perfection in Shen's works, he could not help feel sorry that Shen had been neglected by literary historians. However, Wang was much comforted by A. Cheng's novella "The King of Chess" (*Qiwang*, 1984) and wrote a glowing review, as he saw the lyrical tradition inherited by a younger writer. In his generation, A. Cheng was perhaps one of the most theoretically critical figures of the language reform. In his book *Casual Remarks in Casual Style* (*Xianhua xianshuo*), published in 1994, A. Cheng criticized how the "standard language" (*putonghua*), as an official pedagogical tool after 1949, exerted a bad influence on literary writings, and he expressed his faith in a revival of the secular spirit deeply imbedded in traditional popular literature.

Around this time, butterfly literature, applauded by A. Cheng as exemplary of the secular tradition, was excavated as part of "repressed modernities" by literary historians, and redeemed as equally important as May Fourth literature (Fan Boqun 2010: 1–27). The label attracted contemporary readers with its images of "small lovable animals" suitable for a growing nostalgia for old Shanghai, and the revival of such soft literature was interwoven into the intellectual project of rewriting literary history after the mid-1980s.

When the issue of *wenyan* was raised by those who had experienced political persecution, it reminded them of the violence of language in the Cultural Revolution. In 1988, Ke Ling, a writer of the May Fourth generation, stated that most contemporary *baihua* writings looked "pale and weak" as an anemic patient, and that this "lingering symptom" (*houyizheng*) was left by the May Fourth writers who had brutally amputated *wenyan*. He believed that the phenomenon of an impure mother tongue had caused secret worries among thoughtful folks. But why "secret worries"? Zhou Ruchang asked this question a decade later. He praised Ke Ling's brave challenge to *baihua* and proclaimed, "*Wenyan, wenyan*—a language from the ancient Chinese past and a miracle of human creation—is by no means the 'fierce floods and savage beasts'" to be scared of (Zhou Ruchang 1998: 8).

A more radical critique of *baihua* was made by Shen Xiaolong, a young linguist at Fudan University, who called for a "cultural linguistics" to reshape the study of Chinese language based on its own tradition (1990: 75–106). By targeting *Mr. Ma's Grammar Book* (*Mashi wentong*) published in 1898, which laid a foundation for modernizing

Chinese according to Western linguistics, Shen criticized the Westernization of *Hanyu* since the early twentieth century, from the May Fourth *baihua* movement to the Communist language reform, from the Western systemization of grammar to the romanization of phonetics.

In 1993, Zheng Min, a well-known modernist poet and professor at Beijing Normal University, asked a sharp question: why has modern Chinese poetry failed to produce masterpieces such as those in classical poetry? For her, the Chinese language underwent its modern fate through three phases: first, it was hurt by the May Fourth iconoclasm; after the 1950s, it was further victimized by political homogeneity and populism; and it was after 1979 that its vitality and diversity started to revive, signaled by the emergence of Misty Poetry. She blamed Chen Duxiu and Hu Shi for tyrannically declaring that the classical language was dead. From then on, Chinese culture became a wounded body, and this was responsible for the failure of New Poetry.

In Zheng's diagnosis, what is behind the clear divide between the living and the dead language is a dualist mode of thinking invested with oppression, absolutism, and violence; these binary opposites—vernacular versus classical, proletarian versus capitalist, and traditional versus revolutionary—have occupied intellectual life throughout the modern era and severely damaged the development of Chinese literature and culture. This dualism originated in the May Fourth period, and its violent nature is typically embodied by Chen Duxiu's absolute rejection of *wenyan* in his proclamation of the literary revolution: "There is no room for any discussion."

Furthermore, Zheng argued that both Chen Duxiu and Hu Shi ignored the fact that language, according to Ferdinand de Saussure's concept of *langue*, is a semiotic structure of culture; hence, in their denial of *wenyan*, they absurdly amputated Chinese culture as a living body. Zheng (1993: 9) accused Hu Shi specifically: "From our hindsight, Hu Shi was so erudite and familiar with both Chinese and foreign cultures, but he trashed his own cultural treasures developed over millennia. Such an unhealthy mentality requires our attention, for it is more unexplainable if compared to the Red Guards whose violent destruction was out of ignorance." By citing Ludwig Wittgenstein, Martin Heidegger, Derrida, and Western Sinologists to support her reevaluation of *wenyan*, Zheng delivered a critical message that Chinese culture must heal its wounds and develop as an organic whole in response to a new global situation.

Poetic Language across Transnational Borders

During the 1990s, poetic language stood at the frontier of literary creation, and *Hanyu* was tested for its new mission of bridging the past and present, China and the West. The polemic of poetic language became a transnational and transcultural phenomenon when Bei Dao was blamed by Stephen Owen, a professor at Harvard University, and defended by Rey Chow and Michelle Yeh, all of them based in the United States. Owen's criterion of poetic creativity is less rooted in Western modernism than in Chinese classicism. The English translation of Bei Dao's poetry frustrated Owen's high expectation of the vivacity and potential of the Chinese poetic tradition. The dispute centers on his notion of "world poetry," which captures an intriguing interplay between "local color," the political "other," poetic writing, and the "world audience." For Owen (1990), the aesthetic beauty in Bei Dao's poetry was compromised in a process of writing or translation directed at a world audience, who expects cheap local color and images of an undemocratic China. Rey Chow (1993: 2) ridicules Owen's "orientalist" nostalgia for a classical China, which has led him to overlook the "historical context essential to the writing and reading of contemporary Chinese poetry." Compared with Owen's aesthetic concern, Chow's position is political, and her Chinese context "is an assumed political reality that often frames the reading and promotion of a particular kind of contemporary Chinese poetry in the United States" (Y. Huang, 2002: 165–166).

What is neglected in Owen's essay is a critical insight of contemporary Chinese poetic language under "global influence." Leaving aside his personal judgment of Bei Dao's poetry, Owen reveals that Chinese literature embarking upon the world is constrained by the mechanisms of literary institutions in the West, as the process of making "world poetry" involves interventions of translation, publishing, readership, and even award agencies such as the Nobel Prize committee.

Returning to Zheng Min, her 1993 critique drew the attention of overseas literary scholars. Michelle Yeh (1998: 8–9) criticized Zheng's "simplistic" view of May Fourth language reform for "violently ignoring the Chinese new poetry that has developed over eighty years." Referring to the irony that Zheng justifies *wenyan* by appealing to Western Sinologists, namely the "new international authorities," Yeh revisits the polemic of Owen's book review to which she and Rey Chow had responded earlier. On the linguistic question of "Chineseness" (*Zhonghuaxing*) in modern Chinese poetry, Yeh criticizes Zheng's "static" idea of *wenyan* that denies the historical evolution of modern Chinese poetry. Yeh is inclined to justify *baihua* as a historical necessity and asks: "Is modern Chinese poetry a passive receiver of Western imperial culture, or an active self-reformer? Over the years I have insisted on the latter" (M. Yeh 1998: 9).

In her response to Yeh, Zheng (2002) details the ups and downs of the relationship between *baihua* and *wenyan* since the May Fourth and reaffirms her conclusion that Chinese poetry has been injured by the linguistic turn 80 years ago. Such debates aside, the poetry arena is overshadowed by a longing for the classical tradition, and sometimes similar regret can be heard from younger critics. For example, Liu Xiang (2002) believes that the tradition of lyricism, which was so beautifully developed in classical poetry, has definitely been lost in contemporary Chinese poetry. For Liu, the year 1989 is crucial for the disappearance of a kind of intellectual ideal as well as of real poetry.

The 1990s literary field witnessed the rise of a new generation of poetic writing. An aura was created around the term "1990s poetry," whereby Chinese avant-gardists experimented, reformed, and invented *Hanyu* in theory and practice. Nevertheless, in 1998, the 1990s poets were divided into two camps: the group of "intellectual writing" (*zhishi fenzi xiezuo*) headed by Xi Chuan, Ouyang Jianghe, and Sun Wenbo in Beijing, and the group called "folk position" (*minjian lichang*) led by Yu Jian, Han Dong, and Yang Ke from southern provinces. Identified as the third-generation poets, most of them were friends in the previous decade and showed their devotion to the freedom of art by publishing underground poetry, and then they fell apart, but the division helped them clarify their poetic theories.

The "intellectual poets" claim the legitimacy of 1990s poetry as characterized by textual complexity, Western resources, narrative techniques, individual voice, aesthetic modernity, and assimilation of knowledge. The poets of the "folk position" emphasize intuition, creativity, ordinary life, and oral language, and a strong nativist ethos is implied in their critique of the intellectual poets as "surrendering to the foreign," "colonizing the poetic realm," and "destroying the humanities by equating poetry with knowledge." For the latter group, Yu Jian fervently advocates ordinary language, especially southern dialects, as poetic language. Portraying *putonghua* as the "hard tongue" representative of state ideology, and southern dialects as the "soft tongue" enriched by private, everyday life, Yu describes his painful experiences of speaking and writing in *putonghua*, which his soft tongue could not accommodate. He praises the tradition of southern writings: "In the outer provinces, words such as 'secularized', 'worldly', 'petty urbanite', 'small familial', 'trivial', 'carnal', or 'ordinary' have no bad meanings as in *putonghua*; instead they are taken for granted in the classical writings of the southerners" (Yu 1998: 17). Reluctantly admitting that *putonghua* writing is "healthy" and "necessary" for modern Chinese poetry, Yu claims that it is southern poetry centering on dialects and ordinary language that has truly created new poetry since the 1980s.

Epilogue: *Hanyu* in Global Flux

Nowadays, literary historians barely hold the canonical view that Chinese literary modernity started with May Fourth literary movement; by revising the periodization of the "modern," they generally shared the conception of "twentieth-century Chinese literature" in favor of multiple modernities. This chapter traces the linguistic tension and fusion between literary revolution and the national essence originated from the turn of the twentieth century, and in subsequent decades the literary field was governed, explicitly or implicitly, by the mechanisms of revolution and reformation centered around *baihua* and *wenyan*. Against this historical backdrop, we can better grasp the signification of the reaction to the linguistic turn in 1990s China, when *baihua* was decentered along with the fading revolutionary ideology, and the new consciousness of *Hanyu* arose.

Ironically, many Chinese intellectuals had long aspired to romanization as the destiny for Chinese language, but now this cosmopolitan ideal has lost charm. The intellectual infatuation with post-isms of the West was intended to reenter the world, and it was accompanied with local anxieties as evident in their collective reconfiguration of *Hanyu*, which projects a rejuvenation of the national essence advocated a century earlier. Facing the new global situation, the ethnicity of Han has been conjured up as unified Chinese identity.

Few have ever doubted the achievement of *baihua* and its dominance in everyday life, though, in recent years, *wenyan* has been increasingly articulated in terms of cultural development. In April 2013, many young poets gathered at Yangzhou, led by Yang Lian, a representative of Misty Poetry, and performed the Spring Rite in the literati tradition initiated by Wang Xizhi in the Eastern Jin dynasty. Poetry societies have emerged here and there, and more young people are learning to write poetry in classical forms. Some scholars have argued that classical poems written in the modern time should not be excluded from the history of modern Chinese literature, and that the best of such poems are more aesthetically valuable than *baihua* literature. Nostalgic or not, recent activities of *wenyan* remind us of the literary debate in the early 1920s, but this time historical experiences are associated with national essentialism, the free market ideology, and "old-and-new" cultural politics.

All these events question the globalist prediction that the power of the nation-state would decline in the process of globalization; yet, in China, the theory meets its limits. In a sense, the intellectuals and the nation-state have cooperated once again, as in the 1920s, for making a new myth of *Hanyu*. When the socialist print industry has turned to state capitalism, linguistic debates are still regulated by the state apparatus, so that print culture has by no means reduced its role of reinforcing the "imagined communities" of nation building.

With the ambiguous relations between new nationalist cultural identity, the nation-state, and globalization, the *Hanyu* consciousness has grown into the new millennium, with a clearer stance as it confronts the increasing pressure of globalization. On February 21, 2002, *Social Science Weekly*, a newsletter of the Academy of Social Sciences in Shanghai, organized a forum entitled "*Hanyu*: How to Break Up the Siege of Foreign Languages," to which several scholars at Fudan University contributed. Concentrating on *Hanyu* as the essence of national culture, they worried about the loss of its "purity" in daily use through hybridized foreign words, mainly English, which have flooded into China since the 1980s. Among these forum contributors is a shared fear that losing one's mother tongue is like losing one's homeland.

This yearning for homeland has a larger implication, mirroring our current borderless world in which national identities are now in flux and inevitably linked to the changing condition of native languages. In this global perspective, the new language consciousness of contemporary China interacts with trends of cultural politics in various places, such as multicultural bilingualism or Sinophone studies in North America, or the politics of dialects in Asia Pacific. However, any oral or written form has a temporo-spatial dimension, and the new linguistic consciousness in China will continue to assert itself at both national and international contexts for years to come.

NOTES

This chapter is partly based on Chen Jianhua (2004). All translations in this chapter are mine unless otherwise noted.

1 For a recent study of *The Critical Review*, see Zhang Hemin (2001). In 1922, Lu Xun criticized *Xueheng* writers allying with butterfly writers due to their similar stand for the

national essence and *wenyan*. *The Critical Review* circulated mostly among elites for over a dozen years, and its linguistic and literary discourses more sophisticated than those in the butterfly magazines.

2   Kaske (2008) has substantially documented debates on educational functions of vernacular and classical language between different groups from the late Qing to the early Republican era, though she discusses little about the link between Protestant missionaries and May Fourth. In this latter respect, see Gao Yuanbao (2010) and Dong Yufei (2014).

3   Probably uncomfortable with consequences of the May Fourth literary movement, Bao Tianxiao (1926) pointed out in *The Crystal* that his *Pictorial Story Magazine* had used *baihua* earlier than *New Youth*. See also Fan Boqun (2010: 17) and Chen Jianhua (2014: 50–51).

4   Starting from the late 1980s, the term "Han poetry" (*Hanshi*) has been used by some poets. In 1991, Mang Ke, Tang Xiaodu, and Meng Lang published *Modern Han Poetry* (*Xiandai hanshi*), an unofficial poetry journal circulating nationwide. Thanks to Meng Lang for this information.

References

Bao Tianxiao 包天笑. 1926. "*Baihua* wen zhi shi" 白话文之始 (The origin of the vernacular). *Jingbao* 晶报 (The crystal), 115 (May 27): 2.

Chen, Jianhua. 2003. "Late Qing 'Poetry Revolution': Liang Qichao, Huang Zunxian and Chinese Literary Modernity." In *The Columbia Companion to Modern East Asian Literature*. Edited by Mostow, Joshua S. New York: Columbia University Press. 333–340.

Chen, Jianhua. 2004. "The Linguistic Turn in 1990s China and Globalization." In *Critical Zone: A Forum of Chinese and Western Knowledge*. Edited by Tong, Q. S., Wang Shouren, and Douglas Kerr. Hong Kong: Hong Kong University Press. 119–138.

Chen, Jianhua. 2009. "An Archaeology of Repressed Popularity: Zhou Shoujuan, Mao Dun, and Their 1920s Literary Polemics." In *Rethinking Chinese Popular Culture: Cannibalization of the Canon*. Edited by Rojas, Carlos, and Eileen Cheng-yin Chow. New York: Routledge. 91–114.

Chen Jianhua 陳建華. 2014. "Zhou Shoujua, Mao Dun yu ershiniandai chu xinjiu wenxue lunzhan" 周瘦鵑、茅盾與二十年代初新舊文學論戰 (Zhou Shoujuan, Mao Dun and literary contro-

versy between the old and the new in the early 1920s). *Shanghai wenhua* 上海文化 (Shanghai culture), 110: 38–55.

Chen, Xiaomei. 2014. "Mapping a 'New' Dramatic Canon: Rewriting the Legacy of Hong Shen." In *Modern China and the West: Translation and Cultural Mediation*, eds. Peng Hsiao-yen and Isabelle Rabur. Leiden: Brill. 224–245.

Chow, Rey. 1993. *Writing Diaspora: Tactics of Intervention in Contemporary Cultural Studies*. Bloomington: Indiana University Press.

Denton, Kirk A. Ed. 1996. *Modern Chinese Literary Thought: Writings on Literature, 1893–1945*. Stanford, CA: Stanford University Press.

Dong, Yufei. 2014. *Phoneticizing China: The Politic of the* Pinyin *Reform Movement*. M. Phil Thesis, Hong Kong University,

Fan, Boqun 范伯群. Ed. 2010. *Zhongguo jin xiandai wenxueshi* 中國近現代通俗文學史 (A history of popular literature in modern China). Rev. edition. Nanjing: Jiangsu jiaoyu chubanshe.

Goldman, Merle. 1962. "Left-wing Criticism of the Pai Hua movement." In *Reflections on the May Fourth Movement: A Symposium*. Edited by Schwartz, Benjamin. Cambridge, MA: Harvard University Press. 85–101.

Gao, Yuanbao 郜元寶. 2010. *Hanyu bieshi: xiandai Zhongguo de yuyan tiyan* 漢語別史—現代中國的語言體驗 (An alternative history of *Hanyu*: the language experience in modern China). Ji'nan: Shandong jiaoyu chubanshe.

Hon, Tze-ki. 2013. *Revolution as Restoration: Guocui xuebao and China's Path to Modernity, 1905–1911*. Leiden: Brill.

Hsia, C. T. 1984. "Hsü Chen-ya's *Yuli hun*: An Essay in Literary History and Criticism." In *Chinese Middlebrow Fiction: From the Ch'ing and Early Republican Eras*. Edited by Liu, Ts'un-yan. Hong Kong: Chinese University Press. 199–240.

Huang, Yunte. 2002. *Transpacific Displacement: Ethnography, Translation, and Intertextual Travel in Twentieth-Century American Literature*. Berkeley: University of California Press.

Judge, Joan. 2012. "Everydayness as a Critical Category of Gender Analysis: The Case of *Funü shibao* (The Women's Eastern Times)." *Jindai Zhongguo funü shi yanjiu* 近代中國婦女史研究 (Studies of modern Chinese women), 20: 1–28.

Kaske, Elisabeth. 2008. *The Politics of Language in Chinese Education, 1895–1919*. Leiden: Brill.

Liu, Xiang 劉翔. 2002. "Ganga shidai de shuqing shige—lun zai Zhongguo dangdai shige geju zhong shuqing shi de diwei he yiyi" 尷尬時代的抒情詩歌—論在中國當代詩歌格局中抒情詩的地位和意義 (Lyrical poetry in the time of predicament: On the status and significance of lyrical poetry in contemporary Chinese poetic situation). *Shi tansuo* 詩探索 (Poetry exploration), 45–46: 9–23.

Liu, Xiaoqing 劉小清. 2004. *Hongse kuangbiao: Zuolian shilu* 紅色狂飆—左聯實錄 (The red whirlwind: a factual record of the league of left-wing writers). Beijing: Renmin wenxue chubanshe.

Luo, Zhitian 羅志田. 2001. "Qingji weirao wanguo xinyu de sixiang lunzheng" 清季圍繞萬國新語的思想論爭 (The ideological controversy

about Esperanto in the late Qing dynasty). *Jindaishi yanjiu* 近代史研究 (Studies of early modern Chinese history), 4: 86–144.

Mao, Dun 茅盾. 1921. "Yinian lai de ganxiang yu mingnian de jihua," 一年來的感想與明年的計畫 (My thought of the past year and plan for the next year). *Xiaoshuo yuebao* 小説月報 (Short story magazine), 12 (Dec.): 3.

Martin, W. R. P. 1881. *The Chinese: Their Education, Philosophy, and Letters*. New York: Harper and Brothers.

Owen, Stephen. 1990. "The Anxiety of Global Influence: What Is World Poetry?" *New Republic* (Nov. 19): 28–32.

Seybolt, Peter J., and Gregory Kuei-ke Chiang. Eds. 1979. *Language Reform in China*. New York: M. E. Sharpe.

Shen, Xiaolong 申小龍. 1990. *Zhongguo wenhua yuyanxue* 中國文化語言學 (Chinese cultural linguistics). Changchun: Jilin jiaoyu chubanshe.

Tang, Xiaobing. 2002. "'Poetic Revolution,' Colonization, and Form at the Beginning of Modern Chinese Literature." In *Rethinking the 1898 Reform Period: Political and Cultural Change in Late Qing China*. Edited by Karl, Rebecca and Peter Zarrow. Cambridge, MA: Harvard University Press. 245–268.

Wang, Xiaoming. 1999. "A Journal and a 'Society': On the 'May Fourth' Literary Tradition." *Modern Chinese Literature and Culture*, 11: 1–39.

Wang, Yichuan 王一川. 1994. "Cong lixing zhongxin dao yuyan zhongxin" 從理性中心到語言中心 (From the center of reason to the center of language). *Wenxue pinglun*, 6: 97–107.

Xu, Youyu 徐友漁. 1999. *Gaobie ershi shiji* 告別二十世紀 (Farewell to the twentieth century). Jinan: Shandong jiaoyu chubanshe.

Yeh, Michelle (Xi Mi 奚密). 1998. "Zhongguo shi de houxiandai?" 中國詩的後現代 (Postmodernism of Chinese poetry?). *Zhongguo yanjiu* 中國研究 (China studies), 37: 1–9.

Yu, Jian 于堅. 1998. "Shige zhi she de ying yu ruan: guanyu dangdai shige de lianglei yuyan xiangdu" 詩歌之舌的硬與軟:關於當代詩歌的兩類語言向度 (The hard and soft poetic tongues: two types of language direction in contemporary poetry). *Shi tansuo* 詩探索 (Poetry exploration), 29: 1–12.

Zhang, Binglin 章炳麟. 1985. *Zhang Taiyan quanji* 章太炎全集 (Complete works of Zhang Taiyan). Shanghai: Renmin chubanshe. 4: 337–353.

Zhang, Hemin 張賀敏. 2001. "*Xueheng pai yanjiu shuping*" 學衡派研究述評 (On studies of *Xueheng* school). *Zhongguo xiandai wenxue yanjiu congkan* 中國現代文學研究叢刊 (Modern Chinese literature studies), 4: 271–290.

Zhao, Henry Y. H. 1997. "Post-Isms and Chinese New Conservatism." *New Literary History*, 28.1: 31–44.

Zheng, Min 鄭敏. 1993. "Shiji mo de huigu: Hanyu yuyan biange yu Zhongguo xinshi chuangzuo" 世紀末的回顧—漢語語言變革與中國新詩創作 (A fin-de-siècle reflection on the change of *Hanyu* and new Chinese poetic writing). *Wenxue pinglun*, 3: 5–20.

Zheng, Min 鄭敏. 2002. "Zhongguo xinshi bashi nian fansi" 中國新詩八十年反思 (Reflections on eighty years of Chinese new poetry"). *Wenxue pinglun*, 5: 68–73.

Zhou, Ruchang 周汝昌. 1998. "Baihua yu wenyan" 白話與文言 (The vernacular and the classical language). *Wenhui bao* 文匯報 (Wenhui daily) (June 11): 8.

Zhou, Shoujuan 周瘦鵑. 1921. "Ziyou tan zhi ziyou tan" 自由談之自由談 (Free talk within free talk). *Shenbao* 申報 (Shanghai daily) (March 27): 14.

19
The Significance of the Northeastern Writers in Exile, 1931–1945

Haili Kong

Northeast China, in the eyes of the majority of the Chinese, had remained a mystery for hundreds of years, owing to its geographical remoteness, cultural differences, and historical hostilities between Northeastern ethnic groups and the majority Han people. Since Manchuria became a powerful state that conquered China, and established a new dynasty called the Qing (1644–1911), the barriers between the Manchu and the Han have been gradually eliminated through cultural assimilation, intermarriage, economic exchange, and mass migration. However, for the Sun Yat-sen's Republican Revolution that succeeded in 1911, the number one goal had been "expelling the Manchu and restoring China," which further made the concept of "nation" vague and the identity of Manchuria ambiguous. Even though the Second Sino-Japanese War in 1937–1945 brought the Northeasterners and people in other parts of China together in the common goal of national defense, the real face of Northeast China had never been fully demystified until decades later.

Geographically, Northeast China, formerly also known as Manchuria, now consists of three provinces—Heilongjiang, Jilin, and Liaoning. For centuries, the immense barren steppes of this region were sparsely populated by nomadic tribes and farmers. Local residents were mainly Manchu, Han, and Mongol, among more than 100 ethnic groups. Since the seventeenth century, the Manchu had ruled China, and a great number of Han people had moved into the area to explore better economic opportunities, or simply to survive famines and political persecutions back home. These newcomers brought with them witchcraft and other primitive religious rituals from south of the Great Wall, and these practices merged with local traditions in Northeast China,

A Companion to Modern Chinese Literature, First Edition. Edited by Yingjin Zhang.
© 2016 John Wiley & Sons, Ltd. Published 2016 by John Wiley & Sons, Ltd.

such as the worship of the sun and bird totems and shamanism, to form a unique Northeastern culture and mentality.

The vast natural resources and immense but uncultivated steppes make Northeast China a land of adventure, and often a focal point of interest at home and abroad. During the nineteenth century, foreign powers, especially Russia and Japan, began to exploit Manchuria's vast natural resources. At the turn of the twentieth century, Japan gained dominance and began to exert its influence in Northeast China, particularly in the period of 1931–1945. Foreign invasion and colonization obviously added another exotic flavor to the culture of this region.

The mixture of ethnic elements and strong foreign influences has made Northeast China a multi-cultural, multi-ethnic, and multi-lingual region. Yet, very few literary works explored life in Northeast China prior to the twentieth century. Local writers had little connection with the national literary centers, such as Beijing and Shanghai, due to travel inconvenience and metropolitan cultural arrogance. The consequence is that Northeast literary works were rarely recorded in official literary histories. Such literary isolation was finally overcome by a group of writers who emerged with fascinating works that portray distinctive regional life, express individual sentiments, and highlight resentments toward the regional disintegration caused by foreign invasions.

This chapter investigates the significance of Northeastern writers in exile in four sections: its emergence as a political/patriotic phenomenon through literary presentations (1928–1935); its sensational success as a regional group on the national literary arena (1936–1937); its literary contribution made by individualistic writers, not as a unified group (1938–1945); and its literary significance as reflected in the novelty of epic genre, narrative style, linguistic usage, as well as its impact on subsequent writers.

The Emergence of Northeastern Writers, 1928–1935

As early as 1906, when *Shengjing Times* (*Shengjing shibao*), the first important regional newspaper, started circulation, local writers began their literary activities. Before the end of the 1920s, however, most literary writings remained at the level of introducing new vernacular literature as well as democratic revolutionary thoughts advocated in the May Fourth Movement. Mu Mutian, who studied in Japan and was a member of the Creative Society, was one of the early representatives of symbolist poetry in China and probably the first nationally acclaimed Northeastern writer. During his stay at his hometown, Changchun, between 1930 and 1931, Mu's poems stirred up patriotic passions and inspired creative impulses among many young intellectuals. Almost at the same time, owing to its unique geographic position and cultural diversity, Harbin, the capital of Heilongjiang province, became a more important center for literary activities than Shenyang and Changchun, two cities closely under Japanese control.

In the late 1920s, *International Gazette* (*Guoji xiebao*), a leading liberal newspaper in Harbin, took the initiative in providing space for unknown young writers to publish their works in its weekly literary supplement edited by Zhao Ximeng, a liberal critic and editor. As a byproduct, the Beilei Society (1928–1932) was organized by Chen Jiying and Kong Luosun, who promoted literary prosperity in Northeast China by organizing literary activities and publishing a *Beilei* literary supplement in *International Gazette*. Their society soon attracted amateurs from all three Northeastern provinces and grew into a literary center in Harbin. Prominent Northeaster writers, such as Xiao Jun (born Liu Honglin) and Xiao Hong (born Zhang Naiying), were almost all connected to the newspaper. In 1931, Xiao Jun published his earliest pieces in *International Gazette* and briefly worked for its "children section." When she was caught in a difficult situation in 1931, Xiao Hong wrote an urgent letter to *International Gazette* asking for help. Later, she published her first story there in 1933. In this sense, this newspaper nurtured and assisted Northeastern writers to grow.

The stories of the two Xiaos help us understand the emergence of Northeastern writers in the early 1930s. Xiao Hong was born in 1911 into a wealthy gentry family in Hulan, a town about 30 miles north of Harbin. Her father apparently never liked her because of her rebellious personality and stubbornness. When she reached age 15 in 1926, her father arranged a marriage for her but met with her strong resistance, which irreversibly broke their relationship and played a decisive role in shaping her future. Xiao Hong decided to leave home to study at a prestigious girls' boarding school in Harbin. Her exposure to the sophisticated urban environment and snobbish elitism at school cast a cloud of pessimistic doubt over her candid view of human life and her dream of becoming independent. After Xiao Hong started to live together with Xiao Jun in 1932, her father was so outraged that he removed her name from the family genealogy in 1935.

Xiao Jun came from a well-to-do carpenter family in a tiny village in Liaoning, and the only notable feature of the place was its tendency to produce lawless bandits (Wang Ke and Xu 1995: 1–4). As Xiao Jun says of his hometown, "There were two choices for men, to be a soldier or a bandit. People there all worship heroes" (Liang Shanding 1990: 21). Obviously, Xiao Jun was no exception, as he was determined to be militant and heroic. Xiao Jun's father was ill-tempered, abusive, and patriarchal. What hurt Xiao Jun the most was his father's abusive treatment of his mother, who eventually committed suicide by swallowing opium. Xiao Jun found it impossible to forgive his father. However, his father's beating did not make him a cowardly person; on the contrary, Xiao Jun became rebellious, capricious, stubborn, and was never afraid of fighting against any authority. Similar to Xiao Hong, Xiao Jun was fond of his caring grandma, whose skill in storytelling was the earliest cultivation of his literary imagination and the source of his dream to become a Robin Hood–type hero. Xiao Jun joined the army in 1925, but after the Mukden Incident in September 18, 1931, he quit because his commander did not want to fight the Japanese. Instead of realizing his original plan to organize an anti-Japanese guerrilla in Harbin, Xiao Jun began his literary career in 1932 after publishing essays in a newspaper and working as its editor's assistant.

The story of the two Xiaos sounds quite romantic up to this point: as a heroic young man, Xiao Jun rescued the pregnant and abandoned young woman Xiao Hong from an awkward predicament, and both discovered a common passion for writing. However, their literary incomes were never enough, and they were kicked out from one place after another. As described in Xiao Hong's *Market Street* (*Shangshi jie*, 1936), their life in Harbin between 1932 and 1934 focused on meeting daily needs. In 1933, Xiao Hong and Xiao Jun published a co-authored book, *Trudging* (*Bashe*, 1933), which was soon banned by the Japanese authority. Limited in its circulation, the book demonstrated their unusual literary talent in depicting a realistic picture of mundane daily life in Harbin, a struggle for survival from hunger, poverty, and the humiliation caused by foreign invaders. The banning of this book made them realize that it was impossible for them to have the freedom to write as they wished in Northeast China, so they escaped from Harbin and headed south in June 1934.

As they arrived in Shanghai in November 1934, they found it a miracle that Lu Xun welcomed them with open arms. In 20 days, Lu Xun wrote them five letters, generously sending them 20 yuan and inviting them to dinner. Lu Xun obviously found in this young couple different from the arrogant established writers in Shanghai, many of whom he disliked and openly criticized. In his correspondence with the Xiaos, Lu Xun (1981: 12: 562) admitted, "Shanghai is absolutely not a good place. That does not mean we should consider everyone as a fierce wolf or greedy tiger, but on the other hand, we can never open up our hearts immediately to a stranger."

Apparently, with their candid manner and outsiders' naiveté, the Xiaos had won Lu Xun's immediate trust. With Lu Xun's recommendation, Xiao Hong's *The Field of Life and Death* (1935) was initially accepted by the well-known Shenghuo Bookstore, but was later rejected owing to the censors' disapproval (Ding Yanzhao 1991: 102). In March 1935, Lu Xun encouraged Xiao Hong, Xiao Jun, and Ye Zi (one of Lu Xun's protégées) to start the Slave Society and publish a Slave series at their own expense. Ye Zi's collection of short stories, *Harvest* (*Fengshou*), was published immediately in March, Xiao Jun's *Village in August* in July, and Xiao Hong's *The Field of Life and Death* in December of 1935. Lu Xun himself not only spent time editing the Xiaos' manuscripts but also wrote positive prefaces for all three books. "To this day it is difficult to find a relatively lengthy reference to any of these works that does not cite Lu Xun's prefatory comments as proof of the work's significance and literary excellence" (Goldblatt 1985: 208).

After the three "illegally" published books came out, the Xiaos immediately caught critical attention and became known as the representatives from Northeast China as well as Lu Xun's protégés. *The Field of Life and Death* was reprinted more than 20 times after its first printing in 1935, and *Village in August* five times within 1 year (Wang Ke and Xu 1995: 92). Xiao Jun's direct description of the anti-Japanese force and Xiao Hong's feminine portrayal of small-town life in Northeast China "no doubt gave the Shanghai literary arena quite a big new surprise and shock," as Lu Xun's wife Xu Guangping remarks (Wang Guanquan 1981: 17). Furthermore, the success of the Xiaos not only drew the reader's attention to Northeast China but also paved the way for the emergence of Northeastern writers in exile, including Duanmu Hongliang (original name Cao Hanwen).

Some friends made quite a fuss over Xiao Jun's table manners and rough language at social gatherings. Ye Zi called him "A mulin" (Shanghai dialect for "nitwit"), while Huang Yuan (one of Lu Xun's loyal disciples) considered him "weird, not like a writer at all, and absolutely wild" (Wang Ke and Xu 1995: 89). Xiao Jun was not amused at all, but it was Lu Xun who told him not to bother about his "wildness" because Lu Xun appreciated it for challenging the pretentious literati atmosphere in Shanghai. As Lu Xun (1981: 5: 204) wrote in 1932, "When Mr. Hu Shizhi and some others advocated the New Literary Movement, they entered the literary arena with leather shoes. However, the advocates of the current Proletarian movement even dare to break into the literary arena with bare foot." The 1935 literary debut of Xiao Hong and Xiao Jun initiated a new literary trend in promoting anti-Japanese sentiments, challenging the newly established literary canon after the May Fourth, and beginning to unveil the mysterious Northeast China. Their books blew like a gust of wild wind across the literary field.

The Peak Time for Northeastern Writers, 1936–1937

After Xiao Hong and Xiao Jun's overnight success in 1935, the literary field attracted more educated and ambitious young people from Northeast China, among them Duanmu Hongliang. Duanmu was a lover of literature, although his background was quite different from the two Xiaos. He was a country gentleman rather than a country bumpkin, and well educated outside of Northeast China rather than self-taught. Duanmu soon became another leading figure of the Northeastern writers in 1936.

Duanmu's ancestors were among the earliest residential cultivators in the sparsely populated Korchin Banner Plains, and, over 200 years, became powerful local land-owners. Thanks to the collapse of the Manchu Qing dynasty and the scramble for land in Manchuria between Japan and Russia at the turn of the century, as well as to natural disasters, Duanmu witnessed the decline of his family wealth. However, the family's glorious past became a tremendous resource for his writing, and the search for his lost family history is romanticized with nostalgia.

Duanmu's literary imagination was initiated by his father, Cao Zhongyuan, a picky gourmand and an obsessive philanderer. However, Cao had a hobby of collecting books, from the classics to modern political, historical, and literary works, and even some foreign books and radical newspapers. His book collection attracted Duanmu and stimulated his strong desire for knowledge through reading. Before he reached the age of 10, Duanmu began to read as many books as possible, including *Dream of the Red Chamber*, and became a well-known prodigy in the region. When he entered his teens, Duanmu was encouraged by his mother to write a record of the Cao family, in which she was a concubine. Her storytelling gift inspired in Duanmu a sense of the grandeur and intrigues of his family history. Through his narcissistic, semi-autobiographical "repentant aristocrat" characters in his family sagas, such as *The Korchin Banner Plains* (*Keerqinqi caoyuan*, 1939), we can clearly discern his mixed emotions toward his family.

Another source of inspiration for Duanmu is *Dream of the Red Chamber* and its author Cao Xueqin. Many similarities exist between Cao Xueqin and Duanmu Hongliang. Cao's ancestors were originally from Hebei province and moved to Liaoning, where Duanmu's ancestors lived for more than 200 years. Cao's family also became incorporated into the Pure White Banner (*Zhengbaiqi*), the same group as Duanmu's family in the Manchurian Eight Banner system. Cao Xueqin became a model for Duanmu in his domestic novel with nearly epic proportions and a panoramic vision. He not only wanted to follow in Cao's footsteps but also saw himself in Cao. Furthermore, his admiration for Cao can be considered an extended form of ancestral worship, combined with Duanmu's nostalgic sentiments toward the glorious, even imaginary past of his own Cao family. Therefore, Duanmu's initial literary task had two aspects: writing about his parents—his mother's misery and his father's glory—and about himself. In this sense, he is like Xiao Hong, as both started their literary careers by writing about their families, hometowns, and themselves. A third important source of inspiration was Duanmu's emotional tie to the Korchin Banner Plains, and this native soil consciousness had been strengthened and rationalized as he grew up, giving him a sense of "tenaciousness toward life" (H. Kong 2011: 1), melancholy, and solitude that are all reflected in his writings.

In 1928, Duanmu went to Tianjin to attend the prestigious Nankai Boarding School, where he acquired new knowledge and liberal thought, from Shakespeare to Turgenev, from Marx to Nietzsche, from Lu Xun's *Outcry* to Tolstoy's *Resurrection*. Among all subjects, Duanmu liked literature the best. He became a great movie fan and spent much time in theaters, watching mainly foreign films. He was so fascinated by cinematic narrative that he consciously adopted film techniques in some of his later writings. As C. T. Hsia (2004: 349) remarks, Duanmu was "certainly the first Chinese novelist to openly acknowledge his indebtedness to that [cinematic] medium."

After 3 years of urban school life in Tianjin, a more mature Duanmu claimed that he had never missed home as a youngster and considered "home" to be "a narrow cage" or "feudal shackles." Then, the Mukden Incident suddenly changed him: "I was tortured by thoughts of my hometown, especially during sleepless nights" (Zhong Yaoqun 1988: 205). Similar to Xiao Jun's patriotic attitude at that time, an eagerness to recover the lost territory became Duanmu's commitment, and he made up his mind to participate in the resistance. Duanmu became an activist and organized the "League of Anti-Japanese Aggression and National Salvation" with fellow students at Nankai, where his criticism of school officials and Tianjin's mayor resulted in his expulsion from school in 1931.

In March 1932, Duanmu joined the special students unit in the National Army in Chicheng city and traveled throughout the Hebei and Shanxi provinces to promote the war of resistance. Duanmu only stayed in the troop for 3–4 months, but, as he admitted, this short but exciting period of army life added an authentic dimension to his fictional repertoire. One of his best short stories, "The Faraway Wind and Sand" ("*Yaoyuan de fengsha,*" 1936), captures his military life. His familiarity with the army is also evident in works such as "Snail Valley" (*Luosi gu,* 1938).

In the fall of 1932, Duanmu was admitted to the Department of History at Tsinghua University, where he actively participated in activities of the League of Left-wing Writers, an organization more political than literary, as it advocated that literature and art be totally devoted to a struggle of "victory or death" (Tang Tao 1979: 2: 11). In August 1933, the police rounded up 19 league members at a secret meeting, but Duanmu happened to be absent and left for Tianjin the next day, thus ending his studies at Tsinghua. He felt frustrated and lost in Tianjin: "I lay on the bed like a corpse. ... I didn't know if I could live on" (Duanmu 1980: 106).

During this agonizing period, Duanmu received a letter from Lu Xun, which affected his life greatly:

> This letter made me feel as if I had suddenly seen my lover with whom I had lost touch for years. It seemed that something I had forgotten was [suddenly] recalled. ... Like a ray of sunshine, Lu Hsün [Xun]'s voice beckoned me, and I crawled through the gate of darkness. Like a tide, I could not stop myself and wrote without stop until I finished *The Korchin Banner Plains.* That set my literary career on its right course. (C. T. Hsia 2004: 344)

Duanmu may have exaggerated Lu Xun's power in pushing him onto the literary path, but it was similar to the situation when Xiao Jun and Xiao Hong received their first letter from Lu Xun in 1934. Regardless, within 4 months in 1933, Duanmu finished *The Korchin Banner Plains,* the significance of which was reconfirmed 50 years later: "There have been no other modern Chinese novelists who completed at twenty-one a novel as complex and as long as *The Korchin Banner Plains*" (C. T. Hsia 2004: 346).

The Korchin Banner Plains deals mainly with the fictionalized history of Duanmu's family and events of his hometown. This novel was intended as the first volume of a trilogy, but the sequels were never completed, except for five chapters of the second volume written in the 1940s. For Duanmu (1980: 108), "all the characters and stories are based on real identical models in life." However, it took quite a few years before Duanmu could publish the novel. In December 1933, Zheng Zhenduo, who had read manuscript chapters as they were mailed to him, sent Duanmu an enthusiastic letter:

> When the last part of your manuscript arrived, how happy I was. This is the most out-standing long novel of the past decade, I believe. I must try my best to help publish it. If there are any improper parts that need to be taken out, I wonder if you will agree to do so. ... Such a magnificent work makes me too excited to sleep. The dialogues are especially natural and beautiful. The characterization is profound [and] ... the language used in conversation by the characters in the novel is the real language of the common people. After its publication, I can predict that it will astonish its readers. (Kong 1998: 34)

Zheng's letter sounds very supportive, but the novel was not published until 6 years later. One reason was that Duanmu stubbornly refused Zheng's suggestion to take out "improper parts."

In the meantime, Duanmu came to Shanghai in 1936 and finished his second novel, *The Sea of Earth* (*Dadi de hai*, 1936), in 5 months. He assumed that editors would accept his work right away, so he mailed the manuscript directly to *Writers* (*Zuojia*), a well-known literary journal, without any sponsor's recommendation. The manuscript was returned to him immediately, and apparently was not even read. Angry and disappointed at the elitist literary field, Duanmu wrote to Lu Xun in July 1936 and enclosed two chapters of *The Sea of Earth*. Lu Xun replied promptly and asked for the entire manuscript.

After reading the novel, Lu Xun wrote to say that the novel was good, but he suggested that Duanmu should submit short stories because it was too difficult to publish a novel. Duanmu followed the advice and sent "The Sorrows of Egret Lake" ("*Ciluhu de youyu*") to Zheng Zhenduo, through whose recommendation the story was published in *Literature* (*Wenxue*) in August 1936 and became Duanmu's first publication in a reputable journal. In the meantime, he sent another story to Lu Xun, who thought it was "a little bit too depressing" (Lu Xun 13: 684). However, Lu Xun still recommended the story to *Writers*, which published it in October 1936. Unfortunately, Lu Xun passed away in October 1936, but Duanmu's brief connection with him was sufficient for the literary world. Soon, Lu Xun's disciple Hu Feng became Duanmu's new patron and wrote a positive review of "The Sorrows of Egret Lake," in which he praised the story as "an invaluable harvest from our literary creation of the year" (H. Kong 2011: 2). Hu helped Duanmu publish *The Sea of Earth*, introduced him to Mao Dun, and invited Duanmu to join the editorial board of *July* (*Qiyue*), along with Xiao Jun and Xiao Hong.

During Duanmu's stay in Shanghai between January 1936 and September 1937, Mao Dun often gave him helpful suggestions. For instance, he suggested that Duanmu listen to *pingtan* (storytelling with singing in Suzhou dialect) to become familiar with some southern dialects, and this turned out to be useful in Duanmu's later works. A lover of dialects and local culture, Duanmu used southern dialects to create a special polyphonic environment for his stories, such as "Snake Swallower" ("*Tun she'er*," 1937) and "Nocturne in March" ("*Sanyue yequ*," 1937), and his linguistic talent was unique among his Northeastern counterparts. It was also Mao Dun who finally helped Duanmu get *The Korchin Banner Plains* published in 1939.

After 1936, Duanmu Hongliang, Xiao Hong, and Xiao Jun were called "northeastern writers in exile," who brought "strangers' flavors" and "freshness" to the literary field and made 1936 a year of "big literary harvest" in Hu Feng's judgment (H. Kong 2011: 2). Their works successfully directed attention to Northeast China, further promoted patriotic sentiments, and opened up a new chapter in modern Chinese literary history in which northeastern literature was integrated into national literature.

Ideological Clash and Narcissistic Nostalgia, 1938–1945

The year 1938 was a turning point for Duanmu, the two Xiaos, and other Northeastern writers in exile for they were all facing a challenging dilemma: to maintain their individual voices or to merge them into the revolutionary mainstream after the full-scale

Sino-Japanese War started. In January, Duanmu and the two Xiaos, along with other left-wing writers, were invited to teach at the National Revolutionary University in Linfen, Shanxi. Soon after they arrived at Linfen, the two Xiaos had a heated debate over whether Xiao Jun should stay on as a writer or go directly to fight the Japanese at the front. Xiao Hong insisted that, as a writer, Xiao Jun should use a pen, not a gun, to express his patriotic feeling and serve the war. It would be worthless and wasteful, she felt strongly, if a talented writer such as Xiao Jun died in the battlefield. However, Xiao Jun's pride kept him from listening to her. In fact, the growing emotional gap between them became obvious. In February 1938, Xiao Jun left the school and planned to join the guerrillas to fight the Japanese army. However, he returned from his first brief trip to the Communist base in Yan'an and appeared in Xi'an in late February. In Xi'an, Xiao Jun's rudeness and infidelity made Xiao Hong finally decide to leave him and marry Duanmu, even though she was pregnant with Xiao Jun's child and cherished her feelings toward Xiao Jun until her death.

Despite the disapproval of their friends, Xiao Hong at last made up her mind to travel to Wuhan with Duanmu in April 1938, rather than to Yan'an with Xiao Jun. This became a major reason why Duanmu and Xiao Hong were alienated by their fellow writers who went to Yan'an, and why both their literary works were neglected in mainland China until the 1980s. As Ding Ling remarked in the wartime, Duanmu "was just different" and "how could I have anything in common with him?" (H. Kong 1998: 43); in her memorial essay for Xiao Hong, Ding Ling expressed her regret that she "didn't interfere enough in helping change her lifestyle" (Wang Guanquan 1981: 27). Duanmu was thus viewed by many left-wing writers as a "Satanic" figure who had led vulnerable Xiao Hong astray from the revolution.

On the other hand, Xiao Jun and most of his fellow Northeastern writers, such as Shu Qun, Luo Feng, and Bai Lang, chose to go to Yan'an with their enthusiasm for the revolution. Soon after they arrived there separately in September 1941, Xiao Jun started to organize a "September Eighteenth Literary Society." However, this society was almost immediately ordered to disband, as it presented a potential danger of subversive "regionalism" and "factionalism" to the revolutionary cause (Shen Weiwei 1992: 43–44). Its dismissal signaled a warning to anyone who refused to conform to the Communist authorities, and reaffirmed that Yan'an had no freedom of speech. No writers in Yan'an were allowed to exist as a separate group or faction, and it meant that individuality in literature was not allowed when it differed from Party ideology.

While most of the others obediently gave up their individuality, Xiao Jun stubbornly insisted on having his voice heard. He ignored the warning signals and persisted in his carefree or even reckless behavior. One instance was when Xiao Jun openly expressed his sympathy toward Wang Shiwei, whose articles exposing the dark side of Yan'an had outraged Mao and were partially responsible for the 1942 launch of the Rectification Movement aiming at intellectuals in Yan'an. When Wang Shiwei was not allowed to defend himself, Xiao Jun questioned the format of mass criticism and the unfair treatment of Wang. Xiao Jun immediately became a target himself and was ordered to present self-criticism at a rally of 2,000 people. Xiao Jun's nonchalant behavior, anarchist attitudes, and intractable personality were never welcomed by the Communist authorities. After 1938, Xiao Jun remained a "traveler" without a destination and could hardly write anything significant except the first two parts of his most ambitious novel, *The Third Generation* (*Disandai*).

In contrast, Xiao Hong and Duanmu remained prolific and further developed their literary styles, even though they were constantly on the move. Xiao Hong published her best novel, *Tales of Hulan River* (1941); a collection of short stories, *A Cry in the Wilderness* (*Kuangye de huhan*, 1940); two collections of prose essays, *In Memory of Mr. Lu Xun* (*Huiyi Lu Xun xiansheng*, 1940) and *Prose Writings of Xiao Hong* (*Xiao Hong sanwen*, 1940); in addition to her satirical novel, *Ma Bole* (1941), published in an incomplete form. Duanmu published three novels: *The Korchin Banner Plains*, *The Great River* (*Dajiang*, 1939), and *Sidelight of the New Capital* (*Xindu huaxu*, 1940); two incomplete novels, *The Great Era* (*Dashidai*, 1941) and volume two of *The Korchin Banner Plains* (1943); as well as a novella, many short stories, and plays. Both writers obviously reached the peak of their literary creativity and demonstrated their mastery of a variety of genres and styles.

Xiao Hong's sudden death in Hong Kong from "a throat infection and other complications arising from advanced pulmonary tuberculosis and other debilitating illnesses" (Goldblatt 1976: 115) in 1942 not only cast a lasting shadow over the introverted Duanmu but also drastically changed his writing style. The first two short stories published in 1942, after Duanmu had moved to Southwest China, were "The First Kiss" (*"Chuwen"*) and "Early Spring" (*"Zaochun"*). It is no mere coincidence that these two semi-autobiographical stories deal with the complex psychological moods of adolescent sexual dreams and desires in a retrospective mode. The strong confessional tone of the first-person narrators in both stories convinces the reader that Duanmu was deeply immersed in painful and remorseful memories of his past. His allegorical story "Osprey Village" (*"Diao'e bao,"* 1942) may be also interpreted as his personal response to the unfair treatment from his fellow writers and a plea for understanding. In the story, Shilong "was incorrigibly lazy and, apparently, worthless. He had no talent for being good company or for getting into people's good graces: he was capable neither of bringing a smile to their faces nor of forcing one onto his own" (Duanmu 1988: 285). Shilong was wronged by his fellow villagers because he was different; however, he still sacrificed his life in a vain attempt to challenge the 1,000-year-old custom of the village in order to awaken the fellow villagers. In these stories, Duanmu expresses his personal feelings—confession, remorse, and anger—rather than patriotic concerns. This actually signals his shift from an "obsession with China" to that with the self in the 1940s, and brings his literary style closer to Xiao Hong's.

From 1943 to 1945, Duanmu published 13 short stories in total, and attempted to complete volume two of *The Korchin Banner Plains*. However, he was unable to continue the grand-epic style he had developed in the 1930s due to his stylistic shift in the 1940s. Unlike his pre-1942 corpus, most of his fiction during this later period was either about historical figures from regional legends or was adapted from Greek mythology. They were a continuation of stories such as "The

First Kiss" and "Early Spring" in terms of a thematic concern with nostalgia and the emotional loss of the traumatized self. Obviously, Duanmu was experimenting with a new style modeled on self-consciousness and stream of consciousness in a somewhat pessimistic and remorseful tone. His new style is more modernist than realist. All his writings of this period were about such universal human concerns as good and evil, or the self and the other, which allowed him to maintain a distance from, if not to transcend, contemporary issues.

The Significance of Northeastern Writers

Xiao Hong, Xiao Jun, and Duanmu Hongliang, along with several others, were called "Northeastern writers in exile" after 1936, and in 1951 the term "Northeastern writers group" (*dongbei zuojia qun*) was first used by literary historian Wang Yao (1982: 291). It is convenient to group the Northeastern writers together for analysis in the literary history since they all emerged around 1936. And the "group" as anti-Japanese writers was soon welcomed by the left-wing writers. Although readers may form a misunderstanding of or even underestimate their literary contributions, these writers never really shared overriding literary or aesthetic principles. Therefore, the term "group" refers to a political phenomenon rather than a literary school.

The only common contribution of this group is their literary presentation of the multiple aspects of the natural/human environments in Northeast China to the world for the first time. Particularly their native soil flavor and panoramic description of Northeastern landscape and culture brought in refreshing perspectives and further cultivated patriotism among general readers beyond Northeast China. Xiao Hong, Duanmu, and Xiao Jun best represent the group and were the most idiosyncratic writers at the time. Significantly, Xiao Jun's novel *Village in August*, translated by Edgar Snow and published by Smith & Durrell in the United States in 1942, was the first English translation of a modern Chinese novel in the West. Within 2 years, this novel was printed three times by the World Publishing House in the United States, and Collins Publishing House also published this translation in London and Australia. All this demonstrated the urgent demand and warm welcome of this "China's Great War Novel" (Xiao Jun 1944: cover) during World War II.

Whereas Xiao Hong is concerned more with human existentialistic conditions, especially women caught in the vicious cycle of life and death, than with the Anti-Japanese War, her attention goes beyond gender and class issues. Her short story "Hands" ("*Shou*," 1936) exposes the snobbishness of the elite education and the discrimination against the poor at school, but actually also touches upon a fundamental and universal problem—how to accept and tolerate differences. The story describes how Wang Yaming, whose father is a less privileged dye-factory owner, faces discrimination from fellow students, teachers, school principal, as well as dorm supervisors and the school doorman, simply due to the dark color of her hands, which is an indicator of her difference. What Xiao Hong wants to criticize is the education system that aims at transforming different students into a uniformed "color," so her story goes beyond class and poverty issues.

Duanmu's attention to artistic style and aesthetic harmony is evident in his early fiction with a left-wing tendency. For instance, "The Sorrows of Egret Lake" centers on the most common left-wing theme in the 1930s: poverty, hunger, and growing class conflicts in the countryside. However, the difference here is that the story opens with a strong native soil flavor: natural imagery that only exists in traditional Chinese poetry and paintings (e.g., radiating reflections of the lake, the moonlight, foggy atmosphere, and chirping insects) introduces readers to a harmonious world of human feelings and natural surroundings. When this harmony is suddenly interrupted by two bean thieves, mother and daughter, at midnight, it leads to a sense of awkwardness, regret, and embarrassment for the bean field guards, as well as the reader. However, the contrast between the beauty of natural imagery and the ugliness of human society reaches a new compromise at the end of the story, where sympathy, understanding, and even mutual help exist between the field guards and the thieves. The story is covered by a foggy layer of melancholy, which binds human feelings and the natural surroundings together in a single inextricable entity. The theme of the story seems hidden behind the foggy veil, which gives the reader plenty to ponder on. No wonder Hu Feng praises this story as "a piece of lyrical music" (H. Kong 2011: 2).

Duanmu's more significant contribution is his narrative style. *The Korchin Banner Plains* is an epic novel of regional nativism and a family saga of more than 200 years. The first three chapters started with legends about the history and origin of the region—a group of migrants escaped from a flood back home and moved into the area, becoming the pioneers of the region—and the framework resembles the Biblical Genesis. This epic novel is innovative and distinguishes Duanmu from his contemporaries, with the only exception of Li Jieren, whose trilogy about Chengdu—*Ripples on Dead Water* (1936), *Before the Tempest* (1936), and *The Great Wave* (*Dabo*, 1937)—also contains a strong sense of history but is set in a city rather than the grassland. The feature that distinguishes Duanmu most is nativism, which fills the novel with strong nostalgic sentiments and builds up the interdependence between nature and humans. Duanmu elevates the role of natural landscape, previously idyllic yet unknown, to that of rejuvenation. The very wildness of the landscape is a fundamental force in the making of history, which provides a new vision to transcend the mundane world. Decades later, his legacy is carried on in works such as Mo Yan's *Red Sorghum* (1988) and Lin Yaode's *1947—Lilium Formosanum* (*1947 gaosha baihe*, 1990). Mo Yan not only emphasizes the dynamic power of the wildness as Duanmu did, but also raises the status of natural products, such as red sorghum, to spiritual heights, because his fiction has transformed red sorghum into a spirit. Mo Yan's praise of the wine god is therefore also a praise of the spirit of freedom, which liberates people from man-made restrictions. Similar to the epic beginning of Duanmu's *The Korchin*

Banners Plains, Lin Yaode's *1947 – Lilium Formosanum* narrates the splendid genesis of Taiwan from a mystical viewpoint.

Both Xiao Hong and Duanmu were talented in painting, which gave them a strong sense of colors and of perspectives, and hence their narratives of landscape and space arrangements are visually powerful. In Duanmu's stories, some episodes connecting sections are presented by way of cinematic montages, and he pays attention to sounds and dialects so that his narratives often offer a kind of acoustic pleasure derived from words and their polyphonic effects. After 1938, Duanmu's strong feelings for his lost native place were transformed into a desire to search for the lost self and forgotten past in the 1940s, as in short stories "The First Kiss" and "Early Spring." His literary attention was shifted from Northeast China to Shanghai, Hong Kong, and Southwest China, and his artistic forms from external natural environments to internal human minds with nuance and subtlety. His narrative style became more mature and sophisticated than before.

Similarly, Xiao Hong's *Tales of Hulan River* depicts the small town life near Harbin in vivid detail. Different from her earlier novel *The Field of Life and Death*, this later novel features a narrative voice of the growing young girl, who is a curious observer and naïve witness. The cold and desolate small town provides a background for the young girl to understand society and humanity, as reflected in so many poor residents' tragic stories. Xiao Hong surpasses her contemporaries by distancing herself from current political issues with her literary depiction and philosophical contemplation on the meanings of life and death, which endows her novel with a unique elegiac style.

Duanmu Hongliang, Xiao Hong, and Xiao Jun form a literary trio whose remarkable depictions of Northeastern customs, dialects, legends, religions, culture, and history, and whose sufferings of homesickness and homelessness during their wanderings throughout the wartime, demonstrate a special passion for literature. Obviously, such a passion greatly affected the literary themes, geopolitical consciousness, and artistic styles in their writings. Their fictional worlds not only project their visions of the vast Northeastern plains, the primitive rural life, and the lost past, but also determine the manner in which they express their thoughts, frustrations, and hopes. All this contributes to the significance of the Northeastern writers during the Anti-Japanese War. Their literary works and aesthetic principles have left strong marks in modern Chinese literature, and their influences have gone beyond the regional and national borders. Even today, their romantic and liberal lifestyle and creative writings still attract attention and stimulate imagination. Right after *Xiao Hong* (dir. Huo Jianqi, 2012), a beautifully shot biographical film, *The Golden Era* (*Huangjin shidai*, 2014), which comes from the Hong Kong filmmaker Ann Hui (Xu Anhua), portrays all three Northeastern writers in exile, together with other related writers during the war. These new cinematic representations of the Northeastern writers in exile not only encourage more young readers to explore their literary works and their romantic lives, but also reconfirm an important fact—that people's interest in these writers and their eventful times will never die.

REFERENCES

Ding, Yanzhao 丁言昭.1991. *Xiao Hong zhuan* 蕭紅傳 (A biography of Xiao Hong). Taipei: Yechiang.

Duanmu, Hongliang 端木蕻良. 1980. *Houniao zhiyu* 火鳥之羽 (Phoenix feather). Hong Kong: Xianggang wenxue yanjiushe.

Duanmu, Hongliang. 1988. *Red Night*. Trans Howard Goldblatt. Beijing: Panda Books.

Goldblatt, Howard. 1976. *Hsiao Hung*. Boston: Twayne.

Goldblatt, Howard. 1985. "Lu Xun and Patterns of Literary Sponsorship." In *Lu Xun and His Legacy*. Edited by Lee, Leo Ou-fan. Berkeley: University of California Press. 199–215.

Hsia, C. T. 2004. *C. T. Hsia on Chinese Literature*. New York: Columbia University Press.

Kong, Haili. 1998. "What Did Literary Patronage Mean to an Individualistic Writer in the 1930s: The Case of Duanmu Hongliang." *Journal of Modern Literature in Chinese*, 2.1: 31–51.

Kong, Haili 孔海立. 2011. *Duanmu Hongliang zhuan* 端木蕻良传 (Life of Duanmu Hongliang). Shanghai: Fudan daxue chubanshe.

Liang, Shanding 梁山丁. 1990. *Xiao Jun jinian ji* 蕭軍紀念集 (Collection of memorial essays on Xiao Jun). Shenyang: Chunfeng wenyi chubanshe.

Lu, Xun 魯迅. 1981. *Lu Xun Quanji* 魯迅全集 (Complete works of Lu Xun). 16 vols. Beijing: Renmin wenxue chubanshe.

Shen, Weiwei 沈衛威. 1992. *Dongbei liuwang wenxueshi lun* 東北流亡文學史論 (A history of the exile Northeastern literature). Zhengzhou: Henan renmin chubanshe.

Tang, Tao 唐弢. 1979. *Zhongguo xiandai wenxue shi* 中國現代文學史 (A history of modern Chinese literature). 3 vols. Beijing: Renmin wenxue chubanshe.

Wang, Guanquan 王觀泉. Ed. 1981. *Huainian Xiao Hong* 懷念蕭紅 (In memory of Xiao Hong). Harbin: Heilongjiang remnin chubanshe.

Wang, Ke 王科 and Xu Sai 徐塞. 1995. *Xiao Jun pingzhuan* 蕭軍評傳 (Studies of Xiao Jun). Chongqing: Chongqing chubanshe.

Wang, Yao 王瑤. 1982. *Zhongguo xin wenxue shiliao* 中國新文學史稿 (A draft history of new Chinese literature). Revised edition. 2 vols. Shanghai: Shanghai wenyi chubanshe.

Xiao, 1944. *Village in August*. Trans. Edgar Snow. New York: World Publishing Co.

Zhong, Yaoqun 鍾耀群. Ed. 1988. *Duanmu Hongliang* 端木蕻良. Hong Kong: Sanlian shudian.

20

Writing Cities

Weijie Song

The tension and connection between the city and the country constitute one of the major themes in modern Chinese literature. Because the majority of the Chinese population is peasants and farmers, modern Chinese literature is predominantly out-lined and defined by rural and regional themes where the idea of "native soil" becomes a significant allegory to represent the Chinese nation-state. Nevertheless, as Joseph Esherick (2000: ix) points out, "with Chinese cities entering the new millennium as vibrant centers of economic, social, and cultural change, it is time to seek the origins of this renewed urban vitality by looking back to the transformation of urban space and society in the first half of the twentieth century." Yingjin Zhang (1996: xvii) calls attention to the recurrent city/country antithesis "deeply ingrained in the mentality of modern Chinese writers," and explores the spatial, temporal, and gender configurations and changes in modern Beijing and Shanghai. Leo Lee (1999: xi) challenges the Chinese scholarship in Western academia that is "preoccupied with rural villages" and examines Shanghai's literary sensibility, cultural cartography, modern consciousness, and cosmopolitan imagination. Recently, mainland Chinese scholars (Zhang Hongsheng 2007; Yang Jianlong 2013) have observed that the discursive predominance of twentieth-century revolution and enlightenment defines and determines the nature of modern Chinese literature; that is, peasants and villagers become the dominant images, if not stereotypes, of modern Chinese literary narratives. However, the ongoing modernization process, the rapid development of globalization, and the recent colossal growth of urbanization, particularly in mainland China since the 1990s, among other factors, have changed the ratio, size, and scope of rural and urban population as well as the relation between infrastructure and superstructure, and have

A Companion to Modern Chinese Literature, First Edition. Edited by Yingjin Zhang.
© 2016 John Wiley & Sons, Ltd. Published 2016 by John Wiley & Sons, Ltd.

therefore redefined the literary liaison between the country and the city, and witnessed the booming of literature and literary studies of the cities at the turn of the twentieth-first century.

It is worth noting that *"chengshi wenxue"* (urban literature) is a broad, loosely defined subgenre and literary keyword. The terms *"cheng"* (city, wall), *"shi"* (city, market), *"chengshi"* (city), and *"dushi"* (metropolis) refer to a set of multiple meanings ranging from county administrative centers, small market towns, midsized cities, and large capitals, to major metropolises (including treaty ports and commercial manufacturing centers) in terms of size, population, function, administration, and governance (Y. Zhang 1996: 6–7). *Chengshi wenxue* has also been alternatively mixed with *dushi wenxue* in the heated debates on the rise of literary mappings of Chinese cities and metropolises since the 1990s. Furthermore, the Chinese term *"chengshi wenxue"* vaguely indicates both "cities in literature" and "literature in cities," in which the cities serve as geographical backgrounds, cultural settings, or the subject matter for literary imagination and aesthetical/political investigation. Scholarships of urban literature have focused on, among others, the liaisons between the city and the people (Zhao Yuan 1991); the rise and fall of literary schools and narrative modes (Yan Jiayan 1989; Wu Fuhui 1995; Yang Yi 2003; D. Wang 2006); the configurations of time, space, and gender in urban milieu (Y. Zhang 1996); the new urban culture and alternative modernity in wartime China (L. Lee 1999; Shih 2001); urban imagination and cultural memory (Chen Pingyuan 2008); multimedia, urbanism, and global transformation in Maoist and post-Maoist China (Luo Gang 2006; Braester 2010; Visser 2010); as well as feelings, emotions, and literary topography (W. Song 2016).

This chapter charts literary imaginations and representations of major cities in the Chinese-speaking world from the late nineteenth century to the present. The main issues are literary modernity, urban awareness, historical consciousness, individual/collective memories, and nationalist perceptions regarding the old and new capital, Beijing; the semi-colonial metropolis and socialist Shanghai and its remnants; the traumatized and aloof Nanjing; the abandoned capital, Xi'an; Taipei under Japanese colonial rule and the subsequent Nationalist Party's dominance; and Hong Kong from a British Crown Colony to a Special Administrative Region of China.

Urban Literature in Late Qing and Republican China

Since the Opium War (1840–1842), the opening and growth of Chinese treaty ports to foreign trades brought to light the contacts, confrontations, and juxtapositions of indigenous and foreign cultures in cities such as Shanghai, Ningbo, Hankou (Hankow), Guangzhou (Canton), Shantou (Swatow), Fuzhou (Foochow), Xiamen (Amoy), Tianjin, and Harbin. Shanghai has become the foremost "modern" city and has provided a dynamic context for the development of urban narratives. Han Bangqing's *The Sing-Song Girls of Shanghai* (*Haishanghua liezhuan*, 1892–1894; English, 2005) may well manifest the early achievements of depicting and envisioning a modernized Chinese city in terms of persons and things, emotions and morality, amusement and sorrow, and regional linguistic consciousness (Wu dialect) in the *fin-de-siècle* Shanghai. David Wang (1997: 89–90) observes that Han's urban narrative provides a panoramic portrait of lust, desire, romantic liaisons, and moral dilemma among two dozen courtesans and their male patrons in different social positions in the Shanghai pleasure quarters during the last decades of the nineteenth century, and inquires into the ethical and psychological realities in its pioneering infusion of modernist sensibilities into the traditional genre of courtesan novels.

If Han's tedious and repetitive representation of life and desire in the courtesan house demonstrates an internalized view of the human bondage and the everlasting feelings in the urban milieu, then a grand and transnational "China Dream," or a prolonged fantasy that haunts the Chinese mind, focuses on an imagined World Expo to be held in Shanghai in the paper world. Liang Qichao's *The Future of New China* (*Xin Zhongguo weilai ji*, 1902), Wu Jianren's *The New Story of the Stone* (1905), and Lu Shi'e's *New China* (*Xin Zhongguo*, 1910) imagine and invent scenes about national exhibitions and World Expo, envisioning a modern Shanghai and a strong China standing proudly in the ranks of nation-states. Yet, Lu's utopian narrative suddenly comes into an end when the protagonist wakes up from his daydreaming.

"The ten miles of foreign zone" (*shili yangchang*) and the greater Shanghai glamour and lure provide a fertile land for literary production and consumption, in which popular literature, particularly the butterfly school, emerged and prevailed, and extended from Shanghai and its nearby cities to Beijing and Tianjin. Authors such as Bao Tianxiao, Xu Zhenya, Zhou Shoujuan, Chen Dieyi, and Qin Shouou capture daily scenes, write sentimental stories, and produce popular romance in the changing urban environment. One outstanding writer in this group is Zhang Henshui, arguably the most prolific and popular writer in the first half of the twentieth century, who contributed a genealogy of literary mappings of Shanghai, Nanjing, Xi'an, Chongqing, and, most significantly, Republican Beijing. Zhang's literary topography of modern Beijing—mostly fiction serialized in literature supplements of newspapers and later published as best sellers in book form—captures the fleeting and ephemeral moments in Beijing's everyday life, on the one hand, and seizes the everlasting joys and griefs in the transitional city, on the other hand. Zhang's urban novels became enormously popular between the 1920s and the 1930s and created what I shall call a modern Beijing in the narratives of snapshots and manners (W. Song 2016). The finest achievements of this kind are represented in Zhang Henshui's popular romances—*Unofficial History of Beijing* (*Chunming waishi*, 1924–1929), *Grand Old Family* (*Jinfen shijia*, 1926–1932), *Fate in Tears and Laughter* (1929–1930), and *Deep Darkness of the Night* (Ye shenchen, 1937–1938). From the material culture of everyday life to the cultural debates of the time, from family sagas to street gossip, from warlords' cruelty to chivalric assassination, Zhang has produced not only "fiction for comfort" (Link 1981: 9) and satisfied the demands of the literature market, but he has also registered both the transient and transitional symptoms and the long-lasting pains and sorrows in Republican Beijing (McClellan 2005). Mapping Beijing from the affective, poetic, sonic, spatial, and ethnographic perspectives, Zhang's urban romance provides a sophisticated cityscape in a time when tradition and modernity meet and compete, and personal, familial, social, and national relations are redefined (see Chapter 15 by Yi Zheng).

The 1930s witnessed a peak decade of urban literature in Republican China. Ba Jin's *Family* (serialized in 1931–1932) sets the city of Chengdu as the battlefield between the feudalist authority and the young rebel generation, and launches a severe attack on the "cannibalistic" nature of the Confucian family ethics and hierarchy. Mao Dun's magnum opus *Midnight* (1933), an ambitious and naturalist/realist Shanghai epic, depicts the financial and social crisis, the defeat of Chinese nationalist industries by foreign capitalist exploitation, the struggles of the working class, and the labyrinth of money and desire. A milestone in leftist and revolutionary literature, *Midnight* constructs a profound connection between modern history and class-consciousness in terms of Chinese revolution and urban modernity. Cao Yu, a leading dramatist hailed as "China's Ibsen" (X. Chen 2010: 14), chose Tianjin, Shanghai, and Beijing, respectively, for his *Thunderstorm* (1933), *Sunrise* (*Richu*, 1936), and *Peking Man* (*Beijing ren*, 1940), to cope with the moral degeneration, the corruption of patriarchy, and the destruction of family in the hostile and semi-colonial, semi-feudalist cities.

The fierce debates between the Beijing School and the Shanghai School in the 1930s highlight the contradictory and competitive understanding of Chinese urban culture. The Shanghai writers include Shi Zhecun, Liu Na'ou, Mu Shiying (all three also known as New Sensationalists), Shao Xunmei, Ye Lingfeng, Zhang Ziping, and Du Heng. The Beijing writers consist of Shen Congwen, Zhou Zuoren, Fei Ming, Li Jianwu, Zhang Tianyi, Zhu Guanqian, Xiao Qian, Lu Fen (Shi Tuo), Ling Shuhua, Yang Jiang, and Lin Huiyin. Shanghai modernity is measured by speed, height, and brightness, as conveyed by the neon sign "light, heat, power," which starts Mao Dun's tour de force of Shanghai, *Midnight*. The imagery of Beijing, however, is dominated by ancient city walls, gate towers, the imperial palaces, historical relics, idyllic scenes, and slow yet steady camels, all enhancing a landscape of harmony and tranquility unfolding in a timeless capital. Beijing is eulogized as authentically Chinese, profoundly cultural and aesthetic, rooted in tradition, elegant, serene, and grand (W. Song 2014). In contrast, Shanghai is stereotyped as a demonic metropolis (*modu*), an antithesis of Beijing, as well as an anti-urban non-city. Yingjin Zhang (1996: 15–16) argues that the Beijing–Shanghai opposition is marked by strong emotional attachments that associate Beijing with a native land and cultural heritage and configure Shanghai as a commercial center, a betrayal of ancestral roots. Shu-mei Shih (2001: 175–7) and Robin Visser (2010: 12–13) point out that this anti-urban discourse entertained by May Fourth intellectuals is informed by their anti-imperial and anticolonial cultural standpoint.

On the eve of the Second Sino-Japanese War, Lao She, a preeminent Beijing native writer and Manchu bannerman, presented a set of city-texts witnessing the charming legacy of old Beijing and the problematic encroachment of modernity. His critically acclaimed novel *Rickshaw Boy* (*Luotuo Xiangzi*, 1937), "the finest modern Chinese novel up to that time" (C. T. Hsia 1999: 187), deploys both a "fictional realism" (D. Wang 1992) and a psychological realism (L. Liu 1995) to portray the fate and failure of rickshaw puller Xiangzi, an orphan of Beijing. From Lao She's point of view, Xiangzi attempts to construct a utopian body contact or corporeal linkage with Beijing, yet ends up as a walking beast in the unfathomable darkness of the city. Republican Beijing is configured as the locus of tears and laughter and the struggling site of emotional attachment and detachment. *Rickshaw Boy* demonstrates the metamorphosis of the symbolically homeless orphan who encounters a complete process of dream-making and dream-waking irony in Lao She's literary topography of Xiangzi's urban desires.

During the Second Sino-Japanese war and the Chinese civil war, Eileen Chang appeared as a phenomenal literary legend in wartime Shanghai. Her urban narratives locate at the nexus of a "contrast in de-cadence" (*cenci de duizhao*), a technique of popular fiction, an aesthetics of desolation, as well as a strategy of romancing the ordinary in tumultuous times (L. Lee 1999: 283). Chang's "Blockade" (1943) captures the ambivalent amorous encounter between a female English instructor and a married male accountant trapped in a tramcar in Shanghai during the Japanese occupation. Her novella "The Golden Cangue" (1943), hailed as a masterpiece of all times, portrays the abnormal state of mind of a woman, Cao Qiqiao, desperately confined in the hostile and stressful family hierarchy within a transitional modern Shanghai. Her "Red Rose, White Rose" ("*Hong meigui yu bai meigui*," 1944) provides a nuanced portrait of subtle feelings, confusing romances, calculation, and cynicism firmly situated in an indifferent urban milieu (R. Chow 1999). "Love in a Fallen City" (1943), one of her most popular and representative works, tells a tale of twin cities—Shanghai and Hong Kong—by famously exemplifying the uneven contrast of romance and warfare, twisted love/marriage, and unexpected destruction and catastrophe in her urban world, which is at times enchanting and at times disenchanting.

Other major urban literature in the 1940s includes Qin Shouou's *Begonia* (*Qiuhaitang*, serialized in 1941–1942, the book in 1943), arguably the most popular Shanghai comedy–tragedy about the fate of local opera singers, which established Qin as a leading butterfly writer during the war. Ba Jin's *Cold Nights* (*Hanye*, 1947) captures the melancholia and depression of humble Chinese intellectuals in Chongqing against the great backdrop of the Japanese invasion of China. Lao She also contributes a wartime epic, *Four Generations under One Roof* (*Sishi tongtang*, 1944–1950), which discloses an affective mapping of military violence, family degeneration, urban misery, and national suffering in wartime Beijing, a wounded city under Japanese rule. Wartime feelings, such as nostalgia, mourning, shame, anger, and hatred, mediate the new and modern interactions of family and city, self and society, individual and nation-state, and urban history and traumatic memory in Lao She's wartime atlas of emotions. The Little Sheepfold Lane, a representative alleyway in Beijing, and other real and fictional places and spaces, ranging from a small clandestine room in a family house to the gigantic Tiananmen Square in the heart of the city, display the urban "structure of feelings" and cultural memories shaped by war and violence and invoke a dialectics of pain and catharsis, trauma and redemption, nostalgia and longing, loss and epiphany, and melancholy and hope: modern emotional negotiations between private obsession and public passion, personal desire and collective guilt, and quasi-loyalist affection and nationalist sentiment.

Mapping Mainland Cities after 1949

During the Maoist era from the 17-year period to the Cultural Revolution, the anti-urban bias of Mao's peasant-based Communist revolution "tended to relegate urban history to a subordinate role in the grand narrative of modern China" (Esherick 2000: ix). In the landscape of mainstream socialist realist literature, urban writings were sporadic, marginal, and mainly centered on industrial themes. The cities must undergo a socialist remodeling and reconstruction. Xiao Yemu's short story "Between Husband and Wife" (1950) touches upon the sensitive gap between the country and the city: the wife, from a worker–farmer background, feels discomfort and distress after she is settled in Beijing to reunite with her husband, an intellectual cadre with urban *petit bourgeois* viewpoints and tastes. The severe attack on Xiao's Beijing story set the basic tone for the Maoist urban writing: literature and art should serve workers, peasants, soldiers—rather than exploiters and oppressors—after Mao's Yan'an spirit entered Chinese cities.

Lao She's *Dragon Beard Ditch* (*Longxu gou*, 1951; English, 1956) unveils an intriguing chronotope of the great transformation from pre-Mao "dystopia" to Maoist "paradise" engineered by socialist urban planning. As an unhygienic corner and a figurative miniature of the underprivileged ghetto, the old Dragon Beard Ditch reveals the pre-socialist everyday life of a shabby compound occupied by many households east of the Bridge of Heaven in the southern part of Beijing. As soon as Beijing becomes a socialist capital, the haunting danger of contamination and social sickness in the filthy ditch is cleaned up physically in hygienic sweeping and symbolically in socialist ideological purification. *Dragon Beard Ditch* offers a salient, distorted, and imaginary example of the socialist production of space by physically and psychologically transforming an infamous stinking slum into a wholesome socialist community. The socialist sun shines over Dragon Beard Ditch, where the inhabitants are endowed with new class consciousness and released from their hygienic and political morass, and they warmly welcome baptism and redemption by the newly established socialist regime.

The Yutai Teahouse in Lao She's play *Teahouse* (*Chaguan*, 1957; English, 1980) embodies the decline of the Manchu Empire, the failure of the warlord regime, and the downfall of the Nationalist government, recapitulating and condensing the 50-year history and politics into a pessimistic miniature of old Beijing. The teahouse functions as a physical and psychological place and space, and a warped space–time continuum that presents the interactions between material deformations and emotional vicissitudes (nostalgic sympathy, a sense of loss, as well as melancholia and self-mourning).

Shanghai is depicted in socialist literature as a bygone capitalist center of decadence and appropriation, and a newly established socialist city inhabited by citizens with new class-consciousness. Zhou Erfu's four-volume *Morning in Shanghai* (1958, 1980), "a successor to Mao Dun's *Midnight*" (McDougall and Louie 1997: 241), reveals the disappearance of capitalist forces, the prolonged process of socialist transformation, and the urban planning of new communities for model workers. Ouyang Shan's five-volume *Romance of a Generation* (*Yidai fengliu*, 1959, 1964, 1981, 1983, and 1985)—in particular, the first volume, *Three-Family Lane*, set in a span from the May Fourth Movement to the "Great Revolution" period—chooses Guangzhou as the geographical site for revolutionary and romantic bildungsroman centering on three families with the capitalist, landlord–bureaucrat, and working-class backgrounds (J. Liu 2003: 178). In the field of drama and theater, revolutionary plays such as Shen Ximeng's *Sentinel under the Neon Lights* (*Nihong dengxia de shaobing*, 1963), Chen Yun's *The Young Generation* (*Nianqing de yidai*, 1963), and Cong Shen's *Never Forget* (*Qianwan buyao wangji*, 1964) reflect urban life in Shanghai and Harbin to showcase the ongoing class struggle, the formation of proletarian consciousness, and the critique of bourgeois entertainment and fetishism.

From the post-Mao periods to the present, urban literature has rejuvenated in the 1980s, proliferated in the 1990s, and flourished in the twenty-first century. Lu Wenfu's "The Man from a Peddler's Family" ("*Xiaofan shijia*," 1980) depicts a Suzhou wonton peddler's frustration, pride, and affection for his beloved hometown. Lu's acclaimed "The Gourmet" ("*Meishijia*," 1983) incorporates distinctive culinary experiences, vanishing and reemerging refined lifestyles, and the appreciation of gastronomy into his illustrations of Suzhou. Liu Xinwu, a representative of scar literature, published his Mao Dun Prize–winning novel *The Bell Tower and Drum Tower* (*Zhong gu lou*) in 1985. This Beijing saga colorfully depicts how many Beijingers suffered and survived the catastrophic Cultural Revolution and eventually obtained their urban identity and historical consciousness when they happened to stand in front of the Bell Tower and Drum Tower, the obsolete time-telling center that lost its original function in 1924, the year the last emperor of the Qing Dynasty was forced to leave the Forbidden City. Feng Jicai, a native of Tianjin and a passionate defender and tireless advocate of the indigenous culture of his hometown, contribute his Tianjin-flavor works, including his aesthetic and grotesque representations of martial arts and queue culture in his "Magic Braid" ("*Shenbian*," 1984), and of foot-binding tradition in his *The Three-Inch Golden Lotus* (1986). Other authors labeled as urban writers include Deng Youmei, Wang Zengqi, Chen Jiangong, Su Shuyang, Han Shaohua, Liu Suola, and Xu Xing.

Wang Shuo was a major urban author in the late 1980s and early 1990s, a leading figure of hooligan literature. Considered a contemporary successor of Lao She (Barmé 1999: 72), Wang's poignant Beijing stories include "The Troubleshooters" (1987), *Playing for Thrills* (1989; English, 1997), *No Regrets about Youth* (*Qingchun wuhui*, 1991), and "Wild Beasts" ("*Dongwu xiongmeng*," 1991). Rebellious youth culture and resistance against authorities as well as perplexing configurations of individuality, collectivity, sexual imagination, and political fantasy constitute the major themes of Wang's urban adventures from the military compound to the mean streets, from leisure parks to the political monuments. Wang's Beijing writing is characterized by strong cynicism and dark humor, and is disguised by a fearless use and abuse of Maoist propaganda and revolutionary vocabulary.

Another wave of urban literature emerged and intensified in the 1990s and has continued to flourish since then. Shanghai has been configured as a feminine city by female writers such as Cheng Naishan, Chen Danyan, Wei Hui, Mian Mian, Xu Lan,

Ren Xiaowen (Shi Zhanjun 2006), and, the most prolific and significant writer among them, Wang Anyi. Wang's representative Shanghai narratives include *The Song of Everlasting Sorrow* (1995; English 2008), *Fierce Heroes Everywhere* (*Biandi xiaoxiong*, 2005), *The Era of Enlightenment* (2007), and *Heavenly Fragrance* (2011). Despite Wang's vehement disavowal, she is often compared with Eileen Chang because both writers display a reflection of and obsession with Shanghai, and their urban narratives are characterized by meticulously elaborate and nuanced feminine description of the city. *The Song of Everlasting Sorrow*, which narrates the romance and accidental death of a former beauty pageant winner of Shanghai, is widely hailed as an instant classic in modern Chinese literature. For Xudong Zhang (2000: 369), the novel is "a saga of modern Shanghai told ruthlessly and meticulously from the viewpoint of a class living in the heart of the dreams, fantasies, and everyday rituals of a Shanghai that ceased to exist after 1949." Jin Yucheng's *Blossoms* (*Fanhua*, 2012), first released online and narrated in Shanghai dialect, features an encyclopedic exhibition of memories, emotions, and material life in post-1949 Shanghai. It resurrects the charms of traditional story-telling and combines it with modern, Faulknerian narrative skills so as to exhibit the authentic Shanghai life represented by male characters, which is different from the overwhelming female voices and *petits récits* conceived successfully by woman writers.

Although literature in Shanghai and Shanghai in literature have been mainly determined by female writers and feminine imagination and representation, other literary writings of mainland Chinese cities are mostly defined by male writers and male points of view—for example, the historical memory and "evening glow" of a derelict Xi'an in Jia Pingwa; the romance and nostalgia of a traumatized Nanjing in Ye Zhaoyan and Ge Liang; Suzhou in Zhu Wenying's subtle portraits of the local charms; Chengdu, China's fifth most populous city, in Murong Xuecun's ironic and comic–tragic urban romance, *Leave Me Alone*; Shenzhen in Ding Li's business and workplace novels; and Beijing in Liu Zhenyun's neo-realist representations, Qiu Huadong's up-to-date urban records and romances, and Xu Zechen's youth bildungsroman. The only exception to such male dominance occurs to Wuhan, as two of its major writers are female (Chi Li and Fang Fang).

Jia Pingwa's *The Defunct Capital* (1993), *Old Xi'an* (*Lao Xi'an*, 1999), and *King of Trash* (*Gaoxing*, 2007) reiterate the historical privilege and geographical disadvantage of Xi'an in its dialects, habits, customs, and infrastructure. *The Defunct Capital*, which was banned and only recently reissued, displays the early post-Maoist urban life and its moral corruption, exotic obsession, and everlasting beliefs and superstitions. *Old Xi'an* calls attention to the glorious legacy of Xi'an and its reluctant transformation in modern times, echoing what Lin Yutang (1953: 4) once observed, "the sedate ancient city, the famed capital of the Tang emperors, change hesitantly, unwilling, but perceptibly. 'The Anchor of China's Conservatism' … [Xi'an] would not change gracefully. The changes in men and morals, government and costumes, meant chaos and confusion." Through filters of confusion and chaos brought by the maelstrom of modernization, Jia seeks to exhibit a super-stable Xi'an preserved in words and memories. The spontaneous but erudite essays in *Old Xi'an* demonstrate Jia's impressive familiarity with Xi'an not only as a physical city but as an ancient capital in personal and collective memories that are vital in the establishment of its cultural identity.

Along with Beijing, Xi'an, and Luoyang, Nanjing is one of the top four ancient cultural capitals, and has suffered but survived historical crises and dynastic transformation. Ye Zhaoyan's *Nanjing 1937: A Love Story* (*Yijiusanqi nian de aiqing*, 1996; English, 2002) represents the catastrophic Nanjing Massacre colored by a sentimental romance permeated with mourning and nostalgia by an omnipresent and omnipotent witness and survivor of this calamity, who looks backward at the ruins of a magnificent city, sighing in regret and grief. For Michael Berry (2008: 163), this recollection of the traumatized city constitutes "both a longing for the grandeur and decadence of old Nanjing and a nostalgic gesture of remembering (and re-creating) Republican-era literary texts and traditions." Ye's *Old Nanjing: Reflections of Scenes on the Qinhuai River* (*Lao Nanjing: jiuying qinhuai*, 1999) attempts to invoke the power of photography and the charms of old photos to exhibit the breath and heartbeat of the city's history. Similarly, Ge Liang's *Rosefinch* (*Zhuque*, 2009) demonstrates an obsessive nostalgia for Nanjing. He blends family histories and fictional stories (three generations), blurs the boundaries between tradition and modernity, and thus unfolds the multilayered mysteries and discoveries of Nanjing around the 1920s, 1930s, and 1950s.

When examining the rise of urban literature in the twenty-first century, Chen Xiaoming (2006: 12) points out that urban literature in a strict sense should present the existence of the city, its objective images, the authors' reflections on urban life, and the spiritual contradictions between literary characters and the city. Meng Fanhua (2014) observes that urban literature in the twenty-first century does not lack in writers, works, social issues, or stories, but has not yet provided representative literary characters for the times and therefore remains an incomplete project.

Imagining Taipei, Hong Kong, and Beyond

If we extend our scope of investigation from mainland Chinese cities to Taipei and Hong Kong, then the year 1949 would serve as a key point of departure. In late 1940s, with the founding of PRC and the Nationalists' retreat to Taiwan, millions of people were uprooted from their hometowns and made painstaking efforts to relocate or assimilate into new literary, cultural, and political environments (D. Wang, Chen, and Xu 2010; X. Wang 2013). For writers of mainland origins who migrated to Taiwan, Hong Kong, and other Sinophone regions outside of the newly established Socialist China, literary writings of cities have to counter the memories of recent experiences of a severed nation, as well as rethink, restructure, and reframe their memories— individual, urban, and national—in order to provide their affective mappings of cities, detached and reconnected, near and afar. Some writers attempt to balance and bridge their new urban experiences in Taipei or Hong Kong, and their memories about main- land cities ranging from their old hometowns to their sojourning cities are shaped by unforgettable recollections and creative reinventions. Other writers born after 1949 cannot easily claim themselves as the legitimate native sons or daughters of Taipei or Hong Kong and have engaged and developed sustained dialogues with earlier generations and the legacy of diversified and complicated urban narratives.

By raising the question "Where have all the urban natives gone?" I inquire, for instance, how native Beijing writers who were relocated to Taipei after the 1949 division projected poignant cultural and political implications into their reminiscent writings about a lost hometown. These writers include Qi Rushan, Liang Shiqiu, Tang Lusun, Xia Yuanyu, Ding Bingsui, and Hou Rongsheng. As a Beijing native, Taipei dweller, and veteran writer and scholar, Liang Shiqiu blends food memory and diasporic nostalgia in his depictions and recollections of the long-lasting flavors of Chinese urban food and the lingering aroma of Beijing dishes during his Taipei years in his four-volume collection of essays *From a Cottager's Sketchbook* (*Yashe xiaopin*, 1949, 1973, 1982, 1986; abridged English, 2005). In doing so, Liang contributes subtle and influential articulations, emotional topography, and tangible and symbolic embodiments of Chinese culinary culture (in particular, the delicate tastes of Beijing food) as the incarnation of humanity, the authenticity of individual identity, the tokens of collective memory, the traces of diaspora, the souvenirs of nostalgia, and the aftertaste of hometown cuisine (W. Song 2012).

During the Republican period, Taiwan writers have traveled across the borders and resided in Beijing before returning to Taiwan. These Beijing sojourners include Hong Yanqiu, Zhang Wojun, Zhang Shenqie, Zhong Lihe, and Lin Hai-yin (Lin Haiyin), among others, who later describe their Beijing experiences in their autobiographies or writings in other literary genres. Zhong Lihe and Lin Hai-yin construct contrasting imageries of South Beijing to deal with the intricate relationships between hometown and a strange land, assimilation and dissimilation, as well as dislocation and identity crisis. Zhong Lihe's dystopian novella "Oleander" ("*Jiazhutao*," 1944; English, 2014) portrays a bleak city image and launches cynical criticism of the hygienic morass and moral decline in Beijing's lower-class society on the south side of the city. Lin Hai-yin, once a Taiwan girl in Beijing, published a series of her Beijing memories starting in the 1960s. Her representative *Memories of Peking: South Side Stories* (*Chengnan jiushi*, 1960; English, 2003) presents a beautiful and encouraging image of oleander and some warm and nostalgic imagery of Beijing, and eulogizes her bittersweet childhood memory, lived and imagined, of the south side of Republican Beijing (Mei 2004: 127–55).

Bai Xianyong (Pai Hsien-yung) contributes the well-crafted, psychologically profound *Taipei People* (*Taibei ren*, 1971; English 2000), a collection of 14 short stories that describes not only a bleak Taipei image but also its entangled links with Nanjing, Shanghai, Guilin, Kunming, Beijing, and other mainland cities against the great backdrop of the 1949 divide and the diasporic experiences across the Taiwan Strait. *Taipei People* provides vivid portraitures of melancholic mainland émigrés—including schizophrenic scholars ("Winter Night," 1970), the never-aged high-ranked courtesan lady from Shanghai's Paramount Dance Hall to Taipei's fashionable district ("Eternal Yin Xueyan" ["*Yongyuan de Yin Xueyan*"], 1965), and depressed Nationalist officials and disheartened social ladies ("Wandering in the Garden, Waking from a Dream" ["*Youyuan jingmeng*"], 1966), among many others—in terms of diaspora and exile, as well as physical and psychological deterioration and reorientation (Ko Ching-ming 2006: 199–244). Later, Bai shifts his focus to a local Taipei story in his *Crystal Boys* (*Niezi*, 1983; English, 1990), a pioneering gay novel that deals with the sounds, furies, frustrations, and desires of rebel youths in a local homosexual community.

During the peak Cold War years in the 1960s–1970s, Wang Wenxing's modernist and avant-garde novel *Family Catastrophe* (*Jiabian*, 1973) presented Taipei as the new home for mainland emigrants as well as a battlefield for an ongoing father/son contradiction and an imagined solution to generational, familial, and geopolitical dilemma. Huang Chun-ming's literary Taipei, a city of sadness, emerges from his early stories "My Son's Big Doll" ("*Erzi de da wanou*," 1968), "Xiaoqi's Cap" ("*Xiaoqi de na yiding maozi*," 1974), and, in particular, "Taste of Apples" ("*Pingguo de ziwei*," 1972), which captures the tensions between the country and the city, Taiwan and the United States, in a Taipei morning car accident and its unexpected and bittersweet consequences (Chen Fang-ming 2011: 540–5).

Since the 1980s, urban writing has been flourishing in the landscape of Taiwan literature, thanks to native-born writers and Malaysian émigrés, such as Huang Fan, Zhang Dachun, Lin Yaode, Ping Lu, Yang Zhao, Zhu Tianwen (Chu T'ien-wen), Zhu Tianxin (Chu T'ien-hsin), Su Weizhen, Yuan Qiongqiong, Li Yongping, Wu He, Li Zishu, Ng Kim Chew, and Luo Yijun, to just name a few. Zhang Dachun's *The Great Liar* (*Da shuohuang jia*, 1988–1989), first serialized in newspapers and later published as a book, combines different genres such as news reportage, detective story, political expose, and historical fiction, thereby forcefully presenting an absurd urban reality. Widely regarded as a leading novelist and scriptwriter, Zhu Tianwen reads Taipei as follows: "It is utterly chaotic, but it has a tremendous energy, with every kind of potential" (Hillenbrand 2007: 288). Her "Fin-de-siècle Splendor" ("*Shijimo de huali*," 1990) sees the unseen, presents the unpresentable, and provides a feminist declaration, a redefinition of smell and visuality, and an alternative utopia for redemption. Yvonne Chang (1993: 78) states that the novella "envisions a hollow existential condition that has resulted from the unbridled development of materialist urban culture." Zhu's acclaimed gay novel *Notes of a Desolate Man* (*Huangren shouji*, 1994; English, 1999) inherits Eileen Chang's legacy of desolation and cynicism, and contributes an erotics and aesthetics of decadence in a new *fin de siècle*. Her *Words of a Witch* (*Wuyan*, 2007) reflects the meaning of writing and femininity from the perspective of a solitary woman. Zhu Tianxin, Zhu Tianwen's younger sister and another leading writer in contemporary Taiwan, contributes a vaguely defined but critically acclaimed Taipei trilogy. "Remembering My Brothers from the Military Compound" ("*Xiang wo juancun de xiongdimen*," 1992) touches upon friendship, nostalgia, anxiety, and cultural consciousness among the mainlander military retirees and their second-generation children, cultivated within the unique urban milieu and sociopolitical communities. Her *The Old Capital: A Novel of Taipei* (*Gudu*, 1997; English, 2007) and *The Wanderer* (*Manyouzhe*, 2000) highlight an old soul, or an urban wanderer who relies on imaginary maps, invokes literary geography and cartography

(L. Chen 2007), and observes and participates in the great urban transformation with a post-loyalist complex (D. Wang 2007).

Beginning in 1949, while both Communist and Nationalist political authoritarianism imposed barriers to cultural and economic exchanges across the Taiwan Strait, "Hong Kong has become a unique urban space where forces of politics and commerce, colonialism and nationalism, and modernity and historicity converge. Ever since the early 1950s, Hong Kong has been a haven for émigré writers, dissident critics, and exiled scholars whose voices would otherwise have been muffled by either the Nationalist or the Communist regime. The colony also became an arena where different political forces contested to gain the upper hand in the propaganda war" (P. Chi and Wang 2000: xxi–xxii). Huang Guliu's *The Tale of Shrimpball* (*Xiaqiu zhuan*, 1947–1948) features Hong Kong, Guangzhou, and the guerrilla war zone of South China to tell how a proletarian boy is cultivated into a revolutionary hero. Zhao Zifan's *Semi-Lower-Class Society* (*Banxialiu shehui*, 1953) depicts the misery of unfortunate refugees and diasporic sentiments in the post-1949 Hong Kong ghetto-like resettlement sites and the hostile urban environment at large. Cao Juren's *Hotel* (*Jiudian*, 1954) touches upon the calamity of mainland emigrants in Hong Kong, in particular the madness of the female protagonist trapped in a decadent and immoral nightlife. Liu Yichang's *The Drunkard* (*Jiutu*, 1963), a stream-of-consciousness novel, exhibits an urban professional writer's suffering and pain when he is forced to abandon his beloved serious literature and obliged to write popular literature driven by the urban market and commercial forces (martial arts and even erotic works). Liu's *Intersection* (*Duidao*, 1972) delineates the confusion and intersection of Hong Kong time and space, silence and articulation, and Chinese and British/Western cultural influences.

If Liu Yichang adopts a critical attitude toward Hong Kong popular literature, arguably the mainstream of colonial Hong Kong, then Jin Yong, the most widely read novelist in the Sinophone world since the 1950s, constructs an alternative urban narrative from the 1950s to 1980s by writing about mainland cities in imperial dynasties—Beijing, Hangzhou, Haining, Suzhou, Yangzhou, Nanjing, Luoyang, Kaifeng, Dali, Kunming, Fuzhou, Foshan, and so on—in his Hong Kong martial arts fiction to register an illuminating historical and cultural consciousness. Although written in Hong Kong during the Cold War era, Jin Yong's topography of the imperial cities in the Ming–Qing dynastic transformation blends the real and the imagined, and envisions a dialect of absence and presence. It charts a wide range of chivalric activities: intruding into the political center embodied by the Forbidden City (the "Great Within") and fleeing to peripheral regions such as Xinjiang's Islamic community, the overseas kingdom in Brunei in Southeast Asia, and an unknown place somewhere inside Yangzhou. I mainly consider his three martial arts novels, *Romance of the Book and the Sword* (1955–1956, 1975 revision), *The Sword Stained with Royal Blood* (*Bixue jian*, 1956, 1975 revision), and *The Deer and the Cauldron* (1969–1972, 1981 revision). By rewriting political, ethnic, and cultural crises in dynastic transitions, Jin Yong explores various topics, including gratitude and revenge between Han and non-Han peoples, ambivalent individual identity, and imagined cultural memory against the backdrop of the 1949 Chinese division and the post-1949 migrations in the Sinophone world. By intertwining literary topography and chivalric fantasy, Jin Yong's martial arts narrative from the 1950s to the 1980s inscribes post-loyalist attachments and detachments into the imagery of Beijing, an imperial capital, among other mainland cities, and into Hong Kong, the birthplace of his chivalric geography, thus suggesting a frustrated yet flexible identity and a supplementary yet self-sufficient "republic of letters" in his remapping of Beijing's and China's past for contemporary Hong Kong/Sinophone articulations.

Richard Hughes (1976) once described Hong Kong and its many faces as a "borrowed place" and "borrowed time." Indeed, located in between motherland China and colonizer Britain, Hong Kong literature faces the in-betweenness, and configures its historical consciousness and urban awareness, which bring to light the identity crisis and symbolic resolution starting from the 1970s, a time of rapid economic growth and, more significantly, of growth in self-confidence and the forging of a local identity (Xi Xi 1997). Xi Xi's representative works weave female consciousness, everyday life, and the mood of the city, and contribute a genealogy of Hong Kong images and urban feelings ranging from fear and anxiety to hope, which are vividly demonstrated in her *My City* (*Wocheng*, 1979), the collection of short stories *A Girl Like Me* (*Xiangwo zheyang de yige nüzi*, 1982), the series of allegorical stories of "The Fertile Town" (*Feituzhen*), *Marvels of a Floating City* (*Fucheng zhiyi*, 1988; English, 1997), and *The Beautiful Mansion* (*Meili dasha*, 1977). As Stephen Chan (Chen Qingqiao) puts it (2000: 181), for Xi Xi, "the city offers a unique display of space, with distinct structures, specific postures, particular orientations, and possibilities for boundless imagination."

Other famous Hong Kong narratives in the 1980s–1990s include the talented female writer Zhong Xiaoyang's *Stopping by the Roadside* (*Tingche zan jiewen*, 1982); Yi Shu's dozens of popular urban romances; and prolific and popular writer Li Bihua's (Lillian Lee) sensational *Rouge* (*Yanzhi kou*, 1985), *Farewell My Concubine* (*Bawang bieji*, 1988), and many others. *Rouge* was adapted into a critically acclaimed box-office hit film in 1987 by Stanley Kwan (Guan Jinpeng), marking a crucial moment in Hong Kong literature, cinema, history, and a global trend of Hong Kong nostalgia (Chen Guoqiu 2000).

Taiwanese female writer and Hong Kong sojourner Shi Shuqing (Shih Shu-ch'ing) has composed a Hong Kong trilogy—*Her Name Is Butterfly* (*Ta mingjiao Hudie*, 1993), *Bauhinia Are Everywhere* (*Bianshan yang zijing*, 1995), and *The Lonely Garden* (*Jimo yunyuan*, 1997). The trilogy (abridged English, *City of the Queen: A Novel of Colonial Hong*, 2005) describes Hong Kong as a city of commerce, colonialism, sex, and adventure. The legend of the British Crown Colony is firmly tied with the story of the heroine—a beautiful rural girl who is kidnapped and sold as a prostitute in Hong Kong, but who eventually becomes a rich landowner and grandmother of the first Chinese judge on the Hong Kong Supreme Court.

As a poet, essayist, novelist, translator, cultural critic, and film scholar, Leung Ping-kwan shows a consistent and critical obsession with Hong Kong in his creative and scholarly works. His collections of short stories, *Islands and Continents* (*Dao yu dalu*,

1987), *A City of Memories, a City of Fictions* (*Jiyi de chengshi, xugou de chengshi*, 1994), and *Postcolonial Food and Love* (*Houzhimin shiwu yu aiqing*, 2012), together with his anthologies of poems and essays, display a sophisticated Hong Kong preceding and following the 1997 handover in terms of the poetics and politics of daily objects, and mundane urban spaces and places as well as "old ends" and "new ends" in "a city of transition" (E. Cheung 2012:1).

The new trendsetters in literary Hong Kong are Wong Bik-wan and Dung Kai-cheung (Dong Qizhang). Wong, a unique voice in Hong Kong literature, is usually compared to Lu Xun, Eileen Chang, or Wang Anyi. Her *Tenderness and Violence* (*Wenrou yu baolie*, 1994), *Portraits of Pious Women* (*Lienü tu*, 1999), and *Biographies of Martyred Men* (*Lielao zhuan*, 2012) introduce inscrutable nightmare, unbearable loss and melancholia, abrupt familial and urban violence, unexpected cruelty and ferocity in striking, and depressing metropolitan settings before and after the 1997 handover of Hong Kong. Dung Kai-cheung (2012: xi–xii) compellingly challenges the stereotyped images of Hong Kong:

> There are enough fictitious Hong Kongs circulating around the world. It doesn't matter so much how real or false these fictions are but how they are made up. The Hong Kong of Tai-Pan and Suzie Wong, a mixture of economic adventures, political intrigues, sexual encounters, and romances; the Hong Kong of Bruce Lee, Jackie Chan, and Jet Li kung-fu-fighting their way through to the international scene; the Hong Kong of John Woo's gangster heroes shooting double-handed and Stephen Chow's underdog antiheroes making nonsensical jokes. And yet, in spite of these eye-catching exposures, Hong Kong remains invisible. A large part of the reality of life here is unrepresented, unrevealed, and ignored.

Dung's two early novels, *The Rose of the Name* (*Mingzi de meigui*, 1997) and *Visible Cities* (*V cheng fansheng lu*, 1998), acknowledge Umberto Eco, Italio Calvino, Borges, and Roland Barthes as his sources of inspiration. His recent ambitious works include a trilogy of natural history, *Works and Creation* (*Tiangong kaiwu*, 2005), *Histories of Time* (*Shijian fanshi*, 2007), and *the Age of Learning* (*Wuzhong yuanshi*, 2010), which blends Visible City/Hong Kong and imaginary history, urban objects and family saga, historical events and private letters, and personal feelings and daily minutiae in his creative and distinctive literary narratives.

Dung's avant-garde imaginations/representations of Hong Kong and other (in) visible cities illuminate his unique understanding of urban literature, which is evidenced in his newly written preface for the 2012 English translation of his 1997 fictional account *Atlas: The Archaeology of an Imaginary City* (*Dituji: Yige xiangxiang de chengshi de kaoguxue*). In "An Archaeology for the Future," Dung (2012: xii) states, literature "is not just a different way of world-representing but also a different way of world-building, that is, creating conditions for understanding, molding, preserving, and changing the world that we live in. It is the task of literature to make visible the invisible … [and] to articulate the unarticulated." This literary manifesto invokes and exemplifies mature methods of imagining all Chinese cities.

References

Bai Xianyong (Pai Hsien-Yung). 1990. *Crystal Boys: A Novel*. Trans. Howard Goldblatt. San Francisco: Gay Sunshine Press.

Bai Xianyong. 2000. *Taipei People*. Ed. and Trans. George Kao. Bilingual edition. Hong Kong: Chinese University Press.

Berry, Michael. 2008. *The History of Pain: Trauma in Modern Chinese Literature and Film*. New York: Columbia University Press.

Braester, Yomi. 2010. *Paint the City Red: Chinese Cinema and the Urban Contract*. Durham, NC: Duke University Press.

Chan, Stephen C. K. 2000. "The Cultural Imaginary of a City: Reading Hong Kong Through Xi Xi." In *Chinese Literature in the Second Half of a Modern Century: A Critical Survey*. Edited by Chi, Pang-yuan and David Der-wei Wang. Bloomington: Indiana University Press. 180–192.

Chang, Sung-sheng Yvonne. 1993. *Modernism and the Nativist Resistance: Contemporary Chinese Fiction from Taiwan*. Durham, NC: Duke University Press.

Chen, Fang-ming 陳芳明. 2011. *Taiwan xin wenxueshi* 臺灣新文學史 (A history of modern Taiwanese literature). 2. Vols Taipei: Lianjing.

Chen, Guoqiu 陳國球. Ed. 2000. *Wenxue Xianggang yu Li Bihua* 文學香港與李碧華 (Literary Hong Kong and Lilian Lee). Taipei: Maitian.

Chen, Lingchei Letty. 2007. "Mapping Identity in a Postcolonial City: Intertextuality and Cultural Hybridity in Zhu Tianxin's *Ancient Capital*." In *Writing Taiwan: A New Literary History*. Edited by Wang, David Der-wei, and Carlos Rojas. NC: Duke University Press. 301–323.

Chen, Pingyuan 陳平原. 2008. *Beijing jiyi yu jiyi Beijing* 北京記憶與記憶北京 (Beijing memories). Beijing: Sanlian shudian.

Chen Xiaoming 陳曉明. 2006. "Chengshi wenxue—wufa xianshen de 'tazhe'" 城市文學—無法現身的"他者" (Urban literature: an invisible "other"). *Wenyi yanjiu*, 1: 12–25.

Cheung, Esther M. K. 2012. "Introduction to the New Edition: New Ends in a City of Transition." In *City at the End of Time*. Edited by Leung Ping-kwan. Trans. Gordon T. Osing and Leung Ping-kwan. Hong Kong: Hong Kong University Press. 1–19.

Chi, Pang-yuan, and David Der-wei Wang. Eds. 2000. *Chinese Literature in the Second Half of a Modern Century: A Critical Survey*. Bloomington: Indiana University Press.

Chow, Rey. 1999. "Seminal Dispersal, Fecal Retention, and Related Narrative Matters: Eileen Chang's Tale of Roses in the Problematic of Modern Writing." *Differences: A Journal of Feminist Cultural Studies*, 11.2: 153–176.

Dung, Kai-cheung. 2012. *Atlas: The Archaeology of an Imaginary City*. Trans. Dung Kai-cheung, Anders Hansson, and Bonnie S. McDougall. New York: Columbia University Press.

Esherick, Joseph W. Ed. 2000. *Remaking the Chinese City: Modernity and National Identity, 1900–1950*. Honolulu: University of Hawaii Press.

Han, Bangqing. 2005. *The Sing-Song Girls of Shanghai*. Trans. Eileen Chang; revised and ed. Eva Hung. New York: Columbia University Press.

Hillenbrand, Margaret. 2007. *Literature, Modernity, and the Practice of Resistance: Japanese and Taiwanese Fiction, 1960–1990*. Leiden: Brill.

Hughes, Richard. 1976. *Hong Kong: Borrowed Place, Borrowed Time*. London: Deutsch.

Ko, Ching-ming 柯慶明. 2006. *Tianwan xiandai wenxue de shiye* 臺灣現代文學的視野 (Perspectives on Taiwan literature). Taipei: Maitian.

Lao, She. 1980. *Teahouse: A Play in Three Acts*. Trans. John Howard-Gibbon. Beijing: Foreign Languages Press.

Lao, She. 1956. *Dragon Beard Ditch: A Play in Three Acts*. Trans. John Howard-Gibbon. Beijing: Foreign Languages Press.

Lee, Leo Ou-fan. 1999. *Shanghai Modern: The Flowering of a New Urban Culture in China, 1930–1945*. Cambridge, MA: Harvard University Press.

Liang, Shiqiu. 2005. *From A Cottager's Sketchbook*. Trans. Ta-tsun Chen. 2 vols. Hong Kong: Chinese University Press.

Lin Hai-yin. 2003. *Memories of Peking: South Side Stories*. Trans. Nancy C. Ing and Chi Pang-yuan. Hong Kong: Chinese University Press.

Lin Yutang. 1953. *The Vermillion Gate*. 2nd edition. New York: John Day Company.

Link, E. Perry. 1981. *Mandarin Ducks and Butterflies: Popular Fiction in Early Twentieth-century Chinese Cities*. Berkeley: University of California Press.

Liu, Jianmei. 2003. *Revolution Plus Love: Literary History, Women's Bodies, and Thematic Repetition in Twentieth-Century Chinese Fiction*. Honolulu: University of Hawaii Press.

Liu, Lydia H. 1995. *Translingual Practice: Literature, National Culture, and Translated Modernity—China, 1900–1937*. Stanford, CA: Stanford University Press.

Luo, Gang 羅崗. 2006. *Xiangxiang chengshi de fangshi* 想像城市的方式 (Ways of imagining cities). Nanjing: Jiangsu renmin chubanshe.

McClellan, Thomas Michael. 2005. *Zhang Henshui and Popular Chinese Fiction, 1919–1949*. Lewiston, NY: Edwin Mellen Press, 2005.

McDougall, Bonnie S., and Kam Louie. 1997. *The Literature of China in the Twentieth Century*. New York: Columbia University Press.

Meng, Fanhua 孟繁華. 2014. "Jiangou shiqi de Zhongguo chengshi wenxue—dangxia Zhongguo wenxue zhuangkuang de yige fangmian" 建構時期的中國城市文學—當下中國文學狀況的一個方面 (Chinese urban literature in construction: one aspect of current Chinese literature). *Wenyi yanjiu*, 2: 5–14.

Shi, Zhanjun 施戰軍. 2006. "Lun Zhongguo shide chengshi wenxue de shengcheng" 論中國式的城市文學的生成 (The birth of Chinese-style urban literature). *Wenyi yanjiu*, 1: 4–11.

Shih, Shu-ch'ing. 2005. *City of the Queen: A Novel of Colonial Hong Kong*. Trans. Sylvia Li-chun Lin and Howard Goldblatt. New York: Columbia University Press.

Shih, Shu-mei. 2001. *The Lure of the Modern: Writing Modernism in Semicolonial China, 1917–1937*. Berkeley: University of California Press.

Song, Weijie. 2012. "Emotional Topography, Food Memory, and Bittersweet Aftertaste: Liang Shiqiu and the Lingering Flavor of Home." *Journal of Oriental Studies*, 45.1–2: 89–105.

Song, Weijie. 2014. "The Aesthetic versus the Political: Lin Huiyin and Modern Beijing." *Chinese Literature: Essays, Articles, Reviews (CLEAR)*, 36: 61–94.

Song, Weijie. 2016. *Mapping Modern Beijing: Space, Emotion, and Literary Topography*. Oxford, New York: Oxford University Press.

Visser, Robin. 2010. *Cities Surround the Countryside: Urban Aesthetics in Post-socialist China*. Durham: Duke University Press.

Wang, David Der-wei. 1992. *Fictional Realism in Twentieth-Century China: Mao Dun, Lao She, Shen Congwen*. New York: Columbia University Press.

Wang, David Der-wei. 1997. *Fin-de-siècle Splendor: Repressed Modernities of Late Qing Fiction, 1849-1911*. Stanford, CA: Stanford University Press.

Wang, Dewei 王德威. 2006. *Ruci fanhua* 如此繁華 (Urban splendor). Shanghai: Shanghai shudian.

Wang, Dewei 王德威. 2007. *Hou yimin xiezuo: shijian yu jiyi de zhengzhi xue* 後遺民寫作：時間與記憶的政治學 (Post-loyalist writing: The politics of time and memory). Taipei: Maitian.

Wang, Dewei 王德威, Chen Sihe 陳思和, and Xu Zidong 許子東. Eds. 2010. *Yijiu sijiu yihou* 一九四九以後 (After 1949). Hong Kong: Oxford University Press.

Wang, Shuo. 1997. *Playing for Thrills: A Mystery*. Trans. Howard Goldblatt. New York: William Morrow and Company.

Wang, Xiaojue. 2013. *Modernity with a Cold War Face: Reimagining the Nation in Chinese Literature across the 1949 Divide*. Cambridge, MA: Harvard University Asia Center.

Wu, Fuhui 吳福輝. 1995. *Dushi xuanliu zhong de haipai xiaoshuo* 都市漩流中的海派小說 (Fiction of Shanghai school in urban vortex). Changsha: Hunan jiaoyu chubanshe.

Xi, Xi. 1997. *Marvels of a Floating City and Other Stories*. Ed. and Trans. Eva Hung. Hong Kong: Renditions Paperbacks.

Yan, Jiayan 嚴家炎. 1989. *Zhongguo xiandai xiaoshuo liupai shi* 中國現代小說流派史 (A history of the schools of modern Chinese novel). Beijing: Renmin wenxue chubanshe.

Yang, Jianlong 楊劍龍. 2013. "Lun Zhongguo dushi wenxue yu dushi wenxue yanjiu" 論中國都市文學與都市文學研究 (On Chinese urban literature and urban literary studies). *Jianghan luntan* 江漢論壇 (Jianghan forum), 3: 11–16.

Yang, Yi 楊義. 2003. *Jingpai haipai zonglun* 京派海派綜論 (Beijing school and Shanghai school). Beijing: Zhongguo shehui kexue chubanshe.

Ye, Zhaoyan. 2002. *Nanjing, 1937*. Trans. Michael Berry. New York: Columbia University Press.

Zhang, Dachun 張大春. 1989. *Da shuohuang jia* 大説謊家 (The great liar). Taipei: Yuanliu.

Zhang, Hongsheng 張鴻聲. 2007. "'Wenxue zhong de chengshi' yu 'chengshi xiangxiang' yanjiu" "文學中的城市"與"城市想象"研究 ("The city in literature" and research of "urban imagination"). *Wenxue pinglun*, 1: 116–122.

Zhang, Xudong. 2000. "Shanghai Nostalgia: Postrevolutionary Allegories in Wang Anyi's Literary Production in the 1990s." *Positions*, 8.2: 349–387.

Zhang, Yingjin. 1996. *The City in Modern Chinese Literature and Film: Configurations of Space, Time, and Gender*. Stanford, CA: Stanford University Press.

Zhao, Yuan 趙園. 1991. *Beijing: cheng yu ren* 北京:城與人 (Beijing: the city and its residents). Shanghai: Shanghai renmin chubanshe.

Zhong, Lihe. 2014. *From the Old Country: Stories and Sketches of China and Taiwan*. Ed. and Trans. T. M. McClellan. New York: Columbia University Press.

Zhu, Tianwen. 1999. *Notes of a Desolate Man*. Trans. Howard Goldblatt and Sylvia Li-chun Lin. New York: Columbia University Press.

Zhu, Tianxin. 2007. *The Old Capital: A Novel of Taipei*. Trans. Howard Goldblatt. New York: Columbia University Press.

21
Divided Unities of Modern Chinese Literature and Visual Culture: The Modern Girl, Woodcuts, and Contemporary Painter–Poets

Paul Manfredi

This chapter concerns modern Chinese literature's relationship to visual culture of the past century. In lieu of an attempt at comprehensive treatment, impossible in the space of a single chapter, I will explore the issue from three different perspectives.[1] First, I briefly review verbal visualizations of the Modern Girl/New Woman in literary texts by modern writers Mao Dun and Eileen Chang. Second, I explore a single format, woodblock printing, first as a didactically oriented feature of modernity advocated by writers such as Lu Xun, and then as an important tool for broader artistic–cultural reconfiguration in the aftermath of the Cultural Revolution. Finally, through a thematic lens of visual–verbal landscape, I explore a specific instance of word–image interrelation in the twenty-first century, namely the visual art of poets. I am working through these three dimensions of literary and visual–cultural expressions with "divided unity," a phrase I use to describe the way in which notable forms of Chinese word and image expression have moved from a state of fundamental overlap in literati culture, through a period of nominal division in May Fourth modernity, and back to confluence in the contemporary period.

Chinese literary and visual-art traditions are in large part characterized by the tools used to manifest their expression, namely ink, the brush, and various writing surfaces. These implements are obviously fundamental to the principally visual art of calligraphy, but also inherent to literary media regardless of genre, as well as a host of visual styles of Chinese painting and visual art from landscape to birds and flowers, fruit and nuts to figure painting. Thus, the advent of modernity in Chinese literature and visual art is characterized in part by two fundamental rifts, the first separating their respective

A Companion to Modern Chinese Literature, First Edition. Edited by Yingjin Zhang.
© 2016 John Wiley & Sons, Ltd. Published 2016 by John Wiley & Sons, Ltd.

expressions from premodern models (a rhetorical necessity inherent in the notion of reform), and the second from each other, as the models for innovation of Chinese cultural media originated from the West where no such essential word–image overlap exists.[2]

A complete list of such innovations would be long indeed, but particularly notable examples bear brief review. These include the rise of verse libre as the dominant poetic form, a mode of poetic composition that emerged in self-conscious and, in many respects, hotly contested debates among would-be modern writers in the wake of the literary revolution begun in 1917. Hu Shi's *Experiments*, published in 1920, was the first widely circulated collection of such works, and the origin of what is now generally referred to as New Poetry (see Chapter 9 by Michelle Yeh). At the same time, and from the same coterie of writers, emerged the short story as a coherent literary genre, with Lu Xun's *Outcry*, which contained seminal "Diary of a Madman." Modern Chinese drama came to prominence not long thereafter, with Cao Yu and others writing in a realistic mode that overlapped broadly with the intentional, even didactic tendencies of May Fourth literary practice. Parallel to all of this are the innovations of the visual art realm, equally contested, and in some respects more radically impacted by shifts in tools of production, and mode or manner of exhibition.[3] The advent of oil painting as a principally modern medium and the arrival of photography and film conspire to "make it new," in Pound's famous formulation.

The parallel efforts to advance change in cultural expression of both word and image in the common project of modernity were undoubtedly successful, as the Chinese experience from quotidian to rarefied saw massive transformation in a short period of time. Apart from the developments stemming from concerted study of foreign models, another major dimension spurring change was technological, particularly modern print culture and publishing. Epitomizing modern experience became the project of a number of major periodicals, including *The Young Companion* (*Liangyou*), *Arts and Life* (*Meishu shenghuo*), and *True Face Pictorial* (*Zhenxiang*), all of which provided lines of "new" from every conceivable angle. It is important to recognize that such efforts were more than designed to simply satisfy an appetite for novelty. The imperatives to change grew from an awareness of China's relative weaknesses in global context, and thus even small changes in lifestyle could carry with them the higher purpose of strengthening the nation. This was nowhere more true than for writers and artists of the period, whose commitment to new forms of expression dovetailed with their roles as architects of a new China.

The Modern Girl

For the purpose of seeing modernity in China, perhaps no better object of focus exists than the city of Shanghai, a subject of portraits both urban and visual, an essential site of sociocultural change, and a nexus that emerged through the end of the nineteenth century into the twentieth, both materially and theoretically new. The variegated forms of cultural expression, encompassing but certainly not limited to visual and verbal, should be viewed in a network of interrelated forces—governmental, educational, personal–practical (modern health, modern family)—which collectively constitute Shanghai imaginary. The literary and the visual are but two aspects of the broader managed chaos of modern re-vision, terminology, fashion, and learning, generating images and icons—new building styles, new light cameras, and a wide array of modern actions.

No single image is more indicative of the broad trend of Chinese cultural modernity than the Modern Girl or New Woman. On the strictly visual level, the Modern Girl was new to the landscape on many levels, whether in the unflinching depiction of the female body as in the 1926 Shanghai Academy of Arts exhibition of art works composed from nude models, or the myriad product-oriented advertisements of the new commodity market only recently coming into being, or of course residual exposes of traditional femininity reproduced technologically in photography and other new media (e.g., film). Amidst the tensions surrounding these various depictions of the female, heavily circumscribed by older discourses of propriety and social norms, newly infused with largely male-dominated sphere of political and social reform, and constantly buffeted by advertisements featuring the female body as object and subject of desire, the Modern Girl emerged metonymically as a key figure for modernity in Republican China.

As a literary fact, meanwhile, the Modern Girl is equally operative, if not more so. In Mao Dun's *Midnight* (1933), she actually assaults "the tradition" embodied by Old Man Wu, who is visiting Shanghai from the countryside:

> Wu Jianzhen's heart raced as though a needle were piercing his scattered nerves. His eyes instinctively fell upon Miss Fu Fang's body. Only now did he fully realize her dress. Even though it was only May, because the weather was warm today, she was in full summer attire: She was wearing a pale blue chiffon that wrapped her strong body, a pair of full breasts protruding prominently. Her short-cut sleeves revealed her soft white shoulders entirely. Old Man Wu turned away with a kind of indescribable disgust, only to have his eyes fall upon another semi-nude body wearing only a bright gauzy waistcoat that was nearly transparent. She sat high atop a rickshaw with her bare legs in full view—she seemed to not be wearing any pants. "A myriad wanton minds!" This sentence running incessantly through Old Man Wu's mind. (Mao Dun 1982: 12)

This famous passage marks a kind of pinnacle and also a complex instance of the male gaze, as the author's imagination conjures the embodiment of Chinese patriarchal tradition coming face to face with modernity in the form of the female body and breaking down before it. Mao Dun's vision drives the point clearly enough, but it is also a rather cartoonish look at the more often quite subtle oscillations of modernity expressed in the vision of the Modern Girl.

In fact, Mao Dun's own descriptions of this figure run the gamut and bring out the gaze as both medium and subject of critique. In *Rainbow* (1929–1930), by contrast:

> She looked to be no more than twenty years old, leaning on the ship's railing, looking out towards the sea. She was wearing a satiny white waist-length blouse above a black skirt, both of which caught the wind so as to accentuate her slender figure, making her all the

more captivating. Her hair was cut short, jet-black at the sides framing a soft, oval face, set off by long, slender eyebrows, a straight nose, beautiful sultry eyes, and small, round lips. She was a flawless Oriental beauty. Looking at her from the rear, she was gentleness incarnate; but from the front one could see amidst her tightly closed lips and delicate eyebrows a distinct resolution. She was the kind of girl who knew her direction, and never looked back. (Mao Dun 1951: 2)

The "flawless Oriental beauty" of her backside is dialectically positioned against the resoluteness of her forward-looking eyes. Indeed, self-consciously articulated angles, such as explicit frames of photographs or paintings, often frame the female figure with such unmistakable intentionality, whether it is to sell a product, or to point the way toward new possibilities of social reform. At the same time, however, literary framing of the female figure can be decidedly ambiguous, and this ambiguity can become an essential sign for the contested space that the Modern Girl represents.

The counterpart to Mao Dun's character Mei from *Rainbow* could be Cuiyuan from Eileen Chang's "Blockade" (1943):

She looked something like a church matron, though she was young enough to be unmarried. She wore a knitted white cheongsam with a rolling blue edge—blue and white, giving her entire dress a funereal flavor. She was even carrying a small umbrella that was adorned with blue and white squares. Her hairstyle was entirely nondescript, as if she were afraid to arouse any attention. In fact, she was not in danger of that at all. Her looks were not unattractive, but her prettiness was of the ambiguous sort, as if afraid to cause any offense. Everything about her face was somewhat imprecise, with no strong features or lines. Even her own mother could not say for certain whether she had a long face or a round face. (Zhang Ailing 1991: 224)

Chang's character demonstrates certain features in common with other New Women of the time: she is educated, Westernized, knowledgeable, and well versed in modernity. But her construction is less stable, literally difficult to see. Her widespread circulation in visual culture at the time actually leads to a more amorphous condition, liminally situated in contending waves of expectations and implications.

Eileen Chang's story is a product of 1943, temporally removed from Mao Dun's figures of the preceding decade. This is time enough for the Modern Girl to undergo marked transformation, and more particularized reading of these various images of the female figure in literary texts of the time requires careful schematization.[4] Nonetheless, the literary Modern Girl is a kind of crystallization of modern impulses even when she is difficult to see. She flows in texts of this period because of her passivity, and yet the visualizations of her agency are always the promise of visual consumption. The possibility of the Modern Girl's self-determination is a microcosm of contending forces of Chinese modern experience (see Chapter 25 by Tze-lan Sang).

The Woodcut

The woodcut is both an ancient medium of visual and verbal expression in China and an important, even cutting-edge format for modern literature and art. As early as the late ninth century, its ancestor, the *Diamond Sutra* (*Jingang jing*), had indelibly marked human culture as the first printed book.[5] What followed were centuries of continuous use in the widest array of printing functions. Even so, with the advent of the May Fourth Movement, the woodblock was still fully reinvigorated as the "new woodcut" (*xinxing banhua*), a medium that took the stage as a major cultural force with specifically modernist intentions. The success of the woodcut at this juncture was principally for two reasons. On the one hand, its indigenous origins shielded it from the charge of belatedness and inferiority *vis-à-vis* foreign models that were the source of so much modern media in China; on the other, the ubiquity of woodblock printing in Chinese culture allowed it to more or less transcend "elegant" or "low-brow" distinctions, thereby achieving high status among newly educated elite just when it took effect as a tool for impacting the widest possible audience (the masses). As a consequence of this positionality, the woodcut rose to the occasion of new expectations for artistic endeavors in early-twentieth-century China, when the imperative to reform cast all cultural production in a new, more meaningful light.

The key figure in advocating for the use of woodcut in a more consequential—which is to say socially conscious—art was Lu Xun. The period during which he came to realize the woodcut's potential, moreover, coincided with the ideological debates he was engaged in with other writers and critics in Shanghai, principally those affiliated with the Creation Society (X. Tang 2008: 77). The result of this turbulent exchange was an increasing commitment to a revolutionary literary practice, and the woodcut became, for Lu Xun, a viable medium for pursuing this program. Following models in Japan, which had developed its own woodcut movement earlier in the century, Lu Xun termed the new work "creative print" (*chuangzuo muke*) in order to distinguish it from other forms of reproduction. He introduced many exemplary artists to Chinese audiences starting in 1929, and continued to work on developing woodcut prints as a mode of disseminating new ideas until his death in 1936.[6]

By May 1942, when Mao Zedong presented his seminal "Yan'an Talks," the woodcut had taken central role in propaganda purposes, a weapon as the rhetoric of revolution became increasingly martial in nature. This was because the entire context for literature and art had shifted solely to the project of social and political function. As Mao (1965: 3: 69) put it:

> Comrades! You have been invited to this forum today to exchange ideas and examine the relationship between work in the literary and artistic fields and revolutionary work in general. Our aim is to ensure that revolutionary literature and art follow the correct path of development and provide better help to other revolutionary work in facilitating the overthrow of our national enemy and the accomplishment of the task of national liberation.

This narrowly defined sphere for literature and art became the only possibility for such cultural activity in the years following the establishment of the PRC. In effect, this meant that everything that was culturally produced (and exhibited) was produced officially; from inspiration through delivery, cultural products were to be thoroughly reviewed by a network of censors and cultural programmers whose job it was to evaluate and then sanction or prohibit any artistic project in terms of the value and efficacy of social impact. Such a system was particularly strict during the Cultural Revolution, which coincided, name notwithstanding, with the darkest period in Chinese letters in the twentieth century, culturally speaking.

By the mid-twentieth century, the woodcut had become emblematic of the didactic state, words and images so semiotically fused to their propagandistic purpose that there was no room for interpretative play. Apart from woodcut's inherent suitability to the project, the prominence of this medium was also in part due to the fact that the vice-minister of culture, Zheng Zhenduo, was himself an early proponent of the woodcut along with Lu Xun, and, in the years following their endeavors, grew to become China's foremost scholar on the subject. Through Zheng's leadership, the Rongbaozhai studio in Beijing became the leading producer of images for instructive purposes. By the late 1950s, and particularly with Mao's dictum to "speed up socialist transformation of handicrafts," the studio took a leading role in producing a profusion of "Revolutionary Romanticist" works, namely those that were a "particularly intense and ideal form of socialist realism, rich in detail, truthfulness, vividness, and revolutionary fervor" (Wachs and Finkelstein 2003: 104).

Given the centrality of the woodcut to Chinese visual cultural experience in the modern era, and the ubiquity of its manifestation as a propaganda tool from the beginning of the PRC, reaching its apogee during the Cultural Revolution, it is not really surprising that the woodcut would take a leading role in resignifying the semiotic landscape in the contemporary era. One of the leading examples of this effort is the artist Xu Bing and his 1987 "Book from the Sky." Xu's work, which debuted at the China National Gallery in 1988, is a book of woodblock and moveable type print of 4,000 entirely invented Chinese characters, a process that took him years to complete. Xu's work is but one outstanding example of avant-garde practice that demonstrates the centrality of the word in the Chinese visual-art context, an object of aesthetic value replete with cultural significance even when stripped entirely of its "significance."

The degree to which Xu meditated on the very nature of the words he would go on to display in cities all over the world, becoming in the process something of an iconic figure in the rapidly evolving spectacle of contemporary Chinese art, is typical of the artists of this generation. These artists were fully infused with revolutionary mentality as instilled in them by Maoist propaganda, but now their efforts were entirely repurposed to liberate Chinese society from the shackles of the ideological constraints that strict revolutionary programs had placed upon them. Xu works painstakingly in this project to create a verbal–visual discourse that would first displace and then actually circumvent the establishment of any single authority. The tight bond of progressive politics and woodcut media, forged in the tumult of Chinese literary and visual-art modernity, was ultimately undone by creative reapplication of the very principles of Chinese classical aesthetics, Chinese calligraphy, and the authority of the word.

Poetry and Visual Art: New Landscapes

Coming into the twenty-first century, Chinese word–image confluences such as that used by Xu Bing are increasingly prominent. Of these, perhaps the most notable is the large number of poets who are now engaged in visual-art work. The development of poets turning to visual art, it should also be noted, takes place in the context of a widespread decline in the centrality, if not volume, of poetic production in the Chinese context. In contrast to its pinnacle cultural position of the early 1980s, when poets of the "Misty" generation could lay claim to heroic status as leaders of the unofficial art movement (broadly construed), the opening of the new century has seen rapid decline of the social role of the poet in China. During the same period, visual artists have experienced rather stunning success, taking over from poets in their high-profile and often politicized stratagems (in particular, events and exhibitions organized by Ai Weiwei), but also leading the entire world in terms of the market value of their creative productions. Chinese contemporary visual art emerged as an essential component of global scape, where artists create objects of visual attention that merge with a global awareness of the rise of China as a newly dominating superpower, and thus effectively fuse an array of concomitant concerns and hopes into an integrated body of work that is perpetually on display at biennales and triennales in major cities from Miami to Tokyo, Venice to Dubai (not to mention cities in China).

Landscape is a useful frame for exploring the poet's engagement with visual art in particular. As China rises in prominence globally, visions of place, even abstractly construed, accrue added significance as companions or counterpoints to the widespread global imaging of Chinese locations. Poets, whose genre itself (free verse) is essentially linked to the modern literary project begun in the May Fourth era, are inherently attuned to a modernity in the lyrical expression. At the same time, creative landscape is a principal genre of classical Chinese visual art, one that also has historically demonstrated important confluence with classical verbal media (poetry). Indeed, the very act of aesthetic contemplation of place is a key pose for the literati artist, one rich in philosophical, in addition to strictly aesthetic, underpinnings. With this in mind, the landscape image produced by a Chinese artist of the present provides not only an object of passive contemplation, but an active engagement with the globalized China and re-engagement with the Chinese tradition.[7]

Of the new literati poets, there is perhaps no better example than Mang Ke, not only because Mang had no direct engagement with visual art prior to around 2005, but because he is himself a core figure in the development of contemporary Chinese poetry. Mang Ke, partnered with Bei Dao, was in fact the driving force that moved Chinese poetry out of the ideological confines that had boxed it during the Mao years.

The *Today* (*Jintian*) poets, as they would later be known, were in fact the dominant force of the unofficial contemporary art movement, as the logistics of writing a poem in times of extreme control over any form of expression are more manageable than creating works of visual or other performance art. As a form of poetic landscape, Mang's famous "Sunflower in the Sun" is a case in point:

> Do you see it?
> Do you see that sunflower in the sun?
> You see, it hasn't bowed its head
> But turned to look back
> In order to gnaw through
> That cord, held in the sun's hands,
> Wrapped around its neck.
>
> Do you see it?
> This proud sunflower head held high
> Glaring at the sun?
> Its head blocks all the rays of sunlight
> And even when there is no sun
> Its head emits beams of light
>
> Do you see the sunflower?
> You should approach it
> And as you do you will discover
> That the soil around its feet
> Handful by handful
> Oozes with blood
>   (Mang 1995: 1204–1205; trans.
>   Paul Manfredi)

This defiant flower, pitched in violent struggle, is a typical rhetorical figure for Mang Ke circa 1979, full of revolutionary spirit and willing to sacrifice its life for social change at any cost. Such a posture left an indelible mark on the writers, readers, and artists of all kinds of Mang's generation. Veteran critic and writer Tang Xiaodu, for instance, likens these early contemporary poetic texts to earthquakes. Tang cites the final stanza of Mang's "Sky," once again featuring the sun image, as a case in point: "The sun ascends / The sky— this blood-soaked shield" (X. Liang, Nan, and Liu 2004: 12; trans. Paul Manfredi).

Amidst the still pervasive propaganda machine, Mang Ke and his contemporaries carved out a new space with a messianic sensibility, one that drew upon a cultural logic of individual freedom, a new liberation this time from authoritarian manipulation of art and other forms of human expression. We can view such revision as a key step in the development of contemporary Chinese cultural experience, a virtually ex-nihilo creation posited into the cultural realm by Mang and his contemporaries to counter the socialist reality, which, up until the 1970s, was the only permissible socio-cultural scape that could emerge in the literary field. The image of a defiant sunflower is

Figure 21.1 Mang Ke, "Untitled" (2012), 80 x 80 cm (Sun Lei and Wang n.d.: 17). By permission of Mang Ke.

emblematic of Mang Ke's own social position at the time, a role he shared with fellow poets and visual artists alike. It was not until the year 2005, however, 30 years after his initial poetic performances, that Mang moved to a strictly visual medium.

Figure 21.1 shows one of a series of "Untitled" (Wuti, 2012).

A comparison of these two modes of Mang Ke's expression, poetic and visual, is instructive: in the first case, a verbal landscape is created by individual will, and the figure of sunflowers standing in blood-soaked soil is a patently heroic gesture, one that derives its power from the context of sociocultural struggle within China in the late twentieth century. By contrast, the untitled oil painting of 2010 shows us something very different; here, we have echoes of the literati tradition, invitations not to read images and words for their meaning, but invitations to engage the mind of the artist himself. As veteran art critic Li Xianting (2010) puts it:

> [In Mang Ke's work] a desolate field is not some particular desolate field, and flowers are not of some specific species or breed; it is instead the pure vibrancy that is the sedimentary image deep within Mang Ke's consciousness. This is in fact an expressive method long used by poets.

Mang Ke is painting, then, in part as one would write a poem, with an image drawn from the depths of his psyche, laid upon canvas not in order to depict a meaningful image (e.g., sunflower), or even express something on an individual level. Instead, he reconnects his once verbal artistic sensibility to a generalized landscape that is semantically empty but thus also open to echoes of a tradition (including his own famed poems of previous decades) and also future possibilities. This transition from word to image is significant for two reasons: first, such a move corresponds with the overall drift toward the visual and away from the verbal in expressive art in contemporary China (although Internet poetry may belie this point a bit). Next, by just comparing Mang's experience as a cultural figure late in the twentieth century, when poets were near celebrities, if still greatly constrained by censors determined to stem the flow of new ideas, with Mang's fortunes in the twenty-first century, when simply sustaining a livelihood in a society increasingly focused on material wealth became a major challenge, we glimpse a larger shift in Chinese socio-cultural experience, one that privileges the material over the ideological. In other words, Mang's move to the visual is indicative of China's shift to the consumable and away from the "spiritual" of pure poetry that characterize his early work. In making such a shift, Mang Ke is engaging in a mode of cultural practice that has strong roots in Chinese traditional culture, where literati painters held high prominence in cultural expression.

Mang Ke is not alone. His visual art, when exhibited, appears in the collectivity of the poet–painter genre (*shipai*) or "paintings by poets" (*shiren huihua*), a loosely affiliated group of 15–20 poet–artists comprised of both veteran poets such as Duo Duo and new-generation poets such as Wang Ai. At the center of the operation, however, is a core group of creative artists whose role in a specifically word–image-based poetics goes back to the beginnings of Chinese contemporary art in the 1970s. The principal figure in this respect, both as a poet–painter in his own right, and as an organizer, curator, and driving force of the community of artists whose work is exhibited with increasing frequency in urban centers in China, is Yan Li. Yan was one of the founding members of both the *Today* poets, along with Mang Ke, as well as the Stars art group, another unofficial art movement that also came into being in the pivotal year of 1979.[8]

Although Mang Ke's and Yan Li's careers have been parallel throughout the years, beginning in roughly the same place and the same time, and despite the fact that the two have remained close friends over the years, their sensibilities as artists and poets could not be more different. The essence of this difference can be found in a kind of urbanity that is the core of Yan's creative work. Where Mang's work is pastoral, a landscape of mountains and water, Yan's is determinedly city-focused, and has been from the time he first began creating poetry as a teenager. The most prominent examples of Yan's urban vision are the titular cities, for instance, his nearly 100-line, nine-stanza poem "New York" ("*Niuyue*," 1987). Beyond mere content, though, is Yan's aesthetic–formal engagement with the city, manifest in his characteristically tongue-in-cheek work titled the "Poetry Gum" (*kouxiangtang shi*) series, being ongoing short poetical works of two or three lines that Yan has been composing and publishing in a variety of venues for nearly two decades.[9] These works, which now number in the thousands, address a variety of themes, but do so in a manner commensurate with urban life—fast-paced, and shifting in perspectives, similar to mirrors on a disco ball. Such reflections rarely carry with them reducible ideological messages or even emotional signals. Yan's urban sentiments arise from glimpses of the phenomenal world in

Figure 21.2 Yan Li, "Mother and Child" (2004), 64 x 90 cm (Yan Li 2004: 39). By permission of Yan Li.

transition, with hints of exhilaration and wonder tempered by his skepticism of progress and intention of power brokers who ceaselessly "make it all happen."

The urban themes in Yan's work on the visual and verbal levels lend themselves to each other, incline toward one another, and illustrate one another, as in "Mother and Child" (Muzi, 2002) (Figure 21.2).

And the poem goes: "Parents try to take every single brick of the house and nurture it / Into a memorial plaque" (Yan Li 2004: 38; trans. Paul Manfredi).

This particular urban scene parallels Yan's personal experience—married in 1995, with two children, his daughters are aged 6 and 2 years at the time this image was created. But Yan's urban picture is abidingly larger than this in scope and intent. From his early writings through the present, Yan strives to get to the essence of systems, be they global-financial as in his frequent references to transnational corporations, or ideological, as in frequent borrowings from political discourse, either in the form of slogans or other top-down programs. The approach involves the use of the short, almost epigrammatic poems mentioned earlier, and the establishment of ongoing symbolism, both visual and verbal. Recurrent in the visual realm are the bricks seen in the "Mother and Child" image. On the verbal level, major corporations are often named (Yan Li 2006; trans. Paul Manfredi):

New York washes away the blood in America's heart
And washes off the red
Save for the free flow of Coca-Cola

Appropriate to the city, these landscapes are scenes, snippets, moments with dramatic content. What emerges in word and image is a sustained meditation on desire and consumption (and also environmental degradation), features of our shared world and the powers that drive its material existence. Yan strives in all this to drill down to an essence, a dynamic, an exchange. Yan's urban vision delves deeply into contemporary experience, getting under its skin. Moments of reflection, best manifest in the above-mentioned "Poetry Gum" series, do not keep the lyrical I away long, as he is always returning to the fold of urban engagement. The urban scene melds with the lyrical subject in a manner similar to the interwoven quality of word and image. Yan Li's painting in particular is a symbolist painting, with carefully deployed visual elements: the brick, the balloon, natural figures—birds and trees—all of which speak ideas in a manner words would, as in his "The City Is Her Dressing Table" (*Dushi shi tade shuzhuang tai*, 2008) (Figure 21.3).

Here, the record album theme, begun in 1987 and carried on in the decades since, has accrued meaning as it developed, with a medium (vinyl record), a one-time vehicle for audio expression, fading away from material experience, then fragmenting and

Figure 21.3 Yan Li, "The City Is Her Dressing Table" (2008), 100 x 80 cm (Yan Li 2008: 33). By permission of Yan Li.

reemerging as a sign in Yan's tight semiotic system. The shattered record albums refer to media systems, constantly destroyed and renewed in technology's march toward progress, but all the while permeating the built environment. Similar to the urban landscape he depicts, densely packed, there is little space between Yan's word and image, a kind of media density that comes at the viewer as a completed act—poet–artist, art, word, image, all a single fact.

Compared with Mang Ke and Yan Li, Sun Lei is of a newer generation. Born in 1971, Sun was only into his teens when China's reform was underway. He is also the only professionally trained and employed artist discussed in this chapter, now teaching at the Shandong Art Institute and a member of numerous professional arts organizations. He is, in short, the kind of cultural figure in present-day China who can be considered representative rather than marginal, central rather than peripheral. His choice to operate simultaneously in verbal–visual media is all the more significant because of this.

As a question of visuality, Sun Lei is far closer to Yan Li than Mang Ke regarding an urban scene, as evident in his "Shop Window" (Chuchuang, 2010):

> Walking slowly on the street
> I stop
> Take out a cigarette and light it
> Staring through the window at the silky display
> I tap the glass, it sounds quietly twice.
> I point to flaming colors on silk
> Like a child wild with love.
> Knowing that somewhere on those burning streets resides my lover's breath
> I tremble a bit… after a while,
> I walk on slowly to another window display
>   (Sun Lei and Jiang 2010: 8–9; trans. Paul Manfredi)

The old political engagement of Mang Ke is completely absent this landscape, leaving behind only the phenomenal world of colors arranged behind glass, utterly available but beyond reach. Sun's posture, very often peripatetic, is a quintessentially contemporary pose, set in the Chinese city where the rapidity of building causes shudders, moments of shock or dismay, but only momentarily, between drags on a cigarette.

We see this again in Sun's painting "Purple Boat" (Zihang, 2011) (Figure 21.4).

This is not the only type of painting that Sun Lei produces, often resorting to a typical oil on canvas with a bit of mixed media involved (newsprint, etc.), but here the materials, paper, colored ink, charcoal, combined with the mountains, water, and two deer (a familiar feature topic of classical Chinese painting), register a strong affinity with the classical tradition. In this case, though, the water in the foreground is not a flowing river but a swimming pool, the thatched hut a small factory bound by a high-rise, and of course a boat sailing off into space.

"Not Red" (Feihong, 2011) is another example of the similar style with a greater degree of austerity (Figure 21.5).

Figure 21.4 Sun Lei, "Purple Boat" (2011), 180 x 90 cm (Sun Lei and Wang n.d.: 101). By permission of Sun Lei.

Figure 21.5 Sun Lei, "Not Red" (2011), 70 x 140 cm (Sun Lei and Wang n.d.: 105). By permission of Sun Lei.

As is often the case in a Sun Lei painting, the words emerge here as figures, words we see without reading. They are incantations, evocations of the power of advertisement, suggestions relating to expressions of meaning without meaning. Other semiotic codes are present, snakes and plum blossoms, mountains, temples, and even blocks of color evoking specific landscapes of painting traditions extending back to the mid-twentieth century (Rothko, etc.). Sparse as it is, the image provides something of a catalogue and a critique at once. Such a critique is visible in Sun's work as an artist, but also as curator, editor, and exhibition organizer, extending influence broadly in a mode of new literati expression, a new scene with notably old characteristics.

The cubist and hieratic qualities of Sun's landscapes—where figures are drawn into prominence not as part of a mimetic "scene" but instead by virtue of the artist's own scheme of visual value—are clear indications of modernity in the expressions of poet–painters in contemporary China. Similarly, the poetry written by Sun Lei, Yan Li, and their compatriots cannot be mistaken for classical verse forms. Nonetheless, the landscape structure of Sun's "Purple Boat" is also clearly of the Chinese tradition, reminding viewers that the challenges to one-person perspective and other longstanding strategies grown out of Western perspectivist tradition have been inherent in Chinese art for centuries. Moreover, the posture of the poet in the city, a short sojourn, looking for love or protest, is recast in such an image, suggesting once again the ancient practice of exploring nature, of harmonizing with one's surroundings in the mode of a Tao Qian or Wang Wei, two classical poets whose paradigmatic escapes from the folly of human structures, both literal and figurative, have long since achieved canonical status. This nexus of old and new in contemporary Chinese art and letters is again hardly a novel feature of Chinese modernity. What is novel, though, is the scale of integration of word and image practices we see in Yan's and Sun's work, combined specifically with the pace and scale of China's built environments, material realities that have drawn attention of poets and other creative artists in China and indeed around the world. Articulating the experience of such a massively and rapidly transforming, even transmogrifying, landscape is an essential project for many artists in China today.

The work of poet–artists cannot be considered the mainstream of contemporary Chinese poetry, which is still more concerned with finding a viable language of its own, unimpeded by discourses non-indigenous. Even more so, the art of these poets is not the mainstream of contemporary visual expression, the upper echelons of which fetch the highest prices on global art market. Poet–artists are a niche, but a niche that is rich in cultural implication, a re-synthesis of word and image that harkens back and points forward at once. It is important to see that the visual context for Chinese contemporary art is global in a way that literature cannot be, and thereby relates to the spectacle that China has become on the world stage. By engaging in various visual practices, Chinese poets are actually now only capitalizing on what was once "theirs" in the first place, namely the purview of visual expression. Classical poets were visual artists if in no other realm than in the execution of Chinese writing (calligraphy), a visual art to begin with. Given the long tradition of painting and poetry as sister arts, and the tradition of poems and paintings appearing simultaneously (same canvas or other surface), the points of visual–verbal art connection are arguably more numerous than the realms of discrete performance.

The modern period contains key intersections of the verbal and the visual in Chinese literary expression. In this chapter, I have reviewed three forms of such overlap, each demonstrating its own characteristics, from poignantly social implications of the Modern Girl, to determinedly political purposes of the woodblock print, to aesthetically and philosophically oriented return of literati expression on the part of poet–artists in the twenty-first century. But they also share in the degree to which modern Chinese literature has depended on visual material, which proves indispensable in the development of new forms of literary style.

NOTES

1 Chinese visual culture is a relatively new field, particularly in its relation to literature (Andrews, Shen, and Spence 1998; L. Lee 1998; X. Tang 2000; J. Kuo 2007).

2 There are isolated and even highly important instances of visual–verbal overlap in Western traditions, as the famous phrase *"ut pictura poesis"* demonstrates. However, these are not fundamental to the writing and visual-art tradition in the way they are in China.

3 The Chinese term *"guohua"* (national painting) is most emblematic of these innovations in visual art. The phrase is generated by an essential distinction, placing all former visual art genres in China in a newly localized space, and opening the artistic field to receive modern alternatives.

4 Yingjin Zhang (2007: 123–124) identifies three broad categories of representing the female body: artwork, commodity, and signifier of a culturally significant event, which overlapped in the context of newly emerging technologies and discourses of the early twentieth century.

5 Such claims to origins are always available for criticism, and some scholars (Wachs and Finkelstein 2003: 118) argue that the precedents to Chinese printing are available in the Middle East. By the ninth century, however, it

is clear that Chinese printing industry was quite advanced.

6 The pinnacle of such efforts was the seminar that Lu Xun organized in August 1931 in Shanghai, which featured the Japanese print-maker Uchiyama Kakichi (X. Tang 2008: 113–133).

7 This more active view of the Chinese landscape is also expressed by W. J. T. Mitchell, who sees the word less as a noun than as a verb, "to landscape," and who takes landscape "as a process by which social and subjective identities are formed" (1994: 1–34). For him, landscape has broad implications for global power dynamics (imperialism) and other socio-historical trends.

8 As a question of materials, Yan works in either oil or acrylic, and mostly as a painter, though he has created some small installation works. He is also widely practiced as a verbal artist, writing short stories and even some novellas. During his years in New York (1985–1995), he was the editor of the journal *First Line* (*Yihang*), a Chinese unofficial publication that served to launch the careers of many young writers at a time when publishing in China was still a major challenge.

9 Most notably in a weekly installment in the Shanghai-based *Xinmin Evening News* (*Xinmin*

wanbao) since 2008. "Poetry gum" is a phrase that Yan Li uses informally to describe the works. The only published collection of these poems bears the title *Spinning Polyhedral Mirror* (*Duomianjing xuanzhuanti*, 1999).

REFERENCES

Andrews, Julia F., Kuiyi Shen, and Jonathan D. Spence. 1998. *A Century in Crisis: Modernity and Tradition in the Art of Twentieth-Century China*. New York: Guggenheim Museum.

Kuo, Jason. Ed. 2007. *Visual Culture in Shanghai, 1850–1930*. Washington, D.C.: New Academia Publishing.

Lee, Leo Ou-fan. 1999. *Shanghai Modern: The Flowering of a New Urban Culture in China, 1930–1945*. Cambridge, MA: Harvard University Press.

Li, Xianting 栗憲庭. 2010. "Hua shi Mang Ke de lingwai yizhong shi" 畫是芒克的另外一種詩 (Painting is another kind of poetry for Mang Ke). Mang Ke (blog), *blog.sina.com*. Accessed 25 October 2010.

Liang, Xiaoming 梁曉明, Nan Ye 南野, and Liu Xiang 劉翔. Eds. 2004. *Zhongguo xianfeng shige dangan* 中國先鋒詩歌檔案 (Chinese Avant-garde poetry archive). Hangzhou: Zhejiang wenyi chubanshe.

Mang Ke 芒克. 1995. "Xiang ri kui" 向日葵 (Sunflower). In *Xinshi sanbai shou* 新詩三百首 (300 New Poems). Edited by Xiao Xiao 蕭蕭 and Zhang Mo 張默. Taipei: Jiuge. 1204–1205.

Mao, Dun 茅盾. 1951. *Hong* 虹 (Rainbow). Beijing: Kaiming shudian.

Mao, Dun 茅盾. 1982. *Ziye* 子夜 (Midnight). *Mao Dun quanji* 茅盾選集 (Selected works of Mao Dun). Vol. 1. Chengdu: Sichuan renmin chubanshe.

Mao, Zedong. 1965. *Selected Works of Mao Zedong*. 4 vols. Beijing: Foreign Languages Press.

Mitchell, W. J. T. Ed. 1994. *Landscape and Power*. Chicago: University of Chicago Press.

Sun, Lei 孫磊, and Jiang Nan 姜楠. Eds. 2010. *Xiuci: dangdai shiren huihua zhan* 修辭:當代 詩人繪畫展 (Rhetoric: paintings by contemporary poets). Beijing: Yueren huixin yishupin.

Sun, Lei 孫磊, and Wang Jiaxin 王家新. Eds. n.d. *Huying de hai* 呼應的海 (Echoes of the sea). Beijing: Fangyuan yishu kongjian.

Tang, Xiaobing. 2000. *Chinese Modern: The Heroic and the Quotidian*. Durham, NC: Duke University Press.

Tang, Xiaobing. 2008. *Origins of the Chinese Avant-garde: The Modern Woodcut Movement*. Berkeley, University of California Press.

Wachs, Iris, and Haim Finkelstein. 2003. *Poetry, Painting Politics: Chinese Urban Woodblock Printing Studios in an Age of Revolution, 1949–2000*. Beer-Sheva: Avraham Baron Gallery, Ben-Gurion University of Negev.

Yan, Li 嚴力. 1999. *Duomianjing xuanzhuanti* 多麵鏡旋轉體 (Spinning Polyhedral Mirror). Xining: Qinghai renmin chubanshe.

Yan, Li 嚴力. 2004. *Yan Li shihua ji* 嚴力詩畫集 (Poetry and art of Yan Li). Xinning: Qinghai renmin chubanshe.

Yan, Li 嚴力. 2006. Unpublished Manuscript.

Yan, Li 嚴力. 2008. *Yan Li yishu zuopin ji* 嚴力藝 術作品集 (New art works of Yan Li). New York: Walt Whitman Literature Foundation.

Zhang, Ailing 張愛玲. 1991. "Fengsuo" 封鎖 (Blocade). In *Diyi luxiang* 第一爐香 (The First Brazier). Taipei: Huangguan. 223–230.

Zhang, Yingjin. 2007. "Artwork, Commodity, Event: Representations of the Female Body in Modern Chinese Pictorials." In *Visual Culture in Shanghai, 1850–1930*. Edited by Kuo, Jason. Washington, D.C.: New Academia Publishing. 121–161.

22

All the Literature That's Fit to Print: A Print Culture Perspective on Modern Chinese Literature

Nicolai Volland

The transformation of Chinese print culture since the late nineteenth century has profoundly reshaped the modes of literary production and consumption. The change in the physical appearance of books—from the thread-bound *juan* to the books and journals circulating in the early twenty-first century—is nothing less than revolutionary. The adoption of new printing technologies, the diversification of distribution channels, and the changing economics of publishing have fundamentally altered the reading experience for consumers of literature in China. Yet, the changes that Chinese print culture has undergone since the late nineteenth century had equally thorough-going effects on literary production: new channels of writing, such as newspapers and journals, left an immediate imprint on literary forms and styles. Meanwhile, the rise of new institutions, such as the modern publishing house and the editorial offices of journals, created unprecedented opportunities for writers to interact and participate in the larger processes of literary production and circulation. Most importantly, print culture has directly influenced the aesthetic processes that gave rise to modern Chinese literature, shaping the emerging forms of writing at all critical junctions, from the turn of the twentieth century through the New Culture Movement, the 1920s–1930s, the early socialist period, to the 1980s–1990s. As shown in this chapter, print culture played an essential role in the ongoing processes of defining the formal and aesthetic dimensions of literature in China. I will reassess the importance of print culture for our evolving understanding of modern Chinese literature and offer a chronological examination of some of the key moments in the history of both print culture and modern Chinese literature as a whole.[1]

A Companion to Modern Chinese Literature, First Edition. Edited by Yingjin Zhang.
© 2016 John Wiley & Sons, Ltd. Published 2016 by John Wiley & Sons, Ltd.

Print Culture and the Historiography
of Modern Chinese Literature

Print culture–based approaches to literature cannot replace textual analysis, but they enrich our understanding of the dynamics of literary production and consumption. Only since the 1990s has print culture received wider attention within the larger field of modern Chinese literary studies. Since then, scholars in both China and abroad have produced a growing body of innovative research that complements, corrects, and frequently also challenges the existing knowledge of modern Chinese literature and literary production. In a seminal article, Wang Xiaoming (1991) has pointed out the significance of both literary journals and literary societies for the dynamics of New Literature since the May Fourth Movement. Michel Hockx (2003; also 1999) has picked up from Wang and suggested an approach that builds on a sociology of literature inspired by Bourdieu (1993) and his work on the field of cultural production. Leo Ou-fan Lee (1999) has emphasized the role of print culture within the larger tableau of modern Chinese culture. Independent from Western research, a number of Chinese scholars, most notably Chen Pingyuan (2004) and Xia Xiaohong, have emphasized the transformative role of the new print media in the formation of modern Chinese literature. Research in Chinese print culture has further benefited from the quick growth of studies on the early Chinese press (Judge 1996; Mittler 2004; Wagner 2007). Christopher Reed (2004) is the most complete account yet of the modern Chinese publishing industry. These and other more recent studies have provided the basis for increasingly sophisticated inquiries into the dynamics of literary production (and, to some degree, consumption) in modern China.

Yet, print culture has also played a crucial role in major historiographical developments within the field, reshaping our understanding of the canon. The definition of modern Chinese literature has undergone significant changes since the early 1980s. Both the periodization of the "modern" and its content—the canon and its inclusivity and exclusivity—have shifted in response to new research. Efforts to rewrite literary history got underway in China since the 1980s (Z. Huang, Chen, and Qian 1988), aiming to break through the state-sanctioned, teleological historiography focused on the revolutionary May Fourth tradition. Meanwhile, scholars in the United States and Europe began to move beyond the early canon defined by pioneering studies (C. T. Hsia 1961; Průšek 1980). All the major revisionist projects have relied heavily on print culture and hitherto neglected printed sources to redefine the outlook and shape of modern Chinese literature.

Perry Link's seminal study (1981) restored butterfly popular fiction to its place within modern Chinese literature, drawing to a large extent on popular journals from the 1910s–1920s, and on interviews with the editors and publishers of these journals (many of whom were influential writers in their own right). In a similar vein, the rediscovery of the New Sensationalist school of Shanghai modernism is contextualized in Leo Lee's extensive work (1999) on the vibrant print culture of the 1930s. And David Wang's work (1997) on the "repressed modernities" of late Qing fiction—not until recently acknowledged as a proper part of modern Chinese literature—relies heavily on the rapidly proliferating fiction journals published in the last decade of the Qing. None of these interventions would have been possible without attention to important but hitherto neglected repositories of printed materials, which have allowed and continue to allow us to reimagine both the canon of modern Chinese literature and its periodization.

New Media and New Institutions

The evolution of Chinese print culture has shaped writing and reading practices long before the modern era. During the Ming and Qing eras, in particular, local centers of printing and publication in places such as Suzhou became sites for the negotiation and dissemination of tastes, styles, and emerging genres. The publishing trade in late imperial China was diverse and sophisticated, ranging from large-scale literati-operated publishing concerns, to small, often non-commercial imprints serving the needs of individual writers or local poetry clubs, to highly developed commercial woodblock printers catering to a mass market (Chia 2003; K. Chow 2004; K. Chow and Brokaw 2005; McDermott 2006). The commercial segment of the industry was especially well organized, and operated through far-flung trade networks, giving even readers in remote regions of the empire access to printed literature (Brokaw 2007). The output of this industry was as diverse as the trade itself, including both mass market prints and elaborately illustrated luxury editions of popular fiction (Hegel 1998).

With the introduction of Western printing technologies in the late nineteenth and early twentieth century, Chinese print culture diversified significantly, generating new media for the dissemination of literature. These new media, in turn, had a demonstrable impact on literary production. The earliest new print medium was the newspaper, which started gaining popularity in the 1870s, especially with the founding of *Shenbao* (Mittler 2004). As Patrick Hanan (2004) has shown, the latter—and the early Chinese press in general—played a crucial role in the translation and publication of foreign fiction. More generally, they pioneered the serialization of fiction in the daily press, a practice that became common after 1900. Newspapers were equally suitable to carry other genres, such as poetry. Within the new Chinese newspapers, literary pieces usually retained a peripheral nature, bracketed by—and interacting with—other genres, such as news reports, travelogues, or advertisements. For this reason, plus the space and time constraints of the daily paper, literature after 1900 began to gravitate toward other new media, such as newspaper supplements and literary journals. Newspaper supplements emerged in the 1910s as an increasingly popular space to concentrate and highlight literary writing and debates within the newspaper. Supplements such as the *Shenbao*'s "Free Talk" could gain considerable clout, to the point where warring factions within the literary field competed over their editorship (Tsai 2010). Newspapers remained sites of reading and writing literature, especially in times of high volatility, when the speed and wide reach of newspapers were crucial.[2]

The most influential medium, and the one most consequential for literary production, was the literary journal. The earliest Chinese literary journals can be dated back to the 1870s (Hanan 2004: 85–109), but the genre took off in earnest after the turn of the century. The sheer number of major and minor literary journals in the first half of the twentieth century is staggering, attesting to the vibrancy of literary production. The rise of the periodical press in turn shaped the emergence of modern Chinese literature. The hybrid space of the journal was the prime site of experimentation and negotiation, reconfiguring the aesthetics of about every single genre. As multi-authored texts, journal issues combine disparate contents that contextualize each other, implying innovative reading strategies that in turn stimulate new forms of writing.[3] The seriality of the literary journal offered continuity, especially in times of rupture, such as during the New Culture Movement, and made sure that even ephemeral experiments would reach readers and thus enter a larger consciousness. The compartmentalization of space within the journal further allowed crossover between genres printed side by side, as well as cross-fertilization between literary and non-literary texts, and between literature from different countries (and occasionally in different languages), which all appeared between the covers of a journal. These features of the journal were, of course, by no means exclusive to China, but they played a key role in the transformation of Chinese literature throughout most of the twentieth century.[4] Only in the 1990s did the book displace the literary journal as the prime site of literary circulation.

Books were the oldest medium of literary circulation in China, but their physical shape underwent a dramatic transformation in the twentieth century. The displacement of *juan*, thread-bound volumes collected in boxes (*han*), by industrially produced books, printed on both sides of large sheets that are folded, cut, and bound into volumes of hundreds of pages, not only radically changed the appearance of books, but opened up new possibilities for literary texts: new-style books could accommodate longer consecutive texts while also producing new textual aesthetics, ranging from spatial organization (paragraphs, punctuation) to modern fonts to illustrative material. The book cover in particular emerged as a site of aesthetic and epistemological competition in a crowded literary marketplace.[5] With the commercialization of cultural production in the 1990s, the book achieved unprecedented prominence as an industrially produced and professionally marketized cultural commodity.

Collectanea (*congshu*) are an overlooked medium that has, however, made considerable impact on Chinese literary production. Publishers large and small discovered the advantages offered by serial publishing, giving rise to book series that ranged from three or four titles to hundreds of volumes. The predilection for serial publishing can be seen as a marketing device, but it also impacts the reading of individual texts by contextualizing them, thus linking them with other texts and suggesting reading and interpretive strategies. This sense of bracketing is reinforced by formal constraints that the series imposes on individual texts, such as uniform covers and design, but also paratextual structuring devices such as series forewords. *Congshu* publishing spread quickly in the 1920s and retained its popularity in socialist China after 1949 as well as in the reform era.

With the rise of newspapers, journals, modern books, and collectanea, a range of different spaces for literary production emerged that had a direct impact on the production and consumption of texts. The borders between these media, however, were often fluid.[6] Migration of texts across different media (such as serialization of a novel in a newspaper, followed by its publication as a book, and consequent reprint in a series) was and is common.[7] The implications of such migrations in terms of these texts' economy of meaning, especially in light of their reception in radically different contexts, remains poorly understood.

Literary production in modern China was confronted not only with an unprecedented choice of media, but also operated within a network of institutions that offered new resources to writers. The two most prominent institutions were publishing houses and the editorial offices and boards of literary journals. Modern publishing houses offered many an aspiring writer employment as editors, thus involving these writers on multiple levels in the processes of literary production and circulation. New-style publishers such as the Shenbaoguan provided new career options for the educated and upwardly mobile since the late nineteenth century; these paths gained importance with the abolition of the imperial examination system in 1905 and the transformation of the literati class. With the rise of large concerns such as the Commercial Press, new standards of writing and publishing spread quickly; the large publishers in particular functioned as gatekeepers who could sway the direction of cultural production, as evidenced by the Commercial Press's 1920 decision to change the editorship of *Short Story Monthly*, putting the May Fourth radicals around Mao Dun in charge of one of the key journals of the time. Most important, though, was the constitution of the publishing house as a social space that furthered interaction and debate, and provided an umbrella for the endeavors and cultural enterprises of likeminded writers. Hundreds of small-scale "peer publishers" (*tongren chubanshe*) sprang up in the Republican era, to promote the aesthetic ideologies of usually not more than a small group of owner–investor–editor–writers. Short-lived though many of these ventures proved to be, they had an indelible impact on the writing of these individuals, much of which is remembered in association with such publishing houses, bearing the signatures of the sites of its production even decades later.[8]

Similar functions, in terms of both social organization and textual production, can be observed for literary journals and their offices. While some of the leading Chinese literary journals—often the more enduring and long-lived ones—were published by the nation's most prominent publishing houses, the Republican era saw the proliferation of a staggering variety of literary journals organized, similar to the smaller publishers, as "peer journals" (*tongren zazhi*) (Chen Pingyuan 2005a: 11). As institutions, these journals and their boards (often not more than three or four founders) negotiated textual production by formulating agreed standards of inclusion and exclusion for the texts considered for publication. In the 1920s and 1930s in particular, much of a writer's *habitus* came to depend on the journals in which he or she chose to publish (for established writers) or was given opportunity to publish (for emerging writers) (Hockx 2003). (Dis)association with various literary groups and ideologies was negotiated through journals and their boards, which controlled the aesthetic criteria of textual production under their auspices. With the nationalization of the publishing industry in the early 1950s, both publishing houses and literary journals lost some of their status as autonomous arbiters of literary taste, but they continued to play an important role as employers and sites of socialization for writers–editors throughout the socialist era and beyond.

Print Culture and the Birth of Modern Chinese Literature, 1870–1945

The early stages of the transformation of Chinese print culture are closely intertwined with the name of the Shenbaoguan. Founded in 1872 by the British merchant Ernest Major, the *Shenbao* was China's first modern newspaper to create a wider impact (Mittler 2004). As Hanan (2004: 110–123) has shown, the *Shenbao* began to translate Western fiction almost immediately after its founding. A year later, Major set up *Trifling Notes on the World at Large* (*Yinghuan suoji*), one of the first Chinese periodicals, which also ventured into serialized fiction (Hanan 2004: 85–109). Most importantly, Major saw commercial opportunities for book publishing in Jiangnan, the cultural heartland that had been devastated by the Taiping rebellion a decade earlier. After the loss of countless private libraries, the region's literati were desperate to rebuild their collections. The Shenbaoguan began to cater to this demand beginning from 1873, using its lithographic equipment to produce affordable but high-quality reprints of older editions, ranging from annotated classics to masterpieces of fiction such as *The Scholars* (Wagner 2002). Yet, the Shenbaoguan also started publishing new Chinese fiction, such as the courtesan novel *Illusion of Romance* (*Fengyue meng*) (Hanan 2004: 35). The editions produced by Major's press retained the look and feel of traditional works of print, but took advantage of modern equipment and marketing methods that paved the way for successive waves of innovation in the last decades of the Qing.

The new media and institutions of print culture played a pivotal role in the literary transformation of the first decade of the twentieth century. With the founding of the Commercial Press in 1898, a major new player entered a field that it would dominate until 1949. Organized as a joint stock company, the Commercial Press acquired state-of-the-art printing equipment and ventured into both book and journal publishing. In 1903, the Commercial Press launched *Illustrated Fiction* (*Xiuxiang xiaoshuo*, 1903–1906), a biweekly magazine set up to compete with the popular *New Fiction* (*Xin xiaoshuo*, 1902–1906). The latter had been established in Tokyo by Liang Qichao, as a vehicle to promote its founder's literary reforms, and moved to Shanghai in 1903. To edit its fledgling venture, the Commercial Press appointed Li Boyuan, by then a seasoned journalist, editor, and writer. Li's exposé novel *The Bureaucrats: A Revelation* (1903–1905), had started serialization in *World Vanity Fair* (*Shijie fanhua bao*, 1901–1910), a daily newspaper Li had founded (and kept editing while working for *Illustrated Fiction*). The managers at the Commercial Press roped in Li in the hope of copying the success of its rival, *New Fiction*, which was serializing Wu Jianren's *Strange Events Witnessed Over Twenty Years* (1903–1905), another highly popular exposé novel. *Illustrated Fiction* serialized a number of influential novels, including Li's own *A Brief History of Enlightenment* (1903–1905) and Liu E's *Travels of Lao Can* (1903). The magazine folded after Li's untimely death in 1906, the same year when *New Fiction* shut down. Both were almost immediately replaced by *All-Story Monthly* (*Yueyue xiaoshuo*, 1906–1909) and other fiction magazines catering to a growing market, not least in field of butterfly fiction (Link 1981: 251–260).

By the 1910s, the centrality of literary journals and publishing houses as platforms for literary innovation was well established. It is little surprising that the most radical reformers chose a journal as their mouthpiece, the site to launch both their programmatic declarations and their practical experiments with creating a literature that, they insisted, was a radical departure from the literary practice of the past. *New Youth* (1915–1926) is arguably the most important journal, literary or otherwise, of the Republican period. The New Culture Movement and its self-centered discourses have been successively deconstructed since the late 1980s, but the role of *New Youth* in shaping these very discourses is undeniable (Doleželová-Velingerová 2002; Chen Pingyuan 2005a). It is therefore justified to take a more detailed look at the role of print culture in the making of modern Chinese literature, as manifested on the pages of *New Youth*.

Lu Xun's famous short story "Kong Yiji" was published in the April 1919 issue of *New Youth*, just weeks before the momentous May Fourth demonstrations. Not many of his readers today take the trouble and go to *New Youth* in order to read the story. A canonical piece of modern Chinese literature, "Kong Yiji" has been reprinted and anthologized countless times, first in Lu Xun's own 1923 collection *Outcry*. The removal of the story from its original context, however, comes with a loss of crucial information that reveals the processes at work in the formation of what became known as New Literature, and that show Lu Xun's short story as part of larger intertextual processes within and beyond the confines of the journal.

A quick look at the April 1919 issue reveals, for instance, two advertisements on the page facing "Kong Yiji"—for a chemistry and a physics textbook, respectively (Figure 22.1).[9] This layout—a short story depicting a degenerate old-style scholar printed opposite introductions to modern science, published by the same Qunyi shushe that produced *New Youth*—is a not-so-subtle sign of the editors' proposed reading of Lu Xun's story. More importantly, it alerts us to the expectations of *New Youth*'s intended readers, an audience schooled in modern learning. In this respect, the journal's target audience resembles the author of "Kong Yiji" himself, who had received a medical education in Japan and would have consumed textbooks akin to those in the advertisement—in fact, the advertisement text reveals that both volumes are translations of Japanese textbooks, raising the hypothetical possibility that the advertised books might be just those that had enlightened Lu Xun a decade earlier. On the pages of *New Youth*, "Kong Yiji" was thus not merely a social satire, but a polemic against traditional practices of knowledge production that gained power from the direct contrast (visualized through the advertisement) with the new sciences and modern attitudes that China was importing via Japan from the West.

Figure 22.1 Lu Xun's "Kong Yiji," and advertisements for two science textbooks on the facing page, *New Youth*, April 1919 issue. Courtesy of National University of Singapore Chinese Library.

If the two advertisements create a visible tension with Lu Xun's short story, "Kong Yiji" communicates with other articles in the same issue, drawing on and at the same time feeding into discourses at the heart of the modernizers' agenda. At a prominent location early in the April 1919 issue, readers find an article by Peking University professor Zhu Xizu on "The Value of the Vernacular" (*"Baihuawen de jiazhi"*). *New Youth* had begun its crusade for a new literature in the vernacular several years before, and by 1919 many of Zhu's points are but reiterations of arguments that had been made earlier in the journal, given added punch by stinging denunciations of China's conservatives. The importance attached to writing in the vernacular, however, naturally draws attention to Lu Xun's short story, which is implicitly valorized as an example of exactly the arguments presented by Zhu. In fact, "Kong Yiji" appears as a response, a proof of concept for a radical proposition. And if the reader is still in doubt as to the sources of inspiration for this new departure—promoted by Zhu and practiced by Lu Xun—he is receiving an answer from an advertisement on the page facing Zhu's article. The ad promotes a set of flashcards for students of English, an "indispensible and genial aid" for learners of the foreign language. The new Chinese literature, exemplified by "Kong Yiji," draws on foreign sources of inspiration for both its value system and its linguistic conventions. The short story appearing in *New Youth* is thus enmeshed in a range of intellectual and aesthetic discourses, embedded in a network of reformist agendas spread out across the pages of *New Youth*, covering creative writing, articles, and advertisements. In an ironic indication of the intellectual confusion of the day, all the advertisements are composed in the classical *wenyan* style.

Lu Xun's "Kong Yiji" is but one example among many of how new media and new institutions such as the editorial community behind *New Youth* configured and shaped the processes leading to the formation of modern Chinese literature. In the same issue of *New Youth*, readers would find the following poem by Hu Shi:

一涵!   Yihan!
月亮正在你的房子上,   The moon stands high above your chamber still,
正照在我的窗子上 。   shines right upon my windowsill.
你想我如何能讀書,   Just think, how could I read,
如何能把我的心關在這幾張紙上!   how lock away my heart in pages yet to fill!

(Trans. Nicolai Volland)

Hu's "Yihan" belongs to the first wave of Chinese poems written in the new vernacular.[10] Hu began publishing his *baihua* poems in 1916, many of them on the pages of *New Youth*. Although the author decided not to include "Yihan" in his collection *Experiments* (1919), it bears many of the same features. *Experiments* gains its rhetorical power from the wide range of textual experiments illustrating possible strategies to revolutionize the writing of Chinese poetry. As a collection published within the enclosed space of a book, *Experiments* emphasizes the exploratory nature of Hu's enterprises and the boldness of his departure from tradition. At the same time, the autonomous claims of the medium, a *danxingben* (single-issued volume) obscure the roots and sources of inspiration that fuelled Hu's efforts, and in fact the larger textual economy in which his poetic experiments were rooted.

The same *New Youth* issue that contained "Yihan" offers another contribution by Hu Shi, the translation of a poem by Omar Khayyam:[11]

要是天公換了卿和我,   Ah! Love, could you and I with Him conspire
該把這糊塗世界一齊都打破,   To grasp this sorry Scheme of Things entire,
再團再煉再調和,   Would not we shatter it to bits—and then
好依着你我的安排, 把世界重新造過!   Remould it nearer to the Heart' Desire!

The parallels between Hu's translation and his own poem, quoted in the preceding text, are obvious: as with the former, "Yihan" is a quatrain, with free rhythm and an AABA rhyme scheme. Hu's poetic choices follow closely those of his translation, which in turns attempts to recreate the poetics (minus the iambic meter) of Omar Khayyam's poem. In a discursive introduction, Hu analyzes his source and explains his own choices:[12]

Omar Khayyam, the author of this short poem, comes from the country of Persia. His [writings on] mathematics and astronomy are the pride of the history of Persia's civilization. He was not just a scientist but also a poet. Five hundred of his "jueju"-style poems are very famous (called *Rubivat* [*sic*], these are rhymed quatrains, in which the first, second, and fourth lines are rhymed, but not the third line. They closely resemble the Chinese jueju-form, and that is why I am using this expression). The English poet *Fitzgerald* has translated over a hundred of these, and there are translations from others as well. This is poem no. 108 in the *Fitzgerald* translation. The birth date of the Persian poet is unclear; he died in the year 1123 of the Western calendar, which corresponds to the fifth year of the Xuanhe reign of the Chinese [emperor] Song Huizong.[13]

I quote Hu Shi's introduction at length since it not only details the poetics behind his translation, but also locates it within a larger, transnational web of literary practice. The dating creates an equivalence between Chinese and international time, and implies a parallel with contemporary Chinese poetical practice—*shi* and *ci* poetry of the Song dynasty—that is confirmed by the analogy between the Persian *rubaiyat* and the Chinese *jueju*. What Hu fails to elaborate on is the fact that the equivalence relies on the detour through nineteenth-century Britain, in form of Edward Fitzgerald's free English rendering of the Persian poem. Yet, it is exactly this link that provides the possibility of transculturation, of transnational textuality in the first place.

Hu Shi's translation appears on the page facing his own poem "Yihan" noted earlier (Figure 22.2).[14] This editorial intervention allows the readers of *New Youth* to read the three poems—the one by Omar Khayyam, Hu's translation, and his own poem—in

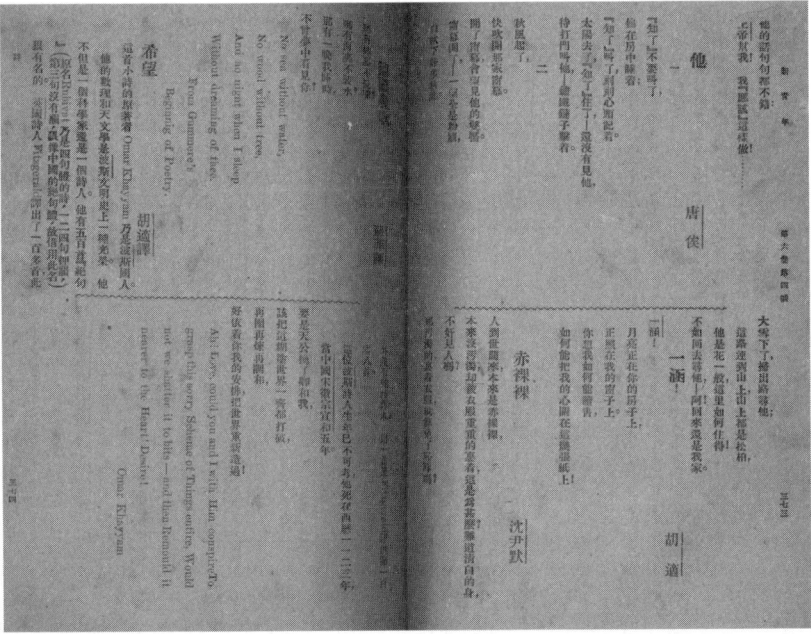

Figure 22.2 Hu Shi's poem "Yihan," and, on the facing page, his introduction to and translation of Omar Khayyam's poem, *New Youth*, April 1919 issue. Courtesy of National University of Singapore Chinese Library.

conjunction with each other, moving back and forth between them. On the pages of *New Youth*, the bold experiments of vernacular poetry thus appear as elements of a transnational literary practice. At the same time, the processes of aesthetic innovation are linked to other intellectual discourses: In his preface to Omar Khayyam's poem, Hu Shi notes the latter's reputation as a polymath. It is no coincidence that the same issue of *New Youth* also contained an article on science,[15] as well as a lengthy treatise on the philosophy of pragmatism, penned by none other than Hu Shi. The author—and by extension the journal itself—place themselves in a tradition of scientific and pragmatist intellectual practice that is linked at multiple points with creative processes past and present, Chinese and foreign.

The journal thus becomes a site of negotiation that allowed translations and original writing, texts in English and Chinese, as well as theoretical, programmatic, and literary texts to appear all in the same space. It breaks down the borderline between these genres, establishing a continuum in which the foreign poem is imported into a new Chinese textual ecology, while the new-style poem acquires a programmatic character of its own, calling for linguistic and literary revolutions. As with many other journals—and, to varying degrees, newspapers, books, and *congshu* series—*New Youth* exposed the very processes of writing, the emergence of novel literary forms at a key junction in modern Chinese literature. The journal emerged as the ground that inspired and made possible the birth of Hu Shi's new poetry and Lu Xun's short fiction, as well as countless literary experiments and innovations throughout the twentieth century.

The ongoing evolution of print technologies provided the ground for continuous innovations in modern Chinese literary practice. New equipment introduced in the late 1920s and the 1930s, for instance, allowed publishers of journals and books alike to greatly reduce the cost of reproducing photographs, illustrations, and other graphic elements, while yielding much higher-quality reproductions than hitherto possible. These developments radically altered the aesthetic dimension of books and journals, triggering an aesthetic revolution in print culture that in turn influenced literary production itself. The contrast between *New Youth*, which contains very little graphic design and no illustrations at all, and the literary magazines of just a decade later, is instructive. The beautifully produced *Camel* (*Luotuo*, 1926), for example, edited by a triumvirate that included Zhou Zuoren, featured a beautifully calligraphed cover on its first and only issue, and contained 11 high-quality black-and-white reproductions of paintings and woodcuts by the French realist master Jean-François Millet.[16] The images in this issue illustrated an eclectic mix of poetry, translations, and essays, as well as a diary-style novel by Xu Zuzheng, one of the journal's editors. The novel, *The Diary of Lan Shengdi* (*Lan Shengdi de riji*, 1926), is one of the earliest examples of this genre in modern Chinese literature. Its sentimentalism was apparently influenced by European romanticism, and Millet's pastoral scenes effectively translate the mood of Xu's novel into a visual language, thus merging word and image into a multi-sensorial experience for the journal's readers. At the same time, the confluence of the written and the visual on the journal's pages is a reminder that new literary sensibilities emerging in the 1920s–1930s were forged by (often external) stimuli that went far beyond the printed word.

One of the most famous examples of the cross-fertilization of textual and visual experimentation is the journal *Les Contemporaines* (1932–1935), founded under the editorship of Shi Zhecun. *Les Contemporaines* combined bold covers, avant-garde design, art deco type fonts, photographic reproductions, line-drawings, cartoons, and illustrated advertisements with a wide range of literary texts, many known today as modernist experiments that brought modern Chinese literature into dialogue with modernism elsewhere in the world (L. Lee 1999: 132–144; Shih 2001: 249–257). The February 1934 issue, for instance, featured fiction by Mu Shiying and Dai Wangshu, poetry by Lin Jinfa and Zhang Kebiao, and an essay by Mu Mutian on his poetic practice, among other contents. This who-is-who of modernist literature is accompanied by a visual cornucopia as bold as the issue's literary contributions. The cover features a painting by the artist and writer Guo Jianying, depicting the stylized silhouette of a woman who sports red lipstick and a perm, and two large, presumably male, hands (Figure 22.3). A four-page insert in the middle of the issue contains a photograph of Zhou Zuoren and a piece of his calligraphy, celebrating the writer's 50th birthday; drawings and film stills from the Hollywood movie *Alice in Wonderland* (dir. Norman

Figure 22.3 Cover of *Les Contemporaines*, Feb. 1934 issue, design by Guo Jianying. Courtesy of National University of Singapore Chinese Library.

Z. McLeod, 1933); and photographs and facsimiles of Dostoyevsky's works. Elsewhere, the issue contains line drawings and illustrated advertisements that enter into dialogue with the literary experiments on the pages of the journal. The printed space of *Les Contemporaines* produces a cross-genre aesthetics that celebrates the hybridity of modernism as a new formal language.

The eruption of the Anti-Japanese War in 1937 dealt a blow to the institutional landscape of Chinese print culture. Countless journals closed down as their editors fled Shanghai, heading to the interior. Some remained in unoccupied Shanghai, known as "orphan island" (1937–1941). The major publishing houses, such as the Commercial Press, hedged their bets by dividing their operations, relocating part of their staff to Chongqing and other wartime cultural centers, while keeping some editors in Shanghai. The latter were forced to cooperate with the Japanese after the occupation of the foreign concessions in December 1941. War and occupation came at a high price for the publishing industry and for China's cultural elite, but also created new opportunities: in Shanghai, emerging writers such as Eileen Chang benefitted from the exodus of established authors, and from new journals eager to cultivate gifted writers. Many new journals, as well as publishing houses, sprang up in unoccupied Chongqing, Guilin, and Kunming, producing a lively patriotic cultural movement. And, in Yan'an, the Communists built their own publishing apparatus, which laid the ground for their overhaul of the publishing industry after 1949. Notably, the wartime disruption did not change the basic patterns of print culture, its main media, or the role of institutions (such as publishing houses and the editorial boards) as the arbiters of modern Chinese literature.

Print Culture in Socialist and Postsocialist China

The marketplace for cultural production underwent major changes in postwar China that affected both the publishing industry and the literary establishment. As I have detailed elsewhere (Volland 2014), the publishing industry experienced a brief postwar boom during which the major publishers, now reunited in Shanghai, tried to recover their dominant position; numerous new publishing houses were founded, and a flurry of new literary journals proliferated. This boom, however, soon gave way to crisis: economic disruptions from the civil war between the Nationalists and the Communists threatened the bottom line of the industry, while censorship took a toll on politically engaged literature. Readers, wary of prolonged turmoil, turned to cheaply produced pulp fiction, fuelling the rise of a new lowbrow culture that would find its fullest expression in Hong Kong, where many writers of popular fiction fled after 1949 (Yung and Rea 2014).

The Communist takeover in mainland China fundamentally transformed the institutional structure of the print industry and its role. In the first half of the 1950s, hundreds of small publishing houses were closed, the larger ones merged into new state-owned entities, and the behemoths—the Commercial Press and Zhonghua

Books—nationalized (Volland 2014). Practically all pre-1949 literary journals were shut down. In their stead, the state created its own flagship publications, which consequently took the lead in the building of a new "people's literature." As Krista Van Fleit Hang (2013: 23–56) has shown, the new journal *People's Literature* (*Renmin wenxue*) played a key role in defining the aesthetic parameters of socialist literary production. The journal's efforts were complemented by those of an eponymous publishing house, both answering to the state-sponsored China Federation of Literary and Art Circles (*Zhonghua quanguo wenxue yishujie lianhehui*). They were flanked by other official publications, such as the biweekly *Literary Gazette* (*Wenyibao*) and, since 1953, by *Translations* (*Yiwen*), a journal featuring translated literature from all over the world, with a focus on the socialist-bloc nations. A steady stream of translations familiarized writers and readers alike with the aesthetic conventions in particular of Soviet literature, which profoundly influenced Chinese literary production in the 1950s (see Chapter 13 by Zha Mingjian).

The reorganization of the literary field and the publishing industry dramatically reduced the number of publishing outlets, but provided much-needed stability to a notoriously volatile sector.[17] It also led to the decentralization of the industry beyond Shanghai and a few other urban centers, as publishing houses and literary journals were set up in provincial capitals across the country, which at times could turn into alternative centers of innovation. As creators of the new people's literature, writers were appointed to the editorial boards of the new journals and at the state-owned publishers, positions that offered them access to the resources of the state, including both funding and prestige, but also made them vulnerable during political campaigns conducted through the organizational nexus of these work units (*danwei*).

At the onset of the Cultural Revolution, all literary journals shut down (with the notable exception of the English-language monthly *Chinese Literature*), and the work of almost all publishing houses was suspended, as their staff engaged in struggle against "capitalist roaders" and representatives of a "bourgeois line in literature and art" within their own ranks. While book publishing resumed around 1970, journals took longer to re-emerge. The resulting gap was taken up by hand-copied or mimeographed unofficial "publications," which were passed on from hand to hand in the cities, but also in the countryside, where many of the educated had been relocated (Link 1989). The instability inherent in the hand-copied medium dramatically reduced authors' control over their texts, and—ironically—accomplished what the Cultural Revolution's promoters had failed to achieve: modes of collective (and often anonymous) literary production. The fluid organization of this emerging unofficial literary scene and its channels of circulation stimulated new forms or creativity and experimentation, most notably in the field of poetry (Crevel 1996: 21–68). In many ways, it echoed the anarchic literary field of the 1920s–1930s, and anticipated trends in literary production and publishing in the late 1970s and 1980s.

Many publishing houses resumed operations in the mid-1970s, and some journals shuttered in 1966 were re-launched in 1977 and 1978, followed by a plethora of old and new journals in the following years. The reinstated print culture of the 1980s, centered around state-sponsored journals and mainstream publishing houses, closely resembled the structures built in the 1950s. A brief proliferation of unofficial literary journals after 1977, often emerging from the unofficial literary scene of the early and mid-1970s, did not last, and *Today*, the last independent literary journal of note, shut down in late 1978 (but was re-launched as an exile overseas journal in 1990). Reform-era China never developed a *samizdat* press akin to the highly influential unofficial publications in the late Soviet Union and Eastern Europe.

The Chinese publishing industry did not experience a fundamental shift until the 1990s, when the onslaught of market forces, within a few years, effectively broke down the existing modes of literary circulation, with concomitant effects on literary production. The broader shift toward a market economy first of all led to the rise of a "second channel" of unlicensed publishers, who operated in the cracks of the system, notably by purchasing book numbers (ISBNs) from cash-starved state-owned publishers for their own ventures (S. Kong 2005: 65–94). By the end of the 1990s, the "second channel" had captured a sizable share of the book market, and forced change upon the publishing industry itself. This came in the form of a policy of "conglomeration" (*jituanhua*), which transformed the nation's publishing houses from old-style state-owned enterprises into profit-driven entities, with access to both the financial and the regulatory resources of the state. By the end of the 2000s, the state-owned publishing houses had recaptured much of the market, driving back the influence of the "second channel" publishers by studying and applying many of their methods (and sometimes entering into joint ventures with them).

The marketization of the publishing industry profoundly reshaped modes of literary production in China. The most conspicuous change is the rise of the book as the leading print medium. Subject to much closer scrutiny than books, journals did not attract the intervention (and investment) of the private "second channel" and went into a decline that was aggravated by shifting audience tastes (in particular, the rise of television). Faced with the erosion of the leading literary journals' prestige and influence, many authors turned to the more lucrative book market. Market-savvy writers such as Wang Shuo found new opportunities in working with private and (later) official publishers (S. Kong 2005: 11–36). Notably, the emergence of the book as the most prestigious medium favored different genres; it is no coincidence that, in the 1990s, the novel rose to unprecedented prominence as writers (e.g., Yu Hua, Su Tong, Mo Yan, or Wang Anyi) who had made their name with short fiction in the 1980s now turned into the nation's leading novelists.

Finally, the proliferation of the Internet and electronic platforms for the dissemination of literature has had a significant impact on the Chinese literary field (see Chapter 23 by Jin Feng). In particular, the Internet allowed for the reemergence of peer platforms, akin to the peer journals of the Republican period and their collectively run boards. At the same time, access to electronic platforms, including blogs and microblogs, greatly reduced the access barriers for burgeoning writers. The availability of vast amounts of literature on the Internet—both genuine Internet literature and works produced for other media that consequently started circulating online—has transformed reading patterns as well, but has not (yet) led to the kind of crisis of the publishing industry seen elsewhere. To the contrary, the rise of online booksellers and vibrant online second-hand marketplaces has made books available in places where readers previously had very limited access to new publications, which has offset (at least temporarily) the migration of readers to new platforms. Fifteen years into the new millennium and the Internet age, the Chinese publishing industry remains vibrant and profitable. The ongoing evolution of Chinese print culture interacts with literary production and will continue to shape what is written and how these works look.

NOTES

1   Much to my regret, it is not possible in the space of this chapter to discuss the print cultures of either Hong Kong or Taiwan, or to delve into the riches of local print cultures in modern China.

2   One notable example is the publication of Lu Xinhua's short story "The Scar," which appeared on August 11, 1978, in *Wenhui Daily* (*Wenhuibao*) and signaled the relaxation of ideological controls after the Cultural Revolution.

3   Hockx (2003: 118–157) has suggested a "horizontal reading" strategy to take account of the multivalent contents and contexts of a single journal issue.

4   Literary journals played key roles in other contexts of innovation and transformation. Compare the Russian "thick journal" of the late nineteenth century (Martinsen 1997) and "small magazines" of the modernist movement in Britain (Churchill and McKible 2008; Brooker and Thacker 2009).

5   This is not to say that the break with older forms of print products was radical. Note, for instance, the double register used by many journals in the 1910s–1920s, which split the printed page in the middle. This bifurcation of the printed space drew on patterns of spatial organization from traditional woodblock prints (e.g., parallel organization of text and commentary).

6   In the 1990s, a hybrid medium of "book series journals" emerged, resulting from publishers' difficulty in obtaining periodical book numbers (ISSN). Numerous *de facto* journals were thus technically published as book series, effectively fusing the characteristics and constraints of the two different media.

7   Such migration could be within or outside the control of the authors, and thus their strategies of textual production (Yung and Rea 2014).

8   For a well-known example, see the memoirs of Bao Tianxiao (1990), a figure typifying the occupational versatility of literary production in the late Qing and Republican era.

9   At least some of the reprints of *New Youth* leave white all advertisements from the journal, depriving modern readers from reconstructing much of the journal's textual practice. I have worked with multiple copies of *New Youth* (both originals and reprints) available in the National University of Singapore's Chinese Library.

10 The title refers to Gao Yihan, a frequent contributor to *New Youth* and Hu's colleague at Peking University, who shared a courtyard house with Hu in Beijing at the time.

11 Chinese text (Hu's translation) and English version both from *New Youth*. Line breaks and orthography follow the text in *New Youth*

(including misspellings or typos in the third and fourth lines: "Remould" instead of "Re-mould;" and "Heart'" instead of "Heart's"). Judging from the text reproduced in *New Youth*, Hu must have relied on either the third (1872) or the fourth (1879) edition of the Fitzgerald translation. Note that both Chinese and English were printed vertically, a practice consistent throughout *New Youth*. I cannot recreate the optical impression of the original, which forces the reader to rotate the journal by 90° to read the English text (but not the Chinese).

12 Expressions in italics appear in English in the original. "*Rubivat*" is a misspelling or typo for "*rubaiyat*."

13 Omar Khayyam was born in 1048 and died in 1131, not in 1123.

14 Hu Shi's poem is preceded by one from Lu Xun (using the pseudonym Tang Yi).

15 "The Origin of Organic Life" ("*Shengwu zhi qiyuan*"), by Zhou Jianren, the younger brother of Lu Xun. A letter by Zhou Zuoren makes complete the family portrait of the Zhou brothers in the April 1919 issue of *New Youth*.

16 *Camel* was published by Beixin shuju in Beijing and printed at Jinghua yinshuaju, a state-of-the-art facility owned by the Commercial Press with some of the best printing equipment available in China. Selling for the steep price of 1 yuan, about three to five times the price of other journals, the journal folded after a single issue.

17 Chen Pingyuan (2005a: 11) notes editorial volatility as one of the characteristics of the numerous peer journals, resulting in many short-lived ventures in the Republican era.

REFERENCES

Bao, Tianxiao 包天笑. 1990. *Chuanyinglou huiyilu* 釧影樓回憶錄 (Reminiscences of the bracelet shadow chamber). Taipei: Longwen chubanshe.

Bourdieu, Pierre. 1993. *The Field of Cultural Production: Essays on Art and Literature*. Edited by Randall Johnson. Cambridge, UK: Polity.

Brokaw, Cynthia J. 2007. *Commerce in Culture: The Sibao Book Trade in the Qing and Republican Periods*. Cambridge, MA: Harvard University Asia Center.

Brooker, Peter, and Andrew Thacker. Eds. 2009. *The Oxford Critical and Cultural History of Modernist Magazines*. Oxford, UK: Oxford University Press.

Chen, Pingyuan 陳平原. 2004. *Wenxue de zhoubian* 文學的周邊 (On the perimeter of literature). Beijing: Xin shijie chubanshe.

Chen, Pingyuan 陳平原. 2005a. "Sixiang shi shiye zhong de wenxue: *Xin qingnian* yanjiu" 思想史視野中的文學:《新青年》研究 (Literature from the perspective of intellectual history: a study of *New Youth*). In *Dazhong meijie yu Zhongguo xiandai wenxue* 大眾媒介與中國現代文學 (Mass media and modern Chinese literature). Edited by Cheng Guangwei 程光煒. Beijing: Renmin wenxue chubanshe. 9–59.

Chia, Lucille. 2003. *Printing for Profit: The Commercial Publishers of Jianyang, Fujian (11th–17th Centuries)*. Cambridge, MA: Harvard University Asia Center.

Chow, Kai-wing. 2004. *Publishing, Culture, and Power in Early Modern China*. Stanford, CA: Stanford University Press.

Chow, Kai-wing, and Cynthia Brokaw. Eds. 2005. *Printing and Book Culture in Late Imperial China*. Berkeley: University of California Press.

Churchill, Suzanne W., and Adam McKible. Eds. 2008. *Little Magazines and Modernism: New Approaches*. London: Ashgate.

Crevel, Maghiel van. 1996. *Language Shattered: Contemporary Chinese Poetry and Duoduo*. Leiden: Research School CNWS.

Doleželová-Velingerová, Milena. Ed. 2002. *The Appropriation of Cultural Capital: China's May Fourth Project*. Cambridge, MA: Harvard University Asia Center.

Hanan, Patrick. 2004. *Chinese Fiction of the Nineteenth and Early Twentieth Centuries: Essays by Patrick Hanan*. New York: Columbia University Press.

Hang, Krista Van Fleit. 2013. *Literature the People Love: Reading Chinese Texts from the Early Maoist Period, 1949–1966*. New York: Palgrave Macmillan.

Hegel, Robert E. 1998. *Reading Illustrated Fiction in Late Imperial China*. Stanford, CA: Stanford University Press.

Hockx, Michel. 2003. *Questions of Style: Literary Societies and Literary Journals in Modern China, 1911–1937*. Leiden: Brill.

Hockx, Michel. Ed. 1999. *The Literary Field in Twentieth-Century China*. Honolulu: University of Hawaii Press.

Hsia, C. T. 1961. *A History of Modern Chinese Fiction, 1917–1957*. New Haven, CT: Yale University Press.

Huang, Ziping 黃子平, Chen Pingyuan 陳平原, and Qian Liqun 錢理群. 1988. *Ershi shiji Zhongguo wenxue san ren tan* 二十世紀文學三人談 (A three way conversation on twentieth-century Chinese literature). Beijing: Renmin wenxue chubanshe.

Judge, Joan. 1996. *Print and Politics: "Shibao" and the Culture of Reform in Late Qing China*. Stanford, CA: Stanford University Press.

Kong, Shuyu. 2005. *Consuming Literature: Best Sellers and the Commercialization of Literary Production in Contemporary China*. Stanford, CA: Stanford University Press.

Lee, Leo Ou-fan. 1999. *Shanghai Modern: The Flowering of a New Urban Culture in China, 1930–1945*. Cambridge, MA: Harvard University Press.

Link, E. Perry. 1981. *Mandarin Ducks and Butterflies: Popular Fiction in Early Twentieth-century Chinese Cities*. Berkeley: University of California Press.

Link, E. Perry. 1989. "Hand-copied Entertainment Fiction from the Cultural Revolution." In *Unofficial China: Popular Culture and Thought in the People's Republic*. Edited by Link, Perry, Richard Madsen, and Paul G. Pickowicz. Boulder: Westview Press. 17–36.

Martinsen, Deborah A. Ed. 1997. *Literary Journals in Imperial Russia*. Cambridge, UK: Cambridge University Press.

McDermott, Joseph P. 2006. *A Social History of the Chinese Book: Books and Literati Culture in Late Imperial China*. Hong Kong: Hong Kong University Press.

Mittler, Barbara. 2004. *A Newspaper for China? Power, Identity, and Change in Shanghai's News Media, 1872–1912*. Cambridge, MA: Harvard University Asia Center.

Průšek, Jaroslav. 1980. *The Lyrical and the Epic: Studies of Modern Chinese Literature*. Ed. Leo Ou-fan Lee. Bloomington: Indiana University Press.

Reed, Christopher A. 2004. *Gutenberg in Shanghai: Chinese Print Capitalism, 1876–1937*. Vancouver: University of British Columbia Press.

Shih, Shu-mei. 2001. *The Lure of the Modern: Writing Modernism in Semicolonial China, 1917–1937*. Berkeley: University of California Press.

Tsai, Weipin. 2010. *Reading Shenbao: Nationalism, Consumerism, and Individuality in China, 1919–1937*. New York: Palgrave Macmillan.

Volland, Nicolai. 2014. "Cultural Entrepreneurship in the Twilight: The Shanghai Book Trade Association, 1945–1957." In *The Business of Culture: Cultural Entrepreneurs in China and Southeast Asia, 1900–65*. Edited by Rea, Christopher G., Rea and Nicolai Volland. Vancouver: University of British Columbia Press. 234–258.

Wagner, Rudolf G. 2002. "Shenbaoguan zaoqi de shuji chuban, 1872–1875" 申報館早期的書

籍出版, 1872–1875 (The early publishing activities of the Shenbaoguan, 1872–1875). In *Wan Ming yu wan Qing: Lishi chuancheng yu wenhua chuangxin* 晚明與晚清: 歷史傳承與文化創新 (The late Ming and the late Qing: Historical dynamics and cultural innovations). Edited by Chen Pingyuan 陳平原, Wang Dewei 王德威, and Shang Wei 商偉. Wuhan: Hubei jiaoyu chubanshe. 169–178.

Wagner, Rudolf G. Ed. 2007. *Joining the Global Public: Word, Image, and City in Early Chinese Newspapers, 1870–1910*. Albany: State University of New York Press.

Wang, David Der-wei. 1997. *Fin-de-siècle Splendor: Repressed Modernities of Late Qing Fiction, 1849–1911*. Stanford, CA: Stanford University Press.

Wang, Xiaoming 王曉明. 1991. "Yifen zazhi he yige 'shetuan:' lun 'wu si' wenxue chuantong" 一份雜誌和一個"社團"—論"五四"文學傳統 (A journal and a "society": on the "May Fourth" literary tradition). *Jintian* 今天 (Today) 3–4: 94–114.

Yung, Sai-shing, and Christopher G. Rea. 2014. "From Print to Screen: The Culture Enterprises of Law Bun." In *The Business of Culture: Cultural Entrepreneurs in China and Southeast Asia, 1900–65*. Edited by Rea, Christopher G., and Nicolai Volland. Vancouver: University of British Columbia Press. 150–177.

23

The Proliferating Genre: Web-Based Time-Travel Fiction and the New Media in Contemporary China

Jin Feng

China is currently the world's largest broadband Internet market (Barboza 2008). As a site of dynamic cultural production, the Chinese Web rivals or surpasses printed channels. By 2000, Web literature, consisting mainly of unedited items, had surpassed the volume of print matter published in China (Linder 2005: 896). The study of Chinese Web literature in China, however, is just emerging from the shadow cast by the scholarly disdain of entertainment-oriented popular literature. Experts such as Ouyang Youquan (2003), one of the premier Chinese scholars in Web studies, have produced seminal articles and monographs. Wang Xiaoming (2011) examines Chinese Web literature in the context of its competition with other modes of cultural production such as "serious literature" (*yansu wenxue*) and "blog literature" (*boke wenxue*). But, as a rule, Chinese scholars limit their analyses to a particular discipline, and have thus fallen short of excavating the dynamic and multi-sited production and consumption of Web literature. Additionally, controversial topics such as homoerotic tales, the impact of state censorship on Web literature, or issues of class and gender usually remain off their scholarly radars.

In English-language scholarship, for a long time, scholars focused on issues of civil liberty and state censorship rather than the cultural production on the Web (Hockx 2005). Haomin Gong and Xin Yang (2010) reveal the "cultural intervention" happening on the Internet when Chinese users employ *egao*, or "technology-enabled parody," to produce fan videos. But the uneven writing quality and ostensibly unprogressive ideologies displayed by Web literature sometimes turn scholars away. For example, Shuyu Kong (2005: 180) summarizes the development of the literature website *Under the Banyan Tree*, and decries Web literature as "at best, simply a form

A Companion to Modern Chinese Literature, First Edition. Edited by Yingjin Zhang.
© 2016 John Wiley & Sons, Ltd. Published 2016 by John Wiley & Sons, Ltd.

of 'literary karaoke' for self-entertainment and, at worst, 'literary detritus' freely and copiously discharged onto the screen. The subject and style of these works tends to be narrow, trite, and monotonous, full of conventional and clichéd expressions of predictable personal sentiments."

Several recent monographs look at Chinese Web literature in a more balanced way. One of the first few scholars in the field, Michel Hockx (2015) gives a general survey of Chinese Web literature and shows how poetry websites promotes community building. Heather Inwood (2014) also devotes several chapters to the dynamic relationship between the "space" afforded by the Internet and the dissemination of modern Chinese poetry. Turning to a different genre, I look at Chinese Web romance, noting new subgenres and pursuing its unique aesthetics and ethos (J. Feng 2013). All three books scrutinize not only the unique forms of various Web genres, but also the circuit of culture that energizes the production and consumption of Web literature. They also employ interdisciplinary methods, integrating media studies and ethnographic fieldwork into literary and discursive analysis.

In this chapter, I use Web-based time-travel fiction as a case to explore the effects of technology and new media on modern Chinese literature and culture. All genres of literature including poetry, fiction, *manga* (comic strips), and essays published on the Web can be regarded as Web or Internet literature. This term can also encompass both works originally published in print form but later digitalized, and creative works especially made for the Web. I focus on the latter group, especially Web fiction, since it embodies revealing and even startling new shifts in ideology and form, garners large followings in China and overseas, and exerts considerable social influence, but has so far been understudied.

In the following, I first trace the origin and evolution of Chinese Web literature, including a discussion of the politics and economics of Web publishing. I then outline some common characteristics of Web novels, such as their shared plots, tropes, and devices. Finally, I examine new writing and reading practices that the Internet has inculcated and the unique aesthetics and ethos that Web fiction embodies. As will be shown, despite the lack of social consciousness and writing skills often associated with Chinese Web fiction, it is characterized by not only the sheer enthusiasm and social energy it generates, but also the narrative innovations and border crossings that it makes possible.

Genealogy

Chinese users access Web literature via both personal computers and cell phones. They can go to work-centered "vertical" (*chuizhi*) literature sites, literary channels housed in portal sites such as Xinlang (sina.com), or BBS discussion forums. In a report issued by China Internet Network Information Center (CNNIC 2013: 39), a state-run research center founded in 1997, by the end of June 2013, 248 million Chinese, or 42.1% users, had used Web literature, a 6.4% increase within 6 months. Another report

(CNNIC 2011b: 37–38) reveals that 56.9% of consumers of Web literature were 24 or younger, while 35.3% (the largest group) had received a college education or higher; 33.9% earned a monthly income between 1,001 and 3,000 yuan, and 89% lived in urban areas. Male users outstripped female users (55.7% versus 44.3%). Science fiction was the most popular genre among males (45.3% of men preferred it), while romance was favored by females (46.9% of women preferred it). Interestingly, home proved to be the most common location of reading for both men and women (almost 90%), for they generally regarded Web literature as "leisure, relaxation, and entertainment." Users of Chinese Web literature thus occupy the sociopolitical location of, for lack of a better word, the middle class.[1]

Chinese Web literature has come a long way from its beginning. In 1989, only a few scientists at prestigious institutions in China had e-mail accounts. It was not until 1994 that China acquired full-function Internet connectivity, and only after 1996 did the Internet become available to the average urban consumer, while the first BBS forum was set up at Tsinghua (Qinghua) University in Beijing in 1995 (G. Yang 2009: 29). In the ensuing years, the number of Web users has increased by leaps and bounds (and is still growing rapidly), paving the way for the birth of literature websites.

It was Chinese students studying in the United States who first launched Chinese Web literature. As early as 1989, a group of students founded *News Digest* (*Xinwen wenzhai*), later known as *China Digest* (*Huaxia wenzhai*), a listserv that accepted submissions of creative writing and was distributed to overseas Chinese students; the venue was closely linked to the student demonstrations at Tiananmen at the time (Li Dajiu 2010a). In 1991, Wang Xiaofei, another overseas Chinese student, established *Chinese Poem Net* (chpoem-1@listserv.acsu.buffalo.edu) at the University of Buffalo (Li Dajiu 2010b). In February 1994, Fangzhou zi and others founded the first literature website based in China, *New Threads* (*Xin yusi*, www.xys.org), to be followed by others such as *Olive Tree* (*Ganlan shu*, www.wenxue.com) in March 1995; *Cute Tricks* (*Hua Zhao*, www.huazhao.com), the first Chinese women's literature website, at the end of 1995; and *Under the Banyan Tree* in 1997.

In 1999, a Web novel titled *First Close Touch* (*Diyi ci de qinmi jiechu*) by Taiwan writer Pizi Cai (a.k.a. Cai Zhiheng or Tsai Chih-Heng) constituted a landmark in Chinese Web literature, for this irreverent yet idealistic work on youthful romance and experience attracted an unprecedented large following in the Chinese-speaking world on both sides of the Taiwan Strait (P. Yin 2005: 31). Cai's novel exerted a strong influence on the development of Chinese Web literature; many of its characteristics are typical of productions and exchanges in Chinese cyberspace today, in particular a playful yet also deliberately prosaic style characterized by a "matter-of-fact approach and a self-conscious avoidance of heroic grandeur" (G. Yang 2009: 29). It is arguable whether Chinese Web literature indeed embraces a utopian impulse such as Guobing Yang (2009: 182) has found in Web-based Chinese activism. Yet, it manifests a new "structure of feelings," that is, "a common set of perceptions and values shared by a particular generation and most clearly articulated in artistic forms and conventions" at a particular historical moment (Taylor 1997), fostered by the larger sociopolitical environment in which it exists.[2]

No discussion of Chinese Web literature can overlook the role of the state, which sees the Internet both as a forum in need of censorship and regulation and as an opportunity for economic development. Before 2013, at least 14 government units, from the Ministry of Culture and the Ministry of Information Technology to offices that oversee films and books, each exerted some control over China's Internet (Wines 2011). The 12th Chinese People's National Congress, which ended its first session in March 2013, passed measures to restructure government ministries and agencies in order to cut red tape. It unveiled plans to integrate the two major media regulators, the General Administration of Press and Publication (GAPP) and the State Administration of Radio, Film and Television, into a ministerial-level body titled State General Administration of Press, Publications, Radio, Film, and Television to oversee those five sectors.[3] What this merger will bring to Internet censorship remains to be seen, but the powerful Chinese Internet surveillance regime already comprises multiple levels of legal regulation and technical control, ranging from various self-censoring practices to the state-sponsored Golden Shield Project, a.k.a. the Great Firewall of China (HBCFIT 2006).

State control has caused China-based literature websites to practice self-censorship in order to avert government shutdown or other forms of punishment. For instance, they use a software that automatically deletes "sensitive words" from published works, leaving blanks where politically forbidden words once existed, such as terms referring to the student demonstration on June Fourth (*liusi*), 1989, or phrases deemed pornographic. Some have also enforced a system of reader reporting. If a reader files a complaint about a certain work, usually alleging "pornographic depiction," the author will be warned and access to the work temporarily blocked until changes are made and approved by Web administrators. Indeed, in his 2006 study that includes several intellectual and military websites, Yongming Zhou (2006) concludes that there is no "public sphere" in the Chinese cyberspace at all due to tight state control.

Yet, the Chinese state also attempts to utilize the Internet to spur economic development. Since China entered the World Trade Organization in 2001, both domestic and foreign corporations have been seeking to tap into the exponential growth of the Chinese Internet market, and the industry is forecast to grow to $57.72 billion in 2016.[4] The CNNIC's reports, issued in January and July annually, shed some light on how the state promotes Internet-driven economic development in order to increase its popularity and public satisfaction. The 27th semiannual report (CNNIC 2011a), dated January 2011, summarizes: "The rapid increase of mobile net citizens and more thorough Internet utilization, as well as the rapid development of information technology in China guided by Internet construction, have strongly promoted the reform of economic development, social progress, and people's living standards." According to the state news agency, Xinhua, the government strives to make the Internet "an impetus in transforming the mode of economic growth and in optimizing industrial structure" by fostering Internet development in four areas: Internet infrastructure; technological progress and application; Internet application in other industries and information; and Internet security management.[5] The CNNIC reports also show strong governmental support for aiding small- and medium-sized enterprises to use the Internet effectively. A report (CNNIC 2012) analyzing the "E-Commerce of Medium-sized and Small Chinese Enterprises in 2011" has attributed the relatively generous Internet access enjoyed by medium-sized and small enterprises in China to the promotion of the state, which provides "a guarantee ... that these enterprises can share Internet services conveniently."

The state's two-pronged approach to the Internet, combining stringent political control with economic stimulation, has borne fruit in Web publishing. In 2010, the GAPP vowed to "remove unwholesome content from the Web," such as matter identified as "pornographic, vulgar, and violent." But the state also defined the "cultural industry" as a "national strategic industry," and, by the end of 2010, had established three "national bases" of digital publishing in Shanghai, Chongqing, and Hangzhou, while pouring funds into their further construction and expansion (CNNIC 2011b).

The Shanghai Shengda Internet Development Company has built its business around Web literature, taking advantage of both state policies and the development of the Chinese market economy. This company started out in the 1990s, specializing in computer games, but in the last 5 years it has spawned Shengda Literature (*Shengda wenxue*), and is the largest publisher of Web literature in contemporary China. In 2008 alone, Shengda invested close to 1 billion yuan to buy out the five most influential literature websites in China, including long-established powerhouses such as *Rongshu xia, Jinjiang*, and *Hongxiu tianxiang*, and incorporated them into Shengda Literature Ltd (Wang Xiaoming 2011: 76). Furthermore, Shengda introduced new profit-making models, such as their notorious pay-per-view system, in which they require readers to pay for access to certain popular works only made available to "VIP" subscribers, while sharing profits with relevant Web authors on the basis of subscription numbers and the length of their works. In its attempt to corner the market on Web literature, Shengda not only collaborates with established authors to digitize their entire print oeuvres, but also integrates multimedia elements into Web literature to attract a younger, more technologically savvy, and adventurous audience, in the process generating new genres in fiction such as Web travel (*wangyou*, short for *wangluo youxi*, Web-based computer games) and fantasy (*xuanhuan*), both with their roots in the fantasy world of computer games. Hou Xiaoqiang, CEO of Shengda Literature, has announced that the company is working with the Chinese Writers Association, the largest national organization of Chinese writers, to mainstream Web literature, forecasting that "the difference between print and Web-based literature will eventually disappear, and 'traditional' and 'Web' literature will be reunited on the platform of the Internet" (Qian Yijiao 2008).

Shengda Literature now owns six literature websites and runs an audiobook website, a digital publishing website, and three brick-and-mortar publications that publish print materials. It plays a crucial role in the commercialization of Chinese Web literature. *Qidian* (Starting point), Shengda's first acquisition, was the first of the literature websites in China to charge users for access to certain popular works. *Qidian* has established an elaborate system of rewards for authors and readers to encourage their output and participation. Web authors are paid for the number of words they produce every day, every month, and every year. They can also earn bonuses if readers show interest through increased subscriptions or in the high number of votes they cast for particular works. As a result, works published at *Qidian* tend to stretch out over months and years before they are finally completed, often reaching several million Chinese characters in length.

New Media, New Platform

Various political, economic, and socio-cultural forces shape the content and audience of Chinese Web literature. Although individual experiences and practices vary, it is helpful to take stock of the broad trends in the cultural production and consumption on the Chinese Web before I delve into specific narrative patterns and reading and writing practices related to Web fiction.

Chinese Web readers occupy the middle section in society, but they have plenty of issues to feed their anxieties and insecurities: the skyrocketing housing prices in Chinese metropolises such as Beijing and Shanghai; the widening gap between the rich and poor; uncertain job prospects after college, now that the state no longer automatically assigns jobs; and food safety incidents that have killed and injured tens of thousands of people. For Chinese women, especially, along with the rise in their level of formal education, literacy, and salary, there has also come discrimination in education and employment, sexual harassment on the job, the commodification of their bodies in the media, and the perennial dilemma that women face about the choice between career and family. Single women have to bear not only the traditional cultural stigma, but also the brunt of countless Web jokes at their expense, as they are all lumped into the category of "leftover women" (*shengnü*) (Lake 2012). Women who choose or are forced to focus their energies on home and family do not fare any better. Other than the ever-thorny issue of extended family versus nuclear family in Chinese culture, crystalized in the struggle between mother-in-law and daughter-in-law, the ghost of the "other woman" (*xiaosan*) always haunts an ostensibly happy marriage. Web users also harbor a gnawing sense of the loss of basic decency among their fellow Chinese. In Foshan, Guangdong, in October 2011, a 2-year-old girl named Little Yueyue (Xiao Yueyue) was hit by two cars and left unattended. Within 7 minutes, 18 people walked by without paying any attention until a garbage collector sent her to a hospital, where she died after a week. With the assistance of the Internet, this incident ignited a nationwide discussion of the decline of morality in contemporary Chinese society.

Perry Link's (1981) analysis of the butterfly fiction popular in the early twentieth century prompts an eerie sense of *déjà vu*. Link characterizes its readership as middle class, and its function as providing comfort to over-stimulated but insecure urban dwellers with rural origins who resented the gaps between their expectations and realities. He also highlights the role of new media (printed newspapers and picture books) in the spread of the romance novels. His observations on romance consumption in early-twentieth-century China could easily apply to Web fiction and its audiences in the twenty-first century.

The feature that distinguishes these two contexts is the Internet. Its characteristics, such as the high speed of dissemination, widespread connectivity, an unprecedented volume of information, and interactive responsiveness, have effected changes in reader psychology and behavior. The Chinese cyberspace has enabled users to rally rescuers and donors in the wake of horrific natural disasters such as the Sichuan earthquake in 2008, whip up nationalist fervor for the 2008 Olympic Games held in Beijing, and instigate boycotts and rallies for a variety of political causes. It has also made obscure figures into media stars overnight: such as a young woman with meager formal education who nevertheless boasted of her own talent and advertised her high standards for potential mates (Fengjie, Sister Phoenix, a.k.a. Luo Yufeng).

On the Internet, a seemingly pointless remark can catch on and go viral immediately, as illustrated by "the curious case of Jia Junpeng." On July 16, 2009, an anonymous user in a Baidu discussion forum posted a message titled "Jia Junpeng, your mother asked you to come home to eat" (*"Jia Junpeng ni mama han ni huijia chifan"*). The message consisted simply of the 12 Chinese characters in its title, without any punctuation marks or accompanying content. Yet, it received 3,000 responses within 5 hours. Within 1 day, it attracted 7 million hits and 300,000 comments. A cryptic posting was turned into a national media event, while "Jia Junpeng" became a household word in Chinese cyberspace overnight. Nobody knows who the sender was or even whether Jia Junpeng was a real person, though Guobing Yang (2011) asserts that this case started out as a form of consumer activism allowing users to vent their frustration over the delayed launch of a computer game. Web users appropriated this particular line to express a variety of social sentiments, from resentment of corrupt officials to loneliness and boredom, and with great alacrity and gusto.

The birth of the so-called "high-speed train genre" (*gaotie ti*) provides yet another example of Web users parodying official discourses to vent their anger with the state.[6] Following the clash of two high-speed trains and the deaths of 40 people in Wenzhou, Zhejiang, in July 2011, Wang Yongping, a spokesperson for China's Ministry of Railways, attempted to explain the government's ineffectual rescue effort at a news conference, uttering the famous line: "Whether you believe it or not, I am convinced [by this explanation] anyway" (*"Zhiyu ni xin buxin, fanzheng wo shi xin le"*). Finding his remarks *leiren* (ridiculous and insensitive), Web users immediately made an image of Wang into a GIF file and incorporated it into an animation clip, which they disseminated online. A T-shirt printed with Wang's famous line was designed and sold on the Web, and a competition asking users to create variations on Wang's original sentence structure was announced. Among the more than 7,000 entries submitted within 3 days, many questioned and criticized the ministry's position and Wang's own truthfulness. Some also expressed discontent over other social issues: "There is no traffic jam in Beijing today. Whether you believe it or not, I am convinced anyway."

The unique platform provided by the Internet enables Chinese users to express their opinions—likes and dislikes—at an unprecedented volume and with unprecedented candor and speed despite the state's censorship attempts. Web literature relies on similar technological features. It is composed, published, distributed, and read differently than earlier forms of print literature. New reading and writing practices have emerged, reshaping the generic conventions of Chinese fiction. Furthermore, Web fiction embodies many irresolvable contradictions of postsocialist China, even as it embraces playfulness and detachment while ostensibly renouncing seriousness and meaning. In his study of Chinese postmodernism, Xiaobin Yang (2002: 23) defines the paradigm of Chinese modernity as a "unified concern for an ultimate, absolute subjectivity" and a belief in technological history. If twentieth-century Chinese literature was driven by the idea of modernization and progress and expressed through the absolute national and historical subject, Web literature in the new millennium displays instead the splintering of univocal subjectivity into various contradictory role-playing games.

Plots, Tropes, and Devices

Although some genres of Web fiction, such as "workplace intrigues" (*zhichang*) and "motivational" (*lizhi*) fiction, adopt a contemporary setting, Web fiction is often set in a premodern era and employs the trope of time travel. Some have ascribed the popularity of time-travel fiction to *Tale of Seeking Qin* (*Xun Qin ji*, ca. 1991), a fantasy written by a male Hong Kong writer named Huang Yi, and adapted into a popular TV series in 2001. This novel tells the story of a special-forces soldier who travels back to the Warring States period (475–221 BCE), and helps the Duke of Qin to establish the first unified Chinese imperial dynasty. The hero's sexual exploits as well as his miraculous deployment of modern knowledge and technology have spurred widespread imitations on the Chinese Web. Women also utilized the trope of time travel to write romances. Xi Juan, a female author from Taiwan, described the romantic adventures of a young woman who travels back to the Song dynasty (961–1279 CE) in her novel, *Love That Crosses Time* (*Jiaocuo shiguang de ailian*, 1993), published to wide commercial success and reader acclaim.

Male Web authors often adopt the following variations on the time-travel plot: (1) stud (*zhongma*) fiction: a man travels back to the past in his own body or adopts the body of another man, changes history by using modern technology, and becomes the object of passion and devotion of multiple beautiful women; (2) farming (*zhongtian*) fiction: a man travels back in history, occupies the lower echelons of society, but gradually rises in status through hard work and keeping a low profile; (3) rebirth: a man travels backward in his own life, (re)awakens in early childhood, and sets about changing his destiny and his family's.

Female authors appropriate popular plots and tropes from male-authored works, even while deriding widespread clichés. They also insert gender-bending themes, creating new subgenres such as: *danmei*, male–male homoerotic tales written mostly by women and for women's consumption; *nüzun*, matriarchal tales; and *tongren*, or fan fiction, which lifts elements from a work without the original author's expressed permission and not for profit, and recasts them through rewriting. Female-authored fiction frequently realizes the theme of redemption, allowing the heroine to redress wrongs suffered in modern times in another, fantastical time and locale, and thus creates an empowered or even masculinized heroine in the process.

Web fiction also adopts narrative devices introduced, enabled, or enhanced by the Internet. A perfect case in point is female authors' use of *fanwai* (*bangai* in Japanese) to insert a chapter that tells the story from the perspective of a character other than the focal narrative voice or central consciousness, usually represented by the heroine. *Fanwai*, which in the context of cinema refers to "special features," denotes scenes that have been shot but edited out of the final version of the film. By using this device, the author creates an interstice in the narrative and invites the reader to identify with another character. Although the flow of the plot seems to be interrupted, *fanwai* allows readers to see the other side of the story. This device can be used to provide a glimpse into male psychology, thereby correcting a fatal flaw in traditional print romances in which the transformation of the hero from a sadistic antagonist to a gentle and caring lover remains unexplained at the time the transformation occurs (Radway 1984: 147). In using *fanwai,* the author can induce affective identification, leading the reader to see the gentler side of the male figure and thus understand, if not endorse, the protagonist's relationship with him. *Fanwai* often becomes not only a teaser to attract readers but also a delaying tactic for authors facing readers' insatiable appetite to read the main story as quickly as possible, for in *fanwai* authors can repeat previous scenes and hint at future developments without actually delivering new chapters of the main story. Further, *fanwai* also attracts readers to participate in the writing of the novel. Some readers post their own *fanwai* chapters in their commentaries, while others individually or collaboratively turn their *fanwai* into fan fiction in a different space, becoming authors themselves.

These characteristics of Web fiction—especially their fantastical settings, prevalent use of time travel, and a heavy dose of gender bending—register the unsettled feel of postsocialist China. This is especially true if we look at the evolution from stud to farming, and then to magic-space (*kongjian*) fiction. Authors of *kongjian* fiction supply the protagonist with a magic space that boasts everything from gold and silver mountains to magic plants, animals, drugs, magnificent buildings and hot springs, and science labs and computers. This space is only accessible to the protagonist, as it can be collapsed into a piece of jade jewelry that he or she wears or is simply conjured up in his or her mind's eye. This genre has incorporated elements from video and computer games. The notoriously popular "Happy Farm" ("*Kaixin nongchang*"), for instance, allows players to cultivate their own piece of virtual land, harvest crops and flowers, raise livestock and poultry, and build houses, while also rising in the ranks based on the time they spend online.

The evolution of time-travel fiction from stud fiction to farming literature and magic-space tales follows a trajectory from the public sphere through the family circle and culminates in the individual as its principal focus. The public prominence and success typical of the first generation of time travelers gives way to more domestic concerns in farming fiction, where familial relationships as well as economic production become the focus of the plot. Novels featuring a magic space, a metaphor for the protagonist's "inscape," mark a further retreat into the sanctity of the interior self. This trend echoes what Shuyu Kong (2005: 104) calls the "personal writing" typical of Chinese fiction since the late 1980s, as authors "turn away from social and historical concerns to emphasize personal and domestic life, and do so to such an extent that even descriptions of collective historical experiences are conveyed through the lenses of personal memory and flawed narrators."

Web fiction reveals deep contradictions in its ethos as it moves farther and farther away from the grand official narrative of nation building even while deploying expansive and aggressive plots such as changing history by using modern technology or upsetting patriarchal rule through creating a matriarchal society. Shuyu Kong (2005: 104) argues that the inward turn in contemporary Chinese fiction "reflects a collective consciousness that is attempting to reconstruct the self as an individual in a postrevolutionary society." The current inward turn in Web fiction similarly reveals shifts in Chinese users' structure of feelings, and thereby redefines their (post)socialist identity.

New Writing and Reading Practices

A casual scan of any Chinese-language literature website yields titles similar to and derivative of one another, and male and female authors freely borrow narrative devices, such as the proliferated trope of time travel, from each other. Indeed, Chinese Web fiction is characterized by the appropriation of heterogeneous elements, for the Internet provides tools for users to borrow and reinvent existing artifacts and tropes, and thereby inculcates new reading and writing practices.

Writers have utilized the Internet to realize their literary dreams, such as the author and dissident Murong Xuecun, a former car salesman who made a name for himself by publishing Web novels (Farrar 2009). More important, the Internet fosters new reader behavior. Interactive features help consumers of Web fiction change into its producers, and they employ the tactics of textual poaching (de Certeau 1984) to appropriate from, challenge, and alter the system and products of the relatively powerful from their position of relative powerlessness.

For example, the commentary space at the women's literature site *Jinjiang*, placed under each chapter of the fictional text, facilitates the free exchange of information and opinions. Web users share among themselves a unique language. They often use the initials of *pinyin* romanization of Chinese characters, words from other languages, or similarly pronounced Chinese characters to replace the correct words (Y. Zhou 2006, marking the boundaries of insiders versus outsiders. The content of their communications, moreover, induces feelings of recognition and identification even more effectively. Because of the serialized nature of the novels, readers' comments and authors' responses often involve negotiations over plot and characterization. But the commentary space combines the functions of a writer's workshop, an opinion column, and a social space. Here, authors and readers discuss novel-writing and rhetorical devices in general. They also express their opinions on a variety of controversial topics such as homosexuality, rape, and polygamy, occasionally branching into political satire with wordplay on current political slogans. Perhaps readers and authors navigate to this space not so much for information and ideas as for the social energy and emotional support that it offers. Authors and readers often exchange holiday greetings and tell each other about changes and problems in their lives, such as unemployment and pregnancy. In return, they receive not only consolation and congratulations, but also practical tips at times.

Furthermore, Web readers share several common interpretive practices. They instantaneously incorporate elements lifted from contemporary, global sociopolitical life into their comments, such as the Jasmine Revolution in the Arab world. This intimate link between fiction and current affairs sometimes causes readers to reflect on controversial historical events, such as the Tian'an men Incident of 1989. Second, readers tend to adopt a biographical or autobiographical way of reading, as demonstrated in their criticism of Qiong Yao, a mainland-born romance writer from Taiwan, as a *xiaosan*, a home wrecker who glorifies extramarital affairs in her romances out of ulterior motives. They also use their own life stories to vouch for or question the plausibility of the plot, and to agree or disagree with their fellow readers. Fiction and real life exist side by side for these readers. Rather than practicing detached aesthetic appreciation, they believe that fiction and life can and should reflect each other, despite many fantastical elements in the Web novel.

Third, while readers often expect Web fiction to be a realistic, transparent representation of their (emotional) life, they also exercise imagination freely to fill out the plot, often reading into the story things that the author has not intended or will not fulfill, and then denounce the author vehemently for failing their expectations. The structure of BBS forums especially provides fertile soil for such behavior. There is no authorial moderation or intervention on a discussion forum, so readers can carry out a trial *in absentia*, while also egging each other on. Faced with the sheer volume of postings, forum moderators get too busy and distracted to curtail readers' enthusiasm and wild accusations. But the repetitive plots and literary devices in a lot of works and pervasive copycat practices on the Web have also preconditioned readers to such an extent that they assume they know what is going to happen next, and thus feel justified about, and indeed enjoy, indulging in wild speculations.

Some argue that this style of reading—extrapolation that draws the reader well beyond the information explicitly presented in the text, the intermingling of personal experience and narrative events, the focus on a narrative's world rather than its plot—reflects a female gendered approach to narrative comprehension.

David Bleich (1986: 239), for example, concludes that men tend to read for authorial meaning, perceiving a "strong narrational voice" shaping events, while women see themselves as participating in and actively contributing to a conversation initiated by the narrative. But the reading practices that some scholars identify as intrinsically feminine in fact reveal strategies that women have adopted to rewrite male-centered narratives in a way that better serves their interests. As Henry Jenkins (1992: 113) points out, such strategies "deflect the focus away from male protagonists and onto the larger sets of social relations constituting the narrative world," "reclaim from the margins the experiences of female characters," and show "alienation and discomfort" rather than acceptance of male-oriented narrative priorities.

Perhaps more important, reading and commenting on Web literature alongside like-minded fellow users is a social process by which individual interpretations are reshaped and reinforced through ongoing discussions with other readers. Such discussions expand the experience of the text beyond its initial consumption. The meanings that emerge from the online community are consequently more fully integrated into the readers' lives, and are fundamentally different from those generated through a casual encounter with an otherwise unremarkable text. Serialized novels on the Chinese Internet produce a unique rhythm of their own. By skillfully timing the release of new installments, authors can whet appetites, build up suspense, and stimulate reader discussion. However, if a work is stretched out too long, readers may complain of boredom and even reproach the author for profiteering by including superfluous plotting. Furthermore, with the encouragement of fellow users, readers also contest or defy authorial intentions and interpretations. Readers' discussions not only excavate and create meanings in the work and influence the author in many ways, but also help them to make sense of their own lives through their acts of extrapolation. They are, especially when reading controversial materials such as homoerotic tales (J. Feng 2009), engaged in creative play through which they express and manage their fears, desires, and fantasies, which they otherwise lack the means and sense of security to explore fully and reveal to the (disapproving) general society.

As a result of the lively conversations between webmasters, authors, and readers, Web works often display extraordinary fluidity. This can be seen, first, in the different kinds of border-crossing that they make possible. Web novels often describe and even celebrate moral and sexual behavior otherwise not condoned by society. Moreover, the creation and adaptation of these works challenge both the traditional demarcation of media and the boundary between author and reader. Since Web fiction often incorporates elements of music, cartoon, and cinema, the boundaries between the literary text and other genres and media become increasingly blurred. Furthermore, each work is in a perpetual state of flux, subject to endless editing, modification, and even deletion. Because authors aspire to high ranking and positive reception, they take pains to respond to comments left by webmasters and readers. The reading community of any work is thus able to produce almost concurrent, "interlinear" (D. Rolston 1997) commentary that can change the shape of the text precisely because of the instantaneity of feedback. Given that high-ranked Web novels often catch the eye of publishers, this malleability on the author's part is not just a good-will gesture to attract a greater following, but also an effective way to adapt to the market, making their manuscripts publishable and profitable (P. Yin 2005: 31–33). The interactive features of literature websites turn readers into authors, and make their identities mutually constitutive. Ultimately, Web literature makes it possible for readers and authors to form what Matt Hills (2002: 180) calls "a community of imagination," which constitutes itself "through a common affective engagement … and similar imaginative experiences."

Conclusion

Chinese Web literature demonstrates an acute sensitivity to contemporary social and cultural trends. Web writing has helped young, obscure authors to realize literary dreams that would have been unattainable without professional help and financial support in traditional print media. Web reading, moreover, provides users with the opportunity to reflect on their own life situations, and to view them in their larger sociopolitical context, in a supportive environment in Chinese cyberspace.

Chinese Web readers are typically young, urban, and relatively well educated. They read and write Web literature in search of entertainment and companionship, and in the process they produce social satire and construct personal and literary identities. The multimedia environment on the Internet has shaped the content and form of Web fiction; it not only incorporates references to current events and Web-induced lingo and writing styles, such as the high-speed train genre, but also utilizes audiovisual elements such as music and images to complement and enhance the reading experience. Web fiction features narrative innovations such as *fanwai*, supplementary chapters that present scenes from another character's point of view. New subgenres inspired by computer games, such as magic-space fiction, or unusual gender benders including matriarchal and homoerotic tales, have also emerged, potentially signaling social as well as literary changes.

The Internet has fostered a general culture of imitation and repetition that enables readers and writers to appropriate and utilize familiar literary tropes such as time travel to address their life concerns and realize the theme of redemption in narratives. Rewriting leads to reinvention as well, and in some cases even allows Web users to explore their gender and cultural identities in a liminal space that pushes against the very boundaries of ethical and social acceptability. Although Web works may display varying literary qualities and controversial ethics, the exchange surrounding these texts ultimately resignifies, reorients, and recharges readers and authors with new relevance and energy. The proliferated Web fiction may turn out not so lacking in narrative innovations or progressive consciousness, after all.

NOTES

1 Karl Gerth (2010: 14) estimates that about a third of the population, or 430 million Chinese, belongs to this category, which is defined as households owning at least six appliances or electronic goods, such as TVs, refrigerators, washing machines, cell phones, DVD players, air conditioners, and microwaves.

2 This concept was first used by Raymond Williams in his *A Preface to Film* (with Michael Orrom, 1954), developed in *The Long Revolution* (1961), and elaborated throughout his work, in particular *Marxism and Literature* (1977). Williams used it to characterize the lived experience or the quality of life at a particular time and place.

3 "China unveils cabinet reshuffle plans," accessed March 17, 2013, http://www.china.org.cn/china/NPC_CPPCC_2013/2013-03/10/content_28191188.htm.

4 "Internet Services in China: China Industry Report," accessed November 20, 2011, http://www.ibisworld.com.cn/industry/default.aspx?indid=805&partnerid=prweb.

5 "China to foster Internet development in four areas," accessed November 23, 2011, http://news.xinhuanet.com/english2010/china/2011-08/23/c_131069427.htm.

6 http://news.sina.com.cn/s/p/2011-07-27/032922881925.shtml. Accessed February 18, 2012.

REFERENCES

Barboza, David. 2008. "China Surpasses U.S. in Number of Internet Users." *New York Times*, July 16.

Bleich, David. 1986. "Gender Interests in Reading and Language." In *Gender and Reading: Essays on Readers, Texts, and Contexts*. Edited by Elizabeth A. Flynn and P. P. Scheweickart. Baltimore, MD: Johns Hopkins University Press. 234–266.

Certeau, Michel de. 1984. *The Practice of Everyday Life*. Trans. Steven Rendall. Berkeley: University of California Press.

CNNIC. 2011a. "Di ershiqi ci Zhongguo hulianwangluo fazhan zhuangkuang tongji baogao (2011 yiyue)" 第27次中國互聯網絡發展狀況統計報告 (The 27th statistical survey report on Chinese Internet development, Jan. 2011). Accessed 23 March 2012. http://www.cnnic.cn/research/bgxz/tjbg/201101/t20110120_20302.html.

CNNIC. 2011b. "Zhongguo wangluo wenxue yonghu diaoyan baogao." 中國網絡文學用户調研報告 (Survey report of users of Chinese Web literature, Dec. 2010). Accessed 16 August 2012. http://www.cnnic.cn/research/bgxz/wmbg/201108/P020110819564826236297.pdf.

CNNIC. 2012. "2011 nian Zhongguo zhongxiao qiye dianzi shangwu diaocha baogao" 2011年中國中小企業電子商務調查報告 (The report on the e-commerce of medium-sized and small Chinese enterprises in 2011). Accessed 16 March 2013. http://www.cnnic.cn/research/bgxz/bgxz_qybg/201206/t20120614_28883.html.

CNNIC. 2013. "Di sanshier ci Zhongguo hulianwangluo fazhan zhuangkuang tongji baogao (2013 nian yiyue)" 第32次中國互聯網絡發展狀況統計報告 (2013年7月) (The 32nd statistical survey report on Chinese Internet development, July 2013). Accessed 22 July 2013. http://www.cnnic.cn/hlwfzyj/hlwxzbg/hlwtjbg/201307/P020130717505343100851.pdf.

Gong, Haomin, and Xin Yang. 2010. "Digitalized Parody: The Politics of *egao* in Contemporary China." *China Information*, 24.1: 3–26.

Farrar, Lara. 2009. "For Many Chinese, Literary Dreams Go Online." Accessed 15 Feb. 2009. http://www.cnn.com/2009/SHOWBIZ/books/02/15/china.publishing/index.html.

Feng, Jin. 2009. "Addicted to Beauty: Web-based *Danmei* Popular Romance." *Modern Chinese Literature and Culture*, 21. 2: 1–41.

Feng, Jin. 2013. *Romancing the Internet: Producing and Consuming Chinese Web Romance*. Leiden and Boston: Brill.

Gerth, Karl. 2010. *As China Goes, So Goes the World: How Chinese Consumers Are Transforming Everything*. New York: Hill and Wang.

Harvard Berkman Center for Internet and Technology (HBCFIT). 2006. *Internet Filtering in China in 2004–2005*. Accessed 23 March 2012. http://opennet.net/studies/china.

Hills, Matt. 2002. *Fan Cultures*. London: Routledge.

Hockx, Michel. 2014. *Internet Literature in China*. New York: Columbia University Press.

Hockx, Michel. 2015. "Virtual Chinese Literature: A Comparative Case Study of Online Poetry Communities." In *Culture in the Contemporary PRC*. Edited by Michel Hockx and Julia C. Strauss. Cambridge, UK: Cambridge University Press. 148–169.

Inwood, Heather. 2014. *Verse Going Viral: China's New Media Scenes*. Seattle: University of Washington Press.

Jenkins, Henry. 1992. *Textual Poachers: Television Fans and Participatory Culture*. London: Routledge.

Kong, Shuyu. 2005. *Consuming Literature: Best Sellers and the Commercialization of Literary Production in Contemporary China*. Stanford, CA: Stanford University Press.

Lake, Roseann. 2012. "All the Shengnu Ladies." Accessed 22 March 2012. http://salon.com/a/sQ769AA.

Li, Dajiu 李大玖. 2010a. "Wangluo wenxue qiyuan de jizhong butong shuofa (yi)" 網絡文學起源的幾種不同説法(一) (Several theories on the origin of Web literature, part 1), published 5 Jan. 2010. In "Li Dajiu de boke" 李大玖的博客 (Li Dajiu's

blog). Accessed 22 Feb. 2012. http://blog.sina.com.cn/s/blog_5223ef410100hiid.html.

Li, Dajiu 李大玖. 2010b. "Zuizao de chunwenxue wangluo meiti shiliao" 最早的純文學網絡媒體史料 (Sources on the earliest pure literature websites), published 13 June 2010. In "Li Dajiu de boke" 李大玖的博客 (Li Dajiu's blog). Accessed 22 Feb. 2012. http://blog.sina.com.cn/s/blog_5223ef410100k7nj.html.

Linder, Birgit. 2005. "Web literature." In *Encyclopaedia of Contemporary Chinese Culture*. Edited by Edward L. Davis. London: Routledge. 895–896.

Ouyang, Youquan 歐陽友權. 2003. "Wangluo wenxue: Minjian huayuquan de huigui" 網絡文學: 民間話語權的回歸 (Web-based literature: The return of civil discourses). *Huaiying shifan xueyuan xuebao* 淮陰師範學院學報, 25.3: 335–340.

Qian, Yijiao 錢亦蕉. 2008. "Wenxue, meng kaishi de defang—Shengda wenxue gongsi CEO Hou Xiaoqiang zhuanfang 文學, "夢開始的地方"—盛大文學公司 CEO 侯小強專訪 (Literature, where the dream starts: An interview of Hou Xiaoqiang, the CEO of Shengda Literature). *Xinmin zhoukan* 新民週刊, 2. Accessed 6 Dec. 2012. http://www.sachina.edu.cn/Htmldata/news/2008/10/4047.html.

Radway, Janice. 1984. *Reading the Romance: Women, Patriarchy, and Popular Literature*. Chapel Hill: University of North Carolina Press.

Rolston, David L. 1997. *Traditional Chinese Fiction and Fiction Commentary: Reading and Writing between the Lines*. Stanford, CA: Stanford University Press.

Taylor, Jenny Bourne. 1997. "Structure of Feelings." In *A Dictionary of Cultural and Critical Theory*, ed. Michael Payne. Blackwell Reference Online. Accessed 23 March 2012. http://www.blackwellreference.com/public/tocnode?id=g9780631207535_chunk_g978063120753522_ss1-37#citation.

Wang, Xiaoming 王曉明. 2011. "Liufen tianxia: Jintian de Zhongguo wenxue" 六分天下:今天

的中國文學 (The world divided into six parts: today's Chinese literature). *Wenxue pinglun*, 5: 75–85.

Wines, Michael. 2011. "China Creates New Agency for Patrolling the Internet." *New York Times* (May 5). Accessed 15 November 2011. http://www.nytimes.com/2011/05/05/world/asia/05china.html.

Yang, Guobing. 2009. *The Power of the Internet in China: Citizen Activism Online*. New York: Columbia University Press.

Yang, Guobing. 2011. "The Curious Case of Jia Junpeng, or The Power of Symbolic Appropriation in Chinese Cyberspace." *The China Beat*. Accessed 23 March 2012. http://www.thechinabeat.org/?p=1010.

Yang, Xiaobin. 2002. *The Chinese Postmodern: Trauma and Irony in Chinese Avant-Garde Fiction*. Ann Arbor: University of Michigan Press.

Yin, Pumin. 2005. "Web Writing." *Beijing Review* (August 25): 31.

Zhou, Yongming. 2006. *Historicizing Online Politics: Telegraphy, the Internet, and Political Participation in China*. Stanford, CA: Stanford University Press.

Part IV
Issues and Debates

24

The Persistence of Form: Nation, Literary Movement, and the Fiction of Ng Kim Chew

Carlos Rojas

"The Disappearance of M" (*M de shizong*, 1994), a short story by Malaysian Chinese author Ng Kim Chew (Huang Jinshu), revolves around the publication of a mysterious novel entitled *Kristmas* that sends shock waves around the world.[1] *Kristmas* is described as a heteroglossic work composed primarily in English but also featuring a variety of other languages ranging from Malay (both modern and classical) to Jawi, Arabic, Bali, German, French, and even ancient Chinese oracle bones script.[2] The novel is enthusiastically compared to *Ulysses*, arouses considerable national pride, and even inspires discussion of the possibility of a Nobel Prize.

The story's description of how this fictional novel generates Nobel Prize buzz is ironic, given that the prize is awarded not to an individual literary work but rather to an author in recognition of his or her entire oeuvre, while Kristmas was published anonymously under the initial "M" and nothing is known for certain about the author. The fact that the original manuscript was mailed to the publisher from a location in West Malaysia, however, suggests that the author was Malaysian, while the fact that the postage had been charged to a Chinese deposit company implies that he or she may have been ethnically Chinese. To determine who wrote the novel and whether it would therefore count as an example of "national literature," a pair of national literature discussion forums are convened in Kuala Lumpur, and are attended by many of Malaysia's ethnically Malay and Chinese authors, respectively. In the second forum, a heated debate erupts between two groups of authors belonging to modernist and realist camps, respectively. For instance, Meng Sha, who is identified as one of the realists, argues that the novel certainly cannot be considered to be an example of Malaysian Chinese literature, given that it is not even written in Chinese; while Tan

A Companion to Modern Chinese Literature, First Edition. Edited by Yingjin Zhang.
© 2016 John Wiley & Sons, Ltd. Published 2016 by John Wiley & Sons, Ltd.

Swie Hian (Chen Ruixian), who is identified as a leading modernist, instead praises the work for its success in "cross[ing] Malaysian literature's ethnic boundaries" and "mix[ing] up many of the world's languages, thereby creating a unique new written language." The conference concludes with the moderator announcing that the next step will be to attempt to track down both the anonymous author as well as the work's original "Chinese edition"—"if, that is, you believe he must have written it in Chinese."

Even as the story's fictional literature forum ostensibly revolves around questions of national identity, it simultaneously underscores a rather different set of categories, in that each of the conference participants is explicitly identified by the literary movement with which they are affiliated. At first glance, these two sets of taxonomical regimes appear to be governed by distinct logics, in that a work's national identity is typically assumed to be determined by its origins and its author's identity, while the work's affiliation with a particular literary movement is instead a function of its formal qualities. A national tradition, moreover, may generate a wide variety of literary movements, even as these same movements may easily cross national borders.

While Ng's story underscores a basic contrast between these two taxonomical systems, it also points to some of the underlying tensions and contradictions implicit in each. First, the category *Malaysian Chinese literature* is actually a curious hybrid, as reflected in the fact that, in the conventional Chinese abbreviation *Mahua wenxue*, the *Ma* is short for "Malaysia" (*Malaixiya*) while the *hua* may refer either the Chinese language (*Huawen*) or for the Chinese people (*Huaren*). Consequently, some critics use *Mahua wenxue* to refer to literature written in Chinese by citizens or residents of Malaysia, while others use it more broadly to refer to all works by ethnically Chinese authors from Malaysia writing in *any* language, including not only Chinese but also English, Malay, and Baba Malay (the latter being a creole written in romanized script and featuring a primarily Malay grammar but with many words derived from the Hokkien dialect of Chinese). The challenge of how to categorize the multilingual *Kristmas*, accordingly, rehearses a set of questions that underlie that category of Mahua literature itself, in that the author is unknown, and it is not even known for certain in what language the heteroglossic work was originally written.

Second, the two literary movements to which the participants in the story's fictional debate nominally belong are themselves fluid and amorphous, with similar designations having been used to refer to movements in other geographic regions and historical periods. Literary modernism, for instance, is a category that first emerged in the late nineteenth and early twentieth century in Europe and North America, but which was quickly adopted in other countries and regions around the world, including China, Taiwan, and Southeast Asia. In each of its various incarnations, literary modernism is not only the symptom of a set of sociocultural transformations associated with modernization and modernity but also the product of a process of imitation and modification. Similarly, the English term *realism* began to gain popularity in the mid-nineteenth century, and ultimately came to be applied to a wide range of representational forms—including poetic realism, socialist realism, and naturalism. As a result, literary realism may be understood as not so much an imitation of reality itself, but rather an imitation of preceding literary models. The taxonomical significance of these sorts of movements, accordingly, lies not only in the way in which they help constrain a set of works that are partially modeled on one another, but also in the way that they open up a creative space within which the form itself can be radically reimagined.

In the following discussion, I use Ng Kim Chew's "The Disappearance of M" to reflect on the relationship between these two sets of taxonomical regimes, focusing on three distinct intertextual moments in the story, each of which invokes a different historical–regional juncture. In historical terms, these three moments proceed from the early-twentieth-century May Fourth period, to the mid-twentieth-century war-time period, to the contemporary moment. In geographic terms, they move from mainland China (and Japan), to Southeast Asia, and finally to Ng's adopted home of Taiwan. I consider how each of these three moments opens up a broader reflection on the relationship between literary taxonomies based on national origin and literary form, respectively, arguing that the *imitative logic* on which literary movements are grounded offers a useful way of reassessing the emphasis on origins and identity that drives many discussions of national literature.

Desire

Ng Kim Chew was born in 1967 in Johor, West Malaysia, and grew up in a poor village in a rubber forest. In 1986, he enrolled in National Taiwan University, eventually receiving his doctorate in Chinese literature. Ng is currently a professor in Taiwan, specializing in Mahua literature, and is also a creative writer in his own right. Virtually all of his stories are set in Malaysia and the surrounding archipelago, and his characters frequently struggle with a sense of cultural alienation as they attempt to negotiate their overlapping relationships with a Chinese cultural heritage and with the Malaysian nation that they call home. His fiction reflects concerns with the diasporic movement of peoples and cultural works, together with related taxonomical considerations of how those peoples and works may be classified. In this respect, his short stories are paradigmatic examples of Mahua literature, even as they simultaneously interrogate some of the taxonomical assumptions on which the category itself is grounded.

Ng's "The Disappearance of M" begins with the description of a journalist named Huang who has embarked on a 3-month investigation to try to track down the anonymous author of *Kristmas*.[3] In the story's opening passage, Huang has just arrived in a remote Malaysian village, where he is attempting to follow up on a recent newspaper report describing how a visitor identified as a "young Singapore man" arrived a few months earlier and built himself a stilt house, but then disappeared again. Having already met with all of the Mahua authors he could find, Huang is now trying to see if he can learn more about this visitor from Singapore, on the off chance that he might be the mysterious "M" who wrote *Kristmas*.

Following an initial discussion of Huang's arrival in the village, the story transitions to an extended flashback that begins with the national literature discussion forum mentioned earlier, followed by a description of a trip that Huang makes to Taiwan to interview the several Mahua authors living there. Huang ultimately concludes, however, that none of these Taiwan-based authors could have authored the novel in question, given that they all have strong Americanized, Sinitic, or nativist tendencies. The implication is that each of these diasporic authors has cultural allegiances to either Taiwan, mainland China, or the United States that would have made it difficult for them to mobilize a multilingual discourse to compose a bona fide Mahua work.

One of the authors Huang meets in Taiwan, for instance, is Li Yongping, who is committed to writing in a version of Chinese that is intended to be even more "pure" than any existing version of the language. Li is openly scornful of *Kristmas*, suggesting that the novel was probably an elaborate stunt by a Chinese author living abroad. The irony, however, is that a similar criticism could also be applied to Li Yongping himself. Originally a Malaysian citizen of Chinese descent, Li Yongping came to the United States for graduate school, where he received a doctorate in comparative literature. He subsequently immigrated to Taiwan and is currently viewed more as a Taiwanese author than a Mahua one. At first glance, his works might appear to be composed in a language that is the precise opposite of that of *Kristmas*, in that he tries to create an impossibly pure version of the Chinese language, while *Kristmas* instead adopts an aggressively heteroglossic approach. At the same time, though, one could also argue that it is precisely in the conjunction of Li's American, Taiwanese, and Chinese connections and sympathies that we may find a displaced articulation of the tensions resulting from his biographical origins as a Chinese ethnic minority in Malaysia. By this reading, Li Yongping's status as a Mahua author—and, by extension, his commonalities with other Mahua authors in Taiwan and elsewhere—are most evident precisely in his apparent attempts to compensate for his diasporic background by reclaiming an idealized version of the language of the Chinese mainland.

Immediately following the description of Huang's trip to Taiwan, Ng's story jumps back to the narrative present with the protagonist dreaming that he is floating in mid-air and peering down at all of the regions he had just visited in his quest, including North Malaysia, South Malaysia, East Malaysia, and Singapore. Huang fantasizes that he is reviewing the works of all known Mahua authors, in an attempt to determine if any of them could be M. It suddenly occurs to him, however, that M might not be ethnically Chinese at all, but rather Malay or Indian. At this point, he walks over to a nearby hut and sees a man whom he believes to be the early-twentieth-century Chinese author Yu Dafu. Alluding to the common belief that Yu Dafu was apprehended and executed by the Japanese military in 1945 while living incognito in a remote Sumatran village, Huang asks in surprise, "Didn't I hear you had been killed by the Japanese?" The other man asks in return, "Who said I died? Did anyone see my corpse? Couldn't I have gone into hiding?" It then occurs to Huang that perhaps Yu Dafu, who was famous for knowing many foreign languages, might have somehow gone on to compose *Kristmas* years after his alleged death. Huang gives the man a copy of the novel, but the other man simply laughs and hands it back to him, at which point Huang abruptly wakes up.

Unlike the other contemporary authors referenced in Ng's story, Yu Dafu was active in the first half of the twentieth century. Born in 1896, Yu Dafu began publishing poetry in 1911, and in 1914 he travelled to Japan with his brother for high school. In 1921, while still in Japan, Yu Dafu helped establish the Creation Society, a literary society inspired by contemporary Western aesthetic trends such as romanticism and neo-romanticism. It was also in 1921 that Yu published his short story collection *Sinking* (*Chenlun*; English 2007), whose title story describes a Chinese student studying in Japan who is fascinated with Western romantic literature (the story quotes several verses from Wordsworth in the original English), suffers from acute hypochondria (the story uses the English term), and feels deeply ashamed of his Chinese nationality. Yu's protagonist masturbates obsessively, though he is tormented by a fear that this will impact his thought processes, and even his ability to write. At one point, he peeks in on his Japanese landlord's daughter while she is in the shower and later visits a local brothel, though these actions merely exacerbate his feelings of inferiority. The story concludes with the protagonist cursing China's weakness while wrestling with an urge to throw himself into the sea.

Given Yu Dafu's explicit focus on his Chinese protagonist's sense of national inferiority *vis-à-vis* the Japanese, it is ironic that "Sinking" itself is directly indebted to the Japanese "I-novel" (*watakushi shōsetsu*)—a genre that emerged in the early twentieth century and was distinguished by its use of a first-person confessional tone to explore a set of inner contradictions within the narrator's psyche. While Yu Dafu's "Sinking" is technically written in a third person voice, it resembles an I-novel in its explicit focus on the protagonist's feelings of estrangement and alienation. The irony, however, is that the presumably quasi-autobiographical story presents these anxieties through a literary genre that itself carries distinctly foreign connotations. In other words, for Yu Dafu, it is precisely through a process of *speaking through* a literary genre with foreign connotations that he is thereby able to express some of the anxieties experienced by contemporary Chinese.

Yu Dafu returned to China in 1922, where he continued his literary activities and became a prominent member of the May Fourth New Culture Movement, which advocated the development of progressive literature written in the vernacular to help strengthen the nation. Similar to Yu Dafu, many other May Fourth authors found inspiration in foreign literary works, and their own compositions often reflected this influence at the level of the works' thematics, narrative structure, and grammatical constructions. As a result, even as these Chinese texts were characterized by what critic C. T. Hsia (1999) has famously described as an "obsession with China," they nevertheless revealed a strong indebtedness to foreign literary models. Their foreignness, in other words, was mobilized in order to help the authors critically address the challenges confronting the Chinese nation, even as this foreign influence *itself* came to be perceived as one of the challenges facing China.

In introducing this spectral appearance of Yu Dafu into his story about a journalist's quest for the author of the mysterious *Kristmas*, Ng Kim Chew tacitly layers one set of early Chinese literary debates onto a set of contemporary concerns with the status of

Mahua literature in an increasingly globalized world. Just as the Mahua authors attending the story's fictional National Literature Discussion Forum debate the taxonomical limits of Mahua literature even as they tacitly reaffirm the plasticity of designations such as modernism and realism, Yu Dafu and other early-twentieth-century May Fourth authors similarly deployed a variety of "foreign" literary forms in their attempts to think through a set of national problematics. For them, the foreign origins of these literary forms offered a useful way of interrogating their understanding of their own national identity and national heritage.

While realism and modernism are presented as being mutually opposed in the discussion of the contemporary literature forum in Ng's story, in the May Fourth context realism and modernism were both perceived as imported representational forms that were used to help articulate a critical and reformist vision of the nation. In this early-twentieth-century period, realism *was* a modernist mode, and the process of creating a verisimilar literary account necessarily involved copying not only external reality itself but also earlier literary *representations* of that same reality—even if those literary representations that came to be perceived as paradigmatic exemplars of literary realism originated from a different national tradition. It was precisely from within the gap between the model and its copy, meanwhile, that a new vision of a modern Chinese literature began to emerge (M. Anderson 1990; D. Wang 1992).

The story's speculation that Yu Dafu—who was born and is assumed to have spent most of his life in mainland China—might have authored a novel with the potential of becoming a defining work of contemporary Malaysian Chinese literature, accordingly, mirrors in reverse the way in which much of the distinctive literary production from early-twentieth-century China's May Fourth Movement was itself directly informed by a set of literary practices and representational strategies that had been recently introduced into China from abroad.

Exile

When Huang awakens from the reverie in which he encounters the man who appears to be Yu Dafu, he finds himself back in the remote Malaysian village in which he had just arrived at the beginning of the story, trying to track down information on the visitor from Singapore. He discovers that the visitor had interacted closely with a local family, including a young boy, the boy's elder sister, and their parents. Huang speaks to each of these family members in turn, and they describe how the visitor appeared to be in his thirties or forties, but note that it was very difficult to judge his age and that he might well have been even older. They describe how he wore "May Fourth–style" glasses, had his hair cut so short that he resembled a student, and was "as thin as a cockroach." The family recalls that the visitor seemed somewhat neurotic, and the family's teenage daughter describes how he appeared to be romantically interested in her and would periodically send her love letters (which she would deliberately ignore).

The family reports that the visitor left behind a collection of manuscript fragments when he departed, from which they concluded that he must have been a writer of some sort. The family's daughter brings Huang some of these documents to look over, explaining:

> "I never knew his [the visitor's] name. ... I once heard him explain that he was constantly changing the pennames under which he wrote his manuscripts, and was always taking other peoples' manuscript fees ... I heard that at one point or other he has 'poached' the name of every Mahua author alive." She handed him a bundle she was carrying in her breast. "These are some documents I saved after he disappeared." (K. C. Ng 1994: 31)

Huang examines each of the documents in turn, and eventually finds a fragment that reads:

> Even a heart that has long been cold still has some impulse. I can't change my old habits. I never expected that even here I would encounter such a pure young girl, like a moonlit flower. But I'm too old. Forget it, forget it. I don't want to harm anyone or anything. I fear attachment, and being bound by beautiful women. (K. C. Ng 1994: 31–32)

Noticing that this passage closely resembles the writings of Yu Dafu—particularly with respect to its fascination with young women, which is a distinguishing characteristic of much of Yu Dafu's writing—Huang speculates that the mysterious visitor could have been the May Fourth Chinese author, who might have somehow survived his abduction in 1945 and possibly even gone on to write the novel *Kristmas*.

Reflecting on the possibility that Yu Dafu might be the author of *Kristmas*, Huang observes that Yu once wrote that "if only there could appear a great author, it would change the fate of Mahua literature." This is an observation that the historical Yu Dafu made after fleeing China in late 1938 and relocating to Singapore, where he quickly became very involved in local literary and cultural affairs. He not only attempted to introduce modern literary models associated with the May Fourth Movement, he also advocated for the development of a distinctive and autonomous body of Chinese-language literature that could represent the Southeast Asia region within which Singapore is located. In particular, he argued that the region needed one or more "great authors" in order to earn broader regional, and even global, recognition. To the extent that Yu Dafu began his literary career in Japan, using a set of representational forms borrowed from abroad to articulate a conflicted sense of ethno-national identity, therefore, it is notable that, three decades later, he became involved in an inverse attempt to introduce literary models from China to help develop a new literary movement by and about overseas Chinese in Southeast Asia. While the May Fourth adoption of foreign literary models was frequently linked to a set of deep-rooted anxieties about national identity, Yu Dafu hoped that a reappropriation of these same models to Southeast Asia might instead help promote a nationalist literature that would help establish Sinophone Southeast Asia as a distinctive para-national region in its own right (Groppe 2010; Tsu 2010).

Yu Dafu's efforts to develop the literary scene in Singapore ended up being short-lived, however, and on the eve of the 1942 Japanese invasion of Singapore he fled again and ended up in a small village in Western Sumatra, where he adopted the fictional identity of a Chinese businessman named Zhao Lian. Even though Yu Dafu had previously been actively involved in anti-Japanese protests during the war, he nevertheless subsequently capitalized on his fluency in Japanese in order to secretly work as an interpreter for the Japanese military police while in Sumatra. One evening in 1945, an unknown visitor came to Yu Dafu's home and led him away, and he was never seen again. It was subsequently reported that he had been executed by the Japanese for revealing military secrets, though the fact that his remains were never recovered leaves open the possibility that he might have somehow survived his abduction. Ng Kim Chew, meanwhile, appears to have been fascinated with this possibility that Yu Dafu might have continued living incognito in Southeast Asia for decades after his reported death. He explores some of the ramifications of this counterfactual scenario not only in "The Disappearance of M" but also in "Death in the South" ("*Si zai nanfang*," 1994), which Ng published in the same collection as "The Disappearance of M," as well as another story, "Supplement" ("*Buyi*," 2001), which Ng published in another collection 7 years later.

"Death in the South" describes the narrator's discovery of an archive of manuscript fragments that appear to have been composed by Yu Dafu following his alleged death, and concludes with the narrator carefully recopying these texts into his notebook and feeling that he is thereby becoming united with the spirit of the legendary author. "Supplement," meanwhile, takes inspiration from a 1990s Taiwan documentary focusing on Yu Dafu's life.[4] The original documentary concludes with Yu Dafu's 1945 execution, but Ng's story describes how the filmmakers are subsequently provided with evidence that Yu Dafu might not have died in 1945 after all, whereupon they decide to travel to Indonesia to determine whether or not it will be necessary to add an addendum (a "supplement") to their original work. The filmmakers are eventually kidnapped and taken to an isolated island where a small community of Chinese, led by an elderly man whom the filmmakers suspect to be Yu Dafu, is observing an almost parodic allegiance to traditional Chinese practices and forms (Groppe 2010).

In both these stories, an inquiry into Yu Dafu's fate ends up revolving around an elaborate process of cultural mimicry. Just as the isolated island community at the end of "Supplement" is found to be carefully imitating traditional Chinese cultural practices, the narrator at the end of "Death in the South" imagines that he is able to meld with Yu Dafu's spirit by copying Yu's manuscripts. In each instance, the process of imitation is viewed as enabling the possibility of a sort of spiritual transference. Mimicry, here, functions as a form of what Derrida describes as a process of iterative citation, wherein the process of repeated citation necessarily entails a potential deviation from that which is being cited, though at the same time it is precisely within this space of deviation and divergence that it becomes possible to establish an identification with earlier cultural models and loci of national identity (Derrida 1988). The imitative logic that underlies literary movements such as realism and modernism, in other words, also structures the discourses of origins and identity on which conceptions of national literature are themselves predicated. It is precisely through the process of copying formal elements from existing literary movements that it thereby becomes possible to create a movement that might come to function as a locus of regional or national identity.

Just as Yu Dafu's embrace of foreign literary forms at the beginning of his career was linked to a set of anxieties about national identity, his advocacy of foreign literary forms in Singapore during the war-time period a couple of decades later reflected an attempt to use literature to promote a diasporic ethno-national identity. A similar effort to envision a national literature from within a diasporic perspective, meanwhile, can be found in post-1949 Taiwan literature. While the 1950s, Taiwan's first full decade under Nationalist rule, was dominated by anti-communist literature, the 1960s was noted for a surge of modernist literature, wherein Taiwan authors drew on literary forms with foreign connotations to interrogate Taiwan's sense of geographic isolation from the mainland. In the 1970s, meanwhile, the pendulum swung the other way, with a surge of nativist literary production that used realism to explore an array of topics grounded in Taiwanese society and culture. Although frequently viewed as mutually opposed movements, Taiwan's modernist and nativist movements both reflected an attempt to articulate a sense of cultural distinctiveness *vis-à-vis* a sense of diasporic dislocation, appealing either to foreign representational forms or to local content in an effort to distinguish contemporary Taiwanese literary production from that which was being produced across the Taiwan Strait in mainland China.

A similar tension may be found, meanwhile, in the debate between the modernists and the realists in the national literature discussion forum described in Ng's "The Disappearance of M"—where the realists claim that the Mahua literature as a national category must be grounded on a tangible link to the socio-cultural conditions of the Mahua experience (such as the use of the Chinese language), while the modernists argue that a set of hybrid representational forms may be used to reflect the more abstract sensibilities associated with Mahua literature as a fundamentally diasporic and hybrid category. In contrast to the abject tenor that characterized the discourse of (Chinese) national identity in Yu Dafu's story "Sinking," however, the discourses of national identity found in both the mid-century Taiwanese modernist/nativist movements and in the contemporary Mahua modernist/realist movements reflect instead the celebratory attitude similar to that which motivated Yu Dafu's attempts to establish an internationally recognized Chinese-language literary tradition in Southeast Asia in the late 1930s.

Metatext

After discovering the manuscript containing the passage apparently composed by Yu Dafu, the reporter Huang in Ng's story identifies additional manuscripts in the same collection that appear to have been written by other identifiable authors. For example, Huang next finds a fragment that begins, "White cloak, you are impossible to forget," and he concludes that it must have been written by the poet Wen Ruian, who regularly invoked the symbol of a "white cloak" in his texts. Huang finds other fragments that seem to have been authored by others, such that "nearly every document offered a different possibility, and every possibility was mutually contradictory." The implication seems to be that the mysterious visitor was indeed extremely adept— as the Malaysian family's daughter put it—in "poaching the name of every Mahua author alive," which leads Huang to reflect that perhaps M is not so much an individual as a compound entity that may be expressed by the (imaginary) mathematical formula: $M_1 + M_2 + M_3 \ldots Mn, n_\in N_0$.

The next day, the daughter hands Huang a newspaper containing a supplementary section labeled "Xiangqing literary prize special issue." Huang opens the supplement, and discovers that one of the essays is titled "The Disappearance of M." The author of the essay is listed simply as "M," and the report notes that the author's actual identity is unknown. Huang looks over the essay, and finds it to be almost identical to his own (as-yet-incomplete) account of his search for "M." Deeply disconcerted by this discovery, Huang begins to suspect that "M" might even be the girl who gave him the newspaper in the first place. As Ng's story puts it (1994: 39):

> How was it that it never occurred to him that M might not be a man, or even a woman, but rather a girl who was both the protagonist and the author? Was it therefore not surprising that the manuscript left behind by the missing author (whom we might call MX?) was full of Yu Dafu's expressions of depression? It finally occurred to him that M was a compound entity, of which he was only one insignificant element. On a sheet of paper, he wrote,
> "Perhaps after not too long someone will discover my own 'disappearance' (that is a structural necessity....)."
> He proceeded to lie down and read the final lines of this "The Disappearance of M":

In this passage, the narrative folds back upon itself as Huang realizes that the essay in the newspaper closely mirrors the text that he himself is in the process of composing, from which he begins to suspect that "M" may not be a single individual but rather a composite figure—a compound entity of which Huang himself was also a single component. He concludes that M's identity may be expressed through a recursive mathematical function, in which he himself is one of the variables. In particular, Huang's knowledge that the Singaporean visitor had been romantically interested in the Malaysian family's teenage daughter, combined with the knowledge that Yu Dafu had been notorious for his attention, in his writings, on beautiful young girls, leads Huang to suspect that the girl might herself have been part of the compound "author function" of the essay itself.

Following the colon at the end of the preceding block quote, there appears a transcript of *another* literary conference that was convened to determine the identity of the author of *Kristmas*. This account of the conference—which presumably corresponds not only to the version of "The Disappearance of M" printed in the newspaper that

Huang has been given, but also to the narrative that Huang is himself in the process of composing to describe his quest for the author of *Kristmas*, as well as to the short story by Ng Kim Chew himself, of which Huang is the protagonist—appears to be heavily redacted. The document quotes many of the authors who participated in the conference, but a series of bracketed notes point out that many of these quotes have either been abridged or deleted altogether at the speakers' request.

One of the conference participants who is quoted repeatedly in this final portion of the text is the contemporary Taiwanese author Zhang Dachun (Chang Ta-chun). Zhang's first remarks that appear in the story are cited as follows (K. C. Ng 1994: 41):

> "I am very familiar with this writing style, which basically uses a fictional plotline to discuss a topic. The author's technique [deleted, at Zhang's request], and addresses a very serious issue: [deleted, at Zhang's request] … [deleted, at Zhang's request]."

Several other participants then add their own observations, whereupon the narrator notes that:

> the conference moderator invited all of the critics to review and revise the portions of the transcript corresponding to their contributions—in order to bring fiction more closely into alignment with reality, while at the same time aligning reality closer to fiction. Zhang Dachun, while reviewing the transcript, beamed with a *Great Liar*-like smile, such that the creases on either side of his mouth danced back and forth like a pair of carp. …
>
> At that point an absurd situation presented itself: A group of Taiwan authors in the work were critiquing characters who shared their name in a work by the same title, even as the characters in the work itself were simultaneously critiquing a work by the same title. In the end, Zhang Dachun couldn't help but sigh:
> "Don't you know, reality itself is actually so fictional!" (K. C. Ng 1994: 42)

Although not a Mahua author, Zhang Dachun is regarded as one of contemporary Taiwan's most original and innovative writers. For instance, Zhang's novel *Great Liar*, which is referenced in the passage cited earlier, adopts a distinctive narrative practice in which every day he would adapt that day's news stories into his own fictional text. He continued this practice for the first 6 months of 1989, but discontinued it in June, after the Chinese government's violent crackdown on the democracy protesters in Beijing's Tiananmen Square rendered the practice of creating a fictionalized version of current events unpalatable. In this way, a literary work that is initially premised on a process of having fiction imitate reality is aborted when reality unexpectedly overtakes fiction.

Ng Kim Chew's decision to foreground this fictionalized version of the author Zhang Dachun at the end of "The Disappearance of M" is ironic, given that Ng has been quite critical of Zhang's habit of deliberately blurring fiction and reality. In an essay published a few years later, for instance, Ng (2000) concludes that Zhang's trademark metafictional style constitutes an abrogation of political responsibility. In particular, he contends that, while Zhang's early works from the 1980s reflect the legacy of Taiwan's 1970s nativism movement, Zhang, beginning with his 1994 collection *Guided Tour of an Apartment Complex* (*Gongyu daoyou*), began adopting a literary approach, which Ng characterizes as cynical and disdainful and which Zhang himself described as "lying." Ng (1997: 261–262, 264) claims that "Zhang's impatience and his obsession with form lead him to constantly assert his position through loquacious mockery," and contends that one result of this "obsession with form" has been a chameleon-like fluidity, with Zhang changing genres "every few years or so … from historical novels, to science fiction, to martial arts novels, to detective stories, to legends, and on to reportage and diary novels."[5]

Ng (1997: 254) argues that Zhang's reluctance to commit himself to any particular literary form parallels his more general ambivalence toward identity politics:

> Zhang's resistance to engaging in identity politics as well as to having his own identity specified—in short, his figurative immunity to issues relating to identity—is, perhaps, ultimately the real problem behind, or the real issue being addressed in, Zhang's novels. Moreover, this "immunity" itself can, perhaps, be seen as a symptom of a larger phenomenon relating to the problems that plague the contemporary Taiwanese cultural scene.

Ng contends that a similar ambivalence toward identity may be found in many of Zhang's own literary works beginning with *Guided Tour of an Apartment Complex*, to the point that "Zhang has inserted himself into the story in a way that raises the question, 'Can you believe that's me (the author)?' In other works, we hear his voice but do not actually see him in the story. … In short, Zhang is present in his works precisely by being absent" (Ng 1997: 255).

In this latter critique of Zhang's metafictional and postmodernist writing style, in turn, we find a potential answer to the riddle posed by Ng's own "The Disappearance of M." That is to say, if Zhang Dachun is in fact "present in his works precisely by being absent," the solution to M's own absence in Ng's story may lie in the fact that he is actually all-too-present—in that the authorial identity behind his novel may be viewed not as an individual but rather as a collective, a product of an iterative mathematical function that includes even the reporter himself. Ironically, it was in 1994—the same year that Zhang Dachun published the *Guided Tour of an Apartment Complex* collection, which Ng identifies as marking the point at which Zhang's literature made its critical turn toward metafiction—that Ng himself published the collection *Dream and Swine and Aurora* (*Meng yu zhu yu liming*), which included his own metafictional explorations such as "Death in the South" and "The Disappearance of M." Ng, however, would presumably contend that his own metafictional turn was intended to help explore the very questions of identity that Zhang, in his metafiction, is allegedly sidestepping.

To the extent that Ng's "The Disappearance of M" stresses that one of the key reasons why Huang and the other Mahua authors are so invested in identifying the identity of "M" is precisely because they hope this might help clarify the novel's status as a work of national literature, the conclusion that M may be viewed not as an individual but rather as a collective suggests that national identity itself may similarly be understood as an aggregate process—a product of a process of iterative citation. By extension, a literature's national identity is best viewed as a function not so much of its origins or the identity of its author, but rather as a product of a process of imitation and reproduction. Literary taxonomies grounded on national identity, in other words, obey a similar imitative logic as those based on form or aesthetics, in that the national literature's distinctiveness is a function of its ability to copy and modify existing precedents, which may include literary works not only from the nation or region in question, but also from other regions. Similar to Ng's assessment of Zhang Dachun, the mysterious "M" in Ng's story symbolizes the possibility of a distinctive and internationally recognized body of Malaysian Chinese literary production. This "M" is present "precisely by being absent"—symbolizing the degree to which a national literature contains at its core an empty kernel that is ultimately shaped by fundamentally iterative processes of identification and disidentification.

NOTES

1 For this and the other two stories by Ng discussed in this chapter, see Ng (2016).

2 The title "*Kristmas*," in Ng's "The Disappearance of M," appears in romanized script in the original Chinese-language story.

3 The protagonist shares the same surname as the work's author. For clarity, however, I will use the standard pinyin transliteration, "Huang," when referring to the protagonist, while using the author's preferred spelling, "Ng," to render his own family name.

4 The story is inspired by an actual documentary that was produced and released as part of a series on Chinese-language authors.

5 The Chinese version in Ng (2000: 253–286).

REFERENCES

Anderson, Marston. 1990. *The Limits of Realism: Chinese Fiction in the Revolutionary Period*. Berkeley: University of California Press.

Derrida, Jacques. 1988. *Limited, Inc*. Trans. Jeffrey Mehlman and Samuel Weber. Evanston, IL: Northwestern University Press.

Groppe, Alison. 2010. "The Dis/Reappearances of Yu Dafu in Ng Kim Chew's Fiction." *Modern Chinese Literature and Culture*, 22.2: 161–195.

Hsia, C. T. 1999. *A History of Modern Chinese Fiction*. 3rd edition. Bloomington: Indiana University Press.

Ng, Kim Chew 黃錦樹. 1994. *Meng yu zhu yu liming* 夢與豬與黎明 (Dream and swine and aurora). Taipei: Jiuge.

Ng, Kim Chew. 1997. "Techniques Behind Lies and the Artistry of Truth: Writing about the Writings of Zhang Dachun." In *Writing Taiwan: A New Literary History*. Edited by Wang, David Der-wei and Carlos Rojas. Durham, NC: Duke University Press. 253–282.

Ng, Kim Chew 黃錦樹. 2000. "Huangyan de jishu yu zhenli de jiyi: Shuxie Zhang Dachun de shuxie" 謊言的技術與真理的技藝:書寫張大春的書寫 (Techniques behind lies and the artistry of truth: Writing about the writings of Zhang Dachun). In *Shuxie Taiwan: wenxueshi, houzhimin yu houxiandai* 書寫臺灣:文學史、後殖民與後現代 (Writing Taiwan: literary history, postcoloniality and postmodernity). Edited by Zhou Yingxiong 周英雄 and Liu Jihui 劉紀蕙. Taipei: Maitian. 253–286.

Ng, Kim Chew. 2016. *Slow Boat to China and Other Stories by Ng Kim Chew*. Edited and Translated by Carlos Rojas. New York: Columbia University Press.

Tsu, Jing. 2010. *Sound and Script in Chinese Diaspora*. Cambridge, MA: Harvard University Press.

Wang, David Der-wei. 1992. *Fictional Realism in Twentieth-Century China: Mao Dun, Lao She, Shen Congwen*. New York: Columbia University Press.

Yu Dafu. 2007. "Sinking." In *The Columbia Anthology of Modern Chinese Literature*. Edited by Lau, Joseph S. M., and Howard Goldblatt. 2nd edition. New York: Columbia University Press. 31–55.

25

The Modern Girl in Modern Chinese Literature

Tze-lan D. Sang

Gender and sexuality in modern Chinese literature is a rich topic that has been approached from a variety of angles. Investigating phenomena from women's literary feminism (Dooling 2005), to the new woman in early-twentieth-century Chinese fiction (Larson 1998; L. Wang 2004), to the crisis of masculinity found in early-twentieth-century literature, which was echoed in the post-Mao period (X. Zhong 2000; Tsu 2006), to the emergence of a modern "structure of feeling" (H. Lee 2007), scholars have sought to shed light on new gender and sexual formations as they were articulated through literature during China's transition from empire to republic. Indeed, any examination of Chinese modernity would be incomplete without venturing into the question of gender and sexual modernity, particularly as it has been refracted—and shaped—through textual representation. How have understandings of same-sex and cross-sex relations changed (Sang 2003; Kang 2009)? How have notions of femininity, masculinity, and gender variance evolved (Louie 2002; Chiang 2012)? What new concepts of sexuality have arisen as both tools for social control and new technologies for self-fashioning (Sang 2003; Chiang and Heinrich 2013)?

In the large body of research on gender and sexuality in modern Chinese literature, the literary representation of the Modern Girl in Republican China stands out as one of the most productive questions. The sophisticated studies notwithstanding (L. Lee 1999; Shih 2001; Stevens 2003; H. Peng 2010), the issue is far from exhausted, and there remain areas that merit further exploration. This chapter, then, will revisit the problem of the Modern Girl and attempt to throw some new light on it. First, the chapter will provide a concise overview of existing scholarly approaches. Second, noting the fact that the representation of the Chinese Modern Girl occurred not only in literature but also in a multiplicity of representational genres and media (e.g., fiction, cartoons, films, advertisement drawings, journalistic reports), the chapter will reestablish the linkages between fictional representation and some of the most common motifs that ran through the cacophonous mass media debate over the Modern Girl during the 1930s–1940s. Only by reestablishing the transgeneric and intermedial linkages can we begin to appreciate the public significance of Shanghai modernist writers' seemingly individualistic psychological obsessions with the Modern Girl.

Throughout, I contend that the Modern Girl was a chameleon-like enigma over whose definition intense ideological struggles were fought out. Although media discussions often portrayed her as a gold-digger, a hedonist, and a lavish consumer who was obsessed especially with fashion and cosmetics, a considerable number of commentators in the press insisted on defining the *true* Modern Girl as a modern woman who was intellectual, socially responsible, and patriotic. Fiction writers played with many of these media motifs. Some fiction writers were highly conscious of how the Modern Girl was stereotyped and even maligned by the mass media; they therefore created plots that commented on the ways in which the Modern Girl was less accurately portrayed than fancifully constructed through the media uproar. In other cases, writers depicted the Modern Girl as an unhappy heterosexual: she is either under pressure to settle for financial security rather than true love, or is betrayed or misunderstood by her male lovers. If the Modern Girl was a product of both capitalist consumer culture and a modern sexual ideology that lionized women's desire for men, Chinese literary depictions of the Modern Girl nevertheless showed up the discontents of both capitalist material culture and modern heterosexual liberation.

To begin with, the Modern Girl had a ubiquitous presence in early-twentieth-century Chinese literature and visual culture. From popular fiction to revolutionary literature, from movie fanzines to more serious varieties of newspapers and magazines, from advertising images to leftist cinema, the Modern Girl appeared as an iconic figure in a wide range of representations from the late 1920s through the 1940s. Generally speaking, she was depicted as glamorous, alluring, and sexually liberated. She was envied and emulated as much as chastised. She symbolized the contradictions of modernity—its inordinate attraction as well as threat. She was frequently a key character in the modern heteronormative narrative that gained increasing dominance in urban public discourse in Republican China, a narrative that promoted the liberalization of cross-sex courtship as a progressive, humane practice that radically departed from restrictive Confucian ritual. Paradoxically, however, narratives about the Modern Girl's liberated interactions with men also often spotlighted the difficulty of true love and trust between the sexes. Frequently in these narratives, the Modern Girl's romantic encounters with men are tumultuous affairs—symptoms abound of insincerity, materialistic calculations, competitions for dominance, and major lapses and breakdowns in communication. What is more, besides being placed at the center of tempestuous heterosexual affairs, the Modern Girl was also sometimes cast as a pivotal character in an alternative erotic narrative that involved at least one unconventional modern woman marked by gender ambiguity, wayward sexuality, and a tendency to opt out of heterosexual marriage. The representation of the Modern Girl's love life instantiated, therefore, a significant departure from the idealization of the heterosexual romance that one finds in depictions of the new woman's pursuit of free love produced during the preceding era—the May Fourth period (from approximately the mid-1910s to the mid-1920s). In other words, an intense ideological struggle over the efficacy of heterosexual love as an emancipating force for the female subject was waged over the body of the Modern Girl. Heteronormativity was at first blush produced through the iconic image of the Modern Girl but frequently undermined, at a deeper level, by her troubled relationships.

The English term "Modern Girl" first surfaced in a small number of Chinese sources such as fiction and journalism at the end of the 1920s. The New Sensationalist writer Xu Xiacun published a short story titled "Modern Girl" (English in the original) in the journal *New Literature* (*Xin wenyi*) in November 1929, and, according to Leo Lee (1999: 198), the previous year the Modern Girl "had already been identified in the North China Herald as a 'Chinese flapper'—a young woman 'dressed in semi-foreign style with bobbed hair ... short skirt ... and powdered face' who 'has come to stay.'" By 1932, both the English term and a variety of Chinese translations, including *modeng nüzi*, *modeng nülang*, *modeng xiaojie*, *shidai guniang*, and *shidai xiaojie* appeared to be in wide circulation. The Chinese fascination with the Modern Girl followed on the heels of a Japanese controversy from the mid–late 1920s. According to Barbara Sato, the term "Modern Girl" first appeared in Japan in its phonetic spelling, *modan garu*, in 1923. In the next several years, as publications proliferated on the *moga*, which was how the *modan garu* was commonly called, contradictory expectations arose. Intellectuals generally expected the *moga* to be an intellectual type, interested in radical politics and the betterment of women's position in society, while other observers equated the *moga* with a group of empty-headed, promiscuous young women preoccupied with trendy clothes and having fun (Sato 2003: 57–59; Silverberg 1991). Regardless of whether the Chinese interest in the Modern Girl was influenced by the earlier Japanese discussion, in the early 1930s the term "Modern Girl" joined other terms that had come into circulation in Chinese earlier in the twentieth century to designate a new kind of woman appearing on China's horizon.

The new-style woman at the dawn of the twentieth century was, to the public mind, typified by female revolutionaries, assassins, anti-footbinding advocates, and women educators and students (Y. Hu 2000; Judge 2008). In the ensuing May Fourth era, she was represented by educated women who strove to save the nation while seeking their own sexual and economic autonomy (Z. Wang 1999; Dooling 2005). However, in the early 1930s, the most powerful icon of new femininity had become movie starlets and other sexually alluring urban women sporting the latest fashion and believed to revel in consumption and other urban amusements. A significant reason for this shift, as Louise Edwards (2000: 123) has argued, is that, whereas previously the conceptualization of the modern woman had largely been the purview of reformist intellectuals, during the 1920s–1930s the modern woman moved into the commercial sector, resulting in the intellectual class's loss of monopolistic control over her definition.

Advertising and Hollywood films created glamorous images of the modern woman, spreading ever-more seductive prototypes of new femininity (Benson 1999; Cochran 1999: 37–58; Laing 2004; Zhou Huiling 2004; Barlow 2008). The shift, then, in the popular image of the modern woman from a reform-minded, patriotic intellectual to a glittering, decadent consumer signaled the commodification of everyday life, a de-radicalization of modernity.

Granted that this interpretation has to be qualified with the observation that modernity, in the first place, was never purely an ideological and political formation but rather had always been actualized in part through commercial practices and material culture, and that unconventional women flaunting extravagant fashions and outrageous sexual behavior—high-class courtesans—had been upheld by Shanghai's entertainment press as icons of modernity in as early as the late nineteenth century (C. Yeh 2006: 32–33), it seems that, by the early 1930s, the commodification of the everyday in China's fledgling capitalist economy reached a new intensity and scope. This, coupled with the nation's deepening sovereign crisis after Japan's 1931 invasion of Manchuria and 1932 bombing of Shanghai, demanded a response. In reaction to the commercialization and de-politicization of modern everyday life, both the political left and right seized on the Modern Girl as a symptomatic impediment to nation building, an object in dire need of reproach and reform (Sang 2008: 179–88).

From the late 1920s to the early 1930s, the Modern Girl made frequent appearances in Chinese modernist literature and art as a femme fatale, a metonymy for the modern metropolis that holds both allure and hidden danger for the (male) explorer (L. Lee 1999; Shih 2001; H. Peng 2010; Zhang Yong 2010). In advertising, she symbolized the luxurious, hygienic, and scientifically advanced lifestyle of the middle class and the super wealthy (Laing 2004; Barlow 2008). In response to these dominant, glamorized images, left-wing filmmakers, critics, and other cultural workers, who were predominantly male, tried to subject the Modern Girl to discipline, some going so far as to advocate that only a desexualized working-class heroine who was single-mindedly dedicated to the cause of the socialist revolution could be called a real modern woman (Y. Zhang 1996: 197–198). Meanwhile, on the political right, the fascistic New Life Movement launched by Chiang Kai-shek, leader of the ruling Nationalist Party, in 1934, also found in the Modern Girl an embodiment of the material and spiritual degeneration of the Chinese that had partly resulted from corrupting foreign influence. Officials in several major cities introduced prohibitions to regulate the Modern Girl's body, by discouraging and penalizing women who wore Western-style clothes, purchased foreign products, or exposed parts of their bodies in public (Yen 2005).

Because of this complex history, current approaches to the Chinese Modern Girl of the 1930s have taken several paths. Some scholars see the Modern Girl as a product of global capitalism. For instance, the collaborative research group Modern Girl Around the World, which includes China historians Tani Barlow (2008) and Madeleine Yue Dong (2008), has maintained that the Chinese Modern Girl was part of the global Modern Girl phenomenon, which, besides being manufactured through the mass media and modernist literary, aesthetic, and political discourses, was to a large degree produced through transnational capitalism inflected by imperial relations, especially through the consumer product campaigns launched by multinational corporations. According to the group, "In cities from Beijing to Bombay, Tokyo to Berlin, Johannesburg to New York ... [w]hat identified Modern Girls was their use of specific commodities and their explicit eroticism." The Modern Girl had a "cosmopolitan look," which they created by combining and reconfiguring "aesthetic elements drawn from disparate national, colonial and racial regimes" (The Modern Girl Around the World Research Group 2005: 245–246). Furthermore, examining the invention and staging of a sexy Modern Girl image in the ads for industrial commodities of multinational brands (such as Flint insect spray, Ditmar Brunner kerosene oil, Sunlight soap, Colgate perfume, Pond's vanishing cream, Cutex nail polish, and Kotex menstrual pads) in simple line drawings placed in Chinese newspapers and opinion magazines in the 1920s and 1930s, Barlow (2008: 289) has found that the repetition of this icon in numerous ads contributed to redefining a luscious, new, and scientific femininity, and that "vernacular theories of social life and advertising iconography sutured modern personhood to visual fantasies about commodity use in an imminent future via the sexy Modern Girl icon."

In contrast to these scholars' emphasis on the instrumental role of global capitalism in the making of the Modern Girl, and vice versa, other scholars have focused on the local political significance of the controversies over the Modern Girl, such as Chinese male intellectuals' debates during the 1930s over what constituted the ideal modern woman (Y. Zhang 1996: 187–207; Edwards 2000; Xu Huiqi 2003; Z. Zhang 2005). Yet another important approach aims to uncover the voices of actual Modern Girls in sites such as women's magazines and women's literary works so as to understand how Modern Girls participated in their self-definition and how they resisted or negotiated with the paternalistic repression coming from both the revolutionary left and the institutionalized power of the right (Larson 1998; Z. Wang 1999; L. Wang 2004; Dooling 2005; Yen 2005).

Productive as these varied approaches have been, more effort could be made to connect fictional representations with the general controversy over the Modern Girl that popped up in the pages of a multitude of newspapers and magazines throughout the 1930s–1940s. This will help us understand that, far from writing in a historical vacuum, Shanghai's modernist writers actively intervened into the public debate. A good case in point is Ye Lingfeng's novel *Modern Girl* (*Shidai guniang*, 1932). Originally serialized in the Shanghai newspaper *Current News* (*Shishi xinbao*) during the last 3 months of 1932, the novel is topically titled "*Shidai guniang*," one of the trendiest terms in the early 1930s used to refer to Modern Girls. Ye himself describes the novel as his "first conscious attempt at popular fiction," an exercise that proved to earn him an enthusiastic following among the newspaper's readers but also provoked some of his friends to reproach him for having "degenerated as a writer" (Ye Lingfeng 1996: 65). In Leo Lee's assessment, the novel is a second-rate work expressly created as pulp fiction to accommodate mass readers' taste. As Lee sees it, the novel is marred by a rigid episodic structure imposed by the exigencies of serialization, and it suffers from the paucity of the author's imagination and his weak fictional technique, which the author compensates only with frequent and explicit evocations of the sights and sounds of the city with which he is familiar. Even more disappointing, the heroine is surprisingly traditional at heart in her "loyalty and subservience to a possessive hero," despite being called a Modern Girl, while the male protagonist seems like "a dandy manqué," who is "hopelessly narcissistic and weak-willed," unlike the "ironic, self-mocking heroes" one finds in the stories by Ye's contemporaries Liu Na'ou and Mu Shiying (L. Lee 1999: 263–264).

While Lee's remarks are perceptive in some respects, I argue his terse and, in fact, dismissive reading largely misses the social relevance of the novel. The novel is a direct response to the lively debate over the Modern Girl that reached a fiery pitch in the Chinese press in the early 1930s when China entered a state of emergency following the Mukden Incident in Manchuria in 1931 and the Japanese bombardment of Shanghai in 1932. Ye Lingfeng not only incorporates several social scandals that involved Modern Girls at the time into his fictional plot (such as a homicide case involving two men's rivalry over the movie starlet Li Minghui), but he also makes his heroine Lily (Qin Lili) a living example of the Modern Girl at the crossroads, a young woman who is enamored with the appellative Modern Girl and intent on becoming one, and yet is unsure of its content and definition at best. Searching for a way to assert her unique individual identity as the human epitome of modern times, Lily weighs her three basic life options as she sees them: loveless bourgeois marriage; faithful, exclusive, and yet restrictive romantic love; and complete self-liberation and sexual abandon. After some vicissitudes, Lily chooses the third option, but not without serious qualms. And, as it turns out, identifying as a Modern Girl initially affords her a sense of empowerment as she seeks self-liberation, but ultimately subjects her to scrutiny and surveillance by the mass media and seriously circumscribes her agency. At the end of the novel, Lily's sexual liberation causes devastating consequences in that her first lover feels betrayed and commits suicide, and she is grief-stricken. The novel ends on an ambiguous note, seeming to argue that uninhibited sexuality cannot be a fulfilling path for the Modern Girl, while refraining from explicitly stating what a more satisfying or appropriate life plan for the Modern Girl should be.

To further demonstrate my point, it is useful to describe the plot in some detail. The story revolves around Lily, the sportive, sexy, and sociable 20-year-old daughter of a politician in Hong Kong. Under her father's arrangement, which was made in order to strengthen his own connections to the financial sector, Lily has been betrothed to a rich banker, Zhang Zhongxian. Because of the Japanese bombing on Shanghai in early 1932 and the damages it caused to the university where Lily was matriculated, Lily has been back at home in Hong Kong for several months. Her father is now pushing her to give up her studies in Shanghai and marry Zhongxian right away. However, Lily loves another young man, Lu Jianxiu, who is handsome and has been madly in love with her for 3 years, but there is no hope that he would be considered an appropriate match for Lily by her family because he is merely an office clerk, a so-called salaryman. Also, Jianxiu is rather temperamental, and since both he and Lily are strong-willed, they each have declared that the other would not make an ideal spouse in marriage. Lily tries to postpone her imminent wedding to Zhongxian by claiming that she desires to return to Shanghai to finish her college degree. Yet, just days before her departure, she decides to seduce Jianxiu and gives him her virginity. To her mind, by doing so she is bestowing her love upon the pitiable Jianxiu and secretly exacting revenge on Zhongxian. Nonetheless, afterwards she writes Jianxiu a letter to ask him to treasure the memory of the consummation of their love but also to forget her from then on, because she will be merely a walking corpse.

During her sea journey to Shanghai, Lily resolves that she will destroy all traces of her past, bury her heart, and live under a brightly painted mask henceforth; she decides that she will "appear to the world like a shallow, hypocritical, and even wanton woman" and that no one will be able to detect the sadness behind her gorgeous mask (Ye Lingfeng 1996: 94). On the ship, she attracts the attention of Xiao Jie, a man who occupies a managerial position at a Shanghai bank. Once arrived in Shanghai, Xiao starts to court Lily in earnest and lies to her that he has never been married.

In Shanghai, Lily delays her return to her university and stays instead in a hotel. While visiting her father's old friend Mr. Chen, she is handed a letter from home that shocks her. Her father asks her to immediately return to Hong Kong and encloses a clip from a Hong Kong tabloid in which her sexual liaison with Jianxiu is reported in a grotesquely exaggerated and salacious fashion; she is described as a glamorous socialite "enchanted with modern ways" and is falsely accused of having been sexually promiscuous since attending college in Shanghai and of frequently meeting Jianxiu in a hotel for sex while she is back in Hong Kong (Ye Lingfeng 1996: 106). Lily is terribly shaken by the slanderous article, but she is reluctant to obey her father's order to return to Hong Kong. She decides that she wants to be a completely free woman—free of the requisite expectations of normative marriage, free of her father's and society's dictates—and writes a letter to Mr. Chen to explain her decision. Furthermore, although she does not exactly like Xiao Jie, she gets physically involved with him in order to seek diversion and numb her pain.

Lily assumes that everything is proceeding according to her plans until she is surprised by Xiao Jie's wife, who comes to her hotel with a little girl in tow. Xiao apologizes profusely to Lily for having lied to her about his marital status but promises to get a divorce. After thinking the matter over, Lily writes Xiao and his wife each a letter telling them that there is no need for them to go to court to get a divorce since she is not interested in marrying Xiao in the first place. Things then take yet another unexpected turn: following the newspaper scandal about their affair, Jianxiu has quit his job in Hong Kong to come to Shanghai to look for Lily, in the hopes of finding and comforting her. However, because Lily never returned to her university, Jianxiu is unable to locate her. While waiting anxiously in Shanghai, by chance he spots an article in *Shishi xinbao* in which Lily's involvement with Xiao and Xiao's pending divorce case are reported. Feeling abandoned by Lily and also interpreting Lily's dissolution as partly caused by him, he commits suicide after sending his last words to Lily in a letter to *Shishi xinbao*. Shaken to the core by Jianxiu's suicide and his abiding love unto the last, Lily weeps hot tears of regret at the morgue where his cold, stiff body lies, realizing that she has made a terrible mistake.

In the plot, Xiao Jie and newspaper reporters repeatedly use the term "Modern Girl" to refer to Lily. Lily also perceives herself as a Modern Girl. Initially, the appellative Modern Girl gives Lily the courage to deviate from the most conservative life option available to her—marriage to a wealthy man, which is loveless and yet would secure her a life of luxury. Moreover, her identifying as an independently minded Modern Girl inspires her to seduce Jianxiu, who has been madly in love with her for 3 years without violating her chastity. After actively seducing Jianxiu, Lily writes him a letter, bids him farewell, and asks him to forget about her, for a number of reasons but in part because she does not want to become bonded to any man—not even Jianxiu—as his long-term sexual and domestic servant. She then leaves Hong Kong to go to Shanghai—the capital of Chinese modernity—to further experiment with her self-fashioning as a Modern Girl. Once in Shanghai, she decides she will stay outside "the net"—bourgeois heteronormative marriage; she reasons that she would rather strip away all facades of respectability and be a free woman than become one particular man's sexual slave. It is also her desire for freedom and supreme confidence that she can achieve it that makes her willing to flirt with Xiao Jie and quickly get sexually involved with him. Lily fancies herself as having total control over Xiao, who is smitten by her physical allure, but she is given a rude awakening when Xiao's wife and daughter appear at her door. She feels humiliated and in fact threatened by Xiao's wife, who occupies the moral high ground and has a legitimate claim to her husband in the eyes of society. Although Lily never expected Xiao to be entirely honest with her, it is then that she realizes that she is not in complete control of either him or the situation after all.

What is highlighted throughout the plot are Lily's yearning for autonomy and, furthermore, her extreme competitiveness with the opposite sex in the form of a desire to achieve domination over her male partners. She loathes marriage in large part because she perceives it as a form of long-term prostitution, which would reduce her to a subservient role. Her strong personality clashes with the equally strong will of Jianxiu, who is of a sentimental and obsessive nature. Although Lily's abandonment of Jianxiu after physically seducing him is somewhat inexplicable, Ye Lingfeng seems to argue that Lily is unwilling to make a commitment to Jianxiu because she has yet to fully explore her potential as a Modern Girl. Modernity promises an entirely new vista, and she is driven to find out what she can achieve by stepping off the beaten paths. That Lily's ambitious scheme to liberate herself from emotional bondage, social conventions, and public opinion eventually collapses upon itself is shown to be not exactly her fault: the mass media's sensationalization and defamation of the Modern Girl is relentless. The label may have been productive for her at one point but is soon revealed to function also as an apparatus for surveillance and discipline. The Modern Girl, similar to "the homosexual" that Foucault (1990) so eloquently theorizes, constitutes a special node in a large social field where multiple forces wrestle with one another. Whoever ascends to the Modern Girl identity and tries to inhabit it is simultaneously subjected to intensified regulation and given power at the same time. Discourse and reverse-discourse plays off of each other. The Modern Girl's personal gains and liabilities, potentialities, and limitations render her an enigmatic figure that fascinates. She stimulated the public's imagination in the 1930s, and her charisma continues to be felt even today.

Although Ye's novel is an especially striking example, he was by no means the only Shanghai writer who intervened into the public debate over how the Modern Girl ought to define herself and what self-fashioning options were actually within her reach. Yu Qie's novel *Miss Stranded* (*Qianshui guniang*), originally serialized in *Short Story Monthly* in 1942–1943, also explicitly foregrounds the discrepancy between the theory of broadened possibilities and the actuality of limited agency enjoyed by modern women. The narrator opens the novel thus (Q. Yu 2008: 3):

> An ordinary life is worth recording and remembering. Now, I am going to tell the reader the story of an ordinary woman.
>
> Before embarking on the narration, I would like the reader to consider: Should a woman have a vocation? Should a woman get married? After getting married should a woman serve society, as does her husband, in order to increase the family's fortune? Should she have children? Do children increase the happiness of the family? All these questions should be answered in the affirmative; and yet sadness and dissatisfaction seem to lie just beneath the surface. If we observe closely, we will detect at least sighs hidden in happiness, and bitter tears moistening smiling eyes!

By opening the novel in this vein, the narrator makes it abundantly clear that the story is not so much about an exceptional case as about the common predicaments faced by many young urban women perched on the threshold of adulthood. They have received a moderate amount of school education and must consider questions such as whether to look for a job upon graduation, whether to enter marriage, and whether to have children. While it is convenient to answer these questions in the affirmative, there is no guarantee that the actual outcomes would be perfect or personally satisfying. The Modern Girl—here represented by an average urban young woman rather than incarnated as an unusually glamorous and willful heiress—must come to terms with the gap between ideal and reality and reconcile herself with the spoiled promise of modern autonomy.

Tellingly, the heroine of Yu Qie's text is not introduced by her formal name but rather by a lament that she repeats after her mother regarding their difficult situation. Having been virtually abandoned by her husband for 7 years, the mother comments: "We cannot ascend to the sky to capture the moon, nor can we descend into the ocean to look for pearls. We can merely drift along in shallow water" (Q. Yu 2008: 4). The narrator therefore nicknames the heroine "Qianshui guniang," meaning that she is adrift, and in a sense stranded, in shallow water. The mother, as a result of her own unhappy marriage, finds men unreliable and has therefore urged the daughter to be self-reliant. What is more, as they are running out of the financial means to put Qianshui through high school, Qianshui must look in earnest for a job. And yet, because she lacks special skills, she cannot find any satisfactory work except through her best friend's personal connections, and even then she has difficulty keeping the position. Later, she meets her best friend's older cousin and develops a lesbian relationship with her, becoming *de facto* a dependent on the older, more educated, and more masculine woman, who has inherited a large estate from her family. They break up some time later, because the lesbian lover is attracted to another girl. Meanwhile, Qianshui succeeds in finding a husband through a family friend's introduction. She becomes the young mistress of a modern household, enjoying a moderately high socio-economic status. Her main duties are to please her husband, take care of their offspring, and supervise the servants. However, after her second child is born, her husband develops an affair with one of her former classmates. It is then that Qianshui becomes utterly embittered and disillusioned about her life.

Throughout the narrative, Qianshui's options at every step are laid out: education, jobs, same-sex relationship, and cross-sex marriage. She moves from option to option, deliberating the pros and cons of each. And yet, ultimately nothing seems to afford her complete satisfaction; there is constantly the shadow of insufficiencies and self-doubt. And this feeling of being stranded is far from unique: in some of the most acclaimed stories written by Eileen Chang in the early 1940s, such as "Love in a Fallen City," "Aloeswood Incense: The First Brazier" ("*Chenxiangxie: diyilu xiang*," 1943), and "Blockade," the heroines are also Modern Girls (of various types) confronted with major life decisions. Whatever they choose—marriage or professions—there lingers the shadow of imperfections and a feeling of entrapment (E. Chang 2007). In "Love in a Fallen City," the divorcee Liusu flees to Hong Kong to explore the possibility of romance and marriage with a returnee man, in order to escape the persecution of her conservative and unkind kinsfolk in Shanghai who are pressuring her to return to her ex-husband's family. After much travail, she succeeds in getting the nuptial vows that she longs for from her lover Liuyuan when the destruction wrought by the Japanese invasion of Hong Kong spurs the rich womanizer to desire stability. Although this outcome appears to be a victory for Liusu on the surface, their matrimony is in reality a product of the circumstances, and no sooner have they settled into conjugal life than Liuyuan begins to make passes at other women, telling them jokes that he previously would have told Liusu in flirtation. Nonetheless, Liusu has no choice except to content herself with her status as a taken-for-granted wife. Weilong, the heroine of "Aloeswood Incense: The First Brazier," is an even more abject prisoner in her marriage: she gives up her education and willingly works as a socialite-cum-prostitute that caters to wealthy male clients in order to support the extravagant lifestyle required by her mixed-race playboy husband George. Although falling for the sexually attractive George and going down this heterodox career path is her voluntary decision, she cannot but feel that she has sold both her body—to the male clients—and her soul—to George, who holds her hostage emotionally. It may seem that, with these stories, Eileen Chang is making a particular statement about marriage as a suffocating jail for modern women seeking autonomy and emotional fulfillment; yet, the unmarried college teacher Cuiyuan in "Blockade" feels no less entrapped in her celibacy and her socially respectable profession. True, Cuiyuan has secured a college teaching position immediately upon graduation, setting a record for women's vocations. And yet, now that she is on the verge of passing her prime, her family are suddenly shifting their expectations and wishing that she had worked harder to find a husband. Her professional achievement seems all but a cruel joke. Realizing that no one genuinely respects her for what she does, she feels a growing emptiness gnawing at her.

The Modern Girl's limited agency, then, stands out in these Shanghai novels and stories of the 1930s–1940s as one of her defining characteristics. The compromised nature of her self-fashioning capability can be discerned in her dilemma of having to choose between marriage and vocations; it is also manifest in her participation in commodity culture, which enables her to pursue the modern good life in some ways but restricts her creativity and individual expression in others. In sum, although the rise of the Modern Girl was a product of global capitalism and liberationist ideologies, modern Chinese literature did not simply reduce the Modern Girl to a one-dimensional figure—the freewheeling vamp and dominatrix. Rather, a significant number of fiction writers and works painted a sobering picture of her partial agency and embattled identity.

REFERENCES

Barlow, Tani. 2008. "Buying In: Advertising and the Sexy Modern Girl Icon in Shanghai in the 1920s and 1930s." In *The Modern Girl Around the World: Consumption, Modernity, and Globalization*. Edited by The Modern Girl Around the World Research Group. Durham, NC: Duke University Press. 288–316.

Benson, Carlton. 1999. "Consumers Are Also Soldiers: Subversive Songs from Nanjing Road during the New Life Movement." In *Inventing Nanjing Road: Commercial Culture in Shanghai, 1900–1945*. Edited by Cochran, Sherman. Ithaca, NY: Cornell University, East Asia Program. 91–132.

Chang, Eileen. 2007. *Love in a Fallen City*. Trans. Karen S. Kingsbury. New York: New York Review Books.

Chiang, Howard. Ed. 2012. *Transgender China*. New York: Palgrave Macmillan.

Chiang, Howard, and Ari Larissa Heinrich. Eds. 2013. *Queer Sinophone Cultures*. New York: Routledge.

Cochran, Sherman. Ed. 1999. *Inventing Nanjing Road: Commercial Culture in Shanghai, 1900–1945*. Ithaca, NY: Cornell University, East Asia Program.

Dong, Madeleine Yue. 2008. "Who Is Afraid of the Chinese Modern Girl?" In *The Modern Girl Around the World: Consumption, Modernity, and Globalization*. Edited by The Modern Girl Around the World Research Group. Durham, NC: Duke University Press. 194–219.

Dooling, Amy. 2005. *Women's Literary Feminism in Twentieth-Century China*. New York: Palgrave.

Edwards, Louise. 2000. "Policing the Modern Woman in Republican China." *Modern China*, 26.2: 115–147.

Foucault, Michel. 1990. *The History of Sexuality, Volume I: An Introduction*. Trans. Robert Hurley. New York: Vintage Books.

Hu, Ying. 2000. *Tales of Translation: Composing the New Woman in China, 1898–1918*. Stanford, CA: Stanford University Press.

Judge, Joan. 2008. *The Precious Raft of History*. Stanford, CA: Stanford University Press.

Kang, Wenqing. 2009. *Obsessions: Male Same-Sex Relations in China, 1900–1950*. Hong Kong: University of Hong Kong Press.

Laing, Ellen Johnston. 2004. *Selling Happiness: Calendar Posters and Visual Culture in Early-Twentieth-Century Shanghai*. Honolulu: University of Hawaii Press.

Larson, Wendy. 1998. *Women and Writing in Modern China*. Stanford, CA: Stanford University Press.

Lee, Haiyan. 2007. *Revolution of the Heart: A Genealogy of Love in China, 1900–1950*. Stanford, CA: Stanford University Press.

Lee, Leo Ou-fan. 1999. *Shanghai Modern: The Flowering of a New Urban Culture in China, 1930–1945*. Cambridge, MA: Harvard University Press.

Louie, Kam. 2002. *Theorising Chinese Masculinity: Society and Gender in China*. Cambridge, UK: Cambridge University.

The Modern Girl Around the World Research Group (Alys Eve Weinbaum, Lynn M. Thomas, Priti Ramamurthy, Uta G. Poiger, Madeleine Yue Dong, and Tani E. Barlow). Eds. 2005. "The Modern Girl Around the World." Special issue. *Gender and History*, 17.2: 245–294.

Peng, Hsiao-yen. 2010. *Dandyism and Transcultural Modernity: The Dandy, the Flâneur, and the Translator in 1930s Shanghai, Tokyo and Paris*. London: Routledge.

Sang, Tze-lan D. 2003. *The Emerging Lesbian: Female Same-Sex Desire in Modern China*. Chicago: University of Chicago Press.

Sang, Tze-lan D. 2008. "Failed Modern Girls in Early Twentieth-Century China." In *Performing "Nation": Gender Politics in Literature, Theater, and the Visual Arts of China and Japan, 1880–1940*. Edited by Croissant, Doris, Catherine Vance Yeh, and Joshua S. Mostow. Leiden: Brill. 179–202.

Sato, Barbara. 2003. *The New Japanese Woman: Modernity, Media, and Women in Interwar Japan*. Durham, NC: Duke University Press.

Shih, Shu-mei. 2001. *The Lure of the Modern: Writing Modernism in Semicolonial China, 1917–1937*. Berkeley: University of California Press.

Silverberg, Miriam. 1991. "The Modern Girl as Militant." In *Recreating Japanese Women, 1600–1945*. Edited by Bernstein, Gail Lee. Berkeley: University of California Press. 239–266.

Stevens, Sarah E. 2003. "Figuring Modernity: The New Woman and the Modern Girl in Republican China." *NWSA Journal*, 15.3: 82–103.

Tsu, Jing. 2006. *Failure, Nationalism, and Literature: The Making of Modern Chinese Identity, 1895–1937*. Stanford, CA: Stanford University Press.

Wang, Lingzhen. 2004. *Personal Matters: Women's Autobiographical Practice in Twentieth-Century China*. Stanford, CA: Stanford University Press.

Wang, Xiaoming. 1999. "A Journal and a 'Society': On the 'May Fourth' Literary Tradition." *Modern Chinese Literature and Culture*, 11: 1–39.

Wang, Zheng. 1999. *Women in the Chinese Enlightenment: Oral and Textual Histories*. Berkeley: University of California Press.

Xu, Huiqi (Rachel Hui-chi Hsu) 許慧琦. 2003. "Nala" zai Zhongguo: Xin nüxing xingxiang de suzao ji qi yanbian (1900s–1930s) "娜拉" 在中國:新女性形象的塑造及其演變 ("Nora" in China: the construction of the new woman image and its evolution, 1900s–1930s). Taipei: Zhengzhi daxue lishixuexi.

Xu, Xiacun 徐霞村. 1985 (1929). "Modern Girl." In *Xin ganjuepai xiaoshuo xuan* 新感覺派小説選 (A selection of New Sensationalist fiction), Edited by Yan Jiayan 嚴家炎. Beijing: Renmin wenxue chubanshe. 30–35.

Ye, Lingfeng 葉靈鳳. 1996. *Shidai guniang* 時代姑娘 (Modern girl). Guangzhou: Huacheng chubanshe. Originally serialized in 1932.

Yeh, Catherine Vance. 2006. *Shanghai Love: Courtesans, Intellectuals, and Entertainment Culture, 1850–1910*. Seattle: University of Washington Press.

Yen, Hsiao-pei. 2005. "Body Politics, Modernity and National Salvation: The Modern Girl and the New Life Movement." *Asian Studies Review*, 29.2: 165–186.

Yu, Qie 予且. 2008 (1942–3). *Qianshui guniang* 淺水姑娘 (Miss stranded). Beijing: Huaxia chubanshe.

Zhang, Yingjin. 1996. *The City in Modern Chinese Literature and Film: Configurations of Space, Time, and Gender*. Stanford, CA: Stanford University Press.

Zhang, Yong 張勇. 2010. *Modeng zhuyi: Shanghai wenhua yu wenxue yanjiu, 1927–1937* 摩登主義: 上海文化與文學研究 (Modernism: Research on Shanghai culture and literature, 1927–1937). Taipei: Renjian chubanshe.

Zhang, Zhen. 2005. *An Amorous History of the Silver Screen: Shanghai Cinema, 1896–1937*. Chicago: University of Chicago Press.

Zhong, Xueping. 2000. *Masculinity Besieged? Issues of Modernity and Male Subjectivity in Chinese Literature of the Late Twentieth Century*. Durham, NC: Duke University Press.

Zhou Huiling (Katherine Hui-ling Chou) 周慧玲. 2004. *Biaoyan Zhongguo: nü mingxing, biaoyan wenhua, shijue zhengzhi, 1910–1945* 表演中國: 女明星, 表演文化, 視覺政治, 1910–1945 (Performing China: actresses, performance culture, visual politics, 1910–1945). Taipei: Maitian.

26

Body as Phenomenon: A Brief Survey of Secondary Literature of the Body in Modern Chinese Literature and Culture

Ari Larissa Heinrich

One of the more provocative claims in secondary studies of the body in Chinese literature and culture is that the body is a relatively new phenomenon: something that did not exist until that episodic and arbitrary determination of contemporary reality we often call "the modern." But to marry the Chinese body to modernity in this sense is also to situate the body in modernity globally. The history of the body in English-language secondary sources on modern Chinese literature and culture is deeply phenomenological.

One of the first essays to make this claim explicitly in the secondary literature in English is by an art historian. In an edited volume (Zito and Barlow 1994) that has remained a touchstone in any genealogy of the modern Chinese body, John Hay argued that the idea of a body defined by the boundary of skin is a red herring, the essential truth of which we take for granted when looking at realist representations of corporeality cross-culturally. His assertion was simple and radical: The reason one finds no tradition of "the nude" in Chinese painting—the reason the body is "invisible" in Chinese art—is that the body "did not exist in the culture" (Hay 1994: 43). Despite its framing within visual cultural materials, the essay spoke to literary studies as well. Indeed, one of Hay's key case studies in clarifying the culturally embedded nature of corporeality came from *Golden Lotus* (*Jinping mei*), a novel perhaps best known for its pornographic representations of corporeality. Pornography magnifies the cultural economics of the exposure of the body as a whole or in its component parts. Thus, Hay observes that descriptions of the heroine's body in *Golden Lotus* do not focus on anatomical detail, but instead work by analogy: Pan Jinlian's body parts (hair, eyebrows, face, torso, fingers, waist, bosom) are compared variously to a raven's plumage, willow

A Companion to Modern Chinese Literature, First Edition. Edited by Yingjin Zhang.
© 2016 John Wiley & Sons, Ltd. Published 2016 by John Wiley & Sons, Ltd.

leaves, almonds, cherries, a silver bowl, a flower, shoots of a young onion, and jade. Consequently, "[t]here is no image of a body as a whole object, least of all as a solid and well-shaped entity whose shapeliness is supported by the structure of a skeleton and defined in the exteriority of swelling muscle and enclosing flesh" (Hay 1994: 50-1). In a system where corporeality is always defined by analogy, Hay concludes, what counts as "real" with respect to the body is always already allegorical. Hay therefore extrapolates that the late-nineteenth-century and early-twentieth-century introduction to China of representational systems that prioritize nakedness and "realistic" descriptions of corporeal phenomena may not have made much sense, at least at first. "Since the idea of 'China' was fundamentally cultural rather than ethnic," Hay writes, "one might suspect that the completely uncoded body would have been felt to be not human, and the naked body not, or not yet, Chinese" (Hay 1994: 60–61).

Regardless of what controversies we might engage in about the existence of any organically empirical and universal object known as "the body," Hay's thesis highlights the phenomenological problem of understanding the relationship between *what* the body may or may not be—how we understand it epistemologically—and the aesthetics of its representation. The significance of this problem for studies of modern Chinese literature and culture is hardly trivial, since Republican writers such as Lu Xun—himself trained in anatomy during his time as a medical student in Japan—were confronting exactly such questions about corporeality and "realism" at the same time they began to experiment with new literary forms. Marston Anderson was among the first wave of scholars to recognize the significance of the relationship between the phenomenology of the body and questions of literary aesthetics for early Chinese literary modernism. He makes the point that "in realist metaphysics it is always the body that is accorded substantiality, and … it is above all, those features of the natural world that invasively trespass the imagined autonomy of the body that achieve status as emblems of the Real" (Anderson 1990: 17). The quote reminds us that literary realism not only is not a methodologically pure and corporeally uninvested aesthetic modality that exists outside of or incidental to the body—but, on the contrary, that realist aesthetics cannot exist *without* the body. According to Anderson, the body, and in particular its mortality, is actually the prime number of realism, since realisms always assume the body's materiality as a starting point for descriptions of "those features of the natural world that invasively trespass" its perceived autonomy. Consider, for instance, that many works of realist fiction in modern China depict intense episodes of suffering, trauma, illness, hunger, ectopic sexual desire, and anxiety. Would realism still count as realistic if it depicted the body's health and well-being? Anderson's work reminds us that what counts as literary "realism," far from objective, is in fact a heavily ideological representational technology, the aesthetics of which are deeply and specifically conditioned by questions of corporeality. For modern Chinese literature and culture studies, then, the combination of Anderson's observation with Hay's comparative study of "allegorical" versus anatomical modes of representing the body highlights the truly radical nature of the Chinese modernists' intervention into literary aesthetics, for not only did they experiment with certain new modes of describing the body and "reality," but by extension they *redefined the phenomenological definition of the human body itself.* As it happened, this new phenomenology aligned more legibly, albeit imperfectly, with Western and other non-Sinitic literary realist practices at the time.

To acknowledge the phenomenological shift from an analogical mode of representing the human body in certain Chinese literary traditions to a more "realistic" model in Chinese early modernist experiments is not to suggest that the Chinese had no understanding of anatomy before modernity, or that they simply failed to investigate physiology, discrete organ structure, or anything resembling "scientific" selfhood; that is a whole separate thread, well discussed in secondary literature on the history of science in China. For literary studies, rather, the aesthetics of corporeality do not always overlap perfectly with taxonomies of corporeality itself. Although not specifically focused on literature and literary usage, Shigehisa Kuriyama (1999) provides, for literature, one example of a helpful comparison of classical Greek and Chinese anatomical traditions that accounts not only for evolutions in etymologies for words describing the human body in both contexts, but also for those same aesthetics of visual representation that so captivate John Hay: the muscular versus the holistic, the illustration versus the map.

My own monograph titled *The Afterlife of Images* (Heinrich 2008) draws on Hay, Anderson, and Kuriyama to look at representations of corporeality not necessarily by comparing Chinese and other cultures directly—although there is some discussion of nineteenth-century medical missionary understandings of corporeality—but by looking at the transitional period between late Imperial medical and literary texts and early modern experiments in realist expression. My work examines those conditions of late-nineteenth-century and early-twentieth-century science, medicine, and cultural exchange related to corporeality that *enabled* and *informed* (or were a precondition for) the development of literary realist aesthetics in early modernity, linking changing understandings of the medical body with changing realist literary aesthetics. A specific example concerns the ideologically complex historiography of dissection-based anatomical practice in China. Conventional post–Cold War mythologies often situate "Chinese" dissection practices along a continuum of scientific and industrial "progress" (as determined by measurables such as weapon production, progress in seafaring and colonial efforts, systematization of pharmacological knowledge, and the like). According to this kind of thinking, dissection was never practiced in "premodern" China—apart from some potentially apocryphal records of the ancient surgeon Hua Tuo—until Western activists forced the introduction of dissection practice first by stealth and then by law in the late nineteenth and early twentieth centuries. *The Afterlife of Images* contextualizes the introduction of dissection practice in China not by arguing that Western medical missionaries such as Benjamin Hobson introduced dissection-based anatomical practice to China, but rather by arguing that what they introduced more crucially was a certain kind of aesthetic vocabulary and conceptual framework for the body—"anatomical aesthetics"—that Republican writers such as Lu Xun drew on when constructing a new method for describing the human body to replace familiar analogical models such as those seen in *Golden Lotus*. Following Hay's logic, in other words, I suggest that, in the transition from earlier forms of literary description of the body to newer ones in a "realist" mode, the likes of which Marston Anderson describes, anatomical science provided key reference material. The book "attempts to provide an important footnote to the medical education of, and cultural sources for, writers of the Republican period, and consequently [tries] to illuminate how these writers arrived at their own influential visions of the (Chinese) world," all while providing a working model of "how to integrate ... medical illustration into a more comprehensive understanding of the transmission of ideas about illness across and within cultures, and indeed of the relationship of medical ideology to aesthetics in general (Heinrich 2008: 10). What I am suggesting here is a framework for understanding changes in literary and cultural representations of corporeality that gives equal weight to science and aesthetics as received, and intertwined, epistemological categories.

Beyond these more holistic interrogations of "the body" as a discrete epistemological unit, scholars of modern Chinese literature may also wish to consult works that treat the body not only as a whole but in terms of its component parts and the social structures that make it legible in the larger world—in other words, studies not only of *parts* of the body, or the body literally compartmentalized, but also studies (themselves sometimes parts of larger works) that address precisely those aspects of corporeality that (to quote Anderson again) "invasively trespass the imagined autonomy of the body": things such as disease, hunger, sexual desire, and even gender. Two volumes of essays bookend, both methodologically and thematically, a range of approaches to corporeality in Chinese literature and culture over 20 years. The first is *Body, Subject, and Power in China* (Zito and Barlow 1994). A milestone in Chinese cultural studies, this important volume sought to engage Chinese studies in deliberate dialogue with larger critical and theoretical trends in humanities at the time, including the nature-versus-culture paradigm, post–Cold War innovations in Chinese studies and methodologies, and cultural constructions of corporeality from science to art to medicine to gender. The volume owed a significant debt to post-structuralist critical theories generally (especially critiques of essentialism and the idea of a "natural" body) and more specifically to Foucauldian understandings of the social construction of bodies and the Althusserian "interpellation" of these bodies through ideology. A key innovation of the volume was to ask Chinese-studies disciplines to divest intellectually of our collective and historical obsession with viewing the body as a "transparent, self-present, stable object ... of analysis" and to see it instead as a nexus of knowledge (and mirror of culture) subject to "historically specific regimes of discourse and social discipline" (Martin and Heinrich 2006: 7). Besides Hay's work noted earlier, other essays in this volume by Tani Barlow (on "Theorizing Woman: Funü, Guojia, Jiating"), by Lydia Liu (on "The Female body and Nationalist Discourse" in a novel by the writer Xiao Hong), and by Ann Anagnost (on "The Politicized Body") are all of direct relevance to modern Chinese literary studies, though the volume as a whole provides a key reference point for studies of Chinese corporeality more generally.

The other volume to present a range of approaches to corporeality in Chinese literature and culture is *Embodied Modernities* (Martin and Heinrich 2006). The volume aimed deliberately to account for the dramatic changes in technology and culture in Chinese societies—as well as in scholarship itself—that had taken place in the years since the publication of Zito and Barlow's book. Indeed, similar to that earlier volume, *Embodied Modernities* sought to incorporate more cutting-edge critical methods into a volume that could span material on diverse aspects of corporeality from the late Imperial up through the contemporary periods. Thus, the volume included essays on modern and contemporary feminist critiques of footbinding (Angela Zito); on the body as both ruin and specter in new cinema (Jami Proctor-Xu and Olivia Khoo); and on the representation of the body in Taiwanese digital video puppetry and COSplay (Teri Silvio). My contribution on the "diasporic body in contemporary Chinese litera-ture and art" looked at ways in which fiction by the author Yu Hua and installations by various experimental artists at the turn of the century used the iconography of the organ trade to explore the fraught relationship between the production of Chinese counter-culture and demand for it in the American and European marketplace.

In addition to following up on feminist and post-colonial critical methods, mean-while, the volume also turned out in the course of production to be more than a little queer. Thematically, this was hardly coincidental. The volume's essays on corporeality complicated the then-current analyses of corporeality in Chinese literary and cultural configurations by moving beyond the heteronormative imperative that had previously been the default for so many critical inquiries into the body in science and medicine as a "generative" or discretely bounded sexual object. The volume thus included essays on the changing conceptualizations of sexed and gendered bodies as seen in Republican-era redactions of an example of late Imperial popular fiction (Maram Epstein); on the transgender body embedded within the fiction that was a source for Ang Lee (Li An) when he directed *Crouching Tiger, Hidden Dragon* (*Wohu canglong*, 2000) (Tze-lan Sang); on masculinity and corporeality in the performances of Mei Lanfang and Bruce Lee (Li Xiaolong) (John Zou and Chris Berry, respectively); on male same-sex prostitution in the late nineteenth and early twentieth centuries (Cuncun Wu and Mark Stevenson); and on the gendered and "stigmatic" body in the work of Taiwanese lesbian writer Qiu Miaojin (Fran Martin).

More recently, two special issues of discipline-based journals have investigated var-ious aspects of the relationships among contemporary constructions of Chinese iden-tity, of corporeality, of disease, and of the human more generally (especially in terms of the moving target in the Republican period of what it meant corporeally to be a human as opposed, say, to an ape, and also what it meant to be part of a new human "universal" that, post-evolution, has its own controversial new genealogies). "China and the Human," a two-volume special issue of the journal *Social Text* (Eng, Ruskola, and Shen 2012a, 2012b), addresses these kinds of questions collectively by looking into the philosophical and comparative implications of juxtaposing the words "China" and "human" in a range of works by scholars from diverse disciplines such as anthropology and comparative literature, law and film, and history and politics. The focus of the two volumes is decidedly *un*corporeal—there are no essays addressing corporeality or embodied humanity *per se*, with the volumes exploring, instead, "cosmologies of the human" and the circulating and mutually constitutive ontologies of "human rights" and "China" globally—yet this *corps-manqué* approach could also be seen as a way of isolating the cultural from the material in determining what counts as human. As the editors (Eng, Ruskola, Shen 2012a: 2) note, "We are quite confident that we know what human beings are, and by definition they are no more or less human whether in China or elsewhere. ... Yet what [we] hope ... to accomplish is, precisely, to place in question the self-evident nature of both terms. By juxtaposing China and the human, we do not assume either concept as a pre-given object of knowledge."

A special issue of *Modern Chinese Literature and Culture*, guest-edited by Carlos Rojas, addresses the corporeal component of the human more explicitly. Specifically, the issue makes the transition from looking at modern Chinese literature as discrete from science and medicine to interrogating the deep structural affinities among models of corporeality and disease, and in particular the notion of virus, alongside the process of literary production itself. Locating the work "precisely in this space between art and science," Rojas (2011a: 5) notes that the volume "takes its starting point from the late-nineteenth-century development of modern biomedicine, but its focus is on the ways medical concepts and assumptions have been appropriated within *cultural* contexts. These cultural contexts provide insight into the popular understanding and imagination of health and disease, even as they play an important role in shaping and transforming those same understandings." One might read, for example, literature scholar Andrew Schonebaum's "Vectors of Contagion and Tuberculosis in Modern Chinese Literature" against the medical historian Bridie Andrews' earlier investigation (1997) of how "tuberculosis" was translated in the late Imperial and early modern periods to see an outstanding example of how medical history *as a discipline* can inform and enable a more nuanced understanding of the literature of the body in China (in this case, by providing a context for, and cross-cultural interpretation of, the vogue for tuberculosis as a literary theme in early modern literature, for which Andrews' essay opened the space, and which Schonebaum's elaborates). Meanwhile, in his individual contributions to the volume—an essay titled "Of Canons and Cannibalism: A Psycho-Immunological Reading of 'Diary of a Madman'"—Rojas (2011b) proposes an immunological model for early modern Chinese literature, looking at sources for "microbiological metaphors" in the early literature of political reform. Moreover, Andrea Bachner's innovative essay (2011) inverts more conventional approaches to virology according to which "virus" exists first and foremost as an objective, scientifically verifiable external phenomenon, and instead explores virus as a metaphor (in line with Rojas' immunological model for literature), and then works outward from there.

To contextualize approaches to theorizing constructions of the "human" in modern Chinese literature still further, it may be worth briefly singling out Rojas' introduction to the special issue and reading it against a work produced nearly contemporaneously that treats an overlapping theme, namely, Lydia Liu's essay "Life as Form: How

Biomimesis Encountered Buddhism in Lu Xun." Both essays examine a heretofore lesser-known 1905 work by Lu Xun, "Zaoren shu," translated by Liu as "Technique for Creating Humans," and by Rojas (2012) as "The Art of Creating Humanity." The source text, a story by an American author named Louise Jackson Strong, tells the story of a scientist who creates life from a few cells, which then replicate beyond his control into a whole lab overrun with frightening little humanoid monsters. In Lu Xun's version, itself a translation of a loosely adapted and truncated Japanese version of Strong's piece, the story ends before things turn sour, just as the scientist has mastered the art of creating a human being. Rojas reads the text's description of the narrator's enthusiasm for creating a "microscopic 'sprout of humanity'" historically, as a displaced expression of an "enthusiasm for the power of modern medicine" and "a powerful affirmation of life over death," emphasizing that the foundations for modern germ theory (bacteriology, virology) were coincident with Lu Xun's maturation and education, informing the author's (and indeed the author's generation's) optimism about the possibility of creating a new humanity, observing that the story thus "bridges scientific and literary concerns" (Rojas 2011a: 3–5). Similar to Rojas' other essay in the special issue, the analysis here "appl[ies] microbiological models to issues of political reform," situating modern Chinese literature within the history of science and medicine (Rojas 2011a: 6). The essay works together with my own conclusion in *The Afterlife of Images* to suggest that the emerging technologies of projection and microbiological metaphors were factors in creating the perfect storm that led to Lu Xun's famous epiphany and subsequent "conversion" to literature from medicine (Heinrich 2008: 149–156).

Lydia Liu's essay, by contrast, expands the question of microbiology as literary inspiration to address the deep structural relationship between mimetic representation of life (in literature, art, and science itself, or what she calls "biomimesis") and the very construction of what counts as "real." Taking Anderson's work further, her critical intervention is to treat realism and its mediums themselves as a kind of technology, not for reproducing merely a *likeness* of life or the body, but rather for *co-creating* understandings of the real. Reading Lu Xun's short stories "Mending the Sky" and "Prayers for Blessing" (commonly also translated in English as "New Year's Sacrifice") alongside "Technique for Creating Humans," Liu reminds us that literature in the early modern period was, among other things, not just a reflection of, but a medium *for* "public awareness of the novel questions raised by evolutionary biology." She suggests by extension that the problem of relating form to content in literature is never more important than when "realism" is invoked as a mode for describing the body (L. Liu 2009: 21). Thus, for Liu, what is happening on the occasion of the creation of the human 'germ' in "Technique for Creating Humans" is not simply a passive reflection or even celebration of contemporaneous developments in science, but rather a literary expression of optimism around the subtle imperative of microbiology that life itself can be generated anew. Liu's readings of the two other stories additionally demonstrate that not just innovations in microbiology and biomimetic technologies but debates about Buddhist metaphysics also played a role in shaping dialogue about the creation of life (and by extension corporeality) in Lu Xun's work and beyond. As case studies, in other words, these examples of tuberculosis, microbial aesthetics, and the literary imagination are important because they help contextualize disease phenomena as morphologies of *culture* rather than strictly of corporeality. Studies such as these special issues of *Social Text* and of *Modern Chinese Literature and Culture*, as well as Liu's essay, open up our understandings of what constitutes the aesthetics and ontologies of the human, the body, and of life itself precisely at a time in modern Chinese literary history when it has become harder and harder to ignore the body's fundamental irreducibility in the face of dramatic technological and cultural incursions on its illusory "autonomy."

Finally, where other works have set the stage for deeper investigations into the origins of the real as it relates to the human body and, indeed, understandings of life itself from microbiology to Buddhist philosophy, Andrew Jones' recent book (2011) successfully integrates many of the approaches I have described earlier—historicizing literary and cultural developments in the late Imperial and early modern periods, providing close readings of individual stories to tease out and illustrate specific scientific and other debates informing them, and providing an overview of secondary literature that itself gets contextualized in the construction of modern Chinese literature (and indeed global modernities) as a "field." Noting the often symbiotic relationship between the implicit narrative structures of "developmental thinking" and fictional narrative itself, one of the book's contributions to studies of the body in Chinese literature is that it reframes the conceptualization of evolution in China in a way that accounts for science as a *part* of literary history (not just a source or inspiration for it, but itself as a form of literature). As Jones (2011: 5) points out, the book "initiates a genealogical critique of developmental thinking by tracing its origins in the translation of evolutionary biology into Chinese letters in the late nineteenth century, tracking its proliferation in the print and media cultures of early-twentieth-century China, and suggesting how it gave rise to new narrative forms, lent its structure to the historical imagination, and tragically limited ideological horizons." The book deftly situates, for instance, what was formerly only treated as a rhetorical figure—the constantly reappearing figure of the child in modern Chinese literature—instead as an avatar of evolution that "stood at the very threshold between progress and activism" and that, in literary terms, "became an object of sustained investment and intense anxiety, a beacon for developmental aspirations shadowed by the brutality of a colonial world order in which heredity seemed tantamount to destiny" (Jones 2011: 5). His chapter on "Lu Xun, Natural History, and Narrative Form" provides a fully realized methodological model of literary analysis incorporating the history of science, as it carefully contextualizes the transmission of ideas about evolution in vernacular media—such as fiction, children's stories, textbooks—against developments in the history of evolutionary and biological sciences not only in China but worldwide. As such, the book documents relationships among translated and global discussions about science and the literary imagination in early modern China, and along the way sets the stage for understanding how present corporeal configurations in Chinese literature came to be.

How can we forge connections among such a diverse genealogy of approaches to the body in modern Chinese literature and more recent literary and cultural phenomena? For Rojas and Liu, at least, questions of corporeality and aesthetics in early modern literature (and specifically in the work of Lu Xun) speak directly to more contemporary developments in science and culture at large. Even as he reflects on translations of early modern fiction, Rojas (2011b: 13) invokes the 2003 SARS outbreak as an example of how "'viral' processes (both literal and metaphorical) [can be] responsible for the constitution not only of life, but also of culture." Meanwhile, in "Biomimesis," Lydia Liu embeds a template for future investigations within her analysis of Lu Xun's work when she observes that all biomimetic technologies, including contemporary ones, to some extent *produce* epistemologies of the "real" in their prime directive to represent the human body in ways that can be used by doctors, scientists, and researchers to diagnose, map, and investigate corporeality today; thus, she links her discussion of Lu Xun to contemporary debates on such topics as stem cells and cloning. What then can scholars of contemporary Chinese literatures and cultures do as we enter a brave new world where what was formerly the stuff of science fiction now becomes "operative fiction" in Chinese and global contexts, paving the way in turn for new collaborations between science fiction and science—a mirror of what happened a century ago, with bacteriology? How can we understand contemporary phenomena historically and contextually, not *ex nihilo* but as deeply connected to intellectual and cultural genealogies of the body and its mutual genesis in both science and literature through time? What critical methods can merge critiques of representations of corporeality more generally with evolving understandings of how scientific information is disseminated and incorporated in (and of course shaped by) literature and culture?

Future generations of scholars of modern Chinese literature must reach even further into interdisciplinarity to use scholarship by authors whose work is not specifically China-centered to consider deeply what the significance of the increasingly compartmentalizable body might be in the age of organ transplant scandals, tainted blood supplies, and familiar and age-old finger-pointing about a perceived Chinese irreverence for the sacredness of the "intact" body. It may be that we need to examine more deeply how the framing of ideas about "human rights abuse in the PRC by its global critics as a problem of political freedom rather than economic equality" (Eng, Ruskola, and Shen 2012a: 17) can in turn come full-circle to provide source material for contemporary Chinese writers and producers. And it may be that we have simultaneously to build bridges across and among disciplines and genres even as we keep our feet grounded firmly in the histories of the body from the late Imperial period and beyond that continue to inform and transform current understandings. In short, as the body simultaneously becomes both more global and more compartmentalized, we need to ask questions not just about Chinese cultural and literary history, but about where the body begins and ends, and where it fits phenomenologically amidst an almost-inconceivable proliferation of modalities.

REFERENCES

Anderson, Marston. 1990. *The Limits of Realism: Chinese Fiction in the Revolutionary Period.* Berkeley: University of California Press.

Andrews, Bridie. 1997. "Tuberculosis and the Assimilation of Germ Theory in China." *Journal of the History of Medicine and Allied Sciences*, 52.1: 114–157. DOI: 10.1093/jhmas/52.1.114.

Bachner, Andrea. 2011. "Graphic Germs: Mediality, Virulence, Chinese Writing." *Modern Chinese Literature and Culture*, 23.1: 197–225.

Eng, David L., Teemu Ruskola, and Shuang Shen. Eds. 2012a. Special issue "China and the Human: Part I." *Social Text*, 109.

Eng, David L., Teemu Ruskola, and Shuang Shen. Eds. 2012b. Special issue "China and the Human: Part II." *Social Text*, 110.

Hay, John. 1994. "The Body Invisible in Chinese Art?" In *Body, Subject, and Power in China*. Edited by Zito, Angela, and Tani Barlow. Chicago: University of Chicago Press. 42–77.

Heinrich, Larissa. 2008. *The Afterlife of Images: Translating the Pathological Body Between China and the West*. Chapel Hill: Duke University Press.

Jones, Andrew F. 2011. *Developmental Fairytales: Evolutionary Thinking and Modern Chinese Cultures*. Cambridge, MA: Harvard University Press.

Kuriyama, Shigehisa. 1999. *The Expressiveness of the Body and the Divergence of Greek and Chinese Medicine*. New York: Zone Books.

Liu, Lydia H. 2009. "Life as Form: How Biomimesis Encountered Buddhism in Lu Xun." *Journal of Asian Studies*, 68.1: 21–54. DOI: 10.1017/S0021911809000047.

Martin, Fran, and Larissa Heinrich. Eds. 2006. *Embodied Modernities: Corporeality, Representation, and Chinese Cultures*. Honolulu: University of Hawaii Press.

Rojas, Carlos. 2011a. "Introduction: 'The Germ of Life.'" *Modern Chinese Literature and Culture*, 23.1: 1–13.

Rojas, Carlos. 2011b. "Of Canons and Cannibalism: A Psycho-immunological Reading of 'Diary of a Madman.'" *Modern Chinese Literature and Culture*, 23.1: 31–60.

Rojas, Carlos. 2012. "The Art of Creating Humanity." Translated into Chinese from the original Louise Jackson Strong story as 造人術 by Suozi [Lu Xun], and retranslated into English by Carlos Rojas (with introduction). *Renditions*, 77–78: 70–77.

Schonebaum, Andrew. 2011. "Vectors of Contagion and Tuberculosis in Modern Chinese Literature." *Modern Chinese Literature and Culture*, 23.1: 17–46.

Zito, Angela, and Tani Barlow. Eds. 1994. *Body, Subject, and Power in China*. Chicago: University of Chicago Press.

27

The Post-Maoist Politics of Memory

Yomi Braester

The popular and critically acclaimed science fiction novel *Fat Years* (*Shengshi: Zhongguo 2013*, 2009; English 2011), authored by Chan Koonchung (Chen Guanzhong), revolves around a case of collective amnesia that affects the entire population of the PRC. Long-term memory lapses also appear frequently in the works of the very popular writer Wang Shuo, including *Playing for Thrills* (1988; English 1997), *No Regrets about Youth* (1991), and "Wild Beasts" (1991). The recurrence of forgetting as a central theme is indicative of the significance of memory in modern Chinese fiction. The role of memory in the protagonists' thoughts and actions is key to many novels, so much so that modern Chinese literature has often been defined by the prominence of memory as a literary trope.

This chapter surveys the role of commemoration—and its mirror image in repressing and overlooking the past—in Chinese literature, with emphasis on the PRC in the post-Maoist period. Writers perceived the need for a modern national literature and associated it with a culture of recollection, recuperating traumatic experiences, and bearing witness. Such literary testimony often takes the paradoxical form of stating the characters' inability to fully access the past. *Fat Years* evidences the sustained interest in collective memory and forgetting. Yet insofar as *Fat Years* presents the case for remembrance, it may be considered naïve compared with other twenty-first-century references to memory. In parallel with the persistence of testimonial literature, public discourse in the PRC since the late twentieth century has also pointed to forgetting as a viable and sometimes desirable process. Wang Shuo's hooligan literature in particular entertains amnesia without condemning it. The divergence between Wang Shuo's and Chan Koonchung's novels reveals a rift in these and other writers' views of the significance of collective memory.

A Companion to Modern Chinese Literature, First Edition. Edited by Yingjin Zhang.
© 2016 John Wiley & Sons, Ltd. Published 2016 by John Wiley & Sons, Ltd.

In their distinct approaches to memory, Wang Shuo's and Chan Koonchung's works illustrate salient traits of post-Maoist memory, namely its privatization and diversification. Rather than subscribing to a collective identity and common memories, post-Maoist writers revert to individual experiences that cannot be reduced to a single shared viewpoint. At issue is not only the collapse of communist ideals, but also the restructuring of social spheres. Aleida Assmann (2006) has distinguished among three forms of collective memory: communicative, cultural, and political. One may argue that during the Maoist period the three forms were conflated. Top-down commemoration (political memory) appropriated all forms of social activities (communicative memory) and textual and visual practices (cultural memory). Post-Maoist collective memory has differentiated among these spheres and often places them at odds with one another. Memory is no longer one; its components are in constant flux, turning literature into a site of contention.

Post-Maoist literature must be understood in the context of the rapid social and political change. In the wake of almost 30 years of Mao's rule, including repressed traumas such as the Cultural Revolution, and at an age of personal insecurity and social uncertainty due to political autocracy and unchecked economic growth, memory has anchored public discourse. Since the late 1980s, writers, thinkers, and activists, especially those associated with the June Fourth protests, have embraced the imperative to remember and commemorate, and deplored a particular "Chinese amnesia." Others, prominently the New Left, contested that the glut of memoirs was playing into the hands of the government's neoliberalism. A rich debate has developed around the post-Maoist politics of memory.

In referring to the politics of memory, I target much more than commemoration and its denial by political powers. Rather, "the politics of memory" denotes here the deployment of memory in the political, social, and cultural realms to further ideological agendas. The prominence of memory in post-Maoist works is part of a larger process, noted in another context by Andreas Huyssen. Huyssen argues that modernist thought, founded on a futurist drive, transformed in the late twentieth century and turned to a preoccupation with the past; by the turn of the twenty-first century, the link between past and present can no longer be taken for granted. The abundance of information, through visual and digital media as well as new scholarship, has led to a crisis in our understanding of memory: "Today, we seem to suffer from a hypertrophy of memory, not history" (Huyssen 2003: 3). To contemplate memory and forgetting is tantamount to acknowledging the temporal and spatial instability of the postindustrial, globalizing world. Huyssen observes the manifestation of the new politics of memory in Germany, Argentina, and the United States, but cognate developments have also been taking place in the PRC.

In addressing the relation between fiction and memory, this chapter provides an additional prism for considering issues and texts addressed in other chapters in this volume. Memory and forgetting touch directly on the relation between literature and nationalism, trauma, modernity, and visual arts. The politics of memory is indeed at the center of the literary imagination in contemporary China.

The Figure of History in Studies of Modern Chinese Literature

The defining role of historical consciousness in modern Chinese literature has drawn much scholarly attention. A quick survey of the academic debates may be helpful, not only for identifying memory as a key literary trope, but also for placing the fiction preoccupied with memory in the context of its institutional reception and canonization. Prominent critics, from C. T. Hsia to David Wang and Rey Chow, have commented on the importance of the figure of history. They have established that modern writings have deployed the past—factual or imaginary—as a key device for defining both national identity and a literature representative of the nation. In other words, modern Chinese literature is founded on—and has significantly contributed to—a politics of memory. The use of memory has been claimed for specific literary, social, and political agendas.

A foundational link between national ideology and literary formation was proposed by C. T. Hsia, who coined the phrase "the obsession with China" in 1971. Hsia not only pioneered the study of modern Chinese literature in the United States but also established its reputation as a humanist endeavor marred only by a left-wing and communist obsession for fitting plots to the perceived goals of the nation-state (C. T. Hsia 1999). Scholars have taken up Hsia's formulation in a broader context, to draw attention to the overarching interest of writers of various convictions who have used literature to redefine a collective Chinese identity and even claim the modern literary idiom as key to the nation's well-being.

Hsia's influence is discernible in the writings of David Wang, which have defined the current scholarship of modern Chinese literature. Wang reinterprets "the obsession with China" in line with Benedict Anderson's suggestion that nations are imagined communities, "as a syndrome that Chinese writers had to come to terms with in imagining their nation as a new political entity of the modern age" (C. T. Hsia 1999: xxii–iii). Wang has constructed genealogies of collective memory: history is remembered (or more accurately, the past is constructed) through depictions of violence and brutality, of "the monster that is history" (D. Wang 2004: 2). Wang's choice of authors—from Lu Xun to Gu Cheng—reinterprets the core texts of modern Chinese literature through their view of the nation. More recently, Wang has noted that post–Cultural Revolution fiction consciously presents itself as the bearer of a historical legacy, involving "a politics of posterity." For Wang, the radical fictionalization of the past, exemplified in Mo Yan's fiction, questions "history"—"be it as an ideology, an episteme, an institution, or a narrative form" (D. Wang forthcoming). The challenge of contemporary writers to accepted historical constructions, as noted by Wang, only further reaffirms the role of historical memory in defining Chinese literature.

The connection between the engineering of national identity and the politics of memory is further explored by Rey Chow, who has criticized the "compulsion to emphasize the Chinese dimension to all universal questions" (Chow 1998: 4). Yet Chow does not ally herself with C. T. Hsia's humanism; rather, she is interested in laying bare the inevitable ideological biases of all parties to the construction of "Chineseness." Chow observes the current trend of chauvinistic Sinocentrism among PRC intellectuals and shows its reliance on what she calls "the logic of the wound" (1998: 6). The collective memory of wrongs done to the body politic by Western imperial powers defines the nation. Chow's refutation of the logic of the wound draws attention to the manipulative nature of the politics of memory. PRC authors—and, to a lesser extent, Sinophone writers as well—often identify themselves, or are identified by scholars, as exponents of a national literature, characterized by collective trauma.

Chinese writers' construction of their own literary genealogy based on wounded memory is also the subject of my book *Witness against History* (Braester 2003). I have noted how literary texts have placed themselves within a retroactively reconstituted tradition, thereby creating a canon based on the memory of historical events. The result is a genealogy of modern Chinese literature that privileges events etched in collective memory and is defined in terms of these events' historical aftermath. Periodical and generic tags are telling: May Fourth literature (after the May 4, 1919, anticolonial demonstrations); literature of resistance to Japan (*kangri wenxue*, in reaction to the Japanese invasion during World War II); scar literature (describing in retrospect the scarring events of the Cultural Revolution); and more, including the more general tag "postsocialist" (referring to literary retrospection as Maoist practices recede into the past and are replaced by neoliberal policies). Much of twentieth-century literature in Chinese is testimonial, focusing on wars, revolutions, and famines as the punctuation marks of history. The texts often stress bodily pain as affective evidence supporting the narrator's account. This thematic concern does not, however, manifest itself only in straightforward accounts. While reportage has been a vital and central trend since the 1940s, other forms have often resorted to allegory. Whether due to political restrictions, lack of a vocabulary to describe extreme trauma, or stylistic considerations, writers from Lu Xun to Yu Hua have often couched their memories in forms that elude direct historical reference (Braester 2003: 4). This resistance to direct testimony may be considered a form of the "obsession with China," but only insofar as it also reflects critically on the role of collective memory.

The scholarly works cited above exemplify the ideological stakes in the construction of specific texts, and of entire literary traditions, around the figures of history and national memory. Through the politics of memory, authors intervene in debates over literary form, nationalism, identity, and cultural policy. The politics of memory have been of special importance in the post-Maoist period, not only because of the debates over the Maoist legacy, but also because of a widespread quest for the ethical significance of collective memory in the present.

The Ethics of Commemoration

At the foundation of the politics of memory lies the assumption that commemoration is a moral act, answering to an ethical imperative. The discourse on memory in the aftermath of atrocities such as the Jewish Holocaust and the Great Famine under Mao (1958–1960) has privileged attempts to preserve personal memory and inscribe it in collective consciousness. Collective memory reinforces a diachronic identity—that is, the perception of one's present identity as an extension of past events, often beyond one's living memory. Collective memory is thereby defined as a safeguard against the decay of individual memory. By the same token, forgetting is condemned as a betrayal of the collective endeavor to keep memory alive. The moral imperative to remember encompasses resistance, not only to erasing the past, but also to any form of relegating the past to irrelevance. Prominent thinkers addressing the twentieth-century crisis of memory have marked the ethical pitfalls of sterile memory. Theodor Adorno has claimed that "all reification is forgetting" (Horkehimer and Adorno 1972: 191); Huyssen has warned against nostalgia, that "the past cannot give us what the future has failed to deliver" (2003: 27); Tony Judt (2008: 3–4) has deplored the "musealization of the past." To counter forgetting, commemoration must be proactive, adaptive, and critical.

In post-Maoist China, the ethical dimension of commemoration has been eroded not only by direct suppression of expression but also by the constant rewriting of the past, in historiography, literature, and film. Arif Dirlik (2005: 151) has noted that revolutionary rhetoric abets forgetting "in the sense of relegating to memory that which obstructs the assimilation of the new." The post-Maoist state has sustained the same rhetoric, producing a semblance of continuity from Maoist revolution to state-sponsored neoliberalism. The current widespread collective amnesia is due not to lack of information about the Maoist period but rather to a more sophisticated regulation of discourse. Descriptions of suffering do not point at the perpetrators; acknowledgment of trauma is not followed by blame. The post-Maoist memory-work resists any reassessment of Maoism at the ideological or institutional level.

Post-Maoist amnesia is not guided by a choice to forgive, as in South Africa for example; nor is it simply an escape from the psychological burden of remembering traumatic events. Rather, it is part of a political struggle for defining the borderlines of public debate in present-day China, a struggle with clear ethical implications. It is in this context that we can evaluate the recent collection of Maoist memorabilia, restaging of the model operas of the Cultural Revolution, the republication of movie oldies, as well as proliferation of scholarship, filmed documentaries, and memoirs about the first 30 years of the PRC. The stakes in reasserting the past may be unstated, but they are clear to all involved parties.

The explosion of Cultural Revolution memoirs since the turn of the twenty-first century exemplifies these intricate interests. Two events loom large in the post-Maoist politics of memory: the Cultural Revolution and June Fourth, also known as the Tiananmen massacre. Unlike June Fourth, discussion of which is banned, the Cultural Revolution has been abundantly explored in semi-official and personal accounts. It nevertheless remains a sensitive topic, especially when implications for present-day China are concerned. Many intellectuals have called for preserving the memory of the Cultural Revolution, most famously the writer Ba Jin (2000: iii–xi), who expressed his hope in 1986 for a museum of the Cultural Revolution (on recent memoirs of the Cultural Revolution, see Davies 2002). Yet much of the debate over the Cultural

Revolution is limited to scholarly venues, and a full reevaluation of the period awaits a different political atmosphere. It should therefore have been a welcome development when fiction and popular media reawakened interest in the subject in the 1990s. Critics have pointed out, however, that the Cultural Revolution revival resulted in distancing the present from the past. Geremie Barmé (1999: 316–321) points to the roots of the new Mao cult in the economic and political crises of the late 1980s. Mao became a symbol of social certainty, order, unity, and equality, giving rise to "totalitarian nostalgia." Meanwhile, the New Left in China has warned against a wholesale repudiation of Maoism. Wang Hui (2008) has credited Mao for his authentic politics of revolutionary utopia. Mobo Gao (2008: 48–64) claims that the memoirs popular in the 1990s depict the Maoist period as chaotic, thereby stressing the present economic affluence and social stability and buttressing the current government's neoliberal agenda. For Gao, the commemoration of the Maoist period is intended to dull historical consciousness rather than enhance it. Either way, memory in contemporary China is imbricated in highly manipulative attempts to engineer perceptions of both past and present.

Serial Amnesia

Despite the political sensitivity of more recent events, debates on their commemoration have also defined public discourse in the PRC. The critic and writer Liu Xiaobo has fought to keep the memory of June Fourth alive. His efforts were acknowledged in diametrically opposite ways: he was jailed for prolonged periods, and received the Nobel Prize for Peace in 2010. When Mo Yan, one of the most prolific and imaginative novelists, was given the Nobel Prize in Literature in 2012, many held against him the fact that he refrained from mentioning political oppression. The attitude of intellectuals and authors toward collective memory has come to identify them in the public mind.

The forced silence around June Fourth has exposed the interests behind the politics of memory. The importance of the Tiananmen incident for understanding historical patterns of memory and forgetting was noticed immediately after its occurrence. Activists in the protest movement felt betrayed, not only by the government and the military, but also by the collective memory that should have prevented the recurrence of Maoist suppression tactics. Fang Lizhi, one of the leading intellectuals associated with the protest movement, sought asylum in the US embassy in Beijing. There, he wrote his essay "The Chinese Amnesia" (Fang 1990). Fang's essay presents in a nutshell the politics of memory in the aftermath of June Fourth. The essay is a plea for remembrance, but more importantly it blames the collective forgetting on deliberate party policies. The events of 1989, argues Fang, are a symptom of the political culture that was established in the 1940s and is likely to be repeated in the future.

Fang's essay identifies a "technique of forgetting" promoted by the Party, leading to the tragic recurrence of clashes between the educated elite and the authorities in 1942, 1957, 1970, and 1989. Each time, the dissidents were unaware of the fate of their predecessors and therefore placed themselves in harm's way. Those who have tried to establish a repository of historical memory—as Fang did in 1987 in an attempt to put on record the Anti-Rightists Campaign of 1957—were persecuted, and their voices suppressed. In other words, what Fang calls amnesia is in fact ignorance due to lack of accessible records of earlier incidents. The cure to the Chinese amnesia lies in resisting the Party's restriction of information and learning about the past.

Fang implies that the history of the PRC has been shaped by cyclical responses to violence and strife at the national level. The Chinese amnesia—and the suggested countermeasure of remembrance—are defined by the individual's (in)ability to draw on collective memory. Memory and forgetting are the vehicles of a well-defined historical narrative, one that sees all events as part of the process of becoming an enlightened nation.

Chinese writers who can address June Fourth, either because they live outside the PRC—such as Hong Ying, the author of *Summer of Betrayal* (*Beipan zhi xia*, 1995), and Ma Jian, the author of *Beijing Coma* (*Rou zhi tu*, 2009)—or because they carry a Hong Kong passport (as does Chan Koonchung), stress the importance of the events of 1989 for collective memory.[1] These novels undertake a moral duty and a historical mission for national enlightenment, but also the more practical task of establishing a repository of knowledge for future reference. In the context of the circumscribed reception of accounts of the Tiananmen incident, every historical and literary text becomes perforce part of a collective memory-work.

Ma Jian's novel in particular foregrounds the testimonial value of such writings. The novel is written from the viewpoint of a participant in the student demonstrations, who was hit by a bullet and spends the following decade bedridden, without any ability to communicate with the world around him. Most of the novel is dedicated to a meticulous recreation of the events of spring 1989 and to tracing the changing fortunes of those who took part in the demonstrations or whose relatives were affected by them. *Beijing Coma* is fictional, in that the narrator's persona is not based on any recorded experience—indeed, no record can exist of the mental processes of a person locked within a vegetative body. Yet the novel is based first and foremost on an impulse to bear witness to June Fourth, map out the memories of the protagonist who functions as the author's double, and document all that deserves to be remembered. The protagonist's death at the novel's ending, without having gained the ability to communicate, may signal the end of personal memory. The novel, however, stores these experiences and juxtaposes them with current conditions in China, thereby acting as a monument in the face of the serial amnesia observed by Fang Lizhi.

The Golden Age of Amnesia

The testimonial literature on June Fourth notwithstanding, it was arguably not until Chan Koonchung's *Fat Years* of 2009 that a novel addressed not the events themselves but rather their aftermath—the scarcity of public knowledge about the protests of 1989 and resulting collective amnesia. *Fat Years* weaves a science fictional plot that takes place in 2013. The protagonist, Lao Chen, realizes that the events of an entire month in 2011 have been wiped out of the memory of almost all Chinese citizens. The mystery is resolved as the Communist Party is discovered to be behind a massive cover-up and drugging of the population to erase the collective memory of a brutal crackdown. The inquiry revolves not only around the events two years back. Instead, the novel focuses on the protagonist's limitations in the aftermath of the event—his lingering amnesia and subsequent social awkwardness. The whodunit targets both the earlier events and their implications for the present. In the tradition of self-implicating detective stories, the protagonist's most formidable enemy is himself. Lao Chen is caught in the self-perpetuating nature of amnesia—to forget, he must also forget that he has forgotten. His first sentence in the novel, "just forget it," alludes to his complicity.

Resonating with Fang Lizhi's observation on serial amnesia, the novel depicts how the earlier political suppressions have also been erased from memory. Lao Chen's romantic interest, Little Xi, has remained impervious to memory loss due to a neuro-chemical coincidence. She tells how, when she asks people about the events of spring 1989, no one seems to remember. She notes: "I don't know if they were feigning ignorance or if they really didn't remember." Her interlocutors avoid talking about June Fourth and remember that the Cultural Revolution was "fun." She adds: "Certain collective memories seemed to have been completely swallowed up by a cosmic black hole, never to be heard of again."[2] The novel anticipates future events to be similarly erased, in the form of the fictional crackdown in 2011. The plot coincides with the attempt to counter that amnesia.

In many aspects, *Fat Years* is an exponent of the "obsession with China." The novel sees historical legacy as defining the nation, and at the same time it also questions who can speak in the name of the nation. Chen Xi's son changes his name from Min (people) to Guo (country), in a symbolic move that reflects his uncritical identification with the Communist state. Meanwhile, the protagonists attempt to "awaken" the nation, resonating with Lu Xun's foundational text, "Preface to *Outcry*" ("*Nahan* zixu," 1921), which identifies the writer's task with waking up the national readership, albeit not without reservation and irony.

In its most general outline, Chan's novel describes a battle of wills between those who wish to remember and those who wish to forget or instill forgetting in others. Lao Chen himself undergoes a transformation, starting in the amnesiac camp and increasingly drawn into Little Xi's struggle to retrieve memory. Little Xi speaks in the name of the need to remember: "Do you remember why we were angry, why we struggled, what our ideals were? Do you remember, Lao Chen?" Chen's response dismisses such remembrance as the vestige of another era: "Little Xi, why can't you forget? This is a different age." Yet Little Xi says, "I don't want to forget anymore." When Chen is convinced by her view, it is because even though he is reluctant to be reminded of "China's painful contemporary history," the idea that the records are erased and falsified unsettles him.

Fat Years is especially preoccupied with June Fourth. The missing month in 2011 is an allegory for the "missing year" of 1989. As the novel remarks, the forced silence about the Tiananmen incident led to it that "everybody joked that in China 1988 was immediately followed by 1990. ... For some people that year was an indelible memory. ... For the great majority of young mainland Chinese, the events of the Tiananmen massacre have never entered their consciousness." Yet the novel emphasizes also that the recurrent repression had started long before 1989. Earlier events have likewise been swept aside: "Not only are there no books that mention that lost month, there are definitely no books about the 1989 Tiananmen Massacre. There aren't even any decent books about the Anti-Rightist Campaign or the Cultural Revolution. They're all a pack of lies." Lao Chen finally discerns a historical pattern of ignorance:

> [P]eople born after 1980 have never even heard of Wei Jingsheng, the early dissident who called for democracy as the Fifth Modernization, or Liu Binyan, the most celebrated *People's Daily* investigative reporter of the 1980s; and no wonder whenever the June 1989 student leader Wang Dan lectures overseas about the Tiananmen massacre, there are always Chinese overseas students in the audience who jeer at him. Today's younger generation has no way of knowing.

Fat Years links the events of 1989 to other challenges to Communist autocracy. Equally important, the novel points out also the selective memory of a hyper-consumerist society integrated into global capitalism. The "fat years" (*shengshi*, literally, a golden age), as most urban Chinese experience the present, are no more than a golden age of forgetting. Insofar as the novel's dystopian fantasy is that of an absolute forgetting, of the kind that could only be imagined for 1989, it is an amnesia enabled by the current emphasis on material comfort and integration with global economy.

Literary and Cinematic Memory

Fat Years also addresses specifically the role of literature and cinema in the politics of memory. The protagonist is an author. In 2008, he plans to write a novel. The examples he gives are *Ulysses* and *In Search of Lost Time*—both stories of attempts to overcome temporal dislocation and retrieve the subject of one's memories. With the loss of his memory, Lao Chen also loses his literary inspiration. His writer's block is experienced as "an overwhelming feeling of good fortune, such as I never had before." Forgetting is associated with a blissful relinquishing of authorial responsibility.

Textual and visual records abound, but they are one-sided, manipulative accounts provided by the state. Wei Guo, Little Xi's son who aspires to a position in the Party, watches documentary films about the Nanjing massacre. The Japanese occupation has in fact become a favorite reference of official propaganda. The immense human suffering has been harnessed to the national cause and brought up whenever nationalist sentiments are required as a bargaining chip in intra-Asian negotiations. The popular reception of works on the War of Resistance against Japan is telling. *The Field of Life and Death*, Xiao Hong's novel of 1935, was adapted into a highly successful stage play by Tian Qinxin in 1999, in conjunction with the official celebrations of the 60th anniversary of the victory over Japan. Jiang Wen's more ironic film, *Devils on the Doorstep* (*Guizi laile*, 2000), raised public outcry and was banned from screening. Wei Guo, sticking to the documentaries on the Nanjing massacre shown on state-run TV, reaffirms the doctrinaire historiography that erases the collective memory.

Lao Chen's literary taste is very different. He looks for prominent memoirs critical of the Maoist period, including Zhang Yihe's *The Past Is Not Fog* (*Wangshi bing buru yan*, 2004), Yang Xianhui's *What Happened at Jiabiangou* (*Jiabiangou jishi*, 2008, first serialized 2000–2003, English as *The Woman from Shanghai*, 2009), and Yang Jiang's *Six Chapters from My Life "Downunder"* (*Ganxiao liuji*, 1981; English 1984). In the fictional 2013, these novels have not only been banned but also erased from public record. No eyewitness accounts are available of the political turmoil associated with the Party and the history of the PRC. *Fat Years* depicts a dystopia where all documentation can be retroactively manipulated and made to disappear, facilitated by the transition to digital archiving. Lao Chen searches for clues in old newspapers, but the library stores them only in digitized format: "The online reports of those twenty-eight days were completely different from my memory of them." Although Lao Chen manages to lay his hands on a few fragments of printed matter, the novel does not subscribe to Mikhail Bulgakov's famous challenge to Soviet censorship, "manuscripts don't burn" (1997: 298). In *Fat Years*, the digital age allows for "total collective amnesia."

The novel lacks nuance in describing the attitude of the authorities to memory. As I mentioned earlier, Mobo Gao regards the popularity of memoirs from the Maoist period as a measure for diverting attention from the ills of the present. Chan Koonchung seems to place unmitigated faith in the testimonial value of literature. The banning of all books of reportage and remembrance is regarded as a complete erasure of collective memory. Chan Koonchung's account of Chinese literature and film in the early twenty-first century resonates with Huyssen's observations. The saturation in historical information goes hand in hand with lack of genuine memory work. It is up to literature and visual arts to create a meaningful connection between past and present.

Whereas *Fat Years* makes few literary allusions, it remarks time and again on the role of cinema in establishing collective memory. Lao Chen regularly views oldies with his friend Jian Lin, who picks the films and pairs them with rare wines. Significantly, the first film they watch together is *Never Forget Class Struggle* (*Qianwan buyao wangji jieji douzheng*, directed by Xie Tieli, 1963). The film's title appropriates memory to the Communist collective and includes an injunction against forgetting. Yet in the twenty-first century, such films are viewed not in the manner intended at the time of their production, but rather as vehicles of nostalgia for a bygone era. *Never Forget Class Struggle*, Chen notes, is considered a "red classic." In the early 2000s, home viewers showed a renewed interest in Maoist movies. These films, now available on DVD, allow viewers to look back nostalgically at Communist heroics without raising the specters of suffering caused by Maoist policies. The films have become ideal tools for amnesia under the semblance of memory.

The excess of written and visual records trivializes them, and allows *Never Forget Class Struggle* to paradoxically take part in instilling amnesia. Jian Lin talks of the film in the same way that he assesses his wines: "Those were good times, 1964." Movies are not viewed for ideological content, and no one takes to heart the exhortation *"Never Forget."* Rather, films have become objects of connoisseurship—collected, appreciated in company, and consumed. Jian Lin easily recalls the context in which *Never Forget Class Struggle* was produced—the film's title reflects Mao's call for perpetual revolution, leading to the Cultural Revolution. Yet the historical moment does not register as relevant for later developments. Historical events are taken out of context and remembered as disconnected trivia. Even as Jian Lin and Old Chen watch red classics, they do not get any wiser about the films' implications for their present lives. The red classics are not the sites of living memory, but rather sterilized versions that have no power to bring to the surface unintended memories. The imperative "never forget," originally invoking the logic of the wound, has been replaced with nostalgia as an effective form of forgetting.

The hollowness of the slogan "never forget" is stressed when juxtaposed with its use by the protagonists who, *1984*-style, challenge the engineering of a submissive citizenship. Fang Caodi, who helps Little Xi in her quest, says: "We absolutely must not forget how lonely we used to be. As long as there might be Chinese people who have not forgotten that month, we definitely have to look for them." Fang uses the same phrase as in the film title, "We absolutely must not forget" (*qianwan buyao wangji*). Again, the novel shows little nuance. There is no implied irony in repurposing the Maoist formulation. Even though Fang and his friends do not identify with Maoist rhetoric, they model their heroic battle against amnesia on the film's Maoist slogan.

The logic of connoisseurship continues as Jian Lin invites Lao Chen to watch *The Second Spring* (*Di'er ge chuntian*, directed by Sang Hu and Wang Xiuwen, 1975). This movie, one of the last produced during the Cultural Revolution, became a curiosity, an irrelevant relic of high Maoism, almost as soon as it was produced. Moreover, the film is little known and was only recently released on DVD. While Jian Lin offers a Château Lafite from 1989—"a good vintage," he remarks—he also knowledgeably notes the director's earlier filmography. Despite the film's strong political connotations, Jian Lin and Lao Chen discuss it in neutral terms, as a specimen to be appreciated for its rarity.

Jian Lin serves again the Château Lafite of 1989, naturally without comment on the year's significance in Chinese history, when showing the film *Sunset Street* (*Xizhao jie*, directed by Wang Haowei, 1983). The movie became well known in China for its depiction of the budding post-Maoist consumer culture, including smuggling merchandize from Hong Kong. After watching the film, Jian Lin and Lao Chen discuss the past 30 years of economic reform. *Sunset Street* occasions a reassessment of the entire post-Maoist period—but again, rather than trigger a critical understanding, it launches a self-congratulatory celebration of the economic reforms that have compensated, at least for China's growing middle class, for any heavy-handed interference with the social fabric.

It is also through watching films that Lao Chen meets He Dongsheng, a high-ranking cadre who later provides the small resistance group with an explanation of how the government erased a month from public memory. Films function as a literal meeting place and a figural middle ground between cynical amnesia and engaged struggle to restore memory. Jian Lin's cinephilia attempts—with a debatable measure of success—to restore credibility to the oldies as a gateway to collective memory.

In the black-and-white world of *Fat Years*, where only film provides temporary respite from a Manichean battle between the evil of amnesia and the heroic resuscitation of memory, one character stands out for her childlike innocence. The artist Miaomiao is exposed to the amnesiac drug while taking other medication, which in combination results in both long-term and short-term memory loss. She is incapable even of recognizing the people around her. She therefore remains aloof, unconcerned with the present machinations of memory. Her condition presents an alternative approach—neither complicity nor resistance, but rather a fundamentally asocial behavior that cannot be subsumed by the politics of memory. But whereas she remains a minor figure in Chan Koonchung's novel, cognate characters are given center stage in the works of Wang Shuo.

The Thrills of Amnesia

The post-Maoist politics of memory vacillates among three main trends, each promoted by its own agents. The state-sponsored media reappropriate remembrance in a highly selective form; dissidents repudiate the collective amnesia brought about by the repeated erasure of public records; yet another approach takes a cynical view, whereby forgetting is playful, noncommittal, but perhaps the only way to cope with an absurd reality. The difference between the two non-official approaches is made clear in the contrast between Chan Koonchung and Wang Shuo.

Fat Years launches criticism of Wang Shuo's "Wild Beasts" and its film adaptation *In the Heat of the Sun* (*Yangguang canlan de rizi*, directed by Jiang Wen, 1994). When Lao Chen, in the censored environment of 2013, looks up materials about the Cultural Revolution, all he finds is "a load of nostalgic guff for an adolescence spent in the brilliant sunshine of the glorious past." The description reproduces the Chinese title of *In the Heat of the Sun* (literally, "the days of brilliant sunshine") and summarizes its plot, about youth enjoying the lawlessness of the Cultural Revolution, as told by a seemingly remorseless narrator. Wang Shuo's fiction was indeed reviled as "hooligan literature," a term that the author appropriated with pride. Jiang Wen's film adaptation sparked an emotionally charged debate. Some saw it as expressing disrespect toward the memory of Maoist atrocities, while others defended the adolescent narrator's point of view as equally valid. Barmé (1999: 317) has summed up the first approach by identifying *In the Heat of the Sun* as a proponent of "totalitarian nostalgia." I have argued elsewhere (Braester 2003: 200–201) that *In the Heat of the Sun*, following Wang Shuo's fiction, does not reaffirm lost innocence but rather underlines the dislocation of the narrator, who must reinvent his memories under the onslaught of present social transformation. Chan Koonchung seems to have little tolerance for Wang Shuo's irony and suspension of judgment.

In the 1980s, Wang Shuo established almost single-handedly a new paradigm in the literary politics of memory. Mocking the official narratives was prevalent in the rock 'n' roll music, painting, and performance art of the decade leading to the

Tiananmen protests. Wang Shuo offered a corresponding literary style. His characters are ordinary people from the margins of society, anti-heroes who try to leverage the little they have through semi-legal scams. Wang's hooligan literature became very popular, as readers found his stories impudent, absurd, and reflective of the anti-establishment mood of the time.

"Wild Beasts" exemplifies Wang Shuo's approach to memory. The first-person narrator is an unreliable witness who cannot cope with the changes since his childhood in the 1970s. His reminiscences are punctuated by occasions in which he drinks himself to stupor and loses his memory. Toward the end of the story, he exclaims, "Can I trust my memory at this point? ... Have I ever said a single truthful word?" (Wang Shuo 2006: 83). The narrator and his narrative hurtle toward self-destruction.

Wang Shuo's texts resist the Maoist politics of memory in a particularly seditious manner. His characters are obsessed with personal memories that they do not share even with their immediate environment, not to mention a national collective. In fact, the characters' ineloquence and asocial behavior renders them incapable of even communicating their memories. Memories are often faked, and true memories lose their significance when they can be—and often are—replaced with new, confabulated versions. Versions change so frequently that eventually the readers may turn indifferent to the story's veracity.

The theme of memory tossed about as a plaything is explored at length in Wang's first novel, *Playing for Thrills*. The first-person narrator, Fang Yan, is told about himself stories that do not fit his experience. He starts doubting his own memories, only to find out that his best friends have framed him in a murder case by attaching a false identity to the victim and by one of the perpetrators' appropriation of Fang Yan's name. They have done so with no motive other than playing a deadly prank on an unsuspecting man, for the thrill of it. Fang must solve the mystery by filling in a week missing from his memory, which took place 10 years earlier. The liquor-loving Fang is especially clueless since he is always in a daze, "like I'm surrounded by fog so thick I can't see the nose on my face, which keeps me from recalling anything I've ever done" (Wang Shuo 1997: 64). The matter is further complicated by the fact that by the time the investigation is initiated, 10 years have passed since the crime. As in Chan Koonchung's later novel, all that the self-appointed detective can hold onto is the temporal discrepancy, the fact that 7 days remain unaccounted for.

Fang's amnesia is never explained. He is simply described as having been "frozen" for 10 years. Fang keeps doubting his memories and the very faculty of his memory. When the police interrogate him, he admits that he does not have a good memory. Fang characterizes his testimony as uninvolved, as if he were not in charge of his own memories: "I described my last meeting with Gao Yang like an eyewitness to history. Truth is, I could have gotten the same impression from someone angling for a promotion or planning to go abroad or whatever. In other words, I couldn't be absolutely sure who I was describing" (Wang Shuo 1997: 14).

Playing for Thrills introduces a twist to the conventional whodunit, in that the detective-cum-suspect is not only amnesiac but also a mythomaniac who takes pride in constantly modifying his accounts and reinventing his past. His constant confabulations leave no one—including himself—able to say when he is telling the truth. The real culprits have good reason to believe that these traits will further ensnare Fang. The noose has already been tied, 10 years earlier. Any recollection is bound to be a false one. Trying to remember, by inventing ever-more implausible stories, can only work against Fang. When he is confronted with discrepancies, he does not acknowledge them as such. Instead, he plays along with his interlocutors, thereby further implicating and incriminating himself.

Fang's mythomaniacal amnesia is an individual condition, but it is one he shares with all those who surround him, as a generational affliction. At times, his friends seem in control, encouraging him to forget as part of their plot. One of them urges Fang: "OK, forget it, just forget it. Gao Yang's dead, let it be. Why try to screw your pals over something that happened years ago? Maybe it's time to forget about settling scores" (Wang Shuo 1997: 142). But the friends' ruse reveals also a profound disregard for truth and for keeping memory untainted. For Fang Yan and his friends, there is no difference between forgetting, cheating, and playing for thrills. Life is a game of liar's poker.

Even when Fang reaches out for a friend's memory (a woman whom he forgot having had an affair with), she answers in a noncommittal manner, dismissing her own memories. Fang asks, "This apartment has a memory, doesn't it? Was some tragedy played out in this room?" (Wang Shuo 1997: 148). The woman gives little away: "She said that they had long since forgotten the place, that the memory of what had happened existed only in cracks between the bricks in the wall." Later, she adds: "I don't want to talk about the past. I'd rather let it lie, since I'm content with my life now" (Wang Shuo 1997: 170). Forgetting is a way to make peace with the present. The woman's response dismisses also a fundamental form of memory, namely associating events with specific locations. Mental mapping of one's experiences is a mnemonic device and a means for anchoring one's identity (Yates 1966; Connerton 2009: 99–125). In fact, it is Fang's spatial memory—his insistence that he had never been to Yunnan, the scene of crime—that gives him confidence. The woman's retort disavows this memory-stabilizing mechanism.

More broadly, the protagonists lack the mnemonic pointers for making sense of their past. Modern collective memory, according to Pierre Nora's (1989) famous formulation, relies on sites of memory (*lieux de mémoire*). In the absence of coherent historical narratives that had bound together premodern communities, sites of memory anchor collective consciousness through disconnected and ambiguous symbols. The characters in *Playing for Thrills* readily relinquish even these shards of temporal and spatial reference in exchange for the thrills of forgetting. Wang Shuo's version of amnesia is the result not of repression but rather of cynicism and indifference on the part of his unheroic characters.

Post-Revolutionary Memory

Forgetting for thrills takes a particular form in Wang Shuo's fiction: the characters' pranks and jocular references mock the revolutionary rhetoric and substitute it with popular culture. Dialogs rely on tongue-in-cheek allusions to films such as the Soviet classic *Lenin in 1918* (*Lenin v 1918 godu*, directed by Mikhail Romm, 1939). It is no coincidence that Fang Yan plays along when mistaken for Zhuo Yue, an army general. Fang is an anti-hero; more importantly, in the 1990s, reminiscing about revolutionary grandeur is outdated. Similar to other novels by Wang Shuo, *Playing for Thrills* brims with puns on Communist lingo, displaced into the hooligans' lifestyle. Maoist symbols are obsolete and serve as the butt of ridicule.

The characters jeer at the idea that revolutionary self-sacrifice will be vindicated by its persistence in collective memory. The friends' prank relies on the willingness of one in their midst to die. Martyrdom is replaced with death for the sake of a senseless hoax. The voluntary victim justifies his choice with repurposed Maoist phrasing: "it was for our great revolutionary pioneers to live for more than ten years in the people's hearts" (Wang Shuo 1989: 227). All he wants, however, is to "be a hot topic of conversation." As befits the age of consumerism, ideologically motivated self-sacrifice is substituted with the desire to be a media celebrity.

Wang Shuo keeps referring to popular media and their version of transitory fame. The murdered person in *Playing for Thrills* is named after the commercially successful TV and film director Feng Xiaogang. The novel's warning, not to confuse the con artist Feng with his namesake, "someone at the TV Arts Center," is no more than another red herring in the novel's wild goose chase. In fact, Feng Xiaogang, the director, was embarking at the time of the novel's publication on a fruitful close collaboration with Wang Shuo that would result in post-Maoist spoof classics.

Playing for Thrills also refers directly, with undisguised mockery, to the role of the writer in creating collective memory in the post-Maoist era. Among his evasions of serious conversation, Fang Yan assumes—with flaunted derision—the persona of an ideologically motivated youth:

> I'm planning to write some memoirs. Haven't you noticed all the handwringing in the papers these days, how the old comrades are dropping like flies? If we don't hurry up and help them write down their experiences, it'll be too late. Their lives are at the core of our revolutionary experience, and recording them for posterity will be invaluable in instructing the younger generation in our nation's history. (Wang Shuo 1997: 74)

Fang parodies the memoir industry and mocks its attempt to preserve the revolutionary spirit. Fang proceeds with his usual fabrications, much like Wang Shuo, who presents in his fiction an alternative to Maoist memory work.

The novel ends with a metafictional note by an authorial persona. The authorial character explains Fang Yan's situation (Wang Shuo 1997: 324): "One day he finds himself suspected of murder. Forced to delve into his memories by calling on old friends, he produces a book of life that is missing seven of its pages." In other words, Fang has engaged with memory against his will. As a result, he "produces a book"— he becomes, at least metaphorically, an author. Playing for thrills is ultimately a writer's game, and post-Maoist literature is founded on forgetting.

Post-Memory

Wang Shuo's novels are preoccupied with memory, but it is a doubly and triply failed memory. The protagonists are unable to process their memories, vouch for their veracity, or even convince the reader of their importance. Wang's fiction points to an important development in the politics of memory at the turn of the twenty-first century, teasing out a less-explored aspect of the process observed by Huyssen, namely that the late twentieth century is characterized by a turn from utopian futurism to memory work. Wang Shuo's fiction, however, points out that once collective memory is appropriated by hegemonic power, new forms must be instated, which accommodate forgetting as an integral and sometimes desirable part of one's relationship to the past. Wang Shuo suggests the possibility of a forgetting that is not post-traumatic, but rather willed and playful. It presents an alternative to both official monumentality and to its mirror image in direct attacks on the system, from Liu Binyan's reportage to Chan Koonchung's resistance to amnesia. Wang Shuo does not subscribe to the high modernism that undergirds both Maoist and dissident writings. In a gesture that some consider immoral, Wang Shuo presents a fiction that does not aspire to commemoration, but is constructed instead around faking memory.

Wang Shuo's contribution to post-Maoist culture is both taken for granted and understated. His works and his influence are mentioned at times in conjunction with the postsocialist turn away from Maoist rhetoric, in response to the burgeoning market economy (Y. Huang 2007: 63–104; McGrath 2008). Yet Wang's overall contribution to contemporary Chinese fiction, and to the literary politics of memory in particular, has remained curiously unnoticed. Yan Lianke, arguably the most prominent novelist to rise to fame in the early twenty-first century, has noted that Wang Shuo, who has puzzlingly been almost absent from the literary scene after the 1990s, has influenced all of China's present-day writers (Yuan Dao 2014). Wang's continuing impact is key to understanding the politics of memory in the second decade of the twenty-first century.

Wang Shuo introduces what may be called post-memory—reimagining the present in disregard of the past. Nicholas Dames (2001: 3–11) asserts that at the center of the modern novel lies the act of expressing and working through memory. Unlike the Victorian novel, modern fiction fashions the past as intruding into the present and providing a gateway to characters' psyche. Modern personae are often burdened by traumatic fixation, which threatens their mental cohesion. Wang Shuo marks an age of post-memory. Temporal ruptures abound; the past haunts the present. Yet Wang's protagonists remain largely indifferent, playing their games of faking identities and inventing memories. They are not quite as cool as they believe themselves to be—but it is the excess of their fabrication, rather than a hidden truth related to their past, that often proves to be their nemesis. Wang's works present an alternative to the "obsession with China" and "the logic of the wound." Wang's post-mnemonic, post-obsession fiction does not even bother to refute the figure of history. Memory simply remains suspended outside time, up for grabs in the breathless race to remain in the present.

Notes

1 Belinda Kong (2012) observes that fiction on Tiananmen has become a diasporic genre.

2 All quotations from this novel are from K. Chan (2011).

References

Assmann, Aleida. 2006. "Memory, Individual and Collective." In *The Oxford Handbook of Contextual Political Analysis*. Edited by Goodin, Robert E., and Charles Tilly. Oxford, UK: Oxford University Press. 210–224.

Ba Jin 巴金. 2000. *Suixiang lu* 随想录 (Random thoughts). Beijing: Renmin wenxue chubanshe.

Barmé, Geremie R. 1999. *In the Red: On Contemporary Chinese Culture*. New York: Columbia University Press.

Braester, Yomi. 2003. *Witness against History: Literature, Film and Public Discourse in Twentieth-Century China*. Stanford, CA: Stanford University Press.

Bulgakov, Mikhail. 1997. *Master and Margarita*. Trans. Richard Pevear and Larissa Volokhonsky. Penguin Books, eBook under Creative Commons.

Chan, Koonchung. 2011. *The Fat Years: A Novel*. Trans. Michael Duke. Random House, Google eBook.

Chow, Rey. 1998. "Introduction: On Chineseness as a Theoretical Problem." *Boundary 2*, 25.3: 6.

Connerton, Paul. 2009. *How Modernity Forgets*. Cambridge, UK: Cambridge University Press.

Dames, Nicholas. 2001. *Amnesiac Selves: Nostalgia, Forgetting, and British Fiction, 1810–1870*. Oxford, UK: Oxford University Press.

Davies, David. 2002. "Remembering Red China: Memory and Nostalgia for the Cultural Revolution in Late 1990s China." Ph.D. dissertation, University of Washington.

Dirlik, Arif. 2005. *Marxism in the Chinese Revolution*. Lanham, MD: Rowman & Littlefield.

Fang, Lizhi. 1990. "The Chinese Amnesia." Trans. Perry Link. *New York Review of Books* (Sept. 27): 31.

Gao, Mobo. 2008. *The Battle for China's Past: Mao and the Cultural Revolution*. London: Pluto Press.

Horkheimer, Max, and Theodor W. Adorno. 1972. *Dialectic of Enlightenment*. Trans. J. Cumming. New York: Herder and Herder.

Hsia, C. T. 1999. *A History of Modern Chinese Fiction*. Third edition. Bloomington: Indiana University Press.

Huang, Yibing. 2007. *Contemporary Chinese Literature: From the Cultural Revolution to the Future*. New York: Palgrave Macmillan.

Huyssen, Andreas. 2003. *Present Pasts: Urban Palimpsests and the Politics of Memory*. Stanford, CA: Stanford University Press.

Judt, Tony. 2008. *Reappraisals: Reflections on the Forgotten Twentieth Century*. New York: Penguin.

Kong, Bellinda. 2012. *Tiananmen Fictions outside the Square: The Chinese Literary Diaspora and the Politics of Global Culture*. Philadelphia: Temple University Press.

McGrath, Jason. 2008. *Postsocialist Modernity: Chinese Cinema, Literature, and Criticism in the Market Age*. Stanford, CA: Stanford University Press.

Nora, Pierre. 1989. "Between Memory and History: Les Lieux de Memoire." *Representations*, 26: 7–24.

Wang, David Der-wei. 2004. *The Monster That Is History: History, Violence, and Fictional Writing in Twentieth-Century China*. Berkeley: University of California Press.

Wang, David Der-wei. Forthcoming. "Red Legacy in Fiction." In *Red Legacies in China: Cultural Afterlives of the Communist Revolution*. Edited by Li, Jie, and Enhua Zhang. Cambridge, MA: Harvard University Press.

Wang, Hui 汪暉. 2008. *Qu zhengzhihua de zhengzhi: duan ershi shiji de zhongjie yu jiushi niandai* 去政治化的政治—短二十世纪的终结与九十年代 (The politics of depoliticization of politics: the end of the short twentieth century and the 1990s). Beijing: Sanlian shudian.

Wang, Shuo 王朔. 1989. "'Wanzhu' xupian: yidian zhengjing meiyou" 《頑主》續篇:一點正經沒有 (Pure nonsense). *Zhongguo zuojia* 中國作家 (Chinese writers), 4: 110–140.

Wang, Shuo. 1997. *Playing for Thrills: A Mystery*. Trans. Howard Goldblatt. New York: William Morrow and Company.

Wang, Shuo 王朔. 2006. *Dongwu xiongmeng* 动物凶猛 (Wild beasts). Beijing: Renmin wenxue chubanshe.

Yang, Jiang. 1984. *Six Chapters from My Life "Downunder."* Trans. Howard Goldblatt. Hong Kong: Chinese University Press.

Yang, Xianhui. 2009. *The Woman from Shanghai*. New York: Anchor Books.

Yates, Frances A. 1966. *The Art of Memory*. Chicago: University of Chicago Press.

Yuan, Dao 远道. 2014. "Wenxue de heliu guaiwan le" 文學的河流拐彎了 (The flow of literature has turned a corner). *Beijing Qingnian bao* 北京青年報 (Beijing youth daily), (Jan. 10): D1–D3.

28

Writing Historical Traumas in the Everyday

Lingchei Letty Chen

Traumatic writings are abundant in modern Chinese literature. We only need to consider how much violence the Chinese people have experienced since mid-nineteenth century, with civil unrests (most notably, the Taiping Rebellion of 1850–1864, and the Boxer Uprising of 1897–1901); the two Opium Wars with the British Empire (1839–1842, 1856–1860); the Xinhai Republican Revolution of 1911 that overthrew the Qing dynasty and ended China's several millennia of feudalism with the establishment of the ROC; military cliques that effectively divided up the country and warlord battles that erupted in confrontation with the central military government (1916–1928); and Japanese aggression that culminated in China's participation in World War II. For 8 years, the Chinese fought the Japanese invasion in the Second Sino-Japanese War (1937–1945) with tremendous costs in terms of human lives and resources. China's victory in this war, however, did not bring peace to the land, as the civil war broke out between the Nationalist and the Communist armies. The result was the Nationalists' relocation of the Republican government to Taiwan and the Communists' founding of the PRC in 1949, under the leadership of Mao Zedong. In spite of the relatively peaceful time thereafter, between 1947 and 1976, incessant political campaigns, erroneous socioeconomic policies, massive abuse of power, and ideological craze continued to wreck havoc in ordinary citizens' lives and produced countless victims and unspeakable suffering (D. Wang 2004; M. Berry 2008). The plights and traumas generated from various Maoist political campaigns include the land reform (1947–1950), the Anti-Rightist Campaign (1957), the Great Leap Forward and the Great Famine (1958–1962), as well as the Cultural Revolution (1966–1976).

A Companion to Modern Chinese Literature, First Edition. Edited by Yingjin Zhang.
© 2016 John Wiley & Sons, Ltd. Published 2016 by John Wiley & Sons, Ltd.

After Mao's death in 1976 and since Deng Xiaoping launched his economic reform policies in late 1970s, China's modernization project has accelerated with unprecedented speed. The Communists certainly spare no effort in encouraging the Chinese people to look forward and build a good life. With focus shifted to individual benefits, looking back at a time of material hardship and ideological treachery would seem unpalatable and unnecessary. If pain can be forgotten, it can certainly be done in a time of peace, progress, and prosperity. With the sanction of the government, painful memories of the recent past would seem to have been swept under the carpet, if not for many ordinary citizens' tenacity to record those traumatic experiences and capture individual memories in literature, arts, films, online blogging, and other available forms of representation.

The 3–4 years subsequent to the end of the Mao regime were a short period of literary vitality and productivity, until the Democracy Wall incident and the arrest of Wei Jingsheng in 1979. This literary wave calmed down considerably when the government officially denounced Bai Hua's screenplay *Unrequited Love* (*Kulian*) in 1981, followed by campaigns against "bourgeois liberalism" and "spiritual pollution." Deng's regime then showed a style of periodic expansion and contraction of political and ideological control (Schell and Shambaugh 1999: 3). Although grips were tightened once again, artistic and intellectual activities continued, albeit with less fervor, until around 1985 when the energy spiked up again in the heated culture fever among the intellectual elite. This new cycle of "emancipation of minds" ended in June 1989 when the military cracked down on the pro-democracy protests in Tiananmen Square.

Beginning in early 2000, there has been an increase of scholarly publications in the West investigating issues such as representations of violence, history and memory, individual human agency in the Maoist collectivism, and so on. Particularly in response to the 40th anniversary of the Cultural Revolution in 2006, there have been growing concerns about the dying off of the Great Famine survivors from the Great Leap Forward period, fading memories of the Cultural Revolution, and younger generations' palpable indifference, ignorance, and misguided perception of the Maoist legacies. A national amnesia thus lies at the core of the challenge facing those who believe that preserving memories of historical traumas is crucial to a better understanding of the past.

Literature produced in the immediate aftermath of the Cultural Revolution, known as "scar literature," has been generally ignored by literary scholars because it is deemed overtly formulaic and dogmatic. Sympathetic with Chinese writers who suffered tremendously during the Cultural Revolution, Michael Duke believes that scar literature is the "heart rending cry of 'the people' bursting forth out of the depths of their hitherto unexpressed pain and anguish," an "angry denunciation by 'the people' against their jailors and persecutors," a "collective purgation and purification" (Duke 1985: 63). But, is it good art? Duke thinks for certain it is not.

I contend that to judge these writings in terms of their "artistic value" while overlooking the heavily traumatized mind behind the literary work is a common oversight.

Duke devalues these writings for being "still primarily tendentious, artificial yet art-
less, and a far cry from the canons of critical realism" (Duke 1985: 67). Duke bases his
evaluation of scar literature on the artistic criteria of realism, comparing it with the
critical realism of the May Fourth era. Herein lies his problem: simply because the
narrative style of scar literature follows that of realism, it does not necessarily mean
that we have to limit our analysis in the same vein. On the contrary, our mode of interpretation should take into account the extreme condition under which such writings
were produced. Because Duke follows the criteria of realism, he inevitably reaches the
conclusion that the sole contribution of scar literature is nothing but sociopolitical
(Duke 1985: 96–97).

Duke's work was published in 1985, a time rather close to the texts he was studying, and it was also during the height of the Cold War. Anti-Communist sentiment
was popular in the West, and pro-democracy, pro-human rights were the thinking of
the day. It is only natural that Duke's moralistic stance was pronounced. With some
distance in time, since 2000 there has appeared more systematic studies on topics relevant to scar literature, such as trauma and violence, and generally speaking these
books have taken a more nuanced and relativistic approach. Xiaobin Yang (2002)
delineates the postmodern narrative techniques as an elusive way to probe into the
traumatic past. Yomi Braester (2003) puts scar literature squarely in the genre of
trauma studies. David Wang (2004) offers a comprehensive study that traces the insufferable human tragedies instigated in the name of history. Ban Wang (2004) focuses
on the dynamics between trauma, memory, and history writing in post-Mao literature.
Sabina Knight (2006) examines the issue of moral agency and subjectivity in post-Mao
writers' reflection on their traumatic experiences. Yibing Huang (2007) argues for
reinstituting the legacy of the Cultural Revolution in studies of contemporary Chinese
literature. Michael Berry (2008) traces the recordings, mainly in films and in literature, of violence and suffering in nineteenth-century and twentieth-century China.

Decades later, now, as we approach post-Mao literature, contextual understanding is
pivotal to our reinterpretation of a collection of writings that was produced under
quite unusual circumstances. An important factor to inspect is the historical and
political condition under which censorship guidelines were created, and how they
might have affected the tone of fictional writings and the trajectory of literary
development in the aftermath of the Cultural Revolution. Political situations in the
immediate post-Mao years were precarious; the Cultural Revolution and particularly
Mao's role in it were extremely controversial and potentially explosive. The Party
directive on the matter was aimed at shaping the public discourse, and therefore it had
to be crafted in such a way that it would satisfy as well as contain the popular sentiment while guiding people's thinking in the direction the Party desired.

As mentioned earlier, several book-length studies of modern Chinese literature published after 2000 by scholars in the West have taken the stance that scar literature
actually reflects a deep concern on how the idea of "history" has been used and abused
by ideologues to serve political interests. These scholars observe that explorations of
the relationship between the individual subjectivity and History (with capital "H")

were a common preoccupation shared by the "scarred" writers who pondered on the possibility of finding humane ways to proceed with revolutionary agendas while treating the notion of "history" correctly. Scholarly treatments of these texts often concentrate on analyzing the formal features of the narrative, interpreting theoretical and philosophical significations spawn from narrative strategies, or documenting topical and stylistic changes in the texts. In other words, attention on traumatic writings has been placed more on the textual, and less on the human and the ethical, aspect.

Experiences, memories, and images of those incredible Mao years have been a consistent source of inspiration for contemporary Chinese writers. One way writers capture the traumatic is by inscribing it in the body—the tormented, mutilated, deformed, and retarded body/bodily parts. This metaphorically deconstructive strategy generates a hidden testimony to the corporeal abjection inherent in the Maoist collective body, raising questions about the brutal erasure of the individual. In many contemporary short stories and novels, Maoist atrocities are mediated solely by their traces in the post-Mao contemporary everyday life.

One of the characteristics of representing the traumatic past in the everyday is returning to a bewildering or veiled past. The story may be about both the traumatic past of the survivor and his/her present-day condition, but the distinction between the two temporalities is made to emphasize the differences between the traumatic experience itself and the contemporary lives of the survivors and their children. What jumps out is the disruption of the temporal equilibrium read as a rejection of dissolving memory into the present life, thus keeping the survivor's traumatic memory as an unresolved issue. Han Shaogong's roots-searching stories such as "Homecoming" ("*Guiqulai*," 1985), "Pa Pa Pa" ("*Bababa*," 1985), and "Woman Woman Woman" ("*Nününü*," 1986) betray the author's continuous struggle with the haunting memory of a horrible past that still exists outside of historical time. Roots represent not the cultural foundation of the ancient civilization but the volatile, unstable, and treacherous milieu of the Maoist past that is the kennel of the haunting memory of a trauma. The final line of "Homecoming" exclaimed by the protagonist—"I am tired, I'll never be able to get away from this gigantic I! Mama!" (M. Cheung 1992: 20)—testifies to the insurmountable existential barrier for the individual to align his split self trapped inside the body: the "I" who lives in the present, and the other "I" who is eternally suspended in the irreconcilable tormenting past.

A particularly poignant issue concerning writings of collective trauma is silence. Silence manifests in many forms—in forgetting, distortion, absence of confession, and perpetuation of (self) censorship. Official rhetoric on the Maoist atrocities such as the Great Famine and the Cultural Revolution has a strong silencing power over public memory discourse. The task for writers is thus to create a language to articulate this silence. Works such as Ha Jin's *The Crazed* (2002) and Han Shaogong's *Dictionary of Maqiao* (1997)—despite these two writers' different geopolitical locations and writing environments—are efforts to disquiet the silence with a "language of silence" that releases the silenced/repressed memories and rearticulates them in a new syntax and lexicon. The oppressed memory of the crazed Professor Yang in *The Crazed* is released and spoken through the language of madness and delusion. After a long literary journey followed by 10 years of silence, Han Shaogong now returns with a dictionary that is filled with words and phrases with meanings, definitions, and usages that run in direct contradiction to present-day Mandarin Chinese. This local language of a remote village is, in essence, an ontological project for Han Shaogong to reclaim the lost self. Having traveled in search for Chu culture via the figure of the great ancient poet Qu Yuan, Han Shaogong now arrives at the lexicography of Maqiao that rewrites the normative codes of the social and the historical, the factual and the truthful, and hence the very constitution of the collective memory of the Maoist revolutionary years.

Another example of articulating silence can be found in Zhang Xianliang's novel titled *My Bodhi Tree* (*Wode putishu*, 1997). This novel is based on the diary Zhang kept in 1960, amidst the Great Famine, when he was in the labor camp in the wake of the Anti-Rightist Campaign. Zhang's cryptic and minimalistic diary entries record only the most inconsequential items of the day—his manual labor, trifle words with fellow inmates or supervisors, scrapes of food he had or he desperately wanted to have, and so on. The physical pain, mental anguish, and the constant hunger that constitute his imprisoned condition—things that Zhang could not write down at that time—speak the profound silence that permeates the entire diary. To reconstruct his memories of the past, Zhang has to navigate through pages and pages of negation—of what is unwritten and unspoken. By attempting to fill the void he was forced to leave in the diary, Zhang has to relieve the traumatic past, almost day by day and sometimes moment by moment, in order to annotate each entry. Contrasting with the briefness of the diary, the lengthy commentaries make the original silence ever more overwhelming. Zhang's language of irony, satire, and self-mockery becomes the only language of testimony tolerable to the Party on the historical Great Famine that has largely remained silenced in the public domain. The double silence here—the individual's and the state's—speaks volumes of the moral deficiency in the Chinese authority's handling of the Maoist atrocities.

The nightmarish world in Can Xue's fictional writing bespeaks the deep emotions in human psyche and the memory traces or imprints that traumatic experiences have left in this psychic level. Can Xue frequently evokes animalistic imageries, dirty and abject objects, irrational human behaviors, and magical transformation of life forms to express the intensity of feelings of fear, paranoia, and aggression in situations that are often unnamable and unnamed but are indicative of disaster and deprivation. In her autobiographical "Beautiful Southern Summer Days" ("*Meili nanfang zhixia*," 2000), Can Xue depicts the extreme hunger during the Great Famine through the figure of her grandmother, a shaman-like old woman who seems to have extraordinary senses of smell, sight, and hearing, and also the uncanny faculty to connect with the natural and the supernatural worlds. She sees ghosts, hears sounds coming from the earth, and is able to find wild herbs and forage them into edible foods—a common practice during the Great Famine—to feed her grandchildren. The grandmother dies of exhaustion and starvation. On her deathbed, she gives the bowl of thin gruel from neighbors to the children: "the gruel tastes sweet; maybe it's grandma's blood, there's sugar in the blood. We drank grandma's blood so that our young lives could go on" (Can Xue 2000: 7).

The blood of her grandmother now flows inside her and occasionally she can still hear her grandmother's heavy footsteps echoing in her veins. With the fusion of her grandmother's blood, the granddaughter inherits the extraordinary sensory abilities and transmutes onto her fictional world what these sensations bring her.

In "The Hut on the Mountain" (1985), Can Xue writes about the terrifying and suffocating atmosphere of the Cultural Revolution. The narrator is a youngster through whose perspective we are presented with a world of uncertainty and paranoia. This short story is important in a number of ways. It marks a drastic departure from the formulaic realistic fiction of scar literature, albeit the common subject matter is still the memory of the Cultural Revolution. Published shortly after scar literature fell out of popular favor, "The Hut on the Mountain" continues the testimonial writing but fills the psychical void of its predecessor by representing the traumatic memories of the Mao regime's last decade of violence and chaos. Praised as one of her most celebrated works, the story also reveals Can Xue's remarkable capability of writing in a style that is uniquely hers, in a language that captures the intangible unconscious thoughts and deeply buried emotions born of traumatic experiences. In an interview, Can Xue says that she writes so as to "release reason and senses" into the plane of the unconscious and to reveal a "dream world" that is "bigger and deeper" than the reality we live in (McCandlish 2002).

As Xiaobin Yang (2002: 90) aptly points out, the psychic disturbances and suggestive fears and paranoia in this short story are emblematic of "the untraceable, traumatized historical experience of psychic assaults from which Can Xue—like all others who underwent the 'proletarian dictatorship'—has suffered." The hut that sits on top of a barren mountain behind the first-person narrator's house represents the narrator's "other" psychic space that traps an unknown person who has the same "dark purple pouches" under the eyes (Can Xue 2007: 326), just like what the narrator sees in her own image reflecting in the mirror after a futile attempt to climb up the hill to find the hut. On two trips up the mountain, the narrator's vision is always blurred by bright light, "seeing nothing but the white pebbles glowing with flames" (Can Xue 2007: 328). Unable to see anything the second time around, the narrator determines, as the narrative ends, that there is simply no hut.

Instead of using the hut on the mountain as the overlooking, observing eye, hence implying the possibility of a detached perspective of the narrator whose vision anchors the development of the narrative, Can Xue obstructs the field of vision by refracting it through the mirror and through the shining white pebbles. The narrator's limited capacity to see reflects the fragmented memories of a child or adolescent survivor. As Can Xue's purpose is never to objectively or realistically represent an empirical experience, her narrative here describes not historical details but subjective impressions and abstract feelings of a certain (traumatic) experience. When the narrator climbs up to the mountain the second time, her vision, once again, is blinded by the white light. Instead of discussing whether the hut is an illusion, more significant in this final scene is the white light that subsumes the narrator and the hut, for this signifies the psychic abyss that forever traps the narrator in her frightful, paranoid, and angry state.

The narrator's suspicion of her environment is revealed through the absence of trust she has for her parents and the lack of security she feels in her home, which she believes is constantly under surveillance. It is important to note that the narrative is framed within the hierarchy of a family, and the narrating perspective is that of a child's (regardless of her age) and not of a parent's. The narrator describes her mother's smile as "forced," her stare "ferocious," and her demeanor deceptive (Can Xue 2007: 325–326). The narrator hears thieves pacing outside her house at night and sees someone poke holes on the window screens. She believes her father is one of those wolves that circle and howl around the house at night. Her personal space, symbolized by her drawer, is always being intruded upon by her family members. The violated subject space of the individual and the torn fabric of her family and community are reminiscent of a past troubled time when there was little trust in the society, when the unbreakable bonds among family members and friends, between teachers and pupils, citizens and their government, were routinely broken.

Children are the quintessential figures that function in the narrative of trauma as the reciprocal of extreme deprivation in the everyday. Mo Yan's trauma has its root in his childhood and adolescence during the years of Great Famine and the subsequent Cultural Revolution. He recalls in numerous interviews, most notably in his Nobel Prize acceptance speech (2012), that memories of his early childhood are filled with excruciating hunger and isolation, and constant violence incurred by desperation. Children in Mo Yan's fiction are often the recipients of extreme deprivation in the everyday. Characters such as the child narrator and his superpower companion in "Iron Child" ("*Tiehai*," 1993) or Blacky in "The Transparent Carrot" ("*Touming de hong luobo*," 1984) often create or live in a magical world as a means of escape and protection. Similar to what Michael Rothberg (2000: 109) calls the "borderland" in a conceptualization of traumatic realism, this magical world of Mo Yan is where the vulnerability of children and their right to grow are slain by extreme conditions of hunger and brutality.

As Mo Yan (2012) admits, Blacky is one character with whom he identifies most closely: "That dark-skinned boy with the superhuman ability to suffer and a superhuman degree of sensitivity represents the soul of my entire fictional output. Not one of all the fictional characters I've created since then is as close to my soul as he is. Or put a different way, among all the characters a writer creates, there is always one that stands above all the others. For me, that laconic boy is the one." Notice the first characteristic that Mo Yan describes in his most beloved character: the child's "superhuman ability to suffer." The underlying tone of trauma and victimhood is discernable. Through a child's body, Mo Yan transcribes the unspeakable suffering of the people during the Great Leap Forward, which created the largest human-made famine in history (Thaxton 2008; Yang Jisheng 2012).

Set against the backdrop of the Great Leap Forward, Blacky's skinny and barely clothed body symbolizes the vulnerable and pathetic existence of the people, children and adults alike. Blacky is the youngest worker, in fact the only child laborer, in the work site. All the adult workers care for this child as if he were their own. It is on this child's body that the collective hardship is exemplified. His fragile body bears excruciating physical injuries from the manual work, and yet the pain he feels often carries him into an imaginary world. Blacky's ability to see beyond the harsh reality and to create a world filled with the beauty and richness in nature provides relief, though imaginary, to the otherwise unbearable grim life of daily toil. It is through such contrast that the sign of trauma is revealed in an otherwise even-toned and undramatic narrative. The epitome of Mo Yan's most beloved character is represented in the final scene in which Blacky's new clothes are taken away by a team leader as a punishment for stealing carrots. The farmer, whose carrots field is ruined by Blacky, pleas with the cadre and weeps at the sight of Blacky's naked body as the boy disappears into the yellow hemp field. The image of this boy's fully naked body, and by extension the image of children, thus becomes the signifier of trauma in Mo Yan's fictional landscape of Gaomi, his hometown.

A child narrator is also the key to many of Su Tong's traumatic writing. Common themes found in Su Tong's "Toon Street" ("*Xiangchunshu jie*") series are recurring images and themes of death and corpses, hunger and preoccupation with food, senseless violence among adolescents, and mock trials or persecutions of children by children. This is a collection of stories that take place on the very street where Su Tong grew up and spent his childhood years roaming around. Every story in the series is narrated in the naive voice of a child or a youngster who is often blasé and uncomprehending of the horrors he witnesses. Whatever the story plot, Su Tong consistently depicts the everyday life full of small cruelties and the slightly twisted psychologies and behaviors of children. This somewhat malicious and absurd quotidian existence represents the imprints or traces of the crazed milieu of the Cultural Revolution left in the mind of Su Tong, who was then a child himself. The aura of violence persists in Su Tong's fictional world, manifested in the failure of rationality and collapse of moral codes of interpersonal relationships. Every child or teenager fends for himself/herself on the street, as their daily life suffers a nearly complete absence of adult supervision. As older children are constantly battling for turfs, younger ones are busy emulating the same violence and brutality. Such is the normative existence for the children in the "Toon Street" series.

The narrative's frustrating ambiguity and lack of closure is reflected through its characters' futile and confused struggle with the vexing presence of the horrific and bewildering past in which family and society were in chaos. The battle with displaced memory and fantasy may also be narrated through split voices, which indicate that the knowledge of trauma is registered in a perpetual troping (or the transmitted or inherited memory) of the event by a torn psyche. *To Live* (1998), a novel probably most representative of Yu Hua's writing on the Maoist past, exemplifies the psychological tug of war of a child survivor's effort to negotiate the tension and discrepancy between memory and reality. In a 1993 "Foreword" to the novel, Yu Hua writes that, no matter how enthralling the past, it inevitably is veiled with a layer of fantasy created through imagination and reasoning. In his "Foreword" to a 1996 Korean edition, Yu Hua explains that the reason for choosing the phrase "to live" as the title is the phrase's many connotations, among which is its implication of the collective endurance by the Chinese people in living through the past decades. He further expounds: "Such is literature—it tells what the writer is conscious of, and at the same time it also tells what the writer is unconscious of—and this is when the reader needs to step forward and speak up" (Yu Hua 1998: 4).

Yu Hua is clearly inviting readers' interpretation of this simple but rich story of testimony to a harsh past. Without a tinge of criticism of the Maoist policies or the Party, *To Live* is an existential revaluation of the human costs from the disasters of Mao's radical social experiments. It is an occasion for readers (and particularly Chinese readers) to reflect from a humanistic perspective on the militant era. But the task of reevaluation is not simply that of the readers'; it is also the writer Yu Hua whose unconscious mind wrestles to speak through. The unconscious mind that Yu Hua speaks of may very well be his fractured memory and impressions of the Cultural Revolution. The struggle between the writer's rational conscious self and his intuitive unconscious mind manifests in the split narrating voices, whereby tensions are constantly felt. The narrative is framed with the narrator's speaking voice whose urban background transmutes the protagonist Fugui and his harrowing experiences and turns them into an everlasting tale of human suffering.

In the process of capturing—and constructing—fragmented memories of the past into a coherent story, forgetting is also taking place. Reliability of memory is what preoccupies Ge Fei's memory writings. In "Remembering Mr. Wuyou" ("*Zhuiyi Wuyou xiansheng*," 1986), the ability to recall is reduced to its very mechanical function, that of memorization. This is the only form of memory that is reliable to Ge Fei. In "Green Yellow" ("*Qinghuang*," 1989), the past, even though it is clearly dated as the year of 1967, at the end is rendered a problematic notion by ways of unreliable memories, legends, local annex, and archival materials. In Ge Fei's look back into the recent past, memory and history are empty signifiers; what remains tangible is language with its multitude of signification. Such is the post-Mao generation writers' acute awareness of the dialectic between memory and history, remembering and forgetting, as well as a profound anxiety about their transmitted memory of the Maoist past.

This alienating feeling is doubled by Ge Fei's typical narrator, such as the one in "Green Yellow," who is always someone from the outside, as if an intruder into a time and place where he obviously does not belong, and yet the irresistible impulse to know (the truth) compels him to carry on with his investigation, despite the incongruent nature of the investigation and constant obstacles. The narrative of "Green Yellow" is propelled by the narrator's many encounters with displaced archival materials or local people's lost memories. Paul Ricoeur (2004: 417) delineates the idea of forgetting as taking two forms: "forgetting through the erasure of traces," and "a reversible forgetting even toward the idea of the unforgettable: this is the reserve of forgetting." What Ge Fei's narrator–investigator encounters throughout the narrative is the first form of forgetting, "erasure of traces," and through this very process, the author Ge Fei hopes to release "the reserve of forgetting" in order to awaken memories, the second form of forgetting. The unforgettable is the kernel manifested in a certain mysterious, unspeakable event that the villagers are reluctant to talk about; the unforgettable is also the lucid nature of the truth that the narrator struggles to find. At the end, he can only "define"—not "find"—the meaning of "Green Yellow" in a dictionary.

Ge Fei's skepticism toward memory and history is not uncommon in the generation of child survivors of the Great Famine or the Cultural Revolution. For them, the "transferred knowledge" (Hoffman 2004: xv) of the Maoist era has been modified by the government, and Mao himself has been both humanized (by historians) and deified (by some sectors of the population) in contemporary China. Questions must be asked about the reliability of memory and history, and that is what preoccupies Ge Fei in his earlier writings. It is only in his "Peach Blossom Beauty" ("*Renmian taohua*") trilogy (2004–2011) that he confronts memory and history in allegorical form. I focus here on the trilogy's second novel, *Dreaming of Mountains and Rivers* (*Shanhe rumeng*, 2007), since it deals with the two major historical events of the Mao era: the Great Leap Forward and the Cultural Revolution. Here, memory does not belong to the characters but to the author. In the novel's postscript, Ge Fei (2007) writes that, even though the story begins in the 1950s before he was born, he has already possessed deep memories of that era because history is not like the page of a book—it cannot be easily turned over; and because imagination is memory, what we can see is only ourselves in front of the mirror of history.

Ge Fei's deep memories of a time before his birth in 1964 imply the transmitted nature of such memories *vis-à-vis* history and imagination. In this postmemorial writing, the irreconcilable space between memory and history, which imagination attempts to bridge, is the utopianism that drives the first two novels of Ge Fei's trilogy. *Dreaming of Mountains and Rivers* is a novel of a double utopian vision—the social utopian vision of Mayor Tan Gongda manifested in his map of a fully modernized Mei County, and the utopian emotive landscape manifested in Tan's relationships with women, in particular with Yao Peipei. Narrated in a style reminiscent of classical Chinese novels, the narrative shows how this double utopian vision gradually develops into a chilling and absurd dystopia of totalitarianism, paranoia, violence of rape and murder, and death through persecution.

The first half of the novel is filled with inferences to the collectivization project, the follies of the Great Leap Forward, and the harsh living conditions it has created. Tan's social experiment projects in Mei County are a microcosm of Mao's utopian plan for the whole China to make a great modernization leap, aimed to get ahead of Britain and the United States. While Tan's modernization projects for his own county end up in complete disaster, he later finds proximity of his social utopian vision in the Hua Family Compound, a fully developed community of modernization and collectivization where everyone is equal and everything is shared, including private thoughts. The depiction of the Hua Family Compound in the second half of the novel clearly mimics the ideal vision of the society to be created through the Great Leap Forward and the Cultural Revolution: an egalitarian society with selfless people who are trained to exercise self-disciplining actions upon any slight ideological mishap.

By giving Tan his naïve idealism, Ge Fei portrays him to be more a Don Quixote-like character than a Mao-like character. But what is most curious is Ge Fei's literary and historical re-visioning of a most horrific era in the PRC. Utopianism as seen through Tan's naïve and idealistic personality and attitude seems to suggest a certain desire of Ge Fei for reconciliation with the Maoist past. This desire for reconciliation is not a happy one but rather one of reluctance and skepticism. Tan's final conversation with the Hua Family Compound's mysterious ruler/controller Guo Congnian on this socialist utopia centers on the question of human nature. A perfect sociopolitical system is one that can predict human nature and regulate it to achieve proper balance. But neither Guo nor Tan is convinced that this socialist utopian vision can ever be achieved and kept alive.

In Ge Fei's fragmented memories of the Maoist past, there are no traces of violence or trauma but instead dreams and idealism. But an inherent suffocation is prevalent in the emotive utopian landscape of Tan's love affair with Yao Peipei, who is on the run after killing her rapist. With the letters Yao has sent to him periodically, Tan is able to map out her escape route but only to discover that Yao is actually running in a circle, with him as the center. Not only is Yao trapped in this circle, Tan is similarly trapped in the mental map of her escape route. Neither one can succeed in this desperate attempt to break free. The failure of the social utopian vision now extends to the decimation of the emotive utopian landscape when Yao is finally captured and prosecuted. The last scene of the novel is chilling and ironic: in his dying moment, Tan sees himself and the already dead Yao fantasize about a fully realized Communist society where there is no more fear and corruption, no more hereditary sin and endless humiliation, and no more ruthless cadres and frightful civilians. Utopia, or at least the Maoist utopia, has died an ironic death in this novel. If Ge Fei is attempting for a sense of reconciliation with the painful Maoist past, he realizes that it must come with a price—that of disillusionment and loss of faith in any sort of social and political system.

The effects of trauma can only be felt belatedly. The Maoist legacy has manifested in various forms for more than three decades after Mao's death: in literature and arts, in media and tourism, in fashion trends, and in "lite" memory writings that are easy to market and consume. The Chinese government certainly has encouraged a "lite" version of such remembrance—one can write about the positive aspects of the experiences or the bitterness of the sufferings so long as the memory narrative adheres to the personal aspects without any apparent attempt to discuss the causes and ramifications of a massive violent event that created tragedies to individuals. More often than not, media representations of the pre-reform era, such as found in popular television series and historical documentaries, are "sanitized" to portray the righteous Communists fighting through hardship to achieve glory; Mao-style performances in variety shows are always "beautified" to evoke shallow resemblance or mimicry in the costume and look of that era—all of which evoke not only nostalgic sentiment among the older generation, they also project to younger generations an exotic appearance of that era. But China's rapid economic development also has made the Chinese society more open, and means of communication more accessible. The wide availability of cell phones, the Internet, and social media such as micro blogging allow information to disseminate quickly and networking to be formed. Although these social media are able to evade government restrictions only temporarily, the resilience of Chinese netizens is not to be underestimated.

Despite its many shapes and forms, the collective traumatic memory is hidden beneath the surface, awaiting us to uncover it. I have demonstrated in this chapter that much of post-Mao literature can and should be read as testimony, so that we are able to establish a systematic understanding of victimhood and a methodology to help reclaim the victim's voice and subjectivity. With the 60th anniversary of the founding of PRC on October 1, 2009, the early Republican era and the years leading up to 1949 have become popular materials for TV mini-series and films, most notably *The Founding of a Republic* (*Jianguo daye*, directed by Han Sanping and Huang Jianxin, 2009), a star-studded film with a team of more than 100 top Chinese actors, filmmakers, news anchors, and comedians for the anniversary celebration (L. Lim 2009). However, in spite of the government's repeated spin control, there remains a body of literature that bears witness, by the survivors and their children, to the calamities of the Maoist past, and it is a moral impediment that our future generations must not overlook this dimension of contemporary Chinese literary writings.

REFERENCES

Berry, Michael. 2008. *The History of Pain: Trauma in Modern Chinese Literature and Film*. New York: Columbia University Press.

Braester, Yomi. 2010. *Paint the City Red: Chinese Cinema and the Urban Contract*. Durham, NC: Duke University Press.

Can Xue 殘雪. 2000. *Meili nanfang zhixia* 美麗南方之夏 (Beautiful southern summer days). Kunming: Yunnan chubanshe.

Cheung, Esther M. K. 2012. "Introduction to the New Edition: New Ends in a City of Transition." In Leung Ping-kwan, *City at the End of Time*. Trans. Gordon T. Osing and Leung Ping-kwan. Hong Kong: Hong Kong University Press. 1–19.

Cheung, Martha, trans. 1992. *Homecoming? And Other Stories by Han Shaogong*. Hong Kong: Chinese University of Hong Kong.

Duke, Michael S. 1985. *Blooming and Contending: Chinese Literature in the Post-Mao Era*. Bloomington: Indiana University Press.

Ge Fei 格非. 2007. *Shanhe rumeng* 山河入夢 (Dreaming of mountains and rivers). Taipei: Renren.

Ha Jin. 2002. *The Crazed*. New York: Pantheon.

Hoffman, Eva. 2004. *After Such Knowledge: Memory, History, and the Legacy of the Holocaust*. New York: Public Affairs.

Huang, Yibing. 2007. *Contemporary Chinese Literature: From the Cultural Revolution to the Future*. New York: Palgrave Macmillan.

Knight, Sabina. 2006. *The Heart of Time: Moral Agency in Twentieth-Century Chinese Fiction*. Cambridge, MA: Harvard University Asia Center.

Lim, Louisa. 2009. "Chinese Moviegoers Get a Blockbuster, With a Spin," NPR.org. Accessed 13 March 2012. http://www.npr.org/templates/story/story.php?storyId=112918961.

McCandlish, Laura. 2002. "Stubbornly Illuminating 'the Dirty Snow that Refuses to Melt':

A Conversation with Can Xue." MCLC Resource Center (11 Dec. 2012). Accessed 1 July 2014. http://mclc.osu.edu/rc/pubs/mccandlish.htm.

Mo Yan. 2012. "Nobel Lecture: Storytellers." Trans. Howard Goldblatt. Nobelprize.org. Accessed 23 June 2013. http://www.nobelprize.org/nobel_prizes/literature/laureates/2012/yan-lecture_en.html.

Ricoeur, Paul. 2004. *Memory, History, Forgetting*. Trans. Kathleen Blamey and David Pellauer. Chicago: University of Chicago Press.

Rothberg, Michael. 2000. *Traumatic Realism: The Demands of Holocaust Representation*. Minneapolis: University of Minnesota Press.

Schell, Orville, and David Shambaugh. Eds. 1999. *China Reader: The Reform Era*. New York: Vintage Books.

Thaxton, Ralph A., Jr. 2008. *Catastrophe and Contention in Rural China: Mao's Great Leap Forward Famine and the Origins of Righteous Resistance in Da Fo Village*. New York: Cambridge University Press.

Wang, Ban. 2004. *Illuminations from the Past: Trauma, Memory, and History in Modern China*. Stanford, CA: Stanford University Press.

Wang, David Der-wei. 2004. *The Monster That Is History: History, Violence, and Fictional Writing in Twentieth-Century China*. Berkeley: University of California Press.

Yang, Jisheng. 2012. *Tombstone: The Great Chinese Famine, 1958–1962*. New York: Farrar, Straus and Giroux.

Yang, Xiaobin. 2002. *The Chinese Postmodern: Trauma and Irony in Chinese Avant-Garde Fiction*. Ann Arbor: University of Michigan Press.

Yu, Hua 余華. 1998. *Huozhe* 活著. Haikou: Nanhai chuban gongsi.

29

A Brief Overview of Chinese-Language Scholarship on Modern Chinese Literature

Chen Sihe (translated by Alvin Ka Hin Wong)

The Development of Scholarship on Modern Chinese Literature in China

In mainland China, "modern Chinese literature" (*Zhongguo xiandai wenxue*) is a specialized discipline covering from the New Culture Movement in 1917 to the establishment of the PRC in 1949. The coverage has gradually expanded to include late Qing literature and contemporary literature, the latter encompassing post-1949 literature. This institutional formation differs from China studies in the United States where Asian studies departments designate modern Chinese literature as the continuation of classical Chinese literature. In the PRC, modern Chinese literature becomes an emerging second-level discipline within the first-level discipline of "Chinese language and literature."[1] Therefore, Chinese-language scholarship on modern Chinese literature comes with a longer trajectory than its counterparts overseas. Its disciplinary lineage can be divided into three phases: New Literature in 1917–1949, modern Chinese literature in 1950–1984, and twentieth-century Chinese literature after 1985. These categories influence how scholars approach modern Chinese literature with specific historical constraints on knowledge production.

A Companion to Modern Chinese Literature, First Edition. Edited by Yingjin Zhang.
© 2016 John Wiley & Sons, Ltd. Published 2016 by John Wiley & Sons, Ltd.

The phase of New Literature

The first phase of New Literature refers to literature and literary criticism proposed by such prominent May Fourth intellectuals and writers as Chen Duxiu, Hu Shi, and Lu Xun. They championed the vernacular as the main linguistic style, modeled on genres of Western literature (e.g., short story, novel, prose, new poetry, and drama); they also critiqued Chinese society and its cultural decline by promoting individual freedom and humane literature. Standing somewhat on the opposite platform is soon-to-be-antiquated elite literature (such as classical poetry and Tongcheng-style classical prose) and academically marginalized popular fiction. The "new" in New Literature represents the concept of modernity, which is symbolic of Chinese subjects marching toward historical progress. Following the patriotic students–led May Fourth Movement in 1919, New Literature gained legitimation in national education sectors. The New Culture Movement has produced many writers and intellectuals, including the afore-mentioned Hu Shi, Lu Xun, as well as Zhou Zouren, Qian Xuantong, Liu Bannong, Guo Moruo, Yu Dafu, Mao Dun, and Zheng Zhenduo. These pioneers published many works that galvanized New Literature and set the stage for the early study of modern Chinese literature.

We can trace the research on New Literature to the 1930s. In 1935, the Liangyou Press published a 10-volume compendium to Chinese New Literature under Zhao Jiabi's general editorship, which for the first time systematically accounts for the emer-gence of New Literature (1917–1927). The compendium consists of one volume on literary theory, one volume on literary debates, three volumes on fiction, two volumes on prose essay, and one volume each on New Poetry, drama, and bibliography. The volume editors Hu Shi, Zheng Zhenduo, Mao Dun, Lu Xun, Zheng Boqi, Zhou Zuoren, Yu Dafu, Zhu Ziqing, Hong Shen, and A Ying each wrote a long introduction to evaluate the achievements of New Literature. This compendium was also endorsed by intellectual pioneer Cai Yuanpei with his long preface. Because these contributors were all at the forefront of the New Culture Movement, their statures confirmed the unique value of the compendium. Around the same time, several well-regarded insti-tutions initiated curriculum on New Literature. The surviving archive retains Wang Zhefu's lectures (1933) at Shanxi Provincial Institute of Education, and Zhu Ziqing's lectures (1982) at Tsinghua University in Beijing. By the early 1930s, scholarship on New Literature gradually stood out from general literary criticism. Although only a few institutions designed curricula on New Literature, this early period saw the incip-ience of New Literature as an academic subject in its own right.

The New Culture Movement also gave rise to the emergence of outstanding literary critics, who belonged to various literary societies that publicized their ideological plat-forms and attacked others. Some prominent critics include Mao Dun and Zheng Zhenduo from the Literary Association; Cheng Fangwu from the Creation Society; Liang Shiqiu from the Crescent Moon Society; Zhou Zuoren from the Yusi Society; and Qu Qiubai, Feng Xuefeng, and Hu Feng from the League of Left-Wing Writers. Their literary criticism influenced the emerging theory of New Literature. By the mid-1930s, professors from institutions such as Peking University, Tsinghua University, and Yenching University also participated in criticism on New Literature, especially in the area of New Poetry. Beijing-style (*Jingpai*) literary critics such as Zhu Guangqian, Liang Zongdai, and Ye Gongchao began to diverge from the parochialism of creative writers' circles and formed more objective criticism on literature and art. The most prolific critic at the time was Li Jianwu (penname Liu Xiwei), whose meticulous interpretations of well-known writers such as Ba Jin, Shen Congwen, Cao Yu, and Bian Zhilin sparked debates among writers themselves. Li's inspirational criticism departed from the increasingly narrow ideological perspectives of leftist criticism and provided a model for subsequent research on these writers.

The phase of modern Chinese literature

The second phase of research on modern Chinese literature (1949–1985) began after China entered into new political configurations in 1949. The "modern" here does not fully correlate with the "modernity" in other parts of the world, nor does it equate to "contemporary." Rather, "modern" here marks a designated political concept between 1919 and 1949, when Maoist politics propagated the idea of "new democracy" (*xin minzhu zhuyi*) during the revolutionary period. Therefore, some literary historiography also refers to literature produced in this period as "literature in the revolutionary period of new democracy." This periodization corresponds to the subsequent categorization of "socialist literature" in the post-1949 context. This revolutionary periodization necessarily compromised intellectual thought, and "modern Chinese literary history" became an integral part of "China's revolutionary history" under the Communist leadership. Dissecting literary history from a broader cultural–historical worldview, it becomes evident that conditions of intellectual mentality were formed under the unique culture of war against imperialism. Even after the end of World War II, the shadow of the civil war between the Nationalists and Communists and the subsequent Cold War continued to hold sway over the collective consciousness of Chinese people. This aspect of war mentality holds true across the Taiwan Straits.

Given the necessity of consolidating political sovereignty, modern literary scholarship was elevated to a crucial platform. Research on modern Chinese literature gained institutional legitimacy as a level-two discipline with substantial funding, which opened the door for future research. However, it is the same historical condition that led to many drawbacks. The most pressing problem was the threat of literary studies becoming a mere tool of ideology. In many political campaigns during the 1950–1960s, writers were silenced, suppressed, sent to labor camps, and subjected to all kinds of personal humiliation. Not only did literary studies fail to protest such injustices, but it became an instrument to erase the names of problematic writers. Given the imperative of politicization, some scholars even misconstrued historical truth in order to collaborate in the state's repression of intellectual thought.

Nonetheless, literary scholarship still carried on its academic mission, especially in the anthologizing of literary history and establishment of research on Lu Xun. Modern Chinese literary history was institutionalized as a legitimate field within higher institutions, and various literary histories edited by scholars such as Wang Yao, Liu Shousong, Zhang Bilai, and Tang Tao have largely converged in their critical appraisals of the characteristics, meanings, and receptions of modern Chinese writers. All this contributed to a particular model of literary history. Wang Yao's history (1953) still employs the concept of New Literature, but it already designates the period of 1919–1949 as a historical watershed. A student of Zhu Ziqing and a specialist of traditional Chinese literature, Wang continued Zhu's tradition of methodological research, and his history provides a concrete foundation for future research.

Equally impressive achievements were made in studies of Lu Xun, who had been controversial before his death in 1936. Specifically, some leftists who proposed the idea of revolutionary literature treated Lu Xun as a *passé* intellectual representative of the declining class. Yet, since he became the titular head of the leftist writers, another group of leftist critics defended him. For example, Qu Qiubai's 1930s works (reprint 1980) traced Lu Xun's maturation from evolutionism to class-based critique, and Qu's works on Lun Xun have a long-lasting impact. Mao Zedong also presented the official accolade to Lu Xun. After 1949, Lu Xun was glorified as "a great revolutionary, thinker, and literary giant." In addition, his close disciples such as Feng Xuefeng, Hu Feng, and Li Helin played important roles in proliferating Lu Xun studies in the early 1950s. Another group of Lu Xun's friends such as Xu Shoushang, Tai Jingnong, and Li Liewen, who had migrated to postwar Taiwan, also disseminated the spirit of Lu Xun and New Literature in a place that experienced 50 years of Japanese colonization. However, under the White Terror imposed through martial law, the Nationalist government suppressed leftist intellectual culture in Taiwan, and the mere name of Lu Xun warranted censorship. Meanwhile, beginning in 1955, the Communist government in the mainland began a series of political persecutions, and several of Lu Xun's former protégés such as Hu Feng, Feng Xuefeng, and Xiao Jun were criticized.

Even under political repressions in the 1950s, most scholars of modern Chinese literature studied Lu Xun in one way or another. Within leftist intellectual work, Ding Jingtang stands out as the most prolific, editing the biographies and bibliography on Qu Qiubai and five other leftist intellectual giants. Under the support of book collectors such as Qu Guangxi and Xie Danru, Ding archived more than 50 different kinds of underground leftist periodicals that existed in the 1930s. Meanwhile, Xue Suizhi at Shandong Normal College was the first to systematically edit a sizable bibliography on modern writers in 1960, which shaped the contour of this field. Other notable studies on modern Chinese writers at that time include Zeng Huapeng and Fan Boqun's research on Yu Dafu, Qian Gurong's on Cao Yu, Yang Feng's on Ba Jin, and Ye Ziming's on Mao Dun. In their scholarship, one finds less ideologically driven contents and more sympathetic readings. Overall, these studies objectively assess the uniqueness of modern Chinese writers.

During the Cultural Revolution when all scholarly activities came to a halt, leftist intellectuals in Japan became serious in their research on modern Chinese literature. Most illustrious is Noboru Maruyama's collection of essays (2005) written from the 1960s to 1995, where he diagnoses the root cause of the Cultural Revolution and the reasons behind the persecution of leftist literary movement. His deep suspicion of the Cultural Revolution is expressed in his sympathy for writers such as Zhou Yang, Ding Ling, Ai Qing, and He Qifang. Noboru also devotes attention to the ways in which Lu Xun carved out a unique position within the debates on revolutionary literature and two different slogans of literature. In postwar Japan, Takeuchi Yoshimi is often credited for the dissemination of modern Chinese literary studies and for his deep thinking on ethnicity, race, culture, and history in China and Japan. Takeuchi's approach is to position Lu Xun within the cultural and historical relations in contemporary East Asia. His student Itō Toramaru (1995) further develops Takeuchi's approach by discussing literary history concerning Lu Xun and modern Chinese literature; informed by Japan's cultural history, Itō reveals a self-reflexive account of Japan's imperialism in Asia. Another scholarly adventurous book comes from Maruo Tsuneki (1995), who employs close reading to unpack the symbolic relation between Ah Q and "ghosts" in Lu Xun's worldview, combining in this hauntological study the intersecting knowledge systems of folk religion, anthropology, and cultural custom.

The phase of twentieth-century Chinese literature

The third phase of modern Chinese literature began in 1985, which saw the turn to twentieth-century Chinese literature. Wang Yao's aforementioned history constructs modern Chinese literature as a discursive terrain covering periods of May Fourth literature in 1919–1949, 1930s leftist literature, and post-1940s art and literature in Yan'an and other liberated areas. However, this periodization quickly reached its limit. After 1978, China experienced various reforms, its cultural thought diverted from the ultra-leftist orientation, and many previously persecuted intellectuals were rehabilitated. Their literary works were re-published, and their important contributions publicly recognized. This postsocialist moment opened up many prohibited zones for new research. Meanwhile, literary productions since 1949 had accumulated a history of over 30 years, and the state of post-Mao literature reached a new level on a broader field. These new conditions eschewed the conventional periodization, which proved to be too narrow. If confined within 30 years, literature would not be able to connect to epochal changes in the early twentieth-century, nor could it account for shifting currents of contemporary literature. Isolationism in literary history would amount to the extinction of the discipline. Modern Chinese literature as a discipline exists as an integral part of the social organization in modern China; therefore, it should not be treated as a separate formation.

The emergence of "twentieth-century Chinese literature" as an analytical category can be traced to May 1985, when three scholars at Peking University—Huang Ziping,

Chen Pingyuan, and Qian Liqun—proposed the concept to replace the category of "modern literature." They wrote:

> Twentieth-century literature marks a literary evolution that began at the end of the last century and the beginning of this century (1900). It is one that witnesses the gradual completion of the transition from traditional Chinese literature to modern Chinese literature; one that chronicles the path of Chinese literature crossing into the total structure of world literature; it is a big bang at the crossroad of Eastern and Western cultures; it traces the formation of modern ethnic, racial, and national consciousness that happens at the crosscurrents of literature with politics, morality, and ethics. Finally, through the art of language and its mediation, the expression of old Chinese ethnic–national spirit finds its new life in the monumental era. (Z. Huang, Chen, and Qian 1988: 1)

"Twentieth-century Chinese literature" as a concept is both capacious and optimistic, embodying the progressive mindset of intellectuals in the 1980s, although this optimism would soon crumble in the aftermath of the June Fourth incident in 1989 as literary history would enter into an unpredictable "nameless" (*wuming*) condition.[2] Still, the concept of "twentieth-century Chinese literature" gives momentum to research on modern Chinese literature. First, this concept links literary works from the late Qing, May Fourth, and contemporary periods together and enables more holistic analyses. A wholesome concept that stresses the internal dynamism of literary progression specific to China, the concept critically dissolves the existing disciplinary boundaries between early modern, modern, and contemporary literature and broadens our scholarly horizon.[3] Second, this broad designation connects literary progression with the actual societal processes of modernity, thus making visible the "modernity" of literature while undermining the ideological domestication of literature under the Communist vision of socialism and revolution. This further expands the conceptual terrains of modern Chinese literature, given that many repressed literary phenomena due to ideological constraints can now be treated in a more objective manner. Third, this capacious concept puts emphasis on "progress" (*jincheng*). Twentieth-century Chinese literature marks a dynamic progression full of mobility and vitality; within this infinite possibility lays the new project of rewriting literary history itself.

An exploratory mood around 1985 in China led to more scholars overcoming the division between pre-1949 literature and contemporary literature, enabling an organic examination of literary history. Specifically, Chen Sihe (1987) proposed "modern and contemporary Chinese literature" (*Zhongguo xiandangdai wenxue*) as an organizing principle, and subsequently published several related articles. Wang Xiaoming likewise situated the post-1985 era as the backdrop for twentieth-century literature and analyzed the psychic ruin prevalent in the works of Lu Xun and Zhang Xianliang. New scholarship similar to this demonstrates that, when we examine modern and contemporary literature systematically, their meanings stretch beyond the previously separate spheres. Many episodes of modern literary history in China can be reexamined anew and obtain new life 30 years after 1949. Consequently, modern Chinese literature continues to find new reasons for its existence in the unfolding historical currents of our time.

Author Studies in the Perspective of "Twentieth-Century Chinese Literature"

Modern Chinese literary studies witnessed a vibrant revival after 1985. Having experienced the painful Cultural Revolution and embarked on the postsocialist path, Chinese intellectuals were ready to critically reassess the ills of authoritarianism. However, the top Party leadership was divided on how to implement "liberation of minds" (*sixiang jiefang*). From the 1979 "campaign against bourgeois liberalization" to the 1983 "anti-spiritual pollution campaign" to the June Fourth incident of 1989—all this cast shadows on literary production to the point that vigorous literary criticism could not carry on. As a result, a group of socially engaged young scholars turned their passion toward late Qing and early Republican culture and literature. On the one hand, this analytical distance allowed them to implicitly critique the contemporary condition of existence; on the other hand, this return to earlier eras achieved a reverse-effect of a more aesthetic platform and a refusal to cooptation by politics.

Research on modern Chinese literature accomplished a great deal in the 1980s, most notably in large-scale editorial projects such as Chen Huangmei's (1982), which comprises three large book series—"Movements, Debates, and Societies of Modern Chinese Literature," "Modern Chinese Writers and Works," and "Books and Periodicals on Modern Chinese Literature"—and which totals more than 100 volumes. Given the gigantic shape of such projects, their complex contents, and extensive materials that had been politically censored, there was an urgent need to recover them. The recovery and publications of these texts represented scholarly erudition and accuracy in methodology, and the unearthing of more research materials provided a solid foundation for modern literary studies as a discipline. What added more symbolic meaning for literary studies is the fact that the editors of these collections would form the backbone of up-and-coming young researchers. Their meticulous work mined archives in a genealogical mode: reading through newspapers and magazines, discriminating between forms of evidential materials, interviewing related people, mastering first-hand materials, and so on.

The collation of new research materials soon altered the research trajectory of more seasoned scholars who had entered the scene during the Cultural Revolution. Most of them had participated in the collective authorship of teaching materials on literary history before the Cultural Revolution, and had joined efforts to edit collected writings by Lu Xun. After the end of the Cultural Revolution, they gradually adopted liberal thinking and propelled the discipline of modern Chinese literature into a purely academic orientation. Some of the notable scholars who contributed to this shift include Yan Jiayan, who assisted with Tang Tao's literary history (1979), an important textbook that helped resurrect the rightly deserved statuses of many writers purged during the socialist period. Fan Jun assisted Wang Yao in launching the Association of Modern Chinese Literature, and Fan himself would become a Lao She specialist. Liu Zaifu, an expert on Lu Xun, revitalized studies on literary aesthetics after his appointment as director of the Institute of Literature at the Chinese Academy of Social Sciences (CASS). In particular, Liu introduced theoretical perspectives from the West and attempted to replace orthodox Marxism with modern scientific methods.

During the "liberation of minds," some scholars even questioned the official canonization of May Fourth literature. Specifically, Xu Zhiying from Nanjing University and Zhu Defa from Shandong Normal University both offered revisionist interpretations of May Fourth literature. Fan Boqun of Suzhou (Soochow) University restored the centrality of popular literature. Lu Yaodong of Wuhan University and Sun Yushi of Peking University studied the aesthetic form of New Poetry. Geng Yunzhi of CASS published research on Hu Shi. Wu Zhongjie and Chen Mingshu of Fudan University revisited Lu Xun. These works represent the exemplary research that takes into account the continuity of literary history.

In the process of rebuilding academia from the late 1970s onward, a group of veteran scholars were indispensable. They include Wang Yao at Peking University, Li Helin at Beijing Normal University, Tang Tao at the CASS, Jia Zhifang at Fudan University, Chen Shouzhu at Nanjing University, Ren Fangqiu at Henan University, Zheng Chaozong at Xiamen University, and Wu Hongcong at Sun Yat-sen University. All of them came of age under the influence of May Fourth literature and often knew important writers of that time personally. Many of them suffered political persecution after 1949, while others continued their work quietly in difficult conditions. Nonetheless, they all shared a sense of intellectual mission and the urgency of carrying on Chinese literary studies. After they regained their status as professors, their first collective achievement was the training of a group of young scholars—who were among the first and second cohorts of college students in 1977–1978—as doctoral students in the 1980s–1990s. These new scholars learned through first-hand account the historical truth and events concerning literature, studied the method of archival research and literary excavation, and began comprehensive writer-oriented research while leaving aside the ideological project of literary historiography. In this vein, many turned to Lu Xun with new interpretive hermeneutics, but there were also a number of studies on writers who were previously censored. Together, they expanded the scope of research in modern Chinese literature.

The new generation of scholars often studied Lu Xun as their rite of passage, but their readings often reflect their own aspirations. Wang Furen's book (1986) contends that the value of Lu Xun's early work lies in its symbolic role as the mirror of China's revolution through ideas; the metaphor of mirror originates from Lenin's theorizing of Leo Tolstoy's work as "the mirror of the Russian Revolution." Qian Liqun's work (1988) focuses on Lu Xun's "selfhood"—his unique method of thinking, psychological quality, and sentiment—and analyzes Lu Xun through what Tolstoy termed "the dialectics of the soul." Wang Hui's book (2000) extends his mentor Tang Tao's method and further links the background of historical progress with intellectual history. After

1989, Wang Hui further elaborates "despair" in Lu Xun's work and rethinks the legacy of May Fourth enlightenment. Wang Xiaoming's biography on Lu Xun (1993b) continues to unpack the analytics of "despair," revealing the writers' painful failures in life and rescuing him from official iconization. Gao Yuanbao (2000) goes further in his focus on Lu Xun's psyche and its cultural embedding.

Beyond Lu Xun studies, the most exciting avenue of research in the 1980s–1990s deals with Hu Feng and Ba Jin. Both writers were mentored by Lu Xun, yet their life journeys were rough and bumpy. Hu Feng edited journals such as *July* and *Hope* (*Xiwang*) and promoted the idea of "subjective fighting spirit." He gathered many writers and poets in his July group. Unfortunately, because Hu Feng's artistic view was at odds with Mao Zedong's "Yan'an Talks," in 1955 he and his associates were branded as the "anti-revolutionary clique" and persecuted. The Hu Feng case involved many intellectuals, and Hu Feng studies required archival materials and biographies. Li Hui's book (1989) is the first to delve into this case and remains the most comprehensive account. Hu Feng's wife Mei Zhi and daughter Zhang Xiaofeng also wrote several biographic pieces and edited Hu's writings. Hu Feng studies tend to focus on his commentary on aesthetics, his confrontations with politics, his editorial career, and materials on writers affiliated with the July group such as Lu Ling, Lü Yuan, and Peng Yanjiao. Japanese scholar Kondō Tatsuya also provides invaluable information on Hu Feng. Another giant in Chinese literary history, Ba Jin, was in charge of the Cultural Life Press in the postwar period, which published many works by outstanding young writers. But, after 1949, his view of anarchism was criticized by the Party. To compromise his views, he tried to publish some works that toed the Party line, but he was still persecuted during the Cultural Revolution. In his later years, he stressed the urgency to "speak the truth" (Ba Jin 1979). Fudan University professor Jia Zhifang trained a number of scholars who went on to write important studies on Hu Feng and Ba Jin, and they include Chen Sihe, Li Hui, Japanese scholars Yamaguchi Mamoru, Sakai Hirobumi, and Shintani Hideaki, and Korean scholars No Chongun and Lee Hee-Kyung.

Other important writers such as Mao Dun, Lao She, Cao Yu, and Yu Dafu represent indispensable parts of literary studies. Mao Dun had long been exalted to a highly venerated status, and the politically correct line of his work had led to his canonization in the PRC, which resulted in the obstacles for scholars to delve beneath official accounts. After the Cultural Revolution, Ye Ziming's student Shen Weiwei (1991) wrote a biography on Mao Dun. Because it touches on the writer's history of apostasy from the Party and his hidden private life, the book was censored in the mainland and released in Taiwan instead. Still, Mao Dun's early fiction serves as a form of narrating China's revolution, and it invites endless refreshing new readings. Research on Lao She has taken on a comparatively smoother path. Lao She wrote memorable novels in his early years, and subsequently led a united front among artists and intellectuals in the anti-war efforts against Japan. In the post-1949 era, he politically endorsed the Communist leadership but felt a great sense of fear and distance from politics. During the Cultural Revolution, Lao She suffered from humiliation and violence, and he drowned himself in a lake. Scholars of Lao She concentrate on his tragic life, his narration of city life, his use of Beijing dialect, his Manchu bloodline, and his Christian belief. Research on Cao Yu is only second to Ba Jin in its academic dominance. Cao Yu's plays such as *Thunderstorm* (1933), *Sunrise* (*Richu*, 1936), and *Wilderness* (*Yuanye*, 1937) have remained enduring classics of modern drama, and they are regularly staged and adapted for various plays and television series. Zhu Donglin and Cao Shujun have made noted contributions in their perceptive analyses of Cao Yu's plays, biographical materials, and theatrical performances adapted from his work. Yu Dafu is a controversial writer who is in a league of his own. Because he is open about sexual desires and makes implicit references to his private life, the receptions of his works have been mixed with debates. After his anti-war efforts in the mainland, he migrated to Hong Kong, Singapore, and Sumatra. Suzuki Masao's excavation of archival materials (1996) confirms that the writer was indeed killed by the Japanese army in Sumatra. Although Yu Dafu's fiction had a great impact during the Republican era, the overall output of his work is sparse compared to other writers. Xu Zidong's book (1984) on Yu Dafu is worth reading.

All writers mentioned in the preceding text, excluding Hu Feng, were officially recognized as important writers after 1949; therefore, before the Cultural Revolution, academics had produced some studies on them. By contrast, the following writers constituted a forbidden zone where scholarly attention was possible only after the Cultural Revolution. At first, the mentioning of their names still invited certain censorship, but since the 1990s their texts have gained popular reception. Although Chen Duxiu, Hu Shi, and Zhou Zuoren were all May Fourth pioneers, their contributions to literature were neglected during 1949–1979. Chen Duxiu was famous for launching the *New Youth* magazine and became the first general secretary of the Chinese Communist Party in the early 1920s. But because of the failure of the 1927 Communist uprising, he became the scapegoat of the Communist International and was arrested by the Nationalists. Official Chinese literary history maintained silence on Chen's later years. However, after the 1980s, scholars began to explore outside the Party confinement. The earliest is Wang Guanquan's book (1996), which was banned in the PRC but published in an abridged version in Taiwan, but the Party has loosened its control since then, and new scholarship includes Tang Baolin's biography of Chen Duxiu (2011). Since Hu Shi was a liberal pioneer of New Literature and an influential cultural figure in the Republican era, scholarship on Hu Shi studies first emerged in Taiwan academia, and most of them are biographies and bibliographies (e.g., works by Li Ao).

While the research on Chen Duxiu and Hu Shi revolve more around political thought and less on literary studies, the studies on Zhou Zuoren are almost exclusively on literature. As a key May Fourth thinker, translator, and prose writer, Zhou's early theoretical essays, his championing of descriptive prose, and his translations of ancient Greek and Japanese literature are all remarkable achievements in modern Chinese literature. But because of his suspected collaborator status in Japanese-occupied Beijing, any publication related to Zhou used to be sensitive or forbidden. Even today, Zhou's work from his controversial period cannot be published, and many scholars carefully skip this part of his life. Still, some characterize Zhou as the quintessential modern intellectual, and through Zhou's biography they project certain idealism onto the author (Qian Liqun 1991; Shu Wu 1986). Other notable studies of Zhou include Ha Yingfei (2007) on Zhou's thought in relation to Confucianism and Buddhism, and Kiyama Hideo (2008) on Zhou's wartime experience, which fills an existing research gap.

In 1979, the Chinese edition of C. T. Hsia's history of modern Chinese fiction (1961) was published in Taiwan, and soon it was circulated privately in the PRC and became widely read. Hsia speaks highly of Qian Zhongshu, Shen Congwen, Eileen Chang, and research on these writers quickly became popular in the mainland. Zheng Chaozong was the first to coordinate research on Qian's philosophical thought. "Qian studies" flowered gradually (Zhang Wenjiang 1993), but research on Qian's novels and classical poetry is lacking. Studies on Shen Congwen took off in the 1980s (Ling Yu 1988) and drew attention to Shen's literary texts and the culture of his hometown region in West Hunan. Since the 1990s, "Shen Congwen fever" has been going strong, and his "latent writing"—letters, diary, and archeological studies—and his private life attract researchers. Literary popularity is more evident with Eileen Chang, who has gathered many fans in the mainland as well as in Taiwan and Hong Kong. Chang's few close friends overseas—such as C. T. Hsia, Stephen Soong (Song Qi), and her ex-husband Hu Lancheng—all provided newly available sources such as unpublished notes and letters, which sustain the liveliness of "Eileen Chang studies." In the mainland, Chen Zishan has done much archival work in this area. Although most books on Chang bespeak a certain fan mentality, one exception is Liu Fengjie (2004), who provides a comprehensive account of various critical interpretations.

From the preceding observation, it is evident that author studies remain the foundation of modern Chinese literary scholarship. In the last 30 years, scholars have consistently edited research materials on prominent authors, such as Bing Xin, Ye Shengtao, Xu Zhimo, Li Jinfa, Dai Wangshu, Xiao Hong, Shi Zhecun, Lu Yin, Ding Ling, Guan Lu, Lu Ling, Ai Qing, Tian Han, Lin Yutang, Mu Dan, Feng Zhi, Xu Xu, and Wumingshi. Most studies on post-1949 contemporary literature also orient toward author studies. Before the Cultural Revolution, literary critics wore professional hats as the cultural bureau officials and leaders of writers' associations, and they were instrumental in the implementation of state policies. Entering the 1990s, state leadership in art and literature has shifted, and ideological criticism has lost much of its appeal. This shift has resulted in the flourishing of creative production, and the legitimacy of literary criticism has shifted from the state-sponsored writers association to that of universities. Contemporary cultural criticism and literary studies have joined force to institute a second-level discipline. Through pedagogical innovation and graduate training, this new round of institutionalization has blazed a new path for contemporary literary scholarship.

Research on contemporary Chinese literature mostly revolves around literary history and author studies. The research undertaken in the 1980–1990s paid some attention to writers before the Cultural Revolution, including Zhao Shuli, Liu Qing, Guo Xiaochuan, and Du Pengcheng. These studies emphasize the creative success and shortcomings of writers and their challenges under extra-leftism. The writers who receive most attention are those who emerged in the 1980s. The emergence of these post-Mao young writers and aspiring critics happened simultaneously. For instance, the 1980s witnessed debates on Misty Poetry, avant-garde fiction, roots-searching literature, "new realist" (*xin xieshi*) fiction, and the subsequent transition toward literature inspired by folk culture. Within these new configurations, writers and critics played collaborative roles and formed the most energizing phenomenon in recent memory. Stepping into the new century, these Chinese writers draw on the previous 30 or so years as their collective experiences, from which they distill a unique clairvoyance and mature platform. Their creative identities now fully constructed, they collectively form the most accomplished group of writers since the May Fourth. Representatives include fiction writers such as Zhang Chengzhi, Shi Tiesheng, Jia Pingwa, Han Shaogong, Wang Anyi, Mo Yan, Fang Fang, Zhang Wei, Yan Lianke, Lin Bai, Yan Geling, Yu Hua, Su Tong, Chi Zijian (see Chapter 12 by Yiyan Wang) as well as poets Bei Dao, Shu Ting, Yu Jian, Zhai Yongming, Yang Lian, and Wang Jiaxin (see Chapter 9 by Michelle Yeh). Their writings have sustained critical attention, and they in turn have drawn from criticism to improve their creative output. In sum, the maturation of contemporary Chinese literature is a result of the concerted efforts of both writers and critics.

Rewriting Literary History: Advocacy and Practice

Since the 1980s, researchers have faced two major issues in modern and contemporary Chinese literature. First, through the solid foundation established in author studies, modern literary scholarship has retrieved a large amount of information and materials that were impossible under the previous ideologically constrained mode of literary historiography. The former politicized function of literature no longer satisfied the thirst of young scholars. From the perspectives of pedagogy and research, literary history after 1949 must take up the challenge of science and technology. Second, with the broadening of scholarly perspectives, many literary phenomena previously ignored by official history have emerged from the horizon. These literary texts raise the following questions: How should we treat the relationship between late Qing literature and May Fourth literature? How should one evaluate the creativity of old-style poetry and classical literature, or the aesthetic value of popular literature? How do we reassess Manchukuo and colonial literature (*wei Man wenxue*) written during the Japanese occupation? Geographically, how can scholars integrate the study of mainland Chinese literature with Taiwan literature and Hong Kong literature? In many ways, these are all central problems under the rubric of rewriting literary history.

The task of "rewriting literary history" is not merely to replace official history or showcase current standards. Rather, it should promote an academic culture that questions the very way literary history is written, and reconceive the relation between literary history and writers in multidirectional modes. While the call for moving beyond a unifying literary history sounds conventional to Western readers, one must bear in mind the often tumultuous and stormy reaction that have come with the invocation of "rewriting literary history" in China, for even today officials maintain a standardized structure of instructing literary history. In 1988–1989, Chen Sihe and Wang Xiaoming were among the first promoters to "rewrite literary history" in the journal *Shanghai Literary Theory* (*Shanghai wenlun*), and contributors reevaluated the contribution from writers such as Zhao Shuli, Liu Qing, Guo Xiaochuan, He Qifang, and Ding Ling. These essays remained within the terrain of author studies; but due to the provocation of rewriting literary history, they sparked heated debates. In the aftermath of the June Fourth of 1989, officials at one point censored the call of rewriting literary history as a measure to counter "bourgeois liberalism," although this time around such censorship did not last long.

Since the 1990s, the project of rewriting literary history has gained popularity, and "twentieth-century Chinese literature," as a new periodization concept, has been widely accepted by academics. This concept is rich in its inclusivity, encompassing late Qing literature, May Fourth literature, and post-1949 mainland literature. Other scholars attempt to include Taiwan and Hong Kong literature within it. Since the 1990s, many research teams have written literary histories of the twentieth century, but they often simply integrate late Qing, early Republican, modern, and contemporary literature together without theorizing them substantively. A more promising exploration has been done on the respective histories of different genres and periods of Chinese literature, some of which are briefly introduced in the following text.

Late Qing Literature

In China, early modern literature (1840–1919) references an earlier encounter of literary modernity that hails back to a long tradition. After the May Fourth, scholars of new and old traditions both turned to the Qing dynasty, especially the late Qing (e.g., Hu Shi 1924; Chen Zizhan 1929; Chen Zizhan 1930; Zhou Zuoren 1932; Qian Jibo 1933; Liang Qichao 1936; A Ying 1937), and they pioneered the scholarship of modern Chinese literature. After the 1980s, the larger category of modern literature that includes the late Qing has matured through the collaboration of research teams across universities, and the most notable effort is from Henan University's Ren Fangqiu, whose work (1988) is credited as filling a much-needed void. Heavily influenced by Zhou Zuoren, Ren has launched other books (1984; 1986) equally instrumental in shaping the research on new, classical, and late Qing literature. Other indispensable studies come from Peking University's Chen Pingyuan (1988), Shandong University's Guo Yanli (1990–1993), and Fudan University's Yuan Jin (2006), among others. In addition, two large series of modern Chinese literature (Ma Xueliang 1990; P. Zhang and Wang 1988–1998) further consolidated the foundation for future scholarship. Since the 1990s, with academia becoming more concerned with the analytical problem of modernity (see Chapter 30 by Yingjin Zhang; also Li Oufan 2000), David Wang (1998b: 23–42) entertains the provocation that there would be no May Fourth without late Qing. Another noticeable development has occurred in late Qing popular literature. Fan Boqun (2000; 2007; 2009) has amassed a large amount of primary resources while rethinking literary history; his view that New Literature and popular literature are in fact "two complementary wings" provides theoretical acumen for later research.

Contemporary Literature

Unlike late Qing literature, "contemporary literature" as a concept is rather fuzzy, for it covers broad terrains such as seventeen-year literature (1949–1966), literature of the Cultural Revolution (1966–1976), and post-Mao literature (since 1976). Some scholars also use the term to refer to literature written in the twenty-first century. Literatures produced in these different stages cannot be easily unified, especially given the divergent receptions of seventeen-year literature. However, several publications in the 1990s mark a new direction. Hong Zicheng (1999) employs comprehensive archives to analyze the structural organizations of post-1949 Chinese literature and provides refreshing readings on seventeen-year literature. Chen Sihe's popular textbook (1999) formulates innovative concepts such as "invisible writing" (*qianzai xiezuo*), "collective naming" (*gongming*), "nameless condition," "cultural psychology in war" (*zhanzheng wenhua xinli*), and "folk realm" (*minjian*), and offers new perspectives on contemporary literature. Both Hong's and Chen's books depart from official history and contribute directly to rewriting literary history. There are also topical studies on theorizing literary history. Among notable achievements, Gao Yuanbao and Gao Yu explore the correlation between literature and language; Ding Fan explicates the concept of "Republican literature" (*minguo wenxue*); Yang Jian and Wang Yao interrogate literature of the Cultural Revolution; Dong Zhilin, He Guimei, and Li Yang discuss seventeen-year literature; Wang Guangdong studies the literary history of folk theories and beliefs; Liu Zhirong further explores the concept of invisible writing; and last but not least, Tang Xiaodu, Wang Guangming, Li Zhensheng, and Li Yi have done considerable research on modern Chinese poetry.

Literary Genres

Beside issues of periodization, research on literary history also covers different genres of literature, regional styles and differences, and related disciplines. Literary historiography of genres includes fiction, poetry, prose, drama, and film, while literary historiography by "regions" includes Taiwan literature, Hong Kong literature, Shanghai-style literature (*Haipai wenxue*), literature of Japanese-occupied areas (*lunxian qu wenxue*), and other literatures affiliated with specific literary societies and styles. Literary historiography informed by "relations" factors into the impact of foreign concepts, Western literary influence, and the circulation of Chinese literature worldwide. Furthermore, it touches on such relational areas as literature and education, literature and publishing (see Chapter 22 by Nicolai Volland), literature and religion, literature and sexuality (see Chapter 25 by Tze-lan Sang), and other interdisciplinary formations.

Each one of the earlier-mentioned three categories—genres, regions, and relations—of literary historiography contains its own diversity. While literary history places the PRC at its center, since the 1990s there has been increasing attention to different territories of literary history that include Taiwan and Hong Kong in their scope. New studies on modern Chinese literature by China studies scholars overseas further give these underexplored topics their overdue examination (see Chapter 8 by Ping-hui Liao).

Given the limited space of this chapter, I can only provide a condensed rather than exhaustive account of Chinese-language research on the development of modern Chinese literature. Tracing the institutionalization of modern Chinese literature, this chapter focuses mainly on the three phases—New Literature, modern Chinese literature, and twentieth-century literature—in China. With regard to publications by representative scholars, only some field-defining works are listed here. One regrettable disclaimer is that the various receptions of post-1949 literature and the divergent literary criticism of contemporary literature cannot be adequately treated within the allocated space here, not to mention the lack of coverage on the literary history of Taiwan and Hong Kong. I hope to elaborate on these aspects in a much more extended fashion in the future.

NOTES

1 The PRC Ministry of Education designates "Chinese language and literature" as a first-level discipline, which subsumes the following eight second-level disciplines: Chinese linguistics and philology, theoretical and applied linguistics, classical Chinese literature, contemporary and modern Chinese literature, literary and art theory (*wenyi xue*), comparative literature, literary bibliography, and ethnic minority languages and literature.

2 A "nameless" condition refers to post-1980s China when multiple values contended with each other for dominance. "Namelessness" does not mean the era's lack of ideas but the coexistence of various structures of feeling.

3 "Early modern" holds specific meaning to Chinese literary studies beyond its conventional English usage. It refers to the "early phase" of modern literature produced from 1840 after the Opium War to 1919 when the May Fourth Movement began. Official historiography designates it as "literature of the old democratic revolution," but this term is outdated.

REFERENCES

A Ying 阿英. 1937. *Wan Qing xiaoshuo shi* 晚清小說史 (A history of late Qing fiction). Shanghai: Shangwu yinshuguan.

Ba Jin 巴金. 2000. *Suixiang lu* 随想录 (Random thoughts). Beijing: Renmin wenxue chubanshe.

Chen, Pingyuan 陳平原. 1988. *Zhongguo xiaoshuo xushi moshi de zhuanbian* 中國小說敘事模式的轉變 (The shift in narrative modes in Chinese fiction). Shanghai: Shanghai renmin chubanshe.

Chen, Sihe 陳思和. 1987. *Zhongguo xinwenxue zhengti guan* 中國新文學整體觀 (A total view of new Chinese literature). Shanghai: Shanghai wenyi chubanshe.

Chen, Sihe 陳思和. Ed. 1999. *Zhongguo dangdai wenxue shi jiaocheng* 中國當代文學史教程 (A textbook history of contemporary Chinese literature). Shanghai: Fudan daxue chubanshe.

Chen, Zizhan 陳子展. 1929. *Zhongguo jindai wenxue zhibianqian* 中國近代文學之變遷 (The transformation of early modern literature in China). Shanghai: Zhonghua shuju.

Chen, Zizhan 陳子展. 1930. *Zuijin sanshi nian Zhongguo wenxue shi* 最近三十年中國文學史 (A history of Chinese literature in past thirty years). Shanghai: Taipingyang shudian.

Fan, Boqun 范伯群. 2009. *Duoyuan gongsheng de Zhongguo wenxue de xiandaihua licheng* 多元共生的中國文學的現代化歷程 (The multiplicity of Chinese literary modernization). Shanghai: Fudan daxue chubanshe.

Fan, Boqun 范伯群. Ed. 2000. *Zhongguo jinxiandai tongsu wenxue shi* 中國近代通俗文學史 (A history of early modern popular literature). Nanjing: Jiangsu jiaoyu chubanshe.

Fan, Boqun 范伯群. Ed. 2007. *Zhongguo xiandai tongsu wenxue shi* 中國現代通俗文學史 (A history of modern Chinese popular literature). Illustrated edition. Beijing: Beijing daxue chubanshe.

Gao, Yuanbao 郜元寶. 2000. *Lu Xun liujiang* 魯迅六講 (Six talks on Lu Xun). Shanghai: Sanlian shudian.

Guo, Yanli 郭延禮. 1990–1993. *Zhongguo jindai wenxue fazhanshi* 中國近代文學發展史 (A history of the development of modern Chinese literature). 3 vols. Ji'nan: Shandong jiaoyu chubanshe.

Ha, Yingfei 哈迎飛. 2007. *Banshi rujia ban shijia: Zhou Zuoren sixiang yanjiu* 半是儒家半釋家: 周作人思想研究 (Half Confucian and half Buddhist: a study of Zhou Zuoren's thought). Beijing: Renmin wenxue chubanshe.

Hong, Zicheng 洪子誠. 1999. *Zhongguo dangdai wenxueshi* 中國當代文學史 (A history of contemporary Chinese Literature). Beijing: Beijing daxue chubanshe.

Hsia, C. T. 1961. *A History of Modern Chinese Fiction, 1917–1957*. New Haven, CT: Yale University Press.

Hu, Shi 胡適. 1924. *Wushinianlai Zhongguo zhiwenxue* 五十年來中國之文學 (Chinese literature in past fifty years). Shanghai: Shenbao guan.

Huang, Ziping 黃子平, Chen Pingyuan 陳平原, and Qian Liqun 錢理群. 1988. *Ershi shiji Zhongguo wenxue sanren tan* 二十世紀中國文學三人談 (Three critics on twentieth-century Chinese literature). Beijing: renmin wenxue chubanshe.

Itō, Toramaru 伊藤虎丸. 1995. *Lu Xun, chuangzaoshe yu Riben wenxue: Zhong Ri jinxiandai bijiao wenxue chutan* 魯迅, 創造社與日本文學: 中日近現代比較文學初探 (Lu Xun, the Creation Society, and Japanese literature: comparative literary studies of modern China and Japan). Trans. Sun Meng. Beijing: Beijing daxue chubanshe.

Kiyama, Hideo 木山英雄. 2008. *Beijing kuzhuanji* 北京苦住庵記 (Notes from Beijing's kuzhu hut). Beijing: Sanlian shudian.

Li, Hui 李輝. 1989. *Hu Feng jituanyuananshimo* 胡風集團冤案始末 (The complete story of the unjust case of the Hu Feng clique). Beijing: Renmin ribao chubanshe.

Li, Oufan 李歐梵. 2000. *Xiandaixing de zhuiqiu: Li Oufan wenhua pinglun jingxuan ji* 現代性的追求: 李歐梵文化評論精選集 (In pursuit of modernity: selected works of cultural criticism by Leo Ou-fan Lee). Beijing: Sanlian shudian.

Liang, Qichao. 1936. *jin sanbai nian xueshu shi* 中國近三百年學術史 (A history of Chinese scholarship in past three hundred years). Shanghai: Zhonghua shuju.

Ling, Yu 凌宇. 1988. *Shen Congwen zhuan* 沈從文傳 (Biography of Shen Congwen). Beijing: Shiyue wenyi chubanshe.

Liu, Fengjie 劉峰傑. 2004. *Xiangxiang Zhang Ailing: guanyu Zhang Ailing de yuedu yanjiu* 想像

張愛玲—關於張愛玲的閱讀研究 (Imagining Zhang Ailing: on approaches of reading Zhang Ailing). Hefei: Anhui jiaoyu chubanshe.

Ma, Xueliang 馬學良. Ed. 1990. *Zhongguo jindai wenxue da xi* 中國近代文學大系 (A compendium of modern Chinese literature). 30 vols. Shanghai: Shanghai shudian.

Maruo, Tsuneki 丸尾常喜. 1995. "Ren" yu "gui" de jiuge: Lu Xun xiaoshuo lunxi "人"與 "鬼" 的纠纠: 魯迅小説論析 (Between human and ghost: analysis of Lu Xun's fiction). Trans. Qin Gong. Beijing: Renmin wenxue chubanshe.

Noboru, Maruyama 丸山升. 2005. *Lu Xun, geming, lishi* 魯迅, 革命, 歷史 (Lu Xun, revolution, history). Trans. Wang Junwen. Beijing: Beijing daxue chubanshe.

Qian, Jibo 錢基博. 1933. *Xiandai Zhongguo wenxue shi* 現代中國文學史 (A modern history of Chinese literature). Shanghai: Shijieshuju.

Qian, Liqun 錢理群. 1988. *Xinling de tanxun* 心靈的探索 (Exploration of the psyche). Shijiazhuang: Hebei jiaoyu chubanshe.

Qian, Liqun 錢理群. 1991. *Zhou Zuorenlun* 周作人論 (A study of Zhou Zuoren). Shanghai: Shanghai renmin chubanshe.

Qu, Qiubai 瞿秋白. Ed. 1980. *Lu Xun zagan xuanji* 魯迅雜感選集 (Selection of Lu Xun's reflections). Shanghai: Shanghai wenyi chubanshe.

Ren, Fangqiu 任訪秋. 1984. *Zhongguo jindai wenxue zuojialun* 中國近代文學作家論 (Essays on modern Chinese writers). Zhengzhou: Henan renmin chubanshe.

Ren, Fangqiu 任訪秋. 1986. *Zhongguo xin wenxue yuanyuan* 中國新文學淵源 (The origins of Chinese new literature). Zhengzhou: Henan renmin chubanshe.

Ren, Fangqiu 任訪秋. Ed. 1988. *Zhongguo jindai wenxue shi* 中國近代文學史 (A history of early modern Chinese literature). Kaifeng: Henan daxue chubanshe.

Shen, Weiwei 沈衛威. 1991. *Jianxin de rensheng: Mao Dun zhuan* 艱辛的人生: 茅盾傳 (A diffi-cult life: a biography of Mao Dun). Taipei: Yeqiang chubanshe.

Shu, Wu 舒蕪. 1986. *Zhou Zuoren gaiguan* 周作人概觀 (An overview of Zhou Zuoren). Changsha: Hunan renmin chubanshe.

Suzuki, Masao 鈴木正夫. 1996. *Sumendala de Yu Dafu* 蘇門答臘的郁達夫 (Yu Dafu in Sumatra). Trans. Li Zhensheng. Shanghai: Shanghai yuandong chubanshe.

Tang, Baolin 唐寶林. 2011. *Chen Duxiu quanzhuan* 陳獨秀全傳 (The complete biography of Chen Duxiu). Hong Kong: Zhongwen daxue chubanshe.

Tang, Tao 唐弢. 1979. *Zhongguo xiandai wenxue shi* 中國現代文學史 (A history of modern Chinese literature). 3 vols. Beijing: Renmin wenxue chubanshe.

Wang, Dewei (David Wang) 王德威. 1998b. *Ruhe xiandai, zengyang wenxue: 19–20 shiji Zhongwen xiaoshuo xinlun* 如何現代, 怎樣文學: 19–20世紀中文小説新論 (How modern, what literature? New studies in nineteenth- and twentieth-century Chinese fiction). Taipei: Maitian.

Wang, Furen 王富仁. 1986. *Zhongguo fan fengjian sixiang geming de yimian jingzi: "Nahan" "Panghuang" zonglun* 中國反封建思想革命的一面鏡子: 《呐喊》、《彷徨》綜論 (The mirror of anti-feudalist and revolutionary thought in China: a discussion on *Call to Arms* and *Wandering*). Beijing: Beijing shifan daxue chubanshe.

Wang, Guanquan 王觀泉. 1996. *Beibang de Puluomixiusi: Chen Duxiu zhuan* 被綁的普羅米修斯—陳獨秀傳 (The tied up Prometheus: biography of Chen Duxiu). Taipei: Yeqiang chubanshe.

Wang, Hui 汪暉. 2000. *Fankang juewang: Lu Xun ji qi wenxue shijie* 反抗絶望—魯迅及其文學世界 (Resisting despair: Lu Xun and his literary world). Shijiazhuang: Hebei jiaoyu chubanshe.

Wang, Xiaoming 王曉明. 1993b. *Wufa zhimian de rensheng* 無法直面的人生—魯迅傳 (A life that cannot be faced directly: biography of Lu Xun). Shanghai: Shanghai wenyi chubanshe.

Wang, Yao 王瑤. 1953. *Zhongguo xin wenxue shigao* 中國新文學史稿: 1919–1950 (A draft history of new Chinese literature). 2 vols. Shanghai: Xin wenyi chubanshe.

Wang, Zhefu 王哲甫. 1933. *Zhongguo xin wenxue yundongshi* 中國新文學運動史 (A history of the new literature movement in China). Beiping: Jiechengyinshuju.

Xu, Zidong 許子東. 1984. *Yu Dafu xinlun* 郁達夫新論 (New interpretation of Yu Dafu). Hangzhou: Zhejiang wenyi chubanshe.

Yuan, Jin 袁進. 2006. *Zhongguo wenxue de jindai biange* 中國文學的近代變革 (Recent transformations of Chinese literature). Guilin: Guangxi shifan daxue chubanshe.

Zhang, Peiheng 章培恒 and Wang Jiquan 王繼權. Eds. 1988–1998. *Zhongguo jindai xiaoshuo daxi* 中國近代小説大系 (A compendium of early modern Chinese fiction). 80 vols. Nanchang: Jiangxi renmin chubanshe.

Zhang, Wenjiang 張文江. 1993. *Wenhua kunlun: Qian Zhongshuzhuan* 文化崑崙: 錢鍾書傳 (The Kunlun mountains of culture: biography of Qian Zhongshu). Taipei: Yeqiang chubanshe.

Zhou, Zuoren 周作人. 1932. *Zhongguo xin wenxue de yuanliu* 中國新文學的源流 (The origins of Chinese new literature). Beijing: Renwen shudian.

Zhu, Ziqing 朱自清. 1982. "Zhongguo xin wenxue yanjiu gangyao" 中國新文學研究綱要 (An outline for research on Chinese new literature). *Wenyi luncong* 文藝論叢 (Literary studies), 14: 1–45.

30

Toward a Typology of Literary Modernity in China: A Survey of English Scholarship on Modern Chinese Literature

Yingjin Zhang

Introduction: Five Phases of Modernity in China

At the turn of the new millennium, English scholarship on modern Chinese literature seemed to have rediscovered modernity and its multiple manifestations in modern China: an exploration of "Shanghai modern" (L. Lee 1999b) was immediately followed by examinations of "Chinese modern" (X. Tang 2000) and "the lure of the modern" (Shih 2001). Although books on Chinese literature that carry "modernity" in their titles had appeared at a steady pace in the 1990s (R. Chow 1991; Hockx 1994; L. Liu 1995; X. Tang 1996; D. Wang 1997), they quickly proliferated at the start of the new millennium (Daruvala 2000; X. Zhong 2000; Gimpel 2001; Jones 2001). To put this proliferation in context, scholars in other disciplines of China studies were equally fond of announcing "modernity" in their book titles around the same time (Dikötter 1995; Hershatter 1997; Oakes 1998; Tsin 1999; Walker 1999; Esherick 2000; W. Yeh 2000; Weili Ye 2001), and discussions of Chinese modernity could be traced to the 1970s (G. Wang 1977; Alitto 1979), while some have pushed the parameters of modernity in China all the way to the seventeenth century (C. Chang and Chang 1992) or even earlier (Porter 2012). In the new millennium, the momentum in the quest for Chinese modernity has been as strong as before, at least in literary studies (Laughlin 2005; S. Lu 2007; Laughlin 2008; McGrath 2008; Rojas 2008; Button 2009; H. Peng 2010; S. Qian 2011; H. Gong 2012; X. Wang 2013).

Given such proliferating research on Chinese modernity, it is a daunting task to assess what modernity has brought to Chinese literary studies since the early 1990s. This chapter takes a typological approach by offering a survey of English scholarship

A Companion to Modern Chinese Literature, First Edition. Edited by Yingjin Zhang.
© 2016 John Wiley & Sons, Ltd. Published 2016 by John Wiley & Sons, Ltd.

on modern Chinese literature and delineating what I call "five phases of modernity" in China since the 1840s. My term intentionally evokes the "five faces" of Western literary modernity (Calinescu 1987), but I prefer the punning "phases" here because, in modern China, synchronic dimensions of modernity are less distinct than diachronic ones, and the "faces" of modernity such as decadence, enlightenment, hybridity, ecstasy, and avant-garde are often subsumed by the outstanding "phases" of Chinese modernity—late Qing, May Fourth, urban, socialist, and postsocialist (see relevant chapters in Part I). This chapter focuses on select recent English scholarship and makes passing references to Chinese scholarship on modernity (which is summarized in Chapter 29 by Chen Sihe). By depicting the contours, connections, and permutations of Chinese modernity through critical lenses, I intend for this chapter to be an exercise in typology of literary scholarship.

May Fourth Modernity: Enlightenment and Its Discontents

In China, modernity is most frequently associated with the May Fourth New Cultural Movement of 1917–1927. "In the popular May Fourth parlance, to be 'modern' means above all to be 'new' (*xin*), to be consciously opposed to the 'old' (*jiu*)" (L. Lee 1990: 110). The explosion of journals bearing the catchy word "new" in the early twentieth century pointed to Chinese intellectuals' urgent desire to be on the cutting edge in a new "epoch" (*shidai*). To be "new" means to acquire new knowledge defined by new terms such as enlightenment, rationality, freedom, liberation, democracy, science, technology, evolution, progress, and revolution. The desire to oppose the old, on the other hand, readily translated into the signature of May Fourth radical iconoclasm and anti-traditionism. As Leo Lee (1990: 122) explains:

> "Modernity" in China was loosely defined as a mode of consciousness of time and history as unilinear progress, moving in a continuous "stream" or "tide" from the past to the present; it also contained the valorized notion of the present as a new "epoch," not only unprecedented and qualitatively different from previous eras but better, which leads prophetically to a purposeful future.

Characteristically, May Fourth intellectuals would position themselves as the vanguards of such "progress" toward a better future, and for that goal they would take on the persona of "the zealously ideological, heroic self" (L. Lee 1990: 120).

Among the most celebrated examples of the heroic self is the protagonist in Lu Xun's "Diary of a Madman" (1918), whose final call—"Save the children"—captures the essence of May Fourth enlightenment. For this reason, Fredric Jameson (1986) promotes Lu Xun as a representative not just of Chinese modernity but also of the "national allegory" that is paradigmatic of all Third World literature. Following Jameson, Xiaobing Tang (2000: 49–73) contends that "Diary of a Madman," with its allegedly inaugural use of the modern vernacular (*baihua*) and its construction of a rebellious subjectivity, announces the birth of a Chinese modernism. A prolific scholar of Lu Xun (L. Lee 1985; L. Lee 1987), Leo Lee is nonetheless sensitive to the complexity of May Fourth modernity. Inasmuch as Lu Xun "openly voiced his belief in evolutionism while at the same time refusing to fuse his self with the onward positive tide of history," he may be considered a great "modernist"; moreover, he "has made a creative paradox out of the double meaning of modernity" (L. Lee 1990: 135).

Three points await further elaboration. First, the "double meaning" of May Fourth modernity in Lee's diagnosis—the paradox of historical progress and individual subjectivity—was subsequently resolved in the triumph of the former over the latter. Due to the urgent projects of national salvation and socialist revolution, discontents about May Fourth modernity did not receive due scholarly attention until the 1980s. To quote a critical reassessment, for scholars such as Li Zehou and Liu Zaifu, "the May Fourth Movement was, in a sense, an abortive revolution, because its intellectual goal of enlightenment remains unrealized" (L. Lee 1991: 173).

Second, due to the Western origins of key concepts such as enlightenment and evolution, May Fourth modernity is inevitably seen as "belated modernity," and Chinese intellectuals are seemingly "doomed" in a game of always catching up with the "new" that is originated in and defined by the West. "Belated modernity is a self-imposed torture by those aware of the hegemony of Western modern discourse who choose nevertheless to dwell within it" (D. Wang 1997: 7). According to this reading, China is forever handicapped by its self-generated "discourse of deficit" (Zou 1998). There is, however, at least one way to reposition China in relation to the global structure of inequality in power and knowledge production: to take "translated modernity"—a deceptively second-order entity—in modern China positively by emphasizing praxis in the target language. By means of "translingual practice," Lydia Liu (Liu He) encourages scholars to investigate the ways in which Chinese intellectuals appropriate and negotiate Western terms in order to better understand "the rhetorical strategies, translations, discursive formations, naming practices, legitimizing processes, tropes, and narrative modes that bear upon the historical conditions of the Chinese experience of the modern" (L. Liu 1995: xviii).

Third, restricted by its vision of history as linear progress and its self-acclaimed elitist position, May Fourth modernity left no room for alternative—in particular, popular—literary practices, such as butterfly literature and martial arts fiction, which mixed the old with the new and adhered to conventional narrative techniques such as linked chapters (see Chapter 15 by Yi Zheng). Indeed, the dominant periodization scheme that neatly charts the May Fourth era as the "beginnings" of modern Chinese literature fails to account not only for "alternative modernity" represented by miscellaneous urban publications but also Lu Xun's translation of foreign literature and his—as well as many others'—poetry compositions in classical Chinese (Kowallis 1996; S. Wu 2014). For a more comprehensive view of the origins of modern Chinese literature, we shall now turn to an argument that late Qing fiction embodied certain "incipient modernities" that had subsequently been "repressed" and written off by the linear mode of official literary historiography, which champions the May Fourth as the first legitimate modernity in China.

Late Qing Modernities: Decadence as De-cadence

David Wang demonstrates the existence of widespread nascent creativity and the formation of a matrix of "incipient modernities" in late Qing cultural production (1849–1911). Through literary translation, fictional renovation, and re-engendering of sexual subjectivity, late Qing fiction entered "the crosscultural and interlingual dialogue we know as modernity" (D. Wang 1997: 4). In a counter-hegemonic move, Wang locates four discursive axes around which a poetics of "repressed modernities" was structured in late Qing fiction.

First, under the pretext of enlightenment, late Qing fiction openly indulged in "decadence." In spite of its negative connotation, if we rethink decadence as "de-cadence," we perceive a hidden dimension—"a falling away of the established order, a displacement of that which has been taken for granted, and an uncanny 'falling together' of conceptual and formal elements that would not have come together at a time of high culture" (D. Wang 1997: 25). Thus retheorized, decadence as de-cadence became an effective means of challenging the elitist tendency to degrade literature and then to sanctify it anew with a new ideology. This elitist tendency was exemplified early by Liang Qichao's criticism of "moral degradation" in late Qing fiction and later by May Fourth critics' accusation of butterfly literature as a form of "literary prostitution" (*wenchang*) (Y. Zhang 1997: 56).

Second, instead of evolution or revolution (both predicated on the necessarily violent "overcoming" of the old by the new), late Qing fiction preferred "involution"—an "introverted tendency" that might lead to unexpected inventions and "generate differences and complexities while remaining inside one's own time and place" (D. Wang 1997: 31, 35). A great number of late Qing literary innovations testified to the success of involution as a particular type of development in literary modernity.

Third, in its quest for rationality, late Qing fiction paradoxically embraced emotive excess, and its unique politics of male "sentimentalism" (*qing*) prefigured the contestation or "alteration" of May Fourth modernity attempted by butterfly literature in the subsequent decades.[1]

Fourth, rather than the ideal of mimesis as manifested in its topical coverage of sociohistorical events, late Qing fiction tended to favor "mimicry" as a "low" form of imitation that relies on cynical repetition and overfamiliarization. By means of exaggeration, distortion, and simplification, late Qing writers were able to turn the "depths" of meaning into an extended surface, thereby foreshadowing the type of urban modernities that would flourish in the 1920s–1930s.

From Wang's four discursive axes, we can see that the dominant cultural logic of late Qing fiction is a heteroglossia of "both/and"—which stands in sharp contrast to the clear-cut binarism of the "either/or" characteristic of May Fourth modernity. Due to its carnivalesque celebration of ambivalence and heterogeneity, late Qing fiction predated the kind of "gendered modernity" that Rey Chow (1991: 55) discerns in butterfly literature. Unabashed in its continuous pouring of tears, late Qing fiction had foreshadowed the willful "feminization" of Chinese cultural tradition in butterfly literature. Seen together, late Qing fiction and butterfly literature constituted "alternative modernities" that questioned the "masculine" features of May Fourth modernity (i.e., features conceptually aligned with rationality and revolution).

"The crucial burst of modernity came in the late Qing, not the May Fourth period" (D. Wang 1997: 8)—with this revisionist statement, Wang has participated in a joint venture in mainland China where the concept of "twentieth-century Chinese literature" was promoted by a new generation of scholars in the late 1980s (Chen Sihe 1987; Z. Huang, Chen, and Qian 1988). The late Qing, in other words, is now regarded as an integral and legitimate part of the modern in Chinese culture (Chen Pingyuan 1989). However, we must recognize that, in spite of its endorsement of involution and decadence in synchronic terms, Wang's historiographical paradigm remains fundamentally linear in its conception of development in diachronic terms. This explains why Wang (1997: 16) conjures that "Late Qing fiction would have led to a very different version of the Chinese modern had it not been rejected by high-minded 'modern' Chinese writers as so obviously 'pre-modern'." To substantiate his conjecture, Wang devotes an entire concluding chapter to locating the continuity in the new *fin de siècle*—between contemporary fiction in mainland China, Hong Kong, and Taiwan and its "late Qing antecedents" (a topic to be resumed later).

Urban Modernities: Cosmopolitanism and Hybridity

As mentioned earlier, "late Qing antecedents" to contemporary Chinese literature were similarly present in butterfly literature, a kind of urban fiction popular in the Republican period (1910s–1940s). David Wang's revisionist scheme—whereby the late Qing is seen as repressed or negated by the May Fourth—brings up an intriguing question: does urban modernity as represented by Leo Lee's "Shanghai modern" constitute a new phase of modernity that somehow bypassed the May Fourth and reconnected itself to the late Qing on the one hand and to the 1990s and after on the other?

On the surface, urban modernities—I specifically employ the plural form here—closely resemble late Qing modernities: both celebrated the heterogeneous surfaces at the expense of the depths of certain presumably unified or unitary meaning. Leo Lee (1999b: 63) thus justifies his new methodology of "cultural history": "we must not neglect the 'surfaces', the images and styles that do not necessarily enter into the deepest of thought but nevertheless conjure up a collective imaginary. In my view, 'modernity' is both idea and imaginary, both essence and surface." Based on this conviction, Lee proceeds to read the imaginary beneath or beyond a dazzling array of surfaces, which range from architectural styles, department stores, coffee houses, dance halls, public parks, the race club, movies theaters, residential structures, to popular magazines, textbooks, and repositories (*wenku*), print advertisements, calendar posters, modern pictorials, foreign books, and fictional characters. Advocating cultural history as "a new approach" to urban modernity, Lee (1999b: 58–60) increasingly indulges in a method of cataloguing that parallels his attention to surfaces and sometimes precludes the necessity of in-depth analysis.

Among English scholarship, Lee's approach is not exactly new, because Perry Link (1981) has earlier attempted to classify urban magazines and popular writers' roles in his "sociological" (R. Chow 1991: 47) study of butterfly literature years. What is significant here is that Lee's supposedly "new" method of cultural history stands in opposition to his previous approach to May Fourth modernity—what he has by now described as "the elitist approach of conventional intellectual history, which tends to discuss only the essential ideas of individual thinkers" (L. Lee 1999b: 63). China historians may point to social history as what is missing in Lee's distinction between "elitist" intellectual history and "populist" cultural history, for social history in fact has dominated historical scholarship on modern China in North America for decades. In this context, it is illuminating to compare Lee's (1990: 121–122) earlier statement in favor of a hermeneutic reading of "depths" in intellectual history: "The treaty-port city, particularly Shanghai, constituted a 'spacialization' of 'modernity'—a configuration of space which crystallized the present moment, a self-contained world cut off and set apart from the traditionalism of the surrounding countryside." Without debating this problematic reading (especially the terms "self-contained" and "cut off"), we detect a crucial difference between late Qing modernities and urban modernities of the Republican era: whereas late Qing modernities appeared to be more *self-oriented* or inward-looking in the appropriation of the foreign into the Chinese (hence an insistence on traditionalism that had unfortunately resulted in the marginalization of the late Qing as the "premodern" or "early modern"), the "Shanghai modern" was more *other-oriented* or outward-looking in its imaginary integration with cosmopolitanism and in its ever-renewed display of hybridity. This difference may have prompted Lee (1999b: 315) to argue that, "if cosmopolitanism means an abiding curiosity in 'looking out'—locating oneself as a cultural mediator at the intersection between China and other parts of the world—then Shanghai in the 1930s was the cosmopolitan city par excellence."

The question remains, however, as to the exact relationship between Shanghai as a cosmopolitan city (Lee's view) and Shanghai as a semicolonial city (Shu-mei Shih's view), for both cosmopolitanism and semicoloniality are seen as part and parcel of the 1930s Shanghai modern, and both are exemplified by the same modernist writers (e.g., Liu Na'ou and Mu Shiying) that Lee and Shih discuss. For Lee (1999b: 312), these writers' "sense of Chinese identity was never in question *in spite of* the Western colonial presence in Shanghai," and "it was only because of their unquestioned Chineseness that these writers were able to embrace Western modernity openly, without fear of colonization." In other words, Lee hypothesizes that these writers' secure sense of Chineseness helped them achieve a genuine type of cosmopolitanism.[2] For Shih, it is precisely the pressures of colonization that drove Liu Na'ou and Mu Shiying into troubling identity crises and eventually made them victims of wartime political assassination. Shih sees the advantage of semicoloniality in these writers' ability to bypass the rigid binary opposition between colonialism and nationalism and to critique Chinese patriarchy through the enigmatic figure of New Woman or Modern Girl (see Chapter 25 by Tze-lan Sang), whose "emancipation" is facilitated by a "denationalized cosmopolitanism" in semicolonial Shanghai. Contrary to Lee's hypothesis of a secure Chineseness, Shih argues that Chinese cosmopolitans such as Mu Shiying, having no clear enemy, lacked the option of direct nationalism and were fundamentally insecure—insecure specifically because Mu was a "semicolonial subject" who resembles the "postmodern subject," for both are troubled by split personality (Shih 2001: 237, 312, 331).

To return to Lee's emphasis on surfaces, it is obvious that he has revised his previous claim that "in the 1920s and 1930s, modernity was more largely an unrealized idea than a tangible reality" (Lee 1990: 127). The abundant signs and images catalogued in his Shanghai book confirm the material existence of modernities in Shanghai. What may have occasioned Lee's revision is his subsequent differentiation of what I call "phases of modernity" in China. If May Fourth modernity—with its aborted project of enlightenment—remained "an unrealized idea," urban modernities—with abundant material signs—were undeniably a tangible reality in Republican Shanghai. In contrast to the May Fourth "bifurcation" of Western modernity into a lofty idea (i.e., cosmopolitanism outside China, as object of emulation) and a threatening reality (i.e., colonial presence in China, as object of resistance), Shanghai modernist writers celebrated the materiality of modernities—visually perceived and graphically represented—with all its unresolved tensions and contradictions (Shih 2001: 36, 304).

However, urban modernities call for further differentiation. For instance, even within Shanghai, the vision of modernity projected by Liu Na'ou and Mu Shiying proved more outward-looking or even intentionally outlandish—as captured in their figures of the dandy and the *flâneur* that links them to their counterparts in Tokyo and Paris in a flamboyant showcase of "transcultural modernity" (H. Peng 2010)—than that contained in Eileen Chang, although they all featured Shanghai hybridity and cosmopolitanism extensively. Besides, the geographic parameters of urban modernities extend far beyond Shanghai. From the perspective of a larger framework of cultural history, Beijing writers would enter the scene as another crucial—albeit often neglected—player in urban modernities of the Republican era (Y. Zhang 1996). Most Beijing writers—not just those classified as the "Beijing style"—were more self-oriented in their cultural stance and less susceptible to the forces of "semicolonial modernity" than their Shanghai counterparts, but they were no less cosmopolitan and modern in their quest for an imaginary fusion of Western and Eastern civilizations (Shih 2001). Moreover, urban modernities were projected not just in popular or modernist fiction but in prose writing as well, and the previously much censured quest for leisurely self-cultivation in writers such as Zhou Zuoren and Lin Yutang are now reinterpreted as representing "a sophisticated way of being modern" (Laughlin 2008: 12), an alternative Chinese response to modernity (Daruvala 2000), and a cosmopolitan way of "middling" Chinese modernity in times of radical extremes (S. Qian 2011).

Socialist Modernity: Revolution as Ecstasy

In an epilogue infused with nostalgia for Shanghai modern, Leo Lee (1999b: 338) imagines himself in Eileen Chang's position and comes to a gloomy conclusion that "half a century of revolution has indeed destroyed *in toto* China's urban culture, together

with its cosmopolitan sensibilities." In a sense, Lee's lament for the loss of Old Shanghai
bears witness to the success of socialist modernity in eliminating the traces of old
cultural imaginaries and in projecting new utopian fantasies. In the "lyrical age" of
socialist revolution, "a sublime heroics" (X. Tang 2000: 192–193) negated and
replaced the type of cultural and aesthetic sensibility fashionable in Old Shanghai.
Such replacement is codified in a picture of the stage set designed for the final scene of
a popular 1963 drama titled *The Young Generation*—a panoramic view of the cityscape
of Shanghai where the red flags fly high on top of some Western-style high-rises.

Thus aestheticized and politicized, socialist modernity relied heavily on the staging
of the nation in the form of a theatrical spectacle. "The theatrical dimension of
The Young Generation revealed the centrality of the stage to the logic of the popular
imagination of this visionary period. It was an age when the stage was expected to be
a truthful mirror of life, and life itself was celebrated as a grand stage for purposeful
action" (X. Tang 2000: 194). Both life and the stage offered enormous pleasure to
actors and audiences, and Tang's statement (2000: 195) that "ecstasy stimulated by
staged life may ignite explosive youthful energy" deserves further investigation. Earlier
in his book, Tang (2000: 58) thus explicates the idea of *kuang* in "Diary of a Madman":

> *Kuang* is the archetypal metaphor for an explosive ecstasy (ex-stasis), a jumping off the
> right track, a transgressive crossing of the boundary—in short, a return to the primal or
> instinctual drive. It captures, to a certain extent, the inner experience of the alterity of
> reason, of what has to be repressed and marginalized as irrational; it acknowledges the
> deep discontents that a civilization necessarily breeds.

In an uncanny and profoundly ironic way, the "ecstasy" experienced by Lu Xun's
madman is intertextually linked to the nearly religious ecstasy the young generation
experienced in socialist China. Indeed, propelled by the dynamics of ecstasy (or
kuang), the explosive youthful energy found its volcanic release during the Cultural
Revolution, a period in which life and the stage were completely integrated, transgression and irrationality became rationalized norms, and the instinctual—in its
extreme sadomasochistic mode—ruled the entire nation. All this is dramatically
captured in Ban Wang's psychoanalytical reading of the Cultural Revolution, and his
chapter's subtitle, "A Terrible Beauty Is Born" (1997: 194), says it all.

Due to its traumatic impact on the national psyche, many scholars used to dis-
qualify socialism as a legitimate type of modernity. However, we should not ignore the
utopian nature of socialist fantasy and its all-powerful rhetoric of enlightenment and
progress: the lyrical age "was apparently an age of great passion and expectations, an
age in which the boldest dreams about human happiness were collectively dreamed,
and the most ordinary moments in life gloriously poeticized" (X. Tang 2000: 165).
As "a coercive state project" (Dirlik and Zhang 1997: 17), socialist modernity is at
once a horrid face and a crucial phase of Chinese modernity, a collapsed utopia that
breeds nightmares and invokes nostalgia, including "totalitarian nostalgia" in post-
Mao China (Barmé 1999: 316–344).

The recent interest in socialist modernity may have derived from a persistent belief in socialism as an alternative to global capitalism, even though it was an unfulfilled one. If both late Qing and May Fourth modernities are unmistakably part of translated or belated modernity, and urban modernities of the Republican era part of hybridized, semicolonial modernity, then socialist modernity may have promised to be China's only chance for an "indigenous" modernity, although the official pledge to Marxism originated in the West makes this claim contradictory. In his exploration of "the genealogy of the aesthetic in China's alternative modernity," Liu Kang (2000: xi–ii) pays close attention to Mao Zedong's "plan for a socialist China as an alternative to both Soviet-style socialism and Western capitalism." As Liu argues elsewhere, "Chinese modernity, as an 'alternative modernity', is first and foremost concerned with the question of revolution"; conversely, it is "China's distinct revolutionary legacy and hegemony [that] constitute an alternative, if not post, modernity" (Liu Kang 1998: 167–169).

Similarly attentive to China's socialism, Arif Dirlik (1989: 380) is nonetheless aware that, "within the context of a capitalist world system, the overall motions of which are shaped by a capitalism that socialism has ceased to challenge but rather seeks to accommodate, socialism can no longer claim to possess a coherent alternative to capitalism." For this reason, Dirlik prefers "postsocialism" (a term to be elaborated later). Similarly, Xudong Zhang's study of Chinese modernism is related to the question of how to define Chinese modernity "not as a duplication of modernity as such but as something more or something else, that is to say, as a potential alternative." A shared interest in envisioning a Chinese *alternative* has thus led Zhang to join Dirlik in conceptualizing postsocialism as "the concrete socioeconomic, political, as well as cultural conditions" that have shaped (post)modernity as a particular type of Chinese experience (X. Zhang 1997: 17–18).

Postsocialist Modernities: Of Intellectualism and Consumerism

Before the recent rethinking of China's socialist utopia and revolutionary legacy (Wang Hui 2009; B. Wang 2011; B. Wang and Lu 2012; X. Zhong and Wang 2014), socialist modernity was judged, by and large, as repressive and destructive, as pertaining to the dark ages rather than an era of enlightenment. In the immediate post-Mao period (the 1980s), many scholars resolutely negated socialist modernity by way of reconnecting themselves to the aborted project of May Fourth modernity. The spirits of enlightenment and humanism were resurrected, and culture was given priority over politics. In a time of "high culture fever" (a term characterizing the cultural reflection or introspection of the 1980s), a new "epochal discourse" emerged to valorize enlightenment, rationality, and subjectivity once again (J. Wang 1996). In an ironic way, postsocialist modernities initially resembled socialist modernity, in that both embraced a modern consciousness and both tended to project utopian visions and excite social fantasies. "Aesthetic modernity" of this period was evident across a wide spectrum: theories of Marxist humanism and literary subjectivity; literary modernisms as in Misty Poetry and stream-of-consciousness fiction; myths of untamed nature, primordial happiness, and raw masculine heroes in roots-searching literature; and the textual politics of resistance (e.g., against the tyrannical Mao style) in avant-garde fiction (X. Zhang 1997).

The elitist tendency of intellectualism in the early post-Mao period collided head-on with "sociocultural modernity," which has been engineered by the Communist leadership's new reforms in increasing complicity with transnational capitalism in the age of globalization. Indeed, literature as we know it rapidly lost its commanding power after the late 1980s, and intellectuals started to lament the downfall of "elite culture" (*jingying wenhua*) and "the humanist spirit" (*renwen jingshen*) in a fast-developing consumer society (Chen Pingyuan 1993; McGrath 2008: 25–58). In the wake of the June Fourth of 1989, the project of reconnecting with May Fourth modernity experienced a complete reversal of fortune. Enlightenment itself became a new target in the 1990s sober negation of the 1980s culture fever. With great reluctance, Li Zehou and Liu Zaifu (1997) bid farewell to revolution in their retrospective view of twentieth-century Chinese culture. Drawing on Jacques Lacan and Jacques Derrida, Zheng Min (1993) accused the May Fourth Movement of inflicting a fundamental rupture in Chinese poetic language (see Chapter 18 by Chen Jianhua). With recourse to the latest postmodern and postcolonial theories, a younger generation of scholars was eager to assume their position as "postcritics" in the age of "postpolitics" (Chen Xiaoming 1997) and openly celebrated the advent of new consumer culture as a long overdue integration of the elite and the popular (Chen Xiaoming 1994). For them, new cultural trends were represented by best-selling decadent novels such as Mo Yan's *The Republic of Wine* (1992) and Jia Pingwa's *The Defunct Capital* (1993) (G. Yue 1999: 262–287; X. Yang 2002: 207–229; Y. Wang 2006: 50–112), and by controversial avant-garde art called "political pop" (*zhengzhi bopu*) (Huot 2000: 126–153; S. Lu 2001: 141–192).

As it gathered momentum, the new tendency to reassess aesthetic modernity of the 1980s was taken to be an alarming sign of the emerging "cultural conservatism" in the 1990s. The heated debate in the Hong Kong journal *Twenty-First Century* during the mid-1990s quickly divided cultural critics in mainland China and overseas into several camps.[3] The catchall label *houxue* (post-isms or postology) indiscriminately applied to a large number of scholars of different ideological persuasions inevitably raises this question: are postsocialist modernities from its second decade (the 1990s) onward already on the brink of postmodernity, if not yet immersed in it? In other words, have we entered an entirely new phase in which we are not just dealing with a new face of modernity but a new entity called "postmodernism"?

The limited space does not allow for an adequate account of postmodernism and postsocialism in this chapter, but their mutual imbrication and the shift in the conceptualization of postsocialism are both unmistakable. For Sheldon Lu (2007: 210, original emphasis), "post*socialism* in the era of cautious reform and openness in the 1980s has transformed into *post*socialism in the age of grandiose transnational capitalism from the 1990s to the present." Treating it simultaneously as "a cultural logic," "a periodizing concept and a historical condition," Lu (2007: 209) is fully aware that postsocialism has constituted "a battlefield of intellectual and ideological contention between different persuasions." As one of its vocal promoter states, given the fact that postmodernism is a "nebulous yet productive discourse," "the empty signifier of Chinese postmodernism can only be filled with the phenomenological richness of Chinese post-socialism" (X. Zhang 1999: 78, 104). I take this statement to mean that it is too early for us— then as now—to commit to a fixed position on postmodernism and postsocialism in China, especially when China's phenomenological richness in the recent decades has tended to spill over our discursive framework.

Conclusion: Modernity *vis-à-vis* Postmodernism and Postsocialism

We can now sum up the salient contours of five phases of modernity in China. First, incipient modernities in the late Qing are marked by its cultural logic of heteroglossia (both/and) and its wishful indulgence in decadence and mimicry. Second, translated modernity of the May Fourth period is characterized by its enlightenment rhetoric and its radical binarism of revolution (either/or). Third, urban modernities of the Republican era—especially in its "semicolonial" configuration in Shanghai—are energized by an ever-renewed fascination with the glossy surfaces of materiality and an unabashed display of hybridity along with cosmopolitan sensibility. Fourth, socialist modernity excels in staging glorious life as a grand spectacle and inducing the ecstatic experience of the revolutionary utopia, thereby aspiring to an alternative to capitalist modernity. Finally, aesthetic modernity of the postsocialist era began in its first decade with a return to the May Fourth rhetoric of enlightenment by championing culture over politics, but only to depart, since its second decade, from utopian intellectualism into a sober, at times cynical or even pessimistic, confrontation with an all-powerful consumer culture.

In terms of literary history, we see that modernity has gone through a tortuous zigzag path of negation, mutation, and transformation in modern China. As indicated in Figure 30.1, we cannot but notice that the movement through "phases" is almost always from heteroglossic surfaces to monolithic ideas and back again, except for a direct transition from socialist modernity to the first decade of post-Mao modernities. This exception near the latest point in the movement seems to indicate that modernity in China has traveled full cycle and has arrived in a situation parallel to its starting point: a period marked by a variety of heteroglossic surfaces of competing cultures, discourses, and values.

Set against Figure 30.1, David Wang's (1997: 313–314) questions appear particularly relevant to our typography here:

> I turn to recent evidence that Chinese literature has returned to the unfinished work of inventing the modern, work begun by the late Qing. If late Qing fiction contains the thwarted beginnings of many kinds of modernity, are its repressed modernities resurfacing

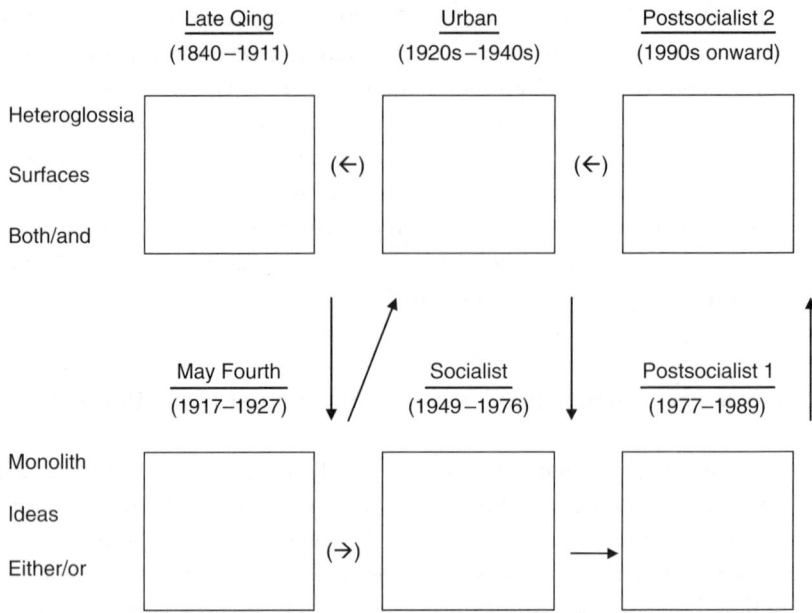

Figure 30.1 Five Phases of Modernity in China.

in late-twentieth-century Chinese fiction? If so, how would this joint rereading of late Qing and late-twentieth-century fiction impinge on the reading of May Fourth modernity? How would it help us reconfigure all the entry points to Chinese modernity—late Qing (premodern, abundance of modernities), May Fourth (modern, restriction to one modernity), and late twentieth century (postmodern, abundance of modernities again)?

Wang's characterization of late-twentieth-century Chinese fiction as "postmodern" with an "abundance of modernities" once again returns us to the apparent contradiction in the naming of the second part of postsocialist modernities. For Chinese postmodern advocates, the 1990s surely cry for a new name—the "post-New Era" (as opposed to the New Era of 1979–1989) (X. Zhang 2008), or "post-Mao-Deng," which eerily sounds like "postmodern" (X. Yang 2000). However, we are cautioned that the charting of "the passage from the modern to the postmodern" in twentieth-century China "may itself betray the same impulse of constructing a rational explanation or seamless horizon of intelligibility" (X. Tang 2000: 342), an impulse that is exactly what Chinese postmodern scholars are fighting against in the first place.

  Nonetheless, postmodernism remains a challenge for several reasons. First, if postmodernity is not treated as a mere periodizing concept, it appears that modernity is still an appropriate concept standing parallel to or even subsuming postmodernity in the new millennium. Leo Lee (1999a) insists on the centrality of modernity in the postmodern era in a lecture at Peking University, and Xiaobing Tang (2000) includes a chapter on postmodernism in his book on Chinese modern. Even the most eager promoters of Chinese postmodernism do not hesitate to use the term "modernity" to describe contemporary Chinese cultural scenes (Chen Xiaoming 1997; Wang Ning 1993). Second, as an equivalent for post-Mao or postrevolution (Dirlik 2011), post-socialism is used to cover a period of the coexistence of modernity and postmodernity (Pickowicz 1994; Dirlik and Zhang 2000), and whether postsocialism, postmodernism, or a new term would acquire more purchase in explicating the evolving sociocultural condition of China in the new millennium remains to be seen. Third, the trajectory of modernity in modern Chinese culture favors a zigzag movement, not a linear progression, in its multiple phases. Given the nature of such movement, "faces" of late Qing modernities such as decadence and mimicry have resurfaced since the late twentieth century, just as Shanghai modern of the 1930s—once imagined to have been lost forever—has been reincarnated into a new cultural dominant in contemporary consumer culture in mainland China (see Chapter 6 by Tao Dongfeng), Hong Kong, and Taiwan. Yet, such reincarnation does not prevent Chinese intellectuals from critiquing both consumer and political cultures and from reclaiming their central role in the unfinished project of modernity.

As this chapter illustrates, after decades of scholarship, there is still no consensus on exactly what modernity is in China. Not long ago, William Rowe (2000: 707) questioned whether modernity had ever existed in Chinese reality: "'modern' as a label has no utility other than in reference to a term in the historical discourse itself; one might even say that 'modernism' has an [sic] historical reality, but 'modernity' does not." Obviously, Rowe's question misses the point because, even construed exclusively as an idea, modernity has a tangible—and highly consequential—existence in modern China. Contrary to Row, Wen-hsin Yeh (2000: 27) sees modernity as not merely tangible but almost pervasive in modern China:

> Modernity is seen … as multifarious and complex. It operates simultaneously on several levels. The topics include projects of intellectual enlightenment, urban cosmopolitanism and consumerism, global enterprises and transnational capitalism, bureaucratic rationalization and industrial technology, the transformation of material culture, municipal planning, urbanization, professionalization, the rise of the nation-state, the disciplining of a new citizenry, and the emergence of a nationalist discourse.

Here, Yeh's preference for the material (fully tangible) over the intellectual (less tangible) is evident in her characterization of Leo Lee's study of Shanghai modern: "Implicit in his approach is the argument that modernity was about business rather than politics, the quest for a good life rather than a just society, the transformative capacity of private enterprises rather than collective action" (W. Yeh 2000: 7). Leo Lee might dispute Yeh's binary characterization of his methodology, but the question for us to pursue further is not so much whether modernity has a historical reality in China, as what kind of reality gives rise to and shapes the particular type of modernity that emerges and prevails in a given historical period; and hence my punning imbrication of "faces" and "phases" of modernity.

In conclusion, I would like to borrow Jameson's argument to locate where we stand in relation to Chinese modernity in the early twenty-first century—just replace his "postmodernism" with "modernity" in the following text:

> As for *postmodernism* itself, I have not tried to systematize a usage or to impose any conveniently coherent thumbnail meaning, for the concept is not merely contested, it is also internally conflicted and contradictory. I will argue that, for good or ill, we cannot *not* use it. But my argument should also be taken to imply that every time it is used, we are under the obligation to rehearse those inner contradictions and to stage those representational inconsistencies and dilemmas; we have to work all that through every time around. (Jameson 1991: xxii)

To paraphrase Jameson's argument, we must always keep in mind those inner contradictions in Chinese modernity and those competing voices of articulating the Chinese experience of modernity, including postmodernism and postsocialism. This chapter is just one such attempt at working through some of the contradictions and representational inconsistencies, and at resituating Chinese modernity as a key concept of cultural historiography that demands our renewed attention.

NOTES

1 For an elaboration of "alteration" as a dynamic of cultural production and its associated motifs of play in modern China, see Y. Zhang 2013.

2 This is a disputable hypothesis because Liu Na'ou's "Chineseness" was questionable at the time because his background as a Taiwan-born, Japan-educated sojourner in Shanghai prompted critics to suspect that he was more comfortable with Japanese than with Chinese in writing.

3 For the pro-modernity position, see Y. H. Zhao (1997); Wang Hui (1998); Ben Xu (1999); and Zhang Longxi (1998). For the postmodern position, see articles (especially those by Chen Xiaoming, Wang Ning, and Zhang Yiwu) in Dirlik and Zhang (2000); S. Lu (2001); X. Zhang (2001); and X. Yang (2002). For critical summaries of some early postmodern debates, see Saussy (1999) and M. Yeh (1999). For other related interventions, see Larson and Wedell-Wedellsborg (1993); R. Chow (2000); and G. Davies (2001).

REFERENCES

Alitto, Guy S. 1979. *The Last Confucian: Liang Shuming and the Chinese Dilemma of Modernity.* Berkeley: University of California Press.

Barmé, Geremie R. 1999. *In the Red: On Contemporary Chinese Culture.* New York: Columbia University Press.

Button, Peter. 2009. *Configurations of the Real in Chinese Literary and Aesthetic Modernity.* Leiden: Brill.

Calinescu, Matei. 1987. *Five Faces of Modernity: Modernism, Avant-Garde, Decadence, Kitsch, Postmodernism.* Durham, NC: Duke University Press.

Chang, Chun-shu, and Shelley Hsueh-lun Chang. 1992. *Crisis and Transformation in Seventeenth-Century China: Society, Culture, and Modernity in Li Yu's World*. Ann Arbor: University of Michigan Press.

Chen, Pingyuan 陳平原. 1989. *Ershi shiji Zhongguo xiaoshuo shi, diyijuan 1897–1916* 二十世紀中國小説史, 第一卷 1897–1916 (A history of twentieth-century Chinese fiction, vol. 1, 1897–1916). Beijing: Beijing daxue chubanshe.

Chen, Pingyuan 陳平原. 1993. "Jin bainian Zhongguo jingying wenhua de shiluo" 近百年中國精英文化的失落 (The downfall of the Chinese elite culture over the past century). *Ershiyi shiji* 二十一世紀 (Twenty-first century), 17: 11–22.

Chen, Sihe 陳思和. 1987. *Zhongguo xinwenxue zhengti guan* 中國新文學整體觀 (A total view of new Chinese literature). Shanghai: Shanghai wenyi chubanshe.

Chen Xiaoming 陳曉明. 1994. "Tianping honggou, huaqing jiexian—'jingying' yu 'dazhong' shutu tonggui de dangdai chaoliu" 填平鴻溝, 劃清界線: "精英" 與 "大衆"殊途同歸的當代潮流 (Fill in the gap, draw the dividing line: a contemporary trend whereby the "elite" and the "popular" converge and move in one direction). *Wenyi yanjiu* 文藝研究 (Literature and art studies), 1: 42–55.

Chen, Xiaoming. 1997. "The Mysterious Other: Postpolitics in Chinese Film." *Boundary 2*, 24.3: 123–141.

Chow, Rey. 1991. *Woman and Chinese Modernity: The Politics of Reading between West and East*. Minneapolis: University of Minnesota Press.

Chow, Rey. Ed. 2000. *Modern Chinese Literary and Cultural Studies in the Age of Theory: Reimagining a Field*. Durham, NC: Duke University Press.

Daruvala, Susan. 2000. *Zhou Zuoren and an Alternative Response to Chinese Modernity*. Cambridge, MA: Harvard University Asia Center.

Davies, Gloria. Ed. 2001. *Voicing Concerns: Contemporary Chinese Critical Inquiry*. Lanham, MD: Rowman and Littlefield.

Dikötter, Frank. 1995. *Sex, Culture, and Modernity in China*. Honolulu: University of Hawaii Press.

Dirlik, Arif. 1989. "Postsocialism? Reflections on 'Socialism with Chinese Characteristics.'" In *Marxism and the Chinese Experience*. Edited by Dirlik, Arif, and Maurice Meisner. Armonk, NY: E. M. Sharpe. 362–384.

Dirlik, Arif. 2011. *Culture and History in Postrevolutionary China: The Perspective of Global Modernity*. Hong Kong: Chinese University Press.

Dirlik, Arif, and Xudong Zhang. 1997. "Introduction: Postmodernism and China." *Boundary 2*, 24.3: 1–18.

Dirlik, Arif, and Xudong Zhang. Eds. 2000. *Postmodernism and China*. Durham, NC: Duke University Press, 2000.

Esherick, Joseph W. Ed. 2000. *Remaking the Chinese City: Modernity and National Identity, 1900–1950*. Honolulu: University of Hawaii Press.

Gimpel, Denise. 2001. *Lost Voices of Modernity: A Chinese Popular Fiction Magazine in Context*. Honolulu: University of Hawaii Press.

Gong, Haomin. 2012. *Uneven Modernity: Literature, Film, and Intellectual Discourse in Postsocialist China*. Honolulu: University of Hawaii Press.

Hershatter, Gail. 1997. *Dangerous Pleasures: Prostitution and Modernity in Twentieth-Century Shanghai*. Berkeley: University of California Press.

Hockx, Michel. 1994. *A Snowy Morning: Eight Chinese Poets on the Road to Modernity*. Leiden: Research School CNWS.

Huang Ziping 黃子平, Chen Pingyuan 陳平原, and Qian Liqun 錢理群. 1988. *Ershi shiji Zhongguo wenxue sanren tan* 二十世紀中國文學三人談 (Three critics on twentieth-century Chinese literature). Beijing: renmin wenxue chubanshe.

Huot, Claire. 2000. *China's New Cultural Scene: A Handbook of Changes*. Durham, NC: Duke University Press.

Jameson, Fredric. 1986. "Third-World Literature in the Era of Multinational Capitalism." *Social Text*, 15: 65–88.

Jameson, Fredric. 1991. *Postmodernism, or, The Cultural Logic of Late Capitalism*. Durham, NC: Duke University Press.

Jones, Andrew F. 2001. *Yellow Music: Media Culture and Colonial Modernity in the Chinese Jazz Age*. Durham, NC: Duke University Press.

Kowallis, Jon Eugene von. 1996. *The Lyrical Lu Xun: A Study of His Classical-Style Verse*. Honolulu: University of Hawaii Press.

Larson, Wendy, and Anne Wedell-Wedellsborg. Eds. 1993. *Inside Out: Modernism and Postmodernism in Chinese Literary Culture*. Aarhus, Denmark: Aarhus University Press.

Laughlin, Charles A. 2008. *The Literature of Leisure and Chinese Modernity*. Honolulu: University of Hawaii Press.

Laughlin, Charles A. Ed. 2005. *Contested Modernities in Chinese Literature*. New York: Palgrave Macmillan.

Lee, Leo Ou-fan. 1987. *Voices from the Iron House: A Study of Lu Xun*. Bloomington: Indiana University Press.

Lee, Leo Ou-fan. 1990. "In Search of Modernity: Some Reflections on a New Mode of Consciousness in Twentieth-Century Chinese History and Literature." In *Ideas across Cultures: Essays on Chinese Thought in Honor of Benjamin I. Schwartz*, eds. Cohen, Paul, and Merle Goldman. Cambridge, MA: Council on East Asian Studies, Harvard University. 109–135.

Lee, Leo Ou-fan. 1991. "Modernity and Its Discontents: The Cultural Agenda of the May Fourth Movement." In *Perspectives on Modern China: Four Anniversaries*. Edited by Lieberthal, Kenneth, Joyce Kallgren, Roderick MacFarquhar, and Frederic Wakeman, Jr. Armonk, NY: M. E. Sharpe. 158–177.

Lee, Leo Ou-fan (Li Oufan 李歐梵). 1999a. "Dangdai Zhongguo wenhua de xiandai xing he hou xiandai xing" 當代中國文化的現代性和後現代性 (Modernity and postmodernity in contemporary Chinese culture). *Wenxue pinglun*, 5: 129–139.

Lee, Leo Ou-fan. 1999b. *Shanghai Modern: The Flowering of a New Urban Culture in China, 1930–1945*. Cambridge, MA: Harvard University Press.

Lee, Leo Ou-fan. Ed. 1985. *Lu Xun and His Legacy*. Berkeley: University of California Press.

Li Zehou 李澤厚, and Liu Zaifu 劉再復. 1997. *Gaobie geming: huiwang ershi shiji Zhongguo* 告別革命: 回望二十世紀中國 (Farewell to revolution: twentieth-century China in retrospect). Hong Kong: Tiandi.

Liu, Kang. 1998. "Is There an Alternative to (Capitalist) Globalization? The Debate about Modernity in China." In *The Cultures of Globalization*. Edited by Jameson, Fredric, and Masao Miyoshi. Durham, NC: Duke University Press. 164–188.

Liu, Kang. 2000. *Aesthetics and Marxism: Chinese Aesthetic Marxists and Their Western Contemporaries*. Durham, NC: Duke University Press.

Liu, Lydia H. 1995. *Translingual Practice: Literature, National Culture, and Translated Modernity— China, 1900–1937*. Stanford, CA: Stanford University Press.

Lu, Sheldon H. 2001. *China, Transnational Visuality, Global Postmodernity*. Stanford, CA: Stanford University Press.

Lu, Sheldon H. 2007. *Chinese Modernity and Global Biopolitics: Studies in Literature and Visual Culture*. Honolulu: University of Hawaii Press.

McGrath, Jason. 2008. *Postsocialist Modernity: Chinese Cinema, Literature, and Criticism in the Market Age*. Stanford, CA: Stanford University Press.

Oakes, Tim. 1998. *Tourism and Modernity in China*. London: Routledge.

Peng, Hsiao-yen. 2010. *Dandyism and Transcultural Modernity: The Dandy, the Flâneur, and the Translator in 1930s Shanghai, Tokyo and Paris*. London: Routledge.

Pickowicz, Paul G. 1994. "Huang Jianxin and the Notion of Postsocialism." In *New Chinese Cinemas: Forms, Identities, Politics*. Edited by

Browne, Nick, Paul G. Pickowicz, Vivian Sobchack, and Esther Yau. New York: Cambridge University Press. 57–87.

Porter, David. Ed. 2012. *Comparative Early Modernities: 1100–1800*. New York: Palgrave Macmillan.

Qian, Suoqiao 錢鎖橋. 2011. *Liberal Cosmopolitan: Lin Yutang and Middling Chinese Modernity*. Leiden: Brill.

Rojas, Carlos. 2008. *The Naked Gaze: Reflections on Chinese Modernity*. Cambridge, MA: Harvard University Asia Center.

Rowe, William. 2000. "Review of *Remaking the Chinese City: Modernity and National Identity, 1900–1950*, Edited by Joseph Esherick." *Journal of Asian Studies*, 59.3: 706–707.

Saussy, Haun. 1999. "Postmodernism in China: A Sketch and Some Queries." In *Cross-Cultural Readings of Chinese: Narratives, Images, and Interpretations of the 1990s*. Edited by Yeh, Wen-hsin. Berkeley: University of California, Institute of East Asian Studies. 128–158.

Shih, Shu-mei. 2001. *The Lure of the Modern: Writing Modernism in Semicolonial China, 1917–1937*. Berkeley: University of California Press.

Tang, Xiaobing. 1996. *Global Space and the Nationalist Discourse of Modernity: The Historical Thinking of Liang Qichao*. Stanford, CA: Stanford University Press.

Tang, Xiaobing. 2000. *Chinese Modern: The Heroic and the Quotidian*. Durham, NC: Duke University Press.

Tsin, Michael Tsang-Woon. 1999. *Nation, Governance, and Modernity in China: Canton, 1900–1927*. Stanford, CA: Stanford University Press.

Walker, Kathy Le Mons. 1999. *Chinese Modernity and the Peasant Path: Semicolonialism in the Northern Yangzi Delta*. Stanford, CA: Stanford University Press.

Wang, Ban. 1997. *The Sublime Figure of History: Aesthetics and Politics in Twentieth Century China*. Stanford, CA: Stanford University Press.

Wang, Ban. Ed. 2011. *Words and Their Stories: Essays on the Language of the Chinese Revolution*. Leiden: Brill.

Wang, Ban, and Jie Lu. Eds. 2012. *China and New Left Visions: Political and Cultural Interventions*. Lanham, MD: Lexington Books.

Wang, David Der-wei. 1997. *Fin-de-siècle Splendor: Repressed Modernities of Late Qing Fiction, 1849–1911*. Stanford, CA: Stanford University Press.

Wang, David Der-wei. 2013. "Post-Loyalism." In *Sinophone Studies: A Critical Reader*. Edited by Shih, Shu-mei, Chien-hsin Tsai, and Brian Bernards. New York: Columbia University Press. 93–116.

Wang, Gungwu. 1977. *China and the World since 1949: The Impact of Independence, Modernity, and Revolution*. New York: St. Martin's Press.

Wang, Hui. 1998. "Contemporary Chinese Thought and the Question of Modernity." *Social Text*, 16.2: 9–44.

Wang, Hui. 2009. *The End of the Revolution: China and the Limits of Modernity*. London: Verso.

Wang, Jing. 1996. *High Culture Fever: Politics, Aesthetics, and Ideology in Deng's China*. Berkeley: University of California Press.

Wang, Ning. 1993. "Constructing Postmodernism: The Chinese Case and Its Different Versions." *Canadian Review of Comparative Literature*, 20: 49–61.

Wang, Xiaojue. 2013. *Modernity with a Cold War Face: Reimagining the Nation in Chinese Literature across the 1949 Divide*. Cambridge, MA: Harvard University Asia Center.

Wang, Yiyan. 2006. *Narrating China: Jia Pingwa and His Fictional World*. London: Routledge.

Wu, Shengqing. 2014. *Modern Archaics: Continuity and Innovation in the Chinese Lyrical Tradition, 1900-1937*. Cambridge, MA: Harvard University Asian Center.

Xu, Ben. 1999. *Disenchanted Democracy: Chinese Cultural Criticism after 1989*. Ann Arbor: University of Michigan Press.

Yang, Xiaobin. 2000. "Answering the Question: What Is Chinese Postmodernism/Post-Mao-Dengism?" In *Chinese Literature in the Second Half of a Modern Century: A Critical Survey*. Edited by Chi, Pang-yuan, and David Der-wei Wang. Bloomington: Indiana University Press. 193–215.

Yang, Xiaobin. 2002. *The Chinese Postmodern: Trauma and Irony in Chinese Avant-Garde Fiction*. Ann Arbor: University of Michigan Press.

Ye, Weili. 2001. *Seeking Modernity in China's Name: Chinese Students in the United States, 1900–1927*. Stanford, CA: Stanford University Press.

Yeh, Michelle. 1999. "Chinese Postmodernism and the Cultural Politics of Modern Chinese Poetry." In *Cross-Cultural Readings of Chinese: Narratives, Images, and Interpretations of the 1990s*. Edited by Yeh, Wen-hsin. Berkeley: University of California, Institute of East Asian Studies. 100–127.

Yeh, Wen-hsin. Ed. 2000. *Becoming Chinese: Passages to Modernity and Beyond*. Berkeley: University of California Press.

Yue, Gang. 1999. *The Mouth That Begs: Hunger, Cannibalism, and the Politics of Eating in Modern China*. Durham, NC: Duke University Press.

Zhang Longxi. 1998. *Mighty Opposites: From Dichotomies to Differences in the Comparative Study of China*. Stanford, CA: Stanford University Press.

Zhang, Xudong. 1997. *Chinese Modernism in the Era of Reforms: Cultural Fever, Avant-garde Fiction, and the New Chinese Cinema*. Durham, NC: Duke University Press.

Zhang, Xudong. 1999. "Postmodernism and Post-Socialist Society: Cultural Politics in China after the 'New Era.'" *New Left Review*, 23.7: 77–105.

Zhang, Xudong. 2008. *Postsocialism and Cultural Politics: China in the Last Decade of the Twentieth Century*. Durham, NC: Duke University Press.

Zhang, Xudong. Ed. 2001. *Whither China? Intellectual Politics in Contemporary China*. Durham, NC: Duke University Press.

Zhang, Yingjin. 1996. *The City in Modern Chinese Literature and Film: Configurations of Space, Time, and Gender*. Stanford, CA: Stanford University Press.

Zhang, Yingjin. 1997. "Building a National Literature in Modern China: Literary Criticism, Gender Ideology, and the Public Sphere." *Journal of Modern Literature in Chinese*, 1.1: 47–74.

Zhang, Yingjin. 2013. "Witness outside History: Play for Alteration in Modern Chinese Culture." *Modernism/Modernity*, 20.2: 349–369.

Zhao, Henry Y. H. 1997. "Post-Isms and Chinese New Conservatism." *New Literary History*, 28.1: 31–44.

Zheng Min 鄭敏. 1993. "Shiji mo de huigu: Hanyu yuyan biange yu Zhongguo xinshi chuangzuo" 世紀末的回顧─漢語語言變革與中國新詩創作 (A fin-de-siècle reflection on the change of *Hanyu* and new Chinese poetic writing). *Wenxue pinglun*, 3: 5–20.

Zhong, Xueping. 2000. *Masculinity Besieged? Issues of Modernity and Male Subjectivity in Chinese Literature of the Late Twentieth Century*. Durham, NC: Duke University Press.

Zhong, Xueping, and Ban Wang. Eds. 2014. *Debating the Socialist Legacy and Capitalist Globalization*. New York: Palgrave Macmillan.

Zou, John Yu. 1998. "Travel and Translation: An Aspect of China's Cultural Modernity, 1862–1926." In *China in a Polycentric World: Essays in Chinese Comparative Literature*. Edited by Zhang, Yingjin. Stanford, CA: Stanford University Press. 133–151.

Bibliography

Abbas, Ackbar. 1997. *Hong Kong: Culture and the Politics of Disappearance.* Minneapolis: University of Minnesota Press.

Bakhtin, Mikhail M. 1993. *Rabelais and His World.* Trans. Hélène Iswolsky. Bloomington: Indiana University Press.

Chen Sihe 陳思和. 1985. "Xin wenxue shi yanjiu zhongde zhengti guan" 新文學史研究中的整體觀 (A total view of research on the history of new literature). *Fudan xuebao* 復旦學報 (Journal of Fudan University), 3: 184–188.

Chen, Xiaomei. 2008. "Tian Han and the Southern Society Phenomenon: Networking the Personal, Communal, and Cultural." In *Literary Societies of Republican China.* Edited by Denton, Kirk A. and Michel Hockx. Lanham, MD: Lexington Books.

CNNIC (China Internet Network Information Center). 2009. "Di ershisan ci Zhongguo hulianwangluo fazhan zhuangkuang tongji baogao (2009 nian yiyue)" 第23次中國互聯網絡發展狀況統計報告 (2009 年1月) (The 23rd statistical survey report on Chinese Internet development, Jan. 2009). Accessed 8 July 2009. http://www.cnnic.cn/research/bgxz/tjbg/200906/t20090615_18388.html.

Dong Jian 董健. 1996. *Tian Han zhuan* 田漢傳 (*A biography of Tian Han*). Beijing: Shiyue wenyi chubanshe.

Duanmu Hongliang 端木蕻良. 1983. *Duanmu Hongliang jinzuo* 端木蕻良近作 (Recent works of Duanmu Hongliang). Guangzhou: Huacheng chubanshe.

Edwards, Louise. 2008. *Gender, Politics and Democracy: Women's Suffrage in China.* Stanford, CA: Stanford University Press.

Fan Jun 樊駿. 2006. *Zhongguo xiandai wenxue lunji* 中國現代文學論集 (Essays on modern Chinese literature). Beijing: Renmin wenxue chubanshe.

Fei Xiaotong. 2008. "Plurality and Unity in the Configuration of the Chinese People." *Chinese Academy of Social Sciences Journal of Humanities*, 1: 1–42.

Ferry, Megan. 2008. "Marketing Chinese Women Writers in the 1990s, or the Politics of Self-Fashioning." In *China's Literary and Cultural Scenes at the Turn of the 21st Century*. Edited by Jie Lu. London: Routledge. 59–79.

Gorky, Maxim. 1945. "How I Learnt to Write." Trans. V. Orfenov. *The Slavic and East European Review*, 23: 2–7.

Huang, Nicole. Forthcoming. "Eileen Chang and Narratives of Cities and Worlds." In *The Columbia Companion to Modern East Asian Literature*. Edited by Kirk Denton. New York: Columbia University Press.

Jia Pingwa. 2001. *Old Xi'an: Evening Glow of an Imperial City*. Trans. Ma Wenqian. Beijing: Foreign Language Press.

Lu, Sheldon H., and Jiayan Mi. Eds. 2009. *Chinese Ecocinema: Nature, Humanity, Modernity*. Hong Kong: Hong Kong University Press.

Lu, Tonglin. 2002. *Contesting Modernity: Cinemas of China and Taiwan*. Cambridge, UK: Cambridge University Press.

Mei Chia-ling 梅家玲. 2004. *Xingbie, haishi jiaguo? Wuling yu bajiuling niandai Taiwan xiaoshuo lun* 性別, 還是家國?五〇與八、九〇年代臺灣小說論 (Gender or nation? Criticism on contemporary Taiwan fiction). Taipei: Maitian.

Ng, Kim Chew 黃錦樹. 2001. *Youdao zhidao* 由島至島 (From island to island). Taipei: Maitian.

Ostrovsky, Nikolai 奧斯特洛夫斯基. 1976. *Gangtie shi zenyang liancheng de* 鋼鐵是怎樣煉成的 (How the steel was tempered). Trans.

Students of Heilongjiang Univeristy. Beijing: Renmin wenxue chubanshe.

Shih, Shu-mei. 2012. "Foreword: The Sinophone as History and the Sinophone as Theory." *Journal of Chinese Cinemas*, 6.1: 5–7.

Song, Weijie 宋偉杰. 1999. *Cong yule xingwei dao wutuobang chongdong: Jin Yong xiaoshuo zaijiedu* 從娛樂行為到烏托邦沖動:金庸小說再解讀 (From entertainment activity to utopian impulse: rereading Jin Yong's martial arts fiction). Nanjing: Jiangsu renmin chubanshe.

Wang Lingzhen, 2007. "Gender Theories in Chinese and Western Literature." In *The Oxford Encyclopedia of Women in World History*. Edited by Bonnie Smith. Oxford, UK: Oxford University Press. 113–117.

Yan Li 嚴力. n.d. *Yan Li shi jingxuan 1974–2008* 嚴力詩精選 1974–2008 (Selection of Yan Li's poems). New York: Walt Whitman Literature Foundation.

Zhou Jianmin 周建民. 2000. "Wangluo wenxue de yuyan yunyong tedian" 網絡文學的語言運用特點 (Characteristics of language used on the Web). *Wuhan jiaoyu xueyuan xuebao* 武漢教育學院學報 (*Journal of Wuhan institute of education*), 19.5: 64–70.

Zhu Hua 朱華. n.d. "Jiekai 1975 nian Mao Zedong ping *Shuihu* neimu" 揭開1975毛澤東評《水滸》內幕 (Unveiling the inside story of Mao Zedong's comments on *Water Margin*." Accessed 26th December 2013. http://club.china.com/data/thread/5688138/2736/59/73/2_1.html.

Glossary

1947 gaosha baihe	1947 高砂百合
41 pao	四十一炮
A. Aodesi'er (b. 1926)	阿·敖德斯爾
Abdullah Talip (1924–2005)	阿卜杜拉塔里甫
Abdurahim Otkur (1923–95)	阿布都熱依穆·烏提庫爾
A Cheng (b. 1949)	阿城
A'ertai (b. 1949)	阿勒泰
Ai Qing (1910–1996)	艾青
"Ai, shi buneng wangjide"	愛, 是不能忘記的
Ai Weiwei (b. 1957)	艾未未
Ai Xila	哀希臘
Akutagawa Ryūnosuke (1892–1927)	芥川龍之介
Aku Wuwu (Luo Qingchun, b. 1964)	阿庫烏霧(羅慶春)
Alai (b. 1959)	阿來
An Mincheng (Marston Anderson)	安敏成
Anni Baobei (b. 1974)	安妮寶貝
"A Q Zhengzhuan"	阿Q正傳
Asu Yue'er (b. 1966)	阿蘇越爾
A Ying (1900–1977)	阿英
"Ba"	跋
"Bababa"	爸爸爸
babu	八不
bai	白

A Companion to Modern Chinese Literature, First Edition. Edited by Yingjin Zhang.
© 2016 John Wiley & Sons, Ltd. Published 2016 by John Wiley & Sons, Ltd.

Baidu	百度
"Baihehua"	百合花
Bai Hua (b. 1929)	白樺
baihua	白話
baihua qifang	百花齊放
baihua shi	白話詩
"Baihuawen de jiazhi"	白話文的價值
baihuawen yundong	白話文運動
baijia zhengming	百家爭鳴
Bai Lang (1912–1994)	白朗
Bailun shixuan	拜倫詩選
Bailu yuan	白鹿原
Baiyangdian shipai	白洋澱詩派
Bai Wei (1894–1987)	白薇
Bai Xianyong (b. 1937)	白先勇
"Baixian zai sushuo shenme"	白鷳再訴說什麼
Bai Youming (Yomi Braester)	柏右銘
Ba Jin (1904–2005)	巴金
Bali chahua nü yishi	巴黎茶花女遺事
Bamo Qubumo (b. 1964)	巴莫曲布嫫
Banxialiu shehui	半下流社會
Banzei	班賊
Ban Zhao (45–ca. 116)	班昭
"Ban zhuren"	班主任
Baofeng zhouyu	暴風驟雨
Baofengyu qian	暴風雨前
baogao wenxue	報告文學
Bao Liying (b. 1968)	包麗英
Bao Tianxiao (1876–1973)	包天笑
Baowei Yan'an	保衛延安
Baoyinhexige (b. 1962)	寶音賀希格
Bashe	跋涉
Bawang bieji	霸王別姬
Ba wo kunzhu	把我捆住
Bayue de xiangcun	八月的鄉村
Bayue weiyuang	八月未央
"Bei aiqing yiwang de jiaoluo"	被愛情遺忘的角落
Bei Dao (b. 1949)	北島
Beijing	北京
Beijing ren	北京人
Beijing zhichun	北京之春
Beiju shengya	悲劇生涯
Beilei she	蓓蕾社

Beipan zhixia	背叛之夏
Bei shamo yanmai de chengshi	被沙漠掩埋的城市
Beishang niliu chenghe	悲傷逆流成河
Beiwanglu	備忘錄
Beixin shuju	北新書局
"Beiying"	背影
Benhua	笨花
ben mo	本末
bensheng ren	本省人
bentuhua chaoliu	本土化潮流
"Biancheng"	邊城
Bianshan yang zijing	遍山洋紫荊
bianwen	變文
Bian Zhilin (1910–2000)	卞之琳
biaoxian zhuyi xiju	表現主義戲劇
Bi Kewei (Paul G. Pickowicz, b. 1945)	畢克偉
Bing Xin (1900–1999)	冰心
Binu	碧奴
Bi Ruxie	畢汝協
"Bishang liangshan"	逼上梁山
bishou	匕首
Bixue jian	碧血劍
Bodong	波動
boke wenxue	博客文學
boluan fanzheng	撥亂反正
"Bo Zhongguo yong wanguo xinyu shuo"	駁中國用萬國新語説
"Budui wenyi gongzuo zuotanhui jiyao"	部隊文藝工作座談會紀要
Bu juanshe yundong	不捲舌運動
"Buli"	布禮
Buluotuo	布洛陀
"Buneng zou natiaolu"	不能走那條路
Burao Yilu (b. 1955)	布饒依露
"Buyi"	補遺
Cai Jianxin (Chien-hsin Tsai, b. 1975)	蔡建鑫
cainü	才女
Cai Peihuo (1893–1933)	蔡培火
Cai Yuanpei (1868–1940)	蔡元培
Cai Zhiheng (Tsai Chih-Heng, b. 1969)	蔡智恆
Caizhu de ernümen	財主底兒女們
caizi jiaren	才子佳人
cangwu nagou	藏污納垢
canku xianshi zhuyi	殘酷現實主義
Can shijie	慘世界

Can Xue (b. 1953)	殘雪
Cao Juren (1900–1972)	曹聚仁
Cao Shujun (b. 1941)	曹樹鈞
Cao Weifeng (1911–1963)	曹未風
Cao Xinzhi (1917–1995)	曹辛之
Cao Xueqin (1715?–1763?)	曹雪芹
Cao Yu (1910–1996	曹禺
cenci de duizhao	參差的對照
Chaguan	茶館
Chamu	查姆
Changhen ge	長恨歌
Changshi ji	嘗試集
"Chaoji nüsheng"	超級女声
Chaoketunaren (b. 1925)	超克圖納仁
chaonü	超女
Chaoxian zu	朝鮮族
Chen'ai luoding	塵埃落定
Chenbao	晨報
Chen Cun (b. 1954)	陳村
Chen Danyan (b. 1958)	陳丹燕
Chen Dawei (Chan Tah-Wei, b. 1969)	陳大為
Chen Dieyi (1907–2007)	陳蝶衣
Chen Dongyuan (1902–1978)	陳東原
Chen Duxiu (1879–1942)	陳獨秀
Chengdu	成都
Chengdu, jinye qing jiang wo yiwang	成都, 今夜請將我遺忘
Cheng Fangwu (1897–1984)	成仿吾
Cheng Ganglong (b. 1970)	陳崗龍
Chengjisi Han (1162–1227)	成吉思汗
Chengnan jiushi	城南舊事
chengshi wenxue	城市文學
Chen Gu	陳嘏
Chen Guanzhong (Chan Koonchung, b. 1952)	陳冠中
Chen Hengzhe (1890–1976)	陳衡哲
Chen Huangmei (1913–1996)	陳荒煤
"Chen Huansheng jincheng"	陳奐生進城
Chen Jiangong (b. 1949)	陳建功
Chen Jianhua (b. 1947)	陳建華
Chen Jingrong (1917–1989)	陳敬容
Chen Jitong (1851–1907)	陳季同
Chen Jiying (1908–1997)	陳紀瀅
Chen Li (b. 1954)	陳黎
Chen Lingqi (Lingchei Letty Chen)	陳綾琪

Chen Mingshu (b. 1931)	陳鳴樹
Cheng Naishan (1946–2013)	程乃姍
Chen Pingyuan (b. 1954)	陳平原
Chen Qingqiao (Stephen C. K. Chan)	陳清橋
Chen Ran (b. 1962)	陳染
Chen Rong (b. 1936)	諶容
Chen Ruixian (Tan Swie Hian, b. 1943)	陳瑞獻
Chen Ruoxi (b. 1938)	陳若曦
Chen Shouzhu (1909–1990)	陳瘦竹
Chen Sihe (b. 1954)	陳思和
"Chenxiangxie: diyilu xiang"	沉香屑: 第一爐香
Chen Xiaomei (b. 1954)	陳小眉
Chen Xiaoming (b. 1959)	陳曉明
Chen Xiefen (1883–1923)	陳擷芬
Chen Xuezhao (1906–1991)	陳學昭
Chen Ying (1907–1986)	沉櫻
Chen Yingzhen (b. 1937)	陳映真
Chen Yinque (1890–1969)	陳寅恪
Chen Youshi (Yu-Shih Chen)	陳幼石
Chen Yun	陳耘
Chenzhong she	沉鐘社
Chen Zhongshi (b. 1942)	陳忠實
Chen Zishan (b. 1948)	陳子善
Chen Zizhan (1898–1990)	陳子展
Chidi zhilian	赤地之戀
Chi Li (b. 1957)	池莉
chi ren xing qing	持人性情
Chi Zijian (b. 1964)	遲子建
chongdan	沖淡
Chongqing	重慶
chongxie wenxue shi	重寫文學史
Choulou de Hanguo ren	醜陋的韓國人
Choushu	仇書
chouti wenxue	抽屜文學
Chuang shiji	創世記
Chuangye shi	創業史
Chuangzao she	創造社
Chuangzao zhoubao	創造週報
chuangzuo muke	創作木刻
Chuanqi	傳奇
"Chuchuang"	櫥窗
Chuci	楚辭
chuizhi	垂直

Chuju	楚劇
Chun	春
Chunfeng yicong	春風譯叢
Chunliu she	春柳社
Chunming waishi	春明外史
chunshi shehui zhuyi	純是社會主義
chun wenxue	純文學
"Chuwen"	初吻
ci	辭
"Ciluhu de youyu"	鷩鷺湖的憂鬱
Cong Shen (1928–2007)	叢深
congshu	叢書
Cong Weixi	從維熙
Cuotuo suiyue	蹉蹉跎歲月
Dabo	大波
Dagongbao	大公報
dahua wenxue	大話文學
Dahua xiyou	大話西遊
Daideng	帶燈
Dai Houying (1938–1996)	戴厚英
Dai Jinhua (b. 1959)	戴錦華
Dai Wangshu (1905–1950)	戴望舒
Dai zu	傣族
Dajiang	大江
dalu ren	大陸人
dan	淡
"Da'nao jishi"	大淖記事
danbo	淡薄
Dangdai Sulian wenxue	當代蘇聯文學
Dangdai waiguo wenxue	當代外國文學
dangdai wenxue	當代文學
danmei	耽美
danwei	單位
danxingben	單行本
danyuan	淡遠
dao minjian qu	到民間去
Dao	道
Daocao ren	稻草人
Dao yu dalu	島與大陸
daqiang wenxue	大牆文學
Da shidai	大時代
Da shuohuang jia	大說謊家
daxia	大俠

Dazhong wenyi	大眾文藝
da Zhongguo zhuyi	大中國主義
dazhongyu	大眾語
De Like (Arif Dirlik)	德里克
"Deng"	燈
Deng Tengke (Kirk Denton, b. 1955)	鄧騰克
Deng Xiaoping (1904–1997)	鄧小平
Deng Youmei (b. 1931)	鄧友梅
"Diao'e bao"	雕鶚堡
Di'er ci woshou	第二次握手
Di'er ge chuntian	第二個春天
Dijiuge guafu	第九個寡婦
Ding Bingsui (1916–1980)	丁秉鐩
Ding Fan (b. 1952)	丁帆
Ding Jingtang (b. 1920)	丁景唐
Ding Ling (1904–1986)	丁玲
Dingzhuang meng	丁莊夢
Disan dai	第三代
disizhong xiju	第四種戲劇
Ditu ji: yige xiangxiang de chengshi de kaoguxue	地圖集:一個想像的城市的考古學
diwang de	帝王的
dixia wenxue	地下文學
Diyi ci de qinmi jiechu	第一次的親密接觸
Dizhi shi	地質師
dongdong	東東
Dong Qizhang (Dung Kai-cheung, b. 1967)	董啓章
"Dongwu xiongmeng"	動物兇猛
"Dongye"	冬夜
Dong Zhilin (b. 1952)	董之林
Dong zu	侗族
Du Aimei (Amy Dooling)	杜愛梅
Duanhong lingyan ji	斷鴻零雁記
Duanmu Hongliang (Cao Hanwen, 1912–1996)	端木蕻良(曹汉文)
Du Boni (Bonnie McDougall, b. 1941)	杜博妮
ducao	毒草
Du Fu (712–770)	杜甫
Du Heng (1916–1980)	杜衡
Duidao	對倒
Duo Duo (b. 1951)	多多
Duomianjing xuanzhuanti	多面鏡旋轉體
Du Pengcheng (1921–1991)	杜鵬程
dushi	都市

Du Yunxie (1915–2002)	杜運燮
"Dushi shi tade shuzhuang tai"	都市是她的梳妝台
E'erguna he you'an	額爾古納河右岸
Er Ma	二馬
Ershinian mudu zhi guai xiangzhuang	二十年目睹之怪現狀
ershi shiji Zhongguo wenxue	二十世紀中國文學
Ershiyi shiji	二十一世紀
ertong wenxue	兒童文學
"Erzi de da wanou"	兒子的大玩偶
Ewenke zu	鄂温克族
Fan Boqun (b. 1931)	范伯群
Fan'elin yu qiangwei	梵峨璘與薔薇
Fang Fang (b. 1955)	方方
Fanhua	繁花
Fang Lizhi (1936–2012)	方勵之
Fangzhou zi (b. 1967)	方舟子
Fan jingshen wuran	反精神污染
Fan Jun (1930–2011)	樊駿
fanlan	泛藍
fanlü	泛綠
"Fannao rensheng"	煩惱人生
fansi wenxue	反思文學
fanwai	番外
fan xiaoshuo	反小説
fanyi wenxue	翻譯文學
Fan ziyouhua	反自由化
Feidu	廢都
feifei	非非
"Fei hong"	非紅
Fei Ming (1901–1967)	廢名
"Feituzhen"	肥土鎮
Feng	楓
feng	諷
fengci xiaoshuo	諷刺小説
Feng Deying (b. 1935)	馮德英
fenggu	風骨
Feng Guifen (1809–74)	馮桂芬
Feng Jicai (b. 1942)	馮驥才
Fengjie	鳳姐
Feng Jin (b. 1971)	馮進
Feng Naichao (1901–1983)	馮乃超
Fengru feitun	豐乳肥臀
fengshui	風水

"Fengsuo"	封鎖
Feng Xiaogang (b. 1958)	馮小剛
Feng xiaoxiao	风萧萧
Feng Xuefeng (1903–1976)	馮雪峰
Feng Yuanjun (1900–1974)	馮沅君
Fengyue bao	風月報
Fengyue meng	風月夢
Feng Zhi (1905–1993)	馮至
feng zi xiu wenyi	封、資、修文藝
Fenjian ji	焚劍記
Fukema (D. W. Fokkema, 1931–2011)	佛克馬
fu	賦
Fucheng zhiyi	浮城誌異
Fu Donghua (1893–1971)	傅東華
Fuermosi zhentan an quanji	福爾摩斯偵探案全集
fugu	復古
Fujii Shōzō (b. 1952)	藤井省三
fukan	副刊
Fu Lan (Nicolai Volland)	傅朗
Fu Lei (1908–1966)	傅雷
fumei	賦魅
Funü shibao	婦女時報
Furong Jiejie (Shi Hengxia, b. 1977)	芙蓉姐姐（史恒俠）
Furong zhen	芙蓉鎮
Futabatei Shimei (1863–1909)	二葉亭四迷
Fuyun	浮雲
Fuzhou	福州
gaige wenxue	改革文學
"Gangdisi de youhuo"	岡底斯的誘惑
Gangtie shi zenyang liancheng de	鋼鐵是怎樣煉成的
Ganlan shu	橄欖樹
Ganxiao liuji	幹校六記
Gao Jianhua (ca. 1890–?)	高劍華
Gao Like (Marián Gálik, b. 1933)	高力克
Gao Xiaosheng (b. 1928)	高曉聲
Gao Xingjian (b. 1940)	高行健
Gao Yihan (1885–1968)	高一涵
Gao Yu (b. 1964)	高玉
Gao Yuanbao (b. 1966)	郜元寶
Gao Yunlan (1910–1956)	高雲覽
gaoshang weida zhi renge	高尚偉大之人格
gaotie ti	高鐵體
Gaoxing	高興

Gaoyang gongzhu	高阳公主
Ge Baoquan (1913–2000)	戈寶權
Ge Fei (b. 1964)	格非
Ge Haowen (Howard Goldblatt, b. 1939)	葛浩文
geju	歌劇
Ge Liang (b. 1978)	葛亮
geming	革命
geming de wenxue	革命的文學
geming wenxue	革命文學
geming xin chuanqi	革命新傳奇
geming yangbanxi	革命樣板戲
genbunichi	言文一致
Geng Jizhi (1899–1947)	耿濟之
Geng Yunzhi (b. 1938)	耿雲志
Geng Dehua (Edward Gunn)	耿德華
Gesaer Wang	格薩爾王
Gong'an	公安
gong'an	公案
Gongkaide qingshu	公開的情書
gongming	共名
Gongyu daoyou	公寓導遊
Gong Zizhen (1792–1841)	龔自珍
Gotō Shinpei (1857–1929)	後藤新平
"Gouri de liangshi"	狗日的糧食
guaidan xianshi zhuyi	怪誕現實主義
"Guanbuzhule"	關不注了
Guanchang xianxing ji	官場現形記
guangchang	廣場
Guangzhou	廣州
guanhua	官話
Guan Lu (1907–1982)	關露
Gu Bin (Wolfgang Kubin, b. 1945)	顧彬
Gu Cheng (1956–1993)	顧城
gudai hanyu	古代漢語
gudao	孤島
Gudu	古都
Gu Hua (b. 1942)	古華
Guiju	桂劇
Guilai	歸來
Guilian	鬼戀
"Guiqulai"	歸去來
guixiu	閨秀
Guizi laile	鬼子來了

Gu Jiegang (1893–1980)	顧頡剛
Gu Long (1938–1985)	古龍
Gulu	古爐
Gu Mingdao (1897–1944)	顧明道
guo	國
guocui	國粹
guohua	國畫
Guo Jianying (1907–1979)	郭建英
Guo Jingming (b. 1983)	郭敬明
Guoji xiebao	國際協報
Guomin dang	國民黨
Guo Moruo (1892–1978)	郭沫若
Guo Qiusheng (1904–1980)	郭秋生
Guo Xiaochuan (1919–1976)	郭小川
Guo Xuebo (b. 1948)	郭雪波
Guo Yanli (b. 1937)	郭延禮
Guoxingye (Koxinga)	國姓爺
guoxue	國學
guoyu	國語
Guoyuancheng ji	果園城記
guoyu de wenxue	國語的文學
guwen	古文
Gu Wenda (b. 1955)	谷文達
guwen yundong	古文運動
"Guxiang"	故鄉
"Guxiang de yecai"	故鄉的野菜
Guxiang, tianxia, huanghua	故鄉, 天下, 黃花
Gu Youcheng	古有成
Gu Zhongyi (1903–1965)	顧仲彝
guzhuang xi	古裝戲
Hai Nan (b. 1962)	海男
Hai Rui baguan	海瑞罷官
Haipai	海派
Haipai wenxue	海派文學
Haishang hua liezhuan	海上花列傳
Haiwai Huarenwenxue	海外華人文學
Haizi (1964–1989)	海子
Ha Jin (b. 1956)	哈金
han	函
Han	漢
Han Bangqing (1856–1994)	韓邦慶
Han Dong (b. 1961)	韓東
Han Han (b. 1982)	韓寒

Hani zu	哈尼族
Hankou	漢口
Hanman lu	汗漫錄
Han Nan (Patrick Hannan, b. 1927)	韓南
Han Rui (Ari Larissa Heinrich)	韓瑞
Han Shaohua (1933–2010)	韓少華
Hanye	寒夜
Ha Sen (b. 1971)	哈森
Han Shaogong (b. 1953)	韓少功
Hanshi	漢詩
Hanshu	漢書
Hanwen	漢文
Hanyu	漢語
Hanzi bu mie, Zhongguo bi wang!	漢字不滅, 中國必亡!
Hao Ran (1932–2008)	浩然
Haowangjiao	好望角
haoxia	豪俠
Harbin	哈爾濱
Ha Yingfei (b. 1969)	哈迎飛
He an	河岸
"Hebiande cuowu"	河邊的錯誤
He Guimei (b. 1970)	賀桂梅
Hehua dian	荷花淀
Heilongjiang	黑龍江
heimu xiaoshuo	黑幕小説
Heinu yutian lu	黑奴籲天錄
He Jingzhi (b. 1924)	賀敬之
"Hei junma"	黑駿馬
Heluo hua (Hoklo)	河洛話
Henhai	恨海
He Qifang (1912–1977)	何其芳
"Hetang yuese"	荷塘月色
He Xiaozhu (b. 1963)	何小竹
He-Yin Zhen (ca. 1884–1920?)	何殷震
Hong	虹
Hong Changtai (Chang-Tai Hung, b. 1949)	洪長泰
"Hongdou"	紅豆
Hong Feng (b. 1959)	洪峰
Hong gaoliang jiazu	紅高粱家族
Honglou meng	紅樓夢
Honglou meng pinglun	紅樓夢評論
Hongloumeng yanjiu	紅樓夢研究
"Hong meigui yu bai meigui"	紅玫瑰與白玫瑰

Hongqi pu	紅旗譜
Hongri	紅日
Hongse niangzi jun	紅色娘子軍
Hong Shen (1894–1955)	洪深
Hongxiu Tianxiang	紅袖添香
Hongyan	紅岩
Hong Yanqiu (1899–1980)	洪炎秋
Hong Ying (b. 1962)	虹影
Hong Zicheng (b. 1939)	洪子誠
Houbei	猴盃
Hougong zhenhuan zhuan	後宮甄嬛傳
Houtu	厚土
Hou Rongsheng (1926–1990)	侯榕生
Hou Xiaoqiang	侯小強
houxue	後學
houyizheng	後遺症
Houzhimin shiwu yu aiqing	後殖民食物與愛情
Hua Tuo (ca. 145–208)	華陀
Hua Zhao	花招
Hua	華
huaju	話劇
Hualian	花蓮
Huancheng	幻城
Huang Biyun (Wong Bik-wan, b. 1961)	黃碧雲
Huang Chun-ming (b. 1935)	黃春明
Huang Fan (b. 1950)	黃凡
Huang Guliu (1908–1977)	黃穀柳
Huang Jingshu (Ng Kim Chew, b. 1967)	黃錦樹
Huang Moxi (1866–1913)	黃摩西
Huangren shouji	荒人手記
Huang Shihui (1900–1945)	黃石輝
Huang Xiang (b. 1941)	黃翔
Huang Xincun (Nicole Huang)	黃心村
Huang Yi (b. 1952)	黃易
Huang Yibing (Mai Mang, b. 1967)	黃亦兵(麥芒)
Huang Yuan	黃源
Huang Yunte (b. 1969)	黃運特
Huang Ziping (b. 1949)	黃子平
Huang Zunxian (1848–1905)	黃遵憲
Huangguan	皇冠
Huangjin shidai	黃金時代
huangse xiaoshuo	黃色小説
huaqiao	華僑

Huaren wenxue	華人文學
Huawen	華文
Huawen wenxue	華文文學
Huaxia wenzhai	華夏文摘
Huayu yuxi	華語語系
"Hudie"	蝴蝶
Hu Feng (1902–85)	胡風
"Huida"	回答
Huijia yihou	回家以後
Huiyi Lu Xun xiansheng	回憶魯迅先生
Hui zu	回族
Hu Lancheng (1906–1981)	胡蘭成
Hulanhe zhuan	呼蘭河傳
humei	護魅
Hung Qisheng (1867–1929)	洪棄生
Huo Da (b. 1945)	霍達
Huo Jianqi (b. 1958)	霍建起
Huodong bianrenxing	活動變人形
Huozhe	活著
Hu Shi (1891–1962)	胡適
Hu Yepin (1903–1931)	胡也頻
Hu Ying (b. 1962)	胡纓
Hu Yuzhi (1896–1986)	胡愈之
Hu Zhide (Theodore Huters)	胡志德
Ishikawa Kin'ichirō (1871–1945)	石川欽一郎
Itō Toramaru (1927–2003)	伊藤虎丸
Jia	家
Jiabiangou jishi	夾邊溝紀事
Jia Baoyu	賈寶玉
Jiabian	家變
Jia Junpeng	賈君鵬
Jia Junpeng ni mama han ni huijia chifan	賈君鵬你媽媽喊你回家吃飯
jiagou ju	佳構劇
"Jianji cuole de gushi"	剪輯錯了的故事
Jiang Guangci (1901–1931)	蔣光慈
Jiang Gui (1908–1980)	姜貴
jianghu	江湖
Jianghu qixia zhuan	江湖奇俠傳
Jiang Jieshi (Chiang Kai-shek, 1887–1975)	蔣介石
Jiang Qing (1914–1991)	江青
Jiang Wen (b. 1963)	姜文
Jiang Zilong (b. 1941)	蔣子龍
Jianguo daye	建國大業

Jianying rushui	堅硬如水
jiao	教
Jiaocuo shiguang de ailian	交錯時光的愛戀
jiaoyu	教育
Jia Pingwa (b. 1952)	賈平凹
Jia Zhifang (b. 1916)	賈植芳
"Jiazhutao"	夾竹桃
Jidi Majia (b. 1961)	吉狄馬加
Ji'e de Guo Su'e	飢餓的郭素娥
Jiehun shinian	結婚十年
"Jieshu"	結束
Ji Jin (b. 1965)	季進
"Jiliu"	激流
Jimo yunyuan	寂寞雲園
Jimu Langge (b. 1963)	吉木狼格
jinbu	進步
jincheng	進程
jindai	近代
jindai shi	近代史
jindai wenxue	近代文學
Jin Fan (b. 1948?)	靳凡
Jinfen shijia	金粉世家
Jingang jing	金剛經
Jingbao	晶報
jingdian xiaofei	經典消費
Jinguang dadao	金光大道
Jinghua yinshuaju	京華印刷局
Jingpai	京派
Jinping mei	金瓶梅
Jingqiaoqiao de zuolun	靜悄悄的左輪
jin gu wen zhi zheng	今古文之爭
jingyinghua	精英化
jingying wenhua	精英文化
Jin Hezai (b. 1977)	今何在
Jin Jiefu (Jeffrey Kinkley, b. 1948)	金介甫
"Jinsuo ji"	金鎖記
Jintian	今天
Jin Wenxue (b. 1962)	金文學
Jin Yong (b. 1924)	金庸
Jin Yucheng (b. 1952)	金宇澄
jituanhua	集團化
jiu	舊
Jiudian	酒店

Jiuguo	酒國
Jiuji lang	九級浪
jiuping zhuang xinjiu	舊瓶裝新酒
jiushi	舊詩
jiuti shi	舊體詩
Jiutu	酒徒
jiuwang	救亡
Jiuye pai	九葉派
Ji Xian (1913–2013)	紀弦
"Ji xiao duzhe"	寄小讀者
Jiyi de chengshi, xugou de chengshi	記憶的城市·虛構的城市
Ji Yihui (1878–1908)	戢翼翬
juan	卷
Juedui xinhao	絕對信號
jueju	絕句
Junma jiang	駿馬獎
Kaixin nongchang	開心農場
Kang Youwei (1858–1927)	康有為
kang Ri wenxue	抗日文學
Karatani Kojin (b. 1941)	柄谷行人
Kawabata Yasunari (1899–1972)	川端康成
Kaynam Orkishi	激流
Keerqinqi caoyuan	科爾沁旗草原
Kejia (Hakka)	客家
Kejia hua (Hakka)	客家話
keju	科舉
Ke Ling (1909–2000)	柯靈
"Kezeng de baihua siliu"	可憎的白話四六
Kikuchi Kan (1888–1948)	菊池寬
Kiyama Hideo (b. 1934)	木山英雄
Kobayashi Takiji (1903–1933)	小林多喜二
kokugo	國語
kominka	皇民化
Kondō Tatsuya (b. 1946)	近藤龍哉
Kong Jiesheng (b. 1952)	孔捷生
Kong Luosun (1912–1996)	孔羅蓀
Kong Haili	孔海立
kongjian	空間
Kongshan	空山
"Kong Yiji"	孔乙己
kouxiangtang shi	口香糖詩
ku	酷
kuaiban	快板

Kuairou yusheng shu	塊肉餘生述
kuang	狂
"Kuangren riji"	狂人日記
Kuangye de huhan	曠野的呼喊
Kucaihua	苦菜花
Kulian	苦戀
Kunan niandai	苦難年代
Kunan shidai	苦難時代
Kun Nan (b. 1935)	崑南
kuso	糞
Lai He (1894–1943)	賴和
Lan Ling (1931–2005)	藍翎
Lan Shengdi de riji	蘭生弟的日記
Lang tuteng	狼圖騰
Lanxing	藍星
Lao Can youji	老殘遊記
Lao Nanjing: jiuying qinhuai	老南京:舊影秦淮
Lao She (1899–1966)	老舍
Lao Xi'an	老西安
Lao Zhang de zhexue	老張的哲學
laosheng	老生
"Laozihao"	老字號
"Lasahe de nüshen"	拉薩河的女神
Lee Hee-Kyung (b. 1973)	李喜卿
Le'e teyi	勒俄特依
leiren	雷人
Leishui dashile Tumenjiang	淚水打濕了圖們江
Leiyu	雷雨
lian	廉
Li An (Ang Lee, b. 1954)	李安
Li Ang (b. 1952)	李昂
liang an san di	兩岸三地
Liang Bin (1914–1996)	梁斌
Liang Bingjun (Leung Ping-kwan, Ye Si, 1948–2013)	梁秉鈞 (也斯)
Liang Hongyu	梁紅玉
Liang Qichao (1873–1929)	梁啓超
Liang Shiqiu (1903–1987)	梁實秋
Liangyou	良友
Liang Yusheng (1924–2009)	梁羽生
Liang Zongdai (1903–1983)	梁宗岱
Lian Heng (Lian Yatang, 1876–1936)	連橫 (連雅堂)
Lian Zhan (b. 1936)	連戰

Lian Zhendong (1904–1986)	連震東
Li Ao (b. 1935)	李敖
Liao Binghui (Ping-hui Liao, b. 1954)	廖炳惠
Liao Hanchen (Yu Wen, 1912–1980)	廖漢臣 (毓文)
libailiu	禮拜六
Li Bihua (Lilian Lee Pik-Wah, b. 1959)	李碧華
Li Boyuan (Li Baojia, 1867–1906)	李伯元 (李寶嘉)
Li Chengpeng (b. 1968)	李承鵬
Li Dechun (Limusishiden, b. 1968)	李得春
Lielao zhuan	烈佬傳
Lienü tu	烈女圖
Li Guangtian (1906–1968)	李廣田
Li Helin (1904–1988)	李何林
Li Hui (b. 1957)	李輝
Li Jianwu (Liu Xiwei, 1906–1982)	李健吾 (劉西渭)
Li Jieren (1891–1962)	李劼人
Li Jinfa (1900–1976)	李金發
Li Liewen (1904–1972)	黎烈文
Li Minghui (1909–2003)	黎明暉
Lin Bai (b. 1958)	林白
Lin Biao (1907–1971)	林彪
Lin Changzhi (b. 1977)	林長治
Lin Chaozhen	林超真
Ling Shuhua (1900–1990)	凌叔華
Ling Yu (b. 1945)	凌宇
Linggong xueshe	伶工學社
Lingshan	靈山
"Ling yu rou"	靈與肉
Linhai xueyuan	林海雪原
Lin Haiyin (Lin Hai-yin, 1918–2001)	林海音
Lin Huiyin (1904–1955)	林徽因
Lin Mohan (1913–2008)	林默涵
Lin Peirui (Perry Link, b. 1944)	林培瑞
Lin Shu (1852–1924)	林紓
Lin Yaode (1962–1996)	林燿德
Lin Yutang (1895–1976)	林語堂
Lin Zexu (1785–1850)	林則徐
Li Oufan (Leo Ou-fan Lee, b. 1942)	李歐梵
Li Ping (b. 1948)	禮平
Li Rui (b. 1950)	李銳
lishi xiaoshuo	歷史小說
Li Shuangshuang	李雙雙
"Li Shuangshuang xiaozhuan"	李雙雙小傳

"Li Shunda zaowu"	李順大造屋
Li Tuo (b. 1939)	李陀
Liu Bannong (1891–1934)	劉半農
Liu Binyan (1925–2005)	劉賓雁
Liudong waishi	留東外史
Liu E (1857–1909)	劉鄂
Liu Fengjie (b. 1953)	劉鋒杰
Liu Fu (1891–1934)	劉復
Liu He (Lydia Liu)	劉禾
Liu Heng (b. 1954)	劉恒
Liu Huiyuan (b. 1948)	劉會遠
Liu Kang (b. 1955)	劉康
Liu Kexiang (b. 1957)	劉克襄
Liu Lianzi (b. 1984)	流瀲紫
Liu Na'ou (1905–1940)	劉吶鷗
liupai	流派
Liu Qing (1916–1978)	柳青
Liu Sanjie	劉三姐
Liu Shaoming (Joseph Lau, b. 1934)	劉紹銘
Liu Shousong (1912–1969)	劉綬松
liusi	六四
Liu Suola (b. 1955)	劉索拉
Liu-Wang Liming (1897–1970)	劉王立明
Liu Xiaobo (b. 1955)	劉小波
Liu Xinglong (b. 1956)	劉醒龍
Liu Xinwu (b. 1942)	劉心武
liuxuesheng wenxue	留學生文學
Liuyan	流言
Liu Yazi (1887–1958)	柳亞子
Liu Yichang (b. 1918)	劉以鬯
Liu Zaifu (b. 1941)	劉再復
Liu Zhenyun (b. 1958)	劉震雲
Liu Zhirong (b. 1973)	劉志榮
Li Xianting (b. 1949)	栗憲庭
Li Xiaojiang (b. 1951)	李小江
Li Xiaolong (Bruce Lee, 1940–1973)	李小龍
Li Xifan (b. 1927)	李希凡
Li Xunhuan	李尋歡
Li Yi (b. 1966)	李怡
Li Yingru (1914–1989)	李英儒
Li Yongping (b. 1947)	李永平
Li Youcai banhua	李有才板話
Li Zehou (b. 1930)	李澤厚

Li Zhensheng (b. 1957)	李振聲
lizhi	勵志
Li Zhun (1928–2000)	李准
Li Zicheng (1606–1645)	李自成
Li Zishu (b. 1971)	黎紫書
Longxu gou	龍鬚溝
Long Yingzong (1911–1999)	龍瑛宗
Lü Bicheng (1883–1943)	呂碧城
Luding ji	鹿鼎記
Lufan yanshi	陸犯焉識
Lu Fen (Shi Tuo, 1910–1988)	蘆焚(师陀)
Lü Heruo (1914–1951)	呂赫若
Luhua dang	蘆花蕩
"Lühua shu"	綠化樹
Lu Juan (b. 1982)	魯娟
Lu Ling (1923–1994)	路翎
Lung Yingzhong (1911–1999)	龍瑛宗
"Lun nüxue"	論女學
Lu Shi'e (1878–1944)	陆士谔
Lu Wenfu (1928–2005)	陆文夫
lunxian qu wenxue	淪陷區文學
"Lun xiaoshuo yu qunzhi zhi guanxi"	論小説與群治之關係
Lunyu	論語
"Lun yuluti zhi yong"	論語錄體之用
Lunyu pai	論語派
Luo Feng (1909–1991)	羅烽
Luo Fu (b. 1928)	洛夫
Luo Guangbin (1924–1967)	羅廣斌
Luo Hong (b. 1910)	羅洪
Luo Longji (1896–1965)	羅隆基
Luo Niansheng (1904–1990)	羅念生
Luo Shu (1903–1938)	羅淑
Luo Yanbin (1869–?)	羅燕斌
Luoyang	洛陽
Luo Yijun (b. 1967)	駱以軍
Luo Yufeng	羅玉鳳
Luo Peng (Carlos Rojas, b. 1970)	羅鵬
"Luosi gu"	螺螄谷
Luotuo	駱駝
Luotuo Xiangzi	駱駝祥子
Luowu Laqie (b. 1958)	俫伍拉且
Lu Xiaopeng (Sheldon Lu, b. 1962)	魯曉鵬
Lu Xinhua (b. 1954)	盧新華

Lu Xun (Zhou Shuren, 1881–1936)	魯迅 (周樹人)
Lu Yanshi	陸焉識
Lu Yanzhou (1928–2006)	魯彥周
Lu Yaodong (1930–2010)	陸耀東
Lu Yin (1898–1934)	盧隱
Luyishi (Lu Yu, 1913–2013)	路易士 (路逾)
Lü Yuan (1922–2009)	綠原
Ma	馬
Ma Bole	馬伯樂
Ma Deqing (b. 1952)	馬德清
Mahua	馬華
Mahua wenxue	馬華文學
Ma Jian (b. 1953)	馬建
Ma Junwu (1881–1940)	馬君武
Ma Lang (b. 1933)	馬朗
Malaixyia	馬來西亞
Malaqinfu (b. 1930)	瑪拉沁夫
Mang Ke (b. 1950)	芒克
Mangmang de caoyuan	茫茫的草原
Manyouzhe	漫遊者
Man zu	滿族
Mao Dun (1896–1981)	茅盾
Mao Dun (Shen Yanbing, 1896–1981)	茅盾 (沈雁冰)
Mao wenti	毛文體
Mao Zedong (1893–1976)	毛澤東
Maqiao cidian	馬橋詞典
Maruo Tsuneki (b. 1937)	丸尾常喜
Mashi wentong	馬氏文通
"Matou qin"	馬頭琴
Ma Xueliang (1913–1999)	馬學良
Ma Yuan (b. 1953)	馬原
mazi gong	碼字工
"M de shizong"	M 的失蹤
Mei Guangdi (1890–1945)	梅光迪
Mei Lanfang (1894–1961)	梅蘭芳
Meili dasha	美麗大廈
Mei Niang (1920–2013)	梅娘
"Meishijia"	美食家
Mei Yici (Yi-tsi Mei Feuerwerker)	梅懿慈
Mei Zhi (1914–2004)	梅志
Meige	梅葛
Meiguo	美國
"Meili nanfang zhixia"	美麗南方之夏

Meishu Shenghuo	美術生活
meiwen	美文
meixue	美學
Meiyu	梅雨
Meiyu	眉語
"Meiyu zhixi"	梅雨之夕
Meizhuo (b. 1966)	梅卓
Memtimin Hoshur (b. 1944)	買買提明·吾守爾
Meng Fanhua	孟繁華
"Menggu ma"	蒙古馬
Menggu zu	蒙古族
Meng-Jiang Nü ku changcheng	孟姜女哭長城
Meng Lang (b. 1961)	孟浪
menglong shi	朦朧詩
Meng Sha (b. 1941)	孟沙
"Meng yu shi"	夢與詩
Meng yu zhu yu liming	夢與豬與黎明
Meng Yue (b. 1956)	孟悦
Mian Mian (b. 1970)	棉棉
miaotang	廟堂
Miao zu	苗族
Miao zu guge	苗族古歌
Micang	迷藏
Miluotou	密洛陀
min	民
mincui zhuyi	民粹主義
minguo wenxue	民國文學
Mingyou zhisi	名優之死
Mingzi de meigui	名字的玫瑰
minjian	民間
minjian lichang	民間立場
minjian xiju	民間戲劇
Minjin dang	民進黨
Minnan hua	閩南話
Minnan yu	閩南語
Minquan bao	民權報
Minzu wenxue yanjiu	民族文學研究
minzu xingshi	民族形式
Miyamoto Yuriko (1899–1951)	宮本百合子
modeng nülang	摩登女郎
modeng nüzi	摩登女子
modeng xiaojie	摩登小姐
Mo Du (b. 1965)	莫獨

modu	魔都
"Moluo shili shuo"	摩羅詩力説
Mori Ogai (1862–1962)	森鷗外
Mo Yan (b. 1955)	莫言
Mu Dan (1918–1977)	穆旦
Mu Mutian (1900–1971)	穆木天
Muqin	母親
Murong Xuecun (b.1974)	慕容雪村
Mushanokōji Saneatsu (1885–1976)	武者小路実篤
Mu Shiying (1912–1940)	穆時英
Musilin de zangli	穆斯林的葬禮
"Muzi"	母子
Muzi Mei (b. 1978)	木子美
Nahan	吶喊
"*Nahan* zixu"	吶喊自序
Nanguo she	南國社
Nanjing	南京
nan Ou bei Mei	南歐北梅
"Nanren de yiban shi nüren"	男人的一半是女人
Nanshe	南社
"Natiao lanse de hada"	那條藍色的哈達
Natsume Sōseki (1867–1916)	夏目漱石
Naxi zu	納西族
nengzhi de kuanghuan	能指的狂歡
Nianqing de yidai	年輕的一代
"Ni biewu xuanze"	你別無選擇
Niehai hua	孽海花
Nie Hualing (Hua-ling Nieh, b. 1925)	聶華苓
Niezi	孽子
Nihong dengxia de shaobing	霓虹燈下的哨兵
Ni Huanzhi	倪煥之
Ningbo	寧波
Nishikawa Mitsuru (1908–1999)	西川滿
"Niuyue"	紐約
Noboru Maruyama (1931–2006)	丸山昇
No Chongun	魯貞銀
Nübao	女報
nüjie	女界
Nü guomin	女國民
"Nününü"	女女女
Nuosu zu	諾蘇族
nüxing wenxue	女性文學
nü xuesheng	女學生

Nüyuhua	女獄花
"Nüzi fuchou lun"	女子復仇論
nüzun	女尊
Ōe Kenzaburō (b. 1935)	大江健三郎
Oshikawa Shunrō (1876–1914)	押川春浪
Ouhua yu	歐化語
Ouyang Jianghe (b. 1956)	歐陽江河
Ouyang Shan (1908–2004)	歐陽山
Ouyang Yuqian (1889–1962)	歐陽予倩
Panghuang	徬徨
Pan Jiaxun (1896–1989)	潘家洵
Pan Jinlian	潘金蓮
Pan Yu-tong (b. 1937)	潘雨桐
Peng Yanjiao (1920–2008)	彭燕郊
pianwen	駢文
pingdan	平淡
"Pingguo de ziwei"	蘋果的滋味
Ping Hu tongche	平滬通車
pinghua	平話
Pingjiang Buxiao Sheng (1889–1957)	平江不肖生
Pingju	平劇
Ping Lu (b. 1953)	平路
pinyin	拼音
Pizi Cai	痞子蔡
pizi wenxue	痞子文學
puji	普及
Pu Shike (Jaroslav Průšek, 1906–1980)	普實克
Pu Songling (1640–1715)	蒲松齡
putonghua	通話
Q ban yuwen	Q版語文
Qiangren Liu (b. 1987)	羌人六
Qian Gurong (b. 1919)	錢谷融
Qiang zu	羌族
Qian Jibo (1887–1957)	錢基博
Qian Liqun (b. 1939)	錢理群
Qian Suoqiao	錢鎖橋
Qianwan buyao wangji	千萬不要忘記
Qianwan buyao wangji jieji douzheng	千萬不要忘記階級鬥爭
Qian Xuantong (1887–1939)	錢玄同
qianzai xiezuo	潛在寫作
qianze xiaoshuo	譴責小説
Qian Zhongshu (1910–1998)	錢鍾書
Qiao changzhang shangren ji	喬廠長上任記

"Qidian"	起點
qimeng	啓蒙
qimeng de wenxue	啓蒙的文學
Qimeng shidai	啓蒙時代
qimeng wenxue	啓蒙文學
Qin	秦
Qing	清
"Qingcheng zhi lian"	傾城之戀
qingchun wenxue	青春文學
Qingchun wuhui	青春無悔
Qingchun zhi e	青春之歌
qingdan	清淡
qingge	情歌
Qinghua	清華
"Qinghuang"	青黃
Qinglong tan	青龍潭
Qinqiang	秦腔
Qin Shouou (1908–1993)	秦瘦鷗
Qin Zihao (1912–1963)	覃子豪
Qiong Yao (b. 1938)	瓊瑤
Qiqie chengqun	妻妾成群
Qi Rushan (1877–1962)	齊如山
Qiu	秋
Qiuhaitang	秋海棠
Qiu Huadong (b. 1969)	邱華棟
Qiu Jin (1875–1907)	秋瑾
Qiu Miaojin (1969–1995)	邱妙津
"Qiwang"	棋王
Qiyue	七月
Qiyue pai	七月派
Qu Bo (1923–2002)	曲波
Qu Guangxi (1911–1968)	瞿光熙
qu jingyinghua	去精英化
qumei	祛魅
qun	群
qunfa	群法
Qunxiang	群象
Qunyi shushe	群益書社
qunzhong	群衆
Qu Qiubai (1899–1936)	瞿秋白
Qu Yuan (343–278 BC)	屈原
Quzi wenxue zhi jingshen	屈子文學之精神
rendao	人道

"Rendao zhongnian"	人到中年
Ren Fangqiu (1909–2000)	任訪秋
Ren Hongjun (1886–1961)	任鴻雋
Renjianshi	人間世
Renmian taohua	人面桃花
Renmin wenxue	人民文學
renwen jingshen	人文精神
Ren Xiaowen (b. 1978)	任曉雯
Richu	日出
Riguang liunian	日光流年
Rongbaozhai	榮寶齋
Rongshu xia	榕樹下
Rou zhi tu	肉之土
Ru Zhijuan (1925–1998)	茹志鵑
Rulin waishi	儒林外史
Sakai Hirobumi (b. 1959)	坂井洋史
Sancong men	三重門
Sancun jinlian	三寸金蓮
san gang	三綱
Sang Hu (1916–2004)	桑弧
"'Sangjia de' 'zibenjia de fa zougou'"	"喪家的" "資本家的乏走狗"
Sanguo yanyi	三國演義
Sang Zilan (Tze-lan D. Sang)	桑梓蘭
Sanjia xiang	三家巷
Sanlian	三戀
San liu jiu xiaobao	三六九小報
Sanliwan	三里灣
sanwen	散文
sanwenshi	散文詩
Sanxia wuyi	三俠五義
"Sanyue yequ"	三月夜曲
Satō Haruo (1892–1964)	佐藤春夫
Satuk Bugra Khan	沙土克·布格拉汗
"Se, jie"	色, 戒
seqing xiaoshuo	色情小說
Seyfeddin Aziz (1915–2003)	賽福鼎·艾則孜
"Shafei nüshi de riji"	莎菲女士的日記
Shahu	沙狐
Sha Ma	沙馬
Shalang	沙狼
Shangguan Wan'er	上官婉兒
Shanghai	上海
Shanghai de zaochen	上海的早晨

Shanghai wenlun	上海文論
"Shanghen"	傷痕
shanghen wenxue	傷痕文學
Shang Qin (1930–2010)	商禽
"Shangshi"	傷逝
Shangshi jie	商市街
Shangwu yinshuguan	商務印書館
Shanhe rumeng	山河入夢
"Shanshang de xiaowu"	山上的小屋
Shantou	汕頭
Shanxiang jubian	山鄉巨變
Shao Nainai de shanzi	少奶奶的扇子
shaoshu minzu	少數民族
Shao Xunmei (1906–1968)	邵洵美
Shediao yingxiong zhuan	射雕英雄傳
shehui heimu	社會黑幕
shehui wenti xiaoshuo	社會問題小説
Shenbao	申報
Shenbaoguan	申報館
"Shenbian"	神鞭
Shen Congwen (1902–1988)	沈從文
Shengda wenxue	盛大文學
Shengjing shibao	盛京時報
shengnü	剩女
Shengshi—Zhongguo 2013	盛世—中國 2013
Shengsi chang	生死場
Shengsi pilao	生死疲勞
Shengtian menkou	聖天門口
Shen Guangwen (1612–1688)	沈光文
"Shengwu zhi qiyuan"	生物之起源
shenmei	審美
shenmei qingcao	審美情操
shenti xiezuo	身體寫作
Shen Weiwei (b. 1962)	沈衛威
Shen Xiaolong (b. 1952)	申小龍
Shen Ximeng (1919–2006)	沈西蒙
Shenzhen	深圳
Shi	蝕
shi	詩
Shi chuangzao	詩創造
shidai	時代
shidai guniang	時代姑娘
shidai xiaojie	時代小姐

Shiga Naoya (1883–1971)	志賀直哉
Shijian fanshi	時間繁史
"Shijian kaishi le"	時間開始了
Shijie fanhua bao	世界繁華報
shijie geming	詩界革命
shijie wenxue	世界文學
Shijie wenxue	世界文學
Shi Jimei (1920–1968)	施濟美
"Shijimo de huali"	世紀末的華麗
Shijing	詩經
Shi Jingyuan (Jing Tsu)	石靜遠
shili yangchang	十里洋場
Shintani Hideaki	新谷秀明
shipai	詩派
Shi Pingmei (1902–1928)	石評梅
Shi Pu (1907–2008)	石璞
shiqing xiaoshuo	世情小說
Shirakaba	白樺派
shiren huihua	詩人繪畫
shishe	詩社
shishi	史詩
Shishi xinbao	時事新報
Shi Shumei (Shu-mei Shih, b. 1961)	史書美
Shi Shuqing (Shih Shu-ch'ing, b. 1945)	施叔青
Shi Tiesheng (1951–2010)	史鐵生
Shi Tuo (1910–1988)	師陀
shiyan wenxue	試驗文學
Shi Yukun	石玉崑
Shi Zhecun (1905–2003)	施蟄存
Shi Zhi (Guo Lusheng, b. 1948)	食指 (郭路生)
shi zhi wei dao	詩之為道
shizhuang xi	時裝戲
"Shou"	手
shouchaoben xiaoshuo	手抄本小說
Shouhuo	收獲
Shouhuo	受活
Shouji	手機
"Shoujie"	受戒
shuang	爽
shufang	書房
Shuihu zhuan	水滸傳
Shujian enchou lu	書劍恩仇錄
shuoli	說理

Shu Qun (1913–1989)	舒群
Shu Ting (b. 1952)	舒婷
Shu Wu (1922–2009)	舒蕪
sichao	思潮
Sigangli	司崗裡
siheyuan	四合院
Sima Qian (145–? BC)	司馬遷
Sishi tongtang	四世同堂
Sishui weilan	死水微瀾
sixiang jiefang	思想解放
siyang buhua	食洋不化
"Si zai nanfang"	死在南方
Song	宋
Song Chunfang (1892–1938)	宋春舫
Song Qi (Stephen Soong, 1919–1996)	宋淇
Song Weijie	宋偉杰
Song Ziheng (Ng Neoh Leng, 1939–2012)	宋子衡
Sulian wenxue	蘇聯文學
Su Manshu (1884–1918)	蘇曼殊
Sun Ganlu (b. 1959)	孫甘露
Sun Lei (b. 1971)	孫磊
Sun Li (1913–2002)	孫犁
Sun Wenbo (b. 1956)	孫文波
Sun Yushi (b. 1935)	孫玉石
Sun Zhongshan (Sun Yat-sen, 1866–1925)	孫中山
Su Qing (1914–1982)	蘇青
Su Shuyang (b. 1938)	蘇叔陽
Su Tong (b. 1963)	蘇童
Sutuke Bugela Han	蘇圖克.布格拉漢
Su Wei (b. 1953)	蘇煒
Su Weizhen (b. 1954)	蘇偉貞
Su Xuelin (1897–1999)	蘇雪林
Suzhou	蘇州
Suzuki Masao (b. 1939)	鈴木正夫
Syman Rapongan (b. 1957)	夏曼.藍波安
Taibei ren	台北人
Tai Jingnong (1903–1990)	台靜農
Taiping hua	太平花
Taiwan huawen yundong	臺灣話文運動
Taiwan ren	臺灣人
Taiwan tongshi	臺灣通史
Taiwan wenhua xiehui	臺灣文化協會
Taiyang buluo	太陽部落

Taiyang she	太陽社
Taiyang zhaozai Sangganhe shang	太陽照在桑幹河上
Taiyu	臺語
Takeo Arishima (1878–1923)	有島武郎
Takeuchi Yoshimi (1908–1977)	竹内好
Ta mingjiao Hudie	她名叫蝴蝶
tanci	彈詞
Tang Baolin (b. 1939)	唐寶林
Tang Haoming (b. 1946)	唐浩明
Tang Lusun (1908–1985)	唐魯孫
Tang Qi (1920–1990)	唐祈
Tang Shi (1920–2005)	唐湜
Tang Song ba dajia	唐宋八大家
Tang Tao (1913–1992)	唐弢
Tang Xiaodu (b. 1954)	唐曉渡
Tang Yi	唐俟
Tang Yue (1891–1987)	唐鉞
Tan Sheying (1891–1978)	談社英
Tansuo	探索
Tanxiang xing	檀香刑
Tao Dongfeng (b. 1959)	陶東風
Tao Qian (365–427)	陶潛
Tao Yuanming (352 or 356–427)	陶淵明
ti	體
Tian Han (1898–1968)	田漢
Tian Jian (1916–1985)	田間
Tian Qinxin	田沁鑫
Tian'an men	天安門
tiandan	恬淡
Tiangong kaiwu	天工開物
Tianjin	天津
Tianxiang	天香
Tianyan lun	天演論
Tianyunshan chuanqi	天雲山傳奇
Tiaoqiao	天橋
Tiedao youjidui	鐵道遊擊隊
"Tiemu qianzhuan"	鐵木前傳
Tie Ning (b. 1957)	鐵凝
tigao	提高
Tingche zan jiewen	停車暫借問
titian xingdao	替天行道
Tixiao yinyuan	啼笑因緣
ti yong	體用

Tokunaga Sunao (1899–1958)	德永直
Tongcheng	桐城
Tonggan gongku	同甘共苦
tongren	同人
tongren chubanshe	同人出版社
tongren zazhi	同人雜誌
tongsu wenxue	通俗文學
"Touming de hong luobo"	透明的紅蘿蔔
Tsubouchi Shōyō (1859–1935)	坪內消遙
Tu	土
"Tu an de laiyuan shi"	圖案的來源史
tuanjie	團結
Tujia zu	土家族
"Tun she'er"	吞蛇兒
Uchiyama Kakichi (1900–1984)	內山嘉吉
Ueda Kazutoshi (1867–1937)	上田萬年
V cheng fansheng lu	V城繁盛錄
Wa	蛙
"Wadi shang de 'zhanyi'"	窪地上的"戰役"
Waiguo wenxue yanjiu	外國文學研究
Waiguo wenyi	外國文藝
waisheng ren	外省人
Wande jiushi xiantiao	玩的就是心跳
Wanfang Lu (b. 1969)	魯萬芳
Wang Ai (b. 1971)	王艾
Wang Anyi (b. 1954)	王安憶
Wang Ban (b. 1957)	王班
Wang Dewei (David Der-wei Wang, b. 1954)	王德威
Wang Furen (b. 1941)	王富仁
Wang Guangdong (b. 1961)	王光東
Wang Guangming (b. 1955)	王光明
Wang Guanquan (b. 1932)	王觀泉
Wang Guowei (1877–1927)	王國維
Wang Haowei (b. 1940)	王好為
Wang Hongsheng	汪宏聲
Wang Hui (b. 1959)	汪暉
Wang Jiaxin (b. 1957)	王家新
Wang Jiquan (b. 1948)	王繼權
wangluo youmin	網絡游民
wangluo youxi	網絡遊戲
Wang Meng (b. 1934)	王蒙
Wang Ning (b. 1955)	王寧
Wang Pengyun (1848–1904)	王鵬運

Wang Runhua (b. 1941)	王潤華
Wangshi bing buru yan	往事並不如煙
Wang Shiwei (1900–1946)	王實味
Wang Shouchang (1863–?)	王壽昌
Wang Shuo (b. 1958)	王朔
Wang Wei (699–761)	王維
Wang Wenxing (b. 1939)	王文興
Wang Xiaofei	王笑飛
Wang Xiaojue	王曉珏
Wang Xiaoming (b. 1955)	王曉明
Wang Xiaoni (b. 1955)	王小妮
Wang Xizhi (303–361 or 321–379)	王羲之
Wang Yangming (147–1529)	王陽明
Wang Xiuwen	王秀文
Wang Yao (1914–1989)	王瑤
Wang Yao (b. 1960)	王堯
Wang Ying (1915–1975)	王瑩
Wang Yiyan	王一燕
Wang Yongping	王勇平
wangyou	網遊
Wang Yunzhang (1884–1942)	王蘊章
Wang Zengqi (1920–1997)	汪曾祺
Wang Zhefu	王哲甫
Wang Zhenhe (Wang Chen-ho, 1940–1990)	王禎和
Wanxia xiaoshide shihou	晚霞消失的時候
"Wanzhu"	頑主
Wa zu	瓦族
Weicheng	圍城
Wei Hui (b. 1973)	衛慧
Wei Jingsheng (b. 1950)	魏京生
wei Man wenxue	偽滿文學
Wei Manzhouguo	偽滿洲國
Weiming she	未名社
Wei Pu (Paul Manfredi)	魏樸
Wei renmin fuwu	為人民服務
Weiwuer zu	維吾爾族
Wei Yi (1880–1930)	魏易
Wei Yuan (1794–1857)	魏源
wen	文
wenchang	文娼
wengai	文丐
Weng Nao (1910–1940?)	翁鬧
wenhuare	文化熱

Wenhuibao	文匯報
Wen Jie	聞捷
wenku	文庫
Wenming xiaoshi	文明小史
wenren	文人
Wenrou yu baolie	溫柔與暴烈
wenru qiren	文如其人
wenti wenxue	問題文學
Wen Ruian (b. 1954)	溫瑞安
Wen Xiangying (Wan Kok Seng, b. 1940)	溫祥英
Wenxuan	文選
wenxue	文學
wenxue de guoyu	文學的國語
Wenxue de qimeng	文學的啓蒙
"Wenxue gailiang chuyi"	文學改良芻議
wenxue geming	文學革命
wenxue shi renxue	文學是人學
"Wenxue xiaoyan"	文學小言
wenxue xing	文學性
Wenxue xunkan	文學旬刊
Wenxue yanjiu hui	文學研究會
wenyan	文言
wenyan wen	文言文
Wenyibao	文藝報
wenyi dazhonghua	文藝大眾化
Wen Yiduo (1899–1946)	聞一多
Wenyi xinchao	文藝新潮
wenyi xue	文藝學
wenyi zaidao	文以載道
wenzhang	文章
wenzhi binbin	文質彬彬
wenzi	文字
Wo ai Meiyuan	我愛美元
Wo bushi Pan Jinlian	我不是潘金蓮
Wocheng	我城
Wode putishu	我的菩提樹
Wohu canglong	臥虎藏龍
Women de ziji pipan	我們的自己批判
"Women fufu zhijian"	我們夫婦之間
"Women zui weida de jieri"	我們最偉大的節日
Wo shi ni baba	我是你爸爸
Wo sinian de changmian zhongde nanguo gongzhu	我思念的長眠中的南國公主
"Wo yong cansun de shouzhang"	我用殘損的手掌

Wo yu ditan	我與地壇
"Wo zai Xiacun de shihou"	我在霞村的時候
Wugen hua	無根花
Wu Guangjian (1867–1943)	伍光健
Wuhan	武漢
Wu Han (1909–1969)	吳晗
Wu He (b. 1951)	舞鶴
Wu Hongcong (1918–2011)	吳宏聰
Wu Jianren (Wo Woyao, 1866–1910)	吳趼人 (吳沃堯)
Wu Jingheng (1865–1953)	吳敬恒
Wukui qiao	五奎橋
"Wuliao"	無聊
wulitou wenxue	無厘頭文學
Wu Mi (1894–1978)	吳宓
wuming	無名
Wumingshi	無名氏
Wu Qiang (1910–1990)	吳強
wusheng	武生
"Wushi nian lai Zhongguo zhi wenxue"	五十年來中國之文學
wusi	五四
wusi wenxue	五四文學
Wu Tao	吳檮
"Wuti"	無題
Wuwangcun guanzhu	無望村館主
wuxia	武俠
Wu xingbie de shen	無性別的神
Wu Xun zhuan	武訓傳
Wuyan	巫言
Wu Zetian	武則天
Wu Zhiying (1868–1934)	吳芝瑛
Wu Zhongjie (b. 1936)	吳中杰
Wuzhong yuanshi	物種源始
Wu Zhuoliu (Wu Chuo-liu, 1900–1976)	吳濁流
Wu Zuxiang (1908–94)	吳組緗
xiahai	下海
Xia Ji'an (Tsi-An Hsia, 1916–1965)	夏濟安
Xiamen	廈門
Xi'an	西安
Xiandai hanshi	現代漢詩
xiandai shi	現代史
Xiandai	現代
xiandaipai	現代派
Xiandaishi	現代詩

xiandaiwenxue	現代文學
xiandangdaiwenxue	現當代文學
xianfeng wenxue	先鋒文學
"Xiangchunshu jie"	香椿樹街
Xianggang (Hong Kong)	香港
Xiang Kairan (1890–1957)	向愷然
"Xiangrikui"	向日葵
"Xiang wo juancun de xiongdimen"	想我眷村的兄弟們
Xiangwo zheyang de yige nüzi	像我這樣的一個女子
"Xiangxin weilai"	相信未來
Xianhua xianshuo	閑話閑説
xianqi liangmu	賢妻良母
xianshi	閒適
"Xianshi yizhong"	現實一種
xiangtu	鄉土
xiangtu wenxue	鄉土文學
xiangtu wenxue yundong	鄉土文學運動
"Xiaobaozhuang"	小鮑莊
Xiaocheng chunqiu	小城春秋
Xiaoerhei jiehun	小二黑結婚
"Xiaofan shijia"	小販世家
"Xiaoqi de na yiding maozi"	小琪的那一頂帽子
Xiao Hei (Tan Kee Keat)	小黑
Xiao Hong (Zhang Naiying, 1911–1942)	蕭紅 (張迺瑩)
Xiao Hong sanwen	蕭紅散文
xiao juchang yundong	小劇場運動
Xiao Jun (Liu Honglin, 1907–1988)	蕭軍 (劉鴻霖)
Xiaonü naier zhuan	孝女耐兒傳
xiaopin sanwen	小品散文
xiaopin wen	小品文
Xiao Qian (1910–1999)	蕭乾
xiaosan	小三
xiaosheng	小生
Xiao shidai	小時代
Xiao Shijun	蕭石君
xiao shimin	小市民
xiaoshuo	小説
Xiaoshuo daguan	小説大觀
Xiaoshuo huabao	小説畫報
Xiaoshuo lin	小説林
"Xiaoshuo tekan"	小説特刊
"Xiaoshuo xiaohua"	小説小話
"Xiaoshuo xiaoyan"	小説小言

Xiaoshuo yuebao	小說月報
xiaoshuojie geming	小說界革命
"Xiaoxiao"	蕭蕭
Xiao Yemu (1918–1970)	蕭也牧
Xiaoyi duohe	小姨多鶴
Xiao Yueyue	小悅悅
Xia Suiqing (1865–1924)	夏穗卿
Xiaqiu zhuan	蝦球傳
"Xia Wusi de banqi"	下五四的半旗
Xia Xiaohong (b. 1953)	夏曉虹
Xia yin ji	俠隱記
Xia Yu (Hsia Yü, b. 1956)	夏宇
Xia Yuanyu (1909–1995)	夏元瑜
Xia Zengyou (1863–1924)	夏曾佑
Xia Zhiqing (C. T. Hsia, 1921–2013)	夏志清
Xi Chuan (b. 1963)	西川
Xie Bingying (1906–2000)	謝冰瑩
Xie Danru (1904–1962)	謝旦如
xieshi zhuyi	寫實主義
xieshou	寫手
Xie Tieli (b. 1925)	謝鐵驪
xiju	戲劇
Xi Juan (b. 1972)	席娟
Xi Mi (Michelle Yeh)	奚密
xin	新
Xin Zhongguo	新中國
Xin Zhongguo weilai ji	新中國未來記
Xi Xi (b. 1938)	西西
Xinan lianda	西南聯大
xin da ya	信達雅
Xin Di (1912–2004)	辛笛
Xindu huaxu	新都花絮
xin ganjue pai	新感覺派
xingling	性靈
Xingqi	星期
Xingyun liushui	行雲流水
Xinjiang	新疆
Xin Jiaozi	新教子
Xinlang	新浪
Xinling shi	心靈史
Xinmin wanbao	新民晚報
xin minzhu zhuyi	新民主主義
xin minzhu zhuyi geming	新民主主義革命

xin nüxing	新女性
Xin qingnian	新青年
xinshi	新詩
Xin shiji	新世紀
Xin shijie	新世界
xin shiqi	新時期
Xin Shitou ji	新石頭記
Xin Taohua shan	新桃花扇
Xinwen wenzhai	新聞文摘
xin wenti	新文體
xin wenxue	新文學
Xin xiaoshuo	新小説
xin xieshi	新寫實
xinxing banhua	新興版畫
xin xinrenlei	新新人類
Xin xin xiaoshuo	新新小説
Xinyue	新月
Xinyue pai	新月派
Xinyue she	新月社
Xin yusi	新語絲
xinziyouzhuyi	新自由主義
xinzuopai	新左派
Xiongdi	兄弟
xiqu	戲曲
xishuo	戲説
Xiuxiang xiaoshuo	繡像小説
Xiwang	希望
xixue	西學
Xiyou ji	西游記
"Xizang, xizai pisheng jieshang de hun"	西藏, 系在皮繩結上的魂
Xizhao jie	夕照街
"Xu"	序
"Xuangao"	宣告
Xu Anhua (Ann Hui, b. 1947)	許鞍華
xuanhuan	玄幻
Xuanwo langhua	漩渦浪花
Xu Bing (b. 1955)	徐冰
Xu Dishan (1893–1941)	許地山
Xue Fucheng (1838–94)	薛福成
Xueheng	學衡
Xue Shaohui (1866–1911)	薛紹徽
Xue Suizhi (1922–1985)	薛綏之
"Xue luozai Zhongguo de tudi shang"	雪落在中國的土地上

xue yu lei de wenxue	血與淚的文學
Xu Guangping (1898–1968)	許廣平
"Xugou"	虛構
Xu Lianshun	許連順
xungen	尋根
xungen wenxue	尋根文學
Xu Kun (b. 1965)	徐坤
Xu Lan (b. 1969)	須蘭
Xu Nianci (1875–1908)	徐念慈
Xun Qin ji	尋秦記
Xu Sanguan maixue ji	許三觀賣血記
Xu Shoushang (1883–1948)	許壽裳
Xu Xiacun (1907–1986)	徐霞村
Xu Xing (b. 1956)	徐星
Xu Xu (1908–1980)	徐訏
Xu Zechen (b. 1978)	徐則臣
Xu Zhenya (1889–1937)	徐枕亞
Xu Zhimo (1897–1931)	徐志摩
Xu Zhiying (1934–2007)	許志英
Xu Zidong (b. 1954)	許子東
Xu Zihua (1875–1935)	徐自華
Xu Zuzheng (1895–1978)	徐祖正
Ya Xian (b. 1932)	瘂弦
Yalu Wang	雅魯王
Yamada Bimyō (1868–1910)	山田美妙
Yamaguchi Mamoru (b. 1953)	山口守
Yamei zu	雅美族
Yan'an	延安
Yan Fu (1854–1921)	嚴復
yangban xi	樣板戲
Yan Geling (b. 1958)	嚴歌苓
Yang Feng	揚風
Yang Gang (1905–1957)	楊剛
Yangge	秧歌
Yangguang canlan de rizi	陽光燦爛的日子
Yang Hui (1899–1983)	楊晦
Yang Jian (b. 1952)	楊健
Yang Jiang (b. 1911)	楊絳
Yang Ke (b. 1957)	楊克
Yang Lian (b. 1955)	楊煉
Yang Limin (b. 1948)	楊利民
Yang Mo (1914–1995)	楊沫
Yang Mu (b. 1940)	楊牧

Yang Quan (1893–1933)	楊銓
Yang Xianhui (b. 1946)	楊顯惠
Yang Yiyan (b. 1925)	楊益言
Yang Zhao (b. 1963)	楊照
Yangzhen (b. 1963)	央珍
Yang Zi (b. 1969)	羊子
"Yanhu"	煙壺
Yan Jiayan (b. 1933)	嚴家炎
Yan Li (b. 1954)	嚴力
Yan Lianke (b. 1958)	閻連科
"Ya nu"	啞奴
yanqing	言情
yanqing xiaoshuo	言情小説
Yashe xiaopin	雅舍小品
yansu wenxue	嚴肅文學
yanwen heyi	言文合一
Yanyang tian	豔陽天
Yanzhi kou	胭脂扣
Yao Ke (1905–1991)	姚克
Yao Wenyuan	姚文元
Yao Xueyin (1910–1999)	姚雪垠
"Yaoyuan de fengsha"	遙遠的風沙
Yao zu	瑤族
Yecao	野草
Ye Gongchao (1904–1981)	葉公超
Yehuo chunfeng dou gucheng	野火春風鬥古城
Ye Lingfeng (1905–1975)	葉靈鳳
Yeren	野人
Ye shenchen	夜深沉
Ye Shengtao (Ye Shaojun, 1894–1988)	葉聖陶（葉紹鈞）
Ye Xin (b. 1949)	葉辛
Ye Zhaoyan (b. 1957)	葉兆言
Ye Zi (1912–1939)	葉紫
Ye Ziming (1935–2005)	葉子銘
yi	義
Yidai fengliu	一代風流
"Yidai ren"	一代人
"Yidi jimao"	一地雞毛
"Yidian zhengjing meiyou"	一點正經沒有
Yihang	一行
Yijing	易經
Yijiusanqi nian de aiqing	一九三七年的愛情
Yiju ding yiwanju	一句頂一萬句

"Yi liyan"	譯例言
yilun wen	議論文
ying gutou	硬骨頭
Yinghuan suoji	瀛寰瑣記
Yingsu zhi jia	罌粟之家
Yi Shu (b. 1946)	亦舒
Yitian tulong ji	倚天屠龍記
Yiwen	譯文
Yizhi xiuhuaxie	一雙繡花鞋
Yi zu	彝族
Yi zu wenxue shi	彝族文學史
yong	用
"Yongyuan de Yin Xueyan"	永遠的尹雪豔
"Youde ren"	有的人
youxia	游俠
youxiu	優秀
"Youyuan jingmeng"	游園驚夢
yuan	元
Yuan Hanyun (1889–1931)	袁寒雲
Yuan Jin (b. 1951)	袁進
Yuan Kejia (1921–2008)	袁可嘉
Yuannü	怨女
Yuan Shikai (1859–1916)	袁世凱
Yuan Zhonglang (1568–1610)	袁中郎
yuanyang hudie	鴛鴦蝴蝶
Yuanye	原野
Yu Dafu (1896–1945)	郁達夫
Yu Daxiong	余大雄
Yue Ye (1920–2001)	岳野
Yueju	粵劇
"Yueliang shan"	月亮山
Yueyue xiaoshuo	月月小説
"Yugong yi shan"	愚公移山
Yu Guangzhong (b. 1928)	余光中
Yu Hua (b. 1960)	余華
Yu Jian (b. 1954)	於堅
Yuli hun	玉梨魂
Yu Ling (1907–1997)	於伶
yuluti	語錄體
Yun Zhaoguang (b. 1929)	雲照光
Yu Pingbo (1900–1990)	俞平伯
Yu Qie (1902–1990)	予且
Yusi	語絲

Yusi pai	語絲派
Yusi she	語絲社
Yuwai xiaoshuo ji	域外小說集
Yu Xiayun	余夏雲
"Yu Xujun lun baihua wenyan shu"	與徐君論白話文言書
yuyan gaige	語言改革
yuyan migong	語言迷宮
Yu Yingshi (b. 1930)	余英時
"Yu zhong tibi"	獄中提筆
Yuzhou feng	宇宙風
zaidao	載道
"Zai xiaohe nabian"	在小河那邊
"Zai Yan'an wenyi zuotanhui shang de jianghua"	在延安文藝座談會上的講話
zaiye de xiju	在野的戲劇
zaju	雜劇
Zang Kejia (1905–2004)	臧克家
Zang zu	藏族
Zang zu wenyi	藏族文藝
"Zaochun"	早春
"Zaoren shu"	造人術
zawen	雜文
zawenxue	雜文學
Zeng Guofan (1811–1872)	曾國藩
Zeng Huapeng (1932–2013)	曾華鵬
Zeng Pu (1872–1935)	曾樸
Zha Jianying (b. 1959)	查建英
Zha Mingjian	查明建
Zhai Yongming (b. 1955)	翟永明
Zhaiyi	摘譯
Zhalagahu (b. 1930)	紮拉嘎胡
Zhan Kai (Siqi Zhai, ca. 1860–ca. 1910)	詹塏（思綺齋）
Zhang Ailing (Eileen Chang, 1920–1995)	張愛玲
Zhang Baorui (b. 1952)	張寶瑞
Zhang Bilai (1914–1991)	張畢來
Zhang Binglin (1868–1936)	章炳麟
Zhang Chengzhi (b. 1948)	張承志
Zhang Dachun (Chang Da-chun, b. 1957)	張大春
Zhang Guixing (b. 1956)	張貴興
Zhang Henshui (1895–1967)	張恨水
Zhang Houzai (1895–1955)	張厚載
zhanghui xiaoshuo	章回小說
Zhang Jie (b. 1937)	張潔
Zhang Jinzhong (Kim Tong Tee, b. 1956)	張錦忠

Zhang Kebiao (1900–2007)	章克標
Zhang Longxi (b. 1947)	張隆溪
Zhang Mo (b. 1931)	張默
Zhang Peiheng (1934–2011)	章培恆
Zhang shao	獐哨
Zhang Shenqie (1904–1965)	張深切
Zhang Songsheng (Sung-sheng Yvonne Chang, b. 1951)	張诵聖
Zhang Tianyi (1906–1985)	張天翼
Zhang Wei (b. 1956)	張煒
Zhang Wenhuan (1909–1978)	張文環
Zhang Wenjiang (b. 1956)	張文江
Zhang Wojun (1902–1955)	張我軍
Zhang Xian (1934–1997)	張弦
Zhang Xianliang (b. 1936)	張賢亮
Zhang Xiaofeng (b. 1939)	張曉風
Zhang Xiguo (b. 1944)	張系國
Zhang Yang (b. 1944)	張揚
Zhang Yihe (b. 1942)	章詒和
Zhang Yimou (b. 1950)	張藝謀
Zhang Yingjin	張英進
Zhang Yiwu	張頤武
Zhang Zhenlü	張枕綠
Zhang Zhidong (1837–1909)	張之洞
Zhang Ziping (1893–1959)	張資平
"Zhanzheng jiaoxiangqu"	戰爭交響曲
zhanzheng wenhua xinli	戰爭文化心理
Zhao Huanting (1877–1951)	趙煥亭
"Zhao hun"	招魂
Zhao Jiabi (1908–1997)	趙家璧
Zhao Mei (b. 1954)	趙玫
Zhao Shaohou (1899–1978)	趙少侯
Zhao Shuli (1906–1970)	趙樹理
Zhao Ximeng (1899–1956)	趙惜夢
Zhao Yanwang	趙閻王
Zhao Yifan	趙一凡
Zhao Yuanren (1892–1982)	趙元任
Zhao Zifan (1924–1986)	趙滋藩
Zhaxi Dawa (Tashi Dawa, b. 1959)	紮西達娃
zhen	貞
Zheng Boqi (1895–1979)	鄭伯奇
Zheng Chaozong (1912–1998)	鄭朝宗
Zheng Chenggong (Koxinga, 1624–1662)	鄭成功

Zheng Chouyu (b. 1933)	鄭愁予
Zheng He (1371–1433)	鄭和
Zheng Min (b. 1920)	鄭敏
Zheng Shusen (William Tay, b. 1948)	鄭樹森
Zheng Yi (b. 1947)	鄭義
Zheng Yi (b. 1961)	鄭怡
Zheng Zhenduo (1898–1958)	鄭振鐸
Zheng Zhengqiu (1895–1935)	鄭正秋
Zheng Zhengyin (1900–1960)	鄭證因
Zhengbaiqi	正白旗
zhengfeng	整風
zhengzhi bopu	政治波普
Zhenxiang	真相
"Zheshi sidian ling bafen de Beijing"	這是四點零八分的北京
zhi	志
zhi	質
zhichang	職場
zhiqing	知青
zhiqing wenxue	知青文學
Zhiqu Weihushan	智取威虎山
Zhishi fenzi xiezuo	知識份子寫作
Zhi Xia (1918–1991)	知俠
Zhiyu ni xin buxin, fanzheng wo shi xin le	至於你信不信, 反正我是信了
zhong	忠
Zhong Dingwen (b. 1904)	鍾鼎文
Zhongguo funü shenghuo shi	中國婦女生活史
Zhongguo funü yundong	中國婦女運動
Zhongguo funü yundong tongshi	中國婦女運動通史
Zhongguo shaoshu minzu zuojia xiehui	中國少數民族作家協會
Zhongguo xiandai wenxue	中國現代文學
Zhongguo xiandangdai wenxue	中國現當代文學
Zhongguo xijujia xiehui	中國戲劇家協會
Zhongguo xinshi	中國新詩
Zhongguo zuojia xiehui	中國作家協會
Zhongguo wenxue	中國文學
Zhongguo xinwenxue daxi	中國新文學大系
Zhongguo zuoyi zuojia lianmeng	中國左翼作家聯盟
Zhonghua quanguo wenyijie kangdi xiehui	中華全國文藝界抗敵協會
Zhonghua quanguo wenxue yishujie lianhehui	中華全國文學藝術界聯合會
Zhonghua	中華
Zhonghuaxing	中華性
Zhong gu lou	鐘鼓樓
Zhong Lihe (Chung Lihe, 1915–1960)	鍾理和

zhongma	種馬
zhong renquan, yi zhuanzhi	重人權, 抑專制
Zhongshen dashi	終身大事
zhongtian	種田
Zhongwen	中文
Zhong Xiaoyang (b. 1962)	鍾曉陽
zhongyi tang	忠義堂
Zhong Yiwen (Choong Yee Voon, b. 1969)	鍾詒雯
Zhou Enlai (1898–1976)	周恩來
Zhou Erfu (1914–2004)	周而復
Zhou Guisheng (1873–1936)	周桂笙
Zhou Jianren (1888–1984)	周建人
Zhou Lei (Rey Chow)	周蕾
Zhou Libo (1908–1979)	周立波
Zhou Ruchang (1918–2012)	周汝昌
Zhou Shoujuan (1895–1968)	周瘦鵑
Zhou Wanyao	周婉窈
Zhou Xingchi (Stephen Chow, b. 1962)	周星馳
Zhou Xuepu (1900–1983)	周學普
Zhou Yang (1908–1989)	周揚
Zhou Zuoren (1885–1967)	周作人
Zhu Defa (b. 1934)	朱德發
Zhu Donglin (b. 1949)	朱棟霖
zhu fu	主輔
Zhu Guangqian (1897–1986)	朱光潛
Zhu Jingnong (1887–1951)	朱經農
Zhuque	朱雀
Zhu Shenghao (1912–1944)	朱生豪
Zhu Tianwen (b. 1956)	朱天文
Zhu Tianxin (Chu T'ien-hsin, b. 1958)	朱天心
Zhu Weizheng	朱維錚
Zhu Wen (b. 1967)	朱文
Zhu Wenying (b. 1984)	朱文穎
Zhu Xizu (1879–1944)	朱希祖
Zhu Ziqing (1898–1948)	朱自清
Zhuang zu	壯族
"Zhuiyi Wuyou xiansheng"	追憶烏攸先生
zhuxiuanlü xiju	主旋律戲劇
"Zihang"	紫航
zijue, yongmeng, fayang, jingjin	自覺, 勇猛, 發揚, 精進
Ziluolan	紫羅蘭
Ziye	子夜

"Ziyou tan" 自由談
Zong Pu (b.1928) 宗璞
zongpai zhuyi 宗派主義
"Zuichun lide yangguang" 嘴唇裏的陽光
"Zuihoude zhaohuan" 最後的召喚
Zuixiao 最小
Zui xiaoshuo 最小説
Zuji 足跡
zuojia 作家
"Zuzhibu xinlai de nianqingren" 組織部新來的青年人

Index

Note: This index includes an individual work under its author.
Page numbers following 'n' refer to notes